HISTORY OF LACE

ANNE, DAUGHTER OF SIR PETER VANLORE, KT.,
FIRST WIFE OF SIR CHARLES CÆSAR, KT., ABOUT 1614.
The lace is probably Flemish, Sir Peter having come from Utrecht.
From the picture the property of her descendant, Captain Cottrell-Dormer.

HISTORY OF LACE

by

Mrs. Bury Palliser

ENTIRELY REVISED, REWRITTEN, AND ENLARGED
UNDER THE EDITORSHIP OF
M. Jourdain and Alice Dryden

Dover Publications, Inc.
New York

Published in Canada by General Publishing Company, Ltd., 30 Lesmill
Road, Don Mills, Toronto, Ontario.
Published in the United Kingdom by Constable and Company, Ltd.

This Dover edition, first published in 1984, is an unabridged republication
of the edition published by Charles Scribner's Sons, New York, in 1911. The
placement of many of the plates has been changed in the present edition, but
nothing has been omitted.

Manufactured in the United States of America
Dover Publications, Inc., 31 East 2nd Street, Mineola, N.Y. 11501

Library of Congress Cataloging in Publication Data

Palliser, Bury, Mrs., 1805-1878.
  History of lace.

  Reprint. Originally published : 4th ed. New York : Scribner, 1911.
  Bibliography : p.
  Includes index.
  1. Lace and lace making—History.   I. Jourdain, Margaret.   II. Dryden,
Alice.   III. Title.
NK9406.P25   1984   746.2'2'09   84-6088
ISBN 0-486-24742-2

PREFACE TO THE FOURTH EDITION

NEARLY thirty years have elapsed since the third edition of the HISTORY OF LACE was published. As it is still the classical work on the subject, and many developments in the Art have taken place since 1875, it seemed desirable that a new and revised edition should be brought out.

The present Revisers have fully felt the responsibility of correcting anything the late Mrs. Palliser wrote ; they have therefore altered as little of the text as possible, except where modern research has shown a statement to be faulty.

The chapters on Spain, Alençon and Argentan, and the Introductory chapter on Needlework, have been almost entirely rewritten. Much new matter has been added to Italy, England and Ireland, and the notices of Cretan and Sicilian lace, among others, are new. The original wood-cuts have been preserved with their designations as in the 1875 edition, which differ materially from the first two editions. Nearly a hundred new illustrations have been added, and several portraits to show different fashions of wearing lace.

The Revisers wish to record their grateful thanks to those who have assisted them with information or lace for illustration ; especially to Mrs. Hulton, Count Marcello and Cavaliere Michelangelo Jesurum in Venice, Contessa di Brazza and Contessa Cavazza in Italy, M. Destrée in Brussels, Mr. Arthur Blackborne, Salviati & Co., and the Director of the Victoria and Albert Museum in London.

M. JOURDAIN.
ALICE DRYDEN.

London, September, 1901.

CONTENTS

LIST OF ILLUSTRATIONS

HISTORY OF LACE

HISTORY OF LACE.

———o⚬⚭⚬o———

CHAPTER I.

NEEDLEWORK.

"As ladies wont
To finger the fine needle and nyse thread."—*Faerie Queene.*

THE art of lace-making has from the earliest times been
so interwoven with the art of needlework that it would be
impossible to enter on the subject of the present work without giving some mention of the latter.

With the Egyptians the art of embroidery was general,
and at Beni Hassan figures are represented making a sort of
net—"they that work in flax, and they that weave network."[1] Examples of elaborate netting have been found in
Egyptian tombs, and mummy wrappings are ornamented
with drawn-work, cut-work, and other open ornamentation.
The outer tunics of the robes of state of important personages
appear to be fashioned of network darned round the hem
with gold and silver and coloured silks. Amasis, King of
Egypt, according to Herodotus,[2] sent to Athene of Lindus a
corslet with figures interwoven with gold and cotton, and to
judge from a passage of Ezekiel, the Egyptians even embroidered the sails of their galleys which they exported to
Tyre.[3]

---

[1] Wilkinson's *Ancient Egyptians*,
vol. iii., p. 134. (See Illustration.)

[2] Herodotus, ii. 182; iii. 47.

[3] Ezekiel, who takes up the cry of
lamentation for "Tyrus, situate at the
entry of the sea," a merchant of the
people for many isles, exclaims, "The
merchants of Sheba, Asshur, and
Chilmad were thy merchants. These
were thy merchants in all sorts of
things, in blue cloths and broidered
works, and in chests of rich apparel."
Another part of the same chapter
mentions galley sails of fine linen
"with broidered work from Egypt."—
Ezekiel xxvii.

The Jewish embroiderers, even in early times, seem to have carried their art to a high standard of execution. The curtains of the Tabernacle were of "fine twined linen wrought with needlework, and blue, and purple, and scarlet, with cherubims of cunning work."[4]　Again, the robe of the ephod was of gold and blue and purple and scarlet, and fine twined linen, and in Isaiah we have mention of women's cauls and nets of checker-work.　Aholiab is specially recorded as a cunning workman, and chief embroiderer in blue, and in purple, and in scarlet, and in fine linen,[5] and the description of the virtuous woman in the Proverbs, who "layeth her hands to the spindle" and clotheth herself in tapestry, and that of the king's daughter in the Psalms, who shall be "brought unto the king in a raiment of needlework," all plainly show how much the art was appreciated amongst the Jews.[6]　Finally Josephus, in his *Wars of the Jews*, mentions the veil presented to the Temple by Herod (B.C. 19), a Babylonian curtain fifty cubits high, and sixteen broad, embroidered in blue and red, "of marvellous texture, representing the universe, the stars, and the elements."

In the English Bible, *lace* is frequently mentioned, but its meaning must be qualified by the reserve due to the use of such a word in James I.'s time.　It is pretty evident that the translators used it to indicate a small cord, since lace for decoration would be more commonly known at that time as *purls*, *points*, or *cut-works*.[7]

"Of lace amongst the Greeks we seem to have no evidence. Upon the well-known red and black vases are all kinds of figures clad in costumes which are bordered with ornamental patterns, but these were painted upon, woven into, or embroidered upon the fabric.　They were not lace.　Many centuries elapsed before a marked and elaborately ornamental character infused itself into twisted, plaited, or looped thread-work.　During such a period the fashion of ornamenting borders of costumes and hangings existed, and underwent a few phases, as, for instance, in the Elgin marbles, where crimped

---

[4] Exodus xxvi.; xxvii.; xxxiv. 2; Isaiah iii. 18; 1 Kings vii. 17.

[5] Exodus xxxviii. 23.

[6] Again, in the song of Deborah, the mother of Sisera says, "Have they not divided the prey? . . . to Sisera a prey of divers colours of needlework, of divers colours of needlework on both sides."—Judges v. 30.

[7] Cantor Lectures on the Art of Lace-making. A. S. Cole (London, 1881).

edges appear along the flowing Grecian dresses." Embroidered garments, cloaks, veils and cauls, and networks of gold are frequently mentioned in Homer and other early authors.[8]

The countries of the Euphrates were renowned in classical times for the beauty of their embroidered and painted stuffs which they manufactured.[9] Nothing has come down to us of these Babylonian times, of which Greek and Latin writers extolled the magnificence ; but we may form some idea, from the statues and figures engraved on cylinders, of what the weavers and embroiderers of this ancient time were capable.[10] A fine stone in the British Museum is engraved with the figure of a Babylonian king, Merodach-Idin-Abkey, in embroidered robes, which speak of the art as practised eleven hundred years B.C.[11] Josephus writes that the veils given by Herod for the Temple were of Babylonian work (πέπλος βαβυλώνιος)—the women excelling, according to Apollonius, in executing designs of varied colours.

The Sidonian women brought by Paris to Troy embroidered veils of such rich work that Hecuba deemed them worthy of being offered to Athene ; and Lucan speaks of the Sidonian veil worn by Cleopatra at a feast in her Alexandrine palace, in honour of Cæsar.[12]

Phrygia was also renowned for its needlework, and from the shores of Phrygia Asiatic and Babylonian embroideries were shipped to Greece and Italy. The *toga picta*, worked with Phrygian embroidery, was worn by Roman generals at their triumphs and by the consuls when they celebrated the games ; hence embroidery itself is styled "Phrygian,"[13]

---

[8] At Athens the maidens who took part in the procession of the Panathenaea embroidered the veil or *peplos* upon which the deeds of the goddess were embroidered. The sacred *peplos* borne on the mast of a ship rolled on wheels in the Panathenaic festival " was destined for the sacred wooden idol, Athene Polias, which stood on the Erechtheus. This *peplos* was a woven mantle renewed every five years. On the ground, which is described as dark violet, and also as saffron-coloured, was inwoven the battle of the gods and the giants." (See page 47, *British Museum Catalogue to the Sculptures of the Parthenon*.)

[9] Pliny, *Hist. Nat.*, viii. 74. "Colores diversos picturae intexere Babylon maxime celebravit et nomen imposuit."
[10] Maspero, *The Dawn of Civilisation in Egypt and Chaldaea* (ed. Prof. Sayce).
[11] Lefébure, *Embroidery and Lace* (trans. A. S. Cole).
[12] Lucan, *Pharsalia*, Book X.
[13] The Romans denominated such embroideries *phrygionae*, and the embroiderer *phrygio*. Golden embroideries were specified as *auriphrygium*. This word is the root of the French *orfroi* (orfreys).

and the Romans knew it under no other name (*opus Phrygianum*).[14]

Gold needles and other working implements have been discovered in Scandinavian tumuli. In the *London Chronicle* of 1767 will be found a curious account of the opening of a Scandinavian barrow near Wareham, in Dorsetshire. Within the hollow trunk of an oak were discovered many bones wrapped in a covering of deerskins neatly sewn together. There were also the remains of a piece of gold lace, four inches long and two and a half broad. This lace was black and much decayed, of the old lozenge pattern,[15] that most ancient and universal of all designs, again found depicted on the coats of ancient Danes, where the borders are edged with an open or net-work of the same pattern.

Fig. 1.

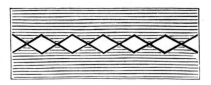

GOLD LACE FOUND IN A BARROW.

Passing to the first ages of the Christian era, we find the pontifical ornaments, the altar and liturgical cloths, and the draperies then in common use for hanging between the colonnades and porches of churches all worked with holy images and histories from the Holy Writ. Rich men chose sacred subjects to be embroidered on their dress, and one senator wore 600 figures worked upon his robes of state. Asterius, Bishop of Amasus, thunders against those Christians "who wore the Gospels upon their backs instead of in their hearts."[16]

In the Middle Ages spinning and needlework were the occupation of women of all degrees. As early as the sixth

---

[14] Mrs. Palliser quotes an extract from the author of *Letters from Italy*, who, speaking of the cabinet at Portici, mentions an elegant marble statue of Diana "dressed after the purple gowns worn by the Roman ladies; the garment is edged with a lace exactly resembling point; it is an inch and a half broad, and has been painted purple." By an Englishwoman (Mrs. Millar) in the years 1770 and 1771 (London, 1777).

[15] Strutt.

[16] Lefébure, *Embroidery and Lace*.

century the nuns in the diocese of St. Césaire, Bishop of Arles, were forbidden to embroider robes enriched with paintings, flowers, and precious stones. This prohibition, however, was not general. Near Ely, an Anglo-Saxon lady brought together a number of maidens to work for the monastery, and in the seventh century an Abbess of Bourges, St. Eustadiole, made vestments and enriched the altar with the work of her nuns. At the beginning of the ninth century St. Viborade, of St. Gall, worked coverings for the sacred books of the monastery, for it was the custom then to wrap in silk and carry in a linen cloth the Gospels used for the offices of the Church.[17] Judith of Bavaria, mother of Charles the Bold, stood sponsor for the Queen of Harold, King of Denmark, who came to Ingelheim to be baptised with all his family, and gave her a robe she had worked with her own hands and studded with precious stones.

"Berthe aux grands pieds," the mother of Charlemagne, was celebrated for her skill in needlework,[18]

> "à ouvrer si com je vous dirai
> N'avoit meillor ouvriere de Tours jusqu'à Cambrai;"

while Charlemagne [19]—-

> "Ses filles fist bien doctriner,
> Et aprendre keudre et filer."

Queen Adelhaïs, wife of Hugh Capet (987-996), presented to the Church of St. Martin at Tours a cope, on the back of which she had embroidered the Deity, surrounded by seraphim and cherubim, the front being worked with an Adoration of the Lamb of God.[20]

Long before the Conquest, Anglo-Saxon women were skilled with the needle, and gorgeous are the accounts of the gold-starred and scarlet-embroidered tunics and violet sacks worked by the nuns. St. Dunstan himself designed the ornaments of a stole worked by the hands of a noble Anglo-Saxon lady, Ethelwynne, and sat daily in her bower with her maidens, directing the work. The four daughters of

---

[17] Mrs. Bury Palliser, "Embroidery," *Encyclopædia Britannica.*

[18] St. Giselle, Berthe's sister, founded many convents in Aquitaine and Provence, and taught the nuns all manner of needlework (Lefébure, *Embroidery and Lace*).

[19] *Chronique Rimée*, by Philippe Mouskés.

[20] Lefébure, *Embroidery and Lace.*

Edward the Elder are all praised for their needle's skill. Their father, says William of Malmesbury, had caused them in childhood " to give their whole attention to letters, and afterwards employed them in the labours of the distaff and the needle." In 800 Denbert, Bishop of Durham, granted the lease of a farm of 200 acres for life to an embroideress named Eanswitha for the charge of scouring, repairing, and renewing the vestments of the priests of his diocese.[21] The Anglo-Saxon Godric, Sheriff of Buckingham, granted to Alcuid half a hide of land as long as he should be sheriff on condition she taught his daughter the art of embroidery. In the tenth century Ælfleda, a high-born Saxon lady, offered to the church at Ely a curtain on which she had wrought the deeds of her husband, Brithnoth, slain by the Danes; and Edgitha, Queen of Edward the Confessor, was "perfect mistress of her needle."

The famous Bayeux Tapestry or embroidery, said to have been worked by Matilda, wife of William the Conqueror, is of great historical interest.[22] It is, according to the chroniclers, " Une tente très longue et estroite de telle a broderies de ymages et escriptaux faisant représentation du Conquest de l'Angleterre "; a needle-wrought epic of the Norman Conquest, worked on a narrow band of stout linen over 200 feet long, and containing 1,255 figures worked on worsted threads.[23] Mr. Fowke gives the Abbé Rue's doubts as to the accepted period of the Bayeux tapestry, which he assigns to the Empress Matilda. Mr. Collingwood Bruce is of opinion that the work is coeval with the events it records, as the primitive furniture, buildings, etc., are all of the eleventh century. That the tapestry is not found in any catalogue before 1369 is only a piece of presumptive evidence against the earlier date, and must be weighed with the internal evidence in its favour.

After the Battle of Hastings William of Normandy, on

---

[21] Mrs. Palliser, " Embroidery," *Encyclopædia Britannica*.

[22] It has been suggested that the embroidery was done by William's granddaughter, the Empress Matilda, widow in 1125 of Henry V., Emperor of Germany, and wife, by her second marriage, of Geoffrey, Count of Anjou (Lefébure).

[23] Mr. Fowke states that the tradition which would make the tapestry the handiwork of Queen Matilda cannot be traced further back than 1803, when the tapestry was sent to Paris for exhibition.

his first appearance in public, clad himself in a richly-wrought cloak of Anglo-Saxon embroidery, and his secretary, William of Poictiers, states that "the English women are eminently skilful with the needle and in weaving."

The excellence of the English work was maintained as time went on, and a proof of this is found in an anecdote preserved by Matthew of Paris.[24] "About this time (1246) the Lord Pope (Innocent IV.) having observed the ecclesiastical ornaments of some Englishmen, such as choristers' copes and mitres, were embroidered in gold thread after a very desirable fashion, asked where these works were made, and received in answer, in England. 'Then,' said the Pope, 'England is surely a garden of delights for us. It is truly a never-failing spring, and there, where many things abound, much may be extracted.' Accordingly, the same Lord Pope sent sacred and sealed briefs to nearly all the abbots of the Cistercian order established in England, requesting them to have forthwith forwarded to him those embroideries in gold which he preferred to all others, and with which he wished to adorn his chasuble and choral cope, as if these objects cost them nothing," an order which, adds the chronicler, "was sufficiently pleasing to the merchants, but the cause of many persons detesting him for his covetousness."

Perhaps the finest examples of the *opus anglicanum* extant are the cope and maniple of St. Cuthbert, taken from his coffin in the Cathedral of Durham, and now preserved in the Chapter library. One side of the maniple is of gold lace stitched on, worked apparently on a parchment pattern. The Syon Monastery cope, in the Victoria and Albert Museum, is an invaluable example of English needlework of the thirteenth century. "The greater portion of its design is worked in a chain-stitch (modern tambour or crochet), especially in the faces of the figures, where the stitch begins in the centre, say, of a cheek, and is then worked in a spiral, thus forming a series of circular lines. The texture so obtained is then, by means of a hot, small and round-knobbed iron, pressed into indentations at the centre of each spiral, and an effect of relief imparted to it. The general

---

[24] Matt. Par., *Hist. Angl.*, p. 473, Edit. Paris, 1644,

practice was to work the draperies in feather-stitch (*opus plumarium*)."[25]

In the tenth century the art of pictorial embroidery had become universally spread. The inventory of the Holy See (in 1293) mentions the embroideries of Florence, Milan, Lucca, France, England, Germany, and Spain, and throughout the Middle Ages embroidery was treated as a fine art, a serious branch of painting.[26] In France the fashion continued, as in England, of producing groups, figures and portraits, but a new development was given to floral and elaborate arabesque ornament.[27]

It was the custom in feudal times[28] for knightly families to send their daughters to the castles of their suzerain lords, there to be trained to spin, weave and embroider under the eye of the lady châtelaine, a custom which, in the more primitive countries, continued even to the French Revolution. In the French romances these young ladies are termed "chambrières," in our English, simply "the maidens." Great ladies prided themselves upon the number of their attendants, and passed their mornings at work, their labours beguiled by singing the "chansons à toile," as the ballads written for those occasions were termed.[29]

---

[25] Mrs. Palliser, "Embroidery," *Encyclopædia Britannica*.

[26] At Verona an artist took twenty-six years to execute in needlework the life of St. John, after the designs of Pollajuolo.

[27] "Gaston, Duke of Orleans, established hot-houses and botanical gardens, which he filled with rare exotics to supply the needle with new forms and richer tints" (Lefébure).

[28] We read, for instance, that Gabrielle de Bourbon, wife of Louis de la Trémouille, "jamais n'estoit oyseuse, mais s'employoit une partie de la journée en broderies et autres menus ouvrages appartenant à telles dames, et y occupoit ses demoyselles dont avoit bonne quantité, et de grosses, riches, et illustres maisons."—*Panegyric de Loys de la Trémoille par Jean Bouchet*.

Again Vecellio dedicates his "Corona" to Signora Nanni, not only on account of the pleasure she takes in works of the needle, but for "il diletto che prende in farne essercitar le donne de casa sua, ricetto delle più virtuose giovani che hoggidì vivono in questa città."

"It is usual here," writes a lady from Madrid in 1679, "for good families to put their daughters to ladies, by whom they are employed to embroider in gold and silver, or various colours, or in silk, about the shift, neck, and hands."

[29] "I jor fist es chambre son pere,
Une estole et i amict pere,
De soie et d'or molt soutilment,
Si i fait ententivement
Mainte croisette et mainte estoile,
Et dist ceste chancon à toile."
—*Roman de la Violette*.

"One day, seated in her father's room, she was skilfully working a stole and amict in silk and gold, and she was making in it, with great care, many a little cross and many a little star, singing all the while this *chanson à toile*."

In the wardrobe accounts of our kings appear constant entries of working materials purchased for the royal ladies.[30] There is preserved in the cathedral at Prague an altar-cloth of embroidery and cut-work worked by Anne of Bohemia, Queen of Richard II.

During the Wars of the Roses, when a duke of the blood royal is related to have begged alms in the streets of the rich Flemish towns, ladies of rank, more fortunate in their education, gained, like the French emigrants of more modern days, their subsistence by the products of their needle.[31]

Without wishing to detract from the industry of mediæval ladies, it must be owned that the swampy state of the country, the absence of all roads, save those to be traversed in the fine season by pack-horses, and the deficiency of all suitable outdoor amusement but that of hawking, caused them to while away their time within doors the best way they could. Not twenty years since, in the more remote provinces of France, a lady who quitted her house daily would be remarked on. " Elle sort beaucoup," folks would say, as though she were guilty of dissipation.

So queens and great ladies sewed on. We hear much of works of adornment, more still of piety, when Katharine of Aragon appears on the scene. She had learned much in her youth from her mother, Queen Isabella, and had probably

---

[30] In one of Edward I. we find a charge of eight shillings for silk bought for the embroidery work of Margaret, the King's daughter, and another for four ounces of silk, two hundred ounces of gold thread, a spindle, etc.—*Liber de Garderoba*, 23 *Edw. I.*, Public Record Office.

In one of Edward III. the sum of £2 7s. 2d. is expended in the purchase of gold thread, silk, etc., for his second daughter Joanna.—*Liber Garderobae*, 12–16 *Edw. III.*, Public Record Office,

Elizabeth of York worked much at her needle. In the account of her household, preserved in the Public Record Office, every page of which is signed by Queen Elizabeth herself, we find—

" To Evan Petreson joiner, for the stuff and making of 4 working stools for the Queen ; price of the stool 16 pence—5s. 4d.

" To Thomas Fissch, for an elne of linen cloth for a samplar for the queen, 8d."

In the Inventory 4 Edward VI., 1552 (Harl. MSS. No. 1419), are entries of—

" Item, XII. samplars " (p. 419).

" Item, one samplar of Normandie canvas, wrought with green and black silk " (p. 524).

" A book of parchment containing diverses patternes " (p. 474), probably purchases for his sisters.

[31] See, for instance, the interesting account of the Countess of Oxford, given by Miss Strickland in her *Life of Queen Elizabeth of York.*

assisted at those "trials" of needlework [32] established by
that virtuous queen among the Spanish ladies :—

"Her days did pass
In working with the needle curiously." [33]

It is recorded how, when Wolsey, with the papal legate
Campeggio, going to Bridewell, begged an audience of Queen
Katharine, on the subject of her divorce, they found her at
work, like Penelope of old, with her maids, and she came to
them with a skein of red silk about her neck. [34]

Queen Mary Tudor is supposed, by her admirers, to have
followed the example of her illustrious mother, though all we
find among the entries is a charge " to working materials for
Jane the Fole, one shilling."

No one would suspect Queen Elizabeth of solacing herself
with the needle. Every woman, however, had to make one
shirt in her lifetime, and the " Lady Elizabeth's grace," on
the second anniversary of Prince Edward's birth, when only
six years of age, presented her brother with a cambric smock
wrought by her own hands.

The works of Scotland's Mary, who early studied all
female accomplishments under her governess, Lady Fleming,

---

[32] These are alluded to in the dialogue between Industria and Ignavia,
as given in Sibmacher's " Modelbuch,"
1601 (French translation) : " La vieille
dame raconte l'histoire des concours
de travail à l'aiguille chez les anciens
Espagnols ; comme Isabelle, femme de
Ferdinand, a hautement estimé les travaux de l'aiguille."

The " Spanish stitch," so often mentioned, was brought in by Katharine,
on her marriage with Prince Arthur,
in 1501. We have constantly in her
wardrobe accounts sheets and pillow-
beres, " wrought with Spanish work of
black silk at the edge."

In the Inventory of Lord Monteagle,
1523 (Public Record Office, are " eight
partlets, three garnished with gold, the
rest with Spanish work."

In 1556, among the New Year's gifts
presented to Queen Mary Tudor, most
of the smocks are " wrought with black
silk, Spanish fashion."

In the Great Wardrobe Accounts of
Queen Elizabeth, 3 & 4, Public Record
Office, we have " sixteen yards of Spanish
work for ruffs."

" Twelve tooth cloths, with the
Spanish stitch, edged with gold and
silver bone lace."—*Ibid.* Eliz. 5 & 6.

The Spanish stitch appears in France
with Henry II., 1557. " Pour la façon
d'ung gaban avec ung grant collet
chamarrez à l'Espaignolle de passement
blanc," etc.—*Comptes de l'Argentier
du Roy.* Archives Nat. K. K. 106.

[33] Taylor, the Water Poet, *Katharine of Aragon.*

[34] The industry of Henry's last queen
was as great as that of his first. Specimens still exist at Sizergh Castle,
Westmoreland, of Katharine Parr's
needlework—a counterpane and a toilet
cover. An astrologer, who cast her
nativity, foretold she would be a queen ;
so when a child, on her mother requiring her to work, she would exclaim, " My
hands are ordained to touch crowns
and sceptres, not needles and spindles."

are too well known to require notice. In her letters are constant demands for silk and other working materials wherewith to solace her long captivity. She had also studied under Catherine de Médicis, herself an unrivalled needle-woman, who had brought over in her train from Florence the designer for embroidery, Frederick Vinciolo. Assembling her daughters, Claude, Elizabeth and Margaret, with Mary Stuart, and her Guise cousins, " elle passoit," says Brantôme, " fort son temps les apres-disnées à besogner apres ses ouvrages de soye, où elle estoit tant parfaicte qu'il estoit possible." [35] The ability of Reine Margot [36] is sung by Ronsard, who exalts her as imitating Pallas in the art. [37]

Many of the great houses in England are storehouses of old needlework. Hatfield, Penshurst, and Knole are all filled with the handiwork of their ladies. The Countess of Shrews-bury, better known as " Building Bess," Bess of Hardwick, found time to embroider furniture for her palaces, and her samplar patterns hang to this day on their walls.

Needlework was the daily employment of the convent. As early as the fourteenth century [38] it was termed " nun's work "; and even now, in secluded parts of the kingdom, ancient lace is styled by that name. [39]

Nor does the occupation appear to have been solely

---

[35] *Dames Illustres.*

[36] The " Reine des Marguerites," the learned sister of Francis I., was not less accomplished with her needle, and entries for working materials appear in her accounts up to the year of her death, 1549.

" Trois marcs d'or et d'argent fournis par Jehan Danes, pour servir aux ouvraiges de la dicte dame."—*Livre de dépenses de Marguerite d'Angoulême,* par le Comte de la Ferrière-Percy. Paris, 1862.

[37] " Elle addonoit son courage
A faire maint bel ouvrage
Dessus la toile, et encor
A joindre la soye et l'or.
Vous d'un pareil exercice
Mariez par artifice
Dessus la toile en maint trait
L'or et la soie en pourtrait."
—*Ode à la Royne de Navarre,* liv. ii., od. vii.

[38] 1380. " Œuvre de nonnain."—*Inventaire de Charles V.*

[39] " My grandmother, who had other lace, called this " (some needlepoint) " nun's work."—*Extract from a letter from the Isle of Man,* 1862.

" A butcher's wife showed Miss O—— a piece of Alençon point, which she called ' nun's work.' "—*Extract from a letter from Scotland,* 1863.

1698, May. In the *London Gazette,* in the advertisement of a sale by auction, among other " rich goods," we find " nun's work," but the term here probably applies to netting, for in the *Protestant Post Boy* of March 15th, 1692, is advertised as lost " A nun's work purse wrought with gold thread."

1763. In the *Edinburgh Advertiser* appears, " Imported from the Grand Canaries, into Scotland, nun's work."

confined to women. We find monks commended for their skill in embroidery,[40] and in the frontispieces of some of the early pattern books of the sixteenth century, men are represented working at frames, and these books are stated to have been written " for the profit of men as well as of women."[41] Many were composed by monks,[42] and in the library [43] of St. Geneviève at Paris, are several works of this class, inherited from the monastery of that name. As these books contain little or no letterpress, they could scarcely have been collected by the monks unless with a view to using them.

At the dissolution of the monasteries, the ladies of the great Roman Catholic families came to the rescue. Of the widow of the ill-fated Earl of Arundel it is recorded : " Her gentlewomen and chambermaids she ever busied in works ordained for the service of the Church. She permitted none to be idle at any time." [44]

Instructions in the art of embroidery were now at a premium. The old nuns had died out, and there were none to replace them.

Mrs. Hutchinson, in her *Memoirs*, enumerates, among the eight tutors she had at seven years of age, one for needlework, while Hannah Senior, about the same period, entered the service of the Earl of Thomond, to teach his daughters the use of their needle, with the salary of £200 a year. The money, however, was never paid ; so she petitions the Privy Council for leave to sue him.[45]

When, in 1614, the King of Siam applied to King James for an English wife, a gentleman of " honourable parentage " offers his daughter, whom he describes of excellent parts for " music, her needle, and good discourse." [46] And these are the sole accomplishments he mentions. The bishops, however,

---

[40] As, for instance, " the imbrothering " of the monks of the monastery of Wolstrope, in Lincolnshire.

[41] *Livre de Lingerie.* Dom. de Sera, 1581. " Donne, donzelle, con gli huomini." — Taglienti, 1530. Patterns which " les Seigneurs, Dames, et Damoiselles ont eu pour agréables."— Vinciolo, 1587.

[42] Jehan Mayol, carme de Lyon ; Fra Hieronimo, dell' Ordine dei Servi ; Père Dominique, religieux carme, and others.

[43] One in the Bibliothèque Impériale is from the " Monasterio St. Germani à Pratis."

[44] He died in 1595. *Lives of the Earl and Countess of Arundel,* from the original MS. by the Duke of Norfolk. London, 1857.

[45] P. R. O. Calendar of State Papers. Domestic. Charles I. Vol. clxix. 12.

[46] P. R. O. Calendar of State Papers. Colonial. No. 789.

PLATE I.

ARGENTAN.—Showing buttonhole stitched
réseau and "brides bouclées."

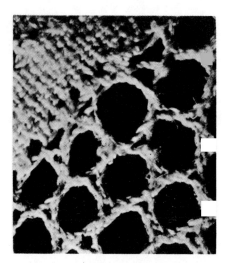

CIRCULAR BOBBIN RÉSEAU.—Variety
of Mechlin.

VENETIAN NEEDLE-POINT.
Portions of lace very much enlarged to show details of stitches.

PLATE II.

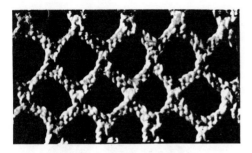

ITALIAN BOBBIN RÉSEAU.

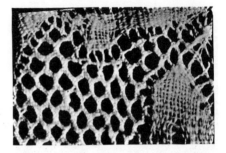

SIX-POINTED STAR-MESHED BOBBIN RÉSEAU.
—Variety of Valenciennes.

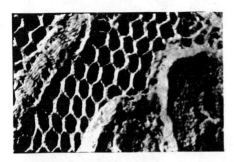

BRUSSELS BOBBIN RÉSEAU.

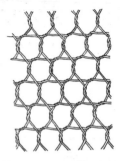

FOND CHANT OF CHANTILLY
AND POINT DE PARIS.

Valenciennes.   Lille.   Toilé.

DETAILS OF BOBBIN RÉSEAU AND TOILÉ.

Alençon réseau.

DETAILS OF NEEDLE RÉSEAU AND BUTTONHOLE STITCHES.

Portions of lace very much enlarged to show details of stitches.

shocked at the proceeding, interfered, and put an end to the projected alliance.

No ecclesiastical objection, however, was made to the epitaph of Catherine Sloper—she sleeps in the cloisters of Westminster Abbey, 1620 :—

" Exquisite at her needle."

Till a very late date, we have ample record of the esteem in which this art was held.

In the days of the Commonwealth, Mrs. Walker is described to have been as well skilled in needlework " as if she had been brought up in a convent." She kept, however, a gentlewoman for teaching her daughters.

Evelyn, again, praises the talent of his daughter, Mrs. Draper. " She had," writes he, " an extraordinary genius for whatever hands could do with a needle."

The queen of Charles I. and the wives of the younger Stuarts seem to have changed the simple habits of their royal predecessors, for when Queen Mary, in her Dutch simplicity, sat for hours at the knotted fringe, her favourite employment, Bishop Burnet, her biographer, adds, " It was a strange thing to see a queen work for so many hours a day," and her homely habits formed a never-ending subject of ridicule for the wit of Sir Charles Sedley.[47]

From the middle of the last century, or rather apparently from the French Revolution, the more artistic style of needle-work and embroidery fell into decadence. The simplicity of male costume rendered it a less necessary adjunct to female or, indeed, male education. However, two of the greatest generals of the Republic, Hoche and Moreau, followed the employment of embroidering satin waistcoats long after they had entered the military service. We may look upon the art now as almost at an end.

---

[47] See his epigram, " The Royal Knotter," about the queen,

" Who, when she rides in coach abroad
Is always knotting threads."

CHAPTER II.

CUT-WORK.

"These workes belong chiefly to gentlewomen to passe away their time in vertuous exercises."

"Et lors, sous vos lacis à mille fenestrages
    Raiseuls et poinct couppés et tous vos clairs ouvrages."
                                        —*Jean Godard*, 1588.

It is from that open-work embroidery which in the sixteenth century came into such universal use that we must derive the origin of lace, and, in order to work out the subject, trace it through all its gradations.

This embroidery, though comprising a wide variety of decoration, went by the general name of cut-work.

The fashion of adorning linen has prevailed from the earliest times. Either the edges were worked with close embroidery—the threads drawn and fashioned with a needle in various forms—or the ends of the cloth unravelled and plaited with geometric precision.

To judge from the description of the linen grave-clothes of St. Cuthbert,[1] as given by an eye-witness to his disinterment in the twelfth century, they were ornamented in a manner similar to that we have described. "There had been," says the chronicler, "put over him a sheet . . . this sheet had a fringe of linen thread of a finger's length; upon its sides and ends were woven a border of projecting workmanship fabricated of the thread itself, bearing the figures of birds and beasts so arranged that between every two pairs there were interwoven among them the representation of a branching tree which divides the figures. This tree, so tastefully depicted, appears to be putting forth its

---

[1] Translated from the *Libellus de Admirandis beati Cuthberti Miraculis* of Reginald, monk of Durham, by Rev. J. Rain. Durham, 1855.

leaves," etc. There can be no doubt that this sheet, for many centuries preserved in the cathedral church of Durham, was a specimen of cut-work, which, though later it came into general use, was, at an early period of our history, alone used for ecclesiastical purposes, and an art which was, till the dissolution of monasteries, looked upon as a church secret.

Though cut-work is mentioned in Hardyng's *Chronicle*,[2] when describing the luxury in King Richard II.'s reign, he says :—

> " Cut werke was greate both in court and townes,
> Both in menes hoddis and also in their gownes,"

yet this oft-quoted passage, no more than that of Chaucer, in which he again accuses the priests of wearing gowns of scarlet and green colours ornamented with cut-work, can scarcely be received as evidence of this mode of decoration being in general use. The royal wardrobe accounts of that day contain no entries on the subject. It applies rather to the fashion of cutting out[3] pieces of velvet or other materials, and sewing them down to the garment with a braid like ladies' work of the present time. Such garments were in general use, as the inventories of mediæval times fully attest.

The linen shirt or smock was the special object of adornment, and on the decoration of the collar and sleeves much time and ingenuity were expended.

In the ancient ballad of "Lord Thomas,"[4] the fair Annette cries :—

> " My maids, gae to my dressing-room,
> And dress me in my smock ;
> The one half is o' the Holland fine,
> The other o' needlework."

Chaucer, too, does not disdain to describe the embroidery of a lady's smock—

> " White was her smocke, embrouded all before
> And eke behynde, on her colar aboute,
> Of cole blacke sylke, within and eke without."

The sums expended on the decoration of this most necessary article of dress sadly excited the wrath of

---

[2] *Chronicle of John Hardyng*, circ. 1470.

[3] Temp. Rich. II. In their garments " so much pouncing of chesell to make holes, so much dragging (zigzagging) of sheers," etc.—*Good Parson*, Chaucer.

[4] Percy, *Reliques of Ancient Poetry*, vol. iii.

Stubbes, who thus vents his indignation : " These shirtes (sometymes it happeneth) are wrought throughout with needlework of silke, and such like, and curiously stitched with open seame, and many other knackes besides, more than I can describe ; in so much, I have heard of shirtes that have cost some ten shillynges, some twenty, some forty, some five pounds, some twenty nobles, and (which is horrible to heare) some ten pound a pece." [5]

Up to the time of Henry VIII. the shirt was " pynched " or plaited—

> " Come nere with your shirtes bordered and displayed,
>   In foarme of surplois." [6]

These,[7] with handkerchiefs,[8] sheets, and pillow-beres,[9] (pillow-cases), were embroidered with silks of various

---

[5] *Anatomie of Abuses*, by Philip Stubbes, 1583.

[6] *The Shyp of Folys of the Worlde*, translated out of Latin by Alex. Barclay, 1508.

[7] The inventories of all nations abound in mention of these costly articles. The "smocks" of Katharine of Aragon "for to lay in," were wrought about the collar with gold and silk. Lord Monteagle, 1523, had " two fine smocks of cambric wrought with gold." (Inv. P. R. O.) Among the New Year's Gifts offered to Queen Mary Tudor by the Duchess of Somerset (1556), we find a smock wrought over with silk, and collar and ruffles of damask, gold purl, and silver. Again, in the household expenses of Marguerite de France, 1545, we find a charge of " 4 livres 12 sols, pour une garniture de chemise ouvré de soye cramoisie pour madicte dame."—(Bib. Imp. MSS. Fonds François, 10,394.) About the same date (G. W. A. Eliz. 1 & 2, 1558–59) appear charges for lengthening one smocke of drawne work, 20s. Six white smockes edged with white needlework lace, 10s. To overcasting and edging 4 smockes of drawn work with ruffs, wristbands, and collars, three of them with black work, and three of them with red, etc. At the funeral of Henry II. of France, 1559, the effigy was described as attired

in " une chemise de toile de Hollande, bordée au col et aux manches d'ouvraige fort excellent."—Godefroy, *Le Céré-monial de France*, 1610.

[8] See FRANCE.

[9] The pillow-bere has always been an object of luxury, a custom not yet extinct in France, where the "taies d'oreiller, brodées aux armes," and trimmed with a rich point, form an important feature in a modern trousseau. In the inventory of Margaret of Austria, the gentle governess of the Low Countries, are noted—

" Quatre toyes d'oraillers ouvrées d'or et de soye cramoysie et de verde.

" Autres quatres toyes d'oraillers faites et ouvrées d'or et de soye bleu à losanges qui ont estées données à Madame par dom Diego de Cabrera." —*Corr. de l'Empereur Maximilien I. et de Marguerite d'Autriche*, par M. Leglay. Paris, 1839.

Edward VI. has (Harl. MSS. 1419) " 18 pillow-beres of hollande with brode seams of silk of sundry coloured needlework." And again, " One pillow-bere of fine hollande wrought with a brode seam of Venice gold and silver, and silk nedlework."

And Lady Zouche presents Queen Elizabeth, as a New Year's gift, with " One pair of pillow-beares of Holland work, wrought with black silk drawne work."—Nichol's *Royal Progresses*.

colours, until the fashion gradually gave place to cut-work, which, in its turn, was superseded by lace.

The description of the widow of John Whitcomb, a wealthy clothier of Newbury, in Henry VIII.'s reign, when she laid aside her weeds, is the first notice we have of cut-work being in general use. "She came," says the writer, "out of the kitchen in a fair train gown stuck full of silver pins, having a white cap upon her head, with cuts of curious needlework, the same an apron, white as the driven snow."

We are now arrived at the Renaissance, a period when so close a union existed between the fine arts and manufactures; when the most trifling object of luxury, instead of being consigned to the vulgar taste of the mechanic, received from artists their most graceful inspirations. Embroidery profited by the general impulse, and books of designs were composed for that species which, under the general name of cut-work, formed the great employment for the women of the day. The volume most generally circulated, especially among the ladies of the French court, for whose use it was designed, is that of the Venetian Vinciolo, to whom some say, we know not on what authority, Catherine de Médicis granted, in 1585, the exclusive privilege of making and selling the *collerettes gaudronnées* [10] she had herself introduced. This work, which passed through many editions, dating from 1587 to 1623, is entitled, "Les singuliers et nouveaux pourtraicts et ouvrages de Lingerie. Servans de patrons à faire toutes sortes de poincts, couppé, Lacis & autres. Dedié à la Royne. Nouvellement inventez, au proffit et contentement des nobles Dames et Demoiselles & autres gentils esprits, amateurs d'un tel art. Par le Seigneur Federic de Vinciolo Venitien. A Paris. Par Jean le Clerc le jeune, etc., 1587."

Two little figures, representing ladies in the costume of the period, with working-frames in their hands, decorate the title-page.[11]

The work is in two books: the first of Point Coupé, or

---

[10] *Goderonné — goudronné*, incorrectly derived from pitch (*goudron*), has no relation to stiffness or starch, but is used to designate the fluted pattern so much in vogue in the sixteenth century—the "gadrooned" edge of silversmiths.

1588. Il avait une fraise empesée et godronnée à gros godrons, au bout de laquelle il y avoit de belle et grande dentelle, les manchettes estoient goudronnées de mesme.

[11] They are introduced into the Title page of this work.

rich geometric patterns, printed in white upon a black ground
(Fig. 2) ; the second of Lacis, or subjects in squares (Fig. 3),
with counted stitches, like the patterns for worsted-work of
the present day—the designs, the seven planets, Neptune,
and various squares, borders, etc.

Vinciolo dedicates his book to Louise de Vaudemont,
the neglected Queen of Henry III., whose portrait, with that
of the king, is added to the later editions.

Various other pattern-books had already been published.

Fig. 2.

POINT COUPÉ.—(Vinciolo.)

The earliest bearing a date is one printed at Cologne in
1527.[12]

These books are scarce ; being designed for patterns, and
traced with a metal style, or pricked through, many perished
in the using. They are much sought after by the collector
as among the early specimens of wood-block printing. We
give therefore in the Appendix a list of those we find recorded,
or of which we have seen copies, observing that the
greater number, though generally composed for one particular
art, may be applied indifferently to any kind of ornamental
work.

Cut-work was made in several manners. The first

---

[12] See APPENDIX.

·consisted in arranging a network of threads upon a small frame, crossing and interlacing them into various complicated patterns. Beneath this network was gummed a piece of fine ·cloth, called quintain,[13] from the town in Brittany where

Fig. 3.

LACIS.—(Vinciolo. *Edition* 1588.)

Ce Pelican contient en longueur 70 mailles et en hauteur 65.

it was made. Then, with a needle, the network was sewn to the quintain by edging round those parts of the pattern that were to remain thick. The last operation was to cut away the superfluous cloth ; hence the name of cut-work.

The author of the *Consolations aux Dames*, 1620, in

---

[13] " Quintain, quintin, French lawne." Randle Cotgrave. *Dictionarie of the French and English tongues.* 1611.

" 26 virges de Kanting pro sudariis pro ille 47/8."—*G. W. A. Charles II.,* 1683-4.

addressing the ladies, thus specially alludes to the custom
of working on quintain :—

> "Vous n'employiez les soirs et les matins
> A façonner vos grotesques quaintains,
> O folle erreur—O despence excessive."

Again, the pattern was made without any linen at all ;
threads, radiating at equal distances from one common
centre, served as a framework to others which were united to
them in squares, triangles, rosettes, and other geometric
forms, worked over with button-hole stitch (*point noué*),
forming in some parts open-work, in others a heavy
compact embroidery.   In this class may be placed the old
conventual cut-work of Italy, generally termed Greek lace,
and that of extraordinary fineness and beauty which is
assigned to Venice. Distinct from all these geometric
combinations was the lacis [14] of the sixteenth century, done
on a network ground (*réseau*), identical with the *opus
araneum* or spider-work of continental writers, the "darned
netting" or modern *filet brodé à reprises* of the French
embroiderers.

The ground consisted of a network of square meshes,
on which was worked the pattern, sometimes cut out of
linen and appliqué,[15] but more usually darned with stitches
like tapestry.   This darning-work was easy of execution, and
the stitches being regulated by counting the meshes,[16]
effective geometric patterns could be produced. Altar-cloths,
baptismal napkins, as well as bed coverlets and table-cloths,
were decorated with these squares of net embroidery. In the
Victoria and Albert Museum there are several gracefully-

---

[14] Lacis, espèce d'ouvrage de fil ou
de soie fait en forme de filet ou de
réseuil dont les brins étaient entre-
lacez les uns dans les autres.—*Dict.
d'Ant. Furetière*, 1684.

[15] Béle Prerie contenant différentes
sortes de lettres, etc., pour appliquer
sur le réseuil ou lassis. Paris, 1601.
See APPENDIX.

[16] So, in the Epistle to the Reader,
in a Pattern-book for Cut-works (London, J. Wolfe & Edward White, 1591),
the author writes of his designs :—

"All which devises are soe framed
in due proportion as taking them in
order the one is formed or made by
the other, and soe proceedeth forward ;
whereby with more ease they may be
sewed and wrought in cloth, and keeping true accompt of the threads, maintaine the bewtey of the worke. And
more, who desyreth to bring the work
into a lesser forme, let them make the
squares lesse. And if greater, then
inlarge them, and so may you worke
in divers sortes, either by stitch, pouncing or pouldering upon the same as
you please. Alsoe it is to be understood
that these squares serve not only for
cut-workes, but alsoe for all other
manner of seweing or stitching."—(See
APPENDIX, No. 72).

designed borders to silk table-covers in this work, made both of white and coloured threads, and of silk of various shades. The ground, as we learn from a poem on lacis, affixed to the pattern-book of " Milour Mignerak,"[1] was made by beginning a single stitch, and increasing a stitch on each side until the required size was obtained. If a strip or long border was to be made, the netting was continued to its prescribed length, and then finished off by reducing a stitch on each side till it was decreased to one, as garden nets are made at the present day.

This plain netted ground was called *réseau, rézel, rézeuil,*[18] and was much used for bed-curtains, vallances, etc.

In the inventory of Mary Stuart, made at Fotheringay,[19] we find, " Le lict d'ouvrage à rezel"; and again, under the care of Jane Kennethee, the " Furniture of a bedd of network and Holland intermixed, not yet finished."

When the *réseau* was decorated with a pattern, it was termed *lacis*, or darned netting, the Italian *punto ricamato a maglia quadra*, and, combined with *point-coupé*, was much used for bed-furniture. It appears to have been much employed for church-work,[20] for the sacred emblems. The Lamb and the Pelican are frequently represented.[21]

---

[17] *Pratique de l'aiguille industrieuse du très excellent Milour Matthias Mignerak*, etc. Paris, 1605. See APPENDIX.

[18] The inventories of Charles de Bourbon, ob. 1613, with that of his wife, the Countess of Soissons, made after her death, 1644 (Bib. Nat. MSS. F. Fr. 11,426), alone prove how much this *réseuil* was in vogue for furniture during the seventeenth century.

" Item un pavillon de thoille de lin à bende de reseuil blang et noir faict par carel prisé, vi. l. t. (livres tournois).

"Item quatre pentes de ciel de cotton blanc à carreaux.

" Item trois pentes de ciel de thoille de lin à carreaux et raiseuil recouvert avec le dossier pareil estoffe, et petit carreau à point couppé garny de leur frange, le fonds du ciel de thoille de lin, trois custodes et une bonne grace et un drap pareille thoille de lin à bandes de reseuil recouvert . . . prisé xviii. l. t."—*Inv. de Charles de Bourbon.*

" Item une autre tapisserie de rezeuil de thoile blanche en huit pièces contenant ensemble vingt aulnes on environ sur deux aulnes trois quarts de haute.

"Item une autre tenture de tapisserie de rézeau tout de leine (lin) appliquée sur de la toille blanche en sept pièces contenant dix-huit aulnes de cours sur trois aulnes de haute.

" Item trois pantes, fonds de dossier, les deux fourreaux de piliers, la converture de parade, le tout en point couppé et toillé.

"Item, une garniture de lict blanc, faict par carré d'ouvrage de poinct couppé, le tout garny avec la couverte de parade, prisé la somme de soixante livres tournois."—*Inv. de la Comtesse de Soissons.*

[19] Dated 20 Feb., 1587. Now in the Record Office, Edinburgh.

[20] 1781. " Dix-huit Pales de differentes grandeurs, tous de toile garnis tant de petite dentelle que de filet brodé."—*Inv. de l'Eglise de S. Gervais.* Arch. Nat. L.L. 654.

[21] *Point and Pillow Lace*, by A. M. S. (London, 1899).

In the inventory of Sir John Foskewe (modern Fortescue),. Knight, time of Henry VIII., we find in the hall, "A hanging of green saye, bordered with darning."

Queen Mary Stuart, previous to the birth of James I. (1560), made a will, which still exists,[22] with annotations in her own handwriting. After disposing of her jewels and objects of value, she concludes by bequeathing "tous mes ouvrages masches et collets aux 4 Maries, à Jean Stuart, et Marie Sunderland, et toutes les filles";—"masches,"[23] with *punti a maglia*, being among the numerous terms applied to this species of work.

These "ouvrages masches" were doubtless the work of Queen Mary and her ladies. She had learned the art at the French court, where her sister-in-law, Reine Margot, herself also a prisoner for many life-long years, appears to have occupied herself in the same manner, for we find in her accounts,[24] "Pour des moulles et esguilles pour faire rezeuil la somme de iiii. L. tourn." And again, "Pour avoir monté une fraize neufve de reseul la somme de X. sols tourn."

Catherine de Médicis had a bed draped with squares of reseuil or lacis, and it is recorded that "the girls and servants of her household consumed much time in making squares of reseuil." The inventory of her property and goods includes a coffer containing three hundred and eighty-one of such squares unmounted, whilst in another were found five hundred and thirty-eight squares, some worked with rosettes or with blossoms, and others with nosegays.[25]

Though the work of Milour Mignerak, already quoted, is dedicated to the Trés-Chrestienne Reine de France et de Navarre, Marie de Médicis, and bears her cipher and arms, yet in the decorated frontispiece is a cushion with a piece of lacis in progress, the pattern a daisy looking at the sun, the favourite impresa of her predecessor, the divorced Marguerite, now, by royal ordinance, "Marguerite Reine,. Duchesse de Valois." (Fig. 4.)

These pattern-books being high in price and difficult to procure, teachers of the art soon caused the various patterns

---

[22] In the Record Office, Edinburgh.

[23] "Mache, the Masches (meshes) or holes of a net between the thread and thread (Cotgrave).

[24] *Comptes de la Reine de Navarre,*. 1577. Arch. Nat. K.K. 162.

[25] *Inventory of Catherine de Médicis,* Bonaffé.

PLATE III.

Altar or Table Cloth of fine linen embroidered with gold thread, laid, and in satin stitches on both sides. The cut out spaces are filled with white thread needle-point lace. The edging is alternated of white and gold thread needle-point lace. Probably Italian. Late sixteenth century.—Victoria and Albert Museum.

Fig. 5.

ELIZABETHAN SAMPLER.

to be reproduced in "samcloths,"[26] as samplars were then termed, and young ladies worked at them diligently as a proof of their competency in the arts of cut-work, lacis and réseuil, much as a dame-school child did her A B C in the country villages some years ago. Proud mothers caused these *chefs-d'œuvre* of their children to be framed and glazed; hence many have come down to us hoarded up in old families uninjured at the present time. (Fig. 5.)

A most important specimen of lacis was exhibited at the Art International Exhibition of 1874, by Mrs. Hailstone, o Walton Hall, an altar frontal 14 feet by 4 feet, executed in point conté, representing eight scenes from the Passion of

Fig. 4.

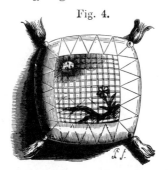

IMPRESA OF QUEEN MARGARET OF NAVARRE IN LACIS.—(Mignerak.)

Christ, in all fifty-six figures, surrounded by Latin inscriptions. It is assumed to be of English workmanship.

Some curious pieces of ancient lacis were also exhibited (*circ.* 1866) at the Museum of South Kensington by Dr. Bock, of Bonn. Among others, two specimens of coloured silk network, the one ornamented with small embroidered shields and crosses (Fig. 6), the other with the mediæval gammadion pattern (Fig. 7). In the same collection was a towel or altar-cloth of ancient German work—a coarse net ground, worked over with the lozenge pattern.[27]

---

[26] Randle Holme, in *The School Mistris Terms of Art for all her Ways of Sewing*, has "A Samcloth, vulgarly, a Samplar."

[27] In the Bock collection, part of which has since been bought for the Victoria and Albert Museum, are specimens of "rézeuil d'or," or network with patterns worked in with gold thread and coloured silks. Such were the richly-wrought "serviettes sur filez d'or" of Margaret of Austria.

"Autre servyette de Cabes (Cadiz) ouvrée d'or, d'argent sur fillez et bordée d'or et de gris.

"Autre serviette à Cabes de soye grise et verde à ouvrage de fillez bordée d'une tresse de verd et gris."—Inventory already quoted.

But most artistic of all was a large ecclesiastical piece, some three yards in length. The design portrays the Apostles, with angels and saints. These two last-mentioned objects are of the sixteenth century.

When used for altar-cloths, bed-curtains, or coverlets, to produce a greater effect it was the custom to alternate the lacis with squares of plain linen.

> "An apron set with many a dice
> Of needlework sae rare,
> Wove by nae hand, as ye may guess,
> Save that of Fairly fair."
> Ballad of Hardyknute.

This work formed the great delight of provincial ladies in

Fig. 6.   Fig. 7.

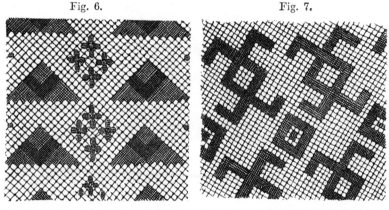

"SPIDERWORK," THIRTEENTH CENTURY.—(Bock   "SPIDERWORK," FOURTEENTH CENTURY.—(Bock
  Coll. South Kensington Museum).   Coll. South Kensington Museum.)

France. Jean Godard, in his poem on the Glove,[28] alluding to this occupation, says :—

> ' Une femme gantée œuvre en tapisserie
> En raizeaux deliez et toute lingerie
> Elle file—elle coud et fait passement
> De toutes les fassons . . . ."

The armorial shield of the family, coronets, monograms, the beasts of the Apocalypse, with fleurs-de-lys, sacrés cœurs, for the most part adorned those pieces destined for the use of the Church. If, on the other hand, intended for a pall, death's-heads, cross-bones and tears, with the sacramental cup, left no doubt of the destination of the article.

---

[28] " Le Gan," de Jean Godard, Parisien, 1588.

As late as 1850, a splendid cut-work pall still covered the coffins of the fishers when borne in procession through the streets of Dieppe. It is said to have been a votive offering worked by the hands of some lady saved from shipwreck, and presented as a memorial of her gratitude.

In 1866, when present at a peasant's wedding in the church of St. Lo (Dép. Manche), the author observed that the " toile d'honneur," which is always held extended over the heads of the married pair while the priest pronounces the blessing, was of the finest cut-work, trimmed with lace.

Both in the north and south of Europe the art still lingers on. Swedish housewives pierce and stitch the holiday collars of their husbands and sons, and careful ladies, drawing the threads of the fine linen sheets destined for the " guest-chamber," produce an ornament of geometric design.

Scarce fifty years since, an expiring relic of this art might be sometimes seen on the white smock-frock of the English labourer, which, independent of elaborate stitching, was enriched with an insertion of cut-work, running from the collar to the shoulder crossways, like that we see decorating the surplices of the sixteenth century.

Drawn-thread embroidery is another cognate work. The material in old drawn-work is usually loosely-woven linen. Certain threads were drawn out from the linen ground, and others left, upon and between which needlework was made. Its employment in the East dates from very early times, and withdrawing threads from a fabric is perhaps referred to in Lucan's *Pharsalia* :—[29]

> " Candida Sidonio perlucent pectora filo,
> Quod Nilotis acus compressum pectine Serum
> Solvit, et extenso laxavit stamina velo."

" Her white breasts shine through the Sidonian fabric, which pressed down with the comb (or sley) of the Seres, the needle of the Nile workman has separated, and has loosened the warp by stretching out (or withdrawing) the weft."

---

[29] Descriptive Catalogue of the in the South Kensington Museum Collections of Tapestry and Embroidery (p. 5).

CHAPTER III.

LACE.

" Je demandai de la dentelle .
Voici le tulle de Bruxelles,
La blonde, le point d'Alençon,
Et la Maline, si légère ;
L'application d'Angleterre
(Qui se fait à Paris, dit-on) ;
Voici la guipure indigène,
Et voici la Valenciennes,
Le point d'esprit, et le point de Paris ;
Bref les dentelles
Les plus nouvelles
Que produisent tous les pays."
Le Palais des Dentelles (Rothomago).

LACE [1] is defined as a plain or ornamental network, wrought
of fine threads of gold, silver, silk, flax, or cotton, interwoven, to which may be added " poil de chèvre," and also
the fibre of the aloe, employed by the peasants of Italy and
Spain. The term *lacez* rendered in the English translation
of the Statutes [2] as " laces," implying braids, such as were
used for uniting the different parts of the dress, appears
long before lace, properly so called, came into use. The
earlier laces, such as they were, were defined by the word
" passament " [3]—a general term for gimps and braids, as
well as for lace. Modern industry has separated these two
classes of work, but their being formerly so confounded
renders it difficult in historic researches to separate one
from the other.

The same confusion occurs in France, where the first lace
was called *passement*, because it was applied to the same

---

[1] Lace. French, *dentelle ;* German,
Spitzen ; Italian, *merletto, trina ;*
Genoa, *pizzo ;* Spanish, *encaje ;*
Dutch, *kanten.*

[2] Statute 3 Edw. IV. c. iii.
[3] " Passement, a lace or lacing."—
Cotgrave.

PLATE IV.

FAN MADE AT BURANO AND PRESENTED TO QUEEN ELENA OF ITALY ON HER MARRIAGE, 1896.
Photo by the Burano School.

PLATE V.

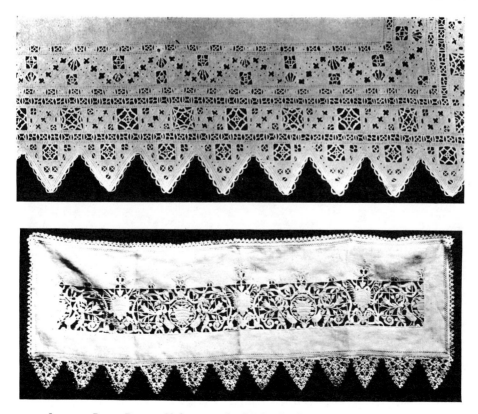

ITALIAN. PUNTO REALE.—Modern reproduction by the Society Æmilia Ars, Bologna.
Photo by the Society.

PLATE VI.

ITALIAN.—Modern reproduction at Burano of Point de Venise à la feuille et la rose, of seventeenth century.
Width, 8 in. Photo by the Burano School.

PLATE VII.

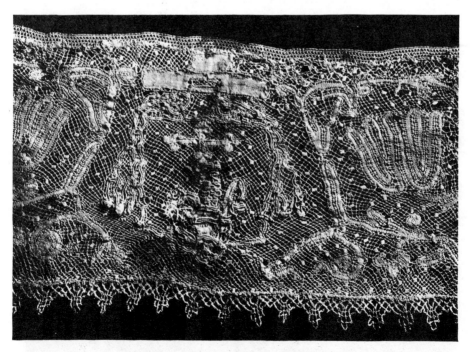

Heraldic (carnival lace), was made in Italy. This appears to be a specimen, through the archaic pattern points to a German origin. The réseau is twisted and knotted. *Circ.* 1700.
The Arms are those of a Bishop.
Photo by A. Dryden from private collection.

use, to braid or lay flat over the coats and other garments. The lace trade was entirely in the hands of the "passementiers" of Paris, who were allowed to make all sorts of " passements de dentelle sur l'oreiller aux fuseaux, aux épingles, et à la main, d'or, d'argent, tant fin que faux, de soye, de fil blanc, et de couleur," etc. They therefore applied the same terms to their different products, whatever the material.

The word *passement* continued to be in use till the middle of the seventeenth century, it being specified as " passements aux fuseaux," " passements à l'aiguille"; only it was more specifically applied to lace without an edge.

The term *dentelle* is also of modern date, nor will it be found in the earlier French dictionaries.[4] It was not till fashion caused the passament to be made with a toothed edge that the expression of " passement dentelé" first appears.

In the accounts of Henry II. of France, and his queen, we have frequent notices of " passement jaulne dantellé des deux costez,"[5] " passement de soye incarnat dentellé d'un costé,"[6] etc., etc., but no mention of the word " dentelle." It does, however, occur in an inventory of an earlier date, that of Marguerite de France, sister of Francis I., who, in 1545, paid the sum of vi. livres " pour soixante aulnes, fine dantelle de Florance pour mettre à des colletz."[7]

After a lapse of twenty years and more, among the articles furnished to Mary Stuart in 1567, is " Une pacque de petite dentelle";[8] and this is the sole mention of the word in all her accounts.

---

[4] Not in those of Rob. Estienne, 1549; Frère de l'Aval, 1549 ; or Nicot, 1606. Cotgrave has, " Dentelle, small edging (and indented), bone-lace, or needlework." In Dict de l'Académie, 1694, we find, " Dentelle, sorte de passement à jour et à mailles tres fines ainsi nommé parceque les premières qu'on fit etoient dentelées."

[5] *Comptes de l'Argentier du Roi*, 1557.—Arch. Nat. K. K. 106. " Passement de fine soie noire dentelle d'un costé." " Passement blanc," " grise," also occur.

[6] *Argenterie de la Reine*, 1556.— Arch. Nat. K. K. 118.

[7] *Dépenses de la maison de Madame Marguerite de France, sœur du Roi.*— Bib. Nat. MSS. F. Fr. 10,394, fol. 62.

[8] " Plus de delivré une pacque de petite dentelle qui est estez cousu ensemble pour mettre sur les coutures des rideaux des ditz litz contenant 80 aunes."—Rec. Off., Edin. This custom of trimming the seams of bed-curtains with a lace indented on both sides was common throughout Europe. In the Chartley Inv. of Mary Stuart, 1586, one of the Vasquines (jackets) is described, " Autre de satin noir descouppée a descouppemie dentelés."

We find like entries in the accounts of Henry IV.'s first queen.[9]

Gradually the passement dentelé subsided into the modern dentelle.

Fig. 8.

GRANDE DANTELLE AU POINT DEVANT L'AIGUILLE.—(Montbéliard, 1598.)

It is in a pattern book, published at Montbéliard in 1598,[10] we first find designs for "dantelles." It contains

---

[9] 1577. "Pour deux aulnes de passement d'argent a hautte dantelle pour mettre à ung renvers, au pris de soixante solz l'aulne.

"Pour une aulne de dentelle pour faire deux cornettes pour servir à la dicte dame, quatre livres."—*Cptes. de la Reine de Navarre.* Arch. Nat. K. K. 162.

[10] See APPENDIX.

twenty patterns, of all sizes, "bien petites, petites" (Figs. 9, 10, 11, 12), "moyennes, et grosses" (Fig. 8).

The word *dentelle* seems now in general use; but Vecellio, in his *Corona*, 1592, has "opere a mazette," pillow lace, and Mignerak first gives the novelty of "passements

<table>
<tr>
<td align="center">Fig. 9.</td>
<td align="center">Fig. 10.</td>
</tr>
<tr>
<td>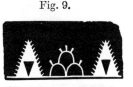</td>
<td></td>
</tr>
<tr>
<td align="center">PETITE DANTELLE.—(1598.)</td>
<td align="center">PETITE DANTELLE.—(1598.)</td>
</tr>
</table>

au fuzeau," pillow lace (Fig. 13), for which Vinciolo, in his edition of 1623, also furnishes patterns (Figs. 14 and 15); and Parasoli, 1616, gives designs for "merli a piombini" (Fig. 16).

In the inventory of Henrietta Maria, dated 1619,[11]

<table>
<tr>
<td align="center">Fig. 11.</td>
<td align="center">Fig. 12.</td>
</tr>
<tr>
<td colspan="2"></td>
</tr>
<tr>
<td align="center">PETITE DANTELLE.—(1598.)</td>
<td align="center">PETITE DANTELLE.—(1598.)</td>
</tr>
</table>

appear a variety of laces, all qualified under the name of "passement"; and in that of the Maréchal La Motte, 1627, we find the term applied to every description of lace.

---

[11] "Petits et grands passements; id. à l'esguille; id. faict au mestier; id. de Flandres à poinctes; id. orangé à jour; id. de Flandres satiné;" with "reseuil, dantelles, grandes et petites, or, argent," etc.—*Inv. de Madame, sœur du Roi.* Arch. Nat. K. K. 234.

So late as 1645, in the inventory of the church of St. Médard at Paris (Arch de l'Emp. L. L. 858), the word is used. We find, "Quatre tours de chaire de thoille baptiste, ung beau surplis pour le predicateur, six autres, cinq corporaulx," all "à grand passement." Also, "deux petits corporaulx à petit passement," and "trois tours de chaire garnyz de grand passement à dentelle."

" Item, quatre paires de manchettes garnyes de passement, tant de Venise, Gennes, et de Malines." [12]

Lace consists of two parts, the ground and the pattern.

The plain ground is styled in French *entoilage*, on account of its containing the flower or ornament, which is called *toilé*, from the flat close texture resembling linen, and also from its being often made of that material or of muslin.

The honeycomb network or ground, in French *fond*,

PASSEMENT AU FUSEAU.—(Mignerak, 1605.)   [PASSEMENT AU FUSEAU.—(Vinciolo, *Edition* 1623.)

champ,[13] *réseau*, *treille*, is of various kinds : wire ground, Brussels ground, trolly ground, etc., *fond clair*, *fond double*, etc.

---

[12] *Inv. apres le decès de Mgr. le Maréchal de La Motte.*—Bib. Nat. MSS. F. Fr. 11,426.

[13] The French terms are more comprehensive :—

Champ, fond travaillé à jour.

Toilé, fleurs entièrement remplies, formant un tissu sans jour.

Grillé, grillage, plein. Also flowers —but distinguished from toilé by having little square spaces between the thread (*grillé*, grating), the work not being so compact.

" On appelle couleuvre, une blond dont le toilé continue serpente entre deux rangs de grillage."—*Roland de la Platière* (the Girondin). Art. Dentelle, *Encyclopédie Méthodique.* Paris, 1780.

Some laces, points and guipures are not worked upon a ground; the flowers are connected by irregular threads overcast (buttonhole stitch), and sometimes worked over with pearl loops (picot). Such are the points of Venice and Spain and most of the guipures. To these uniting threads, called by our lace-makers "pearl ties"—old Randle Holme[14] styles them "coxcombs"—the Italians give the name of "legs," the French that of "brides."[15]

The flower, or ornamental pattern, is either made together with the ground, as in Valenciennes or Mechlin, or separately,

Fig. 15.

Fig. 16.

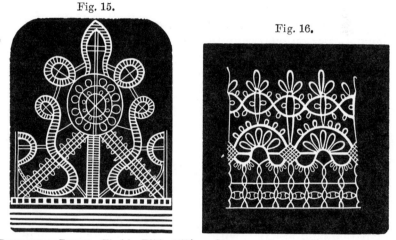

PASSEMENT AU FUSEAU.—(Vinciolo, *Edition* 1623.)   MERLETTI A PIOMBINI.—(Parasole, 1616.)

and then either worked in or sewn on (appliqué), as in Brussels.

The open-work stitches introduced into the pattern are called *modes, jours;* by our Devonshire workers, "fillings."

All lace is terminated by two edges, the pearl, picot,[16] or couronne—a row of little points at equal distances, and the footing or *engrêlure*—a narrow lace, which serves to keep the stitches of the ground firm, and to sew the lace to the garment upon which it is to be worn.

---

[14] *Storehouse of Armory and Blason.* 1688.

[15] "Brides—petits tissus de fil qui servent à joindre les fleurs les unes avec les autres dans l'espèce de dentelle qu'on appelle Point de France, de Venise, de Malines."—*Dict de l'Académie.*

[16] "Une robe et tablier, garnis d'une dentelle d'Angleterre à picot."—*Inv. de décès de la Duchesse de Bourbon.* Arch. Nat. X. 10,064.

Lace is divided into point and pillow (or more correctly bobbin) lace. The term pillow gives rise to misconceptions, as it is impossible to define the distinction between the " cushion " used for some needle-laces and the " pillow " of bobbin-lace. The first is made by the needle on a parchment pattern, and termed needle-point, *point à l'aiguille, punto in aco.*

The word is sometimes incorrectly applied to pillow-lace, as point de Malines, point de Valenciennes, etc.

Point also means a particular kind of stitch, as point de Paris,[17] point de neige, point d'esprit,[18] point à la Reine, point à carreaux, à chaînette, etc.

" Cet homme est bien en points," was a term used to denote a person who wore rich laces.[19]

The mention of point de neige recalls the quarrel of Gros René and Marinette, in the *Dépit Amoureux* [21] of Molière :—

|" Ton beau galant de neige,[21] avec ta nonpareille,
Il n'aura plus l'honneur d'être sur mon oreille."

Gros René evidently returns to his mistress his point de neige nightcap.

The manner of making bobbin lace on a pillow [22] need hardly be described. The " pillow " [23] is a round or oval board, stuffed so as to form a cushion, and placed upon the knees of the workwoman. On this pillow a stiff piece of parchment is fixed, with small holes pricked through to mark the pattern. Through these holes pins are stuck into the cushion. The threads with which the lace is formed are wound upon " bobbins," formerly bones,[24] now small round pieces of wood, about the size of a pencil, having

---

[17] " Une chemisette de toile d'hollande garnye de point de Paris.—*Inv. d'Anne d'Escoubleau, Baronne de Sourdis, veuve de Françcois de Simiane.* 1681. Arch. Nat. M. M. 802.

[18] " Cette dernière sorte de point se fait aux fuseaux."—*Dict. du P. Richelet.* Lyon. 1759.

[19] *Dict. d'Ant. Furetière.* Augmenté par M. Basnage. La Haye, 1727.

[20] 1656.

[21] 1651. " Huit aulnes de toile commune garnies de neige."—*Inv. des emubles de la Sacristie de l'Oratoire*

de Jésus, à Paris. Bib. Nat. MSS. F. Fr. 8621.

" Neuf autres petites nappes ; les deux premières de toile unie ; la troisième à dentelle quallifié de neige." —*Ibid.*

[22] French, *dentelle à fuseaux;* Italian, *merli a piombini;* Dutch, *gespeldewerkte kant;* Old Flemish, *spelle werk.*

[23] French, *carreau, cousin, oreiller;* Italian, *tombolo;* Venice, *ballon;* Spanish, *mundillo.*

[24] See Chapter XXIV.

round their upper ends a deep groove, so formed as to reduce the bobbin to a thin neck, on which the thread is wound, a separate bobbin being used for each thread. By the twisting and crossing of these threads the ground of the lace is formed. The pattern or figure, technically called " gimp," is made by interweaving a thread much thicker than that forming the groundwork, according to the design pricked out on the parchment.[25] Such has been the pillow and the method of using it, with but slight variation, for more than three centuries.

To avoid repetition, we propose giving a separate history of the manufacture in each country ; but in order to furnish some general notion of the relative ages of lace, it may be as well to enumerate the kinds most in use when Colbert, by his establishment of the Points de France, in 1665, caused a general development of the lace manufacture throughout Europe.

The laces known at that period were :—

1. Point.—Principally made at Venice, Genoa, Brussels, and in Spain.

2. Bisette.—A narrow, coarse thread pillow lace of three qualities, made in the environs of Paris[26] by the peasant women, principally for their own use. Though proverbially of little value—" ce n'est que de la bisette "[27]—it formed an article of traffic with the mercers and lingères of the day.

3. Gueuse.—A thread lace, which owed to its simplicity

---

[25] The number of bobbins is generally equal to 50 to each square inch. If the lace be one inch wide, it will have 625 meshes in each square inch, or 22,500 in a yard. The work, therefore, goes on very slowly, though generally performed with the greatest dexterity.

[26] At Gisors, Saint-Denis, Montmorency, and Villiers-le-Bel.—Savary, *Grand Dict. du Commerce*, 1720.

Cotgrave gives, " Bisette, a plate (of gold, silver, or copper) wherewith some kinds of stuffes are stripped." Oudin, " Feuille ou paillette d'or ou d'argent." In these significations it frequently occurs. We find with numerous others :

" 1545. 55 sols pour une once bizette d'argent pour mectre à des colletz."

" Six aulnes bizette de soie noire pour mettre sur une robbe, lv. s.," in the Accounts of Madame Marguerite de France. (Bib. Nat.)

" 1557. Bizette de soye incarnatte et jaulne pour chamarrer ung pourpoint de satin rouge " of Henry II.—*Cptes. de l'Argentier du Roi.* Arch. Nat. K. K. 106.

" 1579. Petite bizette d'or fin dentellez des deux costez pour servir à des manches de satin cramoisy " of Catherine de Médicis.—*Trésorerie de la royne mère du roy.* Arch. Nat. K. K. 115.

In the Chartley Inv. 1586, of Mary Stuart, is mentioned, " Un plotton de bisette noire."

[27] *Dict. de l'Académie.*

the name it bore. The ground was network, the flowers a loose, thick thread, worked in on the pillow. Gueuse was formerly an article of extensive consumption in France, but, from the beginning of the last century, little used save by the lower classes. Many old persons may still remember the term, " beggars' lace."

4. Campane.[28]—A white, narrow, fine, thread pillow edging, used to sew upon other laces, either to widen them, or to replace a worn-out picot or pearl.

Campane lace was also made of gold, and of coloured silks, for trimming mantles, scarfs, etc. We find, in the Great Wardrobe Accounts of George I., 1714,[29] an entry of '"Gold Campagne buttons."

Evelyn, in his " Fop's Dictionary," 1690, gives, " Campane, a kind of narrow, pricked lace ; " and in the " Ladies' Dictionary," 1694, it is described as " a kind of narrow lace, picked or scalloped." [30]

In the Great Wardrobe Account of William III., 1688-9, we have " le poynt campanie tæniæ."

5. Mignonette.[31]—A light, fine, pillow lace, called blonde de fil,[32] also point de tulle, from the ground resembling that

---

[28] Campane, from sonnette, clochette, même grêlot. " Les sonnettes dont on charge les habits pour ornement. Les festons qu'on met aux étoffes et aux dentelles."—*Oudin.*

[29] Public Record Office.

[30] In the last century it was much the fashion to trim the scalloped edges of a broader lace with a narrower, which was called to " campaner."
1720. " Une garniture de teste à trois pièces de dentelle d'Angleterre à raiseau, garni autour d'une campane à dents."—*Inv. de la Duchesse de Bourbon.*
1741. " Une paire de manches à trois rangs de Malines à raizeau campanée."—*Inv. de decès de Mademoiselle Marie Anne de Bourbon de Clermont.* Arch. Nat. X. 11,071. (Daughter of Mademoiselle de Nantes and Louis Duke de Bourbon.)
" Une coëffure de Malines à raizeau à deux pièces campanée."—*Ibid.*
In the lace bills of Madame du Barry, preserved in the Bib. Nat., are various

entries of Angleterre et point à l'aiguille, " campanée des deux côtés " for ruffles, camisoles, etc.
[31] 1759. " Huit palatines tant points que mignonettes."—*Inv. de decès de Louise Henriette de Bourbon-Conty, Princesse du Sang, Duchesse de Orléans.* Arch. Nat. X. 10,077.
" Trente-vingt paires de manchettes, quatre coëffures, le tout tant de differents points qu'Angleterre, mignonettes que tulles."—*Ibid.*
[32] 1758. " Une paire de manchettes à trois rangs de blonde de fil sur entoilage."—*Inv. de Mademoiselle Louise Anne de Bourbon Condé de Charollais* (sister of Mademoiselle de Clermont). Arch. Nat. X. 10,076.
1761. " Fichus garnis à trois rangs de blonde de fil sur entoilage."—*Inv. de Charlotte Aglaë d'Orléans, Princesse du Sang, Duchesse de Modène* (daughter of the Regent).
1789. Ruffles of blonde de fil appear also in the *Inv. de decès de Monseigneur le Duc de Duras.* Bib. Nat. MSS. F. Fr. 11,440.

fabric. It was made of Lille thread, bleached at Antwerp, of different widths, never exceeding two to three inches. The localities where it was manufactured were the environs of Paris, Lorraine, Auvergne, and Normandy.[33] It was also fabricated at Lille, Arras, and in Switzerland. This lace was article of considerable export, and at times in high favour, from its lightness and clear ground, for headdresses [34] and other trimmings. It frequently appears in the advertisements of the last century. In the *Scottish Advertiser*, 1769, we find enumerated among the stock-in-trade, " Mennuet and blonde lace."

6. Point double, also called point de Paris and point des

Fig. 17.

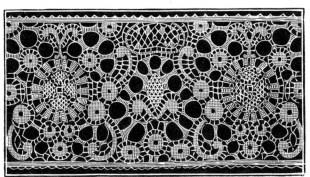

·OLD MECHLIN.

champs : point double, because it required double the number of threads used in the single ground ; des champs, from its being made in the country.

7. Valenciennes.—See Chapter XV.

8. Mechlin.—All the laces of Flanders, with the exception of those of Brussels and the point double, were known in commerce at this period under the general name of Mechlin. (Fig. 17.)

9. Gold lace.

10. Guipure.

---

[33] Mostly at Bayeux.

[34] " On employe aussi pour les coëffures de la mignonette, et on a tellement perfectionné cette dentelle, que estant peu de chose dans son commencement est devenue de consequence et même très chère, j'entends, la plus fine qu'on fait sur de beaux patrons."—*Le Mercure Galant*, 1699.

GUIPURE.

Guipure, says Savary, is a kind of lace or passement made of " cartisane " and twisted silk.

Cartisane is a little strip of thin parchment or vellum, which was covered over with silk, gold, or silver thread, and formed the raised pattern.

The silk twisted round a thick thread or cord was called guipure,[35] hence the whole work derived its name.[36]

Guipure was made either with the needle or on the pillow like other lace, in various patterns, shades and colours, of different qualities and several widths.

The narrowest guipures were called " Têtes de More." [37]

The less cartisane in the guipure, the more it was esteemed, for cartisane was not durable, being only vellum covered over with silk. It was easily affected by the damp, shrivelled, would not wash, and the pattern was destroyed. Later, the parchment was replaced by a cotton material called canetille.

Savary says that most of the guipures were made in the environs of Paris ; [38] that formerly, he writes in 1720, great quantities were consumed in the kingdom ; but since the fashion had passed away, they were mostly exported to Spain, Portugal, Germany, and the Spanish Indies, where they were much worn.[39]

Guipure was made of silk, gold and silver ; from its costliness, therefore, it was only worn by the rich.

At the coronation of Henry II. the front of the high

---

[35] " Guiper. Tordre les fils pendans d'une frange par le moyen de l'instrument qu'on nomme guipoir, fer crochu d'un côté, et chargé de l'autre d'un petit morceau de plomb pour lui donner du poids."—Savary.

[36] " Guipure. A grosse black thread covered or whipped about with silk."—Cotgrave.

" Guipure. Manière de dentelle de soie où il y a des figures de rose ou d'autres fleurs, et qui sert à parer les jupes des dames. . . . Sa jupe est pleine de guipure." — *Dict. du P. Richelet.* 1759.

[37] Roland. We cannot help thinking this a mistake. In the statutes of the Passementiers, we find mention of buttons " à têtes de mort," or would

it rather be " tête de moire," from the black moire hoods (têtes) worn by the Italian women, which were often edged with a narrow guipure ?

[38] Les lieux en France où il se fait le plus de guipures, sont Saint-Denis-en-France, Villiers-le-Bel, Ecouën, Arcelles, Saint-Brice, Groslait, Montmorency, Tremblay, Villepinte, etc.

[39] The sale of Guipures belonged to the master mercers, the workmanship to the passementiers boutonniers. We find in the *Livre Commode ou les Adresses de la Ville de Paris* for 1692, that " Guipures et galons de soye se vendent sur le Petit Pont et rue aux Febvres, où l'on vend aussi des galons de livrées."

PLATE VIII.

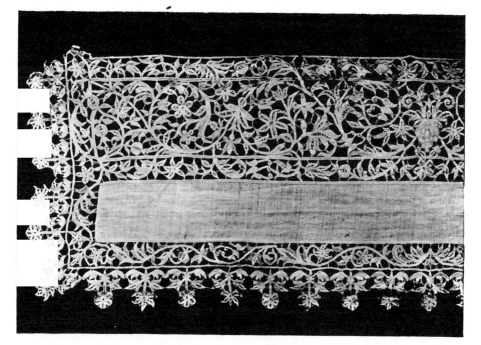

ITALIAN, VENETIAN, FLAT NEEDLE-POINT LACE. "PUNTO IN ARIA."—The design is held together by plain "brides." Date, *circ.* 1645. Width, 11⅝ in.
Victoria and Albert Museum.'

PLATE IX.

PORTION OF A BAND OF NEEDLE-POINT LACE REPRESENTING THE STORY OF JUDITH AND HOLOFERNES.—The work is believed to be Italian, made for a Portuguese, the inscription being in Portuguese. Date, *circ.* 1590. Width, 8 in. The property of Mr. Arthur Blackborne.
Photo by A. Dryden.

PLATE X.

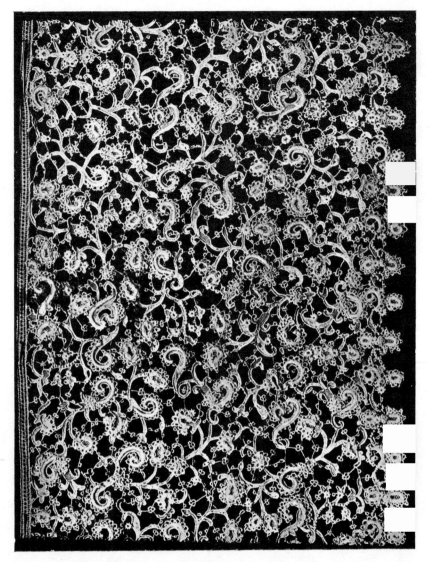

ITALIAN. POINT DE VENISE À LA ROSE. Modern reproduction at Burano of seventeenth century lace. Width, 17 in.

Photo by the Burano School.

altar is described as of crimson velvet, enriched with "cuipure d'or"; and the ornaments, chasuble, and corporaliers of another altar as adorned with a "riche broderie de cuipure."[40]

On the occasion of Henry's entry into Paris, the king wore over his armour a surcoat of cloth of silver ornamented with his ciphers and devices, and trimmed with "guippures d'argent."[41]

In the reign of Henry III. the casaques of the pages were covered with guipures and passements, composed of as many colours as entered into the armorial bearings of their masters; and these silk guipures, of varied hues, added much to the brilliancy of their liveries.[42]

Guipure seems to have been much worn by Mary Stuart. When the Queen was at Lochleven, Sir Robert Melville is related to have delivered to her a pair of white satin sleeves, edged with a double border of silver guipure; and, in the inventory of her clothes taken at the Abbey of Lillebourg,[43] 1561–2, we find numerous velvet and satin gowns trimmed with "gumpeures" of gold and silver.[44]

It is singular that the word guipure is not to be found in our English inventories or wardrobe accounts, a circumstance which leads us to infer, though in opposition to higher authorities, that guipure was in England termed "parchment lace"—a not unnatural conclusion, since we know it was sometimes called "dentelle à cartisane,"[45] from the slips of parchment of which it was partly composed. Though Queen Mary would use the French term, it does not seem to have been adopted in England, whereas "parchment lace" is of frequent occurrence.

From the Privy Purse Expenses of the Princess Mary,[46] we find she gives to Lady Calthorpe a pair of sleeves of "gold,

---

[40] Godefroy. *Le Cérémonial de France*, 1610. *Sacre du Roy Henry II.*, 1547.

[41] In 1549. *Ibid.*

[42] *Traité des Marques Nationales*, dar M. Beneton de Morange de Peyrins. Paris, 1739.

[43] In the Record Office, Edinburgh.

[44] Une robe de velours vert couverte de Broderies, gimpeures, et cordons d'or et d'argent, et bordée d'un passement de même.

Une robe veluat cramoisi bandée de broderie de guimpeure d'argent.

Une robe de satin blanc chamarrée de broderie faite de guimpeure d'or.

Id. de satin jaune toute couverte de broderye gumpeure, etc.

Robe de weloux noyr semée de geynpeurs d'or.

[45] *Dictionnaire de l'Académie.*

[46] 1536–44. Sir Fred. Madden.

2 payr of sleeves whereof one of gold w[h] p'chemene lace, etc.

2 prs. of sleves w[h] pchmyn lase, 8/6.

trimmed with parchment lace," a favourite donation of hers, it would appear, by the anecdote of Lady Jane Grey.

"A great man's daughter," relates Strype [47] "(the Duke of Suffolk's daughter Jane), receiving from Lady Mary, before she was Queen, goodly apparel of tinsel, cloth of gold, and velvet, laid on with parchment lace of gold, when she saw it, said, 'What shall I do with it?' Mary said, 'Gentlewoman, wear it.' 'Nay,' quoth she, 'that were a shame to follow my Lady Mary against God's word, and leave my Lady Elizabeth, which followeth God's word.'"

In the list of the Protestant refugees in England, 1563 to 1571,[48] among their trades, it is stated "some live by making matches of hempe stalks, and parchment lace."

Again, Sir Robert Bowes, "once ambassador to Scotland," in his inventory, 1553, has "One cassock of wrought velvet with p'chment lace of gold." [49]

"Parchment lace [50] of watchett and syllver at 7*s.* 8*d.* the ounce," appears also among the laces of Queen Elizabeth.[51]

King Charles I. has his carpet bag trimmed with "broad parchment gold lace," [52] his satin nightcaps with gold and silver parchment laces,[53] and even the bag and comb case "for his Majesty's barber" is decorated with "silver purle and parchment lace." [54]

Again, Charles II. ornaments the seats on both sides the throne with silver parchment lace.[55] In many of the inventories circ. 1590, "sylke parchment lace" is noted down, and "red" and "green parchment lace," again, appear among the wares found "in y[e] Shoppes." [56]

But to return to the word guipure.

In an inventory of the Church of the Oratoire, at Paris, of the seventeenth century, are veils for the host : one, "de

---

[47] *Ecclesiastical Memoirs*, iii. 2, 167.

[48] State Papers, vol. 82, P. R-O.

[49] Surtees' Society, Durham, "Wills and Inventories."

[50] 1572. Thynne, in his *Debate between Pride and Lowliness*, describes a coat "layd upon with parchment lace withoute."

[51] B. M. Add. MSS. No. 5751.

[52] Roll. 1607. P. R. O.

[53] *Ibid.* 1626. 11 nightcaps of coloured satin, laid on thick, with gold and silver parchment lace, 41. 9. 9.

[54] Roll. 1630.

[55] "Eidem pro novemdecem virg et dim aureæ et argenteæ pergamen laciniæ pondent sexdecim unc $\frac{2}{3}\frac{1}{9}$ venet. . . . pro consuat ad ornand duas sedes utroque latere thronæ in domo Parliament."—*Gt. Ward. Acc.* Car. II. xxx. and xxxi. = 1678-9.

In 1672-73 is an entry for "2 virgis teniæ pergamen."

[56] Surtees' "Inventories."

taffetas blanc garny d'une guipure"; the other, "de satin blanc à fleurs, avec une dentelle de guipure."[57]

These guipures will have also been of silk. When the term was first transferred to the thread passements which are now called guipure, it is difficult to say, for we can find no trace of it so applied.

Be that as it may, the thread guipures are of old date; many of the patterns bear the character of the rich orna-

Fig. 18.

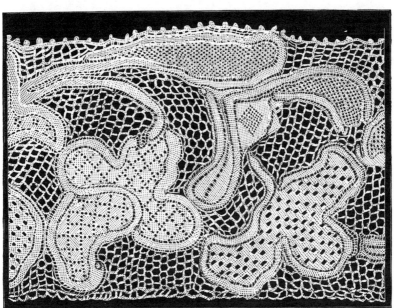

GUIPURE.—(Louis XIV.)

mentation and capricious interlacings of the Renaissance; others, again, are "pur Louis Quatorze" (Fig. 18). The finest thread guipures were the produce of Flanders and Italy. They are most varied in their style. In some the bold flowing patterns are united by brides; in others by a coarse réseau, often circular, and called "round ground."

In that class called by the lace-makers "tape guipure," the outline of the flowers is formed by a pillow or hand-made braid about the eighth of an inch in width (Fig. 19).

---

[57] Bib. Nat. MSS. F. Fr. 8621.

The term guipure is now so extensively applied it is difficult to give a limit to its meaning. We can only define it as lace where the flowers are either joined by "brides," or large coarse stitches, or lace that has no ground at all. The

Fig. 19.

TAPE GUIPURE, BOBBIN-MADE.—(Genoa.)

modern Honiton and Maltese are guipures, so is the Venetian point.

Most of these laces are enumerated in a *jeu d'esprit*, entitled "La Révolte des Passemens," published at Paris in 1661.[58]

---

[58] In the *Recueil de pièces les plus agréables de ce temps, composées par divers autheurs.* Paris, chez Charles Sercy, MDCLXI."

The poem is dedicated to Mademoiselle de la Trousse, cousin of Madame de Sévigné, and was probably written by one of her coterie.

In consequence of a sumptuary edict against luxury in apparel, Mesdames les Broderies—

> " Les Poinctes, Dentelles, Passemens
> Qui, par une vaine despence,
> Ruinoient aujourd'huy la France "—

meet, and concert measures for their common safety. Point de Gênes, with Point de Raguse, first address the company ; next, Point de Venise, who seems to look on Raguse with a jealous eye, exclaims—

> " Encore pour vous, Poinct de Raguse,
> Il est bon, crainte d'attentat,
> D'en vouloir perger un estat.
> Les gens aussy fins que vous estes
> Ne sont bons que, comme vous faites,
> Pour ruiner tous les estats.
> Et vous, Aurillac ou Venise,
> Si nous plions notre valise,"

what will be our fate ?

The other laces speak, in their turn, most despondently, till a " vieille broderie d'or," consoling them, talks of the vanity of this world :—" Who knows it better than I, who have dwelt in kings' houses ? " One " grande dentelle d'Angleterre" now proposes they should all retire to a convent. To this the " Dentelles de Flandres" object ; they would sooner be sewn at once to the bottom of a petticoat.

Mesdames les Broderies resign themselves to become " ameublement ;" the more devout of the party to appear as " devants d'autel ;" those who feel too young to renounce the world and its vanities will seek refuge in the masquerade shops.

" Dentelle noire d'Angleterre" lets herself out cheap to a fowler, as a net to catch woodcocks, for which she felt " assez propre " in her present predicament.

The Points all resolve to retire to their own countries, save Aurillac, who fears she may be turned into a strainer " pour passer les fromages d'Auvergne," a smell insupportable to one who had revelled in civet and orange-flower.

All were starting—

> " Chacun, dissimulant sa rage,
> Doucement ploit son bagage,
> Resolu d'obéir au sort,"

when

> " Une pauvre malheureuse,
> Qu'on apelle, dit on, la Gueuse,"

arrives, in a great rage, from a village in the environs of
Paris. "She is not of high birth, but has her feelings all
the same. She will never submit. She has no refuge—
not even a place in the hospital. Let them follow her advice
and 'elle engageoit sa chaînette,' she will replace them all in
their former position."

Next morn, the Points assemble. "Une grande Cravate [59]
fanfaron" exclaims :—

> "Il nous faut venger cet affront,
> Revoltons-nous, noble assemblée."

A council of war ensues :—

> "La dessus, le Poinct d'Alençon
> Ayant bien appris sa leçon
> Fit une fort belle harangue."

Flanders now boasts how she had made two campaigns under
Monsieur, as a cravat; another had learned the art of war
under Turenne ; a third was torn at the siege of Dunkirk.

> "Racontant des combats qu'ils ne virent jamais,"

one and all had figured at some siege or battle.

> " Qu'avons nous à redouter ? "

cries Dentelle d'Angleterre. No so, thinks Point de Gênes,
" qui avoit le corps un peu gros."

They all swear—
> " Foy de Passement,
> Foy de Poincts et de Broderie,
> De Guipure et d'Orfévrerie,
> De Gueuse de toute façon,"

to declare open war, and to banish the Parliament.

The Laces assemble at the fair of St. Germain, there to
be reviewed by General Luxe.

The muster-roll is called over by Colonel Sotte Depense.
Dentelles de Moresse, Escadrons de Neige, Dentelles de
Hâvre, Escrues, Soies noires, and Points d'Espagne, etc.,
march forth in warlike array, to conquer or to die. At the
first approach of the artillery they all take to their heels,
and are condemned by a council of war—the Points to be
made into tinder, for the sole use of the King's Mousque-
taires ; the Laces to be converted into paper ; the Dentelles,

---

[59] The Cravates or Croates soldiers had a band of stuff round their throats to support an amulet they wore as a charm to protect them from sabre-cuts. What began in superstition ended in fashion.

Escrues, Gueuses, Passemens, and Silk Lace to be made into cordage and sent to the galleys ; the Gold and Silver Laces, the original authors of the sedition, to be " burned alive."

Finally, through the intercession of Love—

" Le petit dieu plein de finesse,"

they are again pardoned and restored to court favour.

The poem is curious, as giving an account of the various kinds of lace, and as a specimen of the taste of the time, but the "ton précieux" of the Hôtel Rambouillet pervades throughout.

The lace trade, up to this period, was entirely in the hands of pedlars, who carried their wares to the principal towns and large country-houses.

" One Madame La Boord," says Evelyn, " a French peddling-woman, served Queen Katherine with petticoats, fans, and foreign laces." These hawkers attended the great fairs [60] of Europe, where all purchases were made.[61]

Even as early as King Henry III.[62] we have a notice " to purchase robes at the fair of St. Ives, for the use of Richard our brother" ; and in the dramas of the sixteenth and seventeenth centuries, we find constant allusion to these provincial markets :—[63]

" Seven
Pedlars' shops, nay all Sturbridge fair,[64] will
Scarce furnish her." [65]

---

[60] These were, in France, Guibray, Beaucaire, and Bordeaux ; in Germany, Frankfort ; in Italy, Novi.

[61] All articles of luxury were to be met with at the provincial fairs. When, in 1671, Catherine of Braganza, the Duchess of Richmond, and the Duke of Buckingham, visited Saffron Walden fair, the Queen asked for a pair of yellow stockings, and Sir Bernard Gascoyne, for a pair of gloves stitched with blue.

[62] 10 Hen. III., Devon's *Issues of the Exchequer.*

[63] " No lace-woman," says Ben Jonson, " that brings French masks and cut-works." That lace was sold by pedlars in the time of Henry VIII., we find from a play, " The Four P's," written in 1544, by John Heywood. Among the contents of a pedlar's box are given " lasses knotted," " laces round and flat for women's heads,"

" sleeve laces," etc.

On opening the box of the murdered pedlar (*Fool of Quality*, 1766), " they found therein silk, linen, laces," etc.

[64] Defoe describes Sturbridge fair as the greatest of all Europe. " Nor," says he, " are the fairs of Leipsig in Saxony, the Mart at Frankfort-on-the-Maine, or the fair of Nuremburg or Augsburg, any way comparable to this fair of Sturbridge."

In 1423, the citizens of London and the suburbs being accused of sending works of " embroidery of gold, or silver, of Cipre, or of gold of Luk, togedre with Spanish Laton of insuffisant stuff to the fayres of Sturesbrugg, Ely, Oxenford, and Salisbury "—in fact, of palming off inferior goods for country use—" all such are forfeited."—*Rot. Parl.*, 2 Hen. VI., nu. 49.

[65] " Lingua, or the Combat of the Tongue." A Comedy. 1607.

The custom of carrying lace from house to house still exists in Belgium, where at Spa and other places, colporteurs,[66] with packs similar to those borne by our pedlars, bring round to the visitors laces of great value, which they sell at cheaper rates than those exposed in the shops.[67]

Many travellers, too, through the counties of Buckingham and Bedford, or the more southern regions of Devon, will still call to mind the inevitable lace box handed round for purchase by the waiter at the conclusion of the inn dinner; as well as the girls who, awaiting the arrival of each travelling carriage or postchaise, climbed up to the windows of the vehicle, rarely allowing the occupants to go their way until they had purchased some article of the wares so pertinaciously offered to their inspection.

In Paris, the lace trade was the exclusive privilege of the passementiers.[68]

---

[66] This system of colporteurs dates from the early Greeks. They are termed both in Greek and Hebrew, " des voyageurs."

[67] " She came to the house under the pretence of offering some lace, holland, and fine tea, remarkably cheap."—*Female Spectator.* 1757.

[68] The centres of the lace manufacture before 1665 were:—

BELGIUM	.	Brussels, Mechlin, Antwerp, Liége, Louvain, Binche, Bruges, Ghent, Ypres, Courtray, etc.
FRANCE	.	(Spread over more than ten Provinces)—
	Artois	Arras (Pas-de-Calais).
	French Flanders	. Lille, Valenciennes, Bailleul (Nord).
	Normandy . .	. Dieppe, Le Hâvre (Seine-Inférieure).
	Ile de France .	. Paris and its environs.
	Auvergne . .	. Aurillac (Cantal).
	Velay . . .	. Le Puy (Haute-Loire).
	Lorraine . .	. Mirecourt (Vosges).
	Burgundy . .	. Dijon (Côte-d'or).
	Champagne . .	. Charleville, Sedan (Ardennes).
	Lyonnais . .	. Lyon (Rhône).
	Poitou . . .	. Loudun (Vienne).
	Languedoc . .	. Muret (Haute-Garonne).
ITALY	. .	Genoa, Venice, Milan, Ragusa, etc.
SPAIN	. .	La Mancha, and in Catalonia especially.
GERMANY	.	Saxony, Bohemia, Hungary, Denmark, and Principality of Gotha.
ENGLAND	.	Counties of Bedford, Bucks, Dorset, and Devon.

CHAPTER IV.

ITALY.

"It grazed on my shoulder, takes me away six parts of an Italian cut-work band I wore, cost me three pounds in the Exchange but three days before."—Ben Jonson—*Every Man Out of His Humour*, 1599.

"Ruffles well wrought and fine falling bands of Italian cut-work."—*Fair Maid of the Exchange*, 1627.

THE Italians claim the invention of point, or needle-made lace.

It has been suggested they derived the art of fine needlework from the Greeks who took refuge in Italy from the troubles of the Lower Empire; and what further confirms its Byzantine origin is, that those very places which kept up the closest intercourse with the Greek Empire are the cities where point lace was earliest made and flourished to the greatest extent.[1]

A modern Italian author,[2] on the other hand, asserts that the Italians learned embroidery from the Saracens of Sicily, as the Spaniards acquired the art from the Moors of Granada or Seville, and brings forward, as proof of his theory, that the word to embroider, both in Italian and Spanish,[3] is derived from the Arabic, and no similar word exists in any other European language.[4] This theory may apply to embroidery, but certainly not to lace; for with the exception of the Turkish crochet "oyah," and some darned netting and drawn-work which occur in Persian and Chinese tissues, there is nothing approaching to lace to be found on any article of oriental manufacture.

---

[1] *Industrial Arts of the Nineteenth Century*, Digby Wyatt.

[2] Francesco Nardi. *Sull' Origine dell' Arte del Ricamo.* Padova, 1839.

[3] *Ricamare. Recamar.*

[4] The traditions of the Low Countries also point to an Eastern origin, assigning the introduction of lace-making to the Crusaders, on their return from the Holy Land.

We proceed to show that evidences of the lace-fabric appear in Italy as early as the fifteenth century.

In 1476, the Venetian Senate decreed that no Punto in Aria whatever, executed either in flax with a needle, or in silver or gold thread, should be used on the curtains or bed-linen in the city or provinces. Among the State archives of the ducal family of Este, which reigned in Ferrara for so many centuries, Count Gandini found mentioned in a Register of the Wardrobe, dated 1476 (A. C. 87), an order given for a felt hat " alla Borgognona," trimmed with a silver and silk gimp made with bobbins. Besides this, in the same document is noted (A. C. 96) a velvet seat with a canopy trimmed at the sides with a frill of gold and silver, made in squares, with bobbins.

The Cavaliere Antonio Merli, in his interesting pamphlet on Italian lace,[5] mentions an account preserved in the Municipal Archives of Ferrara, dated 1469, as probably referring to lace ;[6] but he more especially brings forward a document of the Sforza family, dated[7] 1493, in which the word *trina* (under its ancient form " tarnete ") constantly occurs,[8] together with bone and bobbin lace.

---

[5] *Origine ed Uso delle Trine a filo di refe* (thread), 1864. Privately printed.

[6] 1469.—Io, Battista de Nicollo d'Andrea da Ferrara, debio avere per mia manifatura et reve per cuxere et candelle per inzirare. . . . It. per desgramitare e refilare e inzirare e ripezare e reapicare le gramite a camixi quatordece per li signori calonexi, et per li, mansonarij le qual gramite staxea malissimamente, p. che alcune persone le a guaste, Lire 1 10. It. per reve et p. candelle, L. 0 5.

1469.—I, Baptist de Nicollo of Andrea da Ferrara, having owing to me for my making, and thread to sew, and candles to wax. . . . Item, for untrimming and re-weaving and waxing and refixing and rejoining the trimmings of fourteen albs for the canons and attendants of the church, the which trimmings were in a very bad state, because some persons had spoiled them, L. 1 10. It. for thread and wax, L. 0 5.

These trimmings (gramite), Cav. Merli thinks, were probably " trine."

" At Chicago was exhibited the first kind of net used in Italy as lace on garments. It is made of a very fine linen or silk mesh, stiffened with wax and embroidered in silk thread. It was in use during the fourteenth century, and part of the fifteenth " (*Guide to New and Old Lace in Italy*, C. di Brazza, 1893). This is probably the gramite, or trimmings of the albs, mentioned in the account book formerly belonging to the Cathedral of Ferrara, and now preserved in the Municipal Archives of that city.

[7] See MILAN.

[8] *Trina*, like our word lace, is used in a general sense for braid or passement. Florio, in his Dictionary (*A Worlde of Words*, John Florio, London, 1598), gives *Trine*—cuts, snips, pincke worke on garments ; and *Trinci* —gardings, fringings, lacings, etc., or other ornaments of garments.

Merlo, merletto, are the more modern terms for lace. We find the first as early as the poet Firenzuola (see FLORENCE). It does not occur in any pattern book of an older date than the

PLATE XI.

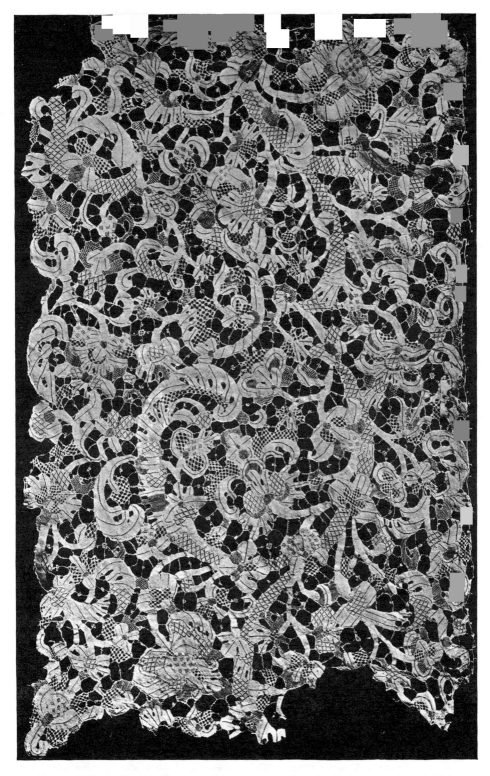

ITALIAN. POINT PLAT DE VENISE. NEEDLE-POINT.—Seventeenth century. Length, 25 in. ; width, 16 in. Victoria and Albert Museum.

PLATE XII.

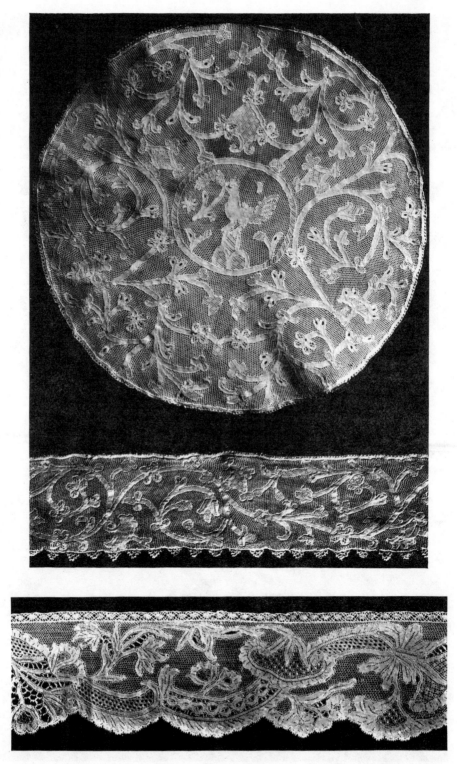

ITALIAN. POINT DE VENISÉ À RÉSEAU.—The upper ones are of yellow silk ; a chalice veil, with dove and olive branch, and possibly an altar border. Probably late seventeenth century. The lower is thread, early eighteenth century. Width, 2 in. In private collections.

Photos by A. Dryden.

Again, the Florentine poet, Firenzuola, who wrote from 1520–30, composed an elegy upon a collar of raised point, made by the hand of his mistress.

Cavaliere Merli cites, as the earliest known painting in which lace occurs, a majolica disc, after the style of the Della Robbia family, in which, surrounded by a wreath of fruit, is represented the half figure of a lady, dressed in a rich brocade, with a collar of white lace. The costume is of the fifteenth century ; but as Luca della Robbia's descendants worked to a later period, the precise date of the work cannot be fixed.

Evidences of white lace, or passement, are said to appear in the pictures of Carpaccio, in the gallery at Venice, and in another by the Gentile Bellini, where the dress of one of the ladies is trimmed round the neck with a white lace.[9] The date of this last painting is 1500.

Lace was made throughout Italy mostly by the nuns,[10] and expressly for the service of the Church. Venice was celebrated for her points, while Genoa produced almost exclusively pillow-lace.

The laces best known in the commercial world in the earlier periods were those of Venice, Milan, and Genoa.

VENICE.

Mrs. Termagant : "I'll spoil your point de Venise for you."—Shadwell, *Squire of Alsatia.*

> "Elle n'avoit point de mouchoir,
> Mais un riche et tres beau peignoir
> Des plus chers de point de Venise
> En negligeance elle avoit mise."
> *Les Combats.* etc., 1663.

The Venetian galleys, at an early period, bore to England " apes, sweet wines," and other articles of luxury. They brought also the gold-work of " Luk," Florence, " Jeane,"

" Fiori da Ricami " of Pasini, and the two works of Francesco de' Franceschi, all printed in 1591.

[9] The laces, both white and gold, depicted in the celebrated picture of the Visit of the Queen of Sheba to Solomon, by Lavinia Fontana, now in the Lambeccari Gallery, executed in the sixteenth century, prove that white lace was in general use in the Italian Courts at that epoch.

[10] At present, if you show an Italian a piece of old lace, he will exclaim, " Opera di monache ; roba di chiesa."

and Venice.[11]   In our early parliamentary records are many statutes on the subject.   The Italians were in the habit of giving short lengths, gold thread of bad quality, and were guilty of sundry other peccadilloes, which greatly excited the wrath of the nation.   The balance was not in England's favour.

> " Thei bare the gold out of this land
> And sowkethe the thrifte out of our hande
> As the waspe sowkethe the honey of the be."

It was these cheating Venetians who first brought over their points into England.

In Venice itself, extravagance in lace was restrained in 1542, by a sumptuary law, forbidding the metal laces embroidered in silk to be wider than *due dita* (*i.e.*, about two inches).   This interference is highly Venetian, and was intended to protect the nobles and citizens from injuring themselves and setting a bad example.

At the coronation of Richard III., " fringes of Venice," and " mantil laces of white silk and Venys gold " appear, and twenty years later Elizabeth of York disburses sundry sums for " gold of Venice " and " other necessaries." [12]   The queen's accounts are less explicit than those of her royal predecessor ; and though a lace is ordered for the king's mantle of the Garter, for which she paid sixteen shillings, the article may have been of home manufacture.

From this time downwards appear occasional mention of partlets,[13] knit caul fashion, of Venice gold, and of white thread,[14] of billament lace of Venice, in silver and black silk.[15] It is not, however, till the reign of Elizabeth [16] that Italian cut-works and Venice lace came into general use.   These points found their way into France about the same period, though we hear little of them.

---

[11] Statute 2, Henry VI., 1423. The first great treaty between the Venetians and Henry VII. was in 1507.

[12] *Privy Purse Expenses of Elizabeth of York*, 1502. P. R. O.   Also published by Sir H. Nicolas.

[13] Inv. Henry VIII.

[14] Gremio, when suing for Bianca, enumerates among his wealth in ivory coffers stuffed, " Turkey cushions bossed with pearl ; valance of Venice gold in needlework."—*Taming of the Shrew.*

[15] " One jerkyn of cloth of silver with long cuts down righte, bound with a billament lace of Venice silver and black silk."—*Robes of the late King* (Edward VI.).

[16] " A smock of cambrik wrought about the collar and sleeves with black silke ; the ruffe wrought with Venice gold and edged with a small bone lace of Venice gold."—*Christmas Presents to the Queen*, by Sir G. Carew.   " 7 ounces of Venice 'laquei bone ' of gold and black silk ; lace ruff edged with Venice gold lace," etc. G. W. A. *Eliz., passim*, P. R. O.

Of " point couppé " there is mention, and enough, in handkerchiefs for Madame Gabrielle, shirts for the king, and fraizes for La Reine Margot ; but whether they be of Venice or worked in France, we are unenlightened. The works of Vinciolo[17] and others had already been widely circulated, and laces and point couppé now formed the favourite occupation of the ladies. Perhaps one of the earliest records of point de Venise will be found in a ridiculous historiette of Tallemant des Réaux, who, gossiping of a certain Madame de Puissieux,[18] writes : " On m'assuroit qu'elle mangeoit du point coupé. Alors les points de Gênes, de Raguse, ni d'Aurillac ni de Venise n'étoient point connus et on dit qu'au sermon elle mangea tout le derrière du collet d'un homme qui etoit assis devant elle." On what strange events hang the connecting threads of history !

By 1626 foreign " dentelles et passements au fuseau " were declared contraband. France paying large sums of money to other countries for lace, the Government, by this ordinance, determined to remedy the evil. It was at this period that the points of Venice were in full use.[19]

> " To know the age and pedigrees
> Of points of Flanders and Venise "[20]

would, in the latter case, have been more difficult, had it not been for the pattern-books so often quoted.

The earliest points, as we already know, soon passed from the stiff formality of the " Gotico " into the flowing lines of the Renaissance, and into that fine patternless guipure which is, *par excellence*, called Point de Venise.[21]

In the islands of the Lagune there still lingers a tale of the first origin of this most charming production.

A sailor youth, bound for the Southern Seas, brought home to his betrothed a bunch of that pretty coralline (Fig. 20) known to the unlearned as the mermaid's lace.[22] The girl, a worker in points, struck by the graceful nature of the seaweed, with its small white knots united, as it were, by

[17] 1587.
[18] Madame de Puissieux died in 1677, at the age of eighty.
[19] Venice points are not mentioned by name till the ordinance of 1654. See GREEK ISLANDS.
[20] *Hudibras.*

[21] Italy we believe to have furnished her own thread. " Fine white or nun's thread is made by the Augustine nuns of Crema, twisted after the same manner as the silk of Bolonia," writes Skippin, 1651.
[22] *Halimedia opuntia*, Linn.

a "bride," imitated it with her needle, and after several unsuccessful trials produced that delicate guipure which before long became the taste of all Europe.

It would be difficult to enumerate the various kinds of lace produced by Venice in her palmy days.

The Cavaliere Merli has endeavoured to classify them according to the names in the pattern-books with which Venice supplied the world, as well as with her points. Out

Fig. 20.

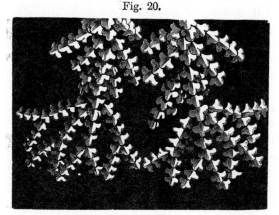

MERMAID'S LACE.

of some sixty of these works, whose names have been collected, above one-third were published in Venice.[23]

1. Punto a reticella.[24]—Made either by drawing the threads of the cloth, as in the samplar already given (Fig. 5), or by working the lace on a parchment pattern in button-hole stitch (punto smerlo). (Fig. 21.) This point is identical with what is commonly called "Greek" lace.

Under this head comes punto reale (the opposite of reticella), where the linen ground is left and the design cut out.* Punto di cartella or cordella (card-work) is similar in effect to reticella, but the button-holing is done entirely over a foundation made by sewing coarse thread and bits of parchment on to the design and covering them with button-hole stitch.

---

[23] That most frequently met with is the Corona of Vecellio. See AP-PENDIX.

[24] First mentioned in the Sforza Inventory, 1493 (see MILAN) ; not in the pattern-books till Vecellio, 1592; but Taglienti (1530) gives "su la rete," and "Il specchio di Pensieri" (1548), "punto in rede."
    * Plate V.

Fig. 21.

RETICELLA.

Fig. 23.

Gros Point de Venise.—From the Collar of a Venetian Nobleman. Musée de Cluny, Paris. 16th century.
N B.—This drawing makes the work and design appear heavier than it is in reality.

2. Punto tagliato.[25]—Cut-work, already described.

3 Punto di Venezia.

4. Punto in aria.[26]—Worked on a parchment pattern, the flowers connected by brides : in modern parlance, Guipure.

5. Punto tagliato a fogliami.[27]—The richest and most complicated of all points, executed like the former, only with this difference, that all the outlines are in relief, formed by means of cottons placed inside to raise them. Sometimes they are in double and triple relief; an infinity of beautiful stitches are introduced into the flowers, which are surrounded by a pearl of geometric regularity, the pearls sometimes in scallops or "campané," as the French term it.[28] This is our Rose (raised) Venice point, the Gros Point de Venise, the Punto a relievo, so highly prized and so extensively used for albs, collerettes, berthes, and costly decoration. We give an example (Fig. 23) from a collar, preserved in the Musée de Cluny, once the property of a Venetian nobleman, worn only on state occasions.

Two elaborate specimens were in the possession of Mr. Webb ; one is a long narrow piece fringed at both ends, which may have served as a maniple (Fig. 26) ; the other, a " pale "[29] for the communion, he has given to the Victoria and Albert Museum.

These two last are made of silk of the natural cream colour. Both silk and thread unbleached appear to have been greatly in favour. At Paris much lace of this colour has been disposed of by its owners since the revolutions in Italy.[30]

Other varieties of so-called rose point are punto neve (point de neige), with its ground of starred threads resembling snowflakes, and the coral point, a small irregular pattern supposed to have been copied from coral.

---

[25] First given in the *Honesto Esempio*. 1550 and *passim*.

[26] Mentioned by Taglienti (1530), and afterwards in the *Trionfo* (1555), and *passim*.

[27] Given in *Il Monte*, circ. 1550, but described by Firenzuola earlier. See FLORENCE.

[28] See Chap. III., notes 28 and 30.

[29] " Toile de la Pale."—A pasteboard about eight inches square, enclosed in cambric or lace, used to cover the paten when laid over the cup.

[30] The whole furniture of a room taken from a palace at Naples, comprising curtains, and vallance of a bed, window curtains, toilet, etc., of straw-coloured laces, reticella, embroidered netting, etc.; the price asked was 18,000 francs = £720. There was also much of the rose point, and a handkerchief bordered with beautiful flat Venetian point of the same colour, forming part of a trousseau. 700 francs = £28.

6. Punto a gropo, or gropari.[31]—Groppo, or gruppo, signifies a knot, or tie, and in this lace the threads are knotted together, like the fringes of the Genoese macramè.[32] After this manner is made the trimming to the linen scarfs or cloths which the Roman peasants wear folded square over the head, and hanging down the back. (Fig. 22.)

Fig. 22.

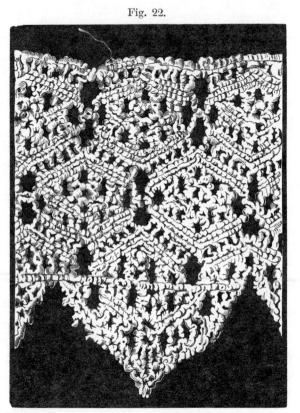

PUNTO A GROPO (Knotted Point).

7. Punto a maglia quadra.—Lacis; square netting,[33] the modano of the Tuscans. (Fig. 24.)

This Tuscan sort was not generally embroidered; the pattern consists in knitting the meshes together in different

---

[31] Taglienti (1530) has *groppi, more-schi,* and *arabeschi;* and *Il Specchio* (1548), *ponti gropposi.* See also the Sforza Inventory, 1493.

[32] See GENOA.

[33] Taglienti (1530) gives *a magliata,* Parasole (1600) *lavori di maglia.*

shapes. It was much used for hangings of beds, and those curtains placed across the windows, called *stores* by the French, and by the Italians, *stuora*.[34]

8. Burato.—The word means a stiff cloth or canvas (*toille clere* of Taglienti, 1527), on which the pattern is embroidered, reducing it to a kind of rude lace. One of the

Fig. 24.

PUNTO A MAGLIA (Lacis)

pattern-books[35] is devoted exclusively to the teaching of this point.

The needle-made laces fabricated at Burano will be noticed later.

9. Punto tirato—Drawn work.[36] Fig. 25 is a lace ground

---

[34] *Punti a stuora* occur in *Il Spec-chio* (1548), *I Frutti* (1564), and in the *Vera Perfettione* (1591) the word *stuora* (modern, *stuoja*) means also a mat of plaited rushes, which some of these interlaced patterns may be intended to imitate.

[35] *Burato.* See APPENDIX.

[36] There are many patterns for this work in *Le Pompe di Minerva*, 1642. Taglienti (1530) has *desfilato* among his *punti*.

made by drawing the threads of muslin (*fili tirati*).[37] The present specimen is simple in design, but some are very complicated and beautiful.

The ordinance of Colbert must have inflicted a serious injury on the Venice lace trade, which, says Daru, " occupoit la population de la capitale." In *Britannia Languens*, a discourse upon trade, London, 1680,[38] it is said that the laces commonly called Points de Venise now come mostly from France, and amount to a vast sum yearly.

Savary, speaking of the thread laces termed Venice point in the early part of the eighteenth century,[39] says, " The

Fig. 25.

PUNTO TIRATO (Drawn Lace).

French no longer purchase these articles, having established themselves manufactures which rival those of the Adriatic."

Still the greater number of travellers [40] make a provision of points in their passage through Venice, and are usually cheated, writes a traveller about this period.[41] He recom-

---

[37] Many other points are enumerated in the pattern-books, of which we know nothing, such as *gasii* (*I Frutti*, 1564), *trezola* (*Ibid*), *rimessi* (*Vera Perfettione*, 1591), *opere a mazzette* (Vecellio, 1591, and Lucretia Romana, N.D.).

[38] *Tracts on Trade of the Seventeenth Century*, published by MacCulloch, at the expense of Lord Monteagle. 1856.

[39] Venice point forms a considerable item in the expenses of Charles II. and his brother James.

[40] Venice noted " for needlework laces, called points."—*Travels Thro' Italy and France*, by J. Ray. 1738.

[41] Misson, F. M., *Nouveau Voyage d'Italie*, 4me édition. La Haye, 1702.

Fig. 26.

POINT DE VENISE À BRIDES PICOTÉES.—Early 18th century.

mends his friend, Mr. Claude Somebody, a French dealer, who probably paid him in ruffles for the advertisement.

Our porte-bouquets and lace-trimmed nosegays are nothing new. On the occasion of the annual visit of the Doge to the Convent delle Vergini, the lady abbess with the novices received him in the parlour, and presented him with a nosegay of flowers placed in a handle of gold, and trimmed round with the finest lace that Venice could produce.[42]

Fig. 27.

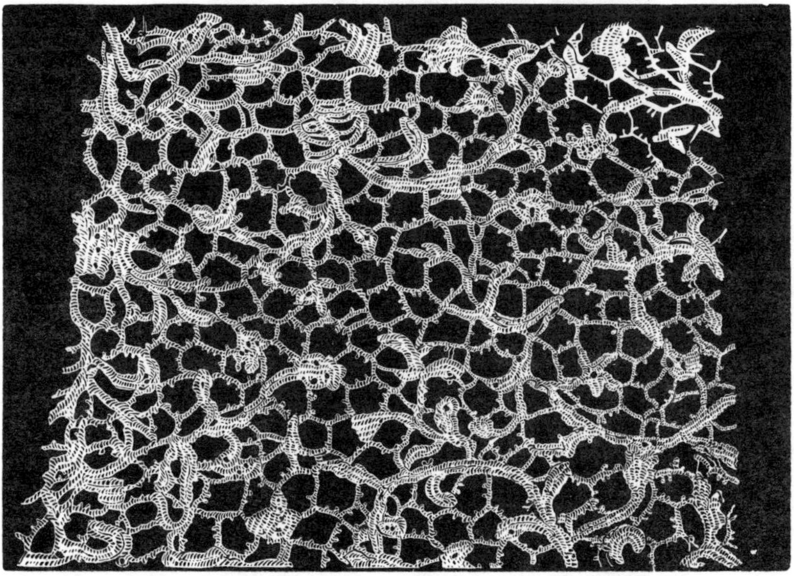

VENICE POINT.

Fynes Moryson[43] is the earliest known traveller who alludes to the products of Venice. "Venetian ladies in general," he says, "wear a standing collar and ruffs close up to the chin ; the unmarried tie their hair with gold and silver lace." Evidently the collars styled "bavari," for which Vecellio[44] gives patterns "all' usanza Veneziana," were

---

[42] *Origine delle Feste Veneziane,* da Giustina R. Michiel.　Milano, 1829.

[43] *An Itinerary, containing his Ten Yeeres Travel through Germany, Boh-* merland, *Switzerland, Netherland, Denmark, Poland, Italy, Turkey, France, England, Scotland, and Ireland.* Lond., 1617.

[44] 1591.

not yet in general vogue.[45]　The Medici collars were supported by fine metal bars called "verghetti," which were so much in demand that the inhabitants of a whole quarter of

Fig. 28.

Gros Point de Venise.—(First half of 17th century.)

Venice were engaged in their production, and the name which it still bears was given to it in consequence.

---

[45] See, in Appendix, designs for *bavari* by Lucrezia.

Fig. 29.

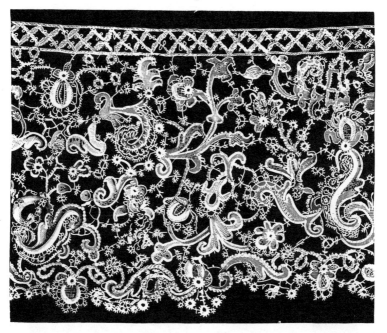

Point de Venise.—End of 17th century.

Fig. 30.

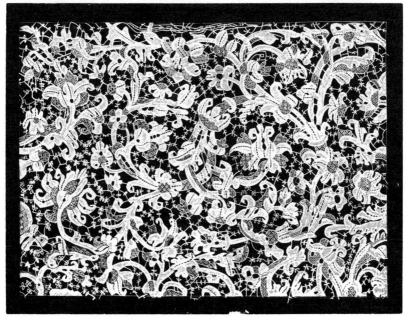

Point Plat de Venise.—Middle of 17th century.

Fig. 31.

Point de Venise à Réseau.—Early 18th century.

N.B.—Mrs. Palliser incorrectly described this as Brussels in her first Editions.

Fifty years later, Evelyn speaks of the veils of glittering taffetas, worn by the Venetian ladies, to the corners of which hang broad but curious tassels of point laces.

According to Zedler, an author who wrote about lace in 1742, the price of Venice point in high relief varied from one to nine ducats per Italian ell.

The Venetians, unlike the Spaniards, thought much of their fine linen and the decorations pertaining to it. " La camicia preme assai più del giubbone," ran the proverb— " La chemise avant le pourpoint." Young nobles were not allowed to wear lace on their garments until they put on the robe, which they usually did at the age of five-and-twenty, on being admitted to the council.[46]

Towards 1770, the Venice ladies themselves commenced to forsake the fabrics of their native islands ; for on the marriage of the Doge's son, in that year, we read that, although the altar was decorated with the richest Venice point, the bride and her ladies wore their sleeves covered up to the shoulders with falls of the finest Brussels lace, and a tucker of the same material.[47]

During the carnival, however, the people, both male and female, wore a camail, or hood of black lace, covering the chin up to the mouth, called a " bauta."[48] It was one of these old black lace hoods that Walpole describes Lady Mary Wortley Montagu as wearing at Florence, 1762, in place of a cap.

Point de Venise à réseau is chiefly distinguished by the conventional treatment of the flowers and ornament, and a general flat look of the work. The outlining thread or cordonnet is stitched to the edge of the pattern and worked in flatly. A minute border to the cordonnet of small meshes intervenes between it and the réseau, which is of square

---

[46] The entry of the Venetian ambassador, Mocenigo, is described in the *Mercure Galant*, 1709 :—

"Il avoit un rabat de point de Venise. . . . Sa robe de damas noir avec des grandes manches qui pendoient par derrière. Cette robe etoit garnie de dentelle noir."

[47] *Letters from Italy*. So, in a play of Goldoni, who wrote in the middle of the last century, the lady has a Brussels (Angleterre) head-dress.

Don Flaminio : " Mi par bellisima cotesto pizzo Barbara : E un punto d'Inghilterra che ha qualche merito." —*Gli Amori di Zelinda e Lindoro.*

In Goldoni's plays all the ladies make lace on the pillow (*ballon*), so the art of making the needle Venice point was probably at an end.

[48] " La plus belle dentelle noire fait l'espèce de camail qui, sous un chapeau noir emplumé, couvre leurs épaules et leur tête."—Madame du Boccage, 1735. *Lettres sur l'Italie.*

" Quella specie de lungo capuocio di finissimo merlo pur nero, chiamato bauta."—Michiel.

meshes and always very fine.   Whether the lace was derived
from the Alençon, and was the result of an attempt to win
back the custom the French manufacturers were taking away
from Venice, or whether it was Alençon that imitated the
Venetian réseau, is a moot point, but certain it is that the
Venetian product surpassed in fineness both Alençon and
Brussels.   Its very delicacy has been its destruction, so that
very few specimens of this lace survive.   Plate XII.

Mezzo Punto, or mixed Venetian guipure, was a mixed
point lace, of which the scrolls and flowers were outlined in
pillow-lace, or by a tape, and the designs filled in with needle
fillings, and connected by pearled brides on a coarse needle-
made réseau.   This variety of lace was sometimes made of
silk.   In point de Venise, flat or raised, the pattern is always
connected by an irregular network of pearled brides.   Real
brides connecting the flowers here and there hardly ever
occur ; and the number of picots attached to one single
branch of the bride network never exceeds two.   The elaborately ornamental detached brides and a multiplicity of picots
are characteristic of " Spanish point " and early point de
France.

The old Burano laces were a coarser outcome of the point
de Venise à réseau, and alone of all Venetian needle laces
survived the dark days of the close of the eighteenth century.
Some fine specimens of these were shown by M. Dupont
d'Auberville in the International Exhibition, and Marini
quotes from a document of the seventeenth century, in which,
speaking of merletti, it is said that " these laces, styled
'punti in aria,' or di Burano, because the greater part of them
were made in the country so called, are considered by Lannoni
as more noble and of greater whiteness, and for excellency of
design and perfect workmanship equal to those of Flanders,
and in solidity superior."

A new departure has been taken in modern times, in
the making of hand-made laces at the island of Burano,
near Venice, where a large number of girls were employed
in the eighteenth century, both in the town and the
convents, in making a point closely resembling that of
Alençon.   Here the art lingered on as late as 1845, when
a superannuated nun of ninety, with whom Mrs. Dennistoun, of Dennistoun, conversed on the subject, said how
in her younger days she and her companions employed

VENICE

their time in the fabric of " punto di Burano " ;[49] how it was
ordered long beforehand for great marriages, and even then
cost very dear. She showed specimens still tacked on paper :
the ground is made right across the thread of the lace.

Burano point had not the extreme delicacy of the
Venetian point à réseau or of Alençon, and the late Alençon
patterns were copied. Though needle-made, it was worked
on a pillow arranged with a cylinder for convenience of
working. The unevenness of the thread gives the réseau
a cloudy appearance, and the cordonnet is, like the Brussels
needlepoint, of thread stitched round the outline instead of
the Alençon button-hole stitch over horse-hair. The mesh
of the réseau is square, as in Alencon.

Fig. 32 is copied from a specimen purchased at Burano
by the Cav. Merli, of the maker, an old woman known by
the name of Cencia Scarpariola. In 1866, the industry
was extinct, and the " Contrada del Pizzo," once the head-
quarters of the lace-makers, was a mystery to the natives,
who could no longer account for the denomination. In the
church is preserved a splendid series of altar-cloths of so-
called Burano point in relief, and a fine *storiato* piece,
representing the mysteries of the Passion. " Venice point
is now no more," writes Mrs. Palliser ; " the sole relic of
this far-famed trade is the coarse torchon lace, of the old
lozenge pattern, offered by the peasant women of Palestrina
to strangers on their arrival at hotels," the same fabric mentioned by Lady Mary Wortley Montagu, when she speaks
of " peddling women that come on pretext of selling
pennyworths of lace."

The formation of the school recently established there,[50]
and the revival of the art of lace-making in Burano, arose
out of the great distress which in 1872 overtook the island.
The extraordinary severity of the winter that year rendered
it impossible for the poor fishermen, who form the population

---

[49] " L'ile de Burano où l'on fabrique
les dentelles."—Quadri, *Huit Jours à
Venise.*

[50] *Technical History of Venetian
Laces,* Urbani de Gheltof. Translated
by Lady Layard. Venice, 1882.

*Origines de la Dentelle de Venise
et l'École de Burano.* Venice, 1897.

Traditions of lace-making were kept

alive in Venice, Cantu and Liguria
during the first half of the nineteenth
century by the manufacture of an
inferior quality of *blonde*, once extensively made at Venice, which has since
died out, owing to the revival in the
production of thread-lace and guipures
at Palestrina.

of the island, to follow their calling. So great was the
distress at that time, while the lagoons were frozen, that the
fishermen and their families were reduced to a state bordering
on starvation, and for their relief contributions were made
by all classes in Italy, including the Pope and the King.

Fig. 32.

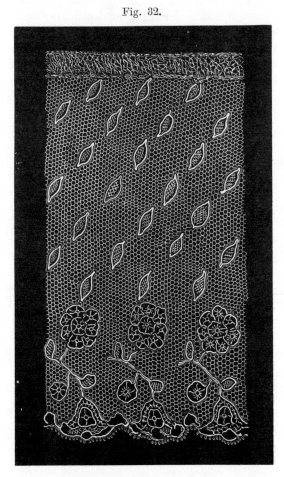

BURANO POINT.—(Late 18th century.)

This charitable movement resulted in the collection of a fund
of money, which sufficed to relieve the immediate distress
and leave a surplus for the establishment of a local industry
to increase the resources of the Burano population.

Unfortunately, the industry at first fixed upon, namely,

PLATE XIII.

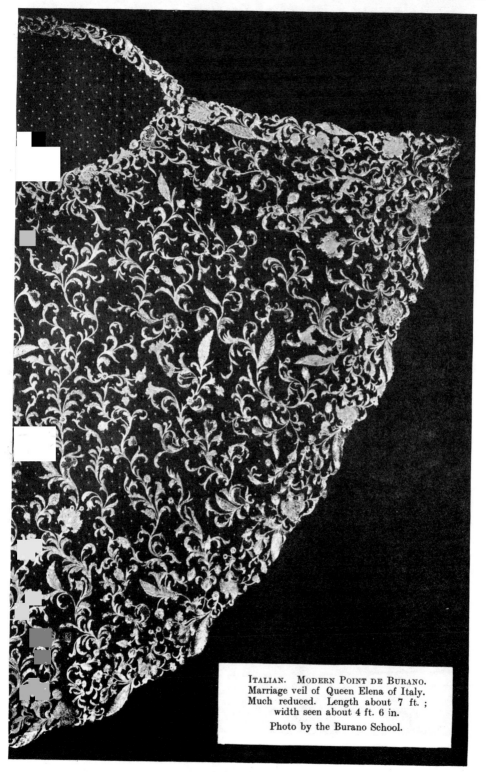

ITALIAN. MODERN POINT DE BURANO.
Marriage veil of Queen Elena of Italy.
Much reduced. Length about 7 ft. ;
width seen about 4 ft. 6 in.

Photo by the Burano School.

PLATE XIV.

ITALIAN.—Modern reproduction at Burano of the flounce now belonging to the Crown of Italy, formerly to Pope Clement XIII., Rezzonico, 1693-1769.   Height, 24 in.

Photo by the Burano School.

that of making fishermen's nets, gave no practical result, the fishermen being too poor to buy the nets. It was then that a suggestion was made by Signor Fambri that an effort should be made to revive the ancient industry of lace-making, and Princess Chigi-Giovanelli and the Countess Andriana Marcello were asked to interest themselves in, and to patronise, a school for this purpose.

To this application these ladies yielded a ready assent, and at a late period Queen Margherita graciously consented to become the president of the institution.

When Countess Marcello, who from that time was the life and soul of the undertaking, began to occupy herself with the foundation of the school, she found an old woman in Burano, Cencia Scarpariola, who preserved the traditions of the art of lace-making, and continued, despite her seventy years and upwards, to make Burano point. As she, however, did not understand the method of teaching her art, the assistance was secured of Madame Anne Bellorio d'Este, a very skilful and intelligent woman, for some time mistress of the girls' school at Burano, who in her leisure hours took lessons in lace-making of Cencia Scarpariola, and imparted her knowledge to eight pupils, who, in consideration of a small payment, were induced to learn to make lace.

As the number of scholars increased, Madame Bellorio occupied herself exclusively in teaching lace-making, which she has continued to do with surprising results. Under Madame Bellorio's tuition, the school, which in 1872 consisted of eight pupils (who received a daily payment to induce them to attend), now, in 1897, numbers four hundred workers, paid, not by the day, but according to the work each performs.

In Burano everything is extremely cheap, and a humble abode capable of accommodating a small family may be had for from six hundred to one thousand Italian lire. It is not a rare occurrence to find a young lace-worker saving her earnings in order to purchase her little dwelling, that she may take it as a dower to her husband. Nearly all the young men of Burano seek their wives from among the lace-women. The school's diploma of honour speaks of the economical importance of the lace-work " to the poor place of Burano," and " the benefit which the gentle industry brings to the inhabitants of the interesting island, whose welfare, having passed through a series of undeserved trials, is due exclusively to the revival of it practised on a large scale."

The lace made in the school is no longer confined, as in the origin it was, to Burano point, but laces of almost any design or model are now undertaken—point de Burano, point d'Alençon, point de Bruxelles, point d'Angleterre, point d'Argentan, rose point de Venise, Italian punto in aria, and Italian punto tagliato a fogliami. The school has been enriched by gifts of antique lace, and Queen Margherita gave the school permission to copy two magnificent specimens of Ecclesiastical lace—now Crown property—that had formerly belonged to Cardinal de Retz, and Pope Clement VII. (Rezzonico).

In order the better to carry out the character of the different laces, the more apt and intelligent of these pupils, whose task it is to trace out in thread the design to be worked, have the advantage of being taught by professional artists.

The four hundred lace-workers now employed are divided into seven sections, in order that each may continue in the same sort of work and, as much as possible, in the same class of lace. By this method each one becomes thoroughly proficient in her own special department, executes it with greater facility, and consequently earns more, and the school gets its work done better and cheaper.

While Countess Marcello was working to re-establish the making of needle-point at Burano, Cav. Michelangelo Jesurum was re-organising the bobbin-lace industry at Pellestrina, a small fishing-town on the Lido. In 1864 the lace of Pellestrina might have been described as an inextricable labyrinth of threads with vaguely distinguishable lines and occasional holes. The lace was so imperfect, and made in such small quantities, that two women who went about selling it in Venice and the country round sufficed to dispose of all that was made. The pricked papers were prepared by an old peasant woman, who made them more and more imperfect at each repetition, losing gradually all trace of the original design. Cav. Jesurum, by a careful copying of the old designs, obtained valuable results, and founded a lace-school and a flourishing industry. About 1875 polychrome lace was introduced in Venice—bobbin-lace worked in colours with designs of flowers, fruits, leaves, arabesques, and animals, with the various tints and shading required. The women who make bobbin-lace now in Venice and in the islands amount to 3,000, but it is difficult to give an exact estimate of their numbers, as many of them are bone-workers, wives and daughters of fishermen, who combine the lace-making with their household duties, with mending of nets and with field-work.

MILAN (" Milano la Grande ").

" Margaret: I saw the Duchess of Milan's gown that they praise so.
" Hero: O that exceeds, they say.
" Margaret: By my troth, it's but a night-gown in respect of yours; cloth o' gold and cuts, and laced with silver."—*Much Ado about Nothing*, iv. 1.

One of the earliest records of Italian lace belongs to Milan, and occurs in an instrument of partition between the sisters Angela and Ippolita Sforza Visconti, dated 1493 (see VENICE).

This document is of the highest interest as giving the inventory of an Italian wardrobe of the fifteenth century. In it, amidst a number of curious entries, are veils of good network, with cambric pillow-cases, linen sheets, mosquito curtains and various articles, worked *a reticella* and *a groppi*, with the needle, bobbins, bones, and other different ways [51] mentioned in the pattern-books of the following century.

Among other items we find, " Half of a bundle containing patterns for ladies' work." [52]

Though the fabric of these fine points dates back for so many centuries, there is little notice of them elsewhere.

---

[51] " Velleto (veil) uno d'oro filato.

" Payro uno fodrete (pillow-case) di cambria lavorate a gugia (à l'aiguille).

" Lenzuolo (sheet) uno di revo di tele (linen thread), cinque lavorato a punto.

" Peza una de tarnete (trina) d'argento facte a stelle.

" Lenzolo uno de tele, quatro lavorato a *radexelo* (reticello).

" Peze quatro de *radexela* per mettere ad uno moscheto (zanzariere, mosquito curtain).

" Tarneta una d'oro et seda negra facta da ossi (bones).

" Pecto uno d'oro facto *a grupi*.

" Lavoro uno de rechamo facto *a grupi* dove era suso le pere de Madona Biancha.

" Binda una lavorata a poncto de doii fuxi (two bobbins) per uno lenzolo."—*Instrumento di divizione tre le sorelle Angela ed Ippolita Sforza Visconti*, di Milano, 1493, Giorno di Giovedì, 12 Settembre.

[52] " La mità de uno fagotto quale aveva dentro certi dissegni da lavorare le donne."

Henry VIII. is mentioned as wearing one short pair of hose of purple silk of Venice gold, woven like a caul, edged with a passamaine lace of purple silk and gold, worked at Milan.[53]

In a wardrobe account of Lord Hay, gentleman of his Majesty's robes, 1606,[54] is noted down to James I., " One suit with cannons thereunto of silver lace, shadowed with silk Milan lace."

Again, among the articles furnished against the " Queen's lying down," 1606, in the bills of the Lady Audrye Walsing-ham,[55] is an entry of " Lace, Milan fashion, for child's waistcoat."

A French edict, dated March, 1613, against superfluity in dress, prohibiting the wearing of gold and silver em-broidery, specially forbids the use of all " passement de Milan, ou façon de Milan " under a penalty of one thousand livres.[56] The expression "à point de Milan" occurs in the statutes of the passementiers of Paris.[57]

" Les galons, passements et broderies, en or et en argent de Milan," says Savary,[58] were once celebrated.

Lalande, who writes some years later, adds, the laces formerly were an object of commerce to the city, now they only fabricate those of an inferior quality.[59]

Much was consumed by the Lombard peasants, the better sorts serving for ruffles of moderate price.[60] So opulent are the citizens, says a writer of the same epoch, that the lowest mechanics, blacksmiths and shoemakers, appear in gold stuff coats with ruffles of the finest point.[61]

And when, in 1767, the Auvergne lace-makers petition for an exemption from the export duty on their fabrics, they state as a ground that the duty prevents them from com-peting abroad, especially at Cadiz, with the lace-makers of Piedmont, the Milanais, and Imperial Flanders. Milan must, therefore, have made lace extensively to a late period.

---

[53] Harl. MS. No. 1419.

[54] Roll. P. R. O.

[55] P. R. O.

[56] De la Mare, *Traité de la Police.*

[57] " Statuts, Ordonnances et Regle-mens de la Communauté des Maistres Passementiers, etc., de Paris, confirmez sur les anciens Statuts du 23 mars 1558." Paris, 1719.

[58] *Grand Dictionnaire Universel du Commerce.* 1723.

[59] *Voyage en Italie.* 1765.

[60] Peuchet, J., *Dictionnaire Univer-sel de la Géographie Commerçante.* Paris, An vii. = 1799.

[61] *Letters from Italy,* by a lady. 1770.

PLATE XV.

ITALIAN.   MILANESE BOBBIN-MADE.— Late seventeenth century.   Width, 12 in.
Photo by A. Dryden from private collection.

PLATE XVI.

PLATE XVII.

ITALIAN, VENETIAN. NEEDLE-MADE.—Very raised and padded. First half of eighteenth century. Width, 3¼ in.

ITALIAN, MILANESE. BOBBIN-MADE.—Early eighteenth century. Width, 5¾ in.

Photos by A. Dryden from private collections.

Fig. 33 is a specimen of what has been termed old Milan point, from the convent of Santa Maria delle Grazie, in that city. It is more often known as Greek lace.

The so-called punti di Milano—points de Milan—were all bobbin-laces, which originated in Milan, and, though imitated by Genoa and Naples, remained unapproached in

Fig. 33.

RETICELLA FROM MILAN.

design and workmanship. After first making passements, Milan imitated the Venetian points, " a fogliami," in which the pattern has the appearance of woven linen, with à jours occasionally introduced to lighten portions of it. The design was at first connected with bars, but later, meshes (in the seventeenth century large meshes, and, still later, smaller meshes) filled the ground. This réseau varies, but most frequently it has four plaited sides to a mesh, as in Valenciennes.

Like other Italian laces, Milanese lace frequently has coats-of-arms or family badges woven in it, such as the Doge's horn, the baldachino (a special distinction accorded to Roman princes), the dogs of the Carrara family, and so on, to commemorate a marriage or some other important event in the family. This sort of lace was known as Carnival lace when made of Venetian point.

Milan lace is now represented by Cantu, near Lake Como, where the making of white and black pillow-lace gives employment to many thousands of women. The torchon lace of the country is original, and in much request with the peasantry.

In the underground chapel of San Carlo Borromeo, in Milan Cathedral, are preserved twenty-six " camicie," trimmed with flounces of the richest point, all more or less splendid, and worked in the convents of the city, but many of the contents of this sumptuous wardrobe have rotted away from the effects of the damp atmosphere.

FLORENCE.

Of Florence and its products we know but little, though the Elegy of Agnolo Firenzuola proves that ladies made raised point at an early period.[62] His expression " scolpì," carved, sculptured in basso rilievo, leaves no doubt upon the matter.

> " This collar was sculptured by my lady
> In bas reliefs such as Arachne
> And she who conquered her could ne'er excel.
> Look on that lovely foliage, like an Acanthus,

---

[62] " Questo collar scolpì la donna mia
De basso rilevar, ch' Aracne mai,
E chi la vinse nol faria più bello.
Mira quel bel fogliame, ch' un acanto
Sembra, che sopra un mur vada car-
poni.
Mira quei fior, ch' un candido ne cade
Vicino al seme, apr' or la bocia l'altro.
Quei cordiglin, che'l legan d'ognitorno,
Come rilevan ben ! mostrando ch' ella
E' la vera maestra di quest' arte,

Com ben compartiti son quei punti !
Ve' come son ugual quei bottoncelli,
Come s' alzano in guisa d'un bel colle
L'un come l' altro ! . . .
Questi merli da man, questi trafori
Fece pur ella, et questo punto a spina,
Che mette in mezzo questo cordoncello,
Ella il fe pure, ella lo fece."
   —*Elegia sopra un Collaretto*,
      Firenzuola (circ. 1520).

Which o'er a wall its graceful branches trails.
Look on those lovely flowers of purest white,
Which, near the pods that open, hang in harmony.
That little cord which binds each one about,
How it projects! proving that she who wrought it
Is very mistress of this art.
How well distributed are all these points!
See the equality of all those little buds
Which rise like many fair proportioned hills,
One like the other. . . .
This hand-made lace, this open-work,
Is all produced by her, this herring-bone,
Which in the midst holds down a little cord,
Was also made by her; all wrought by her."

Henry VIII. granted to two Florentines the privilege of importing for three years' time all " manner of fringys and passements wrought with gold and silver or otherwise," [63] an account of which will be found in the notice of that monarch's reign.

Beyond this, and the statute already mentioned, passed at the " Sute of the Browderers " on account of the " deceyptful waight of the gold of Luk, Florence, Jeane, and Venice," [64] there is no allusion to the lace of Florence in our English records.

In France, as early as 1545, the sister of Francis I. purchases " soixante aulnes fine dantelle de Florence " [65] for her own use, and some years afterwards, 1582, the Queen of Navarre pays 17 écus 30 sols for 10 aulnes et demye of the same passement " faict à l'esguille à haulte dantelle pour mettre à des fraizes." [66] On the marriage of Elizabeth de France with Philip II. in 1559, purchases were made of " passements et de bisette, en fil blanc de Florence."

Seeing the early date of these French accounts, it may be inferred that Catherine de Médicis first introduced, on her arrival as a bride, the Italian points of her own native city.[67]

In Florence, in the fifteenth century, Savonarola, in his sermons (1484–1491), reproached the nuns with " devoting their time to the vain fabrication of gold laces with which to adorn the houses and persons of the rich."

Ray mentions that people of quality sent their daughters

[63] Rymer's *Foedera* (38 Hen. VIII. = 1546).

[64] 4 Hen. VII. = 1488–89.

[65] *Compte des dépenses de la maison de Madame Marguerite de France,* *Sœur du Roi.*—Bib. Nat. MSS. F. Fr. 10,394.

[66] *Comptes de la Reine de Navarre.* —Arch. Nat., K. K. 170.

[67] In 1535.

at eight years old to the Florentine nunneries to be instructed in all manner of women's work.

Lace was also fabricated at Sienna, but it appears to have been the *lavoro di maglia* or lacis, called by the Tuscans *modano ricamato*—embroidered network.

Early in the last century two Genoese nuns, of the Convent Sta. Maria degli Angeli in Sienna, executed pillow laces and gold and silver embroidery of such surpassing beauty, that they are still carefully preserved and publicly exhibited on fête-days. One Francesca Bulgarini also instructed the schools in the making of lace of every kind, especially the Venetian reticella.[68]

THE ABRUZZI.

In the Abruzzi, and also the Province of the Marche, coarse laces are made. These are worked without any drawing, the rude design being made by skipping the pin-holes on a geometrically perforated card. The pattern is surrounded by a heavy thread, and composed of a close stitch worked between the meshes of a coarse net ground. This lace somewhat resembles Dalecarlian lace. In the eighteenth century fine pillow lace was also made in these provinces. The celebrated industry of Offida in the Marche has sunk into artistic degradation.

ROMAGNA.

Lace was made in many parts of Romagna. Besides the knotted lace already alluded to,[69] which is still made and worn by the peasants, the peasant women wore on their collerettes much lace of that large-flowered pattern and fancy ground, found alike in Flanders and on the head-dresses of the Neapolitan and Calabrian peasants.

Specimens of the lace of the province of Urbino resemble in pattern and texture the fine close lace on the collar of Christian IV., figured in our notice of Denmark. The workmanship is of great beauty.

Reticella is made at Bologna, and was revived in January, 1900, by the Aemilia-Ars Co-operative Society. The designs are for the most part taken from old pattern-books, such as Parasole.

---

[68] She died in 1862.   [69] See VENICE, 1.

Fig. 34 represents a fragment of a piece of lace of great interest, communicated by the Countess Gigliucci. It is worked with the needle upon muslin, and only a few inches of the lace are finished. This incompleteness makes it the more valuable, as it enables us to trace the manner of its execution, all the threads being left hanging to its several parts. The Countess states that she found the work at a villa belonging to Count Gigliucci, near Fermo on the Adriatic, and

Fig. 34.

UNFINISHED DRAWN-WORK.

it is supposed to have been executed by the Count's great-grandmother above 160 years ago—an exquisite specimen of " the needle's excellency."

Though the riches of our Lady of Loreto fill a volume in themselves,[70] and her image was fresh clad every day of the year, the account of her jewels and plate so overpower any mention of her laces, which were doubtless in accordance with

---

[70] *Inventaire du Trésor de N. D. de Lorette.*—Bib. Nat. MSS.

the rest of the wardrobe, that there is nothing to tell on the subject.

The laces of the Vatican and the holy Conclave, mostly presents from crowned heads, are magnificent beyond all description. They are, however, constantly in the market, sold at the death of a Cardinal by his heirs, and often repurchased by some newly-elected prelate, each of whom on attaining a high ecclesiastical dignity is compelled to furnish himself with several sets.

A lady [71] describing the ceremony of washing the feet by the Pope, writes, in 1771, " One of his cardinals brought him an apron[72] of old point with a broad border of Mechlin lace, and tied it with a white ribbon round his holiness's waist." In this guise protected, he performed the ceremony.

Clement IX. was in the habit of making presents of Italian lace, at that period still prized in France, to Monsieur de Sorbière, with whom he had lived on terms of intimacy previous to his elevation. " He sends ruffles," cries the irritated Gaul, who looked for something more tangible, " to a man who never has a shirt." [73ᵗʰ]

NAPLES.

When Davies, Barber Surgeon of London,[74] visited Naples in 1597, he writes, " Among the traffic of this city is lace of all sorts and garters."

Fynes Moryson, his contemporary, declares " the Italians care not for foreign apparel, they have ruffles of Flanders linen wrought with Italian cut-work so much in use with us. They wear no lace in gold and silver, but black " ; while Lassels says, all they care for is to keep a coach ; their point de Venise and gold lace are all turned into horses and liveries.[75]

---

[71] *Letters from Italy.*

[72] The *gremial*, or apron, placed on the lap of the Roman Catholic bishops when performing sacred functions in a sitting posture.—Pugin's *Glossary of Ecclesiastical Ornament.*

[73] This reminds one of the lines of Goldsmith, in his poem, " The Haunch of Venison," the giving of venison to hungry poets who were in want of mutton ; he says :

" Such dainties to send them their health it would hurt ;

It's like sending them ruffles when wanting a shirt."

[74] *A true Relation of the Travailes, and most miserable Captivitie of W. Davies.* Lond., 1614.

[75] *An Italian Voyage, or a Complete Journey through Italy*, by Rich. Lassels, Gent. 2nd edit., Lond., 1698. A reprint, with additions by another hand, of the original edition. Paris, 1670. Lowndes' *Bibliographer's Manual.* Bohn's new edit.

Of this lace we find but scanty mention. In the tailor's bill of Sir Timothy Hutton, 1615, when a scholar at Cambridge, a charge is made for " four oz. and a half quarter and dram of Naples lace." And in the accounts of laces furnished for the marriage of the Princess Elizabeth to the Elector Palatine, 1612, is noted " narrow black Naples lace, purled on both sides."

The principal fabric of lace was in the Island of Ischia. Vecellio, in 1590, mentions the ladies' sleeves being trimmed with very fine thread lace.[76] Ischia lace may still be met with, and serves for trimming toilets, table-covers, curtains, etc., consisting generally of a square netting ground, with the pattern embroidered. Black silk lace also used to be made in Ischia.

Much torchon lace, of well-designed patterns, was also made, similar in style to that given in Fig. 40.

Though no longer fabricated in the island, the women at Naples still make a coarse lace, which they sell about the streets.[77]

The *punto di Napoli* is a bobbin lace, resembling the punto di Milano, but distinguished from it by its much rounder mesh and coarser make.

Towards the middle of the last century, many of the Italian sculptors adopted an atrocious system, only to be rivalled in bad taste by those of the Lower Empire, that of dressing the individuals they modelled in the costume of the period, the colours of the dress represented in varied marbles. In the villa of Prince Valguarnera, near Palermo, were some years since many of these strange productions with rich laces of coffee-coloured point, admirably chiselled, it must be owned, in giallo antico, the long flowing ruffles and head-tires of the ladies being reproduced in white alabaster.[78]

---

[76] " Portano alcune vesti di tela di lino sottile, lunghe fino in terra, con maniche larghe assai, attorno alle quali sono attaccati alcuni merletti lavorati di refe sottilissimo."—Habiti di donna dell' Isola d' Ischia. *Degli Habiti Antichi e Moderni di Diverse Parti del Mondo di Cesare Vecellio.* Venezia, 1590.

[77] We have among the points given by Taglienti (1530), " pugliese." Lace is still made in Puglia and the other southern provinces of Naples and in Sicily.

The Contessa di Brazza says that Punto Pugliese resembled Russian and Roumanian embroidery.

[78] Brydone, *Tour through Sicily.* 1773.

GENOA ("Genova la Superba").

"Lost,—A rich needle work called Poynt Jean, a yard and a half long and half quarter broad."—*The Intelligencer*, Feb. 29, 1663.

"Genoa, for points."—*Grand Tour*. 1756.

The art of making gold thread, already known to the Etruscans, took a singular development in Italy during the fourteenth century.

Genoa [79] first imitated the gold threads of Cyprus. Lucca followed in her wake, while Venice and Milan appear much later in the field. Gold of Jeane formed, as already mentioned, an item in our early statutes. The merchants mingled the pure gold with Spanish "laton," producing a sort of "faux galon," such as is used for theatrical purposes in the present day. They made also silver and gold lace out of drawn wire, after the fashion of those discovered, not long since, at Herculaneum.

When Skippin visited Turin, in 1651, he described the manner of preparing the metal wire. The art maintained itself latest at Milan, but died out towards the end of the seventeenth century.

Our earliest mention of Genoa lace is,[80] as usual, to be found in the Great Wardrobe Accounts of Queen Elizabeth, where laces of Jeane of black "serico satten," of colours,[81] and billement lace of Jeane silk, are noted down. They were, however, all of silk.

It is not till after a lapse of nigh seventy years that first Point de Gênes appears mentioned in an ordinance,[82] and in the wardrobe of Mary de Médicis is enumerated, among other articles, a "mouchoir de point de Gennes frisé." [83]

---

[79] From the tax-books preserved in the Archives of S. George, it appears that a tax upon gold thread of four danari upon every lira in value of the worked material was levied, which between 1411 and 1420 amounted to L. 73,387. From which period this industry rapidly declined, and the workers emigrated.—Merli.

[80] Signore Tessada, the great lace fabricant of Genoa, carries back the manufacture of Italian lace as early as the year 1400, and forwarded to the author specimens which he declares to be of that date.

[81] "Laqueo serico Jeano de coloribus, ad 5s. per doz. *G. W. A. Eliz'*—16 & 17 and 19 & 20. P. R. O.

[82] Dated 1639.

[83] *Garderobe de feue Madame.* 1646. Bib. Nat. MSS. F. Fr. 11,426.

Moryson, who visited the Republic in 1589, declares "the Genoese wear no lace or gardes."

As late as 1597, writes Vulson de la Colombière,[84] "ni les points de Gennes, ni de Flandre n'etoient en usage."

It was not before the middle of the seventeenth century that the points of Genoa were in general use throughout Europe. Handkerchiefs, aprons, collars,[85] seem rather to have found favour with the public than lace made by the yard.

No better customer was found for these luxurious articles of adornment than the fair Madame de Puissieux, already cited for her singular taste in cut-work.

"Elle étoit magnifique et ruina elle et ses enfans. On portoit en ce temps-là," writes St. Simon ; "force points de Gênes qui étoient extrêmement chers ; c'étoit la grande parure —et la parure de tout age : elle en mangea pour 100,000 écus (£20,000) en une année, à ronger entre ses dents celle qu'elle avoit autour de sa tête et de ses bras."[86]

"The Genoese utter a world of points of needlework," writes Lassels, at the end of the century, and throughout the eighteenth we hear constantly of the gold, silver and thread lace, as well as of the points of Genoa, being held in high estimation.

Gold and silver lace was prohibited to be worn within the walls of the city, but they wear, writes Lady Mary Wortley Montagu, exceeding fine lace and linen.[87] Indeed, by the sumptuary laws of the Republic, the richest costume allowed to the ladies was black velvet trimmed with their home-made point.

The *femmes bourgeoises* still edge their aprons with point lace, and some of the elder women wear square linen veils trimmed with coarse lace.[88]

---

[84] Le Vray Théatre d'Honneur et de Chevalerie. Paris, 1648.

[85] Queen Christina is described by the Grande Mademoiselle, on the occasion of her visit, as wearing "au cou, un mouchoir de point de Gênes, noué avec un ruban couleur de feu."—*Mém. de Mademoiselle de Montpensier.*

"Item, ung peignoir, tablier et cornette de toile baptiste garnie de point de Gênes."—1644. *Inv. de la Comtesse de Soissons.*

"Un petit manteau brodé et son collet de point de Gênes." — *The Chevalier d'Albret.*

"Linge, bijoux et points de Gênes." —Loret, *Muse Historique.* 1650.

"Item, ung autre mouchoir de point de Gênes."—*Inv. du Maréchal de La Motte.* 1657.

[86] *Mém.*, t. xiv., p. 286.

[87] Signore Tessada has in his possession a pair of gold lappets of very beautiful design, made at Genoa about the year 1700.

[88] *Letters from Italy.* 1770.

"That decayed city, Genoa, makes much lace, but inferior to that of Flanders," states Anderson in his *Origin of Commerce*, 1764.

The Genoese wisely encouraged their own native manufacture, but it was now, however, chiefly for home consumption.

Savary, speaking of the Genoa fabric, says : As regards France, these points have had the same lot as those of Venice —ruined by the act of prohibition.

In 1840, there were only six lace-sellers in the city of Genoa. The women work in their own houses, receiving materials and patterns from the merchant who pays for their labour.[89]

Lace, in Genoa, is called *pizzo*. *Punti in aco* were not made in this city. The points of Genoa, so prized in the seventeenth century, were all the work of the pillow, *a piombini*,[90] or *a mazzetta*, as the Italians term it, of fine. handspun thread brought from Lombardy. Silk was procured from Naples. Of this Lombardy thread were the magnificent collars of which we give an example (Fig. 35), and the fine guipures *à réseau* which were fashioned into aprons and fichus. The old Genoa point still finds favour in the eyes of the clergy, and on fête days, either at Genoa or Savona, may be seen splendid lace decorating the *camicie* of the ecclesiastics.

The Ligurian or Genoese guipures have four entirely distinctive characters. The Hispano-Moresque (or Greek) point de Gênes frisé, the Vermicelli from Rapallo and Santa Margherita, a lace resembling Milanese lace with "brides," and a fourth kind, entirely different from these varieties, called *fugio* (I fly), as it is very soft and airy. It is an adaptation of guipure-like ribbons of weaving, with openwork variations, held together by a very few bars. In all these laces, as in Neapolitan and Milanese lace, a crochet needle is used to join the bars and design by drawing one thread through a pin-hole in the lace and passing a free bobbin through the loop to draw the knot tight.

---

[89] Cavasco. *Statistique de Gênes.* 1840.

[90] The bobbins appear to have been made in Italy of various materials. We have *Merletti a fusi,*, in which case they are of wood. The Sforza inventory gives *a doii fuxi,* "two bobbins," then *a ossi,* "of bone," and, lastly, *a piombini ;* and it is very certain that lead was used for bobbins in Italy. See PARASOLE (1600).

Fig. 35.

GENOA POINT, BOBBIN-MADE.   From a collar in the possession of the Author.
This is an elaborate specimen of Point de Gênes frisé—Italian merletti a piombini.   The plaits almost invariably consist of four threads.

PLATE XVIII.

CUSHION MADE AT THE SCHOOL.—These coloured silk laces are reproductions of the sixteenth century. Size, 20 × 12 in.

PLATE XIX.

ITALY.—Group of workers of the Brazza School, Torreano di Martignacco, Friuli, showing the different kinds of lacework done and pillows in use.

Photos by Contessa di Brazza.

The lace manufacture extends along the coast from Albissola, on the Western Riviera, to Santa Margherita on the eastern. Santa Margherita and Rapallo are called by Luxada[91] the emporium of the lace industry of Genoa, and are still the greatest producers of pillow-lace on the coast. The workers are mostly the wives and daughters of the coral-fishers who support themselves by this occupation during the long and perilous voyages of their husbands. In the archives of the parochial church of Santa Margherita is preserved a book of accounts, in which mention is made, in the year 1592, of gifts to the church, old nets from the coral fishery, together with *pisetti (pizzi)*, the one a votive offering of some successful fishermen, the other the work of their wives or daughters, given in gratitude for the safe return of their relatives. There was also found an old worn parchment pattern for a kind of tape guipure (Fig. 36).[92] The manufacture, therefore, has existed in the province of Chiavari for many centuries. Much of this description of lace is assigned to Genoa. In these tape guipures the tape or braid was first made, and the ground worked in on the parchment either by the needle or on the pillow. The laces consist of white thread of various qualities, either for wear, church decoration, or for exportation to America.

Later, this art gave place to the making of black blonde, in imitation of Chantilly, of which the centres in Italy are now Genoa and Cantu. In the year 1850 the lace-workers began to make guipures for France, and these now form their chief produce. The exportation is very great, and lace-making is the daily occupation, not only of the women, but

---

[91] *Memorie Storiche di Santa Margherita.* Genoese pillow-laces are not made with the réseau, but joined by bars. Of Milan lace it is said, " It resembles Genoese pillow-lace in having the same scrolls and flowers formed by a ribbon in close stitch, with a *mesh* or *tulle* ground, whereas the Genoese lace is held together by bars."—C. di Brazza, *Old and New Lace in Italy* (1893).

[92] Lefébure writes, " A version of these Milanese laces has been produced by using tape for the scroll forms and flowers, and filling in the open portions between the tapes by needlework stitches." The C. di Brazza calls similar lace *Punto di Rapallo* or *Liguria*, a lace formed by a ribbon or braid of close lace following the outline of the design with fancy gauze stitches made by knotting with a crochet needle. The special characteristic of this lace is that the braid is constantly thrown over what has gone before. The design is connected by brides. A modification, where the braid is very fine and narrow, and the turnings extremely complicated, and enriched by no fancy stitches between, is *Punto a Vermicelli.*—*Old and New Lace in Italy.*

of the ladies of the commune.[93] In 1862 Santa Margherita
had 2,210 lace-workers : Rapallo, 1,494. The *maestri*, or

Fig. 36.

LACE PATTERN FOUND IN THE CHURCH AT SANTA MARGHERITA (circ. 1592).

overseers, receive all orders from the trade, and find hands to
execute them.   The silk and thread required for the lace is

---

[93] Communicated by Sig. Gio. Tessada, Junr., of Genoa.

PLATE XX.

ITALIAN. BOBBIN TAPE WITH NEEDLE-MADE RÉSEAU.
Width, 8 in.

Photo by A. Dryden·

PLATE XXI.

ITALIAN, GENOESE. SCALLOPED BORDER OF UNBLEACHED THREADS, TWISTED AND
PLAITED.—Sixteenth or seventeenth century. Width, 5 in.
Victoria and Albert Museum.

PLATE XXII.

PLATE XXIII.

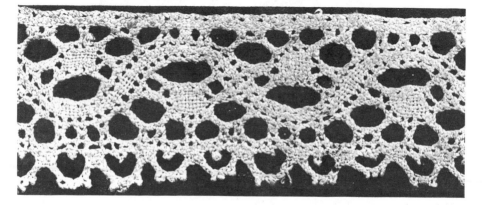

ITALIAN. OLD PEASANT LACES, BOBBIN-MADE.—Actual size.

PLATE XXIV.

ITALIAN. MODERN PEASANT BOBBIN LACE.—Made at the School at Asolo, near Bassano, founded by Browning. Width about 4 in.

Photos by A. Dryden.

weighed out and given to the lace-makers, and the work when completed is re-weighed to see that it corresponds with that of the material given. The *maestri* contrive to realise large fortunes, and become in time *signori* ; not so the poor lace-makers, whose hardest day's gain seldom exceeds a franc and a half.[94] Embroidered lace is also made at Genoa. On a band of tulle are embroidered in darning-stitch flowers or small detached springs, and the ground is sometimes *semé* with little embroidered dots. A coarse thread outlines the embroidery.

The laces of Albissola,[95] near Savona, of black and white thread, or silk of different colours, were once an article of

Fig. 37.

ᴵPARCHMENT PATTERN USED TO COVER A BOOK, BEARING THE DATE 1577. (Reduced.)

considerable exportation to the principal cities of Spain, Cadiz, Madrid and Seville. This industry was of early date. In many of the parochial churches of Albissola are specimens of the native fabric dating from 1600, the work of devout ladies ; and parchment patterns drawn and pricked for pillow-lace, bearing the earlier date of 1577, have been found covering old law books, the property of a notary of Albissola. The designs (Fig. 37) are flowing, but poor, and have probably served for some shawl or apron, for it was a custom long handed down for the daughters of great nobles, previous

---

[94] Gandolfi, *Considerazioni Agrario.*
[95] A small borgo, about an hour's drive from Savona, on the road leading to Genoa.

to their marriage, to select veils and shawls of this fabric, and, in the memory of an aged workwoman (1864), the last of these bridal veils was made for a lady of the Gentili family. Princes and lords of different provinces in Italy sent commissions to Albissola for these articles in the palmy days of the fabric, and four women would be employed at one pillow, with sixty dozen bobbins at a time.[96] The making of this lace formed an occupation by which women in moderate circumstances were willing to increase their incomes. Each of these ladies, called a *maestra*, had a number of workers under her, either at home or out. She supplied the patterns, pricked them herself, and paid her workwomen at the end of the week, each day's work being notched on a tally.[97] The women would earn ʳfrom ten soldi to two lire a day. The last fine laces made at Albissola were bought up by the lace-merchants of Milan on the occasion of the coronation of Napoleon I. in that city.[98]

Among the Alençon laces is illustrated a beautiful lappet sent from Genoa, now in the Victoria and Albert Museum.[99] The pattern is of the Louis Quinze period, and the lovely diapered ground recalls the mayflower of the Dresden and the œil-de-perdrix of the Sèvres china of that time. It was supposed to be of Italian workmanship, though the very fine ground introduced in the *modes* of the riband pattern is the true Alençon réseau stitch. M. Dupont Auberville claimed it for Alençon, asserting he had met with the same ground on point undoubtedly of that manufacture. He named it *réseau rosacé*.

A considerable quantity of lace was formerly made from

---

[96] Cav. Merli.

[97] In the Albert Museum of Exeter are several of these tallies marked with the names of their owners—Bianca, Maria Crocera, and others.

[98] "Many skilful lace-makers in Italy have for some time imitated the old laces and sold them as such to travellers. A Venetian lace-worker, now residing at Ferrara, can copy any old lace known" (Mrs. Palliser, 1864).

[99] This lappet, 357-68, in the Victoria and Albert Museum collection, was described by Mrs. Palliser as "Argen-

tella," and supposed to be of Genoese workmanship. "Formerly much of it was to be met with in the curiosity shops of that city, but now it is of rare occurrence. The Duchess of Genoa possesses a splendid flounce of the same lace, with the Doria eagle introduced into the pattern. It formerly belonged to the Marchesa Barbaretta Saule" (Mrs. Palliser, *History of Lace*, 1864). Contessa di Brazza suggests that Argentella was the Italian for Argentan.

the fibre of the aloe (filo d'erba spada)[100] by the peasants of Albissola, either of its natural cream colour or dyed black. This lace, however, like that fabricated in the neighbourhood of Barcelona, would not stand washing.[101]

There exists a beautiful and ingenious work taught in the schools and convents along the Riviera. It is carried to a great perfection at Chiavari and also at the Albergo de' Poveri at Genoa. You see it in every stage. It is almost the first employment of the fingers which the poor children of either sex learn. This art is principally applied to the ornamenting of towels, termed Macramé,[102] a long fringe of thread being left at each end for the purpose of being knotted together in geometrical designs (Fig. 38). Macramé at the Albergo de' Poveri were formerly made with a plain plaited fringe, till in 1843, the Baroness A. d' Asti brought one from Rome, richly ornamented, which she left as a pattern. Marie Picchetti, a young girl, had the patience to unpick the fringe and discover the way it was made. A variety of designs are now executed, the more experienced inventing fresh patterns as they work. Some are applied to church purposes. Specimens of elaborate workmanship were in the Paris Exhibition of 1867. These richly-trimmed macramé form an item in the wedding trousseau of a Genoese lady, while the commoner sorts find a ready sale in the country, and are also exported to South America and California.[103]

---

[100] Called by the people of the Riviera, *filo del baccalà di Castellaro.* Aloe fibre was formerly used for thread (Letter of Sig. C. G. Schiappapietra). It is also styled *filo di freta* in the Venetian sumptuary ordinances.

[101] The Author has to express her grateful thanks to Signore Don Tommaso Torteroli, librarian to the city of Savona, and the author of an interesting pamphlet (*Storia dei Merletti di Genova lavorati in Albissola,* Sinigaglia, 1863), for specimens of the ancient laces of Albissola, and many other valuable communications.

[102] A word of Arabic derivation, used for denoting a fringe for trimming, whether cotton, thread, or silk.

[103] This custom of ornamenting the ends of the threads of linen was from the earliest times common, and is still occasionally met with both in the north and south of Europe. "At Bayonne they make the finest of linen, some of which is made open like net-work, and the thread is finer than hair" (*Ingenious and Diverting Letters of a Lady's Travels in Spain,* London, 1679).

There is a painting of the "Last Supper" at Hampton Court Palace, by Sebastian Ricci, in which the table-cloth is edged with cut-work; and in the great picture in the Louvre, by Paul Veronese, of the supper at the house of Simon the Canaanite, the ends of the tablecloth are likewise fringed and braided like the *macramé.*

CANTU.

Cantu, a small town near Lake Como, is one of the greatest lace-producing centres in Italy. The lace industry was planted there in the sixteenth century by the nuns of the Benedictine order, and until fifty years ago was confined to simple and rude designs. During the latter half of the nineteenth century, however, the industry has been revived and the designs improved. Thousands of women throughout the

Fig. 38.

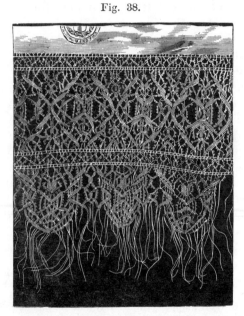

FRINGED MACRAMÉ.—(Genoa.)

province work at it and dispose of their lace independently to travelling merchants, or work under the direction of the Cantuese lace-merchants. The laces are all made with bobbins with both thread and silk.

SICILY.

Sicily was celebrated in olden times for its gold and metal laces, but this fabric has nearly died out. An attempt, however, is now being made to organise a revival of the lace industry as a means of support for the women of Palermo and other populous centres. At Messina, embroidered net (lacis) was made, and bobbin-laces and the antique Sicilian drawn-work are now copied in the women's prison there. Torchon, a lace which is also made in Sicily, has no design worked upon the parchment. The peasant follows the dictates of her fancy, and forms combinations of webs and nets by skipping the holes pricked at regular intervals over the strip of parchment sewed upon the cushion or *ballon*.[104]

There are other variations of old Italian laces and embroideries which have not been mentioned here on account of space ; either they are not often met with—certainly not outside Italy—or in some cases they appear to be only local names for the well-known sorts.

---

[104] LACE SCHOOLS IN ITALY.—At Coccolia, nea: Ravenna, Countess Pasolini founded a school on her property to teach and employ the peasant women and copy antique designs. Another more recently established school near Udine, in the province of Friuli, is under the direction of the Contessa di Brazza. Among charitable institutions which interest themselves in the lace industry are the Industrial School of SS. Ecce Homo at Naples, and San Ramiri at Pisa, which was originally founded by the Grand Dukes of Tuscany in the middle of the eighteenth century to teach weaving. This industry, and that of straw-plaiting, met with no success, and the school gradually developed into an industrial school in the modern sense. There are many schools on the same system in Florence, and one (San Pelegrino) at Bologna. At Sassari, in Sardinia, the deaf and dumb children in the great institution of the " Figlie di Maria " are taught to make net lace. Torchon and Brussels pillow lace is worked under the direction of the Sisters of Providence in the women's prison at Perugia.

CHAPTER V.

GREECE.

" Encor pour vous poincts de Raguse
Il est bon, crainte d'attentat,
D'en vouloir purger un Estat ;
Les gens aussi fins que vous estes
Ne sont bons que comme vous faites
Pour ruiner les Estats."—*La Révolte des Passemens.*

WE have already spoken of Greece as the cradle of embroidery, and in those islands which escaped the domination of the Turks, the art still lingered on. Cyprus, to which in after times Venice gave a queen, was renowned for its gold, its stuffs, and its needlework. As early as 1393, in an inventory of the Dukes of Burgundy, we find noted " un petit pourpoint de satin noir, et est la gorgerette de maille d'argent de Chippre "—a collar of silver network.[1] The peasants now make a coarse thread lace, and some fine specimens have recently been made in white silk, which were exhibited in the Cyprus Court of the Colonial and Indian Exhibition of 1886, and are now in the possession of the Victoria and Albert Museum.

In our own country, in 1423, we have a statute touching the deceitful works of the embroiderers of gold and of silver of Cipre, which shall be forfeited to the king.[2] But the secret of these cunning works became, after a time, known throughout Europe. Of cut-works or laces from Cyprus[3] and the islands of the Grecian seas, there is no mention ; but we hear much of a certain point known to the commerce of the seventeenth century as that of Ragusa, which, after an ephemeral existence, disappears from the scene. Of Ragusa,

---

[1] Laborde, *Glossaire.* Paris, 1853.
[2] Statute 2 Hen. VI., c. x., 1423.

[3] Taglienti (1530) among his *punti* gives *Ciprioto* (an embroidery stitch).

says Anderson, " her citizens, though a Popish state, are manufacturers to a man."

Ragusa, comparatively near the Montenegrin sea-board, and north-western coast of Greece, was, in the fifteenth and early sixteenth centuries, one of the principal Adriatic ports belonging to the Venetian Republic. Certain it is that this little republic, closely allied with the Italian branches of the House of Austria, served them with its navy, and in return received from them protection. The commerce of Ragusa consisted in bearing the products of the Greek islands and Turkey to Venice, Ancona, and the kingdom of Naples ; [4] hence it might be inferred that the fine productions of the Greek convents were first introduced into Italy by the merchants of Dalmatia, and received on that account the denomination of points de Raguse. When Venice had herself learned the art, these cut-works and laces were no longer in demand ; but the fabric still continued, and found favour in its native isles, chiefly for ecclesiastical purposes, the dress of the islanders, and for grave-clothes.

In our English statutes we have no allusion to the point de Raguse ; in those of France [5] it appears twice. " Tallemant des Réaux " [6] and the " Révolte des Passemens " [7] both give it honourable notice. Judging from the lines addressed to it in the last-named *jeu d'esprit*, point de Raguse was of a more costly character, " faite pour ruiner les estats," [8] than any of those other points present. If, however, from this period it did still form an article of commerce, we may infer that it appeared under the general appellation of point de Venise. Ragusa had affronted Louis Quatorze by its attachment to the Austro-Italian princes ; he kicked out her ambassadors, [9] and if the name of the point was unpleasant, we may feel assured it was no longer permitted to offend the royal ears. Though no manufacture of thread lace is known at Ragusa,

---

[4] *Description de Raguse* (Bib. Nat. MSS., F.Fr. 10,772).

[5] Points de Raguse—first mentioned in an Edict of January, 1654, by which the king raises for his own profit one quarter of the value of the " passems, dentelles, points coupez de Flandres, pointinars, points de Venise, de Raguse, de Gênes," etc. (*Recueil des Lois Françaises*). Again, the Ordinance of August, 1665, establishes the points de France, " en la manière des points qui se font à Venise, Gênes, Raguse, et autres pays étrangers," recited in the *Arrêt* of Oct. 12th, 1666.—De Lamare, *Traité de la Police*.

[6] See VENICE.

[7] In 1661.

[8] See head of chapter.

[9] In 1667.

yet much gold and silver lace is made for ornamenting the
bodices of the peasants.　They still also fabricate a kind of
silk lace or gimp, made of twisted threads of cotton covered

Fig. 39.

SILK GIMP LACE.

with metal, which is sewn down the seams of the coats and
the bodices of the peasantry.　The specimen, illustrated in
Fig. 39, may possibly be the old, long-lost point de Raguse.
Its resemblance, with its looped edges, to the pattern given

PLATE XXV.

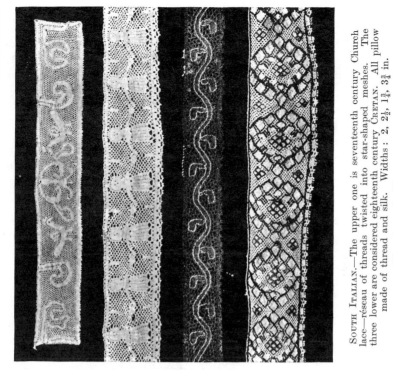

PLATE XXVI.

SOUTH ITALIAN.—The upper one is seventeenth century Church lace—reseau of threads twisted into star-shaped meshes. The three lower are considered eighteenth century CRETAN. All pillow made of thread and silk. Widths : 2, 2½, 1¾, 3¾ in.

Victoria and Albert Museum.

SICILIAN. OLD DRAWN-WORK.—Height, 12 in.

Photo by A. Dryden from Salviati & Co.'s Collection.

Plate XXVIII.

Maltese. Modern, Bobbin made, in Silk.—About two-thirds actual size.

Photos by A. Dryden.

Plate XXVII.

Italian, Rapallo. Modern Peasant Lace, Bobbin
made, in Silk.—Actual size.

from *Le Pompe*,[10] published at Venice in 1557, is very remarkable. We have seen specimens from Italy and Turkey.

The conventionally termed Greek lace is really the Italian *reticella*. "The designs of the earliest Greek laces were all geometrical, the oldest being simple outlines worked over ends or threads left after others had been drawn or cut. Next in date come the patterns which had the outlines further ornamented with half circles, triangles, or wheels. Later, open-work with thick stitches was produced."

Fig. 40.

RETICELLA, OR GREEK LACE.—(Zante.)

The principal seats of the manufacture were the Ionian Isles, Zante, Corfu, Venice, Naples, Rome, Florence and Milan. The Ionian Islands for many years belonged to Venice, which accounts for the similarity in the manufacture. Fig. 40 is from a specimen purchased in the Island of Zante. This lace was much in vogue in Naples for curtains, bed-hangings, and coverlets, and even formed a substitute for

---

[10] See APPENDIX.

tapestry.　A room hung with bands of Greek lace, alternated with crimson or amber silk, has a most effective appearance.

The church lace of the Ionian Isles was not appreciated by the natives, who were only too glad to dispose of it to the English officers in garrison at Corfu.　"Much is still found in Cephalonia : the natives bring it on board the steamers for sale, black with age, and unpleasant to the senses.　This is not to be wondered at when we consider that it is taken from the tombs, where for centuries it has adorned the grave-clothes of some defunct Ionian. This hunting the catacombs has now become a regular trade. It is said that much coarse lace of the same kind is still made in the islands, steeped either in coffee or some drug, and, when thus discoloured, sold as from the tombs " (1869).

The Greek islands now fabricate lace from the fibre of the aloe, and a black lace similar to the Maltese.　In Athens, and other parts of Greece proper, a white silk lace is made, mostly consumed by the Jewish Church.

CRETE.

Pillow-lace making in Crete would seem to have arisen in consequence of Venetian intercourse with the island.　"The Cretan laces [11] were chiefly of silk, which seems to point to a cultivation of silk in the island, as well as to its importation from the neighbouring districts of Asia Minor, when laces were made there, at least one hundred years ago."　In 1875, the South Kensington Museum acquired a collection of Cretan laces and embroideries, some of which (the white thread laces) bear distinct traces of Venetian influence, as, for example, those in which costumed figures are introduced. " As a rule, the motives of Cretan lace patterns are traceable to orderly arrangement and balance of simple geometric and symmetrical details, such as diamonds, triangles and quaint polygonal figures, which are displayed upon groundworks of small meshes.　The workmanship is somewhat remarkable, especially that displayed in the making of the meshes for the grounds.　Here we have an evidence of ability to twist and

---

[11] *A Descriptive Catalogue of the Collections of Lace in the Victoria and Albert Museum*, by the late Mrs. Bury Palliser. Third edition, revised and enlarged by A. S. Cole.

plait threads as marked, almost as that shown by the lace-makers of Brussels and Mechlin. Whether the twisting and plaiting of threads to form the meshes in this Cretan lace was done with the help of pins or fine-pointed bones, may be a question difficult to solve."

The patterns in the majority of the specimens are out-lined with one, two, or three bright-coloured silken threads, which may have been worked in with the other threads as the *cordonnet* in Mechlin. The numerous interlacements which this *cordonnet* makes with the lace point also to the outline having perhaps been run in with a needle.

TURKEY.

"The Turks wear no lace or cut stuff," writes Moryson (1589), winding up with "neither do the women wear lace or cut-work on their shirts"; but a hundred and fifty years later fashions are changed in the East. The Grand Turk now issues sumptuary laws against the wearing gold lace "on clothes and elsewhere." [12]

A fine white silk guipure is now made in modern Turkey at Smyrna and Rhodes, oriental in its style; this lace is formed with the needle or tambour hook. Lace or passe-menterie of similar workmanship, called "oyah" is also executed in colours representing flowers, fruits and foliage, standing out in high relief from the ground. Numerous specimens were in the International Exhibition of 1867.

The point lace manufactured in the harems is little known and costly in price. It is said to be the only silk guipure made with the needle. Edgings of it resemble in workmanship Figs. 121 and 122.

MALTA.

The lace once made in Malta, indigenous to the island, was a coarse kind of Mechlin or Valenciennes of one arabesque pattern.[13] In 1833, Lady Hamilton Chichester

[12] *Edinburgh Advertiser*, 1764.

[13] There is no corroboration of Mrs. Palliser's statement above that lace was ever made in Malta; if so, it would have been of the Genoese geometrical kind, of which Lady Hamilton Chiches-ter adapted the designs and evolved what is now known as Maltese lace by the aid of workers imported from Genoa. The Maltese cross has been introduced into the designs as a dis-tinguishing mark.

induced a woman named Ciglia to copy in white the lace of an old Greek coverlet. The Ciglia family from that time commenced the manufacture of the black and white silk guipures, so generally known under the name of Maltese lace. Much Maltese is made in the orphanage in the little adjacent island of Gozo. Malta has certainly the first claim to the invention of these fine guipures, which have since made the fortune of Auvergne, where they have been extensively manufactured at Le Puy, as well as by our own lace-makers of Bedfordshire and in the Irish schools. The black is made of Barcelona silk, the same used in Catalonia for the fabrication of the black blonde mantillas of the Spanish

Fig. 41.

LOUBEUX DE VERDALE.—(From the cast of his Tomb, Musée de Versailles.)

ladies. Fig. 41 represents the lace round the ecclesiastical robe of Hugues Loubeux de Verdale, Cardinal and Grand Master of the Knights of Malta, who died in 1595, and is buried in the church of St. John, where a magnificent tomb is erected to his memory.

Pillow-laces made by women in Ceylon and Travancore, as well as elsewhere in India,[14] seem to owe more to the instruction of the Portuguese than to the Dutch or English. We mention it in this place because the specimens of thread pillow-lace from Point de Galle and Candy bear a striking

---

[14] " A lace of similar character (Maltese) has also been made successfully in the missionary schools at Madras " (Mrs. Palliser).

resemblance to the Maltese. The specimens of Indian pillow-laces, wrought with white and black threads, in the India Museum, are apparently made in single pieces, and not as in Honiton laces, by separate flowers, which are subsequently placed together for the ground to be worked in between them.[15] "A missionary taught a few Chinese women to make silk lace from the wild silk of this part of China," reports Consul Bullock from Chefoo (at the request of the Nottingham Chamber of Commerce), but the small quantity of lace so produced is sold to Europeans only. The Chinese do not

Fig. 42.

BOBBIN-LACE.—(Ceylon.)

care to buy it. Acting Consul Trotman also reported from Hangkow, that a large quantity of hand-made lace is made in the Roman Catholic orphanages there, but this was entirely for European consumption. White lace in China is not woven by the natives, for white and blue being the national mourning colours, and severe simplicity of dress being *de rigueur* on these occasions, lace of these colours has no sale.[16]

---

[15] Lefébure, *Embroidery and Lace.*
[16] In the Philippine Islands the natives work Manilla grass into a sort of drawn thread-work or tatting.

CHAPTER VI.

SPAIN.

"Of Point d'Espagne a rich cornet,
Two night rails and a scarf beset,
With a large lace and collaret."
　　　　　—Evelyn, *Voyage to Marryland.*

"Hat laced with gold Point d'Espagne."[1]
　　　　　—Wardrobe of a Pretty Fellow, *Roderick Random.*

"The Count: 'Voglio una punta di Spagna, larga, massiccia, ben lavorata. Del disegno, della ricchezza, ma niente di luccicante."—Goldoni, *L'Avaro fastoso.*

SPANISH point, in its day, has been as celebrated as that of Flanders and Italy. Tradition declares Spain to have learned the art from Italy, whence she communicated it to Flanders, who, in return, taught Spain how to make pillow-lace. Though the dress of the Court, guided not by the impulse of fashion, but by sumptuary laws, gave little encouragement to the fabric, on the other hand, the numberless images of our Lady and other patron saints, dressed and re-dressed daily in the richest vestments, together with the albs of the priests and the decorations of the altars, caused an immense consumption of lace for ecclesiastical purposes. "Of so great value," says Beckford, "were the laces of these favoured Madonnas, that in 1787 the Marchioness of Cogalhudo, wife of the eldest son of the semi-royal race of Medino Cœli, was appointed Mistress of the Robes to our Lady of La Solidad, at Madrid, a much-coveted office."

Point d'Espagne, in the usual sense of the word, signifies that gold or silver lace, sometimes embroidered in colours, so largely consumed in France during the earlier years of Louis XIV.'s reign. Ornaments made of plaited and twisted

---

[1] 1756. *Point d'Espagne hats.*—Connoisseur.

gold and silver threads were produced in Spain during the seventeenth century, and mention of them is to be found in the ordinances of that time. Towards the end of the century, Narciso Felin, author of a work published in Barcelona, quoted by M. Aubry, writes that, " edgings of all sorts of gold, silver, silk thread and aloe fibres are made at Barcelona

Fig. 43.

THE WORK-ROOM.—(From an engraving of the Sixteenth Century after Stradan.)

with greater perfection than in Flanders." In the sixteenth century, Flanders was part of the Spanish dominions, and from Flanders Spain imported artistic goods, linen and lace included. Mr. A. S. Cole concludes from this that the Barcelona lace-making was more or less an imitation of that which had previously existed in Spanish Flanders.

Apart from this, the gold and silver lace of Cyprus, Venice, Lucca and Genoa preceded that from Flanders, and it appears that Spain was later in the field of artistic lace-making than either Italy, Flanders or France. Even the celebrity of the gold point d'Espagne is probably due more to the use of gold lace by Spanish grandees,[2] than to the production in Spain of gold lace. The name point d'Espagne was, I think, a commercial one, given to gold lace by French makers.[3]

Dominique de Sera, in his *Livre de Lingerie*, published in 1584, especially mentions that many of the patterns of point couppé and passement given were collected by him during his travels in Spain ; and in this he is probably correct, for as early as 1562, in the Great Wardrobe Account of Queen Elizabeth, we have noted down sixteen yards of black Spanish *laquei* (lace) for ruffs, price 5s.

The early pattern-books contain designs to be worked in gold and silver,[4] a manufacture said to have been carried on chiefly by the Jews,[5] as indeed it is in many parts of Europe at the present time ; an idea which strengthens on finding that two years after the expulsion of that persecuted tribe from the country, in 1492, the most Catholic kings found it necessary to pass a law prohibiting the importation of gold lace from Lucca and Florence, except such as was necessary for ecclesiastical purposes. Mrs. Palliser was of opinion that thread lace was manufactured in Spain at this epoch, for, "in the cathedral of Granada is preserved a lace alb presented to the church by Ferdinand and Isabella, one of the few relics of ecclesiastical grandeur still extant in the country." The late Cardinal Wiseman stated to Mrs. Palliser that he had himself officiated in this vestment, which was valued at 10,000

---

[2] Beckmann, in his *History of Inventions*, says that "It was a fashion to give the name of Spanish to all kinds of novelties, such as Spanish flies, Spanish wax, Spanish green, Spanish grass, Spanish seed, and others.

[3] A. S. Cole. "Cantor Lectures on the Art of Lace-Making."

[4] *Livre Nouveau de Patrons* and *Fleurs des Patrons* give various stitches to be executed "en fil d'or, d'argent, de soie, et d'autres." Both printed at Lyons. The first has no date ; the second, 1549. *Le Pompe*, Venezia, 1559, has "diversi sorti di mostre per poter far, d' oro, di sete, di filo," etc.

[5] "Not many years since, a family at Cadiz, of Jewish extraction, still enjoyed the monopoly of manufacturing gold and silver lace."—*Letter from Spain*, 1863. *Merletto Polichrome*, or parti-coloured lace, was also invented and perfected by the Jews, and was made in silk of various colours, representing fruit and flowers. This industry has been revived in Venice, and carried to great perfection.

crowns. But the following passage from Señor Riano greatly affects the value of what would otherwise be a fact of importance adduced by Mrs. Palliser. "Notwithstanding the opinion of so competent an authority as Mrs. Palliser, I doubt the statement, finding no evidence to support it, that thread lace of a very fine or artistic kind was ever made in Spain, or exported as an article of commerce during early times. The lace alb which Mrs. Palliser mentions to prove this as existing at Granada, a gift of Ferdinand and Isabella in the fifteenth century, is Flemish lace of the seventeenth." [6]

The sumptuous " Spanish point," the white thread heavy arabesque lace, was an Italian production originally. It was imported for the Spanish churches and then imitated in the convents by the nuns, but was little known to the commercial world of Europe until the dissolution of the Spanish monasteries [7] in 1830, when the most splendid specimens of nun's work came suddenly into the market ; not only the heavy lace generally designated as " Spanish point," but pieces of the very finest description (like point de Venise), so exquisite as to have been the work only of those whose " time was not money," and whose devotion to the Church and to their favourite saints rendered this work a labour of love, when in plying their needles they called to mind its destination. Among the illustrations are some photographs received from Rome of some curious relics of old Spanish conventual work, parchment patterns with the lace in progress. They were found in the Convent of Jesù Bambino, and belonged to some Spanish nuns who, in bygone ages, taught the art to the novices. None of the present inmates can give further information respecting them. The work, like all point, was executed in separate pieces given out to the different nuns and then joined together by a more skilful hand. In Fig. 44 we see the pattern traced out by two threads fixed in their places by small stitches made at intervals by a needle and aloe [8] thread working from underneath. The réseau ground is alone worked in. We see the thread left as by Sister Felice Vittoria when she last plied her task.

---

[6] Senor J. F. Riano. *The Industrial Arts in Spain.*—" Lace."

[7] " Spain has 8,932 convents, containing 94,000 nuns and monks."—

Townsend, J., *Journey Through Spain in the Years* 1786 *and* 1787.

[8] The aloe thread is now used in Florence for sewing the straw-plait.

Fig. 45 has the pearled ground, the pattern traced as in the other. Loops of a coarser thread are placed at the corners, either to fasten the parchment to a light frame, like

Fig. 44.

UNFINISHED WORK OF A SPANISH NUN.

a schoolboy's slate, or to attach it to a cushion. In Fig. 46 the pattern is just worked.

A possible reference to lace is found in Father Fr. Marcos

PLATE XXX.

SPANISH, BLONDE.　WHITE SILK DARNING OR MACHINE NET.—Nineteenth century.
Much reduced.

PLATE XXIX.

SPANISH.　MODERN THREAD BOBBIN LACE MADE AT
ALMAGRO.—Slightly reduced.

Photos by A. Dryden from private collections.

PLATE XXXI.

PORTRAIT OF THE DUCHESSE DE MONTPENSIER, INFANTA OF SPAIN, SHOWING MANTILLA.
Middle of nineteenth century.   M. de Versailles.

Antonio de Campos,[9] in his book, *Microscosmia y gobierno Universal del Hombre Crestiano*, when he writes, " I will not be silent, and fail to mention the time lost these last years in the manufacture of *cadenetas*, a work of thread combined with gold and silver; this extravagance and excess reached such a point that hundreds and thousands of ducats were spent in this work, in which, besides destroying the eyesight, wasting away the lives, and rendering consumptive the women who worked it, and preventing them from spending their time with more advantage to their souls, a few ounces of thread

Fig. 45.

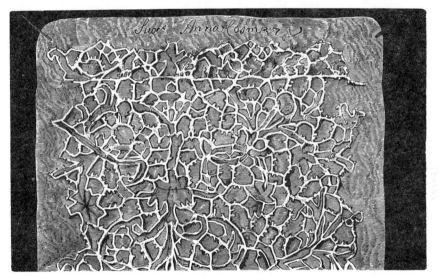

UNFINISHED WORK OF A SPANISH NUN.

and years of time were wasted with so unsatisfactory a result. I ask myself, after the fancy has passed away, will the lady or gentleman find that the chemises that cost them fifty ducats, or the *basquina* (petticoats) that cost them three hundred, are worth half their price ? "

" The most important of Spanish ordinances [10] relating to Spanish art and industry are those which appeared in the

---

[9] Barcelona, 1892, page 225, quoted by Signor J. F. Riano. Date of book 1592.

[10] A. S. Cole, *Ancient Needle-point and Pillow-Lace*.

fifteenth and sixteenth centuries in Toleda and Seville, both
remarkable centres for all kinds of artistic productions.   In
neither of these, nor in the sixteenth and seventeenth century

Fig. 46.

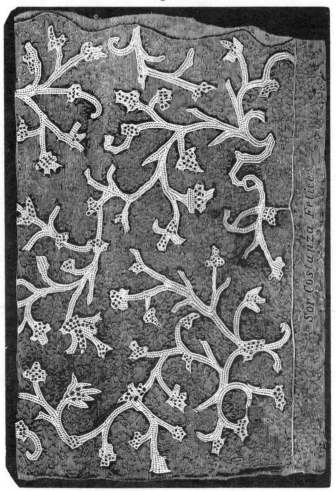

UNFINISHED WORK OF A SPANISH NUN.

ordinances relating to Granada—another art-centre—is there
any mention of lace.

" In the laws which were passed by Ferdinand and Isabella
at the end of the fifteenth and beginning of the sixteenth
centuries, no mention is made of lace, though numerous

details of costumes are named. It will be seen from these remarks on Spanish lace that we give to Italy the credit of producing the artistic and valuable point lace, which unexpectedly came out of Spain after the dissolution of the monasteries."

The ordinance of Philip III, against the wearing of lace, dated 1623, which enjoined "simples rabats, sans aucune invention de point couppé ou passement" for the men, with fraises and manchettes in like trim for the ladies, both too without starch, [11] and which extended to gold and silver lace, was suspended during the matrimonial visit of Prince Charles; [12] indeed, the Queen of Spain herself sent him, on his arrival at Madrid, ten trunks of richly-laced linen. The Prince had travelled incognito, and was supposed to be ill-provided. Whether the surmises of her Majesty were correct, we cannot presume to affirm; we only know that, on the occasion of the Spanish voyage, a charge of two dozen and a half laced shirts, at twelve shillings each, for the Prince's eight footmen, appears in the wardrobe accounts. [13]

The best account of Spanish manners of the seventeenth century will be found in the already-mentioned *Letters of a Lady's Travels in Spain.* "Under the vertingale of black taffety," she writes, "they wear a dozen or more petticoats, one finer than the other, of rich stuffs trimmed with lace of gold and silver, to the girdle. They wear at all times a white garment called *sabenqua*; it is made of the finest English lace, and four ells in compass. I have seen some worth five or six hundred crowns; . . . so great is their vanity, they would rather have one of these lace *sabenquas* than a dozen coarse ones; [14] and either lie in bed till it is washed, or dress themselves without any, which they frequently enough do." A number of portraits exist in the Spanish galleries,

---

[11] This ordinance even extended to foreign courts. We read in the *Mercure Galant*, 1679, of the Spanish ambassadress, " Elle etoit vestue de drap noir avec de la dentelle de soye ; elle n'avait ni dentelle ni linge autour de sa gorge."

[12] *Mercure François.*

[13] They have also provided—
" 14 ruffs & 14 pairs of
    cuffs laced, at 20*s*. . . £14

For lacing 8 hats for the
    footmen with silver
    parchment lace, at 3*s*.. £1 4*s*."
Extraordinary Expenses of his Highness to Spain, 1623. P. R. O.

[14] Doctor Monçada, in 1660, and Osorio, in 1686, reckoned more than three millions of Spaniards who, though well dressed, wore no shirts.—*Townsend's Spain.*

especially by Velasquez and Carrêno, in which these extravagant costumes are fully portrayed, but in very few Spanish portraits of the seventeenth century does thread lace of the kind known to us as point d'Espagne, or de Venise ever appear. Describing her visit to the Princess of Monteleon, the author continues : " Her bed is of gold and green damask, lined with silver brocade, and trimmed with point de Spain.[15] Her sheets were laced round with an English lace, half an ell deep. The young Princess bade her maids bring in her wedding clothes. They brought in thirty silver baskets, so heavy, four women could carry only one basket ; the linen and lace were not inferior to the rest." The writer continues to enumerate the garters, mantle, and even the curtains of the Princess's carriage, as trimmed with fine English thread, black and bone lace.[16]

Judging from this account, Spain at that period received her " dentelles d'Angleterre " from the Low Countries. Spain was early celebrated for its silk,[17] which with its coloured embroidered laces, and its gold and silver points, have always enjoyed a certain reputation. Of the latter, during the seventeenth century, we have constant mention in the wardrobe accounts and books of fashion of the French court. The description of the celebrated gold bed at Versailles, the interior lacings of the carriages, the velvet and brocade coats and dresses, " chamarrés de point d'Espagne," the laces of gold and coloured silk, would alone fill a volume to themselves.[18]

---

[15] Speaking of the apartment of Madame d'Aranda, Beckford writes : " Her bed was of the richest blue velvet, trimmed with point lace."

[16] Our English translation of *Don Quixote* has led some authors into adducing a passage as an evidence that the art of making bone lace was already known in Cervantes' day. " Sanchica," writes Theresa Pança to her husband, the newly-appointed Governor of Baratava, " makes bone lace, and gets eight maravedis a day, which she drops into a tin box to help towards household stuff. But now that she is a governor's daughter, you will give her a fortune, and she will not have to work for it." In referring to the original Spanish we find the words rendered bone lace are " puntas de randas," signifying works of lacis or réseuil — " ouvrage de lacis ou réseuil."—Oudin, *Trésor des Deux Langues Fr. et Esp.* (1660).

[17] As early as the Great Wardrobe Account of Queen Elizabeth, 1587, P. R. O., we have a charge for bobbin lace of Spanish silk, " cum uñ tag," for the mantle, 10s. 8d.

In a letter from Prestwick Eaton to Geo. Willingham, 1631, the writer sends 1000 reals (£25), and in return desires him to send, together with a mastiff dog, some black satin lace for a Spanish suit.—*State Papers, Domestic*, Car. I., P. R. O.

[18] 1697. Marriage of Mademoiselle and the King of Spain. The Queen, says the *Mercure*, wore " une mante de point d'Espagne d'or, neuf aunes de long."

Narciso Felin, writing in the seventeenth century,[19] says that at that time " edgings of all sorts of gold,[20] silver, silk, thread, and aloe, are made there with greater perfection than in Flanders." Campany, another old author, carries the number of lace-makers to 12,000. The Spaniards are said, nevertheless, in 1634, to have derived a great part of their laces from the Île de France, while the French, on their part, preferred those of Flanders.[21] That the lace import was considered excessive is evident by the tariff of 1667 ; the import duty of twenty-five reals per pound on lace was augmented to two hundred and fifty reals. Much point was introduced into Spain at this time by way of Antwerp to Cadiz, under the name of " puntos de mosquito e de transillas."

Madame des Ursins, 1707, in a letter to Madame de Maintenon, ordering the layette of the Queen of Spain from Paris, writes : " If I were not afraid of offending those concerned in the purchase, in my avarice for the King of Spain's money, I would beg them to send a low-priced lace for the linen."

1698. Fête at Versailles on the marriage of the Duc de Bourgogne. " La Duchesse de Bourgogne pourtoit un petit tablier de point d'Espagne de mille pistoles."—*Galérie de l'ancienne Cour, ou Mém. des Règnes de Louis XIV. et Louis XV.*, 1788.

1722. Ball at the Tuileries. " Tous les seigneurs etaient en habits de drap d'or ou d'argent garnis de points d'Espagne, avec des nœuds d'épaule, et tout l'ajustement à proportion. Les moindres etaient de velours, avec des points d'Espagne d'or et d'argent."—*Journal de Barbier*, 1718-62.

1722. " J'ai vu en même temps le carosse que le roi fait faire pour entrer dans Reims, il sera aussi d'une grande magnificence. Le dedans est tout garni d'un velours à ramage de points d'Espagne d'or."—*Ibid.*

1731. Speaking of her wedding-dress, Wilhelmina of Bayreuth, the witty sister of Frederick the Great, writes : " Ma robe étoit d'une étoffe d'or fort riche, avec un point d'Espagne d'or, et ma queue étoit de douze aunes de long."—*Mémoires.*

1751. Fête at Versailles on the birth of the Duc de Bourgogne. The coats of the " gens de cour, en étoffes d'or de grand prix ou en velours de tout couleurs, brodés d'or, ou garnis de point d'Espagne d'or."—*Journal de Barbier.*

[19] *Fenix de Cataluña, compendio desus Antiguas Grandezas y Medio para Renovarlas,*" Barcelona, 1683, p. 75.

[20] In the reign of William and Mary, we find, in a lace-man's bill of the Queen, a charge for forty-seven yards of rich, broad, scalloped, embossed point de Spain ; and her shoes are trimmed with gold and silver lace.— B. M., Add. MSS. ; No. 5751.

At the entry of Lord Stair into Paris, 1719, his servants' hats are described as laced with Spanish point, their sleeves laced with picked silver lace, and dented at the edge with lace.— *Edinburgh Courant.*

In 1740, the Countess of Pomfret, speaking of the Princess Mary's wedding clothes, writes : " That for the wedding night is silver tissue, faced at the bottom before with pink-coloured satin, trimmed with silver point d'Espagne." —*Letters of the Countess of Hartford to the Countess of Pomfret,* 1740.

[21] Marquis de la Gombardière, 1634, *Nouveau Réglement Général des Finances,* etc.

This gold point d'Espagne was much fabricated for home consumption. The oldest banner of the Inquisition—that of Valladolid—is described as bordered with real point d'Espagne, of a curious Gothic (geometric) design. At the Auto-da-fè, the grandees of Spain and officers of the Holy Office marched attired in cloaks, with black and white crosses, edged with this gold lace. Silver point d'Espagne was also worn on the uniform of the Maestranza, a body of nobility formed into an order of chivalry at Seville, Ronda, Valencia and Granada. Even the saints were rigged out, especially St. Anthony, at Valencia, whose laced costume, periwig and ruffles are described as " glorious."

Point d'Espagne was likewise made in France, introduced

Fig. 47.

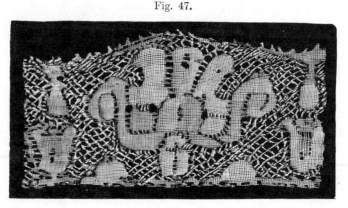

OLD SPANISH PILLOW-LACE.

by one Simon Châtelain, a Huguenot, about 1596, in return for which good services he received more protection than his advanced opinions warranted. Colbert, becoming minister in 1662, guaranteed to Simon his safety—a boon already refused to many by the intolerant spirit of the times. He died in 1675, having amassed a large fortune.[22] That the fabric prospered, the following entry in the wardrobe accounts of the Duke de Ponthièvre, 1732, gives proof:[23] " Un bord de Point d'Espagne d'or de Paris, à fonds de

---

[22] " Eighty children and grandchildren attended his funeral in defiance of the Edict of 19th Sept., 1664, and were heavily fined."—*La France Pro-* *testante,* par M. M. Haag. Paris, 1846–59.

[23] Garderobe de S. A. S. Mgr. le Duc de Penthièvre. Arch. Nat. K. K. 390–1.

réseau." " France," writes Anderson, " exports much lace into Spain."

" The sumptuary law of 1723 has taken away," writes the author of two thick books on Spanish commerce, " all pretence for importing all sorts of point and lace of white and black silk which are not the manufactures of our kingdom. The Spaniards acted on Lord Verulam's policy—that foreign superfluities should be prohibited [24]—for by so doing you either banish them or gain the manufacture." But towards the middle of the eighteenth century there are notices of constant seizures of vessels bound from St. Malo to Cadiz, freighted with gold and silver lace. The *Eagle*, French vessel, taken by Captain Carr, in 1745, bore cases to the value of £150,000.[25] In 1789 we also read that the exports of lace from the port of Marseilles alone to Cadiz exceeded £500,000,[26] and the author of the *Apendice a la Educacion Popular*[27] states that " all the five qualities (of lace) come from foreign lands, and the greater varieties of coarser ones."

Gold and silver lace were made at Barcelona, Talavera de la Reyna, Valencia and Seville. In 1808 that of Seville was flourishing. The gold is badly prepared, having a red cast. The manufacture of blonde is almost entirely confined to Catalonia, where it is made in many of the villages along the sea-coast, and especially in the city of Barcelona. In 1809 it gave employment to 12,000 persons, a number which in 1869 was augmented to 34,000.

There are no large manufactories, and the trade is in the hands of women and children, who make it on their own account, and as they please.[28] Swinburne, who visited Spain in 1775, writes : " The women of the hamlets were busy with their bobbins making black lace, some of which, of the coarser kind, is spun out of the leaf of the aloe. It is curious, but of little use, for it grows mucilaginous with washing." He adds : " At Barcelona there is a great trade in thread lace." [29] Larruga, in his

---

[24] Lord Verulam on the treaty of commerce with the Emperor Maximilian.

[25] *Gentleman's Magazine*, 1745.

[26] Peyron, 1789.

[27] Madrid, 1775.

[28] *Itinéraire de l'Espagne*, Comte Alph. de Laborde, t. v.

[29] Peuchet (*Dictionnaire Universel de la Géographie Commerçante*, An. vii. = 1799), speaking of Barcelona, says their laces are " façon de France,"

Memorias,[30] mentions a manufacture of gold and silver lace which had been set up lately in Madrid, and in another place he [31] mentions lace made at La Mancha,[32] where "the industry of lace has existed at Almagro from time immemorial." Don Manuel Fernandez and Donna Rita Lambert, his wife, natives of Madrid, established in this town in 1766 a manufacture of silk and thread lace. This industry also existed at Granatula, Manzanares and other villages in La Mancha. At Zamora "lace and blonde were made in private houses." In *Sempere Historia del Lujo* [33] we find that in the ordinance issued in 1723 the "introduction of every sort of edgings or foreign laces was prohibited; the only kinds allowed were those made in the country." Cabanillas writes [34] that at Novelda a third part of the inhabitants made lace, and that "more than 2,000 among women and children worked at this industry, and the natives themselves hawked their wares about the country." [35]

The laces of New Castile were exported to America, to which colonies, in 1723, the sumptuary laws were extended, as more necessary than in Spain, "many families having been ruined," says Ustariz, "by the great quantities of fine lace and gold stuffs they purchased of foreign manufacture, by which means Spanish America is drained of many millions of dollars." [36] A Spanish lace-maker does not earn on an average two reals (5*d.*) a day.[37]

The national mantilla is, of course, the principal piece manufactured. Of the three kinds which, *de rigueur*, form the toilette of the Spanish lady, the first is composed of white blonde, a most unbecoming contrast to their sallow, olive complexion ; this is only used on state occasions—birthdays, bull-fights, and Easter Mondays. The second is black

---

but inferior in beauty and quality. The fabrication is considerable, employing 2,000 women in the towns and villages east of Barcelona. They are sold in Castile, Andalusia, and principally in the Indies.

[30] Madrid, 1788. Vol. ii, p. 149.

[31] *Ibid.* Vol. xvii., p. 294.

[32] " The manufacture of silk lace or blonde in Almagro occupies from 12,000 to 13,000 people " (Mrs. Palliser, 1869). Modern torchon laces are still made at Almagro to a very large extent (1901).

[33] Madrid, 1788.

[34] Madrid, 1797.

[35] Senor Juan F. Riano, *The Industrial Arts in Spain*, " Lace " (London, 1879).

[36] *Theory of Commerce*, from the Spanish of Don. Ger. de Ustariz (Lond., 1751).

[37] When the holidays of the Roman Catholic church are deducted, the work-days of the people amount only to 260 in the course of the year—fifty less than in a Protestant country.

blonde, trimmed with a deep lace. The third, " mantilla de tiro," for ordinary wear, is made of black silk, trimmed with velvet. A Spanish woman's mantilla is held sacred by law, and cannot be seized for debt.[38] The silk employed for the lace is of a superior quality. Near Barcelona is a silk-spinning manufactory, whose products are specially used for the blondes of the country. Spanish silk laces do not equal in workmanship those of Bayeux and Chantilly, either in the firmness of the ground or regularity of the pattern. The annual produce of this industry scarcely amounts to £80,000.[39]

Specimens of Barcelona white lace have been forwarded to us from Spain, bearing the dates of 1810, 1820, 1830 and 1840. Some have much resemblance to the fabric of Lille— clear hexagonal ground, with the pattern worked in one coarse thread ; others are of a double ground, the designs flowers, bearing evidence of a Flemish origin.[40]

Spain sent to the International Exhibitions, together with her black and white mantillas, fanciful laces gaily embroidered in coloured silks and gold thread—an ancient fabric lately revived, but constantly mentioned in the inventories of the French Court of the seventeenth century, and also by the lady whose letters we have already quoted. When describing a visit to Donna Teresa de Toledo, who received her in bed, she writes : " She had several little pillows tied with ribbons and trimmed with broad fine lace. She had ' lasses ' all of flowers of point de Spain in silk and gold, which looked very pretty." [41]

The finest specimen of Spanish work exhibited in 1862

---

[38] Ford, *Handbook of Spain.*

[39] 1869.

[40] " Now there are only two kinds of lace made in Spain ; ' encaje de blonda,' mantillas, scarves, lace-ties, etc., in white and black ; these are manufactured in Barcelona, on long pillows stuffed with long straw quite hard, covered with yellow or light blue linen. The lace is worked on a cardboard pattern, and with ' fuseaux ' like the French torchon lace, the only difference being that the pillow is long and narrow and without the revolving cylinder in the centre, so that when making a long piece, or lace by the yard, the pins have to be taken out when you get to the bottom of the pillow, and the work removed to the top and continued. The mantillas, etc., are worked by pieces ; that is to say, the border, flowers, and large designs, and are afterwards joined by the veil stitch.

" The second is ' encaje de Almagro ' —little children of six and seven years old are taught to make it."—*Letter from Spain*, 1901.

[41] " On met de la dentelle brodée de couleur de points d'Espagne aux jupes "—*Mercure Galant.*

was a mantilla of white blonde, the ground a light guipure, the pattern, wreaths of flowers supported by Cupids. In the official report on Lace and Embroidery at the International Exhibition of that year, we read that " the manufacture of black and white Spanish lace shows considerable progress since 1851, both in respect of design and fabrication. The black mantillas vary in value from £4 to £50, and upwards of 20,000 persons are said to be employed in their manufacture."

Before concluding our account of Spanish lace, we must allude to the " dentelles de Moresse," supposed by M. Francisque Michel [42] to be of Iberian origin, fabricated by the descendants of the Moors who remained in Spain and embraced Christianity. These points are named in the above-mentioned " Révolte des Passemens," where the author thus announces their arrival at the fair of St. Germain :—

> " Il en vint que, le plus souvent,
> On disoit venir du Levant ;
> Il en vint des bords de l'Ibère,
> Il en vint d'arriver n'agueres
> Des pays septentrionaux."

What these points were it would be difficult to state. In the inventory of Henry VIII. is marked down, "a purle of morisco work."

One of the pattern-books gives on its title-page—

> " Dantique et Roboesque
> En comprenant aussi Moresque."

A second speaks of " Moreschi et arabesche." [43] A third is entitled, " Un livre de moresque." [44] A fourth, " Un livre de feuillages entrelatz et ouvrages moresques." [45] All we can say on the subject is, that the making cloths of chequered lace formed for a time the favourite employment of Moorish maidens, and they are still to be purchased, yellow with age, in the African cities of Tangier and Tetuan. They may be distinguished from those worked by Christian fingers from

---

[42] *Recherches sur le Commerce, la Fabrication et l'Usage des Etoffes de Soie, etc., pendant le Moyen Âge.* Paris, 1839.

[43] Taglienti, Venice, 1530.
[44] Paris, 1546.
[45] Pelegrin de Florence, Paris, 1530.

PLATE **XXXII.**

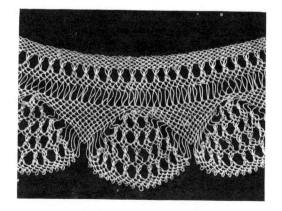

JEWISH. Made in Syria. The pattern is only
modern Torchon, but the knotting stitch is their
peculiar tradition. Same size.

PLATE **XXXIII.**

SPANISH.—The upper one is a copy of Italian lace clumsily made. The lower is probably
a " dentelle de Moresse." Widths about 3½ in.

Photo by A. Dryden from Salviati & Co.'s Collection.

PLATE XXXIV.

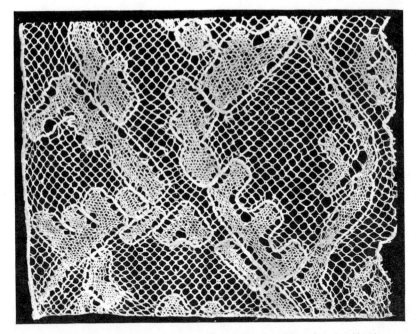

SPANISH.—Pillow made nineteenth century. Réseau of two threads twisted
and crossed. Slightly reduced.

PLATE XXXV.

PARAGUAY. "NANDUTI."—End of nineteenth century. Reduced rather over half.
Photos. by A. Dryden from private collections.

the absence of all animals in the pattern, the representation of living creatures, either in painting, sculpture, or embroidery, being strictly forbidden by Mahommedan law.

PORTUGAL.

Point lace was held in high estimation in Portugal. There was no regular manufacture ; it formed the amusement of the nuns and a few women who worked at their own houses. The sumptuary law of 1749 put an end to all luxury among the laity. Even those who exposed such wares as laces in the streets were ordered to quit the town.[46]

In 1729,[47] when Barbara, sister of Joseph, King of Portugal, at seventeen years of age, married Ferdinand, Prince of Spain, before quitting Lisbon, she repaired to the church of the Madre de Dios, on the Tagus, and there solemnly offered to the Virgin the jewels and a dress of the richest Portuguese point she had worn on the day of her espousals. This lace is described as most magnificent, and was for near a century exhibited under a glass case to admiring eyes, till, at the French occupation of the Peninsula, the Duchesse d'Abrantès, or one of the Imperial generals, is supposed to have made off with it.[48] When Lisbon arose from her ashes after the terrible earthquake of 1755, the Marquis de Pombal founded large manufactures of lace, which were carried on under his auspices. Wraxall, in his *Memoirs*, mentions having visited them.

The fine points in relief of Italy and Spain were the result of such time and labour as to render them too costly for moderate means. Hence they were extensively counterfeited. The principal scroll of the pattern was formed by means of tape or linen cut out and sewn on, and the reliefs were produced by cords fixed and overcast after the work was finished, thus substituting linen and cords for parts of

---

[46] *Magazin de Londres*, 1749.

[47] Mademoiselle Dumont, foundress of the point de France fabric, in the Rue St. Denis, quitted Paris after some years and retired to Portugal : whether she there introduced her art is more than the author can affirm.

[48] It was probably a variety of point de Venise. A few years ago a specimen of point plat was exhibited in London with a Portuguese inscription and designs of figures in costumes of *circ.* 1600.

See Plate IX.

the needlework. These counterfeit points were in France
the occasion in 1669 of an ordinance.

The modern laces of Portugal and Madeira closely
resemble those of Spain; the wider for flounces are of silk;
much narrow lace is made after the fashion of Mechlin.
Both Spain and Portugal enjoy a certain reputation for their
imitation white Chantilly lace. A considerable quantity of
coarse white lace, very effective in pattern, was formerly

Fig. 48.

BOBBIN-LACE.—(Madeira.)

made in Lisbon and the environs; [49] this was chiefly exported,
viâ Cadiz, to South America. Both black and white are

---

[49] The bobbins from Peniche, one
of the few places in Portugal where
pillow-lace is still made, are remarkably pretty. They are of ivory, agree-
ably mellowed by time and constant
handling, and their slender tapering
shafts and bulbous ends are decorated
simply but tastefully with soft-tinted
staining. In size they are small,
measuring from three and a quarter
to three and a half inches long, and
these proportions are extremely good.
Another variety of Peniche bobbin is
made of dark brown, boldly-grained
wood. The lace-makers work on a
long cylindrical cushion—the *almo-
fada*—fastened to a high, basket-work
stand, light enough to be easily moved
from place to place.—R. E. Head,
" Some Notes on Lace-Bobbins," *The
Reliquary*, July, 1900.

extensively made in the peninsula of Peniche, north of Lisbon (Estremadura Province), and employ the whole female population. Children at four years of age are sent to the lace school, and are seated at *almofadas* (pillows) proportioned to their height, on which they soon learn to manage the bobbins, sometimes sixty dozen or more, with great dexterity.[50] The nuns of Odivales were, till the dissolution of the monasteries, famed for their lace fabricated of the fibres of the aloe.

Pillow-lace was made at Madeira at the beginning of the nineteenth century. The coarse kind, a species of *dentelle torchon*, served for trimming pillow-cases and sheets— "seaming lace," as it was called (Fig. 49). Sometimes the

Fig. 49.

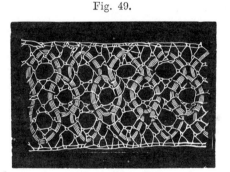

BOBBIN-LACE.—(Brazil.)

threads of the linen were drawn out after the manner of cut-work; but the manufacture had entirely ceased until 1850 (circ. , when it was re-established by Mrs. Bayman.[51]

---

[50] *The Queen*, August, 1872.

"The places in Portugal where the lace industry is chiefly exercised are Peniche, Vianna do Castello, Setubal, a village in Algarve called Faro, and at the present time Lisbon, where, under the help and patronage of H.M. the Queen, a lace dépot has been instituted, in which I have worked for ten years, seeking to raise the Portuguese lace industry to an art. The designs being entirely my own original ones, I am trying to give them a character in unison with the general idea of the architecture throughout the country. I obtained gold medals for my work at the Exhibitions of 1894 at Antwerp and 1900 at Paris, besides others at Lisbon."—Letter from Dona Maria Bordallo Pinheiro, head of the Lace Industry Department at Lisbon, 1901.

[51] "There are now seven families employed in the fabrication of Maltese lace, which is made almost entirely by men; the women occupy themselves in the open-work embroidery of muslin" (1869).

Brazil makes a coarse narrow pillow-lace for home consumption.

The Republics of Central and South America show indications of lace-making, consisting chiefly of darned netting and drawn-work, the general characteristic of the lace of these countries. The lace-bordered handkerchiefs of Brazil, and the productions of Venezuela, with the borders of the linen trousers of the guachos, and the Creva lace of the blacks of the Province of Minas Geraes, are the finest specimens of drawn-work. The lace of Chili is of the old lozenge pattern, and men also appear to be employed on the work. In Paraguay there are two sorts of work—Nanduti or "toile d'arraignée," made in silk or thread by a needle on a cardboard pattern by the copper-coloured natives as an industry ; also embroidery and drawn thread-work on linen, of which there are specimens in the Victoria and Albert Museum—all traditions of the European missionaries and traders who first colonised the country.

CHAPTER VII.

FLANDERS.

"For lace, let Flanders bear away the belle."
—Sir C. Hanbury Williams.

"In French embroidery and in Flanders lace
I'll spend the income of a treasurer's place."
—*The Man of Taste*, Rev. W. Bramstone.

FLANDERS and Italy together dispute the invention of lace. In many towns of the Low Countries are pictures of the fifteenth century, in which are portrayed personages adorned with lace,[1] and Baron Reiffenberg, a Belgian writer, asserts that lace cornettes, or caps, were worn in that country as early as the fourteenth century. As evidence for the early origin of pillow-lace in the Low Countries, Baron Reiffenberg mentions an altar-piece, attributed to Quentin Matsys (in a side chapel of the choir of St. Peter's, at Louvain), in which a girl is represented making lace with bobbins on a pillow with a drawer, similar to that now in use.[2] There exists a series of engravings after Martin de Vos (1580–85), giving the occupations of the seven ages of life : in the third,[3] assigned to *âge mûr*, is seen a girl, sitting with a pillow on her knees, making lace (Fig. 50). The occupation must have been then common, or the artist would scarcely have chosen it to characterise the habits of his country.

Of the two paintings attributed to Matsys—that in St. Peter's, at Louvain, and that in Lierre, only the former is now assigned to the artist. Both pictures are said to be of the end of the fifteenth century or beginning of the sixteenth.

---

[1] Those in the collegiate church of St. Peter's, at Louvain, and in the church of St. Gomar, at Lierre (Antwerp Prov.).—Aubry.

[2] Baron Reiffenberg, in *Mémoires de l'Académie de Bruxelles*. 1820.

[3] Engraved by Collaert. Bib. Nat. Grav.

The triptych at Louvain is reproduced and described in detail by Van Even in his work, *Louvain dans le passé et dans le présent*; [4] it consists of five panels, the centre panel representing " La famille de Sainte Anne"; but among all

Fig. 50.

LACE-MAKING.—(After Martin de Vos.)

the figures none, however, appear to be engaged in making lace or, indeed, in any form of needlework.

---

[4] *Louvain dans le passé et dans le présent formation de la ville, événements, memorables, territoire topo-* *graphie, institutions, monuments, œuvres d'art*, page 330, by Edward van Even, published **1895**.

It has been suggested that the " Lace-maker making lace with bobbins on a pillow with a drawer " (alluded to by Baron Reiffenberg) in the triptych is taken from the above-mentioned engravings by Nicholas de Bruyel and Assuerus van Londonzeel, after the drawings of Martin de Vos.

The historian of the Duke of Burgundy [5] declares Charles the Bold to have lost his *dentelles* at the battle of Granson, 1476; he does not state his authority. Probably they were gold or silver, for no other exist among his relics.

In Vecellio's *Corona* of 1593 and 1596 are two designs of geometrical lace—" ponto fiamengho " and " Manegetti di ponto Fiamengo," point de Flandre.

In 1651, Jacob v. Eyck, a Flemish poet, sang the praises of lace-making in Latin verse. " Of many arts one surpasses all; the threads woven by the strange power of the hand, threads which the dropping spider would in vain attempt to imitate, and which Pallas would confess she had never known;" and a deal more in the same style.[6]

The lace-manufacture of the Netherlands, as Baron Reiffenberg writes, has a glorious past. After exciting the jealousy of other European nations, in the sixteenth century, when every industrial art fled from the horrors of religious persecution, the lace fabric alone upheld itself, and by its prosperity saved Flanders from utter ruin. Every country of Northern Europe,[7] Germany, and England, has learned the art of lace-making from Flanders. After the establishment of the Points de France by Colbert, Flanders was alarmed at the number of lace-makers who emigrated, and passed an act, dated Brussels, December 26th, 1698,

---

[5] M. de Barante.

[6] It goes on: "For the maiden, seated at her work, plies her fingers rapidly, and flashes the smooth balls and thousand threads into the circle. Often she fastens with her hand the innumerable needles, to bring out the various figures of the pattern; often, again, she unfastens them; and in this her amusement makes as much profit as the man earns by the sweat of his brow; and no maiden ever complains at even of the length of the day. The issue is a fine web, open to the air with many an aperture, which feeds the pride of the whole globe; which encircles with its fine border cloaks and tuckers, and shows grandly round the throats and hands of kings; and, what is more surprising, this web is of the lightness of a feather, which in its price is too heavy for our purses. Go, ye men, inflamed with the desire of the Golden Fleece, endure so many dangers by land, so many at sea, whilst the woman, remaining in her Brabantine home, prepares Phrygian fleeces by peaceful assiduity."—*Jacobi Eyckii Antwerpiensis Urbium Belgicarum Centuria.* Antw. 1651. 1 vol., 4to. Bib. Royale, Brussels.

[7] Alençon excepted.

threatening with punishment any who should suborn her workpeople.

Lace-making forms an abundant source of national wealth to Belgium, and enables the people of its superannuated cities to support themselves, as it were, on female industry.[8] One-fourth of the whole population (150,000 women) were said to be thus engaged, in 1861. But a small number

Fig. 51.

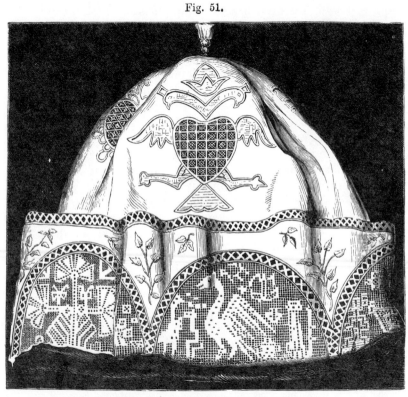

CAP OF THE EMPEROR CHARLES V.—(Musée de Cluny.)
This engraving is not accurately drawn. The spaces contain birds and crosses, and not sprigs.

assemble in the ateliers ; the majority work at home. The trade now flourishes as in the most palmy days of the Netherlands.

Lace forms a part of female education in Belgium.

---

[8] It is said to destroy the eyesight. "I was told by a gentleman well acquainted with Flanders," says McPherson, "that they were generally almost blind before thirty years of age."—*History of Commerce*, 1785.

Fig. 52.

Isabella Clara Eugenia, Daughter of Philip II., Archduchess of Austria, Governess of the Netherlands.—Died 1633.

PLATE XXXVI.

FLEMISH. PORTION OF BED COVER, BOBBIN-MADE.—First half of seventeenth century. This is said to have belonged to Philip IV. of Spain. Above the Austrian eagle and crown is the collar of the Golden Fleece. The workmanship is of great skill.

Victoria and Albert Museum.

Charles V. commanded it to be taught in the schools and convents. Examples of the manufactures of his period may be seen in the cap said to be worn by him under his crown, and in the contemporary portrait of his sister Mary, Queen of Hungary. This cap, long preserved in the treasury of the bishop-princes of Basle, has now passed into the Musée de Cluny (Fig. 51). It is of fine linen; the imperial arms are embroidered in relief, alternate with designs in lacis of exquisite workmanship.[9]

Queen Mary's cuffs (Fig. 53) are of the geometric pattern of the age, and we may presume, of Flanders make, as she was Governess of the Low Countries from 1530 till her death. The grand-daughter of Charles V., the Infanta Isabella, who brought the Low Countries as her dower,[10]

Fig. 53.

MARY, QUEEN OF HUNGARY, GOVERNESS OF THE LOW COUNTRIES. +1558.—(From her portrait, Musée de Versailles.)

appears in her portraits (Fig. 52) most resplendent in lace, and her ruff rivals in size those of our Queen Elizabeth, or Reine Margot.

But to return to our subject. Of the lace schools there were nearly 900 in 1875, either in the convents or founded by private charity. At the age of five small girls commence

---

[9] Together with the cap is preserved a parchment with this inscription: "Gorro que perteneccio à Carlos Quinto, emperad. Guarda lo, hijo mio, es memoria de Juhan de Garnica." ("Cap which belonged to the Emperor Charles V. Keep it, my son, in remembrance of John de Garnica"). J. de Garnica was treasurer to Philip II.

Séguin, however, is of opinion that this cap belonged to one of Charles V.'s successors :—

"Ce bonnet . . . a dû appartenir très certainement à un de ses successeurs (of Charles V.), à cause que ce bonnet se trouve coupé et encadré par un petit entre-deux de guipure au fuseau, façon point de Gênes, qui ne pouvait pas avoir été fait du temps de Charles Quint."—Séguin, *La Dentelle*.

[10] Married, 1599, Albert, Archduke of Austria.

their apprenticeship ; by ten they earn their maintenance ; and it is a pretty sight, an " école dentellière," the children seated before their pillows, twisting their bobbins with wonderful dexterity. (Fig. 54.)

In a tract of the seventeenth century entitled, *England's Improvement by Sea and Land, to outdo the Dutch without Fighting,*[11] we have an amusing account of one of these establishments. " Joining to this spinning school is one for maids weaving bone lace, and in all towns there are schools according to the bigness and multitude of the children. I will show you how they are governed. First, there is a

Fig. 54.

A BELGIAN LACE SCHOOL.

large room, and in the middle thereof a little box like a pulpit. Second, there are benches built about the room as they are in our playhouses. And in the box in the middle of the room the grand mistress, with a long white wand in her hand. If she observes any of them idle, she reaches them a tap, and if that will not do, she rings a bell, which, by a little cord, is attached to the box. She points out the offender, and she is taken into another room and chastised.

---

[1] By Andrew Yarranton, Gent. London, 1677. A proposal to erect schools for teaching and improving the linen manufacture as they do "in Flanders and Holland, where little girls from six years old upwards learn to employ their fingers." Hadrianus Junius, a most learned writer, in his description of the Netherlands, highly extols the fine needlework and linen called cambric of the Belgian nuns, which in whiteness rivals the snow, in texture satin, and in price the sea-silk —Byssus, or beard of the Pinna.

Fig. 55.

OLD FLEMISH BOBBIN LACE.

PLATE XXXVII.

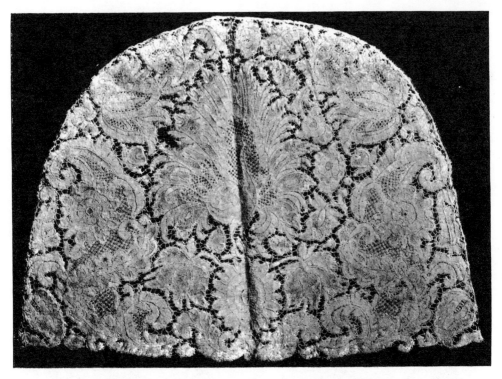

BRUSSELS. POINT D'ANGLETERRE À BRIDES. CROWN OF A CAP.—Last half of seventeenth century.
The property of Mr. Arthur Blackborne.

PLATE XXXVIII

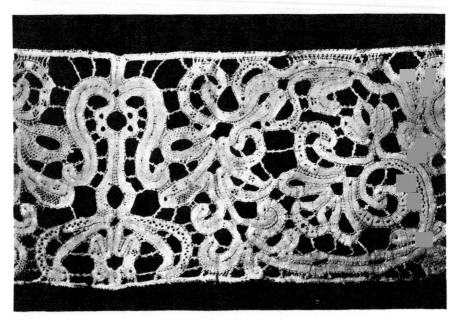

FLEMISH. TAPE LACE, BOBBIN-MADE.—Seventeenth century.
Photos by A. Dryden.

And I believe this way of ordering the young women in Germany (Flanders) is one great cause that the German women have so little twit-twat,[12] and I am sure it will be as well were it so in England. There the children emulate the father—here they beggar him. Child," he winds up, " I charge you tell this to thy wyfe in bed, and it may be that she, understanding the benefit it will be to her and her children, will turn Dutchwoman and endeavour to save

Fig. 56.

OLD FLEMISH (Trolle Kant).

The piece of lace from which this woodcut is taken has five or six different designs all joined together; probably patterns sent round for orders.

moneys." Notwithstanding this good advice, in 1768 England received from Flanders lace-work £250,000 to her disadvantage, as compared to her exports.

The old Flemish laces are of great beauty, some of varied grounds. Fig. 56 represents a description of lace called in the country " Trolle kant," a name which has been transferred to our own lace counties, where lace of a peculiar

---

[12] An old term, still used in Scotland, for gossip, chatter.

make is styled Trolly, with a heavy cordonnet which is called gimp or Trolly. *Kant* in Flemish is " lace."

At one period much lace was smuggled into France from Belgium by means of dogs trained for the purpose. A dog was caressed and petted at home, fed on the fat of the land, then after a season sent across the frontier, where he was tied up, half-starved and ill-treated. The skin of a bigger dog was then fitted to his body, and the intervening space filled with lace. The dog was then allowed to escape and make his way home, where he was kindly welcomed with his contraband charge. These journeys were repeated till the French Custom House, getting scent, by degrees put an end to the traffic. Between 1820 and 1836 40,278 dogs were destroyed, a reward of three francs being given for each.[13]

According to some authorities the earliest lace made in Flanders was of the kind known as Pillow Guipure. The pattern is made as of tape, in flowing Renaissance style, sometimes connected by brides, and sometimes altogether without brides, when the points of the pattern touch each other. In the specimens of this type of lace in the Victoria and Albert Museum there is apparently little in the laces by which the country of their origin may be identified. Sometimes they have been considered French, sometimes Flemish, and sometimes Italian. [See the specimens of tape-lace in the Catalogue of the lace in the Victoria and Albert Museum, p. 49, by A. S. Cole.] (Plate XXXVIII.)

BRUSSELS (BRABANT).

" More subtile web Arachne cannot spin."—Spenser.

" From Lisle I came to Brussels, where most of the fine laces are made you see worn in England."—Lord Chesterfield, 1741.

At what period the manufacture of Brussels lace commenced we are ignorant ; but, judging from the earlier patterns, it may be placed at the beginning of the sixteenth century. The ancient churches of Brabant possess, it is said, many precious specimens, the gifts of munificent princes who have at all periods shown a predilection for Brussels lace, and in every way promoted its manufacture. In usage it is termed

---

[13] These dogs were of large size, and able to carry from 22 to 26 lbs. They also conveyed tobacco. The Swiss dogs smuggle watches.

Point d'Angleterre, an error explained to us by history. In 1662 the English Parliament, alarmed at the sums of money expended on foreign point, and desirous to protect the English bone-lace manufacture, passed an Act prohibiting the importation of all foreign lace. The English lace-merchants, at a loss how to supply the Brussels point required at the court of Charles II., invited Flemish lace-makers to settle in England and there establish the manu-facture. The scheme, however, was unsuccessful. England did not produce the necessary flax, and the lace made was of an inferior quality. The merchants therefore adopted a more simple expedient. Possessed of large capital, they bought up the choicest laces of the Brussels market, and then smuggling them over to England, sold them under the name of point d'Angleterre, or " English Point." [14]

This fact is, curiously enough, corroborated in a second memorandum given by the Venetian ambassador to the English Court in 1695, already mentioned by an informant in London, who states that Venetian point is no longer in fashion, but " that called English point, which, you know, is not made here, but in Flanders, and only bears the name of English to distinguish it from the others." " Questo chiamato punto d' Inghilterra, si sappia che non si fa qui, ma in Fiandra, et porta solamente questo nome d' Inghilterra per distintione dagli altri."

The account of the seizure made by the Marquis de Nesmond of a vessel laden with Flanders lace, bound for England, in 1678 [15] will afford some idea of the extent to which this smuggling was carried on. The cargo comprised 744,953 ells of lace, without enumerating handkerchiefs, collars, fichus, aprons, petticoats, fans, gloves, etc., all of the same material. From this period " point de Bruxelles" became more and more unknown, and was at last effaced by " point d'Angleterre," [16] a name it still retains. [17]

On consulting, however, the English Royal Inventories of

---

[14] Black lace was also imported at this period from the Low Countries. Among the articles advertised as lost, in the *Newsman* of May 26th, 1664, is, " A black lute-string gown with a black Flanders lace."

[15] *Mercure Galant.* 1678.

[16] " Le corsage et les manches étaient bordés d'une blanche et légère dentelle, sortie à coup sûr des meilleures manu-factures d'Angleterre."

[17] We have, however, one entry in the Wardrobe Accounts of the Duc de Penthièvre : " 1738. Onze aunes d'An-gleterre de Flandre."

the time, we find no mention of " English point." In France, on the other hand, the fashion books of the day [18] commend to the notice of the reader, " Corsets chamarrés de point d'Angleterre," with vests, gloves, and cravats trimmed with the same material. Among the effects of Madame de Simiane, dated 1681, were many articles of English point; [19] and Monseigneur the Archbishop of Bourges, who died some few years later, had two cambric toilettes trimmed with the same. [20]

The finest Brussels lace can only be made in the city itself. Antwerp, Ghent, and other localities have in vain tried to compete with the capital. The little town of Binche, long of lace-making celebrity, has been the most successful. Binche, however, now only makes pillow flowers (point plat), and those of an inferior quality.

When, in 1756, Mrs. Calderwood visited the Béguinage at Brussels, she wrote to a friend describing the lace-making. " A part of their work is grounding lace; the manufacture is very curious. One person works the flowers. They are all sold separate, and you will see a very pretty sprig, for which the worker only gets twelve sous. The masters who have all these people employed give them the thread to make them; this they do according to a pattern, and give them out to be grounded; after this they give them to a third hand, who ' hearts' all the flowers with the open work. That is what makes this lace so much dearer than the Mechlin, which is wrought all at once." [21]

The thread used in Brussels lace is of extraordinary fineness. It is made of flax grown in Brabant, at Hal and Rebecq-Rognon. [22] The finest quality is spun in dark underground rooms, for contact with the dry air causes the thread

[18] *Mercure Galant.* 1678.

[19] " Deux paires de manchettes et une cravatte de point d'Angleterre."— *Inventaire d'Anne d'Escoubleau, Baronne de Sourdis, veuve de François de Simiane.* Arch. Nat. M. M. 802.

[20] *Inv. après le decès de Mgr. Mich. Philippine de la Vrillière, Patriarche, Archevêque de Bourges,* 1694. Bib. Nat. MSS. F. Fr. 11,426.

" Une toilette et sa touaille avec un peignoir de point d'Angleterre."—*Inv. de decès de Mademoiselle de Charollais.*

1758. Arch. Nat.

[21] *Mrs. Calderwood's Journey through Holland and Belgium,* 1756. Printed by the Maitland Club.

[22] Flax is also cultivated solely for lace and cambric thread at St. Nicholas, Tournay, and Courtrai. The process of steeping (*rouissage*) principally takes place at Courtrai, the clearness of the waters of the Lys rendering them peculiarly fitted for the purpose. Savary states that fine thread was first spun at Mechlin.

Fig. 57.

Brussels Needle-Point.

Fig. 58

BRUSSELS NEEDLE-POINT.

Fig. 58ᴀ.

BRUSSELS. POINT À L'AIGUILLE.—Formerly belonged to H.M. Queen Charlotte.

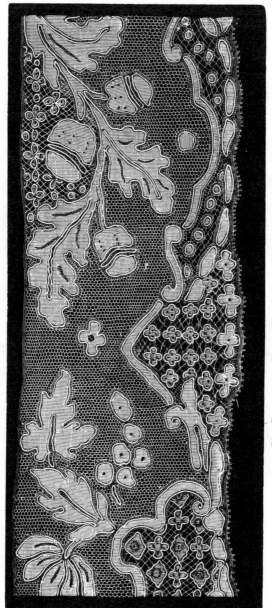

Fig. 59.

Old Brussels. (Point d'Angleterre. Bobbin-made, *circ.* 1750.)

to break, so fine is it as almost to escape the sight. The feel of the thread as it passes through the fingers is the surest guide. The thread-spinner closely examines every inch drawn from her distaff, and when any inequality occurs stops her wheel to repair the mischief. Every artificial help is given to the eye. A background of dark paper is placed to throw out the thread, and the room so arranged as to admit one single ray of light upon the work. The life of a Flemish thread-spinner is unhealthy, and her work requires the greatest skill; her wages are therefore proportionably high.

It is the fineness of the thread which renders the real Brussels ground (*vrai réseau*, called in Flanders, "droschel") so costly.[23] The difficulty of procuring this fine thread at any cost prevented the art being established in other countries. We all know how, during the last fifty years of the bygone century, a mania existed in the United Kingdom for improving all sorts of manufactures. The Anti-Gallican Society gave prizes in London; Dublin and Edinburgh vied with their sister capital in patriotism. Every man would establish something to keep our native gold from crossing the water. Foreign travellers had their eyes open, and Lord Garden, a Scotch Lord of Session, who visited Brussels in 1787, thus writes to a countryman on the subject: "This day I bought you ruffles and some beautiful Brussels lace, the most light and costly of all manufactures. I had entertained, as I now suspect, a vain ambition to attempt the introduction of it into my humble parish in Scotland, but on inquiry I was discouraged. The thread is of so exquisite a fineness they cannot make it in this country. It is brought from Cambrai and Valenciennes in French Flanders, and five or six different artists are employed to form the nice part of this fabric, so that it is a complicated

---

[23] It is often sold at £240 per lb., and in the Report of the French Exhibition of 1859 it is mentioned as high as £500 (25,000fr. the kilogramme). No wonder that so much thread is made by machinery, and that Scotch cotton thread is so generally used, except for the choicest laces. But machine-made thread has never attained the fineness of that made by hand. Of those in the Exhibition of 1862, the finest Lille was 800 leas (a technical term for a reel of 300 yards), the Brussels 600, the Manchester 700; whereas in Westphalia and Belgium hand-spun threads as fine as 800 to 1000 are spun for costly laces. The writer has seen specimens, in the Museum at Lille, equal to 1200 of machinery; but this industry is so poorly remunerated, that the number of skilful hand-spinners is fast diminishing.

art which cannot be transplanted without a passion as strong
as mine for manufactures, and a purse much stronger.   At
Brussels, from one pound of flax alone they can manufacture
to the value of £700 sterling."

There were two kinds of ground used in Brussels lace, the
bride and the réseau.   The bride was first employed, but, even
a century back,[24] had been discontinued, and was then only
made to order.   Nine ells of " Angleterre à bride " appear
in the bills of Madame du Barry.[25]   The lace so made was
generally of most exquisite workmanship, as many magnificent specimens of " bas d'aube," [26] now converted into flounces,
attest.   Sometimes bride and réseau were mixed.[27]   In the
inventories the description of ground is always minutely specified.[28]   (See Plates XXXVII., XLVII., XLVIII., XLIX., LI.)

The réseau was made in two ways,[29] by hand (à l'aiguille),
and on the pillow (au fuseau).   The needleground is worked
from one flower to another, as in Fig. 44.   The pillow is
made in small strips of an inch in width, and from seven to
forty-five inches long, joined together by a stitch long known
to the lace-makers of Brussels and Bayeux only,[30] called
" point de raccroc "—in English, " fine joining "—and

---

[24] *Dictionnaire du Citoyen.*   1761.
[25] *Comptes de Madame du Barry.*
Bib. Nat. MSS. F. Fr. 8157 and 8.
[26] " Trois aubes de batiste garnies
de grande dentelle de gros point d'Angleterre."—*Inv. des Meubles, etc., de
Louis, Duc d'Orléans, decedé 4 fev.*
1752. (Son of the Regent.)   Arch.
Nat. X. 10,075.
" Deux aubes de point d'Angleterre
servant à Messieurs les curez.
" Une autre aube à dentelle de gros
point servant aussy à M. le curé."—
*Inventaire et Description de l'Argen-
terie, Vermeil Doré, Ornemens, Linge,
etc., appartenant à l'Œuvre et Fabrique de l'église Saint-Merry à Paris.*
1714.   Arch. Nat. L.L. 859.
[27] " Une coëffure à une pièce d'Angleterre bride et réseau."—*Comptes de
Madame du Barry.*
" 1 aune et quart d'Angleterre mêlé."
—*Ibid.*
[28] Mrs. Delany writes (" Corr.," vol.
2): The laces " I have pitched on for you
are charming ; it is grounded Brussels."
" Deux tours de gorge à raiseau, un
tour de camisolle à bride."—1720.

Inv. de la Duchesse de Bourbon. Arch.
Nat. X. 10,062–4.
" Six peignoirs de toille fine garnis
par en haut d'une vielle dentelle d'An-
gleterre à raiseau."—*Inv. de deces de
Monsieur Philippe petit fils de France,
Duc d'Orléans, Regent du Royaume,
decedé 2 décembre, 1723.* Arch. Nat.
X. 10,067.
The " fond écaillé " often occurs.
" Une coëffure à une pièce de point
à l'écaille ;
" Une paire de manchettes de cour
de point à raizeau, et deux devants de
corps de point à brides à écailles."—
1761.   *Inv. de la Duchesse de Modène.*
Arch. Nat. X. 10,082.
" Deux barbes, rayon, et fond
d'Angleterre superfin fond écaillé."
—*Comptes de Madame du Barry.*
See her *Angleterre*, Chap. XI. note 26.
[29] To which machinery has added a
third, the tulle or Brussels net.
[30] The needleground is three times
as expensive as the pillow, because the
needle is passed four times into each
mesh, whereas in the pillow it is not
passed at all.

consisting of a fresh stitch formed with a needle between the two pieces to be united. It requires the greatest nicety to join the segments of shawls and other large pieces. Since machine-made net has come into use the "vrai réseau" is rarely made, save for royal trousseaux (Figs. 57 and 58).

There are two kinds of flowers : those made with the needle are called "point à l'aiguille" ; those on the pillow, "point plat."[31] The best flowers are made in Brussels itself, where they have attained a perfection in the relief (point brodé) unequalled by those made in the surrounding villages and in Hainault. The last have one great fault. Coming soiled from the hands of the lace-makers, they have a reddish-yellow cast. In order to obviate this evil the workwoman, previous to sewing the flowers on the ground, places them in a packet of white lead and beats them with the hand, an operation injurious to the health of the lace-cleaner. It also causes the lace to turn black when laid in trunks or wardrobes in contact with flannel or other woollen tissues bleached with sulphur, which discolours the white lead. Bottles containing scent, the sea air, or a heated room, will produce the same disagreeable change, and the colour is with difficulty restored. This custom of powdering yellow lace is of old date. We read in 1782 [32] : "On tolère en même temps les dentelles jaunes et fort sales, poudrez-les à blanc pour cacher leur vetusté, dut la fraude paroître, n'importe, vous avez des dentelles vous êtes bien dispensé de la propreté mais non du luxe." Mrs. Delany writes in 1734 : "Your head and ruffles are being made up, but Brussels always look yellow ; " and she was right, for flax thread soon returns to its natural "crêmée" hue. Yet,

"How curled her hair, how clean her Brussels lace !"

exclaims the poet.[33] Later, the taste for discoloured lace became general. The "Isabelle" or cream-coloured tint was found to be more becoming than a dazzling white, and our coquettish grandmothers, who prided themselves upon the colour of their point, when not satisfied with the richness of its hue, had their lace dipped in coffee.

---

[31] "Trois oreillers, l'un de toille blanche picquée garnis autour de chacun d'un point plat."—*Inv. de la Duchesse de Modène.*

[32] *Tableau de Paris*, par S. Mercier Amsterdam, 1782.

[33] "Fashion." J. Warton.

In the old laces the plat flowers were worked in together with the ground. (Fig. 59.) Application lace was unknown to our ancestors.[34] The making of Brussels lace is so complicated that each process is, as before mentioned, assigned to a different hand, who works only at her special department. The first, termed—

1. Drocheleuse (Flemish, drocheles), makes the vrai réseau.

2. Dentelière (kantwerkes), the footing.

3. Pointeuse (needlewerkes), the point à l'aiguille flowers.

4. Platteuse (platwerkes), makes the plat flowers.

5. Fonneuse (grondwerkes), is charged with the open work (jours) in the plat.

6. Jointeuse, or attacheuse (lashwerkes), unites the different sections of the ground together.

7. Striqueuse, or appliqueuse (strikes), is charged with the sewing (application) of the flowers upon the ground.

The pattern is designed by the head of the fabric, who, having cut the parchment into pieces, hands it out ready pricked. The worker has no reflections to make, no combinations to study. The whole responsibility rests with the master, who selects the ground, chooses the thread, and alone knows the effect to be produced by the whole.

The pattern of Brussels lace has always followed the fashion of the day. The most ancient is in the Gothic style (*Gothique pur*), its architectural ornaments resembling a pattern cut out in paper. This style was replaced by the flowing lines which prevailed till the end of the last century. (Fig. 60.)

In its turn succeeded the *genre fleuri* of the First Empire, an assemblage of flowers, sprigs, columns, wreaths, and *petits semés*, such as spots, crosses, stars, etc. In flowers, the palm and pyramidal forms predominated. Under the Restoration the flowery style remained in fashion, but the palms and pyramids became more rare. Since 1830 great changes have taken place in the patterns, which every year become more elegant and more artistic.

---

[34] Brussels lace-makers divide the plat into three parts, the "mat," the close part answering to the French *toilé* (Chapter III.); *gaze au fuseau*, in which small interstices appear, French *grillé*, and the *jours*, or open work.

The lace industry of Brussels is now divided into two branches, the making of detached sprigs, either point or pillow, for application upon the net ground, and the modern *point à l'aiguille gazée*, also called point de Venise, a needle-work lace in which the flowers are made simultaneously with the ground, by means of the same thread, as in the old Brussels. It is made in small pieces, the joining concealed by small sprigs or leaves, after the manner of the old point, the same lace-worker executing the whole strip from beginning to end. Point gaze is now brought to the highest perfection, and the specimens in the Paris Exhibition of 1867 were remarkable for the precision of the work, the variety and richness of the " jours," and the clearness of the ground.

Brussels point à l'aiguille, point de gaze, is the most filmy and delicate of all point lace. Its forms are not accentuated by a raised outline of button-hole stitching, as in point d'Alençon and point d'Argentan, but are simply outlined by a thread. The execution is more open and slight than in early lace, and part of the *toilé* in made is close, part in open stitch, to give an appearance of shading. The style of the designs is naturalistic. (Plate LII.)

" Point Duchesse " is a bobbin lace of fine quality, in which the sprigs resemble Honiton lace united by " brides." Duchesse is a modern name. The work less resembles the old Brussels laces than the " Guipure de Flandre," made at Bruges in the seventeenth and eighteenth centuries, which was much used for cravats, being exceedingly rich and soft in effect. Bobbin lace is sometimes named point Plat ; the word point in this case signifies the fine quality of the lace, and has nothing to do with the needle-point. Point Plat appliqué is the name given to Belgian bobbin-made sprigs which are afterwards applied to machine-made net. Bobbin lace is not now made in Brussels itself.

Brussels was a favoured lace at the court of the First Empire.[35] When Napoleon and the Empress Marie Louise made their first public entry into the Belgian capital, they

---

[35] The veil presented by the city of Brussels to the Empress Josephine was sold in 1816 by Eugène Beauharnais to Lady Jane Hamilton. It is described to have been of such ample dimensions that, when placed on Lady Jane's head —who was upwards of six feet high— it trained on the ground. The texture of the réseau was exquisitely fine. In each corner was the imperial crown and cypher, encircled with wreaths of flowers. This *chef d'œuvre* passed into the possession of Lady Jane's daughter, the Duchesse de Coigny.

gave large orders for albs of the richest point, destined as a present for the Pope. The city, on its part, offered to the Empress a collection of its finest lace, on vrai réseau, of marvellous beauty ; also a curtain of Brussels point, emblematic of the birth of the King of Rome, with Cupids supporting the drapery of the cradle. After the battle of Waterloo, Monsieur Troyaux, a manufacturer at Brussels, stopped his lace fabric, and, having turned it into a hospital for forty English soldiers, furnished them with linen, as well as other necessaries, and the attendance of trained nurses. His humane conduct did not go unrewarded ; he received a decoration from his sovereign, while his shop was daily crowded with English ladies, who then, and for years after, made a point of purchasing their laces at his establishment when passing through Brussels. Monsieur Troyaux made a large fortune and retired from business.[36]

MECHLIN.

> " And if disputes of empire rise between
> Mechlin, the Queen of Lace, and Colberteen,
> 'Tis doubt, 'tis darkness ! till suspended Fate
> Assumes her nod to close the grand debate."
> —Young, *Love of Fame.*

> " Now to another scene give place ;
> Enter the Folks with silk and lace,
> Fresh matter for a world of chat
> Right Indian this, right Macklin that."
> —Swift, *Journal of a Modern Lady.*

> " Mechlin, the finest lace of all ! "
> —Anderson, *Origin of Commerce.*

> " Rose : Pray, what may this lace be worth a yard ?
> " Balance : Right Mechlin, by this light ! "
> —Farquhar, *The Recruiting Officer.*

Mechlin is the prettiest of laces, fine, transparent, and effective. It is made in one piece, on the pillow, with

---

[36] To afford an idea of the intrinsic value of Brussels lace, we give an estimate of the expense of a fine flounce (*volant*), of *vrai réseau mélangé* (point and plat), 12 metres long by 35 centimetres wide (13¼ yards by 14 inches)—

	Fr.
Cost of the plat	1,885·75
Needle-point	5,000
Open-work, *jours* (*fonnage*)	390
Appliqué (*stricage*)	800
Ground (*réseau*)	2,782
Footing (*engrêlure*)	1·27
Total	10,859·02
= £434 7 6

Equals £36 3s. 9d. the metre, and the selling price would be about £50 16s., which would make the flounces amount to £609 12s.

Fig. 60.

Old Brussels. (Point d'Angleterre. Formerly belonging to Queen Charlotte.)

PLATE XXXIX.

MECHLIN.—Four specimens of seventeenth and eighteenth centuries. Arranged by age, the oldest at the top. The upper one is the end of a lappet, the property of Mr. Arthur Blackborne. Width about 3½ in. Widths of smaller pieces, 1¾ in., lower, 2½ in.

Photos by A. Dryden.

various fancy stitches introduced. Its distinguishing feature is the cordonnet or flat silky thread which outlines the pattern, and gives to this lace the character of embroidery (hence it is sometimes called Broderie de Malines[37]); and secondly, the hexagonal mesh of the réseau. "This is made of two threads twisted twice on four sides, and four threads plaited three times on the two other sides. Thus the plait is shorter and the mesh consequently smaller than that of Brussels lace." Mechlin was sometimes grounded with an ornamental réseau called *Fond de neige*, or *Œil de perdrix*, and also with the six-pointed *Fond Chant*; but these varieties are not common. The earliest Mechlin has the *points d'esprit*, and is very rare. It was made at Mechlin, Antwerp, Lierre and Turnhout, but the manufacture has long been on the decline. In 1834 there were but eight houses where it was fabricated, but at a later date it appears to have partially revived. There was a fine collection of Mechlin lace in the Paris Exhibition of 1867 from Turnhout (Prov. Antwerp), and some other localities. Very little is now manufactured. It is difficult to trace the real point de Malines. Previous to 1665, as elsewhere stated, all Flanders laces, with some exceptions, were known to the French commercial world as "Malines." According to Savary, the laces of Ypres, Bruges, Dunkirk and Courtrai passed at Paris under that name—hence we have in the inventories of the time, "Malines à bride,"[38] as well as "Malines à rézeau."[39]

The statute of Charles II. having placed a bar to the introduction of Flanders lace into England, Mechlin neither appears in the advertisements nor inventories of the time.

We find mention of this fabric in France as early as Anne of Austria, who is described in the memoirs of Marion

---

[37] "Une paire de manchettes de dentelle de Malines brodée."

"Quatre bonnets de nuit garnis de Malines brodée."—*Inv. de decès de Mademoiselle de Charollais.* 1758.

[38] *Inv. de la Duchesse de Bourbon.* 1720.

"1704. Deux fichus garnis de dentelle de Malines à bride ou rézeau.

"Une cravatte avec les manchettes de point de Malines à bride.

"Deux autres cravattes de dentelle de Malines à rézeau et trois paires de manchettes de pareille dentelle."—*Inv. de Franç. Phelypeaux Loisel.* Bib. Nat. MSS. F. Fr. 11,459.

[39] *Inv. de decès de Madame Anne, Palatine de Bavière, Princesse de Condé.* 1723. Arch. de Nat. X. 10,065.

de l'Orme as wearing a veil " en frizette de Malines." [40]
Again, the Maréchal de la Motte, who died in 1657, has,
noted in his inventory,[41] a pair of Mechlin ruffles.

Regnard, who visited Flanders in 1681, writes from this
city : " The common people here, as throughout all Flanders, occupy themselves in making the white lace known
as Malines, and the Béguinage, the most considerable in the
country, is supported by the work of the Béguines, in which
they excel greatly." [42]

When, in 1699, the English prohibition was removed,
Mechlin lace became the grand fashion, and continued so
during the succeeding century.   Queen Mary anticipated
the repeal by some years, for, in 1694, she purchased two
yards of knotted fringe for her Mechlin ruffles,[43] which leads
us to hope she had brought the lace with her from Holland ;
though, as early as 1699, we have advertised in the *London
Gazette*, August 17th to 21st : " Lost from Barker's coach
a deal box containing," among other articles, " a waistcoat
and Holland shirt, both laced with Mecklin lace."   Queen
Anne purchased it largely ; at least, she paid in 1713 [44]
£247 6s. 9d. for eighty-three yards, either to one Margaret
Jolly or one Francis Dobson, " Millenario Regali "—the
Royal Milliner, as he styles himself.   George I. indulges in
a " Macklin " cravat.[45]

" It is impossible," says Savary about this time, " to
imagine how much Mechlin lace is annually purchased by
France and Holland, and in England it has always held the
highest favour."

Of the beau of 1727 it is said :

" Right Macklin must twist round his bosom and wrists."

While Captain Figgins of the 67th, a dandy of the first
water, is described, like the naval puppy of Smollett in
Roderick Random, " his hair powdered with maréchal, a
cambric shirt, his Malines lace dyed with coffee-grounds."
Towards 1755 the fashion seems to have been on the decline

---

[40] In the accounts of Madame du
Barry, we have " Malines bâtarde à
bordure."
[41] *Inv. après le decès de Mgr. le
Maréchal de la Motte.*   Bib. Nat.
MSS. F. Fr. 11,426.   " Quatre paires
de manchettes garnyes de passement
tant de Venise, Gennes, et de Malines."
[42] *Voyage en Flandre.* 1681.
[43] B. M. Add. MSS. No. 5751.
[44] Gr. Ward. Acc. P. R. O.
[45] *Ibid.*

in England. "All the town," writes Mr. Calderwood, " is full of convents ; Mechlin lace is all made there ; I saw a great deal, and very pretty and cheap. They talk of giving up the trade, as the English, upon whom they depended, have taken to the wearing of French blondes. The lace merchants employ the workers and all the town with lace. Though they gain but twopence halfpenny daily, it is a good worker who will finish a Flemish yard (28 inches) in a fortnight."

Mechlin is essentially a summer lace, not becoming in

Fig. 61.

MECHLIN.—(Period Louis XVI.)

itself, but charming when worn over colour. It found great favour at the court of the Regent, as the inventories of the period attest. Much of this lace, judging from these accounts, was made in the style of the modern insertion, with an edging on both sides, "campané," and, being light in texture, was well adapted for the gathered trimmings, later termed [46] "quilles," now better known as "plissés à la

---

[46] " On chamarre les jupes en quiles de dentelles plissées."— *Mercure Galant.* 1678.

" Un volant dentelle d'Angleterre plissée."—*Extraordinaire du Mercure. Quartier d'Esté.* 1678.

vieille." [47]   Mechlin can never have been used as a " dentelle de grande toilette " ; it served for coiffures de nuit, garnitures de corset, ruffles and cravats.[48]

Lady Mary Wortley Montagu, describing an admirer, writes :

" With eager beat his Mechlin cravat moves—
He loves, I whisper to myself, he loves ! "

It was the favourite lace of Queen Charlotte (Fig. 62) and of the Princess Amelia.   Napoleon I. was also a great

Fig. 62.

MECHLIN.—(Formerly belonging to H. M. Queen Charlotte.)

admirer of this fabric, and when he first saw the light Gothic tracery of the cathedral spire of Antwerp, he exclaimed, " C'est comme de la dentelle de Malines."

---

[47] " 1741. Une coiffure de nuit de Malines à raizeau campanée de deux pièces.

" Une paire de manches de Malines brodée à raizeau campanée, un tour de gorge, et une garniture de corset."
—*Inv. de Mademoiselle de Clermont.*

" 1761. Une paire de manches de Malines bridés non campanée, tour de gorge, et garniture de corset."—*Inv. de la Duchesse de Modène.*

[48] " 1720. Une garniture de teste à trois pièces de dentelle de Malines à bride.

" Deux peignoirs de toile d'Hollande garnis de dentelle, l'une d'Angleterre à bride et l'autre de Maline à raiseau."
—*Inv. de la Duchesse de Bourbon.*

ANTWERP.

"At Antwerp, bought some ruffles of our agreeable landlady, and set out at 2 o'clock for Brussels."—*Tour*, by G. L., 1767.

Before finishing our account of the laces of Brabant, we must touch upon the produce of Antwerp, which, though little differing from that of the adjoining towns, seems at one time to have been known in the commercial world.[49] In the year 1560 we have no mention of lace among the fabrics of Antwerp, at that period already flourishing, unless it be classed under the head of " mercery, fine and rare." [50] The cap, however, of an Antwerp lady [51] of that period is decorated with the fine lace of geometric pattern. (Fig. 63.) As early as 1698 the *Flying Postman* advertises as follows : " Yesterday, was dropped between the Mitre Tavern and the corner of Princes-street, five yards and better of Antwerp lace, pinner breadth. One guinea reward."

According to Savary, much lace without ground, " dentelle sans fond," a guipure of large flowers united by " brides," was fabricated in all the towns of Brabant for especial exportation to the Spanish Indies, where the " Gothic " taste continued in favour up to a very late period. These envoys

---

"1750. Une dormeuse de Malines." —*Inv. de Mademoiselle de Charollais.*

" 1770. 5½ grande hauteur de Malines pour une paire de manchettes, 264 francs.

" 1 au. jabot pour le tour de gorge, 16.

" 5 au. ¼ Malines pour garnir 3 chemises au nègre à 12 fr." (The wretch Zamor who denounced her.)— *Comptes de Madame du Barry.*

" 1788. 6 tayes d'oreiller garnies de Malines."—*État de ce qui a été fourni pour le renouvellement de Mgr. le Dauphin.* Arch. Nat. K. 505, No. 20.

" 1792. 2 tayes d'oreillier garnis de maline."—*Notes du linge du ci-devant Roi. Ibid.* No. 8.

" 1792. 24 fichus de batiste garnis de Maline.

"2 taye d'orilier garnis de Maline." —*Renouvellement de M. le Duc. de Normandie. Ibid.*

[49] An Arrêt, dated 14 Aug., 1688, requires that " toutes les dentelles de fil d'Anvers, Bruxelles, Malines et autres lieux de la Flandre Espagnolle," shall enter only by Rousselars and Condé, and pay a duty of 40 livres per lb.—Arch. Nat. *Coll. Rondonneau.*

[5] In the list of foreign Protestants resident in England, 1618 to 1688, we find in London, Aldersgate Ward, Jacob Johnson, born at Antwerp, lace-maker, and Antony du Veal, lace-weaver, born in Turny (Tournay).

[51] This portrait has been engraved by Verbruggen, who gives it as that of Catherine of Aragon.

were expedited first to Cadiz, and there disposed of. In 1696, we find in a seizure made by Monsieur de la Bellière, on the high seas, " 2181 pieces de dentelles grossières à l'Espagnole assorties." [52]   (Plate XLI.)

Since the cessation of this Spanish market, Antwerp lace would have disappeared from the scene had it not been for the attachment evinced by the old people for one pattern, which has been worn on their caps from generation to generation, generally known by the name of "pot lace" (potten kant).   It is made in the Béguinages of three qualities, mostly "fond double."   The pattern has always a

Fig. 63.

A LADY OF ANTWERP.—(Ob. 1598.   After Crispin de Passe.)

vase (Fig. 64), varied according to fancy. [53]   Antwerp now makes Brussels lace.

One of the earliest pattern-books, that printed by Vorsterman [54]—the title in English—was published at Antwerp, but it only contains patterns for Spanish stitch and other embroidery—no lace.   There is no date affixed to the title-page, which is ornamented with six woodcuts representing

---

[52] *Mercure Galant*, 1696.

[53] The flower-pot was a symbol of the Annunciation.   In the early representations of the appearance of the Angel Gabriel to the Virgin Mary, lilies are placed either in his hand, or set as an accessory in a vase.   As Romanism declined, the angel disappeared, and the lily pot became a vase of flowers; subsequently the Virgin was omitted, and there remained only the vase of flowers.

[54] See APPENDIX.

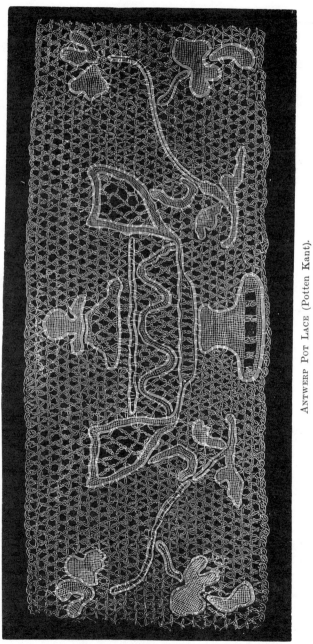

Fig. 64.

Antwerp Pot Lace (Potten Kant).

PLATE XL.

MECHLIN.—Three specimens of last half of eighteenth century.   Photos by A. Dryden from Mrs. Ellis' Collection.

Width, 4 in.

Width, 4½ in.

Victoria and Albert Museum.

Width, 5 in.

women, and one a man, working at frames. This work is most rare ; the only copy known may be found in the Library of the Arsenal at Paris.

Turnhout, which with Antwerp and Mechlin form the three divisions of the modern province of Antwerp, seems to have largely manufactured lace up to the present century ; as we find in 1803, out of forty lace thread and lace fabrics in the province, there were thirteen at Antwerp, twelve at Turnhout, and nine at Malines.[55] Turnhout now produces Mechlin.

FLANDERS (WEST).

The most important branch of the pillow-lace trade in Belgium is the manufacture of Valenciennes, which, having expired in its native city, has now spread over East and West Flanders. The art was originally imported into Flanders from French Hainault in the seventeenth century. As early as 1656, Ypres began to make Valenciennes lace. When, in 1684, a census was made by order of Louis XIV., there were only three forewomen [56] and sixty-three lace-makers. In 1850, there were from 20,000 to 22,000 in Ypres and its environs alone.

The productions of Ypres are of the finest quality and most elaborate in their workmanship. On a piece not two inches wide, from 200 to 300 bobbins are employed, and for the larger widths as many as 800 or more are used on the same pillow. In the exhibition of 1867, one exhibited with the lace in progress had 1,200 bobbins,[57] while in the International Exhibition of 1874 there were no less than 8,000 bobbins on a Courtrai pillow used for making a parasol cover. The ground is in large clear squares, which admirably throws up the even tissue of the patterns. In these there was little variety until 1833, when a manufacturer [58] adopted a clear

---

[55] *Tableau Statistique du Dép. des Deux-Nèthes*, par le Citoyen Herbouville. An X. = 1802.

[56] Their names are given : Veuves Mesele, Papegay, and Turck.

[57] Ypres Valenciennes was exhibited at £80 (the metre). The lace-maker, working twelve hours a day, could scarcely produce one-third of an inch a week. It would take her twelve years to complete a length of six or seven metres, her daily earnings averaging two to three francs. Ypres makes the widest Valenciennes of any manufacture except Courtrai, whence was exhibited a half shawl (pointe) of Valenciennes.

[58] M. Duhayon Brunfaut, of Ypres.

wire ground with bold flowing designs, instead of the thick
treille [59] and scanty flowers of the old laces. (Fig. 65.) The
change was accepted by fashion, and the Valenciennes lace
of Ypres has now attained a high degree of perfection.
Courtrai has made great advances towards rivalling Ypres
in its productions.

Not a hundred years since, when the laces of Valenciennes prospered, those of Belgium were designated as
"fausses Valenciennes." Belgium has now the monopoly
to a commercial value of more than £800,000.[60] The other
principal centres of the manufacture are Bruges, Courtrai,

Fig. 65.

VALENCIENNES LACE OF YPRES.

and Menin in West, Ghent and Alost in East, Flanders.
When Peuchet wrote in the eighteenth century, he cites "les
dentelles à l'instar de Valenciennes" of Courtrai as being in
favour, and generally sought after both in England and
France, while those of Bruges are merely alluded to as
" passing for Mechlin." From this it may be inferred the
tide had not then flowed so far north. The Valenciennes
of Bruges, from its round ground, has never enjoyed a high

[59] *Treille* is the general term for the
ground (*réseau*) throughout Belgium
and the Dép. du Nord.
[60] France alone buys of Belgium
more Valenciennes than all the other
countries united; upwards of 12 millions
of francs (£480,000).—Aubry.

PLATE XLI.

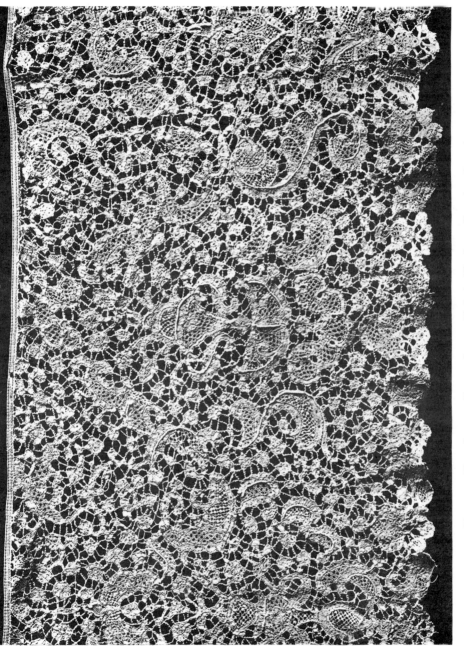

FLEMISH.   FLAT SPANISH BOBBIN LACE.—Made in Flanders.   Seventeenth century.

From a photo the property of A. Dryden.

PLATE XLII.

FLEMISH. GUIPURE DE FLANDRE, BOBBIN-MADE.—Seventeenth century.

In the Musée Cinquantenaire, Brussels.

reputation. In forming the ground, the bobbins are only twisted twice, while in those of Ypres and Alost, the operation is performed four and five times.[61] The oftener the bobbins are twisted the clearer and more esteemed is the Valenciennes. The "guipure de Flandres" made at Bruges in "point plat" is now in high repute, and has proved from its low price a formidable rival to Honiton, which it resembles, but the workmanship is coarser and inferior than in the best Honiton. It is of a brilliant white, and composed of bobbin-made flowers united by *barettes* or *brides à picot*. In the *L'Industrie Dentellière Belge* (1860), it is stated that West Flanders has now 180 fabrics and 400 lace schools. Of these, 157 are the property of religious communities, and number upwards of 30,000 apprentices.[62]

FLANDERS (EAST).

No traveller has passed through the city of Ghent for the last hundred years without describing the Béguinage and its lace school. "The women, "writes the author of the *Grand Tour*, 1756, "number nigh 5,000, go where they please, and employ their time in weaving lace."

Savary cites the "fausses Valenciennes," which he declares to equal the real in beauty. "They are," continues he, "moins serrées, un peu moins solides, et un peu moins chères."

The best account, however, we have of the Ghent manufactures is contained in a letter addressed to Sir John Sinclair by Mr. Hey Schoulthem in 1815. "The making of lace," he writes, "at the time the French entered the Low Countries, employed a considerable number of people of both sexes, and great activity prevailed in Ghent. The lace was chiefly for daily use; it was sold in Holland, France and England. A large quantity of 'sorted' laces of a peculiar quality were exported to Spain and the colonies. It is to be feared that, after an interruption of twenty years, this lucrative branch of commerce will be at an end : the changes of fashion have even reached the West Indian colonists,

---

[61] At Ghent two turns and a half, and at Courtrai three and a half. Each town has its own peculiar stitch.

[62] *L'Industrie Dentellière Belge,* par B. v. d. Dussen, Bruxelles, 1860.

whose favourite ornaments once consisted of Flemish laces[63]
and fringes.   These laces were mostly manufactured in the
charitable institutions for poor girls, and by old women
whose eyes did not permit them to execute a finer work.
As for the young girls, the quality of these Spanish laces,
and the facility of their execution, permitted the least skilful
to work them with success, and proved a means of rendering
them afterwards excellent workwomen.   At present, the best
market for our laces is in France ; a few also are sent to
England." He continues to state that, since the interruption
of the commerce with Spain, to which Ghent formerly belonged, the art has been replaced by a trade in cotton ; but
that cotton-weaving spoils the hand of the lace-makers,
and, if continued, would end by annihilating the lace
manufacture.[64]

Grammont and Enghien formerly manufactured a cheap
white thread lace, now replaced by the making of laces of
black silk.   This industry was introduced towards 1840 by
M. Lepage, and black silk and cotton-thread lace is now
made at Grammont, Enghien, and Oudenarde in the southern
part of Eastern Flanders.   The lace of Grammont is remarkable for its regularity, the good quality of its silk, and its
low price, but its grounds are coarse, and the patterns want
relief and solidity, and the bobbins are more often twisted
in making the ground, which deprives it of its elasticity.
Grammont makes no small pieces, but shawls, dresses, etc.,
principally for the American market.

The "industrie dentellière" of East Flanders is now most
flourishing.   In 1869 it boasted 200 fabrics directed by the
laity, and 450 schools under the superintendence of the nuns.
Even in the poor-houses (hospices) every woman capable of
using a bobbin passes her day in lace-making.

HAINAULT.

The laces of Mons and those once known as "les figures
de Chimay" both in the early part of the eighteenth century
enjoyed a considerable reputation.   Mrs. Palliser, on visiting

---

[63] Robinson Crusoe, when at Lisbon,
sends " some Flanders lace of a good
value " as a present to the wife and
daughter of his partner in the Brazils.

[64] *Answer to Sir John Sinclair*, by
Mr. H. Schoulthem, concerning the
manufactures of Ghent.   1815.

Chimay in 1874, could find no traces of the manufacture beyond an aged lace-maker, an inmate of the hospice, who made black lace—" point de Paris "—and who said that until lately Brussels lace had also been made at Chimay. The first Binche lace has the character of Flanders lace, so it has been supposed that the women who travelled from Ghent in the train of Mary of Burgundy, the daughter of Charles le Téméraire, created the taste for lace at Binche, and that the stay of the great ladies, on their visits to the royal lady of the manor, made the fortune of the lace-makers. Afterwards there was much traffic between the lace-workers of Brussels and Binche, and there is a great resemblance between the laces of the two towns. Sometimes the latter is less light, richer, and more complex in effect, and the design is closely sprinkled with open-work, the ground varied and contrasted.

Binche was, as early as 1686, the subject of a royal edict, leading one to infer that the laces it produced were of some importance. In the said edict, the roads of Verviers, Gueuse, and Le Catelet, to those persons coming from Binche, are pronounced " faux passages." [65] Savary esteems the products of this little village. The same laces, he adds, are made in all the *monastères* of the province, that are partly maintained by the gains. The lace is good, equal to that of Brabant and Flanders. The characteristic peculiarities of Binche are, that there is either no cordonnet at all outlining the pattern, or that the cordonnet is scarcely a thicker thread than that which makes the *toilé*.[66] The design itself is very indefinite, and is practically the same as the early Valenciennes laces. Varieties of the *fond de neige* ground were used instead of the regular *réseau* ground. Dentelle de Binche appears to have been much in vogue in the last century. It is mentioned in the inventory of the Duchesse de Modène,[67] daughter of the Regent, 1761 ; and in that of Mademoiselle de Charollais, 1758, who has a " couvrepied, mantelet, garniture de robe, jupon," etc., all of the same lace. In the *Misérables* of Victor Hugo, the old grandfather routs out

---

[65] Arch. de Nat., Coll. Rondonneau.

[66] *Point and Pillow Lace*, A. M. S. London, 1899.

[67] " Une paire de manchettes de cour de dentelle de Binche ;

" Trois paires de manchettes à trois rangs de dentelle de Binche ;

" Deux fichus de mousseline bordées de dentelle de Binche ;

" Deux devants de corps de dentelle de Binche."—Arch. de Nat. X., 10,082.

from a cupboard " une ancienne garniture de guipure de Binche" for Cosette's wedding-dress.[68] The Binche application flowers have already been noticed.

The lace industry of Binche will soon be only a memory. But before 1830 it " was a hive of lace-makers, and the bees of this hive earned so much money by making lace that their husbands could go and take a walk without a care for the morrow," as it is curiously phrased in an account of Binche and its lace. (Plate XLIII.)

We have now named the great localities for lace-making throughout the Low Countries. Some few yet remain unmentioned.

The needle-point of Liège should be mentioned among the Flanders laces. At the Cathedral of Liège there is still to be seen a flounce of an alb unequalled for the richness and variety of its design and its perfection. Liège in her days of ecclesiastical grandeur carried on the lace trade like the rest.[69] We read, in 1620, of " English Jesuitesses at Liège, who seem to care as much for politics as for lace-making."[70]

An early pattern-book, that of Jean de Glen, a transcript of Vinciolo, was published in that city in 1597. It bears the mark of his printing-press—three acorns with the motto, " Cuique sua præmia," and is dedicated to Madame Loyse de Perez. He concludes a complimentary dedication to the lady with the lines :—

> "Madame, dont l'esprit modestement subtil,
> Vigoureux, se délecte en toutes choses belles,
> Prenez de bonne part ces nouvelles modelles
> Que vous offre la main de ce maistre gentil."

He states that he has travelled and brought back from Italy some patterns, without alluding to Vinciolo. At the end, in a chapter of good advice to young ladies, after exhorting them to " salutairement passer la journée, tant pour l'âme

---

[68] " M. Victor Hugo told the Author he had, in his younger days, seen Binch guipure of great beauty."—Mrs. Palliser, 1869.

[69] Letter of Sir Henry Wotton to Lord Zouch.—State Papers, Domestic, Jas. I., P. R. O.

[70] In the *Bulletin de l'Institut Archéologique*, Liègois XVIII., 1885, is a copy of a contract dated January 23rd, 1634, whereby a lace-maker of Liège, Barbe Bonneville, undertakes for 25 florins, current money, to teach a young girl lace-making.

Again, in the copy of a Namur Act of November, 1701, a merchant of Namur orders from a Liègois " 3 pieces of needle-made lace called Venice point," to sell at the rate of 5½ florins, 4½ florins, and one écu respectively.

que pour le corps," he winds up that he is aware that other exercises, such as stretching the hands and feet, " se frotter un peu les points des bras," and combing the hair, are good for the health ; that to wash the hands occasionally in cold water is both " civil et honnête," etc.

"Dentelles de Liège, fines et grosses de toutes sortes," are mentioned with those of Lorraine and Du Comté (Franche-Comté) in the tariff fixed by a French edict of September 18th, 1664.[71] Mrs. Calderwood, who visited Liège in 1756, admires the point-edging to the surplices of the canons, which, she remarks, " have a very genteel appearance." The manufacture had declined at Liège, in 1802, when it is classed by the French Commissioners among the " fabriques moins considérables," and the lace-makers of the Rue Pierreuse, who made a " garniture étroite "—the " caïeteresses "[72]—had died out in 1881. The same work is now carried on at Laroche.[73]

The lace products of St. Trond, in the province of Limburgh, appear by the report of the French Commission of 1803 to have been of some importance. Lace, they say, is made at St. Trond, where from 800 to 900 are so employed, either at their own homes or in the workshops of the lace-manufacturers. The laces resemble those of Brussels and Mechlin, and although they have a lesser reputation in commerce, several descriptions are made, and about 8,000 metres are produced of laces of first quality, fetching from twelve to fourteen francs the metre. These laces are chiefly made for exportation, and are sold mostly in Holland and at the Frankfort fairs. The report concludes by stating that the vicissitudes of war, in diminishing the demand for objects of luxury, has much injured the trade ; and also suggests that some provisions should be made to stop the abuses arising from the bad faith of the lace-makers, who often sell the materials given them to work with.[74,75]

---

[71] Arch. de Nat., Coll. Rondonneau,
[72] " Caïeteresses," from *caïets.* bobbins.
[73] *Exposition de Liège*, par Chanoine Dubois, 1881.
[74] *Statistique du dép. de la Meuse-Inf.*, par le Citoyen Cavenne. An. X.
[75] Liège in the seventeenth century numbered 1600 workers, and produced black and white laces which it exported to England, Germany and France. The rich clergy of the country also bought a large quantity. At the time of the Exhibition held there in 1881 the fabric had so declined that it was impossible to find a single piece of lace that had been made in the town.

Many of the Belgian churches have lace among the *trésors d'église*. A great number of the convents also possess beautiful lace, for girls who have been educated in them often give their bridal lace, after their marriage, to the chapel of the convent.

At Bruges, an ancient turreted house of the fifteenth century, the Gruuthus mansion, now restored, contains one of the finest collections of lace in the world—a collection of Flemish laces presented to the town by the Baroness Liedts. Bruges itself, and the country round, is full of lace-workers, some working in factories or *ateliers* at the guipure de Flandres, others working at the coarse cheap torchon, sitting in the sun by the quiet canal-sides, or in the stone-cobbled lanes of the old city, where their house-door opens into a room as dark and narrow as a fox-earth, and leading a life so poor that English competition in the cheaper forms of lace is impossible.

Within the last few years the immense development of the Belgian lace trade has overthrown the characteristic lace of each city. Lace, white and black, point and pillow, may at the present time be met with in every province of the now flourishing kingdom of Belgium.[76]

---

[76] *Fil tiré*, drawn and embroidered muslin-work so fine as to be classed with lace, was made in Dinant in the religious communities of the city and the "pays" of Dinant before the French Revolution. At Marche lace with flowers worked directly on the réseau is made, and the lace of Yorck is also imitated—a lace characterised by additions worked on to the lace, giving relief to the flowers.—*Exposition de Liège*, par Chanoine Dubois, 1881. The list of Belgian laces also includes "Les points de Brabant, plus mats, et plus remplis que les points de Flandres; les differentes dentelles de fantaisie, non classées, puis les grosses dentelles de Couvin, en soie noire, qui servaient jadis à garnir les pelisses des femmes de l'Entre Sambre-et-Meuse." —*La Dentelle de Belgique,* par Mme. Daimeries, 1893.

PLATE XLIII.

PLATE XLV.

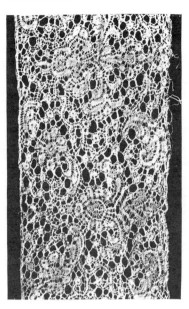

BELGIAN, BOBBIN-MADE.

BINCHE.—WIDTH, 2⅛ in.

PLATE XLIV.

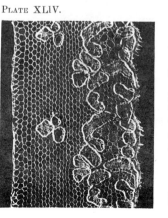

MARCHE.—End of eighteenth century.
In the Musée Cinquantenaire, Brussels.

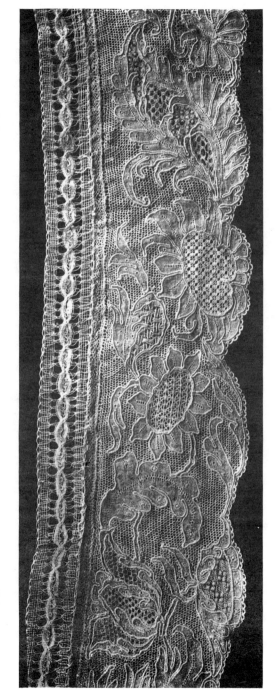

DRAWN AND EMBROIDERED MUSLIN, resembling fine lace.—Flemish work. End of eighteenth century.
Width, 2⅜ in., not including the modern heading.
Photos by A. Dryden from private collections.

PLATE XLVI.

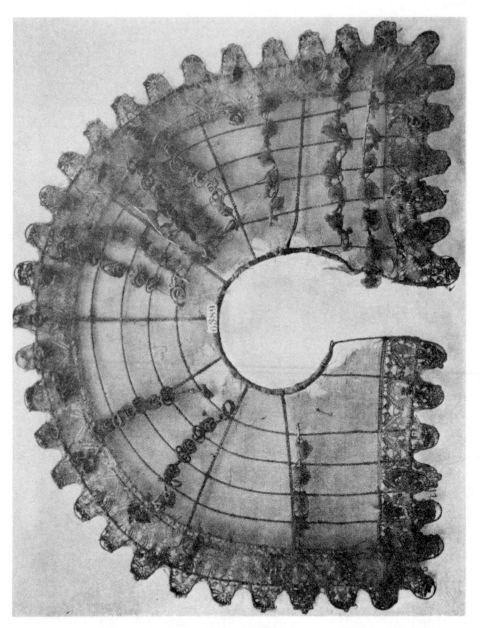

RUFF, EDGED WITH LACE.—In the Musée de Cluny, Paris.

CHAPTER VIII.

FRANCE TO LOUIS XIV.

"Il est une déesse inconstante, incommode,
Bizarre dans ses goûts, folle en ses ornements,
Qui paraît, fuit, revient, et renaît, en tout temps :
Protée était son père, et son nom est la mode."—Voltaire.

" To-day the French
All clinquant, all in gold."—Shakespeare.

To the Italian influences of the sixteenth century France owes the fashion for points coupés and lace.[1] It was under the Valois and the Médicis that the luxury of embroidery, laces of gold, silver, and thread, attained its greatest height, and point coupé was as much worn at that epoch, as were subsequently the points of Italy and Flanders.

Ruffs and cuffs, according to Quicherat, first appeared in France in 1540. The ruff or fraise, as it was termed from its fancied resemblance to the caul [2] or frill of the calf, first

---

[1] Italian fashions appeared early in France. Isabeau de Bavière, wearer of the oriental *hennin*, and Valentine de Milan, first introduced the rich tissues of Italy. Louis XI. sent for workmen from Milan, Venice, and Pistoja, to whom he granted various privileges, which Charles VIII. confirmed.

Lace, according to Séguin, first appears in a portrait of Henri II. at Versailles, a portrait painted in the latter years of his reign.

" Les deux portraits de Francois Ier qui sont au Louvre n'en laissent pas soupçonner l'usage de son temps. Aucun des autres portraits historiques qui y sont, non plus que ceux des galeries de Versailles de la même époque, n'en attestent l'existence, et le premier où on la découvre est un portrait de Henri II à Versailles, qui a dû être peint vers les dernières années de son règne. Le col, brodé d'entrelacs de couleur, est bordé d'une petite dentelle bien simple et bien modeste. Nous possédons des portraits authentiques antérieurs au milieu du XVIe siècle, des specimens incontestés des costumes qui ont précédé cette époque, aucun de ces nombreux témoins n'atteste son existence.

" Il faut reconnaître que l'origine de la dentelle n'est pas antérieure au milieu du XVIe siècle."—Séguin, *La Dentelle.* Paris, 1875.

[2] In Ulpian Fulwell's *Interlude,* 1568, Nichol Newfangle says—

" I learn to make gowns with long
    sleeves and wings,
I learn to make ruffs like calves'
    chitterlings."

adopted by Henry II. to conceal a scar, continued in favour with his sons. The Queen-mother herself wore mourning from the day of the King's death; no decoration therefore appears upon her wire-mounted ruff,[3] but the fraises of her family and the *escadron volante* are profusely trimmed with the geometric work of the period, and the making of laces and point coupé was the favourite employment of her court. It is recorded that the girls and servants of her household consumed much time in making squares of *réseuil*, and Catherine de Médicis had a bed draped with these squares of *réseuil* or *lacis*. Catherine encouraged dress and extravagance, and sought by brilliant fêtes to turn people's minds from politics. In this she was little seconded either by her husband or gloomy son, King Charles; but Henry III. and his "mignons frisés et fraisés" were tricked out in garments of the brightest colours—toques and toquets, pearl necklaces and earrings. The ruff was the especial object of royal interest. With his own hand he used the poking-sticks and adjusted the plaits. "Gaudronneur des collets de sa femme" was the soubriquet bestowed on him by the satirists of the day."[4]

By 1579 the ruffs of the French court had attained such an outrageous size, "un tiers d'aulne,"[5] in depth that the wearers could scarcely turn their heads.[6] "Both men and women wore them intolerably large, being a quarter of a yard deep and twelve lengths in a ruff," writes Stone. In London the fashion was termed the "French ruff"; in France, on the other hand, it was the "English monster." Blaise de Viginière describes them as "gadrooned like organ-pipes, contorted or crinkled like cabbages, and as big as the sails of a windmill." So absurd was the effect, the

---

[3] The Queen was accused by her enemies of having, by the aid of Maître René, "empoisonneur en titre," terminated the life of Queen Jeanne de Navarre, in 1571, by a perfumed ruff (not gloves—*Description de la Vie de Catherine de Médicis*); and her favourite son, the Duke d'Alençon, was said, cir. 1575, to have tried to suborn a valet to take away the life of his brother Henry by scratching him in the back of his neck with a poisoned pin when fastening his fraise.

[4] *Satyre Menippée.* Paris, 1593.

[5] *Chronologie Novenaire*, Vict. P. Cayet.

[6] "S'ils se tournoient, chacun se reculoit, crainte de gater leurs fraizes."
—*Satyre Menippée.*
"Le col ne se tourne à leur aise
Dans le long reply de leur fraise."
—*Vertus et Propriétés des Mignons*, 1576.

journalist of Henry III.[7] declares " they looked like the head of John the Baptist in a charger."

Nor could they eat so encumbered. It is told how Reine Margot one day, when seated at dinner, was compelled to send for a spoon with a handle two feet in length wherewith to eat her soup.[8] These monstrosities, " so stiffened that they cracked like paper," [9] found little favour beyond the precincts of the Louvre. They were caricatured by the writers of the day ; and when, in 1579, Henry III. appeared thus attired at the fair of St. Germain, he was met by a band of students decked out in large paper cuffs, shouting, " À la fraise on connoit le veau "—for which impertinence the King sent them to prison.[10] Suddenly, at the Court of Henry, the fraise gave way to the rabat, or turn-down collar.[11] In vain were sumptuary edicts issued against luxury.[12] The court set a bad example ; and in 1577, at the meeting of the States of Blois, Henry wore on his own dress four thousand yards of pure gold lace. His successor, Henry IV., issued several fresh ordinances [13] against " clin-quants [14] et dorures." Touching the last, Regnier, the satirist, writes :—

" A propos, on m'a dit
Que contre les clinquants le roy faict un edict." [15]

Better still, the King tried the effect of example : he wore a coat of grey cloth with a doublet of taffety, without either

---

[7] " Ces beaux mignons portoient . . . leur fraizes de chemise de toute d'atour empesez et longues d'un demi-pied, de façon qu'à voir leurs testes dessus leurs fraizes, il sembloit que ce fut le chef de Saint Jean dans un plat."—Journal de Henri III., Pierre de l'Estoille.

[8] Perroniana. Cologne, 1691.

[9] Goudronnées en tuyaux d'orgue, fraisées en choux crépus, et grandes comme des meules de moulin."—Blaise de Viginière.

" La fraize veaudelisée à six étages." —La Mode qui Court. Paris, n.d.

[10] " Appelez par les Espagnols ' le-chuguillas ' ou petites laitues, à cause du rapport de ces gaudrons repliées avec les fraisures de la laitue."—His-toire de la Ville de Paris, D. Mich. Félibien.

[11] 1575. Le roy alloit tous les jours faire ses aumônes et ses prières en grande devotion, laissant ses chemises à grands goderons, dont il estoit aupara-vant si curieux, pour en prendre à collet renversé à l'Italienne."—Journal de Henri III., Pierre de l'Estoille.

[12] No less than ten were sent forth by the Valois kings, from 1549 to 1583.

[13] These were dated 1594, 1600, 1601, and 1606.

[14] Copper used instead of gold thread for embroidery or lace. The term was equally applied to false silver thread.

" 1582. Dix escus pour dix aulnes de gaze blanche rayée d'argent clinquant pour faire ung voille à la Boullonnoise." —Comptes de la Reine de Navarre. Arch. Nat. K. K. 170.

[15] Regnier, Math., Ses Satyres. 1642.

trimming or lace—a piece of economy little appreciated by the public. His dress, says an author, " sentait des misères de la Ligue." Sully, anxious to emulate the simplicity of the King, laughed at those " qui portoient leurs moulins et leurs bois de haute futaie sur leurs dos." [16] " It is necessary," said he, " to rid ourselves of our neighbours' goods, which deluge the country." So he prohibited, under pain of corporal punishment, any more dealings with the Flemish merchants.

But edicts failed to put down point coupé ; Reine Margot, Madame Gabrielle, and Bassompierre were too strong for him.

The Wardrobe Accounts of Henry's first queen are filled with entries of point coupé and " passements à l'aiguille " ; [17] and though Henry usually wore the silk-wrought shirts of the day,[18] we find in the inventory of his wife one entered as trimmed with cut-work.[19] Wraxall declares to have seen exhibited at a booth on the Boulevart de Bondy, the shirt worn by Henry when assassinated. " It is ornamented," he writes, " with a broad lace round the collar and breast.

---

[16] The observation was not new. A Remonstrance to Catherine de Médicis, 1586, complains that " leurs moulins, leurs terres, leurs prez, leurs bois et leurs revenuz, se coulent en broderies, pourfilures, passemens, franges, tortis, canetilles, recameurs, chenettes, picqueurs, arrièrepoins, etc., qu'on invente de jour à autre."—*Discours sur l'extrême cherté, etc., presenté à la Mère du Roi, par un sien fidelle Serviteur (Du Haillan)*. Bordeaux, 1586.

[17] " 1579. Pour avoir remonsté trois fraises à poinct couppé, 15 sols.

" Pour avoir monté cinq fraizes à poinct couppé sur linomple, les avoir ourllés et couzeus à la petite cordellière et au poinct noué à raison de 30 sols pour chacune.

" Pour la façon de sept rabatz ourllés à double arrièrepoinct et couzu le passement au dessus.

" 1580. Pour avoir faict d'ung mouchoir ouvré deux rabatz, 20 sols.

" Pour deux pieces de poinct couppé pour servir à ladicte dame, VI livres.

" Pour dix huict aulnes de passement blanc pour mestre à des fraizes à trois escus l'aulne."

1582. The account for this year contains entries for " passement faict à lesguille," "grand passement," " passement faict au mestier," etc.— *Comptes de la Reine de Navarre*. Arch. Nat.

[18] " Vingt trois chemizes de toile fine à ouvrage de fil d'or et soye de plusieurs coulleurs, aux manchettés coulet et coutures.

" Ung chemize à ouvrage de soye noire.

" Quatre chemizes les trois à ouvrage d'or et d'argent et soye bleu."—*Inv. des meubles qui ont estés portés à Paris*. 1602. Arch. Nat.

[19] " 1577. A Jehan Dupré, linger, demeurant à Paris, la somme de soixante douze livres tournois à luy or donnée pour son payement de quatre layz d'ouvraige à poinct couppé pour faire une garniture de chemise pour servir à mon dict segneur, à raison de 18 liv. chacune."—*Comptes de la Reine de Navarre*. Arch. Nat. K. K. 162, fol. 655.

The two wounds inflicted by the assassin's knife are plainly visible." [20]

In the inventory [21] made at the death of Madame Gabrielle, the fair Duchesse de Beaufort, we find entered sleeves and towels of point couppé, with fine handkerchiefs, gifts of the King to be worn at court, of such an extraordinary value that Henry requires them to be straightway restored to him. In the same list appears the duchess's bed of ivory,[22] with hangings for the room of rézeuil.[23]

The Chancellor Herault,[24] who died at the same period, was equally extravagant in his habits ; while the shirts of the combatants in the duel between M. de Crequy and Don Philippe de Savoie are specially vaunted as " toutes garnies du plus fin et du plus riche point coupé qu'on eust pu trouver dans ce temps là, auquel le point de Gennes et de Flandres n'estoient pas en usage." [25]

The enormous collarette, rising behind her head like a

---

[20] "This shirt," he adds, "is well attested. It became the perquisite of the king's first valet de chambre. At the extinction of his descendants, it was exposed to sale."—*Memoirs*.

A rival shirt turned up (c. 1860) at Madame Tussaud's with "the real blood" still visible. Monsieur Curtius, uncle of Madame Tussaud, purchased it at an auction of effects once the property of Cardinal Mazarin. Charles X. offered 200 guineas for it.

[21] " Item, cinq mouchoirs d'ouvrages d'or, d'argent et soye, prisez ensemble cent escuz.

" Item, deux tauayelles aussi ouvrage d'or, d'argent et soye, prisées cent escuz.

" Item, trois tauayelles blanches de rezeuil, prisées ensemble trente escuz.

" Item, une paire de manches de point coupé et enrichies d'argent, prisez vingt escuz.

" Item, deux mouchoirs blancz de point coupé, prisez ensemble vingt escuz.

" Toutes lesquelles tauayelles et mouchoirs cy dessus trouvez dans un coffre de bahu que la dicte defunte dame faisoit ordinairement porter avec elle a la court sont demeurez entre les mains du Sr de Beringhen, suivant le commandement qu'il en avoit de sa

majesté pour les representer à icelle, ce qu'il a promis de faire."—*Inventaire apres le decès de Gabrielle d'Estrées.* 1599. Arch. Nat. K. K. 157, fol. 17.

[22] " Item, un lit d'yvoire à filletz noirs de Padoue, garny de son estuy de cuir rouge."—*Ibid.*

[23] " Item, une autre tenture de cabinet de carré de rezeau brodurée et montans recouvert de feuillages de fil avec des carrez de thoile plaine, prisé et estimé la somme de cent escus Soleil.

" Item, dix sept carrez de thoile de Hollande en broderie d'or et d'argent fait a deux endroictz, prisez et estimez à 85 escus.

" Item, un autre pavillon tout de rezeil avec le chapiteau de fleurs et feuillages. . . .

" Item, un autre en neuf fait par carrez de point coupé."—*Ibid.* fols. 46 and 47.

[24] " Manchettes et collets enrichys de point couppé."—*Inventaire apres le decès de Messire Philippe Herault, Comte de Cheverny, Chancelier de France.* 1599. Bib. Nat. MSS. F. 11,424.

[25] In 1598. Vulson de la Colombière, *Vray Théatre d'Honneur et de Chevalerie.* 1647.

fan, of Mary de Médicis, with its edgings of fine lace, are
well known to the admirers of Rubens :—

> " Cinq colets de dentelle haute de demy-piè
> L'un sur l'autre montez, qui ne vont qu'à moitié
> De celuys de dessus, car elle n'est pas leste,
> Si le premier ne passe une paulme la teste." [26]

On the accession of Louis XIII. luxury knew no bounds.
The Queen Regent was magnificent by nature, while Richelieu,
anxious to hasten the ruin of the nobles, artfully encouraged
their prodigality. But Mary was compelled to repress this
taste for dress. The courtiers importuned her to increase
their pensions, no longer sufficient for the exigencies of the
day. The Queen, at her wits' end, published in 1613 a
" Réglement pour les superfluités des habits," prohibiting
all lace and embroidery. [27]

France had early sent out books of patterns for cut-work
and lace. That of Francisque Pelegrin was published at
Paris in the reign òf Francis I. Six were printed at Lyons
alone. The four earlier have no date, [28] the two others bear
those of 1549 [29] and 1585. [30] It was to these first that
Vinciolo so contemptuously alludes in his dedication, " Aux
Benevolles Lecteurs," saying, " Si les premiers ouvrages que
vous avez vus ont engendré quelque fruit et utilité je
m'assure que les miens en produiront davantage." Various
editions of Vinciolo were printed at Paris from 1587 to 1623 ;
the earlier dedicated to Queen Louise de Lorraine ; a second
to Catherine de Bourbon, sister of Henry IV. ; the last to
Anne of Austria. The *Pratique de Leguille de Milour
M. Mignerak* was published by the same printer, 1605 ; and
we have another work, termed *Bèle Prerie*, also printed at
Paris, bearing date 1601. [31]

The points of Italy and Flanders now first appear at

---

[26] *Satyrique de la Court.* 1613.
[27] *Histoire de la Mère et du Fils,*
from 1616 to 19. Amsterdam, 1729.
[28] *Livre nouveau dict Patrons de
Lingerie, etc.*
Patrons de diverses Manières, etc.
(Title in rhyme.)
*S'ensuyvent les Patrons de Mesire
Antoine Belin.*
Ce Livre est plaisant et utile. (Title
in rhyme.)

[29] *La Fleur des Patrons de Lingerie.*
[30] *Tresor des Patrons.* J. Ostans.
[31] *Le Livre de Moresques* (1546),
Livre de Lingerie, Dom. de Sera
(1584), and *Patrons pour Brodeurs*
(no date), were also printed at Paris.
The last book on this kind of work
printed at Paris is styled, *Méthode pour
faire des Desseins avec des Carreaux,*
etc., by Père Dominique Donat, religieux carme. 1722.

PLATE XLVII.

BRUSSELS. FLOUNCE, BOBBIN-MADE.—Late seventeenth century. Given by Madame de
Maintenon to Fénélon, Archbishop of Cambrai. Now in the Victoria and Albert Museum.
Height, 2 ft. 2 in.

PLATE XLVIII.

BRUSSELS. BOBBIN-MADE.—Period Louis XIV., 1643–1715.
In the Musée Cinquantenaire, Brussels.

PLATE XLIX.

BRUSSELS. POINT D'ANGLETERRE À RÉSEAU.—Eighteenth century. Widths, 2 in. and 3½ in.
Photo by A. Dryden.

court, and the Church soon adopted the prevailing taste for the decoration of her altars and her prelates.[32]

The ruff is finally discarded and replaced by the " col rabattu," with its deep-scalloped border of point. The "manchettes à revers" are trimmed in the same manner, and the fashion even extends to the tops of the boots. Of these lace-trimmed boots the favourite, Cinq-Mars, left three hundred pairs at his death, 1642. From his portrait, after

Fig. 66.

CINQ-MARS.—(M. de Versailles.)

Lenain, which hangs in the Gallery of Versailles, we give one of these boots (Fig. 66), and his rich collerette of Point de Gênes (Fig. 67).

The garters, now worn like a scarf round the knee, have the ends adorned with point. A large rosette of lace completes the costume of the epoch (Fig. 68).

---

[32] A point de Venise alb, of rose point, said to be of this period, is in the Musée de Cluny.

Gold lace shared the favour of the thread fabric on gloves,[33] garters and shoes.[34]

"De large taftas la jartière parée
Aux bouts de demy-pied de dentelle dorée."[35]

The cuffs, collars of the ladies either falling back or rising behind their shoulders in double tier, caps, aprons

Fig. 67.

CINQ-MARS.—(After his portrait by Le Nain.   M. de Versailles.)

descending to their feet (Fig. 69), are also richly decorated with lace.

The contemporary engravings of Abraham Bosse and Callot faithfully portray the fashions of this reign.   In the Prodigal Son, of Abraham Bosse, the mother, waiting his

---

[33] "Quelques autres de frangez Bordent leur riche cuir, qui vient des lieux estranges."
—*Le Gan,*
de Jean Godard, Parisien, 1588

[34] "1619. Deux paires de rozes à soulliers garnies de dentelle d'or."—*Inv. de Madame Sœur du Roi.* (Henrietta Maria.)   Arch. Nat.
[35] *Satyrique de la Court.*

return, holds out to her repentant boy a collar trimmed with the richest point. The Foolish Virgins weep in lace-trimmed handkerchiefs, and the table-cloth of the rich man, as well as his dinner-napkins, are similarly adorned. Again, the Accouchée recovers in a cap of Italian point under a coverlet of the same. At the Retour de Baptême, point adorns the christening-dress of the child and the surplice of the priest.

When, in 1615, Louis XIII. married Anne of Austria, the collerettes of the Queen-Mother were discarded—the

Fig. 68.

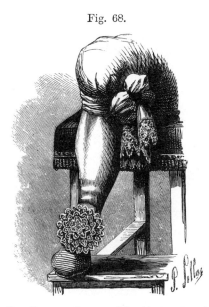

LACE ROSE AND GARTER.—(After Abraham Bosse.)

reign of Italy was at an end—all was now à l'éspagnole and the court of Castile.

The prodigality of the nobles [36] having called down royal ordinances on their heads,[37] these new edicts bring forth

---

[36] The inventory of the unfortunate Maréchal de Marillac, beheaded 1632, has "broderye et poinctz d'Espagnes d'or, argent et soye; rabats et collets de point couppé; taffetas nacarat garnye de dantelle d'argent; pourpoinct passementé de dantelle de canetille de Flandre," etc.—Bib. Nat. MSS. F. Fr. 11,426.

[37] 1620, Feb. 8th. "Déclaration portant deffenses de porter des clinquants, passements, broderies," etc.—Arch. Nat. G. G. G.

1623, March 20th. "Déclaration qui defend l'usage des étoffes d'or," etc.—*Recueil des anciennes Lois Françaises.* T. 16, 107.

1625, Sept. 30th. Déclaration pro-fresh satires, in which the author deplores the prohibition of cut-work and lace :—

> " Ces points couppez, passemens et dentelles,
> Las ! que venaient de l'Isle et de Bruxelles,
> Sont maintenant descriez, avilis,
> Et sans faveur gisent ensevelis ; "[38]

but

> " Pour vivre heureux et à la mode
> Il faut que chacun accommode
> Ses habits aux editz du roi."

Edict now follows on edict.[39] One known as the Code Michaud, entering into the most minute regulations for the toilet, especially excited the risibility of the people. It was

Fig. 69.

YOUNG LADY'S APRON, TIME OF HENRY III.—(After Gaignières. Bib. Nat. Grav.)

never carried out. The caricatures of this period are admirable : one represents a young courtier fresh rigged in his

---

hibits the wearing of "collets, fraizes, manchettes, et autres linges des passements, Point coupez et Dentelles, comme aussi des Broderies et Decoupures sur quentin ou autre toile."— Bib. Nat. L. i. 8.

[38] *Consolation des Dames sur la Reformation des passemens.* 1620.

[39] Again, 1633, Nov. 18th. Déclaration restricts the prohibition ; permits "passements manufacturés dans le royaume qui n'excederont 9 ll. l'aune." —Arch. Nat. G. G. G.

1634, May 30th. "Lettres patentes pour la reformation du luxe des habits," prohibits "dentelles, passements et broderies" on boots, carriages, etc. (British Museum).

1636, April 3rd. "Déclaration contre le Luxe." Again prohibits both foreign and home-made points coupés, etc., under pain of banishment for five years, confiscation, and a fine of 6000 francs.—De la Mare, *Traité de la Police.*

1639, Nov. 24th. Fresh prohibition, points de Gênes specially mentioned. Not to wear on the collar, cuffs, or boots, "autres choses que de la toile simple sans aucune façon."—Arch. Nat. G. G. G.

plain-bordered linen, according to the ordinance. His *valet de chambre* is about to lock up his laced suit :—

> " C'est avec regret que mon maître
> Quitte ses beaux habillemens
> Semés de riches passemens." [40]

Another engraving of Abraham Bosse shows a lady of fashion with her lace discarded and dressed in plain linen cuffs and collar :—

> " Quoique l'âge assez de beauté
> Pour asseurer sans vanité
> Qu'il n'est point de femme plus belle
> Il semble pourtant, à mes yeux,
> Qu'avec de l'or et la dantelle
> Je m'ajuste encore bien mieux."

Alluding to the plain-bordered collars now ordered by the prohibition of 1639, the " Satyrique de la Court" sings :—

> " Naguères l'on n'osoit hanter les damoiselles
> Que l'on n'eust le colet bien garni de dentelles ;
> Maintenant on se rit et se moque de ceux là
> Qui desirent encore paroistre avec cela.
> Les fraises et colets à bord sont en usage,
> Sans faire mention de tous en dentellage."

France at this time paying large sums to Italy and Flanders for lace, the wearing of it is altogether prohibited, under pain of confiscation and a fine of 6,000 livres.[41] The Queen-Mother, regardless of edicts, has over *passements d'or* and all sorts of forbidden articles, " pour servir à la layette que sa majesté à envoyé en Angleterre." [42] Within scarce one year of each other passed away Marie de Médicis, Richelieu, and Louis XIII. The King's effigy was exposed on its " lit de parade vêtue d'une chemise de toile de Hollande avec de tres belles dantelles de point de Gennes au collet et aux manches." [43]—So say the chroniclers.

---

[40] *Le Courtisan Reformé, suivant l'Edit. de l'année* 1633 ; and again, *Le Jardin de la Noblesse Françoise dans lequel ce peut cueillir leur manière de Vettement.* 162
[41] April, 1636.
[42] 16?¹ *l'résorerie de la Reine Mari de Mé .cis.*—Arch. Nat. K. K. 191.
[43] Vulson de la Colombière, *Pompe qu'on pratique aux obséques des Rois de France.*

CHAPTER IX.

LOUIS XIV.

THE courtiers of the Regency under Anne of Austria vied with the Frondeurs in extravagance. The latter, however, had the best of it. " La Fronde," writes Joly, " devint tellement à la mode qu'il n'y avoit rien de bien fait qu'on ne dist être de la Fronde. Les étoffes, les dentelles, etc., jusqu'au pain,—rien n'estoit ni bon, ni bien si n'estoit à la Fronde." [1]

Nor was the Queen Regent herself less profuse in her indulgence in lace. She is represented in her portraits with a berthe of rich point, her beautiful hand encircled by a double-scalloped cuff (Fig. 70). The boot-tops had now reached an extravagant size. One writer compares them to the farthingales of the ladies, another to an inverted torch. The lords of the Regent's court filled up the apertures with two or three rows of Genoa point (Fig. 71).

In 1653,[2] we find Mazarin, while engaged in the siege of a city, holding a grave correspondence with his secretary Colbert concerning the purchase of some points from Flanders, Venice, and Genoa. He considers it advisable to

---

[1] *Mémoires de Guy Joly*, from 1648 to 1665.

[2] About this period a special Act had confirmed the Statutes of the Maîtres Passementiers of Paris. By Article 21, they are privileged to make every sort of passement or lace, " sur l'oreiller, aux fuzeaux, aux épingles, et à la main," on condition the material, gold, silver, thread, or silk, be " de toutes fines ou de toutes fausses." The sale of thread and lace was allowed to the Lingères, but by an Arrêt of the Parliament of Paris, 1665, no one could be a marchande lingère unless she had made profession of the " religion catholique, apostolique, et romaine," a condition worthy of the times. " Il n'y fut," writes Gilles de Felice, in his *Histoire des Protestants de France*, " pas jusqu'à la corporation des lingères qui ne s'en allât remontrer au conseil que leur communauté, ayant été instituée par saint Louis, no pouvait admettre d'hérétiques, et cette réclamation fut gravement confirmée par un arrêt du 21 août, 1665."

advance thirty or forty thousand livres " à ces achapts,"
adding, that by making the purchases in time he will derive
great advantage in the price ; but as he hopes the siege will
soon be at an end, they may wait his arrival at Paris for his
final decision.[3]   Colbert again writes, November 25th,

Fig. 70.

ANNE OF AUSTRIA.—(M. de Versailles.)

pressing his Eminence on account of the " quantité de
mariages qui se feront l'hyver." A passage in Tallemant
des Réaux would lead one to suppose these laces were
destined as patterns for the improvement of French manufactures. " Per mostra di farne in Francia," as the Cardinal
expressed himself. Certainly in the inventory of Mazarin [4]
there are no mention of Italian points, no lace coverlets to
his " Lict d'ange moire tabizée, couleur de rose chamarrée de

---

[3] Dated November 19th, 1653. The
letter is given in full by the Marquis
de Laborde in *Le Palais Mazarin.*
Paris, 1845.

[4] *Inv. fait apres la mort du Cardinal Mazarin,* 1661.—Bibl. Nat.
MSS. Suite de Mortmart, 37.

dentelles d'or et d'argent." We may almost imagine that the minister and his secretary combined were already meditating the establishment of Points de France.

In this reign, fresh sumptuary ordinances are issued. That of November 27th, 1660, is the most important of all,[5] and is highly commended by Sganarelle in the "Ecole des Maris" of Molière which appeared the following year :—

> " Oh ! trois et quatre fois soit béni cet édit,
> Par qui des vêtemens le luxe est interdit ;
> Les peines des maris ne seront pas si grandes,
> Et les femmes auront un frein à leurs demandes.
> Oh ! que je sais au roi bon gré de ses décrets;
> Et que, pour le repos de ces mêmes maris,
> Je voudrais bien qu'on fit de la coquetterie
> Comme de la guipure et de la broderie."

Fig. 71.

A COURTIER OF THE REGENCY.—(After Abraham Bosse)

This ordinance, after prohibiting all foreign "passemens, points de Gênes, points coupés," etc., or any French laces or passements exceeding an inch in width, allows the use of the "collerettes and manchettes" persons already possess for the space of one year, after which period they are only to be trimmed with a lace made in the kingdom, not exceeding an

---

[5] It is to be found at the Archives National, or in the Library of the Cour de Cassation. In the Archives National is a small collection of ordinances relative to lace collected by M. Rondonneau, extending from 1666 to 1773. It is very difficult to get at all the ordinances. Many are printed in De la Mare (*Traité de la Police*); but the most complete work is the *Recueil général des anciennes Lois françaises, depuis l'an 420 jusqu'à la Révolution de* 1789, par MM. Isambert, Ducrusy, et Taillandier. Paris, 1829. The ordinances bear two dates, that of their issue and of their registry.

inch in width. The ordinance then goes on to attack the
" canons," which it states have been introduced into the
kingdom, with " un excès de dépense insupportable, par la
quantité de passemens, points de Venise et Gênes," with
which they are loaded.[6] Their use of them is now entirely
prohibited, unless made of plain linen or of the same stuff as
the coat, without lace or any ornament. The lace-trimmed
" canons " of Louis XIV., as represented in the picture of his
interview with Philip IV., in the Island of Pheasants,
previous to his marriage, 1660 (Fig. 72), give a good idea of
these extravagant appendages. These

" Canons à trois étages
A leurs jambes faisoient d'ombrages." [7]

And, what was worse, they would cost 7,000 livres a pair.
" At the Court of France," writes Savinière, " people think
nothing of buying rabats, manchettes, or canons to the value
of 13,000 crowns." [8] These canons, with their accompanying
rheingraves, which after the prohibition of Venice point
were adorned with the new productions of France, suddenly
disappeared. In 1682, the *Mercure* announces, " Les
canons et les rheingraves deviennent tout à fait hors de
mode."

At the marriage of the young King with the Infanta,
1660, black lace,[9] probably in compliment to the Spanish [10]

---

[6] This "canon," originally called
" bas de bottes," was a circle of linen
or other stuff fastened below the knee,
widening at the bottom so as to fill
the enlargement of the boot, and when
trimmed with lace, having the appearance of a ruffle.

[7] *Dictionnaire des Précieuses.* 1660.
Molière likewise ridicules them :—
" Et de ces grands canons, où, comme
  des entraves,
  On met tous les matins les deux
  jambes esclaves."
  —*L'École des Maris.*
And again, in *L'École des Femmes :*
" Ils ont de grands canons, force
  rubans et plumes."

[8] *Les Délices de la France*, par M.
Savinière d'Alquié. 1670.

[9] The fashion of wearing black lace
was introduced into England in the
reign of Charles II. " Anon the house

grew full, and the candles lit, and it
was a glorious sight to see our Mistress
Stewart in black and white lace, and
her head and shoulders dressed with
diamonds."—Pepys's *Diary*.
" The French have increased among
us many considerable trades, such as
black and white lace."—*England's
Great Happiness*, etc. Dialogue between Content and Complaint. 1677.
" Item, un autre habit de grosse
moire garny de dantelle d'Angleterre
noire."—1691. *Inv. de Madame de
Simiane.* Arch. Nat., M. M. 802.

[10] " Of this custom, a relic may still
be found at the Court of Turin, where
ladies wear lappets of black lace. Not
many years since, the wife of a Russian
minister, persisting to appear in a suit
of Brussels point, was courteously requested by the Grand Chamberlain to
retire " (1869).

court, came into favour, the nobles of the King's suite wearing doublets of gold and silver brocade, "ornés," says the *Chronique*,[11] "de denteiles noires d'un point recherché."[12]   The same writer, describing the noviciate of La Vallière at the Carmelites, writes, "Les dames portoient des robes de brocard d'or, d'argent, ou d'azur, par dessus lesquelles elles avoient jetées d'autres robes et dentelles noires transparentes."[13]   Under Louis XIV., the gold and silver points of Spain and Aurillac rivalled the thread fabrics of Flanders and Italy; but towards the close of the century,[14] we are informed, they have fallen from fashion into the "domaine du vulgaire."

The ordinance of 1660 had but little effect, for various others are issued in the following years with the oft-repeated prohibitions of the points of Genoa and Venice.[15]   But edicts were of little avail.   No royal command could compel people to substitute the coarse inferior laces of France[16] for the fine artistic productions of her sister countries.   Colbert therefore wisely adopted another expedient. He determined to develop the lace-manufacture of France, and to produce fabrics which should rival the coveted points of Italy and Flanders, so that if fortunes were lavished upon these luxuries, at all events the money should not be sent out of the kingdom to procure them.

He therefore applied to Monseigneur de Bonzy, Bishop of Béziers, then Ambassador at Venice, who replied that in Venice "all the convents and poor families make a living out of this lace-making."   In another letter he writes to the minister, "Je vois que vous seriez bien aise d'establir dans le royaume la manufacture des points de Venise, ce qui se pourrait faire en envoyant d'icy quelques filles des meil-

---

[11] *Chroniques de l'Œil-de-Bœuf.*

[12] Madame de Motteville is not complimentary to the ladies of the Spanish Court: "Elles avoient peu de linge," she writes, "et leurs dentelles nous parurent laides."—*Mémoires pour servir à l'histoire d'Anne d'Autriche.*

[13] Madame de Sévigné mentions these dresses: "Avez-vous ouï parler des transparens? . . . de robes noires transparentes ou des belles dentelles d'Angleterre."—*Lettres.*

[14] 1690. *Chroniques de l'Œil-de-Bœuf.*

[15] 1661, May 27; 1662, Jan. 1; 1664, May 31, Sept. 18, and Dec. 12.

[16] "On fabriquait précédemment ces espèces de dentelles guipures, dont on ornait les aubes des prêtres, les rochets des évêques et les jupons des femmes de qualité."—*Roland de la Platière.*   The articles on lace by Roland and Savary have been copied by all succeeding writers on the subject.

Fig. 72.

CANONS OF LOUIS XIV.—(M. de Versailles. 1660.)

Plate LI.

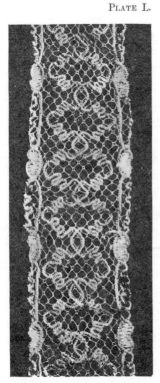

Plate L.

CHENILLE RUN ON A BOBBIN GROUND.—Taken from an early eighteenth century Court dress, and typical of a French dress passementerie of that date. About half-size.

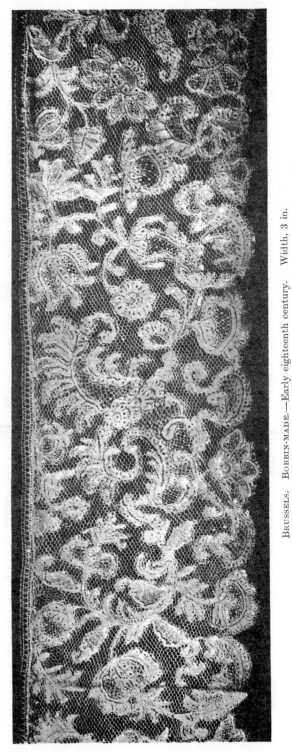

BRUSSELS. BOBBIN-MADE.—Early eighteenth century. Width, 3 in.

Photos by A. Dryden from private collections.

leures ouvrières qui pussent instruire celles de France avec le temps." [17]

Monseigneur de Bonzy's suggestion was accepted, and a few years later (1673) Colbert writes to M. le Comte d'Avaux, who succeeded M. de Bonzy as ambassador at Venice : " I have gladly received the collar of needlepoint lace worked in relief that you have sent me, and I find it very beautiful. I shall have it compared with those new laces being made by our own lace-makers, although I may tell you beforehand that as good specimens are now made in this kingdom." [18] Alençon, an old lace-making centre, was chosen as the seat of the new manufacture. [19] Favier-Duboulay writes to Colbert that, before the introduction of the new points de France, lace-making was to the peasants " une manne, et une vraie bénédiction du ciel, qui s'est espandue sur tout ce pays." The art had spread far and wide through the district about Alençon ; children of seven years of age and aged men earned their daily bread by it, and the shepherdesses worked at their lace while herding their flocks.

M. Odolent Desnos gives the following account of the invention and establishment of point d'Alençon :— [20]

" In 1665, at the recommendation of the Sieur Ruel, he (Colbert) selected a Madame Gilbert, a native of Alençon, already acquainted with the manner of making Venice

---

[17] Mgr. de Bonzy, Dec. 20, 1664. *Correspondance administrative sous Colbert;* vol. 3.

[18] Lefébure.

[19] " Il y a très longtemps que le point coupé se faict icy, qui a son débit selon le temps ; mais qu'une femme nommée La Perrière (*sic*), fort habile à ces ouvrages, trouva il y a quelques années le moyen d'imiter les points de Venise, en sorte qu'elle y vint à telle perfection que ceux qu'elle faisoit ne devaient rien aux estrangers. Pour faire ces ouvrages il luy falloit enseigner plusieurs petites filles auxquelles elle montroit à faire ce point . . . . à présent je vous puis asseurer qu'il y a plus de 8,000 personnes qui y travaillent dans Alençon, dans Seèz, dans Argentan, Falaise . . . .

" Monseigneur, c'est une manne, et une vraie bénédiction du ciel qui s'est espandue sur tout ce pays, dans lequel les petitz enfants mesmes de sept ans trouvent moyen de gaigner leur vie. Les vieillards y travaillent et les petites bergerettes des champs y travaillent mêmes."—*Letter from Favier-Duboulay, intendant d'Alençon since* 1644. Correspondance administrative sous le règne de Louis XIV (quoted by Madame Despierres), vol. 3.

[20] In 1842 M. Joseph Odolant Desnos, grandson of this author, writes, " Ce fut une dame Gilberte, qui avait fait son apprentissage à Venise, et était native d'Alençon. Dès qu'elle fut à ses ordres, ce ministre (Colbert) la logea dans le magnifique château de Lonrai, qu'il possédait près d'Alençon."—*Annuaire de l'Orne.*

point, and making her an advance of 50,000 crowns, established her at his château of Lonrai (Fig. 73), near Alençon, with thirty forewomen, whom he had, at great expense, caused to be brought over from Venice.   In a short time Madame Gilbert arrived at Paris with the first specimens of her fabric.   The king, inspired by Colbert with a desire to see the work, during supper at Versailles announced to his courtiers he had just established a manufacture of point more beautiful than that of Venice, and appointed a day

Fig. 73.

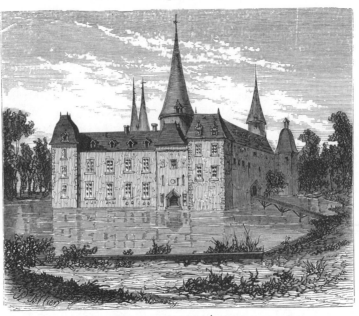

CHÂTEAU DE LONRAI, DÉP. ORNE.

when he would inspect the specimens.   The laces were artistically arranged over the walls of a room hung with crimson damask, and shown to the best advantage.   The king expressed himself delighted.   He ordered a large sum to be given to Madame Gilbert, and desired that no other lace should appear at court except the new fabric, upon which he bestowed the name of point de France.[21]   Scarcely

---

[21] *Mémoires historiques sur la ville d'Alençon*, M. Odolant Desnos. Alençon, 1787.

had Louis retired than the courtiers eagerly stripped the room of its contents. The approval of the monarch was the fortune of Alençon : point de France adopted by court etiquette, the wearing of it became compulsory. All who had the privilege of the casaque bleue '—all who were received at Versailles or were attached to the royal household, could only appear, the ladies in trimmings and head-dresses, the gentlemen in ruffles and cravats of the royal manufacture."

Unfortunately for this story, the Château de Lonrai came into the family of Colbert fourteen years after the establishment of the lace-industry at Alençon,[22] and the name of Gilbert is not found in any of the documents relating to the establishment of point de France, nor in the correspondence of Colbert.[23]

An ordinance of August 5th, 1665, founded upon a large scale the manufacture of points de France,[24] with an exclusive privilege for ten years and a grant of 36,000

---

[22] " Le château de Lonrai ne passa dans la maison de Colbert que par le mariage de Catherine Thérèse de Matignon, Marquise de Lonrai, avec Jean-Baptiste Colbert, fils ainé du grand Colbert, le 6 septembre 1678 " (*i.e.*, fourteen years after the establishment of points de France at Alençon) —Madame Despierres, *Histoire de point d'Alençon.*

[23] Madame Despierres, after an exhaustive study of the mass of documentary evidence on this point, gives as her opinion that—

" (1) La première personne qui à Alençon imita le point de Venise, et par conséquent créa le point d'Alençon, fut Mme La Perrière, vers 1650, et non Mme Gilbert.

" (2) La préposée-directrice des manufactures de point de France des différentes villes du royaume qui a établi les bureaux à Alençon, fut Catherine de Marcq, et non pas une dame Gilbert.

" (3) Les préposées mises à la tête de l'établissement d'Alençon étaient Mme Raffy et Marie Fillesae, dont les noms ne répondent pas à celui d'une dame Gilbert."—Madame Despierres, *Histoire de point d'Alençon.*

[24] Mrs. Palliser sought in vain for this ordinance in the Library of the Cour de Cassation, where it is stated to be, by the authors of the " Recueil général des anciennes Lois françaises, depuis l'an 420 jusqu'à la Révolution de 1789 " ; but fortunately it is recited in a subsequent act, dated Oct. 12, 1666 (Arch. Nat., Coll. Rondonneau), by which it appears that the declaration ordered the establishment in " les villes de Quesnoy, Arras, Reims, Sedan, Château-Thierry, Loudun, Alençon, Aurillac, et autres du royaume, de la manufacture de toutes sortes d'ouvrages de fil, tant à l'éguille qu'au coussin, en la manière des points qui se font à Venise, Gennes, Raguse, et autres pays estrangers, qui seroient appellés points de France," by which it would appear the term point de France did not exclusively belong to the productions of Alençon. After the company was dissolved in 1675 the name of point de France was applied to point d'Alençon alone. In a subsequent arrêt it is set forth that the entrepreneurs have caused to be brought in great numbers the best workers from Venice and other foreign cities, and have distributed them over Le Quesnoy and the above-mentioned towns, and that now are made in

francs.   A company was formed,[25] its members rapidly increased, and in 1668 the capital amounted to 22,000 livres. Eight directors were appointed at salaries of 12,000 livres a year to conduct the manufacture, and the company held its sittings in the Hôtel de Beaufort at Paris.   The first distribution of profits took place in October, 1669, amounting to fifty per cent. upon each share.   In 1670 a fresh distribution took place, and 120,000 livres were divided among the shareholders.   That of 1673 was still more considerable.   In 1675 the ten years' privilege ceased, the money was returned, and the rest of the profits divided. Colbert likewise set up a fabric at the Château de Madrid, built by Francis I., on the Bois de Boulogne.   Such was the origin of point lace in France.

The difficulties met by Colbert in establishing his manufactories can only be estimated by reading his correspondence, in which there are no less than fifty letters on the subject. The apathy of the town authorities and the constant rebellions of the lace-workers who preferred their old stitch were incessant sources of trouble to him, but eventually Colbert's plan was crowned with success.   He established a lucrative manufacture which brought large sums of money into the kingdom [26] instead of sending it out.   Well might he say that [27] "Fashion was to France what the mines of Peru were to Spain." [28]

France " des ouvrages de fil si exquis, qu'ils esgallent, mesme surpassent en beauté les estrangers."—*Bibl. de la Cour de Cassation.*

What became of these manufactures at Le Quesnoy and Château-Thierry, of which not a tradition remains ?

[25] Talon, " secrétaire du cabinet," was one of the first members.   We find by an arrêt, Feb. 15, 1667, that this patent had already been infringed.   On the petition of Jean Pluymers, Paul, and Catherine de Marcq, " entrepreneurs " of the fabric of points de France, his Majesty confirms to them the sole privilege of making and selling the said points.— Arch. Nat., Coll. Rondonneau. Nov. 17 of the same year appears a fresh prohibition of wearing or selling the passements, lace, and other works in thread of Venice, Genoa, and other

foreign countries (British Museum), and March 17, 1668, " Itératives " prohibitions to wear these, either new or " commencé d'user," as injurious to a manufacture of point which gives subsistence to a number of persons in the kingdom.—*Ibid.*   Again, Aug. 19, 1669, a fresh arrêt in consequence of complaints that the workers are suborned and work concealed in Paris, etc.—Arch Nat., Coll. Rondonneau.

[26] Colbert said to Louis XIV. : " There will always be found fools enough to purchase the manufactures of France, though France should be prohibited from purchasing those of other countries."   The King agreed with the minister, whom he made chief director of the trade and manufactures of the kingdom.

[27] A favourite saying of Colbert.

[28] The artists who furnished designs

Boileau alludes to the success of the minister in his " Epistle to Louis XIV " :—

> " Et nos voisins frustrés de ces tributs serviles
> Que payait à leur art le luxe de nos villes." [29]

The point de France supplanted that of Venice,[30] but its price confined its use to the rich, and when the wearing of lace became general those who could not afford so costly a production replaced it by the more moderate pillow-lace. This explains the great extension of the pillow-lace manufacture at this period—the production did not suffice for the demand. Encouraged by the success of the royal manufactures, lace fabrics started up in various towns in the kingdom. The number of lace-workers increased rapidly. Those of the towns being insufficient, they were sought for in the surrounding country, and each town became the

---

for all works undertaken for the court of Louis XIV. must have supplied designs for the lace manufactures : " In the accounts of the King's buildings is the entry of a payment due to Bailly, the painter, for several days' work with other painters in making designs for embroideries and points d'Espagne " (Lefébure).

[29] The principal centres of lace-making were Aurillac, Sedan, Rheims, Le Quesnoy, Alençon, Arras, and Loudun, and the name " Points de France " was given without distinction to all laces made at these towns ; preference was given in choosing these centres to those towns already engaged in lace-making. Alençon produced the most brilliant results, for from the beginning of the seventeenth century the town had been engaged in needle-point lace, and some of the lace-makers earned high wages, and showed great aptitude for the art. In her *Histoire du Point d'Alençon*, Madame Despierres has made some interesting extracts from various marriage contracts and wills :—

" A notable instance is that of a family named Barbot, the mother having amassed 500 livres. Her daughter, Marthe Barbot, married Michel Mercier, sieur de la Perrière, and brought him a wedding-portion of 500 livres, the earnings of her industry ; while her sister Suzanne Barbot's wedding-portion, upon her marriage with Paul Ternouillet, amounted to 6,000 livres, earned in making cut-works and works *en velin* (needle-point lace done on a parchment pattern), which command a high price " (Lefébure).

[30] The Venetian Senate, according to Charles Yriarte, regarded this emigration of workers to France as a crime against the State, and issued the following decree :—

" If any artist or handicraftsman practises his art in any foreign land to the detriment of the Republic, orders to return will be sent him ; if he disobeys them, his nearest of kin will be put into prison, in order that through his interest in their welfare his obedience may be compelled. If he comes back, his past offence will be condoned, and employment for him will be found in Venice ; but if, notwithstanding the imprisonment of his nearest of kin, he obstinately decides to continue living abroad, an emissary will be commissioned to kill him, and his next of kin will only be liberated upon his death."

centre of a trade extending round it in a radius of several miles, the work being given out from the manufactory to be executed by the cottagers in their own homes.[31]

---

[31] To afford an idea of the importance of the lace trade in France at the beginning of the eighteenth century, and of the immense consumption of lace in France, we give the following statistics :—In 1707, the collection of the duties of lace was under-farmed to one Étienne Nicolas, for the annual sum of 201,000 livres. The duty then was of 50 livres per lb. weight of lace, so that there entered annually into France above 400,000 lbs. of lace, which, estimating at the lowest 1,000 lbs. of lace to be worth 1,000 livres, would represent 4 millions of that epoch. Taking into calculation that fraud was extensively practised, that the points of Venice and Genoa, being prohibited, could not appear in the receipts ; and that, on the other part, the under-farmer did not pay the farmer-general the 201,000 livres without the certainty of profit to himself, we must admit that the figure, though high, is far from representing the value of the foreign laces which entered France at that period. We think that 8 millions (£320,000) would be below the true figure.—*Rapport sur les Dentelles fait à la Commission française de l'Exposition Universelle de Londres*, 1851. Felix Aubry. The best history of lace published.

CHAPTER X.

LOUIS XIV.—*continued.*

"Tout change : la raison change aussi de méthode ;
Écrits, habillemens, systèmes : tout est mode."
Racine fils, *Epitre à Rousseau.*

POINT DE FRANCE continued to be worn in the greatest
profusion during the reign of Louis XIV. The King
affected his new-born fabric much as monarchs of the
present day do their tapestries and their porcelains. It
decorated the Church and her ministers. Ladies offered
"tours de chaire à l'église de la paroisse."[1] Albs, "garnies
d'un grand point de France brodé antique";[2] altar-cloths
trimmed with Argentan[3] appear in the church registers.[4]
In a painting at Versailles, by Rigaud, representing the
presentation of the Grand Dauphin to his royal father,
1668, the infant is enveloped in a mantle of the richest point
(Fig. 74); and point de France was selected by royal
command to trim the sheets of holland used at the ceremony
of his "nomination."[5] At the marriage of the Prince de
Conti and of Mademoiselle de Blois the toilette[6] presented

---

[1] " Deux tours de chaire de point de France donnez depuis quelques années par deux dames de la paroisse."—*Inv. de l'église de Saint-Merry, à Paris.* Arch. Nat. L. L. 859.

[2] *Inv. de Madame Anne Palatine de Bavière, Princesse de Condé.*—*Ibid.* X. 10,065.

[3] *Inv. de l'église de Saint-Gervais, à Paris.*—*Ibid.* L. L. 854.

[4] The saints, too, came in for their share of the booty.

" There was St. Winifred," writes a traveller of the day, " in a point commode with a large scarf on and a loup in hand, as tho' she were going to mass. St. Denis, with a laced hat and embroidered coat and sash, like a captain of the guards."—*Six Weeks in France.* 1691.

[5] " Toille de Hollande, avec des grands points de France."—*Le Cérémonial de la Nomination de Monseigneur le Dauphin.* 1668. Arch. Nat. K. K. 1431.

[6] *Le Mercure Galant.* Juillet, 1688. This periodical, which we shall have occasion so frequently to quote, was begun in 1672, and continued to July, 1716. It comprises, with the *Extraordinaires,* 571 vols. in 12mo.

Le Mercure de France, from 1717 to 1792, consists of 777 vols.—Brunet. Manuel de Libraire.

by the King was "garnie de point de France si haut qu'on ne voyait point de toile."[7] The valance, too, and the coverlet of the bed were of the same material.[8]

In this luxury, however, England followed her sister kingdom, for we read in the *Royal Magazine* of 1763 that on the baptism of the young prince, afterwards Duke of York, the company went to the council chamber at St. James's, where a splendid bed was set up for the Queen to sit on, the counterpane of which is described as of inimitable workmanship, the lace alone costing £3,783 sterling.[9] "What princes do themselves, they engage others to do," says Quintilian, and the words of the critic were, in this case, fully verified: jupes,[10] corsets, mantles, aprons with their bibs,[11] shoes,[12] gloves,[13] even the fans were now trimmed with point de France.[14]

At the audience given by the Dauphine to the Siamese ambassadors, " à ses relevailles," she received them in a bed " presque tout couvert d'un tres beau point de France, sur lesquels on avoit mis des riches carreaux."[15] On the occasion of their visit to Versailles, Louis, proud of his fabric, pre-

---

[7] *Le Mercure Galant.*

[8] It was the custom, at the birth of a Dauphin, for the papal nuncio to go to the palace and present to the new-born child " les langes benites," or consecrated layette, on behalf of his Holiness the Pope. The shirts, handkerchiefs, and other linen, were by half-dozens, and trimmed with the richest point. This custom dates as early as the birth of Louis XIII. Mercier describes the ceremony of carrying the layette to Versailles in the time of Louis XV.—*Vie du Dauphin, père de Louis XVI.* Paris, 1858.

[9] In the Lancaster state bedroom, at Fonthill, was sold in 1823: "A state bed quilt of Brussels point, for 100 guineas, and a Brussels toilet cover for 30 guineas."—*Fonthill. Sale Catalogue.*

" 1694. Une toilette de satin violet picquée garny d'un point d'Espagne d'or à deux carreaux de mesme satin et aussi piqué."—*Inv. de Mgr. de la Vrillière, Patriarche, Archéveque de Bourges.* Bib. Nat.

" 1743. Une toilette et son bonhomme garnie d'une vieille dentelle d'Angleterre."—*Inv. de la Duchesse de Bourbon.*

" 1758. Une toilette avec sa touaille de point fort vieux d'Alençon."—*Inv. de Mademoiselle de Charollois.*

" 1770. Une tres belle toilette de point d'Argentan, en son surtout de 9,000 livres.

" Une tres belle toilette d'Angleterre, et son surtout de 9,000."—*Cptes. de Madame du Barry.*

[10] " On voit toujours des jupes de point de France."—*Mercure Galant.* 1686.

" Corsets chamarrés de point de France." *Ibid.*

[11] Madame de Sévigné describes Mademoiselle de Blois as " belle comme un ange," with " un tablier et une bavette de point de France."—*Lettres.* Paris, 27 Jan., 1674.

[12] " Garnis de point de France formant une manière de rose antique."—*Mercure Galant.* 1677.

[13] In the Extraordinaire du *Mercure* for 1678, we have, in " habit d'este," gloves of " point d'Angleterre."

[14] *Mercure Galant.* 1672.

[15] *Ibid.* 1686.

Fig. 74.

Le Grand Bébé. (M. de Versailles.)

sented the ambassadors with cravats and ruffles of the finest point.[16] These cravats were either worn of point, in one piece, or partly of muslin tied, with falling lace ends.[17] (Fig. 75.)

In 1679 the king gave a fête at Marly to the élite of his brilliant court. When, at sunset, the ladies retired to repair their toilettes, previous to the ball, each found in her dressing-room a robe fresh and elegant, trimmed with point of the most exquisite texture, a present from that gallant monarch not yet termed " l'inamusable."

Nor was the Veuve Scarron behind the rest. When, in

Fig. 75.

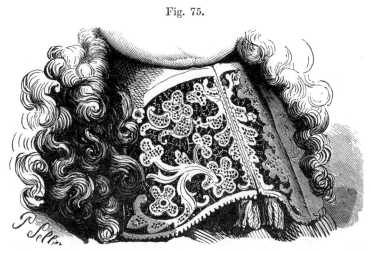

LOUVOIS. 1691.—(From his statue by Girardon. M. de Versailles.)

1674, she purchased the estate from which she afterwards derived her title of Maintenon, anxious to render it productive, she enticed Flemish workers from the frontier to establish a lace manufacture upon her newly-acquired marquisate. How the fabric succeeded history does not relate, but the costly laces depicted in her portraits (Fig. 76) have not the appearance of home manufacture.

Point lace-making became a favourite employment among ladies. We have many engravings of this reign ; one, 1691, of a " fille de qualité " thus occupied, with the motto, " Apres

---

[16] *Mercure Galant.* Fév. 1685.   [17] *Ibid.* 1678.

dîner vous travaillez au point." Another,[18] an engraving of Le Paultre, dated 1676, is entitled "Dame en Déshabille de Chambre" (Fig. 77).

"La France est la tête du monde" (as regards fashion), says Victor Hugo, "cyclope dont Paris est l'œil"; and writers of all ages seem to have been of the same opinion. It was about the year 1680 that the

> " Mode féconde en mille inventions
> Monstre, prodige étrange et difforme,"

was suddenly exemplified in France.

All readers of this great reign will recall to mind the

Fig. 76.

MADAME DE MAINTENON.—(From her portrait. M. de Versailles.)

story of the "Fontanges." How in the hurry of the chase the locks of the royal favourite burst from the ribbon that bound them—how the fair huntress, hurriedly tying the lace kerchief round her head, produced in one moment a coiffure so light, so artistic, that Louis XIV., enchanted, prayed her to retain it for that night at court. The lady obeyed the royal command. This mixture of lace and ribbon, now worn for the first time, caused a sensation, and the next day all

---

[18] At the Mazarin Library there are four folio volumes of engravings, after Bonnard and others, of the costumes of the time of Louis XIV.; and at the Archives Nat. is a large series preserved in cartons numbered M. 815 to 823, etc., labelled "Gravures de Modes."

the ladies of the court appeared " coiffées à la Fontange."
(See Madame du Lude, Fig. 79.)

But this head-dress, with its tiers of point mounted on
wires,[19] soon ceased to be artistic; it grew higher and
higher. Poets and satirists attacked the fashion much as

Fig. 77.

A LADY IN MORNING DÉSHABILLE.—(From an engraving by Le Paultre. 1676.)

they did the high head-dresses of the Roman matrons more
than a thousand years ago.[20] Of the extinction of this mode

---

[19] *La Fontange altière.*—Boileau.

[20] The wife of Trajan wore this coiffure, and her sister Marcina Faustina, wife of Antoninus, much regretted

the fashion when it went out. Speaking of this head-dress, says a writer in the *Bibliothèque Universelle* of 1693, " On regarde quelque fois des certaines

we have various accounts, some asserting it to have been preached down by the clergy, as were the *hennins* in the time of Charles VI.; but the most probable story is that which relates how, in October, 1699, Louis XIV. simply observed, " Cette coiffure lui paroissoit désagréable." The ladies worked all night, and next evening, at the Duchess of Burgundy's reception,[21] appeared for the first time in a low head-dress. Fashion,[22] which the author of the before-quoted *Consolation* would call *pompeux*, was " aujourd'hui en reforme." Louis XIV. never appreciated the sacrifice; to the day of his death he persisted in saying, " J'ai eu beau crier contre les coiffures trop hautes." No one showed the slightest desire to lower them till one day there arrived " une inconnue, une guenille d'Angleterre " (Lady Sandwich, the English Ambassadress!!), " avec une petite coiffure basse—tout d'un coup, toutes les princesses vont d'une extrémité à l'autre." [23] Be the accusation true or not, the *Mercure* of November, 1699, announces that " La hauteur des anciennes coiffures commence á paroître ridicule "; and St. Simon, in his *Memoirs*, satirises the fontange as a " structure of brass wire, ribbons, hair, and baubles of all sorts, about two feet high, which made a woman's face look as if it were in the middle of her body."

In these days lace was not confined to Versailles and the Court.[24]

" Le gentilhomme," writes Capefigue, " allait au feu en manchettes poudré à la maréchale, les eaux se senteur sur son mouchoir en point d'Angleterre, l'élégance n'a jamais fait tort au courage, et la politesse s'allie noblement à la bravoure."

But war brings destruction to laces as well as finances,

---

[22] choses comme tout à fait nouvelles, qui ne sont que des vieilles modes renouvellées. L'auteur en appelle un exemple dans les coiffures elevées que portent les femmes aujourd'hui, croyant ajouter par là quelque chose à leur taille. Les dames Romaines avaient la même ambition et mettaient des ajustemens de tête tout semblables aux Commodes et aux Fontanges de ce temps. Juvenal en parle expressément dans sa Satire VI."

[21] *Galerie de l'ancienne Cour.*

[22] " 1699. Oct. Le Vendredi 25, il y eut grande toilette chez Madame la Duchesse de Bourgogne où les dames parurent, pour la première fois, en coiffures d'une forme nouvelle, c'est à dire beaucoup plus basses."—*Mercure Galant.*

[23] " Corr. de la Duchesse d'Orléans, Princesse Palatine, mère du Régent."

[24] Speaking of the Iron Mask, Voltaire writes:—" His greatest passion was for linen of great fineness and for lace."—*Siècle de Louis XIV.*

〉

and in 1690 the loyal and noble army was found in rags. Then writes Dangeau : "M. de Castanaga, à qui M. de Maine et M. de Luxembourg avoient demandé un passeport pour fair venir des dentelles à l'armée, a refusé le passeport, mais il a envoyé des marchands qui ont porté pour dix mille écus de dentelles, et après qu'on les eut achetées, les marchands s'en retournèrent sans vouloir prendre d'argent, disant qu'ils avoient cet ordre de M. de Castanaga."

"J'avois une Steinkerque de Malines," writes the Abbé de Choisy, who always dressed in female attire. We hear a great deal about these Steinkirks at the end of the seventeenth century. It was a twisted lace necktie, and owed its origin to the battle of that name in 1692,[25] when the young French Princes of the Blood were suddenly ordered into action. Hastily tying their lace cravats—in peaceful times a most elaborate proceeding—they rushed to the charge, and gained the day. In honour of this event, both ladies and cavaliers wore their handkerchiefs knotted or twisted in this careless fashion.

"Je trouve qu'en été le Steinkerque est commode,
J'aime le falbala,[26] quoiqu'il soit critiqué,"

says somebody. Steinkirks became the rage, and held good for many years, worn alike in England[27] and France by the women and the men. Fig. 78 represents the Grand Dauphin in his "longue Steinkerque à replis tortueux";[28] Fig. 79 the Duchesse du Lude[29] in similar costume and high Fontange, both copied from prints of the time.

We find constant mention now of the fashion of wearing a lace ruffle to the ladies' sleeves, concerning the wearing of which "à deux rangs," or "à trois rangs," there was much etiquette.

The falbalas were not given up until after the Regency ; the use of them was frequently carried to such an excess

---

[25] Fought by Marshal Luxembourg —vieux tapissier de Notre-Dame— against William of Orange.

[26] Falbala—a deep single flounce of point or gold lace. The *Mercure Galant*, 1698, describing the Duchess of Burgundy " à la promenade," states : " Elle avoit un habit gris de lin en falbala, tout garny de dentelles d'ar-gent."

" Femme de qualité en Steinkerke et Falbala."—Engraving of 1693.

[27] See ENGLAND.—WILLIAM III.

[28] Regnard.

[29] Dame du palais to Queen Marie Thérèse, and afterwards first lady of honour to the Duchess of Burgundy. She died 1726.

that a caricaturist of that period drew a lady so enveloped in them that she "looked like a turkey shaking its feathers and spreading its comb." This caricature gave rise to a popular song called "La Dinde aux Falbalas"; but in despite of song and caricature, the flounce continued in popularity.

"Les manches plates se font de deux tiers de tour, avec une dentelle de fil de point fort fin et fort haut. On nomme ces manches Engageantes."[30]

This fashion, though introduced in 1688, continued in vogue till the French Revolution. We see them in the portrait of Madame Palatine, mother of the Regent (Fig. 80), and in that of Madame Sophie de France, daughter of Louis XV., taken in 1782 by Drouais.

Before finishing with point de France, we must allude to the équipage de bain, in which this fabric formed a great item. As early as 1688, Madame de Maintenon presents Madame de Chevreuse with an "équipage de bain de point de France" of great magnificence. It consisted not only of a peignoir, but a broad flounce, which formed a valance round the bath itself. You can see them in old engravings of the day. Then

---

[30] *Mercure Galant.* 1683.

Again, in 1688, he says: "Les points de Malines sont fort en regne pour les manches qu'on nomme engageantes. Ou y met des points très-hauts, fort plissés, avec des pieds."

"Ladies trimmed their *berthes* and sleeves with lace; when the sleeves were short they were called *engageantes;* when long, *pagodes.* Upon skirts laces were worn *volantes* or as flounces, whence the name *volant* or flounce, which has come into use for all wide laces; these flouncings were draped either in *tournantes* or *quilles,* the former laid horizontally, the latter vertically upon skirts; but in either case these were stitched down on each edge of the lace, whereas flounces were fastened to dresses by the *engrêlure* or footing. Lace *barbes* and *fontanges* were used as head-dresses."

They appear to have been soon introduced into England, for Evelyn, in his *Mundus Muliebris,* 1690, says: "About her sleeves are engageants;" and the *Ladies' Dictionary* of nearly

the same date gives: "Ængageants, double ruffles that fall over the wrist."

In the lace bills of Queen Mary II., we find—

	£ s. d.
"1694. 1¾ yd. Point for a broad pair of Engageants, at £5 10s.	9 12 6
3½ for a double pair of ditto, at £5 10s.	19 5 0
1 pair of Point Engageants	30 0 0

—(B. M., Add. MSS. No. 5751.)

"1720. Six pairs d'engageantes, dont quatre à un rang de dentelle, et les autres paires à double rang, l'une de dentelle d'Angleterre à raiseau et l'autre de dentelle à bride."—*Inv. de la Duchesse de Bourbon.* Arch. Nat.

"1723. Une paire d'engageantes à deux rangs de point plat à raiseau."—*Inv. d'Anne de Bavière, Princesse de Condé.*

"1770. Six rangs d'engageantes de point à l'aiguille," with the same of point d'Argentan and Angleterre, appear in the lace bills of Madame du Barry.

Fig. 78.

LE GRAND DAUPHIN EN STEINKERQUE.

Fig. 79.

MADAME DU LUDE EN STEINKERQUE.

PLATE LII.

BRUSSELS.   MODERN POINT DE GAZE.—Actual size.
Photo by A. Dryden.

there were the towels and the *descente*, all equally costly,[31] for the French ladies of the seventeenth and eighteenth centuries admitted their *habitués* not only to the *ruelle*,[32]

Fig. 80.

MADAME PALATINE (ELIZ. CHARLOTTE DE BAVIÈRE), DUCHESSE D'ORLÉANS.
(By Rigaud. M. de Versailles.)

but also to the bath-room.[33]   In the latter case the bath

---

[31] " 1725. Deux manteaux de bain et deux chemises, aussi de bain, garnis aux manches de dentelle, l'une à bride, et l'autre à raiseau."—*Inv. d'Anne de Bavière, Princesse de Condé.*

" 1743. Ung Tour de baignoir de bazin garny de vieille dentelle.

" Trois linges de baignoire garnis de dentelle."—*Inv. de la Duchesse de Bourbon.*

[32] Describing the duties of the " critic of each bright ruelle," Tickell says :—

" Oft with varied art, his thoughts digress
On deeper themes—the documents of dress ;
With nice discernment, to each style of face

Adapt a ribbon, or suggest a lace ;
O'er Granby's cap bid loftier feathers float,
And add new bows to Devon's petticoat."—*Wreath of Fashion.*

[33] In the spring of 1802, Mr. Holcroft, when in Paris, received a polite note from a lady at whose house he visited, requesting to see him. He went, and was informed by her maid the lady was in her warm bath, but she would announce his arrival. She returned, and led him to a kind of closet, where her mistress was up to her chin in water. He knew the manners of the place, and was not surprised.—*Travels.*

was *au lait, i.e.,* clouded by the mixture of some essence. " Aux autres temps, autres mœurs."

The " fameuse poupée " of the reign of Louis XIV. must not be forgotten. The custom of dressing up these great dolls originated in the salons of the Hôtel Rambouillet, where one, termed " la grande Pandore," at each change of fashion was exhibited " en grand tenue " ; a second, the little Pandore, in morning *déshabille.* These dolls were sent to Vienna and Italy, charged with the finest laces France could produce. As late as 1764 we read in the *Espion Chinois,* " Il a débarqué à Douvres un grand nombre de poupées de hauteur naturelle habillées à la mode de Paris, afin que les dames de qualité puissent régler leurs goûts sur ces modèles." [34] Even when English ports were closed in war-time, a special permission was given for the entry of a large alabaster doll four feet high, the Grand Courrier de la Mode.[35] In the war of the First Empire this privilege was refused to our countrywomen ; and from that time Englishwomen, deprived of all French aid for a whole generation, began to dress badly. Pitt has much to answer for. With this notice finishes our account of the reign of Louis XIV.

---

[34] Mercier also mentions, in his *Tableau de Paris,* la poupée de la rue Saint-Honoré: " C'est de Paris que les profondes inventions en modes donnent des loix à l'univers. La fameuse poupée, le mannequin precieux, affublé des modes les plus nouvelles . . . passe de Paris à Londres tous les mois, et va de là répandre ses graces dans toute l'Europe. Il va au Nord et du Midi, il pénètre à Constantinople et à Petersbourg, et le pli qu'a donné une main françoise se répète chez toute les nations, humbles observatrices du goût de la rue Saint-Honoré."

[35] The practice was much more ancient. M. Ladomie asserts that in the Royal expenses for 1391, figure so many livres for a doll sent to the Queen of England; in 1496 another, sent to the Queen of Spain; and in 1571 a third, to the Duchess of Bavaria.

Henry IV. writes in 1600, before his marriage to Marie de Médicis : " Frontenac tells me that you desire patterns of our fashion in dress. I send you, therefore, some model dolls."—Miss Freer's *Henry IV.*

It was also the custom of Venice, at the annual fair held in the Piazza of St. Mark, on the day of the Ascension (a fair which dates from 1180), to expose in the most conspicuous place of the fair a rag doll, which served as a model for the fashions for the year.— Michiel, *Origine delle Feste Veneziani.*

CHAPTER XI.

LOUIS XV.

"Le luxe corrompt tout, et le riche qui en jouit, et le pauvre qui le convoite."
—J. J. Rousseau.

Louis XIV. is now dead, to the delight of a wearied nation : we enter on the Regency and times of Louis XV.—that age of "fourchettes," manchettes, and jabots—in which the butterfly abbés, "les porte-dentelles par excellence," played so conspicuous a part.

The origin of the weeping ruffles, if Mercier[1] is to be credited, may be assigned to other causes than royal decree or the edicts of fashion. "Les grandes manchettes furent introduites par des fripons qui voulaient filouter au jeu et escamoter des cartes." It never answers to investigate too deeply the origin of a new invented mode,—sufficient to say, ruffles became a necessary adjunct to the toilet of every gentleman. So indispensable were they, the Parisians are accused of adopting the custom of wearing ruffles and no shirts.

"Les Parisiens," writes Mercier, "achètent quatre ajustemens contre une chemise. Un beau Monsieur se met une chemise blanche tous les quinze jours. Il coud ses manchettes de dentelle sur une chemise sale," and powders over his point collar till it looks white.[2] This habit passed into a proverb. The Maréchal de Richelieu, who, though versed in astronomy, could not spell, said of himself, "Qu'on ne lui avoit pas fourni des chemises, mais qu'il avoit acheté des

---

[1] *Tableau de Paris.* 1782.

[2] "The French nation are eminent for making a fine outside, when perhaps they want necessaries, and indeed a gay shop and a mean stock is like the Frenchman with his laced ruffles without a shirt."—*The Complete English Tradesman.* Dan. Defoe. Lond., 1726. Foote, in his Prologue to the *Trip to Paris*, says, "They sold me some ruffles, and I found the shirts."

manchettes." [3] This account tallies well with former accounts [4] and with a letter of Madame de Maintenon to the Princess des Ursins, 1710. [5]

At this period it was the custom for grisettes to besiege the Paris hotels, bearing on their arms baskets decked out with ruffles and jabots of Malines, Angleterre, and point. What reader of Sterne will not recollect the lace-seller in his *Sentimental Journey?*

The jabot and manchettes of points were the customary " cadeau de noces" of the bride to her intended for his wedding dress—a relic of which practice may be found in the embroidered wedding shirt furnished by the lady, in the North of Europe. [6] The sums expended in these articles would now appear fabulous. The Archbishop of Cambray [7] alone possessed four dozen pairs of ruffles, Malines, point, and Valenciennes. The Wardrobe Bills of the Duke de Penthièvre of 1738 make mention of little else. An ell and a quarter of lace was required for one pair of ruffles. A yard, minus $\frac{1}{16}$, sufficed for the jabot. [8] There were manchettes de jour, manchettes tournantes, [9] and manchettes de nuit : these last-named were mostly of Valenciennes. [10] The

---

[3] *Souvenirs de la Marquise de Créquy.* 1710–1802.

[4] Clement X. was in the habit of making presents of Italian lace, at that time much prized in France, to M. de Sabière. " He sends ruffles," said the irritated Frenchman who looked for something more tangible, " to a man who never has a shirt."

[5] " M. de Vendôme, at his marriage, was quite astonished at putting on his clean shirt a-day, and fearfully embarrassed at having some point lace on the one given him to put on at night. Indeed," continues she, " you would hardly recognise the taste of the French. The men are worse than the women. They wish their wives to take snuff, play, and pay no more attention to their dress." The exquisite cleanliness of Anne of Austria's court was at an end.

[6] In the old Scotch song of Gilderoy, the famous highwayman, we have an instance :—

" For Gilderoy, that luve of mine,
    Gude faith, I freely bought

A wedding sark of Holland fine,
    Wi' silken flowers wrought."

And in an account quoted in the *Reliquary*, July, 1865, is the charge on Feb. 16, of " six shillings for a cravat for hur Vallentine."

[7] *Inv. après le decès de Mgr. C. de Saint-Albin, Archevesque de Cambray.* (Son of the Regent.) 1764. Arch. Nat. M. M. 718.
  Louis XVI. had 59 pairs the year before his death : 28 of point, 21 of Valenciennes, and 10 of Angleterre.— *Etat des Effets subsistant et formant le fond de la garderobe du Roi au 1er Janvier,* 1792. Arch. Nat. K. 506, No. 30.

[8] *Etat d'un Trousseau.* Description des Arts et Métiers. Paris, 1777.

[9] " Deux aunes trois quarts d'Angleterre à bride pour deux paires de manchettes tournantes, à 45 livres l'aune."
  —*Garderobe de S. A. S. Mgr. le Duc de Penthièvre.* 1738. Arch. Nat. K. K. 390.

[10] *Ibid.* The laces for ruffles were of various kinds : point brodé, point à bride, point à raiseau, point à bride à

point d'Alençon ruffles of Buffon, which he always wore, even when writing, were exhibited in 1864 at Falaise, being carefully preserved in the family to whom they have descended.

Even, if a contemporary writer may be credited, " Monsieur de Paris," the executioner, mounted the scaffold in a velvet suit, powdered, with point lace jabot and ruffles.

" Les rubans, les miroirs, les dentelles sont trois choses sans lesquelles les François ne peuvent vivre. Le luxe démesuré a confondu le maître avec le valet,"[11] says an unknown writer, quoted by Dulaure.[12] The servants of the last century had on their state liveries lace equal in richness to that worn by their masters.[13] Of a Prussian gentleman, we read, " His valets, who according to the reigning tastes were the prettiest in the world, wore nothing but the most costly lace."[14] This custom was not confined, however, to France or the Continent. " Our very footmen," writes the angry *World*, " are adorned with gold and

---

écaille, point superfin, point brillant, Angleterre à bride à raiseau, and one pair of point d'Argentan; Valenciennes pour manchettes de nuit à 42 livres l'aune.

The Duke's wardrobe accounts afford a good specimen of the extravagance in the decoration of night attire at this period :—

4 au. de point pour collet et manchettes de la chemise de nuit et garnir la coëffe, à 130 ll.	520 ll.
3 au. ¾ dito pour jabot et fourchettes de nuit et garnir le devant de la camisole, à 66 ll.	247 ll. 1Cs.
Sept douze de point pour plaquer sur les manches de camisolle, à 55 ll.	32 ll. 1s.

Then for his nightcaps :—

3 au. Toile fine pour Coëffes de Nuit	27 ll.
4 au. Dentelles de Malines pour les tours de Coëffes, à 20 ll.	80 ll.
5 au. ½ Valenciennes, à 46 ll.	253 ll.
52 au. dito petit point, pour garnir les Tours, à 5 ll. 5s.	273 ll.

Pour avoir monté un bonnet de nuit de point	1 l.	5s.
7 au. de campanne de point pour chamarrer la camisolle et le bonnet de nuit, à 10 ll. 10s.	73 ll.	10s.

The Marquise de Créquy speaks of a night-cap, " à grandes dentelles," offered, with la robe de chambre, to the Dauphin, son of Louis XV., by the people of the Duke de Grammont, on his having lost his way hunting, and wandered to the Duke's château.

[11] " Le Parisien qui n'a pas dix mille livres de rente n'a ordinairement ni draps, ni lit, ni serviettes, ni chemises ; mais il a une montre à repetition, des glaces, des bas de soie, des dentelles." —*Tableau de Paris.*

[12] *Histoire de Paris.*

[13] " Ordinairement un laquais de bon ton prend le nom de son maître, quand il est avec d'autres laquais, il prend aussi ses mœurs, ses gestes, ses manières. . . . Le laquais d'un seigneur porte la montre d'or ciselée, des dentelles, des boucles à brillants," etc.—*Tableau de Paris.*

[14] *Amusemens des Eaux de Spa.* Amsterdam, 1751.

" Les manches qu'à table on voit tâter la sauce."—*École des maris.*

silver bags and lace ruffles. The valet is only distinguished from his master by being better dressed;" while the *Connoisseur* complains of "roast beef being banished from even 'down stairs,' because the powdered footmen will not touch it for fear of daubing their lace ruffles." [15]

But the time, of all others, for a grand display of lace was at a visit to a Parisian lady on her "relevailles," or "uprising," as it was called, in the days of our third Edward. Reclining on a chaise longue, she is described as awaiting her visitors. Nothing is to be seen but the finest laces, arranged in artistic folds, and long bows of ribbon. An attendant stationed at the door asks of each new arrival, "Have you any perfumes?" She replies not, and passes on—an atmosphere of fragrance. The lady must not be spoken to, but, the usual compliments over, the visitors proceed to admire her lace. "Beautiful, exquisite!"—but, "Hist! speak low," and she who gave the caution is the first, in true French style, to speak the loudest. [16]

Lace "garnitures de lit" were general among great people as early as 1696. The *Mercure* speaks of "draps garnis d'une grande dentelle de point d'Angleterre." In 1738 writes the Duc de Luynes, [17] "Aujourd'hui Madame de Luynes s'est fait apporter les fournitures qu'elle avoit choisies pour la Reine, et qui regardent les dames d'honneur. Elles consistent en couvrepieds [18] garnis de dentelle pour le grand lit et pour les petits, en taies d'oreiller [19] garnies du

---

[15] The state liveries of Queen Victoria were most richly embroidered in gold. They were made in the early part of George II.'s reign, since which time they have been in use. In the year 1848, the servants appeared at the royal balls in gold and ruffles of the richest gros point de France, of the same epoch as their dresses. In 1849, the lace no longer appeared—probably suppressed by order. Queen Anne, who was a great martinet in trifles, had her servants marshalled before her every day, that she might see if their ruffles were clean and their periwigs dressed.

[16] *Tableau de Paris.*

[17] *Mémoires.*

[18] "1723. Un couvrepied de toile blanche, picqure de Marseille, garni autour d'un point en campane de demie aune de hauteur."—*Inv. d'A. de Bavière, Princesse de Condé.*

"1743. Un couvrepied de toile picquée, brodée or et soye, bordé de trois côtés d'une grande dentelle d'Angleterre et du quatrième d'un moyen dentelle d'Angleterre à bords.

"Un autre, garni d'une grande et moyenne dentelle de point d'Alençon.

"Un autre, garni d'un grand point de demie aune de hauteur, brodé, garni d'une campane en bas.

"Un autre, 'point à bride,'" and many others.—*Inv. de la Duchesse de Bourbon.*

[19] "1704. Deux taies d'oreiller garnies de dentelle, l'une à raiseau, et l'autre à bride."—*Inv. de F. P. Loisel.* Bib. Nat. MSS. F. Fr. 11,459.

"1723. Quatre taies d'oreiller, dont trois garnies de differentes dentelles, même point d'Angleterre, etc. Cette fourniture coûte environ 30,000 livres, quoique Madame de Luynes n'ait pas fait renouveler les beaux couvrepieds de la Reine." These garnitures were renewed every year, and Madame de Luynes inherited the old ones.

Madame de Créquy, describing her visit to the Duchesse

Fig. 81.

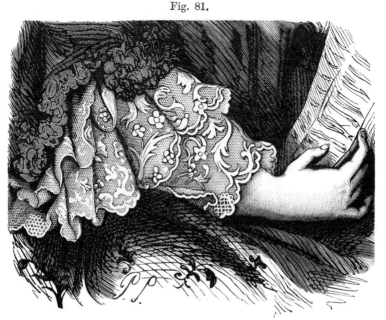

MADAME SOPHIE DE FRANCE, 1782, DAUGHTER OF LOUIS XV. By Drouais. M. de Versailles.
(In this picture the hexagonal brides and heavy relief of Point d'Argentan are clearly to be seen.)

Douairière de La Ferté, says, when that lady received her, she was lying in a state bed, under a coverlet made of point de Venise in one piece. " I am persuaded," she adds, " that

et l'autre de Point."—*Inv. d'Anne de Bavière, Princesse de Condé.*

" 1755. Deux taies d'oreiller garnies de point d'Alençon."—*Inv. de Mademoiselle de Charollais.*

" 1761. Trois taies d'oreiller de dentelle de point à brides."—*Inv. de la Duchesse de Modène.*

" 1770. 7 au. 1/8 vraie Valenciennes pour garnir une taie d'oreiller, à 60 ll. . . 427 10."
—*Comptes de Madame du Barry.*

" 1707. 7 au. tournante d'Angleterre pour garnir des plottes (pincushions) à 50 . 350 00."
—*Comptes de Madame du Barry.*

" 1788. 12 Pelottes garnies de dentelle."—*Ibid.*

" 6 trousses à peigne garnies de dentelle." — *Fourni pour Mgr. le Dauphin.* Arch. Nat.

" 1792. 6 Pelottes garnies de dentelle." — *Linge du çi-devant Roi. Ibid.*

the trimming of her sheets, which were of point d'Argentan, were worth at least 40,000 écus." [20]   To such a pitch had the taste for lace-trimmed linen attained, that when, in 1739, Madame, eldest daughter of Louis XV., espoused the Prince of Spain, the bill for these articles alone amounted to £25,000 ; and when Cardinal Fleury, a most economical prelate, saw the trousseau, he observed, " Qu'il croyait que

Fig. 82.

MADAME ADÉLAÏDE DE FRANCE, DAUGHTER OF LOUIS XV.—(M. de Versailles.)

c'etait pour marier toutes les sept Mesdames." [21]   (Figs. 81, 82).   Again, Swinburne writes from Paris : [22] " The trousseau of Mademoiselle de Matignon will cost 100,000 crowns (£25,000).   The expense here of rigging [23] out a bride is equal to a handsome portion in England.   Five

---

[20] Souvenirs.
[21] *Mémoires du Duc de Luynes.*
[22] 1786.   *Courts of Europe.*
[23] It may be amusing to the reader to learn the laces necessary for l'État d'un Trousseau, in 1777, as given in the *Description des Arts de Métiers :* " Une toilette de ville en dentelle ; 2 jupons garnis du même.   Une coif-

fure avec tour de gorge, et le fichu plissé de point d'Alençon.   Un idem de point d'Angleterre.   1 id. de vraie Valenciennes.   Une coiffure dite ' Battant d'œil ' de Malines brodée, pour le negligé.   6 fichus simples en mousseline à mille fleurs garnis de dentelle pour le negligé.   12 grands bonnets garnis d'une petite dentelle pour la

thousand pounds' worth of lace, linen, etc., is a common thing among them."

The masks worn by the ladies at this period were of black blonde lace [24] of the most exquisite fineness and

Fig. 83.

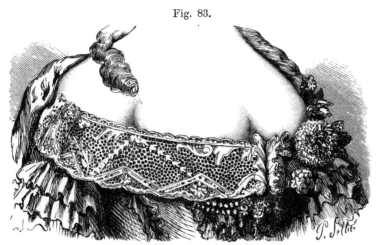

MARIE THÉRÈSE ANT. RAPH., INFANTA OF SPAIN, FIRST WIFE OF LOUIS DAUPHIN, SON OF LOUIS XV.
—By Tocqué. Dated 1748. M. de Versailles.

design.[25] They were trimmed round the eyes, like those described by Scarron :—

> " Dirai-je comme ces fantasques
> Qui portent dentelle à leurs masques,
> En chamarrent les trous des yeux,
> Croyant que le masque en est mieux."

In the reign of Louis XV., point de France was rivalled

nuit. 12 à deux rangs, plus beaux, pour le jour, en cas d'indisposition. 12 serres-tête garnis d'une petite dentelle pour la nuit. 2 taies d'oreiller garnies en dentelle. 12 pièces d'estomach garnies d'une petite dentelle. 6 garnitures de corset. 12 tours de gorge. 12 paires ce manchettes en dentelle. Une toilette ; les volants, au nombre de deux, sont en dentelle ; ils ont 5 aunes de tour. Dessus de pelotte, en toile garnie de dentelle, etc. La Layette : 6 paires de manches pour la mère, garnies de dentelle. 24 bonnets ronds de 3 ages en dentelle. 12 bavoirs de deux ages, garnis en dentelle." The layette was furnished together with the trousseau, because, says a fabricant, "les enfans se font plus vite que les points."

[24] " 1787. Pour achat de 11 au. blonde noire, à 6 10 . . . 71 livres 10 sous."
—*Comptes de Monsieur Hergosse.*
Bib. Nat. MSS., F. Fr. 11,447.

[25] When the Empress Joséphine was at Frankfort-on-the-Maine, a masked ball was given on the occasion. The ladies, says Mademoiselle Avrillion, wore short dominoes with their faces covered with a mask, " le tour des yeux garni d'une petite dentelle noire."—*Mém. de Mademoiselle Avrillion, première femme de chambre de l'Impératrice.* Paris, 1833.

by the productions of Angleterre [26] and Malines.   Argentan
and Alençon (Fig. 83) were declared by fashion to be " dentelles d'hiver : " each lace now had its appointed season.[27]
" On porte le point en hiver," says the Dictionary of the
Academy.

There was much etiquette, too, in the court of France, as
regards lace, which was never worn in mourning.   Dangeau
chronicles, on the death of the Princess of Baden, " Le roi
qui avoit repris les dentelles et les rubans d'or et d'argent,
reprend demain le linge uni et les rubans unis aussi." [28]

" Madame " thus describes the " petit deuil " of the Margrave of Anspach : " Avec des dentelles blanches sur le noir,
du beau ruban bleu, à dentelles blanches et noires.   C'etoit
une parure magnifique." [29]

---

[26] A few extracts from Madame du
Barry's lace accounts will furnish an
idea of her consumption of point
d'Angleterre :—
Une toilette d'Angle-
  terre complette de . 8823 livres.
Une parure composée de
  deux barbes, rayon et
  fond, 6 rangs de man-
  chettes, 1 1/2 au. de
  ruban fait exprès, 1/3
  jabot pour le devant
  de tour. Le tout d'An-
  gleterre superfin de . 7000 —
Un ajustement e d'Angle-
  terre complet de . . 3216 —
Une garniture de peig-

noir d'Angleterre de . 2342 livres.
Une garniture de fichu
  d'Angleterre . . . 388 —
8 au. d'Angleterre
  pour tayes d'oreil-
  ler 240
9 1/2 au. dito pour
  la tête . . . 76
14 au. pied dito pour
  la tête 140
        —— 456 livres.
[27] " Les dentelles les plus précieuses
pour chaque saison." — (Duchesse
d'Abrantès.)
[28] *Mémoires.*
[29] *Mém. de la Princesse Palatine,
veuve de Monsieur.*

Plate LIII.

Madame Louise de France.—Trimmings and tablier of Point d'Argentan.
Painted by Nattier at the age of eleven, 1748. M. de Versailles.

PLATE LIV.

FRENCH. Border of POINT PLAT DE FRANCE to a baptismal veil of embroidered muslin. – The orderly arrangement of the "brides" differs from the Venetian, and foreshadows the "grande maille picotée."

In the Musée Cinquantenaire, Brussels.

CHAPTER XII.

LOUIS XVI. TO THE EMPIRE.

"Proud Versailles! thy glory falls."—Pope.

In the reign of Louis XVI. society, tired out with ceremony and the stately manners of the old court, at last began to emancipate itself. Marie-Antoinette (Fig. 84) first gave the

Fig. 84.

Marie-Antoinette.—From a picture by Madame Le Brun. M. de Versailles.

signal. Rid herself of the preaching of "Madame Etiquette" she could not on state occasions, so she did her best to amuse herself in private. The finest Indian muslin now supplanted the heavy points of the old court. Madame du Barry, in her *Memoirs*, mentions the purchase of Indian muslin so fine that the piece did not weigh fifteen ounces, although sufficient to make four dresses. " The ladies looked," indignantly observed the Maréchale de Luxembourg, " in their muslin aprons and handkerchiefs like cooks and convent porters." [1] To signify her disapproval of this new-fangled custom, the Maréchale sent her grand-daughter, the Duchesse de Lauzun, an apron of sailcloth trimmed with fine point and six fichus of the same material similarly decorated. Tulle and marli [2] were much worn during the latter years of the Queen's life, and entries of tulle, marli, blondes, and embroidered linens occur over and over again in Madame Eloffe's accounts with the Queen. The richer ornamental laces were not worn, and one reads of items such as " a gauze fichu trimmed with white *prétention*."

On leaving Versailles for the last time (October 6th, 1789), Marie Antoinette distributed among her suite all that remained of her fans and laces.

The arrangement of the lace lappets was still preserved by rule. " Lappets to be pinned up "—lappets to be let down on grand occasions. [3] Later Madame de Staël, like a true *bas-bleu*—without speaking of her curtsey to Marie Antoinette, which was all wrong—on her first visit of ceremony to Madame de Polignac, in defiance of all etiquette, left her lace lappets in the carriage.

The democratic spirit of the age now first creeps out in

---

[1] " Cuisinières et Tourières." The joke formed the subject of some clever verses from the Chevalier de Boufflers.

[2] *Marli*, which takes its name from the village between Versailles and St. Germain, is tulle dotted with small square spots. See page 225.

[3] The *barbe*, or lappet, of whatever form it be, has always, in all ages and all countries, been a subject of etiquette. At the interment of Queen Mary Tudor, December 14th, 1558, it is told how the ladies in the first and second chariots were clad in mourning apparel, according to their estates, "their barbes above their chynes." "The 4 ladies on horseback in like manner had their barbes on their chynes." In the third chariot, "the ladies had their barbes under their chynes."—State Papers, Domestic,

Eliz., vol. 32.

See also the curious extract from Madame de Campan's *Mémoires*:—

" Madame de Noailles était remplie de vertus ; mais l'etiquette était pour elle une sorte d'atmosphère. Un jour je mis, sans le vouloir, cette pauvre dame dans une angoisse terrible ; la reine recevait je ne sais plus qui. Tout était bien, au moins je le croyais. Je vois tout-à-coup les yeux de Madame de Noailles attachés sur les miens, et puis ses deux sourcils se levent jusqu'au haut de son front, redescendent, remontent. L'agitation de la Comtesse croissait toujours. La reine s'aperçut de tout ceci . . . et me dit alors à mi-voix : 'Detachez vos barbes, où la comtesse en mourra.' L'etiquette du costume disait : ' Barbes pendentes.' "

the fashions. Among the rich *parures* of Du Barry [4] we find " barbes à la paysanne "—everything now becomes " à coquille," " à papillon."

Even the Queen's hairdresser, Léonard, " qui

" Portait jusques au ceil l'audace de ses coiffures,"

did not venture to introduce much lace.

The affected phraseology of the day is very " precious " in its absurdity. We read of the toilette of Mademoiselle Duthé in which she appeared at the opera. She wore a robe " soupirs étouffés," trimmed with " regrets superflus " ; a point of " candeur parfaite, garnie en plaintes indiscrètes " ; ribbons en " attentions marquées " ; shoes " cheveux de la reine," [5] embroidered with diamonds, " en coups perfides " and " venez-y-voir " in emeralds. Her hair " en sentiments soutenus," with a cap of " conquête assurée," trimmed with ribbons of " œil abattu " ; a " chat [6] sur le col," the colour of " gueux nouvellement arrivé," and upon her shoulders a Médicis " en bienséance," and her muff of " agitation momentanée."

In the accounts of Mademoiselle Bertin, the Queen's milliner, known for her saying, " Il n'y a rien de nouveau dans ce monde que ce qui est oublié," we have little mention of lace. [7]

---

[4] Only in her last lace bill, 1773 :

" Une paire de barbes plattes longues de 3/4 en blonde fine à fleurs fond d'Alençon, 36.

" Une blonde grande hauteur à bouquets détachés et à bordure riche.

" 6 au. de blonde de grande hauteur façon d'Alençon à coquilles à mille poix, à 18.

" Une paire de sabots de comtesse de deux rangs de tulle blonde à festons, fond d'Alençon."—*Comptes de la Comtesse du Barry.* Bib. Nat. F. Fr. 8157.

Madame du Barry went to the greatest extravagance in lace ajustements, barbes, collerettes, volants, quilles, coëffes, etc., of Argentan, Angleterre, and point à l'aiguille.

[5] The great fashion. The shoes were embroidered in diamonds, which were scarcely worn on other parts of the dress. The back seam, trimmed with emeralds, was called " venez-y-voir."

[6] *Souvenirs du Marquis de Valfons*, 1710–1786. A " chat," tippet or Palatine, so named after the mother of the Regent.

[7] In the National Archives, formerly preserved with the *Livre Rouge* in the Armorie de Fer, is the *Gazette pour l'année*, 1782, of Marie Antoinette, consisting of a list of the dresses furnished for the Queen during the year, drawn up by the Comtesse d'Ossune, her dame des atours. We find—grands habits, robes sur le grand panier, robes sur le petit panier, with a pattern of the material affixed to each entry, and the name of the couturière who made the dress. One " Lévite " alone appears trimmed with blonde. There is also the *Gazette* of Madame Elizabeth, for 1792.

"Blond à fond d'Alençon semé à poix, à mouches," now usurps the place of the old points.   Even one of the "grandes dames de la vieille cour," Madame Adélaïde de France herself, is represented in her picture by Madame Guiard with a spotted handkerchief, probably of blonde (Fig. 85).

The Church alone protects the ancient fabrics.   The lace of the Rohan family, almost hereditary Princes Archbishops of Strasburg, was of inestimable value.   "We met," writes

Fig. 85.

MADAME ADÉLAÏDE DE FRANCE.—After a picture by Madame Guiard, dated 1787.   M. de Versailles.

the Baroness de Oberkirch, "the cardinal coming out of his chapel dressed in a soutane of scarlet moire and rochet of English lace of inestimable value.   When on great occasions he officiates at Versailles, he wears an alb of old lace ' en point à l'aiguille' of such beauty that his assistants were almost afraid to touch it.   His arms and device are worked in a medallion above the large flowers.   This alb is estimated at 100,000 livres.   On the day of which I speak he wore the rochet of English lace, one of his least beautiful, as his secretary, the Abbé Georget, told me."[8] On his elevation to the see of Bourges (1859), Monseigneur de La Tour d'Auvergne celebrated mass at Rome arrayed with all the sacerdotal ornaments of point d'Alençon of the finest workmanship. This lace descended to him from his uncle, Cardinal de La Tour d'Auvergne, who had inherited it from his mother, Madame d'Aumale, so well known as the friend of Madame de Maintenon. Under the first Empire, a complete suit of lace was offered to the prelate for sale, which had belonged to Marie-Antoinette. This lace is described as formed of squares of old point d'Angleterre or de Flandre, each representing a different subject. The beauty of the lace and its historic interest decided his Eminence to speak of it to his colleague, Cardinal de Bonald, and these two prelates united their resources, bought the lace, and divided it.

But this extravagance and luxury were now soon to end. The years of '92 and '93 were approaching. The great nobility of France, who patronised the rich manufactures of the kingdom at the expense of a peasantry starving on estates they seldom if ever visited, were ere long outcasts in foreign countries. The French Revolution was fatal to the lace trade. For twelve years the manufacture almost ceased, and more than thirty different fabrics entirely disappeared.[9] Its merits were, however, recognised by the Etats Généraux in 1789, who, when previous to meeting they settled the costume of the three estates, decreed to the *noblesse* a lace cravat. It was not until 1801, when Napoleon wished to " faire revenir le luxe," that we again find it chronicled in the annals of the day : " How charming Caroline Murat looked in her white mantelet of point de Bruxelles et sa robe garnie des mêmes dentelles," etc. The old laces were the work of years, and transmitted as heirlooms[10] from generation to generation.

---

[8] *Mémoires sur la Cour de Louis XVI.*

[9] Among these were Sedan, Charleville, Mézières, Dieppe, Havre, Pontl'Évêque, Honfleur, Eu, and more than ten neighbouring villages. The points of Aurillac, Bourgogne, and Murat disappeared ; and worst of all was the loss of the manufacture of Valenciennes.

Laces were also made in Champagne, at Troyes and Domchéry, etc.

[10] 1649. Anne Gohory leaves all her personals to Madame de Sévigné except her " plus beau mouchoir, le col de point fin de Flandres, et une juppe de satin à fleurs fond vert, garnye de point fin d'or et de soie."

1764. Geneviève Laval bequeaths to

They were often heavy and overloaded with ornament. The ancient style was now discarded and a lighter description introduced. By an improvement in the point de raccroc several sections of lace were joined together so as to form one large piece ; thus ten workers could now produce in a month what had formerly been the work of years.

Napoleon especially patronised the fabrics of Alençon, Brussels, and Chantilly. He endeavoured, too, without success, to raise that of Valenciennes. After the example of Louis XIV., he made the wearing of his two favourite points obligatory at the Court of the Tuileries, and it is to his protection these towns owe the preservation of their manufactures. The lace-makers spoke of the rich orders received from the imperial court as the most remarkable epoch in their industrial career. Never was the beauty and costliness of the laces made for the marriage of Marie-Louise yet surpassed. To reproduce them now would, estimates M. Aubry, cost above a million of francs. Napoleon was a great lover of lace : he admired it as a work of art, and was proud of the proficiency of his subjects Mademoiselle d'Avrillion relates the following anecdote :—The Princess Pauline had given orders to the Empress Joséphine's lace-maker for a dress and various objects to the value of 30,000 francs. When the order was completed and the lace brought home, the Princess changed her mind and refused to take them. Madame Lesœur, in despair, appealed to the Empress. She, thinking the price not unreasonable, considering the beauty of the points, showed them to Napoleon, and told him the circumstance. " I was in the room at the time," writes the authoress of the *Mémoires*. The Emperor examined minutely each carton, exclaiming at intervals, " Comme on travaille bien en France, je dois encourager un pareil commerce. Pauline a grand tort." He ended by paying the bill and distributing the laces among the ladies of the court.[11] Indeed, it may be said that never

---

her sister " une garniture de dentelle de raiseau à grandes dents, valant au moins quinze livres l'aune."—Arch. de Nat. Y. 58.

1764. Anne Challus leaves her " belle garniture de dentelle en plein, man-chettes, tour de gorge, palatine et ond."—*Ibid.*

1764. Madame de Pompadour, in her will, says, " Je donne à mes deux femmes de chambre tout ce qui con-cerne ma garderobe . . . . y compris les dentelles."

[11] *Mém. de Mademoiselle d'Avrillion.*

was lace more in vogue than during the early days of the Empire.

The morning costume of a French duchesse of that court is described in the following terms:—" Elle portait un peignoir brodé en mousseline garni d'une Angleterre très-belle, une fraise en point d'Angleterre. Sur sa tête la duchesse avait jeté en se levant une sorte de ' baigneuse,' comme nos mères l'auraient appelée, en point d'Angleterre, garnie de rubans de satin rose pâle." [12]   The fair sister of Napoleon, the Princess Pauline Borghese, " s'est passionnée," as the term ran, " pour les dentelles." [13]

That Napoleon's example was quickly followed by the *élégantes* of the Directory, the following account, given to the brother of the author by an elderly lady who visited Paris during that very short period [14] when the English flocked to the Continent, of a ball at Madame Récamier's, to which she had an invitation, will testify.

The First Consul was expected, and the *élite* of Paris early thronged the *salons* of the charming hostess, but where was Madame Récamier? " *Souffrante*," the murmur ran, retained to her bed by a sudden indisposition. She would, however, receive her guests *couchée*.

The company passed to the bedroom of the lady, which, as still the custom in France, opened on one of the principal *salons*. There, in a gilded bed, lay Madame Récamier, the most beautiful woman in France. The bed-curtains were of the finest Brussels lace, bordered with garlands of honey-suckle, and lined with satin of the palest rose. The *couvrepied* was of the same material; from the pillow of embroidered cambric fell " des flots de Valenciennes."

The lady herself wore a *peignoir* trimmed with the most exquisite English point. Never had she looked more lovely —never had she done the honours of her hotel more grace-fully. And so she received Napoleon—so she received the heroes of that great empire. All admired her " fortitude," her *dévouement*, in thus sacrificing herself to society, and on the following day " tout Paris s'est fait inscrire chez elle." Never had such anxiety been expressed—never had woman gained such a triumph.

---

[12] *Mémoires sur la Restauration*, par Madame la Duchesse d'Abrantès.

[13] *Ibid.* T. v., p. 48.

[14] After the Peace of Amiens, 1801.

The Duchesse d'Abrantès, who married in the year 1800, describing her trousseau,[15] says she had " des mouchoirs, des jupons, des canezous du matin, des peignoirs de mousseline de l'Inde, des camisoles de nuit, des bonnets de nuit, des bonnets de matin, de toutes les couleurs, de toutes les formes, et tout cela brodé, garni de Valenciennes ou de Malines, ou de point d'Angleterre." In the corbeille de mariage, with the cachemires were " les voiles de point d'Angleterre, les garnitures de robes en point à l'aiguille, et en point de Bruxelles, ainsi qu'en blonde pour l'été. Il y avait aussi des robes de blonde blanche et de dentelle noire," etc. When they go to the Mairie, she describes her costume : " J'avais une robe de mousseline de l'Inde brodée au plumetis et en points à jour, comme c'était alors la mode. Cette robe était à queue, montante et avec de longues manches, le lé de devant entièrement brodé ainsi que le tour du corsage, le bout des manches, qu'on appelait alors amadis. La fraise était en magnifique point à l'aiguille, sur ma tête j'avais un bonnet en point de Bruxelles. . . . Au sommet du bonnet était attachée une petite couronne de fleurs d'oranger, d'où partait un long voile en point d'Angleterre qui tombait à mes pieds et dont je pouvais presque m'envelopper." Madame Junot winds up by saying that " Cette profusion de riches dentelles, si fines, si déliées ne semblaient être qu'un réseau nuageux autour de mon visage, où elles se jouaient dans les boucles de mes cheveux."

Hamlet always used to appear on the stage in lace cravat and ruffles, and Talma, the French tragedian, was very proud of his wardrobe of lace. Dr. Doran relates of him that on one occasion, when stopped by the Belgian custom-house officers at the frontier, an official, turning over his wardrobe, his stage costumes, etc., contemptuously styled them " habits de Polichinelle." Talma, in a rage exclaimed, " Habits de Polichinelle ! Why, the lace of my jabot and ruffles alone is worth fifty louis a yard, and I wear it on my private costume." " And must pay for it accordingly," added the official. " Punch's clothes might pass untaxed, but Monsieur Talma's lace owes duty to our king." Talma was forced to submit.

The French lace manufacture felt the political events of

---

[15] *Mémoires de Madame la Duchesse d'Abrantès.*

1813 to 1817, but experienced a more severe crisis in 1818, when bobbin net was first made in France. Fashion at once adopted the new material, and pillow lace was for a time discarded. For fifteen years lace encountered a fearful competition. The manufacturers were forced to lower their prices and diminish the produce. The marts of Europe were inundated with tulle; but happily a new channel for exportation was opened in the United States of North America. In time a reaction took place, and in 1834, with the exception of Alençon, all the other fabrics were once more in full activity.[16] But a cheaper class of lace had been introduced. In 1832–33 cotton thread first began to be substituted for flax.[17] The lace-makers readily adopted the change; they found cotton more elastic and less expensive It gives, too, a brilliant appearance, and breaks less easily in the working. All manufacturers now use the Scotch cotton, with the exception of Alençon, some choice pieces of Brussels, and the finer qualities of Mechlin and Valenciennes. The difference is not to be detected by the eye; both materials wash equally well.

We now turn to the various lace manufactures of France, taking each in its order.

---

[16] The revival first appeared in the towns which made the cheaper laces: Caen, Bayeux, Mirecourt, Le Puy, Arras, etc.   [17] "Fil de mulquinerie."

CHAPTER XIII.

THE LACE MANUFACTURES OF FRANCE.

FRANCE is a lace-making, as well as a lace-wearing, country.

Of the half a million of lace-makers in Europe, nearly a quarter of a million are estimated as belonging to France.

Under the impulse of fashion and luxury, lace receives the stamp of the special style of each country. Italy furnished its points of Venice and Genoa. The Netherlands, its Brussels, Mechlin, and Valenciennes. Spain, its silk blondes. England, its Honiton. France, its sumptuous point d'Alençon, and its black lace of Bayeux and Chantilly. Now, each style is copied by every nation; and though France cannot compete with Belgium in the points of Brussels, or the Valenciennes of Ypres, she has no rival in her points of Alençon and her white blondes, or her black silk laces. To begin with Alençon, the only French lace not made on the pillow.

ALENÇON (DÉP. ORNE), NORMANDY.

> " Alenchon est sous Sarthe assis,
> Il luic divise le pays."—*Romant de Rou.*

We have already related how the manufacture of point lace was established by Colbert. The *entrepreneurs* had found the lace industry flourishing at the time of the point de France. (Page 155.)

Point d'Alençon is mentioned in the *Révolte des Passe-mens*, 1661, evidently as an advanced manufacture; but the monopoly of the privileged workmen—the new-comers—displeased the old workwomen, and Colbert[1] was too despotic

---

[1] The name *point Colbert*, adopted in memory of the great Minister, is applied to point laces in high relief.

" La brode a toujours existé dans le point d'Alençon, aussi que dans le point de Venise, seulement dans le

in his orders prohibiting to make any kind of point except that of the royal manufactory, and made the people so indignant that they revolted. The intendant, Favier-Duboulay, writes to Colbert, August 1665, that one named Le Prevost, of this town, having given suspicion to the people that he was about to form an establishment of "ouvrages de fil," the women to the number of above a thousand assembled, and pursued him so that, if he had not managed to escape their fury, he would assuredly have suffered from their violence. "He took refuge with me," he

Fig. 86.

COLBERT + 1683.—M. de Versailles.

writes, "and I with difficulty appeased the multitude by assuring them that they would not be deprived of the liberty of working. It is a fact that for many years the town of Alençon subsists only by means of these small works of lace : that the same people make and sell, and in years of scarcity they subsist only by this little industry, and that wishing to

point d'Alençon les reliefs étaient moins énlevés. On ne mettait pas seulement un fil, mais trois, cinq, huit ou dix fils, suivant l'épaisseur du relief que l'on voulait obtenir puis, sur ce bourrage, se faisaient des points bouclés très serrés de façon que la boucle fut presque sous les fils formant le relief. C'est ce point que certains fabricants nomment point Colbert."—Madame Despierres, *Histoire du Point d'Alençon.*—Page 228, *post*.

take away their liberty, they were so incensed I had great difficulty in pacifying them."

The Act, it appears, had come from the Parliament of Paris, but as Alençon is in Normandy, it was necessary to have the assent of the Parliament of Rouen.

The remonstrance of the intendant (see his letter in Chap. IX., page 155) met with the attention it deserved.

On September 14th following, after a meeting headed by Prevost and the Marquis de Pasax, intendant of the city, it was settled that after the king had found 200 girls, the rest were at liberty to work as they pleased ; none had permission to make the fine point of the royal pattern, except those who worked for the manufactory ; and all girls must show to the authorities the patterns they intended working, " so that the King shall be satisfied, and the people gain a livelihood."

The " maîtresse dentellière," Catherine Marcq, writes to Colbert, November 30th, 1665, complaining of the obstiracy of the people, who prefer the old work. " Out of 8,000 women, we have got but 700, and I can only count on 250 who at least will have learnt to perfection the Venetian point, the remainder merely working a month and then leaving the establishment."

The new points are duly chronicled.[2]   In 1677 the *Mercure* announces, " They make now many points de France without grounds, and ' picots en campannes ' to all the five handkerchiefs.   We have seen some with little flowers over the large, which might be styled ' flying flowers,' being only attached in the centre."

In 1678 it says : " The last points de France have no brides, the fleurons are closer together.   The flowers, which are in higher relief in the centre, and lower at the edges, are united by small stalks and flowers, which keep them in their places, instead of brides.   The manner of disposing the branches, called ' ordonnances,' is of two kinds : the one is a twirling stalk, which throws out flowers ; the other is regular —a centre flower, throwing out regular branches on each side."   In October of the same year, the *Mercure* says :

---

[2] In 1673, July, we read in the *Mercure* :—" On fait aussi des dentelles à grandes brides, comme aux points de fil sans raiseau, et des dentelles d'Espagne avec des brides claires sans picots ; et l'on fait aux nouveaux points de France des brides qui en sont remplies d'un nombre infini."

" There has been no change in the patterns," and it does not allude to them again. What can these be but Venice patterns? The flower upon flower—like " fleurs volantes "— exactly answers to the point in high relief (Fig. 87).

A memoir drawn up in 1698 by M. de Pommereu[3] is the next mention we find of the fabric of Alençon. " The manufacture of the points de France is also," he says, " one of the most considerable in the country. This fabric began at Alençon, where most of the women and girls work at it, to the number of more than eight to nine hundred, without counting those in the country, which are in considerable

Fig. 87.

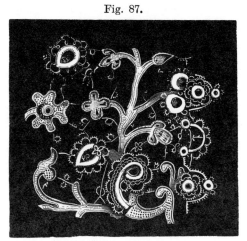

VENICE POINT.—" Dentelle Volante.

numbers. It is a commerce of about 500,000 livres per annum. This point is called ' vilain '[4] in the country ; the principal sale was in Paris during the war, but the demand increases very much since the peace, in consequence of its exportation to foreign countries." The number of lace-workers given by M. Pommereu appears small, but Alençon

[3] *Mémoire concernant le Généralité d'Alençon*, dressé par M. de Pommereu. 1698. Bib. Nat. MSS. Fonds Mortemart, No. 89.

[4] Vilain, velin, vellum, from the parchment or vellum upon which it is made.

" La manufacture des points de France, appelés dans le pays velin."— Savary, Vol. I., p. 108.

" The expression is still used. When the author inquired at Alençon the way to the house of Mr. R., a lace manufacturer, she was asked in return if it was ' Celui qui fait le velin ? ' "— Mrs. Palliser.

manufacture was then on the decline. The death of its protector, Colbert (1683), and the Revocation of the Edict of Nantes, which reduced the population one-third, the industrial families (qui faisaient le principal commerce) retiring to England and Scotland, the long wars of Louis XIV., and, finally, his death in 1715, all contributed to diminish its prosperity.[5]

Savary, writing in 1726, mentions the manufacture of Alençon as not being so flourishing, but attributes it to the long wars of Louis XIV. He adds, " It still, however, maintains itself with some reputation at Alençon ; the magnificence, or, if you like, the luxury of France, sufficing to keep it up even in war-time ; but it flourishes principally in peace, in consequence of the large exports to foreign countries." Russia and Poland were its great marts : and before the Revolution, Poland estimates the annual value of the manufacture at 11,000,000 to 12,000,000 livres.[6] The workwomen earned from three sous to three livres per day.

In 1680, in *Britannia Languens*, a discourse upon trade, it states that " the laces commonly called points de Venise now come mostly from France, and amount to a vast sum yearly."

Point d'Alençon is made entirely by hand, with a fine needle, upon a parchment pattern, in small pieces, afterwards united by invisible seams. There are twelve processes, including the design, each of which is executed by a special workwoman. These can again be subdivided, until the total number of processes is twenty or twenty-two.[7] The design,

---

[5] In 1788 Arthur Young states the number of lace-makers at and about Alençon to be from 8,000 to 9,000."— *Travels in France*.

Madame Despierres, however, states that only 500 or 600 lace-workers left Alençon on the Revocation of the Edict of Nantes, *as there were not 4,000 lace-workers then in the town*.

[6] He deducts 150,000 livres for the raw material, the Lille thread, which was used at prices ranging from 60 to 1,600 livres per pound ; from 800 to 900 livres for good fine point ; but Lille at that time fabricated thread as high as 1,800 livres per pound.

[7] In 1705 there were ten processes :—(1) Le dessin ; (2) le picage ; (3) la trace ; (4) les fonds ; (5) la dentelure ou bride à picots ; (6) la brode ; (7) l'enlevage ; (8) l'éboulage ; (9) le régalage ; (10) l'assemblage.

Mrs. Palliser gives eighteen processes, and states that this number is now reduced to twelve. The workwomen were :—(1) The piqueuse ; (2) traceuse ; (3) réseleuse ; (4) remplisseuse ; (5) fondeuse ; (6) modeuse ; (7) brodeuse ; (8) ébouleuse ; (9) régaleuse ; (10) assembleuse ; (11) toucheuse ; (12) brideuse ; (13) boucleuse ; (14) gazeuse ; (15) mignonneuse ; (16) picoteuse ; (17) affineuse ; (18) affiquese.

PLATE LV.

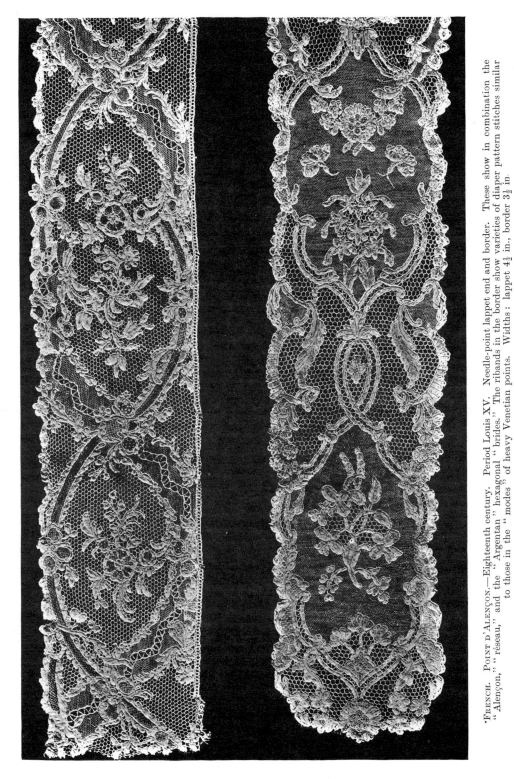

'FRENCH. POINT D'ALENÇON.—Eighteenth century. Period Louis XV. Needle-point lappet end and border. These show in combination the "Alençon," "réseau," and the "Argentan" hexagonal "brides." The ribands in the border show varieties of diaper pattern stitches similar to those in the "modes" of heavy Venetian points. Widths: lappet 4½ in., border 3½ in.

Victoria and Albert Museum.

Fig. 88.

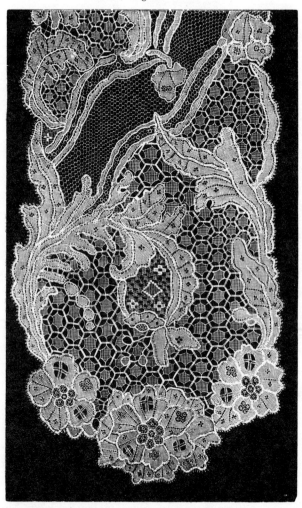

ARGENTELLA, OR POINT D'ALENÇON À RÉSEAU ROSACÉ.—Period
Louis XV.

engraved upon a copper plate, is printed off in divisions upon pieces of parchment ten inches long, each numbered according to its order. Green parchment is now used, and has been in vogue since 1769, at which date it is noted in an inventory of Simon Geslin (April 13th, 1769). The worker is better able to detect any faults in her work than on white. The pattern is next pricked upon the parchment, which is stitched to a piece of very coarse linen folded double. The outline of the pattern is then formed by two flat threads, which are guided along the edge by the thumb of the left hand, and fixed by minute stitches passed, with another thread and needle, through the holes of the parchment. When the outline is finished, the work is given over to the "réseleuse" to make the ground, which is of two kinds, bride and réseau. The delicate réseau is worked backwards and forwards from the footing to the picot—of the bride, more hereafter. Besides the hexagonal bride ground, and the ground of meshes, there was another variety of grounding used in Alençon lace. "This ground consists of buttonhole-stitched skeleton hexagons, within each of which was worked a small solid hexagon connected with the surrounding figure by means of six little tyes or brides." Lace with this particular ground has been called Argentella.[8] In making the flowers of Alençon point, the worker supplies herself with a long needle and a fine thread; with these she works the "point noué" (buttonhole stitch) from left to right, and when arrived at the end of the flower, the thread is thrown back from the point of departure, and she works again from left to right over the thread. This gives a closeness and evenness to the work unequalled in any other point. Then follow the "modes," and other different operations, which completed, the threads which unite lace,

---

[8] "The origin of this name Argentella is obscure, but it was presumed to imply that the lace was worked in Genoa or Venice. There is, however, no evidence of this type of lace being made there. Another theory is that Argentella is an Italianised title for the more delicate examples of point d'Argentan. The character of the lace and the style of the floral patterns worked upon mesh grounds are those of Alençon laces." In Specimen 1,373-74 in the Victoria and Albert Museum collection the cordonnet is done in buttonhole stitches closely cast over a thread which outlines various forms in the design—a distinctive mark of point d'Alençon. And the hexagonal wheel device in this example is often to be seen introduced into flounces of point d'Aleıçon, of which other portions are composed of the ordinary Alençon ground or réseau. —A. S. Cole. Fig. 88 and Plate LVII.

parchment and linen together, are cut with a sharp razor passed between the two folds of linen, any little defects repaired, and then remains the great work of uniting all these segments imperceptibly together. This task devolves upon the head of the fabric, and is one requiring the greatest nicety. An ordinary pair of men's ruffles would be divided into ten pieces; but when the order must be executed quickly, the subdivisions are even greater. The stitch by which these sections are worked is termed "assemblage," and differs from the "point de raccroc," where the segments are united by a fresh row of stitches. At Alençon they are joined by a seam, following as much as possible the outlines of the pattern. When finished, a steel instrument, called a picot, is passed into each flower, to polish it and remove any inequalities in its surface. The more primitive lobster-claw or a wolf's tooth was formerly used for the same purpose.

Point d'Alençon is of a solidity which defies time and washing, and has been justly called the Queen of Lace. It is the only lace in which horsehair is introduced along the edge to give firmness and consistency to the cordonnet, rendered perhaps necessary to make the point stand up when exposed to wind, mounted on the towering fabrics then worn by the ladies. The objection to horsehair is that it shrinks in washing and draws up the flower from the ground. It is related of a collar made at Venice for Louis XIII. that the lace-workers, being unsuccessful in finding sufficiently fine horsehair, employed some of their own hair instead, in order to secure that marvellous delicacy of work which they aimed at producing. The specimen, says Lefébure, cost 250 golden écus (about sixty pounds). In 1761, a writer, describing the point de France, says that it does not arrive at the taste and delicacy of Brussels, its chief defect consisting in the thickness of the cordonnet, which thickens when put into water. The horsehair edge also draws up the ground, and makes the lace rigid and heavy. He likewise finds fault with the "modes" or fancy stitches of the Alençon, and states that much point is sent from there to Brussels to have the modes added, thereby giving it a borrowed beauty; but connoisseurs, he adds, easily detect the difference.[9]

When the points of Alençon and Argentan dropped their

---

[9] *Dictionnaire du Citoyen*, Paris, 1761.

general designations of " points de France "[10] it is difficult to say. An eminent writer states the name was continued till the Revolution, but this is a mistake. The last inventory in which we have found mention of point de France is one of 1723,[11] while point d'Argentan is noted in 1738,[12] and point d'Alençon in 1741, where it is specified to be " à réseau." [13]

In the accounts of Madame du Barry, no point d'Alençon is mentioned—always point à l'aiguille—and "needle point" is the name by which point d'Alençon was alone known in England during the last century. The purchases of needle point of Madame du Barry were most extensive. Sleeves (engageantes) and lappets for 8,400 livres ; court ruffles at 1,100 ; a mantelet at 2,400 ; a veste at 6,500 ; a grande coëffe, 1,400 ; a garniture, 6,010, etc.[14]

In the description of the Department of the Orne drawn up in 1801, it is stated, " Fifteen years back there were from 7,000 to 8,000 lace-workers at Alençon and its environs : the fabric of Argentan, whose productions are finer and ·more costly, had about 2,000." Almost all these lace-makers, some of whom made réseau, others the bride ground, passed into England, Spain, Italy, Germany, and the courts of the north, especially to Russia. These united fabrics produced to the annual value of at least 1,800,000 fr., and when they had extraordinary orders, such as " parures " for beds and other large works, it increased to 2,000,000 fr. (£80,000). But this commerce, subject to the variable empire of fashion, had declined one-half even before the Revolution. Now it is almost nothing, and cannot be estimated at more than 150,000 to 200,000 fr. per annum. " It supported three

---

[10] Madame Despierres writes on this head that entries of point d'Alençon occur as early as 1663 :—

" 1663, 9 juin—contrat entre Georges Rouillon, Greffier, et Marie Leroy. . . .

" 1900 liv. gagnées par son industrie à faire des ouvrages de point d'Alençon."

[11] *Inv. de Madame Anne Palatine, Princesse de Condé.* See chap. x. note 2.

[12] In the Inventory of the Duc de Pen hièvre, 1738. See chap. xi.

[13] " Une coiffure de point d'Alençon à raiseau."—*Inv. de decès de Mademoiselle de Clermont*, 1741. Again, 1743, *Inv. de la Duchesse de Bourbon*. Bib. Nat.

[14] Among the objects of religious art exhibited in 1864 at the General Assembly of the Catholics of Belgium at Malines was a " voile de bénédiction," the handkerchief used to cover the ciborium, of point d'Alençon, with figures of the Virgin, St. Catherine, St. Ursula, and St. Barbara. It belonged to the Church of St. Christopher at Charleroi.

cities and their territory, for that of Séez [15] bore its part. Some black laces are still made at Séez, but they are of little importance.—P.S. These laces have obtained a little favour at the last Leipsic fair." [16]

The manufacture of Alençon was nearly extinct when the patronage of Napoleon caused it to return almost to its former prosperity. Among the orders executed for the Emperor on his marriage with the Empress Marie Louise, was a bed furniture of great richness. Tester, curtains, coverlet, pillow-cases. The principal subject represented the arms of the empire surrounded by bees. From its elaborate construction, point d'Alençon is seldom met with in pieces of large size; the amount of labour therefore expended on this bed must have been marvellous. Mrs. Palliser, when at Alençon, was so fortunate as to meet with a piece of the ground powdered with bees, bought from the ancient fabric of Mercier, at Lonray, when the stock many years back was sold off and dispersed (Fig. 89). The point d'Alençon bees are appliqué upon a pillow ground, " vrai réseau," executed probably at Brussels. Part of the " équipage " of the King of Rome excited the universal admiration of all beholders at the Paris Exhibition of 1855.

Alençon again fell with the empire. No new workers were trained, the old ones died off, and as it requires so many hands to execute even the most simple lace, the manufacture again nearly died out. In vain the Duchesse d'Angoulême endeavoured to revive the fabric, and gave large orders herself; but point lace had been replaced by blonde, and the consumption was so small, it was resumed on a very confined scale. So low had it fallen in 1830, that there were only between 200 and 300 lace-workers, whose products did not exceed the value of 1,200 francs (£48). Again, in 1836, Baron Mercier, thinking by producing it a lower price to procure a more favourable sale, set up a lace school, and caused the girls to work the patterns on bobbin net, as bearing some resemblance to the old " point de bride," but fashion did not favour " point de bride," so the plan failed.

In 1840 fresh attempts were made to revive the manu-

---

[15] Séez has now no records of its manufacture.

[16] *Descr. du Dép. de l'Orne.* An IX. Publiée par ordre du ministre de l'intérieur.

facture. Two hundred aged women—all the lace-makers remaining of this once flourishing fabric—were collected and again set to work. A new class of patterns was introduced, and the manufacture once more returned to favour and prosperity. But the difficulties were great. The old point was made by an hereditary set of workers, trained from their earliest infancy to the one special work they were to follow

Fig. 89.

BED MADE FOR NAPOLEON I.

for life. Now new workers had to be procured from other lace districts, already taught the ground peculiar to their fabrics. The consequence was, their fingers never could acquire the art of making the pure Alençon réseau. They made a good ground, certainly, but it was mixed with their own early traditions: as the Alençon workers say, " Elles bâtardisent les fonds."

In the Exhibition of 1851 were many fine specimens of

the revived manufacture. One flounce, which was valued at 22,000 francs, and had taken thirty-six women eighteen months to complete, afterwards appeared in the " corbeille de mariage " of the Empress Eugénie.

In 1856 most magnificent orders were given for the imperial layette, a description of which is duly chronicled.[17] The young Prince was " voué au blanc " ; white, therefore, was the prevailing colour in the layette. The curtains of the Imperial infant's cradle were of Mechlin, with Alençon coverlet lined with satin. The christening robe, mantle, and head-dress were all of Alençon ; and the three *corbeilles*, bearing the imperial arms and cipher, were also covered with the same point. Twelve dozen embroidered frocks, each in itself a work of art, were all profusely trimmed with Alençon, as were also the aprons of the Imperial nurses.

A costly work of Alençon point appeared in the Exhibition of 1855—a dress, purchased by the Emperor for 70,000 francs (£2,800), and presented by him to the Empress.

A few observations remain to be made respecting the dates of the patterns of Alençon point, which, like those of other laces, will be found to correspond with the architectural style of decoration of the period. The " corbeilles de mariage " preserved in old families and contemporary portraits are our surest guides.

In the eighteenth century the réseau ground was introduced, and soon became universally adopted. After carefully examining the engravings of the time, the collection of historical portraits at Versailles and other galleries, we find no traces of Point d'Alençon with the réseau or network ground in the time of Louis XIV. The laces are all of the Venetian character, à bride, and Colbert himself is depicted in a cravat of Italian design ; while, on the other hand, the daughters of Louis XV. (Mesdames de France) and the " Filles du Régent " all wear rich points of Alençon and Argentan.[18] The earlier patterns of the eighteenth century are flowery and undulating [19] (Fig. 91), scarcely

---

[17] *Illustrated News*, March 22, 1856.
[18] It only requires to compare Figs. 74, 75, 76, and 80, with Figs. 82 and 83 to see the marked difference in the character of the lace.

[19] " Sous Louis XIV. il y avaient de magnifiques rinceaux, guirlandes, et cornes d'abondance d'où s'échappent de superbes fleurs. Sous Louis XV. les fabricants changèrent encore

begun, never ending, into which haphazard are introduced patterns of a finer ground, much as the medallions
of Boucher or Vanloo were inserted in the gilded panellings
of a room. Twined around them appear a variety of *jours*,
filled up with patterns of endless variety, the whole wreathed
and garlanded like the decoration of a theatre. Such was
the taste of the day. "Après moi le déluge"; and the
precept of the favourite was carried out in the style of
design : an *insouciance* and *laisser-aller* typical of a people
regardless of the morrow.

Towards the latter end of the reign a change came over
the national taste. It appears in the architecture and
domestic decoration. As the cabriole legs of the chairs are
replaced by the " pieds de daim," so the running patterns of
the lace give place to compact and more stiff designs. The
flowers are rigid and angular, of the style called *bizarre*, of
almost conventional form. With Louis XVI. began the
ground *semé* with compact little bouquets, all intermixed
with small patterns, spots (*pois*), fleurons, rosettes, and
tears (*larmes*) (Fig. 90), which towards the end of the
century entirely expel the bouquets from the ground. The
semés continued during the Empire.

This point came into the highest favour again during
the Second Empire. Costly orders for trousseaux were given
not only in France, but from Russia and other countries. One
amounted to 150,000 francs (£6,000)—flounce, lappets and
trimmings for the body, pocket-handkerchief, fan, parasol, all
en suite, and, moreover, there were a certain number of metres
of *aunage*, or border lace, for the layette. The making of
point d'Alençon being so slow, it was impossible ever to
execute it " to order " for this purpose.

Great as is the beauty of the workmanship of Alençon,
it was never able to compete with Brussels in one respect :
its designs were seldom copied from nature, while the fabric
of Brabant sent forth roses and honeysuckles of a correctness
worthy of a Dutch painter.

---

leurs dessins pour prendre les fleurs
qui s'épanouent et s'ensoulent capri-
cieusement les unes aux autres.

" Le style de Louis XVI. n'a rien de
l'ampleur ni de l'élégance des styles
précédents. Les formes sont arrondies ;

des guirlandes et des fleurettes sont
la base des dessins de cette époque.

" Sous la république et le premier
empire, les dessins deviennent raides "
(Madame Despierres.)

This defect is now altered.   The designs of the lace are
admirable copies of natural flowers, intermixed with grasses
and ferns, which give a variety to the form of the leaves.

Alençon point is now successfully made at Burano near
Venice, in Brussels, at Alençon itself, and at Bayeux, where

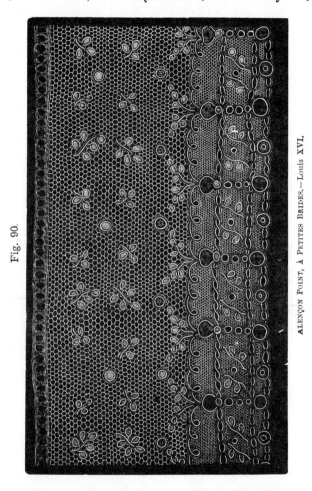

Fig. 90.

ALENÇON POINT, À PETITES BRIDES.—Louis XVI.

the fabric was introduced, in 1855, by M. Auguste Lefébure,
a manufacturer of that town.   Departing from the old
custom of assigning to each lace-maker a special branch
of the work, the lace is here executed through all its stages
by the same worker.   Perhaps the finest example of point
d'Alençon exhibited in 1867 was the produce of the

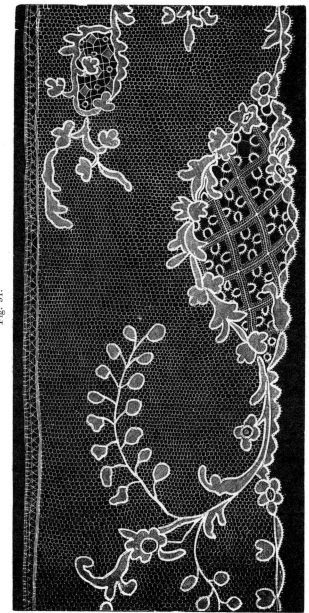

Fig. 91.

Point d'Alençon.—Louis XV. period.

POINT D'ARGENTAN.—Modern reproduction at Burano of the flounce now belonging to the Crow
wrong, as the design and execution is of fifty years later da

Photo

PLATE LVI.

f Italy, said formerly to have belonged to Paul de Gondy, Cardinal de Retz 1614-79. This is evidently
ut it is a fine specimen of an ecclesiastical flounce. Height, 24 in.
Burano School.

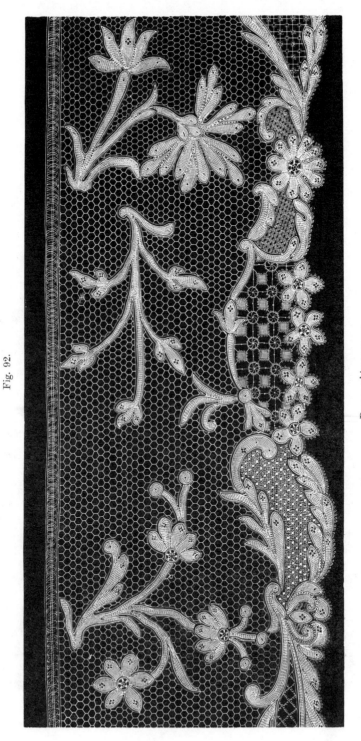

Fig. 92.

Point d'Argentan.

Bayeux fabric; a dress consisting of two flounces, the pattern, flowers, and foliage of most artistic and harmonious design, relieved by the new introduction of shaded tints, giving to the lace the relief of a picture.[20] The ground (point à l'aiguille) was worked with the greatest smoothness and regularity, one of the great technical difficulties when such small pieces have to be joined together. The price of the dress was 85,000 francs (£3,400). It took forty women seven years to complete.

In the Exhibition of 1889 in Paris, Alençon itself showed the best piece of lace that had taken 16,500 working days to make.

---

[20] This effect is produced by varying the application of the two stitches used in making the flowers, the *toilé*, which forms the close tissue, and the *grillé*, the more open part of the pattern. The system has been adopted in France, Belgium, and England, but with most success in France.

CHAPTER XIV.

ARGENTAN (Dép. Orne).

"Vous qui voulez d'Argentan faire conte,
    A sa grandeur arrêter ne faut ;
    Petite elle est, mais en beauté surmonte
    Maintes cités, car rien ne lui defaut ;
    Elle est assise en lieu plaisant et haut,
    De tout côtè à prairie, à campaigne,
    Un fleuve aussi, où maint poisson se baigne,
    Des bois épais, suffisans pour nourrir
    Biches et cerfs qui sont prompts à courir ;
    Plus y trouvez, tant elle est bien garnie,
    Plus au besoin nature secourir
    Bon air, bon vin, et bonne compagnie ! "
                        —*Des Maisons.* 1517.

THE name of the little town of Argentan, whose points long rivalled those of Alençon, is familiar to English ears as connected with our Norman kings. Argentan is mentioned by old Robert Wace as sending its sons to the conquest of England.[1] It was here the mother of Henry II. retired in 1130 ; and the imperial eagle borne as the arms of the town is said to be a memorial of her long sojourn. Here the first Plantagenet held the " cour plénière," in which the invasion of Ireland was arranged ; and it was here he uttered those rash words which prompted his adherents to leave Argentan to assassinate Thomas à Becket.[2]

But, apart from historic recollections, Argentan is celebrated for its point lace. A " bureau " for points de France was established at Argentan at the same time as the bureau at Alençon (1665), and was also under the direction of Madame Raffy. In a letter dated November 23rd, 1665, she writes to Colbert : " Je suis très satisfaite de la publication à son de trompe d'un arrêt qui ordonne aux ouvrières

---

[1] " Li boen citean de Roem,
        E la Jovante de Caem,
        E de Falaise e d'Argentoen."
                —*Roman de Rou.*

[2] Henry founded a chapel at Argentan to St. Thomas of Canterbury.

d'Argentan de travailler uniquement pour la bureau de la manufacture royale."

Point d'Argentan has been thought to be especially distinguished by its hexagonally-arranged brides; but this has also been noticed as a peculiarity of certain Venetian point laces. The bride ground, to which we have before alluded in the notice of Alençon, was of very elaborate construction, and consists of a large six-sided mesh, worked over with the buttonhole stitch. It was always printed on the parchment pattern, and the upper angle of the hexagon is pricked. After the hexagon is formed, by passing the needle and thread round the pins in a way too complicated to be worth explaining, the six sides are worked over with seven or eight buttonhole stitches in each side. The bride ground was consequently very strong. It was much affected in France; the réseau was more preferred abroad.[3] At the present time, it is usual to consider the point d'Alençon as a lace with a fine réseau, the mesh of which is more square than hexagonal in form, worked by looped stitches across horizontal lines of thread, with the flower or ornament worked in fine point stitches, closely resembling the gimp or ornament in the point de Venise à réseau, and outlined by a cordonnet of the finest buttonhole stitches worked over a horsehair or threads, while point d'Argentan is a lace with similar work as regards flower, ornament, and cordonnet, but with a hexagonal bride ground, each side of the hexagon being of the finest buttonhole stitchings. Regarding the date of the introduction of the réseau, the large hexagonal " grande bride" would appear to follow from the points de Venise, Argentan being named before Alençon à réseau. Madame Despierres, however, is of opinion that Argentan simplified the usual réseau by adopting the bride tortillé (*i.e.*, twisting the threads round each mesh instead of the more arduous buttonhole stitching). Alençon would then

---

[3] "The average size of a diagonal, taken from angle to angle, in an Alençon or so-called Argentan hexagon was about $\frac{1}{6}$ of an inch, and each side of the hexagon was about $\frac{1}{10}$ of an inch. An idea of the minuteness of the work can be formed from the fact that a side of a hexagon would be overcast with some nine or ten buttonhole stitches" (A. S. Cole). " So little is the beautiful workmanship of this ground known or understood, that the author has seen priceless flowers of Argentan relentlessly cut out and transferred to bobbin net, 'to get rid of the ugly, old, coarse ground'" (Mrs. Palliser, 1869).

have copied back the petites brides of small hexagonal twisted or buttonholed meshes in Louis XVI.'s reign. To this again succeeded the looped réseau of very thick thread.

With the view of showing that Alençon and Argentan were intimately connected the one with the other in the manufacture of lace, M. Dupont says that, whereas considerable mention has been made in various records of the establishment at Alençon of a lace factory, trace of such records with regard to Alençon cannot be found. A family of thread and linen dealers, by name Monthulay, are credited with the establishment of a branch manufactory or *succursale* for lace at Argentan.

The Monthulays, then, sowed Alençon seeds at Argentan, which developed into the so-called Argentan lace. In almost all respects it is the same as Alençon work.[4] The two towns, separated by some ten miles, had communications as frequent as those which passed between Alençon and the little village of Vimoutier, eighteen miles distant, where one workman in particular produced what is known as the true Alençon lace. If a work were made at Argentan, it was called Argentan, if at Alençon, Alençon, though both might have been produced from the same designs.

In 1708, the manufacture had almost fallen to decay, when it was raised by one Sieur Mathieu Guyard, a merchant mercer at Paris, who states that " his ancestors and himself had for more than 120 years been occupied in fabricating black silk and white thread lace in the environs of Paris." He applies to the council of the king for permission to re-establish the fabric of Argentan and to employ workwomen to the number of 600. He asks for exemption from lodging

---

[4] " Les trois sortes de brides comme champ sont exécutées dans ces deux fabriques, et les points ont été et sont encore faits par les mêmes procédés de fabrication, et avec les mêmes matières textiles," writes Madame Despierres. Mrs. Palliser, on the other hand, was of opinion that the two manufactures were distinct, "though some lace-makers near Lignères-la-Doucelle worked for both establishments. Alençon made the finest réseau; Argentan specially excelled in the bride. The flowers of Argentan were bolder and larger in pattern, in higher relief, heavier and coarser than those of Alençon. The toilé was flatter and more compact. The workmanship differed in character. On the clear bride ground this lace was more effective than the minuter workmanship of Alençon; it more resembled the Venetian. Indeed, so close is its resemblance that many of the fine garnitures de robe, aprons, and tunics that have survived the revolutionary storm would be assigned to Venice, did not their pedigree prove them to be of the Argentan fabric " (Mrs. Palliser, 1869).

soldiers, begs to have the royal arms placed over his door, and stipulates that Monthulay, his draughtsman and engraver, shall be exempted from all taxes except the capitation. The Arrêt obtained by Guyard is dated July 24th, 1708.

Guyard's children continued the fabric. Monthulay went over to another manufacturer, and was replaced in 1715 by Jacques James, who, in his turn, was succeeded by his daughter, and she took as her partner one Sieur De La Leu. Other manufactures set up in competition with Guyard's; among others that of Madame Wyriot, whose factor, Du Ponchel, was in open warfare with the rival house.

The marriage of the Dauphin, in 1744, was a signal for open hostilities. Du Ponchel asserted that Mademoiselle James enticed away his workmen, and claimed protection, on the ground that he worked for the king and the court. But on the other side, " It is I," writes De La Leu to the intendant, on behalf of Mademoiselle James, " that supply the ' Chambre du Roi ' for this year, by order of the Duke de Richelieu. I too have the honour of furnishing the ' Garderobe du Roi,' by order of the grand master, the Duke de La Rochefoucault. Besides which, I furnish the King and Queen of Spain, and at this present moment am supplying lace for the marriage of the Dauphin." [5] Du Ponchel rejoins, " that he had to execute two ' toilettes et leurs suites, nombre de bourgognes [6] et leurs suites ' for the Queen, and also a cravat, all to be worn on the same occasion." Du Ponchel appears to have had the better interest with the controller-general ; for the quarrel ended in a prohibition to the other manufacturers to molest the women working for Du Ponchel, though the Maison Guyard asked for reciprocity, and maintained that their opponents had suborned and carried off more than a hundred of their hands.[7]

The number of lace-makers in the town of Argentan and its environs at this period amounted to nearly 1,200. In a list of 111 who worked for the Maison Guyard appear the

---

[5] Letter of September 19th, 1744.

[6] " Burgoigne, the first part of the dress for the head next the hair."— *Mundus Muliebris.* 1609. " Burgoigin, the part of the head-dress that covers up the head."—*Ladies' Dictionary.* 1694. In Farquhar's comedy of " Sir Harry Wildair," 1700, Parley, when asked what he had been about, answers, " Sir, I was coming to Mademoiselle Furbelow, the French milliner, for a new Burgundy for my lady's head."

[7] The offenders, manufacturers and workwomen, incurred considerable fines.

names of many of the good bourgeois families of the county of Alençon, and even some of noble birth, leading one to infer that making point lace was an occupation not disdained by ladies of poor but noble houses.

De La Leu, who, by virtue of an ordinance, had set up a manufacture on his own account, applies, in 1745, to have 200 workwomen at Argentan, and 200 at Carrouges, delivered over to his factor, in order that he may execute works ordered for the King and the Dauphin for the approaching fêtes of Christmas. This time the magistrate resists. " I have been forced to admit," he writes to the intendant, " that the workmen cannot be transferred by force. We had an example when the layette of the Dauphin was being made. You then gave me the order to furnish a certain number of women who worked at these points to the late Sieur de Monthulay. A detachment of women and girls came to my house, with a female captain (capitaine femelle) at their head, and all with one accord delared that if forced to work they would make nothing but cobbling (bousillage). Partly by threats, and partly by entreaty, I succeeded in compelling about a dozen to go, but the Sieur de Monthulay was obliged to discharge them the next day.[8] I am therefore of opinion that the only way is for M. De La Leu to endeavour to get some of the workwomen to suborn others to work for him under the promise of higher wages than they can earn elsewhere. M. De La Leu agrees with me there is no other course to pursue ; and I have promised him that, in case any appeal is made to me, I shall answer that things must be so, as the work is doing for the king." From this period we have scarcely any notices concerning the fabric of Argentan.

In 1763 the widow Louvain endeavoured to establish at Mortagne (Orne) a manufacture of lace like that of Alençon and Argentan, and proposed to send workers from these two towns to teach the art gratuitously to the girls of Mortagne. We do not know what became of her project ; but at the same period the Epoux Malbiche de Boislaunay applied for permission to establish an office at Argentan, with the ordinary exemptions, under the title of Royal Manufacture. The title and exemptions were refused. There were then

---

[8] Nov. 12th, 1745.

Fig. 93.

POINT D'ARGENTAN.—Grande bride ground.   Eighteenth century.

PLATE LVII.

FRENCH. POINT D'ARGENTAN.— Eighteenth century. Period Louis XV. Needle-point borders. Both these have the hexagonal ground of the genre "Argentan." The upper one is chiefly filled in with the "oeil de perdrix" or "réseau rosacé." Width, $3\frac{3}{8}$ in. The lower one has been pieced together. Width, 7 in.

Victoria and Albert Museum.

(1763) at Argentan three manufactures of point de France, without counting the general hospital of St. Louis, in which it was made for the profit of the institution, and evidently with success; for in 1764, a widow Roger was in treaty with the hospital to teach her two daughters the fabrication of point d'Argentan. They were to be boarded, and give six years of their time. The fine on non-performance was 80 livres. In 1781, the Sieur Gravelle Desvallées made a fruitless application to establish a manufacture at Argentan; nor could even the children of the widow Wyriot obtain a renewal of the privilege granted to their mother.[9] Gravelle was ruined by the Revolution, and died in 1830.

Arthur Young, in 1788, estimates the annual value of Argentan point at 500,000 livres.

Taking these data, we may fix the reigns of Louis XV. and Louis XVI. as the period when point d'Argentan was at its highest prosperity. It appears in the inventories of the personages of that time; most largely in the accounts of Madame du Barry (from 1769 to 1773), who patronized Argentan equally with point d'Angleterre and point à l'aiguille. In 1772, she pays 5,740 francs for a complete garniture. Lappets, flounces, engageantes, collerettes, aunages, fichus, are all supplied to her of this costly fabric.[10]

One spécialité in the Argentan point is the "bride picotée," a remnant, perhaps, of the early Venetian teaching. It consists of the six-sided button-hole bride, fringed with a little row of three or four picots or pearls round each side. It was also called "bride épinglée," because pins were pricked in the parchment pattern, to form these picots or boucles (loops) on; hence it was sometimes styled "bride bouclée."[11]

---

[9] In 1765, under the name of Duponchel.

[10] 1772. Un ajustement de point d'Argentan—
Les 6 rangs manchettes.
1/3 pour devant de gorge.
4 au. 1/3 festonné des deux costés, le fichu et une garniture de fichu de nuit . . . . . . 2,500 livres.
1 au 3/4 ruban de point d'Argentan, à 100 . . 175 —
Une collerette de point d'Argentan . . . . 360 —
—(*Comptes de Madame du Barry.*)

1781. "Une nappe d'autel garnie d'une tres belle dentelle de point d'Argentan."—*Inv. de l'Eglise de St. Gervais.* Arch. Nat. L. 654.

1789. "Item, un parement de robe consistant en garniture, deux paires de manchettes, et fichu, le tout de point d'Argentan." (Dans la garderobe de Madame.)—*Inv. de decès de Mgr. de Duc de Duras.* Bib. Nat. MSS. F. Fr. 11,440.

[11] "Une coiffure bride à picot complete."—*Inv. de decès de Mademoiselle de Clermont,* 1741.

The "écaille de poisson" réseau was also much used at Alençon and Argentan.

The manner of making "bride picotée" is entirely lost. Attempts were made to recover the art some years since (1869), and an old workwoman was found who had made it in her girlhood, but she proved incapable of bringing the stitch back to her memory, and the project was given up.[12]

Point d'Argentan disappeared, and was re-established in 1708; but though a few specimens were produced at the Exhibition of Industry in 1808, the industry died out in 1810.[13] It was again revived with some success by M. M. Lefébure in 1874. In January 1874, with the assistance of the mayor, he made a search in the greniers of the Hôtel Dieu, and discovered three specimens of point d'Argentan in progress on the parchment patterns. One was of bold pattern with the "grande bride" ground, evidently a man's ruffle; the other had the barette or bride ground of point de France; the third picotée, showing that the three descriptions of lace were made contemporaneously at Argentan.

The author of a little pamphlet on Argentan, M. Eugène[14] de Lonlay, remembers having seen in his youth in the Holy week, in the churches of St. Martin and St. Germain, the statues of the apostles covered from head to foot with this priceless point.

Argentan is now much made at Burano. Plate LVI. illustrates one of their fine reproductions.

---

[12] These details on the manufacture of Argentan have been furnished from the archives of Alençon through the kindness of M. Léon de la Sicotière, the learned archæologist of the Department of the Orne (Mrs. Palliser, 1869).

[13] Embroidery has replaced this industry among the workers of the town and the hand-spinning of hemp among those of the country.

[14] *Légende du point d'Argentan.* M. Eugène de Lonlay.

CHAPTER XV.

ISLE DE FRANCE.—PARIS (Dép. Seine).

"Quelle heure est-il ?
Passé midi.
Qui vous l'a dit ?
Une petite souris.
Que fait-elle ?
De la dentelle.
Pour qui ?
La reine de Paris."—*Old Nursery Song.*

EARLY in the seventeenth century, lace was extensively made in the environs of Paris, at Louvres, Gisors, Villiers-le-Bel, Montmorency, and other localities. Of this we have confirmation in a work[1] published 1634, in which, after commenting upon the sums of money spent in Flanders for " ouvrages et passemens,[2] tant de point couppé que d'autres," which the king had put a stop to by the sumptuary law of 1633, the author says :—" Pour empescher icelle despence, il y a toute l'Isle de France et autres lieux qui sont remplis de plus de dix mille familles dans lesquels les enfans de l'un et l'autre sexe, dès l'âge de dix ans ne sont instruits qu'à la manufacture desdits ouvrages, dont il s'en trouve d'aussi beaux et bien faits que ceux des étrangers ; les Espagnols, qui le sçavent, ne s'en fournissent ailleurs."

Who first founded the lace-making of the Isle de France it is difficult to say ; a great part of it was in the hands of the Huguenots, leading us to suppose it formed one of the numerous " industries " introduced or encouraged by

---

[1] *Nouveau Réglement Général sur toutes sortes de Marchadises et Manufactures qui sont utiles et necessaires dans ce Royaume*, etc., par M. le Marquis de la Gomberdière. Paris, 1634. In 8vo.

[2] M. Fournier says that France was at this time tributary to Flanders for " passemens de fil," very fine and delicately worked. Laffemas, in his *Réglement Général pour dresser les Manufactures du Royaume*, 1597, estimates the annual cost of these " passemens " of every sort, silk stockings, etc., at 800,000 crowns. Montchrestien, at above a million.

Henry IV. and Sully Point de Paris, mignonette, bisette, and other narrow cheap laces were made, and common guipures were also fabricated at St. Denis, Écouen, and Groslay.   From 1665 to the French Revolution, the exigencies of fashion requiring a superior class of lace, the workwomen arrived gradually at making point of remarkable fineness and superior execution.   The lappet (Fig. 94) is a good example of the delicacy of the fine point de Paris.

Fig. 94.

Point de Paris.—Reduced.

The ground resembles the fond chant, the six-pointed star meshed réseau.

Savary, who wrote in 1726, mentions how, in the Château de Madrid, there had long existed a manufacture of points de France.[3]   A second fabric was established by the Comte de Marsan,[4] in Paris, towards the end of the same century.   Having brought over from Brussels his nurse,

---

[3] This was established by Colbert, and there they made, as well as at Aurillac, the finest pillow lace in the style of point d'Angleterre.   This manufacture was encouraged by the King and the Court, and its productions were among the choicest of the points de France.

[4] Youngest son of the Comte d'Harcourt.

Fig 95.

POINT DE FRANCE.—Bobbin lace.   Seventeenth century.   With portraits of Louis XIV. and Marie Thérèse.

Mrs. Palliser gives this illustration the above designation in her last edition; in her former ones, that of Flemish lace. The lace has lately come into the possession of Mr. Arthur Blackborne. It appears to be Flemish work made for the French Queen.

PLATE LVIII.

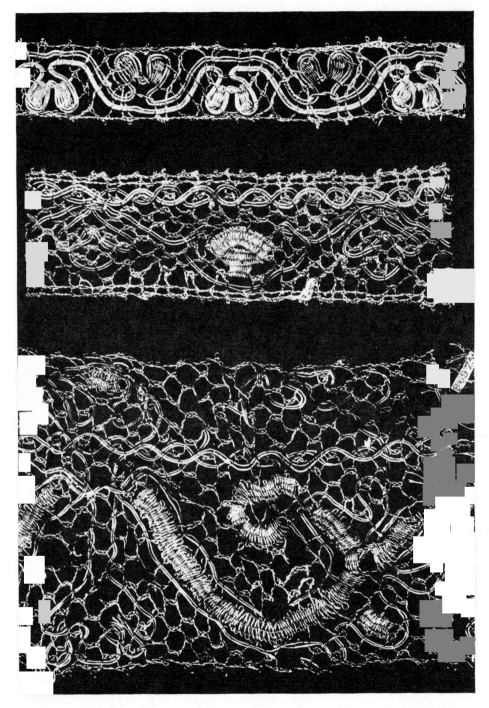

FRENCH (OR DUTCH).—Borders of gold and silver thread and gimp lace. Eighteenth century. From the Treasury of St. Mary's Church, Dantzig. Widths: $1\frac{1}{8}$, $1\frac{3}{4}$ and $4\frac{1}{4}$ in.

Victoria and Albert Museum.

named Dumont, with her four daughters, she asked him, as a reward for the care she had bestowed upon him in his infancy, to obtain for her the privilege of setting up in Paris a manufactory of point de France. Colbert granted the request : Dumont was established in the Faubourg St. Antoine—classic land of embroidery from early times— cited in the " Révolte des Passemens," " Telle Broderie qui n'avoit jamais esté plus loin que du Faubourg S. Antoine au Louvre." A " cent Suisse " of the king's was appointed as guard before the door of her house. In a short time Dumont had collected more than 200 girls, among whom were several of good birth, and made beautiful lace called point de France. Her fabric was next transferred to Rue Saint Sauveur, and subsequently to the Hôtel Saint-Chaumont, near the Porte St. Denis. Dumont afterwards went to Portugal, leaving her fabric under the direction of Mademoiselle de Marsan. But, adds the historian, as fashion and taste often change in France, people became tired of this point. It proved difficult to wash ; the flowers had to be raised each time it was cleaned ; it was thick and unbecoming to the face. Points d'Espagne were now made instead, with small flowers, which, being very fine, was more suitable for a lady's dress. Lastly, the taste for Mechlin lace coming in, the manufacture of Dumont was entirely given up.[5]

In the time of Louis XIV. the commerce of lace was distributed in different localities of Paris, as we learn from the " Livre Commode "[6] already quoted. The gold laces, forming of themselves a special commerce, had their shops in the " rue des Bourdonnais (in which silk laces were especially sold) and the rue Sainte-Honoré, entre la place aux Chats et les piliers des Halles," while the rue Bétizy retained for itself the spécialité of selling " points et dentelles."

The gold and silver laces of Paris, commonly known as points d'Espagne,[7] often embellished with pearls and other

---

[5] Vie de J.-Bap. Colbert. (Printed in the *Archives Curieuses*.)

[6] " Livre commode ou les Adienes de la Ville de Paris " for 1692.

[7] For the introduction of the gold point of Spain into France, see SPAIN.

The manufacture of gold lace in Paris was, however, prior to Colbert.

" 1732, un bord de point d'Espagne d'or de Paris, à fonds de réseau."— *Garderobe de S. A. S. Mgr. le Duc de Penthièvre*. Arch. Nat. K. K. 390-1.

ornaments, were for years renowned throughout all Europe ; and, until the revocation of the Edict of Nantes, an object of great commerce to France. Its importance is shown by the sumptuary edicts of the seventeenth century forbidding its use, and also by its mention in the *Révolte des Passemens.* It was made on the pillow. Much was exported to Spain and the Indies. How those exiled workmen were received by the Protestant princes of Europe, and allowed to establish themselves in their dominions, to the loss of France and the enrichment of the lands of their adoption, will be told in due time, when we touch on the lace manufactures of Holland and Germany. (Plate LVIII.)

Since 1784, little lace has been made in Paris itself, but a large number of lace-makers are employed in applying the flowers of Binche and Mirecourt upon the bobbin-net grounds.

CHANTILLY (Dép. Oise).

" Dans sa pompe élégante admirez Chantilli,
De héros en héros, d'âge en âge embelli."
—Delille. *Les Jardins.*

Although there long existed lace-makers in the environs of Paris, the establishment for which Chantilly was celebrated owes its formation to Catherine de Rohan, Duchesse de Longueville, who sent for workwomen from Dieppe and Havre to her château of Étrepagny, where she retired at the beginning of the seventeenth century, and established schools.

The town of Chantilly, being the centre of a district of lace-makers, has given its name to the laces of the surrounding district, the trade being distributed over more than a hundred villages, the principal of which are Saint-Maximien, Viarmes, Méric, Luzarches, and Dammartin. The proximity to Paris, affording a ready sale for its productions, caused the manufacture to prosper, and the narrow laces which they first made—gueuse and point de Paris— were soon replaced by guipures, white thread, and black silk lace.[8] Some twenty years since there dwelt at Chantilly

---

[8] In *Statistique de la France*, 1800, the finest silk lace is said to be made   at Fontenay, Puisieux, Morges, and Louvres-en-Parisis. The coarse and

an elderly lady, grand-daughter of an old proprietor, who had in her possession one of the original pattern-books of the fabric, with autograph letters of Marie Antoinette, the Princess de Lamballe, and other ladies of the court, giving their orders and expressing their opinion on the laces produced. We find in the inventories cf the last century, " coëffure de cour de dentelle de soye noire," " mantelet garni de dentelles noires," a " petite duchesse et une respectueuse," and other " coëffes," all of " dentelle de soye noire." [9]

White blonde appears more sparingly. The Duchesse de Duras has " une paire de manchettes à trois rangs, deux fichus et deux paires de sabots en blonde." [10] The latter to wear, probably, with her " robe en singe." Du Barry purchases more largely. [11] See pages 181, 182, and 224.

Fig. 96 is a specimen taken from the above-mentioned pattern-book ; the flowers and ground are of the same silk, the flowers worked en grillé (see Chap. III., grillé), or open stitch, instead of the compact tissue of the " blondes mates," of the Spanish style. The cordonnet is a thicker silk strand, flat and untwisted. This is essentially " Chantilly lace." The fillings introduced into the flowers and other ornaments in Chantilly lace are mesh grounds of old date, which, according to the district where they were made, are called vitré, mariage, and cinq trous. Chantilly first created the black silk lace industry, and deservedly it retains her name, whether made there or in Calvados. Chantilly black lace has always been made of silk, but from its being a grenadine, not a shining silk, a common error prevails that it is of thread, whereas black thread lace has never been made

---

common kinds at Montmorency, Villiers-le-Bel, Sarcelles, Écouen, Saint-Brice, Groslay,, Gisors, Saint-Pierre-les-Champs, Étrepagny, etc. Peuchet adds : " Il s'y fait dans Paris et ses environs une grande quantité de dentelles noires dont il se fait des expéditions considérables." It was this same black silk lace which raised to so high a reputation the fabrics of Chantilly.

[9] *Inv. de decés de la Duchesse de Modène.* 1761.

[10] *Inv. de decés du Duc de Duras.* 1789.

[11] " Une fraise à deux rangs de blonde tres fine, grande hauteur, 120 l.

" Une paire de sabots de la même blonde, 84 l.

" Un fichu en colonette la fraise garnie à deux rangs d'une tres belle blonde fond d'Alençon, 120 l.

" Un pouff bordé d'un plissé de blonde tournante fond d'Alençon, à bouquets tres fins et des bouillons de même blonde." This wonderful coiffure being finished with " Un beau panache de quatre plumes couleur impériales, 108 l."

either at Chantilly or Bayeux. The distinguishing feature of this lace is the *fond chant* (an abbreviation of Chantilly), the six-pointed star réseau, or, as it is better described, a diamond crossed by two horizontal threads.

Chantilly fell with '93. Being considered a Royal fabric, and its productions made for the nobility alone, its unfortunate lace-workers became the victims of revolutionary fury, and all perished, with their patrons, on the scaffold. We hear no more of the manufacture until the Empire, a period during which Chantilly enjoyed its greatest prosperity. In 1805, white blonde became the rage in Paris, and the work-women were chiefly employed in its fabrication. The Chantilly laces were then in high repute, and much exported,

Fig. 96.

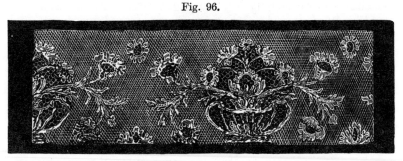

CHANTILLY.—Reduced.—From one of the Order Books, temp. Louis XVI.

the black, especially, to Spain and her American colonies; no other manufactories could produce mantillas, scarfs, and other large pieces of such great beauty. It was then they made those rich large-patterned blondes called by the French " blondes mates," by the Spaniards " trapeada," the prevailing style since the First Empire.

About 1835 black lace again came into vogue, and the lace-makers were at once set to work at making black silk laces with double ground, and afterwards they revived the nexagonal ground of the last century, called fond d'Alençon,[12] for the production of which they are celebrated.

The lace industry has been driven away from Chantilly by the increase in the price of labour consequent on its vicinity to the capital. The lace manufacturers, unable to

---

[12] See preceding note.

pay such high salaries, retired to Gisors, where in 1851 there were from 8,000 to 9,000 lace-makers. They continued to make the finest lace some years longer at Chantilly ; but now she has been supplanted by the laces of Calvados, Caen, and Bayeux, which are similar in material and in mode of fabrication. The generally so-called Chantilly shawls are the production of Bayeux.

CHAPTER XVI.

NORMANDY.

"Dangling thy hands like bobbins before thee."
—Congreve, *Way of the World.*

SEINE INFÉRIEURE.

LACE forms an essential part of the costume of the Normandy peasants. The wondrous " Bourgoin," [1] with its long lappets of rich lace, descended from generation to generation, but little varied from the cornettes of the fourteenth and fifteenth centuries (Fig. 97). The countrywomen wore their lace at all times, when it was not replaced by the cotton nightcap, without much regard to the general effect of their daily clothes. " Madame the hostess," writes a traveller in 1739, " made her appearance in long lappets of bone lace, with a sack of linsey wolsey."

The manufactures of the Pays de Caux date from the beginning of the sixteenth century. It appears to have been the first centre in Normandy, as in 1661 Havre laces occur in the *Révolte des Passemens.* Lace-making was the principal occupation of the wives and daughters of the mariners and fishermen. In 1692, M. de Sainte-Aignan, governor of Havre, found it employed 20,000 women.[2]

---

[1] " The bourgoin is formed of white, stiffly-starched muslin, covering a paste-board shape, and rises to a great height above the head, frequently diminishing in size towards the top, where it finishes in a circular form. Two long lappets hang from either side towards the back, composed often of the finest lace. The bourgoins throughout Normandy are not alike."
—*Mrs. Stothard's Tour in Normandy.*

[2] This must have included Honfleur and other surrounding localities.

By a paper on the lace trade (*Mém.* *concernant le Commerce des Dentelles,* 1704. Bib. Nat. MSS. F. Fr. 14,294), we find that the making of " dentelles de bas prix," employed at Rouen, Dieppe, Le Havre, and throughout the Pays de Caux, the Bailliage of Caen, at Lyons, Le Puy, and other parts of France, one quarter of the population of all classes and ages from six to seventy years. These laces were all made of Haarlem thread. See HOL-LAND.

" The lace-makers of Havre," writes Peuchet, " work both in black and

It was in the province of Normandy, as comprised in its ancient extent, that the lace trade made the most rapid

Fig. 97.

CAUCHOISE.—From an engraving of the eighteenth century.

increase in the eighteenth century. From Arras to St.

white points, from 5 sous to 30 francs the ell. They are all employed by a certain number of dealers, who purchase the produce of their pillows.

Much is transported to foreign countries, even to the East Indies, the Southern Seas, and the islands of America."

Malo more than thirty centres of manufacture established themselves, imitating with success the laces of Mechlin ; the guipures of Flanders ; the fond clair, or single ground, then called point de Bruxelles ; point de Paris ; black thread laces, and also those guipures enriched with gold and silver, so much esteemed for church ornament. The manufactures of Havre, Honfleur, Bolbec, Eu, Fécamp, and Dieppe were most thriving. They made double and single grounds, guipure, and a kind of thick Valenciennes, such as is still made in the little town of Honfleur and its environs. In 1692 the number of lace-makers at Havre and its environs was not less than 22,000. Corneille,[3] 1707, declares the laces of Havre to be " très recherchées " ; and in an engraving, 1688, representing a " marchande lingère en sa boutique,"[4] among the stock in trade, together with the points of Spain and England, are certain " cartons " labelled " Point du Havre." It appears also in the inventory of Colbert, who considered it worthy of trimming his pillow-cases and his camisoles ;[5] and Madame de Simiane[6] had two " toilettes garnies de dentelle du Hâvre," with an " estuy à peigne," en suite.

Next in rank to the points du Havre came the laces of Dieppe and its environs, which, says an early writer of the eighteenth century, rivalled the " industrie " of Argentan and Caen. The city of Dieppe alone, with its little colony of Saint-Nicolas-d'Aliermont (a village two leagues distant, inhabited by the descendants of a body of workmen who retired from the bombardment of Dieppe),[7] employed 4,000 lace-makers. A writer in 1761[8] says, " A constant trade is that of laces, which yield only in precision of design and fineness to those of Mechlin ; but it has never been so consider-

---

[3] *Dictionnaire Géographique.* T. Corneille. 1707.

[4] *Gravures de Modes.* Arch. Nat. M., 815–23.

[5] " 1683. Deux housses de toille piquée avec dentelle du Havre deux camisolles de pareille toille et de dentelle du Havre."—*Inv. fait après le decedz de Monseigneur Colbert.* Bib. Nat. MSS. Suite de Mortemart, 34.

[6] " 1651. Un tour d'autel de dentelle du Havre."—*Inv. des meubles de la Sacristie de l'Oratoire de Jesus, à Paris.* Bib. Nat. MSS. F. F. 8621.

" 1681. Une chemisette de toile de Marseille picquée garnye de dentelle du Havre."—*Inv. d'Anne d'Escoubleau de Sourdis, veuve de François de Simiane.* Arch. Nat. M. M. 802.

[7] " Les ouvriers n'étant apparemment rappelés par aucune possession dans cette ville, lorsqu'elle fut rétablie, ils s'y sont établis et ont transmis leur travail à la postérité."—Peuchet.

[8] Point de Dieppe appears among the already-quoted lace boxes of 1688.

PLATE LIX.

FRENCH, CHANTILLY. FLOUNCE, BLACK SILK, BOBBIN-MADE.—Much reduced.

PLATE LX·

FRENCH, LE PUY. BLACK SILK GUIPURE, BOBBIN-MADE.
Photos by A. Dryden from laces the property of Mr. Arthur Blackborne.

PLATE LXI.

FRENCH. BLONDE MATE, IN SPANISH STYLE.—Nineteenth century.
Photo by A. Dryden.

able as it was at the end of the seventeenth century. Although it has slackened since about 1745 for the amount of its productions, which have diminished in value, it has not altogether fallen. As this work is the occupation of women and girls, a great number of whom have no other means of subsistence, there is also a large number of dealers who buy their laces, to send them into other parts of the kingdom, to Spain, and the islands of America. This trade is free, without any corporation ; but those who make lace without being mercers cannot sell lace thread, the sale of which is very lucrative." [9]

About twenty years later we read, "The lace manufacture, which is very ancient, has much diminished since the points,

Fig. 98.

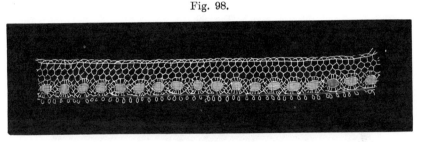

PETIT POUSSIN.—Dieppe.

embroidered muslins, and gauzes have gained the preference ; yet good workers earn sufficient to live comfortably ; but those who have not the requisite dexterity would do well to seek some other trade, as inferior lace-workers are unable to earn sufficient for a maintenance." [10] M. Feret writes in 1824,[11] "Dieppe laces are in little request ; nevertheless there is a narrow kind, named 'poussin,' the habitual resource and work of the poor lace-makers of this town, and which recommends itself by its cheapness and pleasing effect when used as a trimming to collars and morning dresses. Strangers who visit our town make an ample provision of this lace" (Fig. 98). The lace-makers of Dieppe love to give their own

---

[9] *Mémoires pour servir à l'Histoire de la Ville de Dieppe*, composés en l'année 1761, par Michel-Claude Gurbert. P. 99.
[10] *Mémoires Chronologiques pour*
servir à l'Histoire de Dieppe, par M. Desmarquets. 1785.
[11] *Notices sur Dieppe, Arques*, etc., par P. J. Feret. 1824.

names to their different laces—vierge, Ave Maria, etc. (Fig. 99)
—and the designation of Poussin (chicken) is given to the lace
in question from the delicacy of its workmanship.

Point de Dieppe (Fig. 100) much resembles Valenciennes,
but is less complicated in its make. It requires much fewer
bobbins, and whereas Valenciennes can only be made in
lengths of eight inches without detaching the lace from the
pillow, the Dieppe point is not taken off, but rolled.[12] It is
now no longer made. In 1826 a lace school was established
at Dieppe, under the direction of two sisters from the Convent
of La Providence at Rouen, patronized by the Duchesse
de Berri, the Queen of the French, and the Empress
Eugénie. The exertions of the sisters have been most
successful. In 1842 they received the gold medal for

Fig. 99.

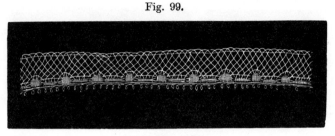

AVE MARIA.—Dieppe.

having, by the substitution of the Valenciennes for the old
Dieppe stitch, introduced a new industry into the department. They make Valenciennes of every width, and are
most expert in the square grounds of the Belgian Valenciennes, made entirely of flax thread, unmixed with cotton,
and at most reasonable prices.[13]

A very pretty double-grounded old Normandy lace, greatly
used for caps, was generally known under the name of
" Dentelle à la Vierge " (Fig. 101). We find only one
mention of a lace so designated, and that in the inventory
made in 1785, after the death of Louis-Philippe, Duke of

---

[12] Peuchet, of Dieppe, says: " On
ne fait pas la dentelle en roulant les
fuseaux sur le coussin, mais en l'y
jetant."

[13] *Almanach de Dieppe pour* 1847.

The Author has to express her
thanks to Sœur Hubert, of the École
d'Apprentissage de Dentelle, and M. A.
Morin, Librarian at Dieppe, for their
communications.

Orleans, the father of Egalité, where in his chapel at Villers-Cotterets is noted, " Une aube en baptiste garnie en gros point de dentelle dite à la Vierge." [14]

The lace of Eu, resembling Valenciennes, was much

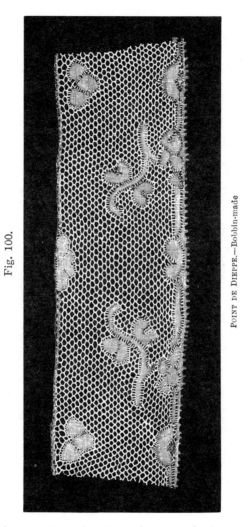

Fig. 100.

POINT DE DIEPPE.—Bobbin-made

esteemed. Located on the site of a royal château, the property of the Duc de Penthièvre, himself a most enthusiastic lover of fine point, as his wardrobe accounts testify, the

---

[14] Arch. Nat. X. 10,086.

lace-makers received, no doubt, much patronage and encouragement from the seigneur of the domain. In the
family picture by Vanloo, known as the " Tasse de Chocolat,"
containing portraits of the Duc de Penthièvre, his son, and

Fig. 101.

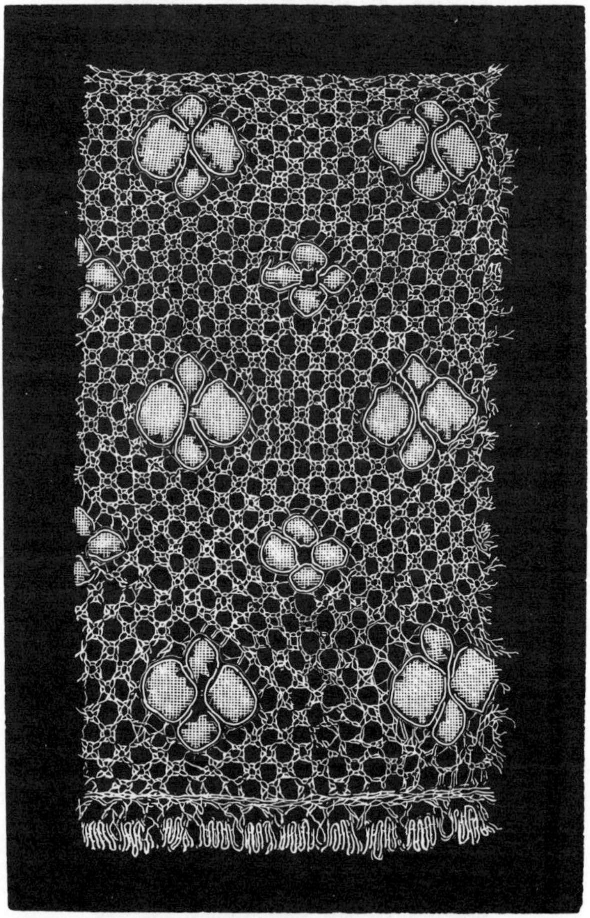

DENTELLE À LA VIERGE

the unfortunate Princesse de Lamballe, together with his
daughter, soon to be Duchess of Orleans, the duke, who is
holding in his hand a medal, enclosed in a case, wears a lace
ruffle of Valenciennes pattern, probably the fabric of his own
people (Fig. 102).

Arthur Young, in 1788, states the wages of the lace-makers seldom exceed from seven or eight sous per day ; some few, he adds, may earn fifteen.   Previous to the Revolution, the lace made at Dieppe amounted to 400,000 francs annually.   But Normandy experienced the shock of 1790.   Dieppe had already suffered from the introduction of foreign lace when the Revolution broke out in all its fury. The points of Havre, with the fabrics of Pont-l'Evêque (Dép.

Fig. 102.

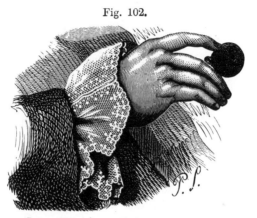

Duc de Penthièvre.—Vanloo. M. de Versailles.

Calvados), Harfleur, Eu, and more than ten other neighbour-ing towns, entirely disappeared.   Those of Dieppe and Hon-fleur alone trailed on a precarious existence.

CALVADOS.

The principal lace centres in the department of Calvados are Caen and Bayeux.

From an early date both black and white thread laces were made, of which the former was most esteemed.   It was not until 1745 that the blondes made their appearance.   The first silk used for the new production was of its natural colour, " écrue," hence these laces were called " blondes." [15]

---

[15] " The silk came from Nankin by way of London or the East, the black silk called ' grenadine ' was dyed and prepared at Lyons, the thread was from Haarlem."—Roland de la Platière.

The blonde of the time of Marie Antoinette is a very light fabric with spots or outline threads of thicker silk forming a pattern. Later, in the time of the Empire, the Spanish style came into vogue. The eighteenth-century patterns were again copied at Caen in the middle of the nineteenth century. After a time silk was procured of a more suitable white, and those beautiful laces produced, which before long became of such commercial importance. A silk throwster, M. Duval, was in a great degree the originator of the success of the Caen blondes, having been the first to prepare those brilliant white silks which have made their reputation. The silk is procured from Bourg-Argental, in the Cevennes. The Caen workers made the Chantilly lace, " Grillé blanc," already described,[15a] and also the " blonde de Caen," in which the flower is made with a different silk from that which forms the réseau and outlined with a thick silk strand. The réseau is of the Lille type, fond simple. It is this kind of blonde which is so successfully imitated at Calais.

Lastly the " blonde mate," or Spanish, already mentioned. In no other place, except Chantilly, have the blondes attained so pure a white, such perfect workmanship, such lightness, such brilliancy as the " Blondes de Caen." They had great success in France, were extensively imported, and made the fortune of the surrounding country, where they were fabricated in every cottage. Not every woman can work at the white lace. Those who have what is locally termed the " haleine grasse," are obliged to confine themselves to black. In order to preserve purity of colour, the lace-makers work during the summer months in the open air, in winter in lofts over their cow-houses : warmed by the heat of the animals, they dispense with fire and its accompanying smoke.[16] Generally, it was only made in summer, and the black reserved for winter work. Peuchet speaks of white lace being made in Caen from the lowest price to twenty-five livres the ell.[17] According to Arthur Young, the earnings

---

[15a] Page 213.

[16] Letter from Edgar McCulloch, Esq., Guernsey.

[17] Blondes appear also to have been made at Le Mans :—

" Cette manufacture qui etoit autre-fois entretenue à l'hôpital du Mans, lui rapportoit un benefice de 4,000 à 5,000 fr. Elle est bien tombée par la dispersion des anciennes sœurs hospitalières."—*Stat. du Dép. de la Sarthe*, par le Citoyen L.-M. Auvray. An X.

of the blonde-workers were greater than those of Dieppe or Havre, a woman gaining daily from fifteen to thirty sous. The silk blonde trade did not suffer from the crisis of 1821 to '32 : when the thread-lace-makers were reduced to the brink of ruin by the introduction of bobbin net, the demand for blonde, on the contrary, had a rapid increase, and Caen exported great quantities, by smuggling, to England. The blonde-makers earning twenty-five per cent. more than the thread-lace-makers, the province was in full prosperity. The competition with the machine-made blondes of Calais and Nottingham has caused the manufacture of the white blondes to be abandoned, and the Caen lace-makers have now confined themselves to making black lace. Caen also produces gold and silver blondes, mixed sometimes with pearls. In 1847 the laces of Caen alone employed more than 50,000 persons, or one-eighth of the whole population of Calvados.

Bayeux formerly made only light thread laces—mignonette, and what Peuchet calls[18] " point de Marli." " On ne voit dans ces dentelles," he writes, " que du réseau de diverses espèces, du fond et une canetille à gros fil, qu'on conduit autour de ces fonds." Marli, styled in the Dictionary of Napoléon Landais a " tissu à jour en fil et en soie fabriqué sur le métier à faire de la gaze," was in fact the predecessor of tulle. It was invented about 1765,[19] and for twenty years had great success, and was much worn by Marie Antoinette. When the mesh ground with an edging of loops, which constituted this lace in the decadence of Louis XVI., had a pattern, it was pois, rosettes, or the spots of point d'esprit. In the *Tableau de Paris*, 1782, we read that Marli employed a great number of workpeople, " et l'on a vu des soldats valides et invalides faire le marli, le promener, l'offrir, et le vendre eux-mêmes. Des soldats faire le marli ! " It was to this Marli, or large pieces of white thread net, that Bayeux owed its reputation. No other fabric could produce them at so low a price. Bayeux alone made albs, shawls, and other articles of large size, of thread lace.

---

[18] The handkerchief of " Paris net " mentioned by Goldsmith.

[19] In the Dép. du Nord, by Jean-Ph. Briatte. " Its fall was owing to the bad faith of imitators, who substituted a single thread of bad quality for the double twisted thread of the country."—Dieudonné, *Statistique de Dép. du Nord.*

In the *Mercure Galant* for June, 1687, we find the ladies wear cornettes à la jardinière " de Marly."

Lace was first made at Bayeux in the convents and schools, under the direction of the nuns of " La Providence." The nuns were sent there at the end of the seventeenth century, to undertake the supervision of the work-room founded by the Canon Baucher, in the old church f S. George. In 1747 the Abbé Suhard de Loucelles provided additional rooms for them in a house in the Faubourg St. Loup, close by the church of Notre Dame de la Poterie. In a short time more than 400 young women were employed at the two sets of work-rooms, and in 1758 the aldermen of the town presented to the intendant of the province a pair of thread lace cuffs, which, according to the accounts of the municipality, cost 144 livres. It was not until 1740 that a commercial house was established by M. Clément; from which period the manufacture has rapidly increased, and is now one of the most important in France. The black laces of Caen, Bayeux, and Chantilly, are alike; the design and mode of fabrication being identical, it is almost impossible, for even the most experienced eye, to detect the difference. They are mostly composed of " piece goods," shawls, dresses, flounces, and veils, made in small strips, united by the stitch already alluded to, the *point de raccroc*, to the invention of which Calvados owes her prosperity. This stitch, invented by a lace-maker named Cahanet, admits of putting a number of hands on the same piece, whereas, under the old system, not more than two could work at the same time. A scarf, which would formerly have taken two women six months to complete, divided into segments, can now be finished by ten women in one. (Plate LIX.)

About 1827, Madame Carpentier caused silk blonde again to be made for French consumption, the fabric having died out. Two years later she was succeeded by M. Auguste Lefébure, by whom the making of " blondes mates " for exportation was introduced with such success, that Caen, who had applied herself wholly to this manufacture, almost gave up the competition. Mantillas (Spanish, Havanese, and Mexican), in large quantities, were exported to Spain, Mexico and the Southern Seas, and were superior to those made in Catalonia. This manufacture requires the greatest care, as it is necessary to throw aside the French taste, and adopt the heavy, overcharged patterns appropriate to the costumes and fashions of the countries for which they are destined. These mantillas have served as models for the imitation made at Nottingham. (Plate LXI.)

To the exertions of M. Lefébure is due the great improve-

Fig. 103.

MODERN BLACK LACE OF BAYEUX.—Much reduced.

ment in the teaching of the lace schools. Formerly the apprentices were consigned to the care of some aged lace-maker, probably of deficient eyesight; he, on the contrary, placed them under young and skilful forewomen, and the result has been the rising up of a generation of workers who have given to Bayeux a reputation superior to all in Calvados. It is the first fabric for large pieces of extra fine quality and rich designs ; and as the point d'Alençon lace has also been introduced into the city, Bayeux excels equally at the pillow and the needle (Figs. 103 and 104).

Messrs. Lefébure have also most successfully reproduced the Venetian point in high relief; the raised flowers are executed with great beauty and the picots rendered with great precision. The discovery of the way in which this complicated point lace was made has been the work of great patience. It is called " Point Colbert." See page 188.

In 1851 there were in Calvados 60,000 lace-workers, spread along the sea-coast to Cherbourg, where the nuns of La Providence have an establishment. It is only by visiting the district that an adequate idea can be formed of the resources this work affords to the labouring classes, thousands of women deriving from it their sole means of subsistence.[20]

Bayeux is now the centre for high-class lace-making in France. M. Lefébure considers that the fichus, mantillas, etc., that are made of fine white thread in the country round Bayeux have all the suppleness and softness which contribute to the charm of Mechlin lace, to which they have a close affinity.

BRETAGNE.

No record of lace-making occurs in Bretagne, though probably the Normandy manufacturers extended westward along the coast. At all events, the wearing of it was early adopted.

---

[20] *L'Industrie Française depuis la Révolution de Février et l'Exposition de 1848,* par M. A. Audiganne.

M. Aubry thus divides the lace-makers of Normandy :—

Department of Calvados—
Arrondissement of Caen . . 25,000
Arr. of Bayeux 15,000
Arr. of Pont-l'Evêque, Falaise,*
    and Lisieux 10,000
Departments of La Manche and

Seine-Inférieure 10,000
                                        ———
                                        60,000

The women earn from 50 sous to 25 sous a day, an improvement on the wages of the last century, which, in the time of Arthur Young, seldom amounted to 24 sous.

Their products are estimated at from 8 to 10 millions of francs (£320,000 to £400,000).

---

* " Falaise, dentelles façon de Dieppe."—Peuchet.

Fig. 104.

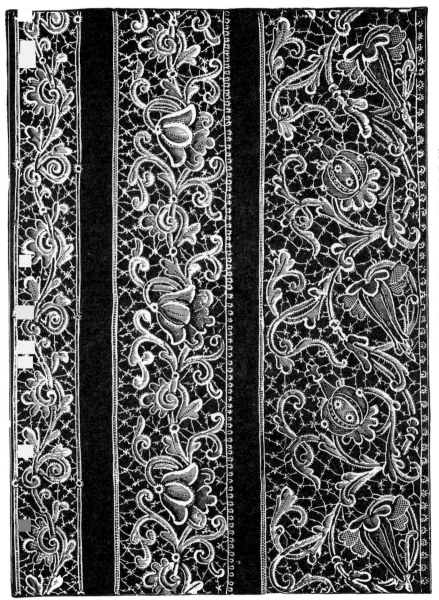

POINT COLBERT.—Venetian point in relief reproduced by M. Lefébure.

Fig. 105.

VALENCIENNES.—1650-1730.

Embroidered tulle or point d'esprit was made in Brittany as in Denmark, and around Genoa, where its production still continues. Embroidered muslins with open-work lace stitches were also made in Brittany during the eighteenth century, and called Broderie des Indes, after the Indian muslin scarfs that were brought to Europe at that date, and set the fashion.

There is a popular ballad of the province, 1587, on " Fontenelle le Ligueur," one of the most notorious partizans of the League in Bretagne. He has been entrapped at Paris, and while awaiting his doom, sends his page to his wife, with these words (we spare our readers the Breton dialect) :—

" Page, mon page, petit page, va vite à Coadelan et dis à la pauvre héritière [21] de ne plus porter des dentelles.

" De ne plus porter des dentelles, parce que son pauvre époux est en peine. Toi, rapporte-moi une chemise à mettre, et un drap pour m'ensevelir." [22]

One singular custom prevails among the ancient families in Bretagne ; a bride wears her lace-adorned dress but twice —once on her wedding-day, and only again at her death, when the corse lies in state for a few hours before its placing in the coffin. After the marriage ceremony the bride carefully folds away her dress [23] in linen of the finest home-spun, intended for her winding sheet, and each year, on the anniversary of the wedding-day, fresh sprigs of lavender and rosemary are laid upon it until the day of mourning.

---

[21] He had run away with the rich heiress of Coadelan.

[22] *Chants populaires de la Bretagne,* par Th. Hersart de la Villemarqué.

[23] The bringing home of the wedding dress is an event of solemn importance. The family alone are admitted to see it, and each of them sprinkles the orange blossoms with which it is trimmed with holy water placed at the foot of the bed whereon the dress is laid, and offers up a prayer for the future welfare of the wearer.

CHAPTER XVII.

VALENCIENNES (Dép. du Nord).

" Ils s'attachoient à considerer des tableaux de petit point de la manufacture
de Valencienne qui representoient des fleurs, et comme ils les trouvoient
parfaitement beaux, M. de Magelotte, leur hôte, vouloit les leur donner, mais
ils ne les acceptèrent point."—1686. *Voyage des Ambassadeurs de Siam.*

PART of the ancient province of Hainault, Valenciennes,
together with Lille and Arras, is Flemish by birth, French
only by conquest and treaty.[1]

Its lace manufacture has been supposed to date from the
fifteenth century, its first productions being attributed to
Pierre Chauvin and Ignace Harent, who employed a three-
thread twisted flax. This early date, however, is probably
not correct. It is more probable that Valenciennes
developed from and took the place of the lace-making
foundation of Colbert at Le Quesnoy. The lace of Le
Quesnoy is never mentioned after Louis XIV., whereas
after that reign Valenciennes comes into notice. It reached
its climax from 1725 to 1780, when there were from 3,000
to 4,000 lace-makers in the city alone.

One of the finest known specimens of the earlier fabric is
a lace-bordered alb,[2] belonging to the ladies of the Convent
of the Visitation,[3] at Le Puy. The lace is 28 inches wide,
consisting of three breadths, entirely of white thread, very
fine, though thick. The solid pattern, which with its flowers
and scrolls partakes of the character of the Renaissance,
comes out well from the clear réseau ground.

---

[1] French Hainault, French Flanders
and Cambrésis (the present Dép. du
Nord), with Artois, were conquests of
Louis XIII. and Louis XIV., confirmed
to France by the treaties of Aix-la-
Chapelle (1668) and Nimeguen (1678).

[2] Photographed in the *Album d'Ar-
chéologie Religieuse*. It is supposed
to have been made towards the end of
the seventeenth century.

[3] Founded 1630.

From 1780 downwards, fashion changed. The cheaper and lighter laces of Brussels, Lille, and Arras, obtained the preference over the costly and more substantial products of Valenciennes—les éternelles Valenciennes, as they were called—while the subsequent disappearance of ruffles from the costume of the men greatly added to the evil. Valenciennes fell with the monarchy. During the war of liberty, foreign occupation decimated its population, and the art became nearly lost. In 1790, the number of lace-workers had diminished to 250 ; and, though Napoleon used every effort to revive the manufacture, he was unsuccessful. In 1851 there were only two lace-makers remaining, and they both upwards of eighty years of age.

The lace made in the city alone was termed " Vraie Valenciennes," and attained a perfection unrivalled by the productions of the villages beyond the walls. In the lace accounts of Madame du Barry we find constant mention of this term.[4] "Vraie Valenciennes" appears constantly in contradistinction to " bâtarde "[5] and " fausse," simply leading us to suppose that the last-mentioned appellations signify the laces fabricated in the neighbourhood. In support of this assertion, M. Dieudonné writes :[6] " This beautiful manufacture is so inherent in the place, that it is an established fact, if a piece of lace were begun at Valenciennes and finished outside the walls, the part which had not been made at Valenciennes would be visibly less beautiful and less perfect than the other, though continued by the same lace-maker with the same thread, and upon the same pillow."[7]

---

[4] "1772. 15 aunes 3-16ᵐᵉˢ jabot haut de vraie Valencienne, 3,706 livres 17 sous"; and many other similar entries.

[5] " 5/8 Bâtarde dito à bordure, à 60 ll., 37 ll. 10 s."—*Comptes de Madame du Barry*.

[6] *Statistique du Dép. du Nord*, par M. Dieudonné, Préfet en 1804.

[7] " Among the various fabrics having the same process of manufacture, there is not one which produces exactly the same style of lace. The same pattern, with the same material, whether executed in Belgium, Saxony, Lille, Arras, Mirecourt, or Le Puy, will always bear the stamp of the place where it is made. It has never been possible to transfer any kind of manufacture from one city to another without there being a marked difference between the productions."—Aubry.

" After the French Revolution, when so many lace-makers fled to Belgium, Alost, Ypres, Bruges, Ghent, Menin, and Courtrai became the centres of this industry, and the lace produced in each town has a distinctive feature in the ground. That made in Ghent is square-meshed, the bobbins being twisted two and a half times. At Ypres, which makes a better quality

The extinction of the fabric and its transfer to Belgium has been a great commercial loss to France. Valenciennes, being specially a "dentelle linge," is that of which the

Fig. 106.

VALENCIENNES.—Period Louis XIV.

greatest quantity is consumed throughout the universe. Valenciennes lace is altogether made upon the pillow, with

of Valenciennes, the ground is also square-meshed, but the bobbins are twisted four times. In Courtrai and Menin the grounds are twisted three and a half times, and in Bruges, where the ground has a circular mesh, the bobbins are twisted three times."

one kind of thread for the pattern and the ground (Fig. 106). No lace is so expensive to make, from the number of bobbins required, and the flax used was of the finest quality. The city-made lace was remarkable for the beauty of its ground, the richness of its design, and evenness of its tissue. Its mesh is square or diamond-shaped, and it has no twisted sides ; all are closely plaited. The ornament is not picked out with a cordonnet, as is the case with Mechlin ; but, like Mechlin, the ground went through various modifications, including the " fond de neige," before the réseau was finally fixed. From their solidity, " les belles et éternelles Valenciennes " became an heirloom in each family. A mother bequeathed them to her daughter as she would now her jewels or her furs.[8] The lace-makers worked in underground cellars, from four in the morning till eight at night, scarcely earning their tenpence a day. The pattern was the especial property of the manufacturer ; it was at the option of the worker to pay for its use and retain her work, if not satisfied with the price she received. This lace was generally made by young girls ; it did not accord with the habits of the " mère bourgeoise " either to abandon her household duties or to preserve the delicacy of hand requisite for the work. It may be inferred, also, that no eyes could support for a number of years the close confinement to a cellar : many of the women are said to have become almost blind previous to attaining the age of thirty. It was a great point when the whole piece was executed by the same lace-worker. " All by the same hand," we find entered in the bills of the lace-sellers of the time.[9]

The labour of making " vraie Valenciennes " was so great that while the Lille lace-workers could produce from three to five ells a day, those of Valenciennes could not complete more than an inch and a half in the same time. Some lace-workers only made half an ell (24 inches) in a

---

[8] In the already quoted *Etat d'un Trousseau*, 1771, among the necessary articles are enumerated : " Une coëffure, tour de gorge et le fichu plissé de vraie Valencienne." The trimming of one of Madame du Barry's pillow-cases cost 487 fr. ; her lappets, 1,030. The ruffles of the Duchesse de Modène and Mademoiselle de Charollais are valued at 200 livres the pair. Du Barry, more extravagant, gives 770 for hers.

[9] " 2 barbes et rayon de vraie valencienne ; 3 au. 3/4 collet grande hauteur ; 4 au. grand jabot ; le tout de la même main, de 2,400 livres."—*Comptes de Madame du Barry.* 1770.

year, and it took ten months, working fifteen hours a day, to finish a pair of men's ruffles—hence the costliness of the lace.[10]   A pair of ruffles would amount to 4,000 livres, and the "barbes pleines," [11] as a lady's cap was then termed, to 1,200 livres and upwards.

The Valenciennes of 1780 was of a quality far superior

Fig. 107,

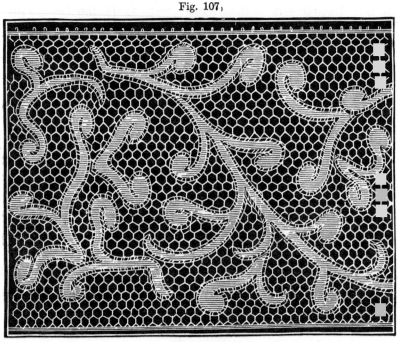

VALENCIENNES.

to any made in the present century.   The réseau was fine and compact, the flower resembling cambric in its texture; the designs still betraying the Flemish origin of the fabric—tulips, carnations, iris, or anemones—such as we

---

[10] Arthur Young, in 1788, says of Valenciennes : " Laces of 30 to 40 lines' breadth for gentlemen's ruffles is from 160 to 216 livres (£9 9s.) an ell.   The quantity for a lady's head-dress from 1,000 to 24,000 livres.   The women gain from 20 to 30 sous a day. 3,600 persons are employed at Valenciennes, and are an object of 450,000 livres, of which the flax is not more than 1/30.   The thread costs from 24 to 700 livres the pound."

[11] The "barbes pleines " consisted of a pair of lappets from 3 to 5 inches wide each, and half an ell (20 inches) long, with a double pattern of sprigged flowers and rounded at the ends.   A narrow lace 1½ ell long, called the *Papillon*, with the bande or passe, and the fond de bonnet, completed the suit.

Fig. 108.

VALENCIENNES LAPPET.—Period Louis XVI.

PLATE LXII.

VALENCIENNES.—Three specimens of seventeenth and eighteenth century. Arranged by age, the oldest at the top, which was made for a royal personage, with the initials E.P. ; it is now the property of Mr. Arthur Blackborne. Widths of the middle and lower pieces 1½ and 2½ in.

Photos by A. Dryden.

see in the old Flemish flower-pieces, true to nature, executed with Dutch exactness (Fig. 108). The city owed not its prosperity to the rich alone ; the peasants themselves were great consumers of its produce. A woman laid by her earnings for years to purchase a " bonnet en vraie Valenciennes," some few of which still appear in the northern provinces of France at church festivals and holidays. These caps are formed of three pieces, " barbes, passe, et fond." The Norman women also loved to trim the huge fabric with which they overcharge their heads with a real Valenciennes ; and even in the present day of " bon marché " a peasant woman will spend from 100 to 150 francs on a cap which is to last her for life.

The last important piece made within the city walls was a head-dress of " vraie Valenciennes " presented by the city to the Duchesse de Nemours, on her marriage in 1840. It was furnished by Mademoiselle Ursule Glairo, herself an aged lady, who employed the few old lace-workers then living, with the patriotic wish of exhibiting the perfection of the ancient manufacture.[12]

LILLE (Dép. du Nord).

" Ces points couppés, passements et dentelles,
Las ! qui venoient de l'Isle et de Bruxelles."
—*Consolation des Dames.* 1620.

The fabrics of Lille and Arras are identical ; both make white lace with single grounds (fond simple) ; but the productions of Lille are far superior to those of Arras in quality. The manufacture of the capital of French Flanders vies with those of the Netherlands in antiquity. As early as 1582 its lace-makers are described, at the entry of the Duke of Anjou into the city, " as wearing a special costume. A gown of striped stuff, with a cap of fine linen plaited in small flutes." A silver medal suspended from the neck by a black ribbon completed a dress which has descended to the nineteenth century.[13] The peace of Aix-la-Chapelle having transferred Lille to France, many of its artizans retired to

---

[12] The fault of the old Valenciennes lace is its colour, never of a clear white, but inclining to a reddish cast.

[13] " Les dentelières avaient adopté un par-dessus de calamande rayée, un bonniquet de toile fine plissé à petits

Ghent; they are described at that period as making both white and black lace.[14] The art, however, did not die out, for in 1713,[15] on the marriage of the Governor, young Boufflers, to Mademoiselle de Villeroi, the magistrates of Lille presented him with lace to the value of 4,000 livres.[16]

Fig. 109.

LILLE.

The beauty of the Lille lace is its ground, called " Point de Lille," or fond clair, " the finest, lightest, most trans-

---

canons. Une médaille d'argent, pendue au cou par un petit liseré noir, complétait leur costume, qui est arrivé jusqu'à nous; car nous l'avons vu, il n'y a pas trente ans."—*Hist. de Lille*, par V. Derode. Paris et Lille, 1848.

[14] *Mémoires sur l'Intendance de Flandre.*—MS. Bib. de Lille.

[15] Period of the peace of Utrecht, when Lille, which had been retaken by Prince Eugène, was again restored to France.

[16] *Histoire Populaire de Lille.* Henri Brunet. Lille, 1848; and *Histoire de Lille.* V. Derode.

parent, and best made of all grounds."[17] The work is simple, consisting of the ground, with a thick thread to mark the pattern[18] (Fig. 109). Instead of the sides of the mesh being plaited, as in Valenciennes, or partly plaited, partly twisted, as in Brussels and Mechlin, four of the sides are formed by twisting two threads round each other, and the remaining two sides by simple crossing of the threads over each other. In the eighteenth century more than two-thirds of the lace-making population of Europe made it under the name of mignonettes and blondes de fil.

The "treille"[19] was finer in the last century; but in 1803 the price of thread having risen 30 per cent.,[20] the lace-makers, unwilling to raise the prices of their lace, adopted a larger treille, in order to diminish the quantity of thread required.

The straight edge and stiff pattern of the old Lille lace is well known (Fig. 110).

The laces of Lille, both black and white, have been much used in France: though Madame Junot speaks disparagingly of the fabric,[21] the light clear ground rendered them especially adapted for summer wear.

They found great favour also in England, into which country one-third of the lace manufactured throughout the Département du Nord was smuggled in 1789.[22] The broad black Lille lace has always been specially admired, and was extensively used to trim the long silk mantles of the eighteenth century.[23]

---

[17] *Report of the Commissioners for* 1851.

[18] As late as 1761 Lille was considered as "foreign" with respect to France, and her laces made to pay duty according to the tariff of 1664.

In 1708 (31st of July) we have an Arrest du Conseil d'Estat du Roy, relative to the seizure of seventeen cartons of lace belonging to one "Mathieu, marchand à l'Isle." Mathieu, in defence, pretends that "les dentelles avoient esté fabriquées à Haluin (near Lille), terre de la domination de Sa Majesté."—Arch. Nat. Coll. Rondonneau.

[19] See FLANDERS (WEST), *treille*.

[20] In 1789, thread was 192 francs the kilogramme.

[21] Describing her trousseau, every article of which was trimmed with Angleterre, Malines, or Valenciennes, she adds: "A cette époque (1800), on ignorait même l'existence du tulle, les seules dentelles communes que l'on connût étaient les dentelles de Lille et d'Arras, qui n'étaient portées que par les femmes les plus ordinaires."—*Mém. de Madame la Duchesse d'Abrantès.* T. iii. Certainly the laces of Lille and Arras never appear in the inventories of the "grandes dames" of the last century.

[22] Dieudonné.

[23] Peuchet states much "fausse Valenciennes, très rapprochée de la vraie," to have been fabricated in the hospital at Lille, in which institution there were, in 1723, 700 lace-workers.

In 1788 there were above 16,000 lace-makers at Lille, and it made 120,000 pieces [24] of lace, representing a value of more than £160,000. In 1851 the number of lace-makers was reduced to 1,600; it is still gradually diminishing, from the competition of the fabric of Mirecourt and the numerous other manufactures established at Lille, which offer more lucrative wages than can be obtained by lace-making.

Fig. 110.

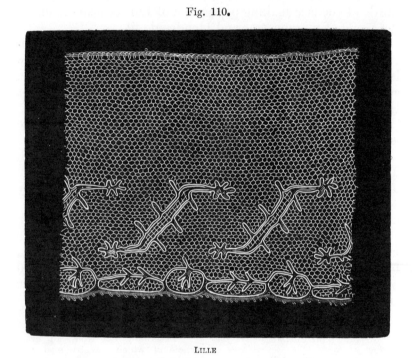

LILLE

The old straight-edged is no longer made, but the rose pattern of the Mechlin is adopted, and the style of that lace copied: the semé of little square dots (*points d'esprit*) on the ground—one of the characteristics of Lille lace—is still retained. In 1862 Mrs. Palliser saw at Lille a complete garniture of beautiful workmanship, ordered for a trousseau at Paris, but the commercial crisis and the revolutions of 1848 virtually put an end to the lace industry of Lille and Arras.

---

[24] A piece of Lille lace contains from 10 to 12 ells.

ARRAS (Artois) (Dép. Pas-de-Calais).

"Arras of ryche arraye,
Fresh as floures in Maye."—Skelton.

Arras, from the earliest ages, has been a working city. Her citizens were renowned for the tapestries which bore their name : the nuns of her convents excelled in all kinds of needlework. In the history of the Abbaye du Vivier,[25] we are told how the abbess, Madame Sainte, dite la Sauvage, set the sisters to work ornaments for the church :—

> "Les filles dans l'ouvroir tous les jours assemblées
> N'y paroissent pas moins que l'Abbesse zelées,
> Celle cÿ d'une aiguille ajuste au petit point
> Un bel etuy d'autel que l'eglise n'a point,
> Broche d'or et de soÿe un voile de Calice ;
> L'autre fait un tapis du point de haute lice,
> Dont elle fait un riche et precieux frontal ;
> Une autre coud une aube, ou fait un corporal ;
> Une autre une chasuble, ou chappe nompareille,
> Où l'or, l'argent, la soÿe, arrangés à merveille,
> Representant des saints vestus plus richement
> Que leur eclat n'auroit souffert de leur vivant ;
> L'autre de son Carreau detachant la dentelle,
> En orne les surplis de quelque aube nouvelle."

Again, among the first rules of the institution of the "Filles de Sainte-Agnès," in the same city, it is ordained that the girls "aprendront a filer ou coudre, faire passement, tapisseries ou choses semblables." [26]

The Emperor Charles V. is said, however, to have first introduced the lace manufacture into Arras.[27] Arras was one of the seats of Colbert's manufactures, probably of the Flemish bobbin lace. It flourished in the eighteenth century, when, writes Arthur Young, in 1788, were made "coarse thread laces, which find a good market in England. The lace-workers earn from 12 to 15 sous." Peuchet corroborates this statement. "Arras," he says,

---

[25] "L'Abbaye du Vivier, etablie dans la ville d'Arras," Poëme par le Père Dom Martin du Buisson, in *Mémoires et Pièces pour servir à l'Histoire de la Ville d'Arras.*—Bib. Nat. MSS., Fonds François, 8,936.
[26] Bib. Nat. MSS., Fonds François, 8,936.
[27] We find in the Colbert Correspondence (1669), the directors of the General hospital at Arras had enticed lace-workers of point de France, with a view to establish the manufacture in their hospital, but the jealousy of the other cities threatening to overthrow their commerce, they wrote to Colbert for protection.

"fait beaucoup de mignonette et entoilage, dont on consomme boucoup en Angleterre." The fabric of Arras attained its climax during the Empire (1804 to 1812), since which period it has declined. In 1851 there were 8,000 lace-makers in a radius of eight miles round the city, their salary not exceeding 65 centimes a day. In 1881, however, the trade had enormously decreased, only one house making a speciality of the old patterns. The old Arras laces are now no more.

There is little, or, indeed, no variety in the pattern of Arras lace ; for years it produced the same style and design.

Fig. 111.

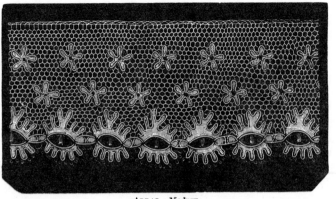

ARRAS.—Modern.

As a consequence of this, the lace-makers, from always executing the same pattern, acquired great rapidity. Though not so fine as that of Lille, the lace of Arras has three good qualities : it is very strong, firm to the touch, and perfectly white ; hence the great demand for both home and foreign consumption, no other lace having this triple merit at so reasonable a price (Fig. 111).

The gold lace of Arras appears also to have had a reputation. We find among the coronation expenses of George I. a charge for 354 yards of Arras lace " atrebaticæ lacinæ." [28]

---

[28] Gt. Ward. Acc. Geo. I. 1714–15 (P. R. O.), and Acc. of John, Duke of Montagu, master of the Great Wardrobe, touching the expenses of the funeral of Queen Anne and the coronation of George I. (P.R.O.)

In 1761 an Act was passed against its being counterfeited, and a vendor of " Orrice lace " (counterfeit, we suppose) forfeits her goods.

BAILLEUL (Dép. du Nord).

As already mentioned, up to 1790 the "vraie Valenciennes" was only made in the city of that name. The same lace manufactured at Lille, Bergues, Bailleul, Avesnes, Cassel, Armentières, as well as that of Belgium, was called "Fausses Valenciennes." "Armentières et Bailleul ne font que de la Valencienne fausse, dans tous les prix," writes Peuchet. "On nomme," states another author,[28] "fausses Valenciennes la dentelle de même espèce, inférieure en qualité, fabriquée moins serrée, dont le dessin est moins recherché et le toilé des fleurs moins marqué." Of such is the lace of Bailleul,[29] whose manufacture is the most ancient and most important, extending to Hazebrouck, Bergues, Cassel, and the surrounding villages.[30]

Previous to 1830, Bailleul fabricated little besides straight edges for the Normandy market. In 1832 the scalloped edge was adopted, and from this period dates the progress and present prosperity of the manufacture. Its laces are not much esteemed in Paris. They have neither the finish nor lightness of the Belgian products, are soft to the touch, the mesh round, and the ground thick; but it is strong and cheap, and in general use for trimming lace. The lace, too, of Bailleul, is the whitest and cleanest Valenciennes made; hence it is much sought after, for exportation to America and India. The patterns are varied and in good taste; and there is every reason to expect that in due time it may attain the perfection, if not of the Valenciennes of Ypres, at least to that of Bruges, which city alone annually sends to France lace to the value of from £120,000 to £160,000.

---

[28] *Statistique des Gens de Lettres.* 1803. Herbin. T. ii.

[29] A museum of lace has been established at Bailleul.

[30] In 1788, Bailleul, Cassel, and the district of Hazebrouck, had 1351 lace-makers. In 1802 the number had diminished; but it has since gradually increased. In 1830 there were 2,500. In 1851 there were already 8,000, dispersed over twenty communes.

CHAPTER XVIII.

AUVERGNE AND VÉLAY.

LE PUY (Dép. Haute-Loire).

As early as the fifteenth century the countrywomen from the mountains of the Vélay would congregate together during the winter within the walls of the neighbouring cities, and there, forming themselves into companies, gain their subsistence by making coarse lace to ornament the albs of the priests, the rochets of the bishops, and the petticoats of ladies of quality. And very coarse and tasteless were these early products, to judge from the specimens which remain tacked on to faded altar-cloths, still to be met with in the province, a mixture of netting and darning without design. They also made what was termed "dentelles de menage" with the coarse thread they used for weaving their cloth. They edged their linen with it, and both bleached together in the wearing.

The lace region of Central France, of which Le Puy is the centre, is considered to be the most ancient and considerable in France. It is distributed over the four departments,[1] and employs from 125,000 to 130,000 women. It forms the sole industry of the Haute-Loire, in which department alone are 70,000 lace-makers.

The lace industry of Le Puy, like all others, has experienced various changes; it has had its trials[2] and its periods of great prosperity.[3] In the chronicles of Le Puy of the sixteenth century[4] we read that the merciers of Notre-Dame

---

[1] Haute-Loire, Cantal, Puy-de-Dôme, and Loire.
[2] 1640.
[3] 1833 and 1848.
[4] By Médecis.

des Anges " qui, suivant l'usage faisaient dans notre ville le commerce des passementeries, broderies, dentelles, etc., comptaient alors quarante boutiques, et qu'ils figurent avec enseignes et torches au premier rang dans les solennités religieuses."

Judging from local documents, this manufacture has for more than two centuries back formed the chief occupation of the women of this province.

It suffered from the sumptuary edicts of 1629, 1635 and 1639, and in 1640 threatened to be annihilated altogether. In the month of January of that year, the Seneschal of Le Puy published throughout the city a degree of the Parliament of Toulouse, which forbade, under pain of heavy fine, all persons of whatever sex, quality, or condition, to wear upon their vestments any lace " tant de soie que de fil blanc, ensemble passement, clinquant d'or ni d'argent fin ou faux ; " thus by one ordinance annihilating the industry of the province. The reason for this absurd edict was twofold ; first, in consequence of the large number of women employed in the lace trade, there was great difficulty in obtaining domestic servants ; secondly, the general custom of wearing lace among all classes caused the shades of distinction between the high and low to disappear. These ordinances, as may be imagined, created great consternation throughout Le Puy. Father Régis, a Jesuit, who was then in the province, did his best to console the sufferers thus reduced to beggary by the caprice of Parliament. " Ayez confiance en Dieu," he said ; " la dentelle ne perira pas." He set out to Toulouse, and by his remonstrances obtained a revocation of the edict. Nor did he rest satisfied with his good work. At his suggestion the Jesuits opened to the Auvergne laces a new market in Spain and the New World, which, until the year 1790, was the occasion of great prosperity to the province. The Jesuit Father, who died in December 1640, was later canonised for his good deeds ; and under his new appellation of Saint François Régis, is still held in the greatest veneration by the women of Auvergne—as the patron saint of the lace-makers.

Massillon, when bishop of Clermont (1717), greatly patronised the lace-makers of his diocese, and, anxious that the province should itself furnish the thread used in the manufacture, he purchased a quantity of spinning-wheels, which he distributed among the poor families of Beauregard, the village in which the summer palace of the bishop, previous to the Revolution, was situated.

The lace trade of this province frequently appears on the scene during the eighteenth century. In 1707 the manufacturers demand a remission of the import duties of 1664 as unfair,[5] and with success. Scarce ten years afterwards,[6] notwithstanding the privilege accorded, we again find them in trouble ; whether their patterns did not advance with the fashions of the day, or the manufacturers deteriorated the quality of the thread—too often the effect of commercial prosperity—the shops were filled with lace, " propres, les unes pour l'Italie, d'autres pour les mers du Sud," which the merchants refused to buy. To remedy this bad state of affairs, the commissioners assembled at Montpelier coolly decide that the diocese should borrow 60,000 livres to purchase the dead stock, and so clear the market. After some arguments the lace was bought by the Sieur Jerphanion, Syndic of the diocese.

Prosperity, however, was not restored, for in 1755 we again hear of a grant of 1,000 livres, payable in ten years by the States of Vélay, for the relief of the distressed lacemakers, and again a fresh demand for exemption of the export duty.[7] This is declared in a memorial of 1761 to be the chief cause of the distress, which memorial also states that, to employ the people in a more lucrative way, a manufacture of blondes and silk laces had been introduced. This distress is supposed to have been somewhat exaggerated by the merciers of Le Puy, whose profits must have been very considerable ; the women, according to Arthur Young, earning only from four to eight sous daily.

Peuchet, with his predecessor, Savary, and other writers on statistics, describe the manufacture of Le Puy as the most flourishing in France. " Her lace," writes Peuchet, " resembles greatly that of Flanders ; much is consumed in the

---

[5] They represent to the king that the laces of the " diocèse du Puy, du Vélay et de l'Auvergne, dont il se faisait un commerce très considérable dans les pays étrangers, par les ports de Bordeaux, La Rochelle et Nantes," ought not to pay the import duties held by the " cinq grosses fermes."— *Arrest du Conscil d'Estat du Roy,*

6 August, 1707. Arch. Nat. Coll. Rond. They ended by obtaining a duty of five sous per lb., instead of the 50 livres paid by Flanders and England, or the ten livres by the laces of Comtè, Liège, and Lorraine

[6] 1715 and 1716.

[7] See MILAN.

French dominions, and a considerable quantity exported to Spain, Portugal, Germany, Italy and England. Much thread lace is also expedited by way of Cadiz to Peru and Mexico. The ladies of these countries trim their petticoats and other parts of their dress with such a profusion of lace as to render the consumption 'prodigieuse.'" "Les Anglois en donnent des commissions en contrebande pour l'Isthmus de Panama. Les Hollandois en demandent aussi et faisaient expédier à Cadiz à leur compte."[8] We read, however, after a time, that the taste for a finer description of lace having penetrated to Mexico and Peru, the commerce of Le Puy had fallen off, and that from that epoch the work-people had supported themselves by making blondes and black lace. The thread used in Auvergne comes from Haarlem, purchased either from the merchants of Rouen or Lyons. In the palmy days of Le Puy her lace-workers consumed annually to the amount of 400,000 livres. The laces made for exportation were of a cheap quality, varying from edgings of 30 sous to 45 livres the piece of 12 ells; of these the annual consumption amounted to 1,200,000 livres.[9] It may indeed be said that, with the exception of the period of the French Revolution to 1801, the lace trade of Le Puy has ever been prosperous.

Formerly they only made at Le Puy laces which had each a distinctive name—ave, pater, chapelets, mie, serpent, bonnet, scie, etc.

Le Puy now produces every description of lace, white and coloured, silk, thread, and worsted, blondes of all kinds, black of the finest grounds, application, double and single grounds; from gold and silver lace to edgings of a halfpenny a yard, and laces of goats' and Angora rabbits' hairs.

In 1847 more than 5,000 women were employed in making Valenciennes. They have also succeeded in producing admirable needle-points, similar to the ancient Venetian. A dress of this lace, destined to adorn an image of the Virgin, was shown in the French Exhibition of 1855.

---

[8] Roland de la Platière.

[9] Three-fourths were consumed in Europe in time of peace:—Sardinia took 120,000 francs, purchased by the merchants of Turin, once a year, and then distributed through the country: Florence and Spain, each 200,000; Guyenne exported by the merchants of Bordeaux 200,000; 500,000 went to the Spanish Indies. The rest was sold in France by means of colporteurs.—Peuchet.

In 1848 commerce and trade languished, and a cheaper lace was produced, made of worsted, for shawls and trimmings. This lace was not long in fashion, but it re-appeared a few years later under the name of " lama," or " poil de chèvre," when it obtained a great success. The hair of the lama has never been used.

Le Puy now offers to the market an infinite variety of lace, and by means of these novelties her laces successfully compete with those of Saxony, which alone can rival her in cheapness ; but as the patterns of these last are copied from the laces of Le Puy and Mirecourt, they appear in the foreign market after the originals.

The finest collection of Auvergne lace in the International Exhibition (1867) was from the fabric of Crâponne (Haute-Loire),[10] established in 1830 by M. Théodore Falcon, to whom Le Puy is indebted for her " musée de dentelles," containing specimens of the lace of all countries and all ages, a most useful and instructive collection for the centre of a lace district. Le Puy has also a lace school, numbering a hundred pupils, and a school of design for lace patterns, founded in 1859.[11]

AURILLAC AND MURAT (Dép. Cantal).

" L'on fait à Orillac les dentelles quit ont vogue dans le royaume," writes, in 1670, the author of the *Délices de la France.*[12] The origin of the fabric is assigned to the fourteenth century, when a company of emigrants established themselves at Cuença and Valcameos, and nearly all the points of Aurillac were exported into Spain through this company. In 1688 there was sold on the Place at Marseilles annually to the amount of 350,000 livres of the products of Aurillac, with other fine laces of Auvergne.[13] In 1726 the

---

[10] In Auvergne lace has preserved its ancient names of " passement " and " pointes," the latter applied especially to needle-made lace. It has always retained its celebrity for passements or guipures made in bands. The simplicity of life in the mountains has doubtless been a factor in the unbroken continuity of the lace-trade.

[11] Le Puy in recent years has named some of its coarse patterns " guipure de Cluny," after the museum in Paris —a purely fanciful name.

[12] Savinière d'Alquie.

[13] Savary. Point d'Aurillac is mentioned in the *Révolte des Passemens.*

PLATE LXIII.

PLATE LXIV.

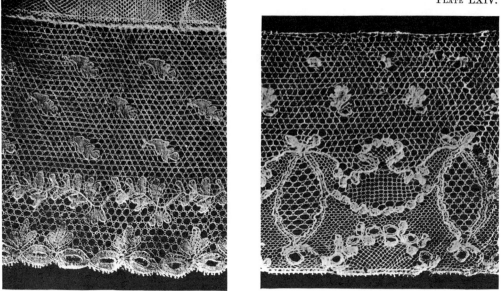

FRENCH.—Two specimens bought in France as Cambrai. They are typical of Northern French laces that became naturalised in England after the French Revolution. Widths, 2½ and 3½ in.

Photos by A. Dryden from private collection.

PLATE LXV.

FRENCH. BOBBIN-MADE.—From the environs of Le Puy.
Period Louis XIII.–Louis XIV.
Now made and called Guipure de Cluny.

In the Musée Cinquantenaire, Brussels.

produce was already reduced to 200,000 livres. The finest "points de France," writes Savary, were made at Aurillac and Murat, the former alone at one time producing to the annual value of 700,000 francs (£28,000), and giving occupation to from 3,000 to 4,000 lace-workers.

An attempt to establish a "bureau" for Colbert's new manufacture of points de France was at first opposed, as we read : "Les trois femmes envoyées par les entrepreneurs pour établir cette manufacture furent attaqués dans les rues d'Aurillac. Les ouvrières de cette ville leur disait 'qu'elles prouvaient s'en retourner, parce qu'elles savaient mieux travailler qu'elles.' "[14]

The lace-makers would not give up what the intendant terms "the wretched old point," which M. Henri Duref, the historian of the Département de Cantal, describes, on the contrary, as consisting of rich flowered designs, such as may be seen by studying the portraits of many Auvergnat noblemen of the period. There are various letters on the subject in the Colbert Correspondence ; and in the last from Colbert, 1670, he writes that the point d'Aurillac is improving, and there are 8,000 lace-women at work. It appears that he established at Aurillac a manufactory of lace where they made, upon "des dessins flamands modifiés," a special article, then named "point Colbert," and subsequently "point d'Aurillac."

In the Convent of the Visitation at Le Puy is shown the lace-trimming of an alb, point d'Angleterre. It is 28 inches wide, of white thread, with brides picotées, of elegant scroll design. If, as tradition asserts, it was made in the country, it must be the produce of this manufactory.

It appears that rich "passements," as they are still called in the country, of gold and silver were made long before the period of Colbert. We find abundant mention of them in the church inventories of the province, and in the museum are pieces of rich lace said to have belonged to Francis I. and his successors which, according to tradition, were the produce of Aurillac. They are not of wire, but consist of strips of metal twisted round the silk.

In the inventory of the sacristy of the Benedictine monastery at St. Aligre, 1684, there is a· great profusion of

---

[14] *Histoire du point d'Alençon*, Madame Despierres.

lace. " Voile de brocard, fond d'or entouré d'un point d'Espagne d'or et argent ;" another, " garni de dentelles d'or et argent, enrichi de perles fines " ; " 20 aubes à grandes dentelles, amicts, lavabos, surplis," etc., all " à grandes ou petites dentelles." [15]

In the inventory of Massillon's chapel at Beauregard, 1742, are albs trimmed with " point d'Aurillac " ; veils with " point d'Espagne or et argent." [16]

Lacis was also made at Aurillac, and some specimens are still preserved among the old families there. The most interesting dates from the early seventeenth century, and belongs to the Chapel of Notre Dame at Thierzac, where Anne of Austria made a pilgrimage in 1631, and which, by the mutilated inscription on a piece of the work, would appear to refer to her.

Mazarin held the Aurillac laces in high estimation, and they are frequently met with in the inventory of the effects he left on his death in 1660. Again, in the account of a masked ball, as given in the *Mercure Galant* of 1679, these points find honourable mention. The Prince de Conti is described as wearing a "mante de point d'Aurillac or et argent." The Comte de Vermandois, a veste edged with the same ; while Mademoiselle de Blois has " ses voiles de point d'Aurillac d'argent," and of the Duchesse de Mortemart it is said, " On voyait dessous ses plumes un voile de point d'Aurillac or et argent qui tomboit sur ses ' épaules.' " The Chevalier Colbert, who appeared in an African costume, had " des manches pendantes " of the same material.

The same *Mercure* of April, 1681, speaking of the dress of the men, says, " La plupart portent des garnitures d'une richesse qui empeschera que les particuliers ne les imitent, puisqu'elles reviennent à 50 louis. Ces garnitures sont de point d'Espagne ou d'Aurillac." From the above notices, as well as from the fact that the greater part of these laces were sent into Spain, it appears that point d'Aurillac was a rich gold and silver lace, similar to the point d'Espagne.

The laces of Murat (Dép. Haute-Garonne) were " façon de

---

[15] " Voile de toile d'argent, garni de grandes dentelles d'or et argent fin, donné en 1711 pour envelopper le chef de S. Gaudence."—*Inventaire du Monastère des Bénédictines de St. Aligre.*

[16] In the convents are constantly noted down " point d'Espagne d'or et argent fin," while in the cathedral of Clermont the chapter contented itself with " dentelles d'or et argent faux."

Malines et de Lille." They were also made at La Chaise Dieu, Alenches, and Verceilles. Those points were greatly esteemed, and purchased by the wholesale traders of Le Puy and Clermont, who distributed them over the kingdom through their colporteurs.

The fabrics of Aurillac and Murat ended with the Revolution. The women, finding they could earn more as domestic servants in the neighbouring towns, on the restoration of order, never again returned to their ancient occupation.

CHAPTER XIX.

LIMOUSIN.

IN the seventeenth and eighteenth centuries, a kind of pillow net (torchon entoilage, Mr. Ferguson calls it)[1] for women's sleeves was manufactured at Tulle (Corrèze) and also at Aurillac. From this circumstance many writers have derived tulle, the French name for bobbin net, from this town. M. Lefébure is of this opinion, and adduces in favour of it the fact that lace was made at Tulle in the eighteenth century, and that an account of 1775 mentions certain Mesdemoiselles Gantes as lace-makers in that town.

The first dictionary in which the word "tulle" occurs is the French Encyclopædia of 1765, where we find, "Tulle, une espèce de dentelle commune mais plus ordinairement ce qu'on appelait entoilage."[2] Entoilage, as we have already shown, is the plain net ground upon which the pattern is worked[3] or a plain net used to widen points or laces, or worn as a plain border. In Louis XV.'s reign Madame de Mailly is described, after she had retired from the world, as "sans rouge, sans poudre, et, qui plus est, sans dentelles, attendu qu'elle ne portait plus que de l'entoilage à bord plat."[4] We read in the *Tableau de Paris* how "Le tul, la gaz et le marli ont occupés cent mille mains." Tulle was made on the pillow in Germany before lace was introduced. If tulle derived its name from any town, it would more probably be from Toul, celebrated, as all others in Lorraine, for its embroidery; and as net resembles the stitches made in embroidery by separating the threads (hemstitch, etc.), it

---

[1] "1773. 6 au. de grande entoilage de belle blonde à poix."

[2] "16 au. entoilage à mouches à 11 l., 1761."—*Comptes de Madame du Barry.*

[3] "7 au. de tulle pour hausser les manchettes, à 9 l., 63 l."—1770. *Cptes. de Madame du Barry.*

[4] *Souvenirs de la Marquise de Créquy.*

may have taken its French name, Tulle, German Tüll, from the points de Tulle of the workwomen of the town of Toul, called in Latin Tullum, or Tullo.[5]

The lace[6] manufactures of Lorraine flourished in the seventeenth century. Mirecourt (Dép. Vosges) and the villages of its environs, extending to the department of Meurthe, was the great centre of this trade, which formed the sole occupation of the countrywomen. For some centuries the lace-workers employed only hempen thread, spun in the environs of Épinal, and especially at Châtel-sur-Moselle.[7] From this they produced a species of coarse guipure termed "passament," or, in the patois of the province, "peussemot."[8]

As early as the seventeenth century they set aside this coarse article and soon produced a finer and more delicate lace with various patterns : they now made double ground and mignonette ; and at Lunéville (Dép. Meurthe), "dentelles à l'instar de Flandre." In 1715 an edict of Duke Leopold regulates the manufacture at Mirecourt.[9] The lace was exported to Spain and the Indies. It found its way also to Holland, the German States, and England, where Randle Holme mentions "Points of Lorraine, without raisings."[10]

The Lorraine laces were mostly known in commerce as

---

[5] In an old geography we find, "Tulle, Tuille three hundred years ago."

The word Tule or Tuly occurs in an English inventory of 1315, and again, in "Sir Gawayn and the Green Knight"; but in both cases the word seems not to indicate a stuff but rather a locality, probably Toulouse.—Francisque Michel.

In Skelton's *Garland of Lawrell*, we find, "A skein of tewly silk"; which his commentator, the Rev. A. Dyce, considers to be "dyed of a red colour."

[6] As early as 1615 there appears to have been a traffic with Italy in laces, the painter Claude Lorraine being taken to Italy in that year by his uncle, a carrier and dealer in laces.

[7] Neufchâteau.

[8] The trader who purchases the lace is called "peussemotier."

[9] The Lorraine laces could only enter France by the bureau of Chaumont, nor could they leave the country without a formal permit delivered at Monthureux-le-Sec.—Arch. Nat., Coll. Rondonneau.

[10] In a catalogue of the collection of objects of religious art, exhibited at Mechlin in 1864, we find noticed, "Dentelle pour rochet, point de Nancy," from the church of St. Charles at Antwerp, together with various "voiles de bénédiction," laces for rochets and altar-cloths, of "point de Paris."

"Les dentelles de Saint-Mihiel," from the town of that name, one of the chief places of the fabric. These last-named laces were much esteemed on their first appearance. Previous to the union of Lorraine to France in 1766, there were scarcely 800 lace-makers in Mirecourt. The number amounted to nearly 25,000 in 1869.[11]

Early in the nineteenth century the export trade gave place to more extensive dealings with France. "Point de Flandres" was then very much made, the patterns imported by travelling merchants journeying on their way to Switzerland. Anxious to produce novelty, the manufacturers of Mirecourt wisely sent for draughtsmen and changed the old patterns. Their success was complete. They soon became formidable rivals to Lille, Geneva, and the Val de Travers (Switzerland). Lille now lowered her prices, and the Swiss lace trade sank in the contest.

Scarcely any but white lace is made; the patterns are varied and in excellent taste, the work similar to that of Lille and Arras.

Some few years since the making of application flowers was attempted with success at Mirecourt, and though it has not yet attained the perfection of the Brussels sprigs, yet it daily improves, and bids fair to supply France with a production for which she now pays Belgium £120,000 annually. The Lorraine application possesses one advantage over those of Flanders, the flowers come from the hands of the lace-makers clean and white, and do not require bleaching.[12] The price, too, is most moderate. The production which of late years has been of the most commercial value is the Cluny lace, so called from the first patterns being copied from specimens of old lace in the Musée de Cluny. The immense success of this lace has been highly profitable to Mirecourt and Le Puy.

---

[11] The *Tableau Statistique du Dép. des Vosges*, by Citoyen Desgoulles, An X, says: "Mirecourt is celebrated for its lace fabrics. There are twenty lace merchants; but the workers are not attached to any particular house. They buy their own thread, make the lace, and bring it to the merchants of Mirecourt to purchase. The women follow this occupation when not engaged in field work; but they only earn from 25 to 40 centimes a day. Before the Revolution, 7/8 of the coarse lace was exported to Germany towards Swabia. Of the fine qualities, France consumed 2/3. The remainder went to the colonies."

[12] So are those of Courseulles (Calvados).

The wages of the 24,000 lace-workers averaging eight-pence a day, their annual products are estimated at £120,000. Much of the Lorraine lace is consumed at Paris and in the interior of France ; the rest is exported to America, the East Indies, and the different countries of Europe.

CHAMPAGNE.

The Ardennes lace was generally much esteemed, especially the " points de Sedan," which derived their name from the city where they were manufactured.[13] Not only were points made there, but, to infer from the Great Wardrobe Account of Charles I., the cut-work of Sedan had then reached our country, and was of great price. We find in one account [14] a charge for " six handsome Sedan and Italian collars of cut-work, and for 62 yards of needlework purl for six pairs of linen ruffs" the enormous sum of £116 6s. And again, in the last year of his reign, he has " six handsome Pultenarian Sedan collars of cut-work, with the same accompaniment of 72 yards of needlework purl" amounting to £106 16s.[15] What these Pultenarian collars may have been we cannot, at this distance of time, surmise ; but the entries afford proof that the excellency of the Sedan cut-work was known in England. Rheims, Château-Thierry and Sedan are mentioned among the other towns in the ordinance establishing the points de France in 1665. In less than four months Rheims numbered a hundred and forty workers, consisting of Venetians and Flemings, with seven from Paris and the natives of the place. In 1669 the number had fallen to sixty, in consequence of the price demanded for their board and lodging. Their lace was remarkable for its whiteness. Lace was made in the seventeenth century at Sedan, Donchéry, Charleville, Mézières, Troyes and Sens.

The thread manufacturers of Sedan furnished the material

---

[13] Savary. Sedan was ceded to Louis XIII. in 1642.

[14] " Eidem pro 6 divit Sedan et Italic colaris opere sciss et pro 62 purles opere acuo pro 6 par manic lintear eisdem, £116 6s."—Gt. Ward.

Acc. Car. I., ix. to xi. P. R. O.

[15] " Eidem pro 6 divit Pultenarian Sedan de opere sciss colaris et pro 72 purles divit opere acuo pro manic lintear eisdem, £106 16s."—Gt. Ward. Acc. Car. I., xi. to xii.

necessary for all the lace-workers of Champagne. Much point de Sedan was made at Charleville, and the laces of this last-named town [16] were valued at from four up to fifty livres the ell, and even sometimes at a higher rate. The greater part of the produce was sold in Paris, the rest found a ready market in England, Holland, Germany, and Poland. [17] Pignariol de la Force, writing later, says the manufacture of points and laces at Sedan, formerly so flourishing, is now of little value. [18]

Most of its lace-makers, being Protestants, emigrated after the Edict of Revocation. Château-Renaud and Mézières were chiefly employed in the manufacture of footings (*engrêlures*). [19] The laces of Donchéry were similar to those of Charleville, but made of the Holland thread. They were less esteemed than those of Sedan. A large quantity were exported to Italy and Portugal; some few found their way to England and Poland. Up to the Revolution Champagne employed from 5000 to 6000 lace-workers, and their annual products were estimated at 200,000 fr. During the twelve years of revolutionary anarchy, all the lace manufactures of this province disappeared.

There are differences of opinion as to the exact character of Sedan lace. M. Séguin considers it to have been a lace inferior in design and workmanship to point de Venise à réseau. A single thread intervenes between the pattern and the réseau, instead of the overcast cordonnet of Alençon, and in other respects it resembles late Venetian needle-point. Certain authorities in Brussels, again, claim the point de Sedan as a needle-made production of Brabant or Liège. M. Lefébure, on the other hand, considers it as an important variety of Alençon. " The floral devices in points de Sedan, which are somewhat large and heavy in execution, spring from bold scroll forms, and in between them are big meshes of the ' grande maille picotée' of the point de France. Instead of an even and slightly raised stitching along their contours, these big flowers are accentuated here and there in well chosen parts by raised stitching, worked somewhat

---

[16] In 1700 there were several lace manufacturers at Charleville, the principal of whom was named Vigoureux.— *Hist. de Charleville.* Charleville, 1854.

[17] Savary. Ed. 1726.

[18] *Description de la France.* Ed. 1752.

[19] Savary.

with the effect of vigorous touches of rather forced high lights in a picture. These recurrent little mounds of relief, as they may be called, are frequently introduced with admirable artistic result. The finest bishops' rochets which appear in the later portraits by Hyacinthe Rigaud and de Larguillière are of point de Sedan."

It is possible that both types of lace mentioned— the heavy kind, and the lace with the réseau—are the productions of Sedan.

BURGUNDY.

Colbert was proprietor of the terre de Seignelay, three leagues from Auxerre, which caused him to interest himself in establishing manufactories, and especially that of point de France. In his Correspondence are twelve letters relating to this manufacture for 1667–74, but it did not succeed. At last, worn out, he says " the mayor and aldermen will not avail themselves of the means of prosperity I offer, so I will leave them to their bad conduct."

Specimens of a beautifully fine well-finished lace, resembling old Mechlin, are often to be met with in Belgium (Fig. 112), bearing the traditional name of "point de Bourgogne," but no record remains of its manufacture. In the census taken in 1571, giving the names of all strangers in the City of London, three are cited as natives of Burgundy, knitters and makers of lace.[20] In the eighteenth century, a manufactory of Valenciennes was carried on in the hospital at Dijon, under the direction of the magistrates of the city. It fell towards the middle of the last century, and at the Revolution entirely disappeared.[21] "Les dentelles sont grosses," writes Savary, "mais il s'en débite beaucoup en Franche-Comté."

---

[20] John Roberts, of Burgundy, eight years in England, " a knitter of knotted wool."

Peter de Grue, Burgundian, " knitter of cauls and sleeves."

Callys de Hove, " maker of lace," and Jane his wife, born in Burgundy.— State Papers, Dom., Eliz. Vol. 84. P.R.O.

[21] M. Joseph Garnier, the learned Archiviste of Dijon, informed Mrs. Palliser that " les archives de l'hospice Sainte-Anne n'ont conservé aucune trace de la manufacture de dentelles qui y fut établie. Tout ce qu'on sait, c'est qu'elle était sous la direction d'un sieur Helling, et qu'on y fabriquait le point d'Alençon."

LYONNOIS.

Lyons, from the thirteenth century, made gold and silver laces enriched with ornaments similar to those of Paris.

The laces of St. Etienne resembled those of Valenciennes, and were much esteemed for their solidity. The finest productions were for men's ruffles, which they fabricated of exquisite beauty.

A considerable quantity of blonde was made at Meran, a village in the neighbourhood of Beauvoisin, but the commerce had fallen off at the end of the last century. These blondes go by the familiar name of " bisettes."

ORLÉANOIS.

Colbert's attempts at establishing a manufactory of point de France at Montargis appear by his letters to have been unsuccessful.

BERRY.

Nor were the reports from Bourges more encouraging.

POITOU.

Lace was made at Loudun, one of Colbert's foundations, in the seventeenth century, but the fabric has always been common. " Mignonettes et dentelles à poignet de chemises, et de prix de toutes espèces," from one sol six deniers the ell, to forty sols the piece of twelve ells.

Children began lace-making at a very early age. " Loudun fournit quelques dentelles communes," says the Government Reporter of 1803.[22]

Peuchet speaks of lace manufactories at Perpignan, Aix,

---

[22] *Descr. du Dép. de la Vienne,* par le Citoyen Cochon. An X.

Fig. 112.

Point de Bourgogne.—Bobbin-made.

PLATE LXVI

WILLIAM, PRINCE OF ORANGE, FATHER OF WILLIAM III., 1627–1650. School of Van Dyck.
The collar is edged with Dutch lace. National Portrait Gallery.
Photo by Walker and Cockerell.

Cahors, Bordeaux,[23] etc., but they do not appear to have been of any importance, and no longer exist.[24]

---

[23] " Ce n'est pas une grande chose que la manufacture de points qui est établie dans l'hôpital de Bourdeaux."— Savary. Edit. 1726.

[24] Table of the Number of Lace-workers in France in 1851. (From M. Aubry.)

Manufacture of Chantilly and Alençon:—

Orne	
Seine-et-Oise	
Eure	12,500
Seine-et-Marne . . .	
Oise	

Manufacture of Lille, Arras, and Bailleul:—

Nord.	18,000
Pas-de-Calais	

Manufacture of Normandy, Caen, and Bayeux:—

Calvados	
Manche	55,000
Seine-Inférieure . .	

Manufacture of Lorraine, Mirecourt:—

Vosges	22,000
Meurthe	

Manufacture of Auvergne, Le Puy:—

Cantal	
Haute Loire	130,000
Loire	
Puy-de-Dôme	

Application-work at Paris and Lace-makers . . .	2,500

Total	240,000

In his *Report on the Universal Exhibition of* 1867, M. Aubry estimates the number at 200,000—their average wages from 1 to $1\frac{1}{2}$ francs a day of ten hours' labour; some earn as much as $3\frac{1}{2}$ francs. Almost all work at home, combining the work of the pillow with their agricultural and household occupations. Lace schools are being founded throughout the northern lace departments of France, and prizes and every kind of encouragement given to the pupils by the Empress, as well as by public authorities and private individuals.

CHAPTER XX.

HOLLAND, GERMANY, SWITZERLAND, AUSTRIA AND HUNGARY.

HOLLAND.

"A country that draws fifty feet of water,
In which men live as in the hold of nature,
And when the sea does in them break,
And drowns a province, does but spring a leak."—*Hudibras.*

WE know little of the early fabrics of this country. The laces of Holland, though made to a great extent, were overshadowed by the richer products of their Flemish neighbours. "The Netherlanders," writes Fynes Moryson, who visited Holland in 1589, "wear very little lace,[1] and no embroidery. Their gowns are mostly black, without lace or gards, and their neck-ruffs of very fine linen."

We read how, in 1667, France had become the rival of Holland in the trade with Spain, Portugal and Italy ; but she laid such high duties on foreign merchandise, the Dutch themselves set up manufactures of lace and other articles, and found a market for their produce even in France.[2] A few years later, the revocation of the Edict of Nantes[3] caused 4,000 lace-makers to leave the town of Alençon alone. Many took refuge in Holland, where, says a writer of the day, "they were treated like artists." Holland gained more than she lost by Louis XIV The French refugees founded a manufactory of that point lace

---

[1] In the Census of 1571, giving the names of all strangers in the city of London, we find mention but of one Dutchman, Richard Thomas, "a worker of billament lace."

[2] In 1689 appears an " Arrest du Roi qui ordonne l'exécution d'une sentence du maître de poste de Rouen, portant confiscation des dentelles venant d'Amsterdam."—Arch. Nat. Coll. Rondonneau.

[3] 1685.

called "dentelle à la Reine"[4] in the Orphan House at Amsterdam.[5]

A few years later, another Huguenot, Zacharie Châtelain,[6] introduced into Holland the industry, at that time so important, of making gold and silver lace.

The Dutch possessed one advantage over most other nations, especially over England, in her far-famed Haarlem[7] thread, once considered the best adapted for lace in the world. "No place bleaches flax," says a writer of the day,[8] "like the meer of Haarlem."[9]

Still the points of Holland made little noise in the world. The Dutch strenuously forbade the entry of all foreign lace, and what they did not consume themselves they exported to Italy, where the market was often deficient.[10] Once alone in England we hear tell of a considerable parcel of Dutch lace seized between Deptford and London from the Rotterdam hoy. England, however, according to Anderson, in 1764, received in return for her products from Holland "fine lace, but the balance was in England's favour."

In 1770 the Empress Queen (Marie Theresa) published a declaration prohibiting the importation of Dutch lace into any of her Imperial Majesty's hereditary dominions in Germany.[11]

As in other matters, the Dutch carried their love of lace

---

[4] We have frequent mention of dentelle à la reine previous to its introduction into Holland.

1619. "Plus une aulne ung tiers de dentelle à la reyne."—*Trésorerie de Madame, Sœur de Roi.* Arch. Nat. K. K. 234.

1678. "Les dames mettent ordinairement deux cornettes de Point à la Reyne ou de soie écrue, rarement de Point de France, parce que le point clair sied mieux au visage."—*Mercure Galant.*

1683. "Deux Aubes de toille demie holande garnis de point à la Reyne." —*Inv. fait apres le decedz de Mgr. Colbert.* Bib. Nat. MSS. Suite de Mortemart, 34.

[5] C. Weisse. *History of the French Protestant Refugees from the Edict of Nantes.* Edinburgh, 1854.

[6] Grandson of Simon Châtelain. See Chap. VI.

[7] In the paper already referred to

(see NORMANDY) on the lace trade, in 1704, it is stated the Flemish laces called "dentelles de haut prix" are made of Lille, Mons and Mechlin thread, sent to bleach at Haarlem, "as they know not how to bleach them elsewhere." The "dentelles de bas prix" of Normandy and other parts of France being made entirely of the cheaper thread of Haarlem itself, an Act, then just passed, excluding the Haarlem thread, would, if carried out, annihilate this branch of industry in France.—*Commerce des Dentelles de Fil.* Bib. Nat. MSS. F. Fr. 14,294.

[8] And. Yarranton. 1677.

[9] "Flax is improved by age. The saying was, 'Wool may be kept to dust, flax to silk.' I have seen flax twenty years old as fine as a hair."— *Ibid.*

[10] *Commerce de la Hollande.* 1768.

[11] *Edinburgh Amusement.*

to the extreme, tying up their knockers with rich point to announce the birth of an infant. A traveller who visited France in 1691, remarks of his hotel . " The warming-pans and brasses were not here muffled up in point and cut-work, after the manner of Holland, for there were no such things to be seen." [12]

The Dutch lace most in use was thick, strong and serviceable (Fig. 113). That which has come under our notice resembles the fine close Valenciennes, having a pattern often of flowers or fruit strictly copied from nature. " The ladies wear," remarks Mrs. Calderwood, " very good lace mobs." The shirt worn by William the Silent when he fell by the assassin is still preserved at The Hague ; it is trimmed with a lace of thick linen stitches, drawn and worked over in a style familiar to those acquainted with the earlier Dutch pictures.

SAXONY.

" Here unregarded lies the rich brocade,
　There Dresden lace in scatter'd heaps is laid ;
　Here the gilt china vase bestrews the floor,
　While chidden Betty weeps without the door."
　　　　　—" Eclogue on the death of Shock, a pet lapdog."
　　　　　Ladies' Magazine. 1750.

" His olive-tann'd complexion graces
　With little dabs of Dresden laces ;
　While for the body Mounseer Puff
　Would think e'en dowlas fine enough."
　　　　　—*French Barber.* 1756.

The honour of introducing pillow lace into Germany is accorded by tradition to Barbara Uttman. She was born in 1514, in the small town of Etterlein, which derives its name from her family. Her parents, burghers of Nuremburg, had removed to the Saxon Hartz Mountains, for the purpose of working some mines. Barbara Etterlein here married a rich master miner named Christopher Uttmann, of Annaberg. It is said that she learned lace-making from a native of Brabant, a Protestant, whom the cruelties of the Spaniards had driven from her country. Barbara had observed the mountain girls occupied in making a

---

[12] *Six Weeks in the Court and Country of France.* 1691.

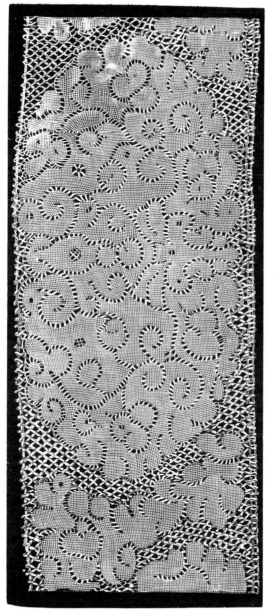

Fig. 113.

Dutch Bobbin-Lace.—Eighteenth century.

Fig. 114A.

BARBARA UTTMANN, WHO INTRODUCED THE LACE MANUFACTURE INTO THE ERZGEBIRGE.—From an Ivory statuette by Koehler, Green Vault, Dresden.

network for the miners to wear over their hair : she took
great interest in the work, and, profiting by the experience
derived from her Brabant teacher, succeeded in making her
pupils produce first a fine knotted tricot, afterwards a kind
of plain lace ground.   In 1561, having procured aid from
Flanders, she set up, in her own name of Barbara Uttmann,
a workshop at Annaberg, and there began to make laces of
various patterns.   This branch of industry soon spread from
the Bavarian frontier to Altenberg and Geissing, giving

Fig. 114.

TOMB OF BARBARA UTTMANN, AT ANNABERG.

employment to 30,000 persons, and producing a revenue of
1,000,000 thalers.   Barbara Uttmann died in 1575, leaving
sixty-five children and grandchildren, thus realising a pro-
phecy made previous to her marriage, that her descendants
would equal in number the stitches of the first lace ground
she had made : such prophecies were common in those days.
She sleeps in the churchyard of Annaberg, near the old
lime-tree.   On her tomb (Fig. 114) is inscribed : " Here lies
Barbara Uttmann, died 14 January, 1575, whose invention

of lace in the year 1561 made her the benefactress of the Erzgebirge."

> " An active mind, a skilful hand,
> Bring blessings down on the Fatherland."

In the Green Vault at Dresden is preserved an ivory statuette of Barbara Uttmann, four and a half inches high, beautifully executed by Koehler, a jeweller of Dresden, who worked at the beginning of the eighteenth century. It is richly ornamented with enamels and precious stones, such figures (of which there are many in the Green Vault) being favourite articles for birthday and Christmas gifts.

Previous to the eighteenth century the nets of Germany had already found a market in Paris.[13] " On vend," says the *Livre Commode des Adresses* of 1692, " le treillis d'Allemagne en plusieurs boutiques de la rue Béthizy."

" Dresden," says Anderson, " makes very fine lace," the truth of which is confirmed by nearly every traveller of the eighteenth century. We have reason to believe the so-called Dresden lace was the drawn-work described in Chapter II., and which was carried to great perfection.

" Went to a shop at Spaw," writes Mrs. Calderwood, " and bought a pair of double Dresden ruffles, which are just like a sheaf, but not so open as yours, for two pounds two."

" La broderie de Dresde est très connue et les ouvriers très habiles," says Savary.

This drawn-work, for such it was, excited the emulation of other nations. The Anti-Gallican Society in 1753 leads the van, and awards three guineas as their second prize for ruffles of Saxony.[14]

Ireland, in 1755, gave a premium of £5 for the best imitation of " Dresden point," while the Edinburgh Society,

---

[13] Treillis d'Allemagne is early mentioned in the French inventories :—

1543. " Pour une aulne deux tiers trillist d'Allemagne."—*Argenterie de la Reine (Eléonore d'Autriche)*. Arch. Nat. K. K. 104.

1557. " Pour une aulne de treilliz noir d'Allemagne pour garnir la robbe de damars noir ou il y a de la bizette."—*Comptes de l'Argentier du Roi (Henry II.)*. Arch. Nat. K. K. 106.

[14] " At a meeting of the Society of Polite Arts, premiums were given to a specimen of a new invention imitating Dresden work. It is done with such success as to imitate all the various stitches of which Dresden work is composed, with such ingenuity as to surpass the finest performance with the needle. This specimen, consisting of a cap and a piece for a long apron, the apron, valued by the inventress at £2 2s., was declared by the judges worth £56."—*Annual Register.* 1762.

following in the wake, a year later presents to Miss Jenny Dalrymple a gold medal for "the best imitation of Dresden work in a pair of ruffles."

In the *Fool of Quality*,[15] and other works from 1760 to 1770, we have "Dresden aprons," "Dresden ruffles," showing that point to have been in high fashion. Wraxall, too, 1778, describes a Polish beauty as wearing "a broad Medicis of Dresden lace." As early as 1760 "Dresden work" is advertised as taught to young ladies in a boarding-school at Kelso,[16] together with "shell-work in grottoes, flowers, catgut, working lace on bobbins or wires, and other useful accomplishments."

The lace of Saxony has sadly degenerated since the eighteenth century. The patterns are old and ungraceful, and the lace of inferior workmanship, but, owing to the low price of labour, they have the great advantage of cheapness, which enables them to compete with France in the American and Russian markets. In all parts of Germany there are some few men who make lace. On the Saxon side of the Erzgebirge many boys are employed, and during the winter season men of all ages work at the pillow; and it is observed that the lace made by men is firmer and of a superior quality to that of the women. The lace is a dentelle torchon of large pattern, much in the style of the old lace of Ischia.[17]

The Saxon needle-lace of the present day is made in imitation of old Brussels, with small flowers on a réseau. Some is worked in coloured thread, and also black silk lace of the Chantilly type is made: of this the Erzgebirge is the chief centre. This lace is costly, and is sold at Dresden and other large towns of Germany, and particularly at Paris, where the dealers pass it off for old lace. This fabric employed, in 1851, 300 workers. A quantity of so-called Maltese lace is also made, but torchon predominates.

The Museum for Art and Industry, opened at Vienna in 1865, contains several pattern-books of the sixteenth century, and in it has been exhibited a fine collection of ancient lace belonging to General von Hauslaub, Master-General of the Ordnance.

---

[15] "Smash go the glasses, aboard pours the wine on circling laces, Dresden aprons, silvered silks, and rich brocades." And again, "Your points of Spain, your ruffles of Dresden."—*Fool of Quality.* 1766.

[16] *Caledonian Mercury.* 1760.

[17] Letter from Koestritz. 1863.

GERMANY (NORTH AND SOUTH).

Germany in the sixteenth and seventeenth centuries was renowned for its lacis, cut-work, and embroidery with thread on net, of which there are several good examples in the Victoria and Albert Museum, together with specimens of early Flemish work from their colonies on the Elbe, established in the twelfth century by various German rulers. The work of these towns is of later date—of the fifteenth century—and has continued to the nineteenth century, when they made cambric caps, embroidered or ornamented with drawn-work, and edged with bobbin-made Tönder lace, in the style of eighteenth century Valenciennes.

"Presque dans toutes sortes d'arts les plus habiles cuvriers, ainsi que les plus riches négociants, sont de la religion prétendue réformée," said the Chancellor d'Aguesseau;[18] and when his master, Louis XIV., whom he, in not too respectful terms, calls "le roi trop crédule," signed the Act of Revocation (1685), Europe was at once inundated with the most skilful workmen of France. Hamburg alone of the Hanse Towns received the wanderers. Lubec and Bremen, in defiance of the remonstrances of the Protestant princes, allowed no strangers to settle within their precincts. The emigrants soon established considerable manufactures of gold and silver lace, and also that now extinct fabric known under the name of Hamburg point.[19]

Miss Knight, in her *Autobiography*, notes : "At Hamburg, just before we embarked, Nelson purchased a magnificent lace trimming for Lady Nelson, and a black lace cloak for another lady, who, he said, had been very attentive to his wife during his absence."

On the very year of the Revocation, Frederic William, Elector of Brandenburg, anxious to attract the fugitive workmen to his dominions, issued from Potsdam an edict[20] in their favour. Crowds of French Protestants responded to the call, and before many years had passed Berlin alone boasted 450 lace manufactories.[21] Previous to this emigration she had none. These "mangeurs d'haricots," as the Prussians

---

[18] In 1713.　　　　　[20] Dated Oct. 29, 1685.
[19] Weisse.　　　　　[21] Anderson.

PLATE LXVIII.

PLATE LXIX.

GERMAN, NUREMBERG.—Used by the peasants on their caps. The cordonnet suggests a Mechlin influence, whilst the heavy réseau is reminiscent of some Antwerp and Flemish and Italian village laces of the end of the seventeenth century.

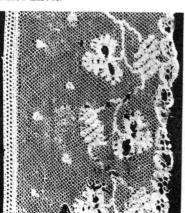

SWISS.—From near Neichatel, Early nineteenth century. Similar in make to Lille and some Devon lace.

ENGLISH, BUCKS.—A unique piece designed and made by the lace-makers for Queen Victoria in the early years of her reign; from her lady-in-waiting Emma, Lady Portman, it has descended to the present owner, Mrs. Lloyd Baker. The above is a complete section of the design, which is outlined with gold thread.

Photos by A. Dryden from private collections.

PLATE LXX.

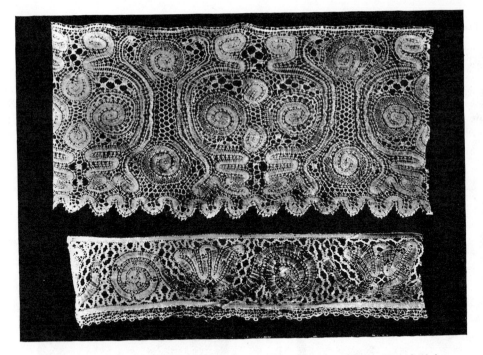

HUNGARIAN. BOBBIN LACE.—Latter half of nineteenth century. Widths, 6¼ and 2½ in.
Victoria and Albert Museum.

PLATE LXXI.

AUSTRO-HUNGARIAN, SOUTH SLAVONIAN. CUFF OF LINEN EMBROIDERED IN SATIN STITCH
IN WHITE SILK. WHITE SILK BOBBIN LACE.—Eighteenth century. Width, 7½ in.
Victoria and Albert Museum.

styled the emigrants, soon amassed large fortunes, and exported their laces to Poland and to Russia. The tables were turned. France, who formerly exported lace in large quantities to Germany, now received it from the hands of her exiled workmen, and in 1723 and 1734 we find " Arrêts du Conseil d'Etat," relative to the importation of German laces.[22]

The Landgrave of Hesse also received the refugees, publishing an edict in their favour.[23] Two fabrics of fine point were established at Hanover.[24] Leipsic, Anspach,[25] Elberfeld, all profited by the migration. " On compte," writes Peuchet, " à Leipsig cinq fabriques de dentelles et de galon d'or et argent."

A large colony settled at Halle, where they made " Hungarian " lace—" Point de Hongrie,[26] a term more generally applied to a stitch in tapestry.[27] The word, however, does occasionally occur :—

> " Your Hungerland [28] bands and Spanish quellio ruffs,
> Great Lords and Ladies, feasted to survey." [29]

All these various fabrics were offsets of the Alençon trade.

Fynes Moryson expresses surprise at the simplicity of the German costume—ruffs of coarse cloth, made at home. The Dantzickers, however, he adds, dress more richly. " Citizens' daughters of an inferior sort wear their hair woven with lace stitched up with a border of pearl. Citizens' wives wear much lace of silk on their petticoats." Dandyism began in Germany, says a writer,[30] about 1626, when the women first wore silver, which appeared very remarkable, and " at last indeed white lace." A century later luxury at the baths of Baden had reached an excess unparalleled in the

---

[22] Arch. Nat. Coll. Rondonneau.
[23] " Commissions and Privileges granted by Charles I., Landgrave of Hesse, to the French Protestants, dated Cassel, Dec. 12, 1685."
[24] Peuchet.
[25] Anderson.
[26] *La France Protestante*, par M. M. Haag. Paris 1846-59.
[27] " Item. Dix carrez de tapisserye a poinctz de Hongrye d'or, d'argent et soye de differends patrons."—1632.

[Inv. après le décès du Maréchal de *Marillac*. Bib. Nat. MSS. F. Fr. 11,424.
[28] Hungary was so styled in the seventeenth century. In a *Relation of the most famous Kingdoms and Common Weales through the World*, London, 1608, we find " Hungerland."
[29] " City Madam." Massinger.
[30] *Pictures of German Life in the Fifteenth, Sixteenth, and Seventeenth Centuries*, by Gustaf Freytag.

present day.   The bath mantles, " équipage de bain," of both
sexes are described as trimmed with the richest point, and
after the bath were spread out ostentatiously as a show on the
baths before the windows of the rooms.   Lords and ladies,
princesses and margraves, loitered up and down, passing
judgment on the laces of each new arrival.[31]

This love of dress, in some cases, extended too far, for
Bishop Douglas [32] mentions how the Leipsic students " think
it more honourable to beg, with a sword by their side, of all
they meet than to gain their livelihood.   I have often," he
says, " given a few groschen to one finely powdered and
dressed with sword and lace ruffles."

Concerning the manufactures of the once opulent cities of
Nuremburg and Augsburg we have no record.   In the first-
mentioned was published, in 1601, the model book, engraved
on copper, of Sibmacher.[33]   On the frontispiece is depicted a
garden of the sixteenth century.   From the branches of a
tree hangs a label, informing the world " that she who loves
the art of needlework, and desires to make herself skilful,
can here have it in perfection, and she will acquire praise,
honour, and reward."   At the foot of the tree is seated a
modest young lady yclept Industria ; on the right a second,
feather-fan in hand, called Ignavia—Idleness ; on the left a
respectable matron named Sofia—Wisdom.   By way of a
preface the three hold a dialogue, reviewing, in most
flattering terms, the work.

A museum was founded in 1865 at Nuremburg for
works and objects connected with the lace manufacture and
its history.   It contains some interesting specimens of
Nuremburg lace, the work of a certain Jungfrau Pickleman,
in the year 1600, presented by the widow Pfarrer Michel, of
Poppenreuth.[34]   The lace is much of the Venetian character.
One specimen has the figures of a knight and a lady, resembling the designs of Vecellio.   The museum also possesses
other curious examples of lace, together with a collection of
books relative to the lace fabric.   (Plate LXVIII.)

" In the chapel of St. Egidius at Nuremburg," writes one

---

[31] *Merveilleux   Amusements   des
Bains de Bade.*   Londres, 1739.
[32] Bishop of Salisbury.   " Letters."
1748-9.

[33] *Modelbuch in Kupfen gemacht.*
Nürnberg, 1601.
[34] Poppenreuth is about a German
mile from Nuremberg.

of our correspondents, " we were led to make inquiries concerning sundry ponderous-looking chairs, bearing some resemblance to confessionals, but wanting the side compart-
ments for the penitents. We learned that they belonged to
the several guilds (Innung), who had undertaken to collect
money for the erection of a new church after the destruction
of the old by fire. For this end the last members sworn in
of every trade sat in their respective chairs at the church
doors on every Sunday and holiday. The offerings were
thrown into dishes placed on a raised stand on the right of
the chair, or into the hollow in front. The devices of each
trade were painted or embossed on circular plates, said to be
of silver, on the back of each chair. One Handwerksstuhl
in particular attracted our attention ; it was that of the
passmenterie-makers (in German, Portenmacher or Posa-
mentier Handwerk), which, until the handicrafts became
more divided, included the lace-makers. An elegant scroll-
pattern in *rilievo* surrounds the plate, surmounted by a
cherub's head, and various designs, resembling those of the
pattern-books, are embossed in a most finished style upon
the plate, together with an inscription dated 1718."

Misson, who visited Nuremberg in 1698, describes the
dress of a newly-married pair as rich in the extreme—that
of the bridegroom as black, " fort chargé de dentelles " ; the
bride as tricked out in the richest " dentelle antique," her
petticoat trimmed with " des tresses d'or et de dentelle noire."

In the Victoria and Albert Museum there are two
women's ruffs from Nuremberg belonging to the latter part
of the sixteenth or early seventeenth century, and embroidered
in blue and black silk and white cotton, and edged with
a coarse thread Mechlin lace with a large meshed irregular
plaited réseau, probably late seventeenth century.

Perhaps the finest collection of old German point is
preserved, or rather was so, in 1840, in the palace of the
ancient, but now extinct, Prince-Archbishops of Bamberg.

Several more pattern-books were published in Germany.
Among the most important is that printed at Augsburg, by
John Schwartzenburg, 1534. It is printed in red, and the
patterns, mostly borders, are of delicate and elegant design.
(See APPENDIX.)

Secondly comes one of later date, published by Sigismund
Latomus at Frankfort-on-the-Main, 1605 ; and lastly, that

of " Metrepière Quinty, demorāt dempre leglīe de iii roies,"
a culōge (Cologne), 1527.

In Austria, writes Peuchet, " les dentelles de soie et de
fil ne sont pas moins bien travaillées." Many of the Protestant lace-workers took refuge in the cities of Freyburg
and Altenburg.

There is a collection in the Victoria and Albert Museum of
cuffs embroidered in satin stitch, and edged with bobbin-lace
" torchon " of the peasants' work in Slavonia in the eighteenth
century. The patterns resemble Cretan and Russian laces.

There is a comparatively modern variety of lace made in
Austria and Bohemia which resembles the old Italian bobbin-
lace ; the school where it is taught is under Government
patronage. This industry was established as a means of
relieving the distress of the Tyrol in 1850, and continues to
flourish.

Austria sent to the International Exhibition of 1874
specimens of needle-point and point plat made in the school
of the Grand Duchess Sophie, and specimens of border laces
in the style of the Auvergne laces were exhibited from the
Erzgebirge and Bohemia.

At the Paris Exhibition, Austria and Vienna both
exhibited copies of old needle-point laces.

At Laybach, in Austria, there was at one time a bobbin-
lace factory which produced lace much esteemed in the
eighteenth century.

The collection of Hungarian peasant lace in the Victoria
and Albert Museum collection contains specimens of coarse
modern pillow-made lace, with rude floral designs worked in
thick thread or yellow silk.

The modern laces of Bohemia are tasteless in design.
The fabric is of early date. " The Bohemian women," writes
Moryson, " delight in black cloth with lace of bright colours."
In the beginning of the nineteenth century upwards of 60,000
people, men, women and children, were occupied in the
Bohemian Erzgebirge alone in lace-making. Since the
introduction of the bobbin-net machine into Austria, 1831,
the number has decreased. There were in 1862 scarcely
8,000 employed in the common laces, and about 4,000 on
Valenciennes and points.[35]

---

[35] " Austria."—*Report of the International Exhibition of* 1862.

SWITZERLAND.

"Dans un vallon fort bien nommé Travers,
S'élève un mont, vrai séjour des hivers."—*Voltaire.*

In the Preface of the *Neues Modelbuch of Froschowern*, printed at Zurich (see APPENDIX), occurs the following :— " Amongst the different arts we must not forget one which has been followed in our country for twenty-five years. Lace-making was introduced in 1536 by merchants from Italy and Venice. Many women, seeing a means of livelihood in such work, quickly learned it, and reproduced lace with great skill. They first copied old patterns, but soon were enabled to invent new ones of great beauty. The industry spread itself about the country, and was carried to great perfection : it was found to be one specially suitable for women, and brought in good profits. " In the beginning these laces were used solely for trimming chemises and shirts ; soon afterwards collars, trimmings for cuffs, caps, and fronts and bodies of dresses, for napkins, sheets, pillow-cases and coverlets, etc., were made in lace. Very soon such work was in great demand, and became an article of great luxury. Gold thread was subsequently introduced into some of it, and raised its value considerably ; but this latter sort was attended with the inconvenience that it was more difficult to clean and wash than laces made with flax threads only." [36]

The above account is interesting, not only in its reference to Switzerland, but from its corroborative evidence of the Italian origin of lace.

In 1572, one Symphorien Thelusson, a merchant of Lyons, having escaped from the massacre of St. Bartholomew, concealed himself in a bale of goods, in which he reached Geneva, and was hospitably received by the inhabitants. When, after the lapse of near a hundred and twenty years, crowds of French emigrants arrived in the city, driven from their homes on the Revocation of the Edict of Nantes, a descendant of this same Thelusson took a body of 2,000 refugees into his service, and at once established a manufacture of lace. [37] The produce of this industry was smuggled

[36] As quoted in Lefébure's *Embroidery and Lace.*

[37] Haag. *La France Protestante.*

back into France, the goods conveyed across the Jura over passes known only to the bearers, by which they avoided the custom-house duties of Valence. " Every day," writes Jambonneau, himself a manufacturer, " they tell my wife what lace they want, and she takes their orders." Louis XIV. was furious.[38]

Though lace-making employed many women in various parts of the country, who made a common description while tending their flocks in the mountains, Neufchâtel has always been the *chef-lieu* of the trade. " In this town," says Savary, " they have carried their works to such a degree of perfection, as to rival the laces of Flanders, not only in beauty but in quality." We have ourselves seen in Switzerland guipures of fine workmanship that were made in the country, belonging to old families, in which they have remained as heirlooms; and have now in our possession a pair of lappets, made in the last century at Neufchâtel, of such exquisite beauty as not to be surpassed by the richest productions of Brussels.

Formerly lace-making employed a large number of workwomen in the Val de Travers, where, during his sojourn at Moutiers, Jean-Jacques Rousseau tells us he amused himself in handling the bobbins.

In 1780 the lace trade was an object of great profit to the country, producing laces valuing from 1 batz to upwards of 70 francs the ell, and exporting to the amount of 1,500,000 francs; on which the workwomen gained 800,000, averaging their labour at scarcely 8 sols per day. The villages of Fleurens and Connet were the centre of this once flourishing trade,[39] now ruined by competition with Mirecourt. In 1814 there were in the Neufchâtel district, 5628 lace-makers; in 1844 a few aged women alone remained. The modern laces of Neufchâtel resemble those of Lille, but are apt to wash thick. (Plate LXVII.)

In 1840, a fabric of " point plat de Bruxelles dite de Genève " was established at Geneva.

By the sumptuary laws of Zurich,[40] which were most

---

[38] The Neufchâtel trade extended through the Jura range from the valley of Lake Joux (Vaud) to Porentruy, near Bâle.

[39] *Statistique de la Suisse.* Picot, de Genève. 1819.

[40] A curious pattern-book has been sent to us, belonging to the Antiquarian Society of Zurich, through the kindness of its president, Dr. Ferd.

severe, women were especially forbidden to wear either blonde or thread lace, except upon their caps. This must have been a disadvantage to the native fabrics, "for Zurich," says Anderson, "makes much gold, silver, and thread lace."

Several pattern-books for lace were published in Switzerland in the later years of the sixteenth century ; one, without a date, but evidently printed at Zürich about 1540, by C. Froschowern, is entitled, *Nüw Modelbüch allerley Gattungen Däntel*, etc. Another one, entitled *New Model-buch*, printed by G. Strauben, 1593, at St. Gall, is but a reprint of the third book of Vecellio's *Corona*. Another, called also *Sehr Newe Model-Buch*, was published at Basle in 1599, at the printing-house of Ludwig Künigs.

Keller. It contains specimens of a variety of narrow braids and edgings of a kind of knotted work, but only a few open-work edgings that could be called lace.

CHAPTER XXI.

DENMARK, SWEDEN AND RUSSIA.

DENMARK.

"Eraste.—Miss, how many parties have you been to this week?
"Lady.—I do not frequent such places; but if you want to know how
much lace I have made this fortnight, I might well tell you."
　　　　　　　　　　—Holberg. *The Inconstant Lady.*

"The far-famed lace of Tönder."

"A certain kind of embroidery, or cut-work in linen, was much used in Denmark before lace came in from Brabant," writes Professor Thomsen. "This kind of work is still in use among the peasants, and you will often have observed it on their bed-clothes."

The art of lace-making itself is supposed to have been first brought over by the fugitive monks at the Reformation, or to have been introduced by Queen Elizabeth,[1] sister of Charles V., and wife of Christian II., that good queen who, had her husband been more fortunate, would, says the chronicler, "have proved a second Dagmar to Denmark."

Lace-making has never been practised as a means of livelihood throughout Denmark. It is only in the province of North Schleswig (or South Jutland, as it is also called) that a regular manufacture was established. It is here that King Christian IV. appears to have made his purchases; and while travelling in Schleswig, entries constantly occur in his journal book, from 1619 to 1625, such as, "Paid to a female lace-worker 28 rixdollars—71 specie to a lace-seller for lace for the use of the children," and many similar

---

[1] On her marriage, 1515.

notices.[2] It was one of those pieces of Tönder lace that King Christian sends to his Chamberlain, with an autograph letter, ordering him to cut out of it four collars of the same size and manner as Prince Ulrik's Spanish. They must contrive also to get two pairs of manchettes out of the same.

In the museum of the palace at Rosenborg are still preserved some shirts of Christian IV., trimmed with Schleswig lace of great beauty (Fig. 115), and in his portrait,

Fig. 115.

SHIRT COLLAR OF CHRISTIAN IV.—(Castle of Rosenborg, Copenhagen.)

which hangs in Hampton Court Palace, the lace on his shirt is of similar texture.

It was in the early part of this monarch's reign [3] that the celebrated Golden Horn, so long the chief treasure of the Scandinavian Museum at Copenhagen, was found by a young

---

[2] "1619. Sept. 11. Paid for a lace, 63 rixd. 11 skillings.

"1620. Oct. 11. Paid to a female lace-worker, 28 rixd.

"Nov. 4. Paid 10 rixd. to a female lace-worker who received her dismissal.

"Nov. 11. Paid 71 specie dollars to a lace-seller for lace for the use of the children.

"Paid 33 specie dollars and 18 skill. Lubec money, to the same man for lace and cambric.

"1625. May 19. Paid 21 rixd. for lace.

"Dec. 20. Paid 25 specie dollars 15 skill. Lubec money, for taffetas and lace."

[3] 1639.

lace-maker on her way to her work. She carried her prize
to the king, and with the money he liberally bestowed upon
her she was enabled, says tradition, to marry the object of
her choice.

The year 1647 was a great epoch in the lace-making of
Jutland. A merchant named Steenbeck, taking a great
interest in the fabric, engaged twelve persons from Dort-
mund, in Westphalia, to improve the trade, and settled them
at Tönder, to teach the manufacture to both men and
women, rich and poor. These twelve persons are described
as aged men, with long beards, which, while making lace,
they gathered into bags, to prevent the hair from becoming
entangled among the bobbins. The manufacture soon made
great progress under their guidance, and extended to the
south-western part of Ribe, and to the island of Romö.[4] The
lace was sold by means of "lace postmen," as they were
termed, who carried their wares throughout all Scandinavia
and parts of Germany.

Christian IV. protected the native manufacture, and in
the Act of 1643,[5] "lace and suchlike pinwork" are described
as luxurious articles, not allowed to be imported of a higher
value than five shillings and sixpence the Danish ell.[6] A
later ordinance, 1683, mentions "white and black lace which
are manufactured in this country," and grants permission to
the nobility to wear them.[7]

Christian IV. did not patronise foreign manufactures.
"The King of Denmark," writes Moryson, "wears but little
gold lace, and sends foreign apparel to the hangman to be
disgraced, when brought in by gentlemen."

About the year 1712 the lace manufacture again was
much improved by the arrival of a number of Brabant
women, who accompanied the troops of King Frederick IV
on their return from the Netherlands,[8] and settled at Tönder.
We have received from Jutland, through the kind exertions
of Mr. Rudolf Bay, of Aalborg, a series of Tönder laces, taken

---

[4] *Rawert's Report upon the Industry in the Kingdom of Denmark.* 1848.

[5] "The Great Recess."

[6] Two-thirds of a yard.

[7] Dated 1643.

[8] "Tönder lace, fine and middling, made in the districts of Lygum Kloster, keeps all the peasant girls employed. Thereof is exported to the German markets and the Baltic, it is sup-posed, for more than 100,000 rixdollars (£11,110), and the fine thread must be had from the Netherlands, and sometimes costs 100 rixdollars per lb." —*Pontoppidan. Economical Balance.* 1759.

Fig. 116.

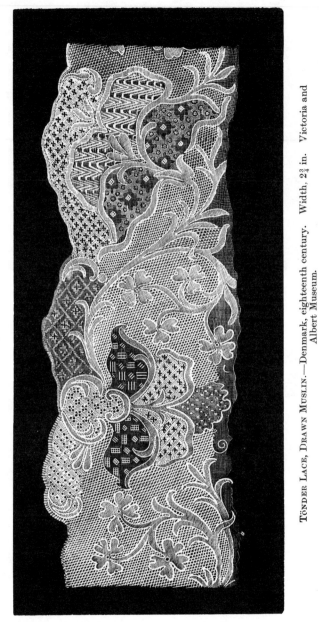

Tönder Lace, Drawn Muslin.—Denmark, eighteenth century.   Width, $2\frac{3}{4}$ in.   Victoria and
Albert Museum.

PLATE LXXII.

RUSSIAN.—The upper piece of lace is needle-point " à brides picotées."   Modern reproduction
of a sixteenth century design.   Width, 3⅜ in.
GERMAN, SAXON.—The lower piece bobbin-made by the peasants of the Erzgebirge.
Nineteenth century.   Width, 3¼ in.
Victoria and Albert Museum.

PLATE LXXIII.

RUSSIAN.—Old bobbin-made with coloured silk outlines.   The property of
Madame Pogosky.
Photo by A. Dryden.

from the pattern-books of the manufacturers. The earlier specimens are all of Flemish character. There is the old Flanders lace, with its Dutch flowers and double and trolly grounds in endless variety. The Brabant, with fine ground, the flowers and *jours* well executed. Then follow the Mechlin grounds, the patterns worked with a coarse thread, in many, apparently, run in with the needle. There is also a good specimen of that description of drawn muslin lace, commonly known under the name of "Indian work," but which appears to have been very generally made in various manners. The leaves and flowers formed of the muslin are worked round with a cordonnet, by way of relief to the thick double ground (Fig. 116).[9] In the Scandinavian Museum at Copenhagen is a pair of lappets of drawn muslin, a fine specimen of this work.

The modern laces are copied from French, Lille, and Saxon patterns; there are also imitations of the so-called Maltese. The Schleswig laces are all remarkable for their fine quality and excellent workmanship. Guipure, after the manner of the Venice points, was also fabricated. A fine specimen of this lace may be seen decorating the black velvet dress of the youthful daughter of Duke John of Holstein. She lies in her coffin within the mortuary chapel of her family, in the castle of Sonderborg. Lace was much used in burials in the seventeenth and eighteenth centuries, when it really appears people were arrayed in more costly clothing than in their lives. The author of *Jutland and the Danish Islands* has often seen mummies in the Danish churches exposed to view tricked out in points of great richness.

The lace industry continued to increase in value till the beginning of the present century. The year 1801 may be considered its culminating point. At that period the number of peasants employed in Tönder and its neighbourhood alone was 20,000. Even little boys were taught to make lace till strong enough to work in the fields, and there was scarcely a house without a lace-maker, who would sit before her

---

[9] " In the Victoria and Albert Museum collection, Denmark is represented by a few skilful embroideries done on and with fine linen, muslin and suchlike, which are somewhat similar in appearance to lace fabrics of Mechlin design."—(A. S. Cole.)

cottage door, working from sunrise till midnight, singing the ballads handed down from their Brabant teachers.[10]

" My late father," [11] writes Mr. F. Wulff, of Brede, " who began the lace trade the end of the last century, first went on foot with his wares to Mecklenburg, Prussia and Hanover: we consigned lace to all parts of the world.　Soon he could afford to buy a horse ; and in his old age he calculated he had travelled on horseback more than 75,000 English miles, or thrice round the earth.　In his youth the most durable and prettiest ground was the old Flemish, much used by the peasants in Germany.　It was solid, and passed as an heir-loom through several generations.　Later, the fine needle ground came in, and lastly, the fond clair, or point de Lille, far less solid, but easier to work ; hence the lace-makers became less skilful than of old."

They had not many models, and the best workwomen were those who devoted their whole life to one special pattern.　Few were found so persevering.　One widow, how-ever, is recorded who lived to the age of eighty and brought up seven children on the produce of a narrow edging, which she sold at sixpence a yard.

Each pattern had its proper name—cock-eye, spider, lyre, chimney-pot, and feather.

The rich farmers' wives sat at their pillows daily, causing their household duties to be performed by hired servants from North Jutland.　Ladies also, a century and a half ago, made it their occupation, as the motto of our chapter, from the drama of Holberg, will show.　And this continued till the fashion of " hvidsom "—white seaming—the cut-work already alluded to, was for a time revived.　This work was, however, looked upon as *infra dig.* for the wives of functionaries and suchlike, in whom it was unbecoming to waste on such employment time that should be devoted to household matters.　Our informant tells of a lady in the

---

[10] " The lace fabric in North Sles-wick in 1840 was divided into two districts—that of Tönder and Lygum Kloster on the western coasts, and that of Haderslaben and Apenraade on the east.　The quality of the lace from these last localities is so bad that no Copenhagen dealers will have it in their shops."—*Report of the Royal Sleswick-Holstein Government.* 1840.

[11] Mr. Jens Wulff, an eminent lace-dealer, Knight of the Danebrog, who has made great exertions to revive the lace industry in Denmark.

north who thus embroidered the christening robe of her child by stealth in the kitchen, fearing to be caught by her visitors—cookery had in those days precedence over embroidery. Among the hoards of this child, born 1755, was found a most exquisite collection of old Tönder lace, embracing all the varieties made by her mother and herself, from the thick Flemish to the finest needle-point.

The fashion of cut-work still prevails in Denmark, where collars and cuffs, decorated with stars, crosses, and other mediæval designs, are exposed in the shop-windows of Copenhagen for sale—the work of poor gentlewomen, who, by their needle, thus add a few dollars yearly to their income.

From 1830 dates the decline of the Tönder lace. Cotton thread was introduced, and the quality of the fabric was deteriorated.[12] The lace schools were given up; and the flourishing state of agriculture rendered it no longer a profitable employment either for the boys or the women.[13] The trade passed from the manufacturers into the hands of the hawkers and petty dealers, who were too poor to purchase the finer points. The "lace postmen" once more travelled from house to house with their little leathern boxes, offering these inferior wares for sale.[14] The art died out. In 1840 there were not more than six lace manufacturers in Schleswig.

The old people, however, still believe in a good time coming. "I have in my day," said an aged woman, "sold point at four thalers an ell, sir; and though I may never do so again, my daughter will. The lace trade slumbers, but it does not die."

SWEDEN.

At a very early period the Scandinavian goldsmith had learned to draw out wires of gold and twine them round threads either of silk or flax—in fact to *guiper* them.

---

[12] Tönder lace was celebrated for its durability, the best flax or silk thread only being used.

[13] "A lace-maker earns from $3\frac{1}{2}d$. to $4\frac{1}{2}d$. per day of sixteen hours."— *Rawert's Report.* 1848.

[14] The Tönder lace-traders enjoy the privilege of offering their wares for sale all over Denmark without a license (concession), a privilege extended to no other industry.

Wadstena, where lies Queen Philippa of Lancaster, daughter of Henry IV., is celebrated for its lace. The art, according to tradition, was introduced among the nuns of the convent by St. Bridget on her return from Italy. Some even go so far as to say she wrote home to Wadstena, ordering lace from Rome; but, as St. Bridget died in 1335, we may be allowed to question the fact: certain it is, though, the funeral coif of the saint, as depicted in an ancient portrait, said to have been taken at Rome after death, is ornamented with a species of perforated needlework.[15] By the rules of the convent, the nuns of Wadstena were forbidden to touch either gold or silver, save in their netting and embroidery. There exists an old journal of the Kloster, called *Diarium Vadstenænse*, in which are, however, no allusions to the art; but the letters of a Wadstena nun to her lover *extra muros*, published from an old collection [16] of documents, somewhat help us in our researches.

"I wish," she writes to her admirer, "I could send you a netted cap that I myself have made, but when Sister Karin Andersdotter saw that I mingled gold and silver thread in it, she said, 'You must surely have some beloved.' 'Do you think so?' I answered. 'Here in the Kloster, you may easily see if any of the brethren has such a cap, and I dare not send it by anyone to a sweetheart outside the walls.' 'You intend it for Axel Nilson,' answered Sister Karin. 'It is not for you to talk,' I replied. 'I have seen you net a long hood, and talk and prattle yourself with Brother Bertol.'"

From netted caps of thread, worked in with gold and silver, the transition to lace is easy, and history tells that in the middle ages the Wadstena nuns "Knit their laces of

---

[15] The early perfection of Bridget herself in this employment, if we may credit the chronicle of the Abbess Margaretha, 1440–46, may be ascribed to a miraculous origin.

When, at the age of twelve, she was employed at her knitted lacework, a fear came over her that she should not finish her work creditably to herself, and in her anxiety she raised her heart above. As her aunt came into the chamber she beheld an unknown maiden sitting opposite to her niece, and aiding her in her task; she vanished immediately, and when the aunt asked Bridget who had helped her she knew nothing about it, and assured her relation she had seen no one.

All were astonished at the fineness and perfection of the work, and kept the lace as of miraculous origin.

[16] *Wadstena Past and Present* (Förr och Nu).

gold and silk." We may therefore suppose the art to have flourished in the convents at an early date.

At the suppression of the monasteries, under Charles IX., a few of the nuns, too infirm to sail with their sisters for Poland, remained in Sweden. People took compassion on the outcasts, and gave them two rooms to dwell in, where they continued their occupation of making lace, and were able, for a season, to keep the secret of their art. After a time, however, lace-making became general throughout the town and neighbourhood, and was known to the laity previous to the dissolution of Wadstena—a favoured convent which survived the rest of the other monasteries of Sweden.

" Send up," writes Gustaf Vasa, in a familiar letter [17] to his Queen Margaret, " the lace passement made for me by Anne, the smith's daughter, at Upsala; I want it : don't neglect this." [18]

In an inventory of Ericksholm Castle, drawn up in 1548, are endless entries of " sheets seamed with cut-work, half worn-out sheets with open border of cut-work, towels with cut-work and with the king's and queen's arms in each corner, blue curtains with cut-work seams," etc.

The style of Wadstena lace changed with the times and fashion of the national costume. Those made at present are of the single or double ground, both black and white, fine, but wanting in firmness. They also make much dentelle torchon, of the lozenge pattern, for trimming the bed-linen they so elaborately embroider in drawn-work.

In 1830 the products in value amounted to 30,000 rix-dollars. They were carried to every part of Sweden, and a small quantity even to foreign parts. One dealer alone, a Madame Hartruide, now sends her colporteurs hawking Wadstena lace round the country. The fabric, after much depression, has slightly increased of late years, having received much encouragement from her Majesty Queen

---

[17] The letter is dated March 20th, 1544.

[18] In the detailed account of the trousseau furnished to his daughter, there is no mention of lace ; but the author of *One Year in Sweden* has seen the body of his little granddaughter, the Princess Isabella, daughter of John III., as it lies in the vault of Strengnäs, the child's dress and shoes literally covered with gold and silver lace of a Gothic pattern, fresh and untarnished as though made yesterday.

Louisa. Specimens of Wadstena lace—the only lace manufactory now existing in Sweden—were sent to the Great International Exhibition of 1862.

Hölesom, or cut-work, is a favourite employment of Swedish women, and is generally taught in the schools.[19] At the various bathing-places you may see the young ladies working as industriously as if for their daily sustenance ; they never purchase such articles of decoration, but entirely adorn their houses by the labours of their own hands. It was by a collar of this hölesom, worked in silk and gold, that young Gustaf Erikson was nearly betrayed when working as a labourer in the barn of Rankhytta, the property of his old college friend, Anders Petersen. A servant girl observed to her master, " The new farm-boy can be no peasant ; for," says she, " his linen is far too fine, and I saw a collar wrought in silk and gold beneath his kirtle."

Gold lace was much in vogue in the middle of the sixteenth century, and entries of it abound in the inventory of Gustavus Vasa and his youngest son, Magnus.

In an inventory of Ericksholm, 1536, is a pair of laced sheets. It is the custom in Sweden to sew a broad border of seaming lace between the breadths of the sheets, sometimes wove in the linen. Directions, with patterns scarcely changed since the sixteenth century, may be found in the *Weaving Book* published at Stockholm in 1828.[20]

Towards the end of 1500 the term " passement " appears in general use, in an inventory of " Pontus de Gardia."

In the neighbourhood of Wadstena old soldiers, as well as women, may be seen of a summer's evening sitting at the cottage doors making lace. Though no other lace manufactory can be said to exist in Sweden beyond that of Wadstena, still a coarse bobbin lace is made by the peasantry for home consumption. The author has received from the Countess Elizabeth Piper, late Grande Maîtresse to her Majesty the Queen of Sweden, specimens of coarse pillow laces, worked by the Scanian peasant women, which, she writes, " form a favourite occupation for the women of our province."

---

[19] In the Victoria and Albert Museum there is a collection of Norwegian cutwork of the eighteenth century.

[20] Weber. *Bilderbuch.*

Leipzig, 1746. *Handbok for unga Fruntimmer*, by Ekenmark. Stockholm, 1826–28.

Latterly this manufacture has been protected and the workwomen carefully directed.

Far more curious are the laces made by the peasants of Dalecarlia, still retaining the patterns used in the rest of Europe two hundred years since. The broader [21] kinds, of which we give a woodcut (Fig. 117), are from Gaguef, that part of Dalecarlia where laces are mostly made and used. Married women wear them on their summer caps, much starched, as a shelter against the sun. Others, of an

Fig. 117.

DALECARLIAN LACE.

unbleached thread, are from Orsa. This lace is never washed, as it is considered an elegance to preserve this coffee-coloured tint. The firmness and solidity of these last laces are wonderful.

The specimens from Rättwik are narrow "seaming" laces of the lozenge pattern.

There is also a sort of plaiting used as a fringe, in the style of the Genoese macramè, from the ends of a small

---

[21] Some are twice the width of Fig. 117.

sheet which the peasants spread over their pillows. No improvement takes place in the designs. The Dalecarlian women do not make a trade of lace-making, they merely work to supply their own wants.[22]

Fig. 118 represents a lace collar worn by Gustavus Adolphus, a relic carefully preserved in the Northern Museum at Stockholm. On it is inscribed in Swedish : " This collar was worn by Gustaf Adolf, King of Sweden, and presented, together with his portrait, as a remembrance, in 1632, to Miss Jacobina Lauber, of Augsburg, because she was the most beautiful damsel present." In addition to this collar, there is preserved at the Royal Kladskammar at Stockholm a blood-stained shirt worn by Gustavus at the Battle of Dirschau, the collars and cuffs trimmed with lace of rich geometric pattern, the sleeves decorated with " seaming " lace.

In an adjoining case of the same collection are some splendid altar-cloths of ancient raised Spanish point, said to have been worked by the Swedish nuns previous to the suppression of the monasteries. A small escutcheon constantly repeated on the pattern of the most ancient specimens has the semblance of a water-lily leaf, the emblem of the Stures, leading one to believe they may have been of Swedish fabric, for many ladies of that illustrious house sought shelter from troublous times within the walls of the lace-making convent of Wadstena.

In the same cabinet is displayed, with others of more ordinary texture, a collar of raised Spanish guipure, worked by the Princesses Catherine and Marie, daughters of Duke Johan Adolf (brother of Charles X.). Though a creditable performance, yet it is far inferior to the lace of convent make. The making of this Spanish point formed a favourite amusement of the Swedish ladies of the seventeenth century : bed-hangings, coverlets, and toilets of their handiwork may still be found in the remote castles of the provinces. We have received the photograph of a flower from an old bed of Swedish lace —an heirloom in a Smaland castle of Count Trolle Bonde.

---

[22] For this information, with a collection of specimens, the author has to thank Madame Petre of Gefle.

Fig. 118.

Collar of Gustavus Adolphus.

PLATE LXXIV.

RUSSIAN.—Part of a long border setting forth a Procession.   Laces and embroidery in silk.
The lace is bobbin-made in thread.   Réseau similar to Valenciennes.   The Russian thread
is good quality linen.   Size of portion shown 18½ × 14 in.
The property of Madame Pogosky.

Photo by A. Dryden.

RUSSIA.

After his visit to Paris early in the eighteenth century, Peter the Great founded a manufacture of silk lace at Novgorod, which in the time of the Empress Elizabeth fell into decay. In the reign of Catherine II. there were twelve gold lace-makers at St. Petersburg, who were scarcely able to supply the demand. In Russia lace-making and embroidery go hand in hand, as in our early examples of embroidery, drawn-work, and cut-work combined. Lace-making was not a distinct industry ; the peasants, especially in Eastern Russia, made it in their houses to decorate, in conjunction with embroidery, towels, table-linen, shirts, and even the household linen, for which purpose it was purchased direct from the peasants by the inhabitants of the towns. Many will have seen the Russian towels in the International Exhibition of 1874, and have admired their quaint design and bright colours, with the curious line of red and blue thread running through the pattern of the lace. Darned netting and drawn-work appear, as elsewhere, to have been their earliest productions. The lace is loosely wrought on the pillow, the work simple, and requiring few bobbins to execute the vermiculated pattern which is its characteristic (Fig. 119, and Plates LXXII.–IV.).

The specimens vary very much in quality, but the patterns closely resemble one another, and are all of an oriental and barbaric character (Fig. 119).

In Nardendal, near Abo, in Finland, the natives offer to strangers small petticoats and toys of lace—a relic of the time when a nunnery of Cistercians flourished in the place.

Much of a simple design and coarse quality is made in Belev, Vologda, Riazan, Mzeresk. At Vologda a lace resembling torchon is made, with colours introduced, red, blue, and écru and white.[23] In some laces silks of various colours are employed. Pillow-lace has only been known in Russia for over a hundred years, and although the

[23] The Russian bobbins are interesting by reason of their archaic simplicity. Lacking any trace of decoration, whether suggested by sentimental fancy or artistic taste, they are purely utilitarian, mere sticks of wood, more or less straight and smooth, and six or seven inches long.

lace produced is effective, it is coarse in texture and crude in pattern. Late in the nineteenth century the Czarina gave her patronage to a school founded at Moscow, where Venetian needle-point laces have been copied, using the finest English thread, and needle-laces made after old Russian designs of the sixteenth century,[24] called *Point de Moscou.*

---

[24] A depôt has been opened in London, where Russian laces and embroidery of all kinds are shown.

Fig. 119.

RUSSIA.—Bobbin-made nineteenth century.

PLATE LXXV.

CAP. (FLEMISH OR GERMAN.)—The insertion is cut-work and needle-point. The lace is bobbin-made, and bears a resemblance to Plate XXVI., South Italian. Late seventeenth century. Length of lace about 12 in.

Photo by A. Dryden from private collection.

CHAPTER XXII.

ENGLAND TO QUEEN ELIZABETH.

" We weare most fantastical fashions than any nation under the sun doth, the French only excepted."—*Coryat's Crudities.* 1611.

IT would be a difficult matter for antiquaries to decide at what precise time lace, as we now define the word, first appears as an article of commerce in the annals of our country.

As early as the reign of Edward III.,[1] the excessive luxury of veils, worn even by servant girls, excited the indignation of the Government, who, in an Act, dated 1363, forbade them to be worn of silk, or of any other material, " mes soulement de fil fait deinz le Roialme," for which veils no one was to pay more than the sum of tenpence. Of what stuff these thread veils were composed we have no record ; probably they were a sort of network, similar to the caul of Queen Philippa, as we see represented on her tomb.[2] That a sort of crochet decoration used for edging was already made, we may infer from the monumental effigies of the day.[3] The purse of the carpenter is described, too, in Chaucer, as " purled with latoun," a kind of metal or wire lace, similar to that found at Herculaneum, and made in some parts of Europe to a recent period.

M. Aubry refers to a commercial treaty of 1390, between England and the city of Bruges, as the earliest mention of lace. This said treaty we cannot find in Rymer, Dumont,

---

[1] *Rot. Parl.* 37 *Edw. III.* Printed. P. 278, Col. 2, No. 26.

[2] See her monument in Westminster Abbey.—Sandford's *Genealogical History*.

[3] " Blanche, Duchess of Lancaster, wife of John of Gaunt, wears a quilted silk cap with a three-pointed border of broad lace network." (Sandford. St. Paul's monument, after Dugdale.) " Elizabeth, Duchess of Exeter, died 1425 (Sandford, p. 259), wore also a caul of network with a needlework edging."

or anywhere else. We have, as before alluded to, constant edicts concerning the gold wires and threads of " Cipre, Venys, Luk, and Jeane," of embroideries and suchlike, but no distinct allusion to " lace." [4]

According to Anderson, the first intimation of such an occupation being known in England is the complaint, made in 1454, by the women of the mystery of thread-working in London, in consequence of the importation of six foreign women, by which the manufacture of needlework [5] of thread and silk, not as yet understood, was introduced. These six women, probably Flemings, had brought over to England the cut-work or darning of the time, a work then unknown in this country.

All authors, up to the present period, refer to the well-known Act of Edward IV., [6] 1463, in which the entry of " laces, corses, ribans, fringes, de soie and de file, laces de file soie enfile," etc., are prohibited, as the first mention of " lace " in the public records.

The English edition of the Fœdera, as well as the statutes at large, freely translate these words as laces of thread, silk twined, laces of gold, etc. ; and the various writers on commerce and manufactures have accepted the definition as " lace," without troubling themselves to examine the question. [7] Some even go so far as to refer to a MS. in the Harleian Library, [8] giving " directions for making many sorts of laces, [9] which were in fashion in the times of King Henry VI.

---

[4] In the Statute 2 Rich. II. = 1378, merchant strangers are allowed to sell in gross and in retail " gold wire or silver wire " and other such small ware." Neither in this nor in the Treaty 13 Rich. II. = 1390, between England, the Count of Flanders, and " les bonnes Gentz des Trois bonnes villes de Flandres Gand, Brugges et Ipre (see Rymer), is there any mention of lace, which, even if fabricated, was of too little importance as an article of commerce to deserve mention save as other " small wares."

[5] Pins not yet being in common use, any lace would be called " work of the needle."

[6] 3 Edw. IV., cap. iv.

[7] " 1463. John Barett bequeaths to ' My Lady Walgrave, my musk ball of gold with ple and lace.

" ' Item, to John Eden, my o gr. of tawny silk with poynts of needle work —*opus punctatum.*' "—*Bury Wills and Inventories.*

[8] Bib. Harl. 2,320.

[9] Such as " Lace Bascon, Lace endented, Lace bordred on both syde, yn o syde, pykke Lace bordred, Lace Condrak, Lace Dawns, Lace Piol, Lace covert, Lace coverte doble, Lace compon coverte, Lace maskel, Lace cheyne brode, Las Cheveron, Lace Oundé, Grene dorge, Lace for Hattys," etc.

Another MS. of directions for making these same named laces is in the possession of the Vicar of Ipsden, Oxfordshire, and has been examined by the author through the kindness of Mr. W. Twopenny.

and Edward IV.," as a proof that lace was already well known, and formed the occupation of the "handcraftry"—as those who gained their livelihood by manual occupation were then termed—of the country. Now, the author has carefully examined this already quoted MS., in the principal letter of which is a damaged figure of a woman sitting and "making of lace," which is made by means of "bowys." [10] As regards the given directions, we defy anyone, save the most inveterate lover of crochet-work, to understand one word of its contents, beyond that it relates to some sort of twisted thread-work, and perhaps we might, in utter confusion of mind, have accepted the definition as given, had not another MS. of similar tenor, bearing date 1651, been also preserved in the British Museum. [11]

This second MS. gives specimens of the laces, such as they were, stitched side by side with the directions, which at once establishes the fact that the laces of silk and gold, laces of thread, were nothing more than braids or cords—the laces used with tags, commonly called "poynts" (the "ferrets" of Anne of Austria)—for fastening the dresses, as well as for ornament, previous to the introduction of pins.

In the Wardrobe Accounts of the time we have frequent notice of these "laces" and corses. "Laces de quir" (cuir) also appear in the Statutes, [12] which can only mean what we now term bootlaces, or something similar.

---

[10] Bows, loops.

[11] Additional MSS. No. 6,293, small quarto, ff. 38. It contains instructions for making various laces, letters and "edges," such as "diamond stiff, fly, cross, long S, figure of 8, spider, hart," etc., and at the end :—

" Heare may you see in Letters New
The Love of her that honoreth you.
    My love is this,
    Presented is
    The Love I owe
    I cannot showe,
    The fall of Kings
    Confusion bringes
Not the vallyou but the Love
When this you see
    Remember me."

In the British Museum (Lansdowne Roll, No. 22) is a third MS. on the same subject, a parchment roll written about the time of Charles I., contain-

ing rules and directions for executing various kinds of sampler-work, to be wrought in letters, etc., by means of coloured strings or bows. It has a sort of title in these words, " To know the use of this Booke it is two folkes worke," meaning that the works are to be done by two persons.

Probably of this work was the " Brede (braid) of divers colours, woven by Four Ladies," the subject of some verses by Waller begin-ning :—

"Twice twenty slender Virgins'
    Fingers twine
This curious web, where all their
    fancies shine.
As Nature them, so they this
    shade have wrought,
Soft as their Hands, and various
    as their Thoughts," etc.

[12] 1 Rich. III. = 1483. Act XII.

In the "Total of stuffs bought" for Edward IV.,[13] we have entries: "Laces made of ryban of sylk; two dozen laces, and a double lace of ryban"—"corses of sylk with laces and tassels of sylk," etc. Again, to Alice Claver, his sylkwoman, he pays for "two dozen laces and a double lace of sylk." These double laces of ribbon and silk were but plaited, a simple ornament still used by the peasant women in some countries of Europe. There must, however, be a beginning to everything, and these tag laces—some made round, others in zigzag, like the modern braids of ladies' work, others flat—in due course of time enriched with an edging, and a few stitches disposed according to rule, produced a rude lace; and these patterns, clumsy at first, were, after a season, improved upon.

From the time of Edward IV. downwards, statute on apparel followed upon statute, renewed for a number of years, bearing always the same expression, and nothing more definite.[14]

The Venetian galleys at an early period bore to England the goldwork of "Luk," Florence, "Jeane" and Venice. In our early Parliamentary records are many statutes on the subject. It is not, however, till the reign of Henry VII. that, according to Anderson, "Gold and thread lace came from Florence, Venice, and Genoa, and became an article of commerce. An Act was then passed to prevent the buyers of such commodities from selling for a pound weight a packet which does not contain twelve ounces, and the inside of the said gold, silver, and thread lace was to be of equal greatness of thread and goodness of colour as the outside thereof." [15]

The Italians were in the habit of giving short lengths, gold thread of bad quality, and were guilty of sundry other misdemeanours which greatly excited the wrath of the nation. The balance was not in England's favour. It was the cheating Venetians who first brought over their gold lace into England.

A warrant to the Keeper of the Great Wardrobe, in the

---

[13] *Privy Purse Expenses of Elizabeth of York*, and *Wardrobe Accounts of King Edward IV.*, by Sir H. Nicolas.

[14] 1 Rich. III. renews 3 Edw. IV.

for ten years, and that of Richard is continued by 19 Henry VII. for twenty years more.

[15] 4 Hen. VII. = 1488-9.

eighteenth year of King Henry's reign,[16] contains an order for "a mauntel lace of blewe silk and Venys gold, to be delivered for the use of our right dere and well-beloved Cosyn the King of Romayne"—Maximilian, who was made Knight of the Garter.[17]

If lace was really worn in the days of Henry VII., it was probably either of gold or silk, as one of the last Acts of that monarch's reign, by which all foreign lace is prohibited, and "those who have it in their possession may keep it and wear it till Pentecost,"[18] was issued rather for the protection of the silk-women of the country than for the advantage of the ever-complaining "workers of the mysteries of thread-work."

On the 3rd of October, 1502, his Queen Elizabeth of York pays to one Master Bonner, at Langley, for laces, rybands, etc., 40*s.*; and again, in the same year, 38*s.* 7*d.* to Dame Margrette Cotton, for "hosyn, laces, sope, and other necessaries for the Lords Henry Courtenay, Edward, and the Lady Margrette, their sister." A considerable sum is also paid to Fryer Hercules for gold of Venys, gold of Danmarke, and making a lace for the King's mantell of the Garter.[19]

It is towards the early part of Henry VIII.'s reign that the "Actes of Apparell"[20] first mention the novel luxury of shirts and partlets, "garded and pynched,"[21] in addition to clothes decorated in a similar manner, all of which are

---

[16] P.R.O. The same Warrant contains an order to deliver "for the use and wearing of our right dere daughter the Lady Mary," together with a black velvet gown, scarlet petticoat, etc., "a nounce of lace for her kyrtel," and a thousand "pynnes."

[17] In the list of the late King Henry's plate, made 1543, we have some curious entries, in which the term lace appears :—

"Item, oone picture of a woman made of erthe with a carnacion Roobe knitt with a knott in the lefte shoulder and bare hedid with her heere rowlid up with a white lace sett in a boxe of wodde.

"Item, oone picture of a woman made of erthe with a carnacōn garment after the Inglishe tyer and bareheddid with her heare rowled up with a white lace sett in a boxe of wodde."— P. R. O.

[18] 19 Hen. VII. = 1504.

[19] Sir H. Nicolas.

[20] Statute 1 Hen. VIII. = 1509-10. An act agaynst wearing of costly Apparell, and again, 6 Hen. VIII. = 1514-15.

[21] "Gard, to trim with lace."— Cotgrave.

"No less than crimson velvet did him grace,
All garded and regarded with gold lace."—Samuel Rowlands, *A Pair of Spy-Knaves.*

"I do forsake these 'broidered gardes,
And all the fashions new."
—The Queen in *King Cambisis,*
circ. 1615.

forbidden to be worn by anyone under the degree of a knight.[22] In the year 1517 there had been a serious insurrection of the London apprentices against the numerous foreign tradesmen who already infested the land, which, followed up by the never-ending complaints of the workers of the mysteries of needlework, induced the king to ordain the wearing of such " myxte joyned, garded or browdered "[23] articles of lynnen cloth be only allowed when the same be wrought within " this realm of England, Wales, Berwick, Calais, or the Marches." [24]

The earliest record we find of laced linen is in the Inventory of Sir Thomas L'Estrange, of Hunstanton, County of Norfolk, 1519, where it is entered, " 3 elles of Holland cloth, for a shirte for hym, 6 shillings," with " a yard of lace for hym, 8*d*."

In a MS. called " The Boke of Curtasye "—a sort of treatise on etiquette, in which all grades of society are taught their duties—the chamberlain is commanded to provide for his master's uprising, a " clene shirte," bordered with lace and curiously adorned with needlework.

The correspondence, too, of Honor. Lady Lisle, seized by Henry VIII.[25] as treasonous and dangerous to the State, embraces a hot correspondence with one Sœur Antoinette de Sevenges, a nun milliner of Dunkirk, on the important subject of nightcaps,[26] one half dozen of which, she complains, are far too wide behind, and not of the lozenge (cut) work pattern she had selected. The nightcaps were in consequence to be changed.

Anne Basset, daughter of the said Lady Lisle, educated in a French convent, writes earnestly begging for an " edge

---

[22] Under forfeiture of the same shirt and a fine of 40 shillings.

[23] 7 Hen. VIII. = 1515–16.—"Thacte of Apparell."

[24] 24 Hen. VIII. = 1532–33.—" An Act for Reformation of excess in Apparel."

[25] In 1539.

[26] Lisle. *Corr.* Vol. i., p. 64. P.R.O. Lord Lisle was Governor of Calais, whence the letter is dated. Honor. Lylle to Madame Antoinette de Sevenges, à Dunkerke.

" Madame,—Je ne vous eusse vollu envoier ceste demi dousaine pour changier nestoit que tous celles que menvoiez dernierement sont trop larges, et une dousaine estoit de cestuy ouvrage dont jestis esmerveillé, veu que je vous avois escript que menvoissiez de louvrage aux lozenges, vous priant que la demy dousaine que menvoierez pour ceste demy dousaine soient du dict ouvrage de lozenge, et quil soient plus estroictes mesmement par devant nonobstant que lexemple est au contraire."

of perle [27] for her coif and a tablete (tablier) to ware." Her sister Mary, too, gratefully expresses her thanks to her mother, in the same year,[28] for the "laced gloves you sent me by bearer." Calais was still an English possession, and her products, like those of the Scotch Border fortresses, were held as such.[29]

Lace still appears but sparingly on the scene. Among the Privy Purse expenses of the king in 1530,[30] we find five shillings and eightpence paid to Richard Cecyll,[31] Groom of the Robes, for eight pieces of " yelowe lace, bought for the King's Grace." We have, too, in the Harleian Inventory,[32] a coif laid over with passamyne of gold and silver.

These " Acts of Apparell," as regards foreign imports, are, however, somewhat set aside towards the year 1546, when Henry grants a licence in favour of two Florentine merchants to export for three years' time, together with other matters, " all manner of fryngys and passements wrought with gold or silver, or otherwise, and all other new gentillesses of what facyon or value soever they may be, for the pleasure of our dearest wyeff the Queen, our nobles, gentlemen, and others." [33] The king, however, reserves to himself the first view of their merchandise, with the privilege of selecting anything he may please for his own private use, before their wares were hawked about the country. The said " dearest wyeff," from the date of the Act, must have been Katherine Parr ; her predecessor, Katherine Howard, had for some four years slept headless in the vaults of the White Tower chapel. Of these " gentillesses " the king now began to avail himself. He selects " trunk sleeves of redd cloth of gold with cut-work ; " knitted gloves of silk, and " handkerchers " edged with gold and silver ; his towels are

---

[27] Among the marriage clothes of Mary Neville, who espoused George Clifton, 1536, is :—

" A neyge of perle, £1 4s. 0d.

In the pictures, at Hampton Court Palace, of Queens Mary and Elizabeth, and another of Francis II., all as children, their ruffs are edged with a very narrow purl.

[28] 1538. Lisle. *Corr.* (P.R.O.)

[29] See Note 24.

[30] Privy Purse Ex. Hen. VIII. 1529-32. Sir H. Nicolas.

[31] Father of Lord Burleigh. There are other similar entries :—" 8 pieces of yellow lace, 9s. 4d." Also, " green silk lace."

1632, " green silk lace " occurs again, as trimming a pair of French shoes in a " Bill of shoes for Sir Francis Windebank and family."—State Papers Dom. Vol. 221. P.R.O.

[32] " Inv. of Hen. VIII. and 4 Edw. VI." Harl. MS. 1419, A and B.

[33] 38 Hen. VIII.=1546. Rymer's *Fœdera.* Vol. xv., p. 105.

of diaper, " with Stafford knots," or " knots and roses ;" he
has " coverpanes of fyne diaper of Adam and Eve garnished
about with a narrow passamayne of Venice gold and silver ;
handkerchers of Holland, frynged with Venice gold, redd
and white silk," others of " Flanders worke," and his shaving
cloths trimmed in like fashion.[34] The merchandise of the
two Florentines had found vast favour in the royal eyes.
Though these articles were imported for " our dere wyeff's
sake," beyond a " perle edging " to the coif of the Duchess
of Suffolk, and a similar adornment to the tucker of Jane
Seymour,[35] lace seems to have been little employed for female
decoration during the reign of King Henry VIII.

That it was used for the adornment of the ministers of

Fig. 120.

FISHER, BISHOP OF ROCHESTER. + 1535.—(M. de Versailles.)

the Church we have ample evidence.   M. Aubry states having
seen in London lace belonging to Cardinal Wolsey.   On this
matter we have no information ; but we know the surplices
were ornamented round the neck, shoulders, and sleeves with
" white work " and cut-work [36] at this period.   The specimens
we give (Figs. 120, 121) are from a portrait formerly in
the Library of the Sorbonne, now transferred to Versailles,
of Fisher, Bishop of Rochester, Cardinal Fisher as he is
styled—his cardinal's hat arriving at Dover at the very
moment the head that was to wear it had fallen at Tower
Hill.

About this time, too, lace gradually dawns upon us in

[34] Harl. MS. 1419. *Passim.*   mont and Fletcher. *The Spanish*
[35] See Holbein's portraits.   *Curate.*
[36] " The old cut-work cope."—Beau-

PLATE LXXVI.

ENGLISH. CUT-WORK AND NEEDLE-POINT.—Cross said
to have belonged to Cardinal Wolsey.

PLATE LXXVII.

ENGLISH. DEVONSHIRE " TROLLY."—First part of nineteenth century.
Photos by A. Dryden from private collection.

PLATE LXXVIII.

MARIE DE LORRAINE, 1515–1560.   DAUGHTER OF DUC DE GUISE, MARRIED JAMES V.
OF SCOTLAND, 1538.—This picture was probably painted before she left France, by an
unknown French artist.   National Portrait Gallery.

Photo by Walker and Cockerell.

the church inventories. Among the churchwardens' accounts of St. Mary-at-Hill, date 1554, we find entered a charge of 3*s.* for making " the Bishopp's (boy bishop) myter with stuff and lace." [37] The richly-laced corporax cloths and church linen are sent to be washed by the " Lady Ancress," an ecclesiastical washerwoman, who is paid by the churchwardens of St. Margaret's, Westminster, the sum of 8*d.* ; this Lady Ancress, or Anchoress, being some worn-out old nun who, since the dissolution of the religious houses, eked out an existence by the art she had once practised within the walls of her convent.

At the burial of King Edward VI., Sir Edward Waldgrave

Fig. 121.

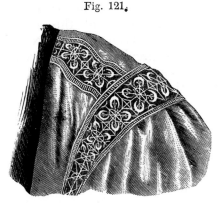

FISHER, BISHOP OF ROCHESTER.—(M. de Versailles.)

enters on his account a charge of fifty yards of gold passement lace for garnishing the pillars of the church.

The sumptuary laws of Henry VIII. were again renewed by Queen Mary : [38] in them ruffles made or wrought out of England, commonly called cut-work, are forbidden to anyone under the degree of a baron ; while to women of a station beneath that of a knight's wife, all wreath lace or passement lace of gold and silver with sleeves, partlet or linen trimmed

---

[37] We read, too, of " 3 kyrcheys y' was given to the kyrk wash," large as a woman's hood worn at a funeral, highly ornamented with the needle by pious women, and given to be sold for the good of the impoverished church, for which the churchwardens of St. Michael, Spurr Gate, York, received the sum of 5*s.*

[38] 1 and 2 Ph. and Mary.

with purles of gold and silver, or white-works, alias cut-works, etc., made beyond the sea, is strictly prohibited.   These articles were, it seems, of Flemish origin, for among the New Year's Gifts presented to Queen Mary, 1556, we find enumerated as given by Lady Jane Seymour, " a fair smock of white work,[39] Flanders making."   Lace, too, is now in more general use, for on the same auspicious occasion, Mrs. Penne, King Edward's nurse, gave " six handkerchers edged with passamayne of golde and silke." [40]   Two years previous to these New Year's Gifts, Sir Thomas Wyatt is described as wearing, at his execution, " on his head a faire hat of velvet, with broad bone-work lace about it." [41]

Lace now seems to be called indifferently purle, passamayne or bone-work, the two first-mentioned terms occurring most frequently.   The origin of this last appellation is generally stated to have been derived from the custom of using sheep's trotters previous to the invention of wooden bobbins.   Fuller so explains it, and the various dictionaries have followed his theory.   The Devonshire lace-makers, on the other hand, deriving their knowledge from tradition, declare that when lace-making was first introduced into their county, pins,[42] so indispensable to their art, being then sold at a price far beyond their means, the lace-makers, mostly the wives of fishermen living along the coast, adopted the

---

[39] " White work " appears also among Queen Elizabeth's New Year's Gifts:—
" 1578.   Lady Ratcliff.   A veil of white work, with spangles and small bone lace of silver.   A swete bag, being of changeable silk, with a small bone lace of gold.
" 1589.   Lady Shandowes (Chandos). A cushion cloth of lawne wrought with whitework of branches and trees, edged with bone work, wrought with crowns."
—Nichols' *Royal Progresses.*
[40] Roll of New Year's Gifts.   1556.
[41] Stowe.   *Queen   Mary.*   An. 1554.
[42] It is not known when brass wire pins were first made in England, but it must have been before 1543, in which year a Statute was passed (35 Hen. VIII.) entitled, " An Act for the True Making of Pynnes," in which the price is fixed not to exceed 6s. 8d. per 1,000.

By an Act of Rich. III. the importation of pins was prohibited.   The early pins were of boxwood, bone, bronze or silver.   In 1347 (*Liber Garderobœ*, 12–16 Edw. III. P. R. O.) we have a charge for 12,000 pins for the trousseau of Joanna, daughter of Edward III., betrothed to Peter the Cruel.   The young Princess probably escaped a miserable married life by her decease of the black death at Bordeaux when on her way to Castille.

The annual import of pins in the time of Elizabeth amounted to £3,297.
—State Papers, Dom., Eliz.   Vol. viii. P. R. O.

In Eliz., Q. of Bohemia's Expenses, we find: " Dix mille espingles dans un papier, 4 florins."—Ger. Corr. No. 41.   P. R. O.

" In Holland pillow-lace is called Pinwork lace—Gespelde-werkte kant." —Sewell's *Eng. and Dutch Dict.*

bones of fish, which, pared and cut into regular lengths, fully answered as a substitute. This explanation would seem more probable than that of employing sheep's trotters for bobbins, which, as from 300 to 400 are often used at one time on a pillow, must have been both heavy and cumbersome. Even at the present day pins made from chicken bones continue to be employed in Spain ; and bone pins are still used in Portugal.[43]

Shakespeare, in *Twelfth-Night*, speaks of

> " The spinsters and the knitters in the sun,
> And the free maids that weave their threads with bone."

" Bone " lace [44] constantly appears in the wardrobe accounts, while bobbin lace [45] is of less frequent occurrence.

Among the New Year's Gifts presented to Queen Elizabeth, we have from the Lady Paget "a petticoat of cloth of gold stayned black and white, with a bone lace of gold and spangles, like the wayves of the sea"; a most astounding article, with other entries no less remarkable, but too numerous to cite.

---

[43] An elderly woman informed the author that she recollects in her youth, when she learned to make Honiton point of an ancient teacher of the parish, bone pins were still employed. They were in use until a recent period, and renounced only on account of their costliness. The author purchased of a Devonshire lace-maker one, bearing date 1829, with the name tatooed into the bone, the gift of some long-forgotten youth to her grandmother. These bone or wood bobbins, some ornamented with glass beads — the more ancient with silver let in—are the calendar of a lace-worker's life. One records her first appearance at a neighbouring fair or May meeting ; a second was the first gift of her good man, long cold in his grave ; a third the first prize brought home by her child from the dame school, and proudly added to her mother's cushion : one and all, as she sits weaving her threads, are memories of bygone days of hopes and fears, of joys and sorrows; and, though many a sigh it calls forth, she cherishes her well-worn cushion as an old friend, and works away, her present labour lightened by the memory of the past.

[44] Surtees' *Wills and Inv.*

" Hearing bone lace value 5*s.* 4*d.*" is mentioned " in y⁰ shoppe of John Johnston, of Darlington, merchant."

[45] 1578. " James Backhouse, of Kirby in Lonsdale. Bobbin lace, 6*s.* per ounce."

1597. " John Farbeck, of Durham. In y⁰ Shoppe, 4 oz. & ½ of Bobbing lace, 6*s.* 4*d.*"—*Ibid.*

" Bobbin" lace is noted in the Royal Inventories, but not so frequently as " bone."

" Laqueo. . . . fact. super lez bobbins."—G. W. A. Eliz., 27 and 28. P. R. O.

" Three peces teniar bobbin."—*Ibid.* Car. I., vi.

" One pece of bobin lace, 2*s.*," occurs frequently in the accounts of Lord Compton, afterwards Earl of Northampton, Master of the Wardrobe of Prince Charles.—Roll, 1622-23, Extraordinary Expenses, and others. P. R. O.

In the marriage accounts of Prince Charles [46] we have charged 150 yards of bone lace [47] for six extraordinary ruffs and twelve pairs of cuffs, against the projected Spanish marriage. The lace was at 9s. a yard. Sum total, £67 10s. [48] Bone lace is mentioned in the catalogue of King Charles I.'s pictures, drawn up by Vanderdort, [49] where James I. is described " without a hat, in a bone lace falling band." [50]

Setting aside wardrobe accounts and inventories, the term constantly appears both in the literature and the plays of the seventeenth century.

" Buy some quoifs, handkerchiefs, or very good bone lace, mistress ? "

cries the pert sempstress when she enters with her basket of wares, in Green's *Tu Quoque*, [51] showing it to have been at that time the usual designation.

" You taught her to make shirts and bone lace,"

says someone in the *City Madam*. [52]

Again, describing a thrifty wife, Loveless, in *The Scornful Lady*, [53] exclaims—

" She cuts cambric to a thread, weaves bone lace, and quilts balls admirably."

The same term is used in the *Tatler* [54] and *Spectator*, [55]

---

[46] In the Ward. Acc. of his brother, Prince Henry, 1607, and the Warrant to the G. Ward., on his sister the Princess Elizabeth's marriage, 1612–13, " bone " lace is in endless quantities.

Bobbin lace appears invariably distinguished from bone lace, both being mentioned in the same inventory. The author one day showed an old Vandyke Italian edging to a Devonshire lace-worker, asking her if she could make it. " I think I can," she answered ; " it is bobbin lace." On inquiring the distinction, she said : " Bobbin lace is made with a coarse thread, and in its manufacture we use long bobbins instead of the boxwood of ordinary size, which would not hold the necessary quantity of this thread, though sufficient for the quality used in making Honiton flowers and Trolly lace."—Mrs. Palliser.

[47] Randle Holme, in his enumeration of ' terms used in arts, gives : " Bone lace, wrought with pegs."

The materials used for bobbins in Italy have been already mentioned.

[48] Lord Compton. " Extraordinary Expenses of the Wardrobe of K. Charles, before and after he was King."—Roll, 1622–26. P. R. O.

[49] An. 1635.

[50] A miniature of Old Hilliard, now in the possession of his Grace the Duke of Hamilton.

[51] 1614.

[52] Massinger. 1612.

[53] Beaumont and Fletcher.

[54] " The things you follow and make songs on now, should be sent to knit, or sit down to bobbins or bone-lace."— *Tatler*.

[55] " We destroy the symmetry of the human figure, and foolishly combine to call off the eye from great and real beauties to childish gewgaw ribbands and bone-lace."—*Spectator*.

and in the list of prizes given, in 1752, by the Society of Anti-Gallicans, we find, " Six pieces of bone lace for men's ruffles." It continued to be applied in the Acts of Parliament and notices relative to lace, nearly to the end of the eighteenth century.[56] After a time, the sheep's trotters or bones having been universally replaced by bobbins of turned box-wood, the term fell into disuse, though it is still retained in Belgium and Germany.

From the reign of Queen Mary onwards, frequent mention is made of parchment lace (see pp. 297–298), a term most generally associated with gold and silver, otherwise we should consider it as merely referring to needle-made lace, which is worked on a parchment pattern.

But to return to Queen Mary Tudor. We have among the " late Queen Mary's clothes " an entry of " compas "[57] lace ; probably an early name for lace of geometric pattern. Open-work edging of gold and passamaine lace also occur ; and on her gala robes lace of " Venys gold," as well as " vales of black network," a fabric to which her sister, Queen Elizabeth, was most partial ; partlets,[58] dressings, shadowes, and pynners " de opere rete," appearing constantly in her accounts.[59]

It was at this period, during the reign of Henry VIII. and Mary, a peculiar and universally prevalent fashion, varying in degrees of eccentricity and extravagance, to slash the garment so as to show glimpses of some contrasting underdress. Dresses thus slashed, or puffed, banded, " pinched," stiff with heavy gold and metal braid or embroidery, required but little additional adornment of lace.[60] The falling collar, which was worn in the early part of the sixteenth century, before the Elizabethan ruff (introduced from France about 1560), was, however, frequently edged with lace of geometric pattern.

Early in the sixteenth century the dresses of the ladies

---

[56] It is used in Walpole's *New British Traveller*. 1784.

[57] Haliwell gives compas as " a circle ; Anglo-Norman."

[58] Partlet, a small ruff or neck-band.

[59] " Eidem pro 4 pec' de opera Rhet' bon' florat' in forma oper' sciss' ad 24s., £4 16s."—G. W. A. Eliz., 43 to 44.

1578–79. New Year's Gifts. Baroness Shandowes. "A vail of black network flourished with flowers of silver and a small bone-lace."—Nichols.

[60] *Encyclopædia Britannica.* Art. *Costume.* Sixteenth Century.

fitted closely to the figure, with long skirts open in front to display the underdress ; and were made low and cut square about the neck. Sometimes, however, the dresses were worn high with short waists and a small falling collar. Somewhat later, when the dresses were made open at the girdle, a partlet—a kind of habit-shirt—was worn beneath them, and carried to the throat.[61]

Entries of lace in the wardrobe accounts are, however, few and inconsiderable until the reign of Queen Elizabeth.

---

[61] *Encyclopædia Britannica.* Art. *Costume.* Sixteenth century.

CHAPTER XXIII.

QUEEN ELIZABETH.

"By land and sea a Virgin Queen I reign,
And spurn to dust both Antichrist and Spain." –Old Masque.

"Tell me, Dorinda, why so gay?
Why such embroidery, fringe and lace?
Can any dresses find a way
To stop the approaches of decay
And mend a ruined face?"—Lord Dorset

UP to the present time our mention of lace, both in the Statutes and the Royal Wardrobe Accounts, has been but scanty. Suddenly, in the days of the Virgin Queen, both the Privy Expenses and the Inventories of New Year's Gifts overflow with notices of passaments, drawn-work, cut-work, crown lace,[1] bone lace for ruffs, Spanish chain, byas,[2] parchment, hollow,[3] billament,[4] and diamond

---

[1] Crown lace—so called from the pattern being worked on a succession of crowns sometimes intermixed with acorns or roses. A relic of this lace may still be found in the "faux galon" sold by the German Jews, for the decoration of fancy dresses and theatrical purposes. It is frequently mentioned. We have:—

"12 yards laquei, called crown lace of black gold and silk."—G. W. A. Eliz. 4 & 5.

"18 yards crown lace purled with one wreath on one side."—*Ibid.* 5 & 6.

[2] "11 virgis laquei Byas."—*Ibid.* 29 & 30.

[3] Hemming and edging 8 yards of ruff of cambric with white lace called hollow lace, and various entries of Spanish lace, Fringe, Black chain, Diamond, knotted, hollow, and others, are scattered through the earlier

Wardrobe Accounts of Queen Elizabeth.

The accounts of the Keepers of the Great Wardrobe, which we shall have occasion so frequently to cite, are now deposited in the Public Record Office, to which place they were transferred from the Audit Office in 1859. They extend from the 1 Elizabeth = 1558 to Oct. 10, 1781, and comprise 160 volumes, written in Latin until 1730–31, when the account appears in English, and is continued so to the end. 1748–49 is the last account in which the items are given.

[4] Eliz. 30 & 31. Billament lace occurs both in the "shoppes" and inventories of the day. Among the list of foreigners settled in the City of London in 1571 (State Papers, Dom., Eliz. Vol 84. P.R.O.), are : William Crutall, "useth the craft of making

lace [5] in endless, and to us, we must own, most incomprehensible variety.

The Surtees' *Wills and Inventories* add to our list the laces Waborne [6] and many others. Lace was no longer confined to the court and high nobility, but, as these inventories show, it had already found its way into the general shops and stores of the provincial towns. In that of John Johnston, merchant, of Darlington, already cited, we have twelve yards of " loom " lace, value four shillings, black silk lace, " statute " lace, etc., all mixed up with entries of pepper, hornbooks, sugar-candy, and spangles. About the same date, in the inventory taken after the death of James Backhouse, of Kirby-in-Lonsdale, are found enumerated " In y[e] great shoppe," thread lace at 16*s.* per gross ; four dozen and four " pyrled " lace, four shillings ; four quarterns of statching (stitching or seaming ?) lace ; lace edging ; crown lace ; hollow lace ; copper lace ; gold and silver chean (chain) lace, etc. This last-mentioned merchant's store appears to have been one of the best-furnished provincial shops of the period. That of John Farbeck, of Durham, mercer, taken thirty years later, adds to our list seventy-eight yards of velvet lace, coloured silk, chayne lace, "coorld" lace, petticoat lace, all cheek by jowl with Venys gold and turpentine.

To follow the " stitches " and " works " quoted in the Wardrobe Accounts of Elizabeth—all made out in Latin, of which we sincerely trust, for the honour of Ascham, the

---

byllament lace " ; Rich. Thomas, Dutch, " a worker of Billament lace."

In 1573 a country gentleman, by his will deposited in the Prerogative Court of Canterbury (Brayley and Britton's *Graphic Illustrations*), bequeaths : " To my son Tyble my short gown faced with wolf skin and laid with Billements lace."

In John Johnston's shop we have : " 3 doz. of velvet Billemunt lace, 12*s.*" In that of John Farbeck, 9 yards of the same. (Surtees' *Wills and Inv.*) Widow Chapman of Newcastle's inventory, 1533, contains : " One old cassock of broad cloth, with billements lace, 10*s.*" (*Ibid.*)

[5] 95 dozen rich silver double diamond and cross laces occur also in the *Extraordinary Expenses for Prince Charles's Journey to Spain.* 1623.— P. R. O.

[6] 1571. " In y[e] Great Shop, 8 peces of ' waborne ' lace, 16*d.*"—*Mr. John Wilkinson's Goods, of Newcastle, Merchant.*

1580. " 100 Gross and a half of ' waborne ' lace."—*Inv. of Cuthbert Ellyson.*

1549. John de Tronch, Abbot of Kilmainham Priory, is condemned to pay 100 marks fine for detaining 2 lbs. of Waborne thread, value 3*s.*, and other articles, the property of W. Sacy.

Queen herself was guiltless—would be but as the inventory of a haberdasher's shop.

We have white stitch, "opus ret' alb," of which she had a kirtle, "pro le hemmynge et edginge" of which, with "laqueo coronat' de auro et arg'"—gold and silver crown lace—and "laqueo alb' lat' bon' operat' super css'"—broad white lace worked upon bone—she pays the sum of 35s.[7]

Then there is the Spanish stitch, already mentioned as introduced by Queen Katherine, and true stitch,[8] laid-work,[9] net-work, black-work,[10] white-work, and cut-work.

Of chain-stitch we have many entries, such as Six caules of knot-work, worked with chain-stitch and bound "cum tapem" (tape), of sister's (nun's) thread.[11] A scarf of white stitch-work appears also among the New Year's Gifts.

As regards the use, however, of these ornaments, the Queen stood no nonsense. Luxury for herself was quite a different affair from that of the people ; for, on finding that the London apprentices had adopted the white stitching and garding as a decoration for their collars, she put a stop to all such finery by ordering[12] the first transgressor to be publicly whipped in the hall of his Company.

Laid-work, which maybe answers to our modern plumetis, or simply signified a braid-work, adorned the royal garters, "Frauncie," which worked "cum laidwork," stitched and trimmed "in ambobus lateribus" with gold and silver lace, from which hung silver pendants, "tufted cum serico color," cost her Majesty thirty-three shillings the pair.[13]

---

[7] G. W. A. Eliz. 16 & 17.

[8] "Eidem pro 6 manuterg' de camerick operat' cum serico nigra trustich," etc.—G. W. A. Eliz. 41 & 42, and, again, 44.

[9] 1572. Inventory of Thomas Swinburne of Ealingham, Esq.

"His Apparell."

"A wellwett cote layd with silver las.

"A satten doullet layd with silver las.

"A payr of wellwett sleeves layd with silver las."—Surtees' *Wills and Inv.*

[10] New Year's Gifts. Lady Mary Sidney. "A smock and two pillow beres of cameryck wrought with black-work and edged with a broad bone-lace of black sylke."

[11] "Eidem pro 6 caules alb' nodat opat' cu' le chainestich et ligat' cu' tape de filo soror, ad 14s., 4l. 4s."—G. W. A. Eliz. 41 & 42.

Also in the last year of her reign (1602) we find :—

"Six fine net caules flourished with chaine stitch with sister's thread."—Wardrobe Accounts. B. M. Add. MSS. No. 5751.

[12] In 1583.

[13] G. W. A. Eliz. 38 & 39. We have it also on ruffs.

"Eidem pro 2 sutes de lez ruffs bon' de la lawne operat' in le laid work et edged cum ten' bon' ad 70s. per pec', 7l."—G. W. A. Eliz. 43 & 44.

The description of these right royal articles appears to have given as much trouble to describe as it does ourselves to translate the meaning of her accountant.

The drawn-work, "opus tract'," seems to have been but a drawing of thread worked over silk. We have smocks thus wrought and decorated " cum lez ruffs et wrestbands." [14]

In addition to the already enumerated laces of Queen Elizabeth are the bride laces of Coventry blue,[15] worn and given to the guests at weddings, mentioned in the *Masques* of Ben Jonson : [16]—

"CLOD.—And I have lost, beside my purse, my best bride-lace I had at Joan Turnips' wedding.
"FRANCES.—Ay, and I have lost my thimble and a skein of Coventry blue I had to work Gregory Litchfield a handkerchief."

When the Queen visited Kenilworth in 1577, a Bridall took place for the pastime of her Majesty. "First," writes the Chancellor, "came all the lusty lads and bold bachelors of the parish, every wight with his blue bridesman's bride lace upon a braunch of green broom." What these bride laces exactly were we cannot now tell. They continued in fashion till the Puritans put down all festivals, ruined the

---

[14] G. W. A. Eliz., last year of her reign. Again—
1600. " Drawing and working with black silk drawne worke, five smocks of fine holland cloth."—B. M. Add. MSS. No. 5751.
" These Holland smocks as white as snow,
And gorgets brave with drawn-work wrought."
—*Pleasant Quippes for Upstart New-fangled Gentlewomen.* 1596.
[15] As early as 1485 we have in the inventory of St. Mary-at-Hill, " An altar cloth of diaper, garnished with 3 blue Kays (St. Peter's) at each end." All the church linen seems to have been embroidered in blue thread, and so appears to have been the smocks and other linen.
Jenkin, speaking of his sweetheart, says: " She gave me a shirt collar, wrought over with no counterfeit stuff."
GEORGE: " What ! was it gold ? "
JENKIN: " Nay, 'twas better than gold."

GEORGE : " What was it ? "
JENKIN : " Right Coventry blue."—*Pinner of Wakefield.* 1599.
" It was a simple napkin wrought with Coventry blue."—*Laugh and Lie Downe, or the Worlde's Folly.* 1605.
" Though he perfume the table with rose cake or appropriate bone-lace and Coventry blue," writes Stephens in his *Satirical Essays.* 1615.
In the inventory of Mary Stuart, taken at Fotheringay, after her death, we have: " Furniture for a bedd of black velvet, garnished with Bleue lace. In the care of Rallay, *alias* Beauregard."
This blue lace is still to be found on baptismal garments which have been preserved in old families on the Continent and in England.
[16] The widow of the famous clothier, called Jack of Newbury, is described when a bride as "led to church between two boys with bride laces and rosemary tied about their sleeves."

commerce of Coventry, and the fabric of blue thread ceased for ever. It was probably a showy kind of coarse trimming, like that implied by Mopsa in the *Winter's Tale*, when she says—

"You promised me a tawdry lace: "[17]

articles which, judging from the song of Autolycus—

"Will you buy any tape,
Or lace for your cape?"

were already hawked about among the pedlars' wares throughout the country : one of the "many laces" mentioned by Shakespeare.[18]

Dismissing, then, her stitches, her laces, and the 3,000 gowns she left in her wardrobe behind her—for, as Shakespeare says, "Fashion wears out more apparel than the man"[19]—we must confine ourselves to those articles immediately under our notice, cut-work, bone lace, and purle.

Cut-work—"opus scissum," as it is termed by the Keeper of the Great Wardrobe—was used by Queen Elizabeth to the greatest extent. She wore it on her ruffs, "with lilies of the like, set with small seed pearl"; on her doublets, "flourished with squares of silver owes"; on her forepart of lawn, "flourished with silver and spangles";[20] on her cushion-

---

[17] "Tawdry. As Dr. Henshaw and Skinner suppose, of knots and ribbons, bought at a fair held in St. Audrey's Chapel; fine, without grace or elegance."—*Bailey's Dict.* 1764.

Southey (*Omniana.* Vol. i., p. 8) says :—

"It was formerly the custom in England for women to wear a necklace of fine silk called Tawdry lace, from St. Audrey.

"She had in her youth been used to wear carcanets of jewels, and being afterwards tormented with violent pains in the neck, was wont to say, that Heaven, in his mercy, had thus punished her for her love of vanity. She died of a swelling in her neck. Audry (the same as Ethelrede) was daughter of King Anna, who founded the Abbey of Ely."

Spenser in the *Shepherd's Calender*, has :—

"Bind your fillets faste
And gird in your waste
For more fineness with a tawdry lace; "

and in the *Faithful Shepherdess* of Beaumont and Fletcher, Amaryllis speaks of

"The primrose chaplet, tawdry lace and ring."

[18] A passage already quoted in *Much Ado about Nothing* shows us that, in Shakespeare's time, the term "to lace" was generally used as a verb, denoting to decorate with trimming. Margaret, the tiring woman, describes the Duchess of Milan's gown as of "Cloth o' gold, and cuts, and laced with silver."

[19] *Much Ado about Nothing.*

[20] New Year's Gifts of Mrs. Wyngfield, Lady Southwell, and Lady Willoughby. — *Nichols' Royal Progresses.*

cloths,[21] her veils, her tooth-cloths,[22] her smocks and her nightcaps.[23] All flourished, spangled, and edged in a manner so stupendous as to defy description. It was dizened out in one of these last-named articles [24] that young Gilbert Talbot, son of Lord Shrewsbury, caught a sight of the Queen while walking in the tilt-yard. Queen Elizabeth at the window in her nightcap! What a goodly sight! That evening she gave Talbot a good flap on the forehead, and told her chamberlain how the youth had seen her "unready and in her night stuff," and how ashamed she was thereof.

Cut-work first appears in the New Year's Offerings of 1577–8, where, among the most distinguished of the givers, we find the name of Sir Philip Sidney, who on one occasion offers to his royal mistress a suit of ruffs of cut-work, on another a smock—strange presents according to our modern ideas. We read, however, that the offering of the youthful hero gave no offence, but was most graciously received. Singular enough, there is no entry of cut-work in the Great Wardrobe Accounts before that of 1584–5, where there is a charge for mending, washing and starching a bodice and cuffs of good white lawn, worked in divers places with broad spaces of Italian cut-work, 20 shillings,[25] and another for the same operation to a veil of white cut-work trimmed with needle-work lace.[26] Cut-work was probably still a rarity; and really, on reading the quantity offered to Elizabeth on each recurring new year, there was scarcely any necessity for her to purchase it herself. By the year 1586–7 the Queen's stock had apparently diminished. Now, for the first time, she invests the sum of sixty shillings in six yards of good ruff lawn, well worked, with cut-work, and edged with good white lace.[27]

---

[21] " Mrs. Edmonds. A cushion cloth of lawn cutwork like leaves, and a few owes of silver."—New Year's Gifts.

" Eidem pro le edginge unius panni vocat' a quishion cloth de lawne alb' operat' cum spaces de opere sciss' et pro viii. virg' de Laquei alb' lat' operat' sup' oss' 33*s*. 4*d*."—G. W. A. Eliz. 31 & 32.

[22] " Mistress Twist, the Court laundress. Four toothcloths of Holland wrought with black silk and edged with bone lace of silver and black silk."—New Year's Gifts.

[23] " Lady Ratcliffe. A night coyf of white cutwork flourished with silver and set with spangles."—*Ibid.*

[24] " Cropson. A night coyf of cameryk cutwork and spangells, with a forehead cloth, and a night border of cutwork with bone lace."—*Ibid.* 1577–8.

[25] " Eidem pro emendac̄ lavacione et starching unius par' corpor' (stays) et manic' de lawne alb' bon' deorsum operat' in diversis locis cum spaciis Lat' de operibus Italic' sciss̄ 20*sh*."—G. W. A. Eliz. 26–27.

[26] *Ibid.*

[27] *Ibid.* 28–29.

From this date the Great Wardrobe Accounts swarm with entries such as a "sut' de lez ruffes de lawne," with spaces of "opere sciss'," [28] "un' caule de lawne alb' sciss' cum le edge," of similar work; [29] a "toga cum traine de opere sciss';" [30] all minutely detailed in the most excruciating gibberish. Sometimes the cut-work is of Italian [31] fabric, sometimes of Flanders; [32] the ruffs edged with bone lace, [33] needle lace, [34] or purle. [35]

The needle lace is described as "curiously worked," "operat' cum acu curiose fact'," at 32s. the yard. [36] The dearest is specified as Italian. [37] We give a specimen (Coloured Plate XV.) of English workmanship, said to be of this period, which is very elaborate. [38]

The thread used for lace is termed "filo soror," or nun's thread, such as was fabricated in the convents of Flanders and Italy. [39] If, however, Lydgate, in his ballad of "London Lackpenny," is an authority, that of Paris was most prized :—

> "Another he taked me by his hand,
> Here is Paris thredde, the finest in the land."

Queen Elizabeth was not patriotic; she got and wore her

---

[28] G. W. A. Eliz. 29-30.

[29] *Ibid.* 35-36.

[30] *Ibid.* 43-44. " A round kyrtle of cutwork in lawne."—B. M. Add. MSS. No. 5751.

[31] " One yard of double Italian cut-work à quarter of a yard wide, 55s. 4d." G. W. A. Eliz. 33 and 34.

" Una virga de opere sciss' lat' de factura Italica, 26s. 8d."—*Ibid.* 29 & 30.

[32] " For one yard of double Flanders cutwork worked with Italian purl, 33s. 4d."—*Ibid.* 33 & 34.

[33] " 3 suits of good lawn cutwork ruffs edged with good bone lace ' operat' super oss'," at 70s., 10l. 10s."—*Ibid.* 43 & 44.

[34] " 7 virg' Tenie lat' operis acui, ad 6s. 8d., 46s. 8d."—*Ibid.* 37-38.

[35] " Eidem pro 2 pectoral' de ope' sciss' fact' de Italic' et Flaundr' purle, ad 46s."—*Ibid.* 42 & 43.

" Eidem pro 1 virg' de Tenie de opere acuo cum le purle Italic' de cons' ope' acuo 20s."—G. W. A. Eliz. 40 & 41.

[36] Eliz. 44 = 1603.

[37] " 3 yards broad needlework lace of Italy, with the purls of similar work, at 50s. per yard, 8l. 15s."—*Ibid.* 41-42.

Bone lace varies in price from 40s. the dozen to 11s. 6d. the yard. Needle made lace from 6s. 8d. to 50s.—G. W. A. *Passim.*

[38] Lace is always called " lacqueus " in the Gt. Wardrobe Accounts up to 1595-6, after which it is rendered " tænia." Both terms seem, like our " lace " to have been equally applied to silk passements.

" Galons de soye, de l'espèce qui peuvent être dénominés par le terme latin de ' tæniola.' "

" Laqueus, enlassements de diverses couleurs, galons imitation de ces chaînes qui les Romains faisoient peindre, dorer et argenter, pour les rendre plus supportables aux illustres malheureux que le sort avoit réduit à les porter." — *Traité des Marques Nationales.* Paris, 1739.

[39] " Fine white or nun's thread is made by the Augustine nuns of Crema," writes Skippin, 1631.

From the Great Wardrobe Accounts

bone lace from whom she could, and from all countries. If she did not patronize English manufacture, on the other hand, she did not encourage foreign artizans; for when, in 1572, the Flemish refugees desired an asylum in England, they were forcibly expelled from her shores. In the census of 1571, giving the names of all the strangers in the City of London,[40] including the two makers of Billament lace already cited, we have but four foreigners of the lace craft : one described as " Mary Jurdaine, widow, of the French nation, and maker of purled lace " ; the other, the before-mentioned " Callys de Hove, of Burgundy." [41]

Various Acts [42] were issued during the reign of Elizabeth in order to suppress the inordinate use of apparel. That of May, 1562,[43] though corrected by Cecil himself, less summary than that framed against the " white-work " of the apprentice boys, was of little or no avail.

In 1568 a complaint was made to the Queen against the frauds practised by the " 16 appointed waiters," in reference to the importation of haberdashery, etc., by which it appears that her Majesty was a loser of " 5 or 600 l. by yere at least " in the customs on " parsement, cap rebone bone lace, cheyne lace," etc.,[44] but with what effect we know not. The annual import of these articles is therein stated at £10,000, an enormous increase since the year 1559, when, among the " necessary and unnecessary wares" brought into the port of London,[45] together with " babies " (dolls), " glasses to looke in," " glasses to drinke in," pottes, gingerbread, cabbages, and other matters, we find enumerated, " Laces of all sortes, £775 6s. 8d.," just one-half less than the more necessary, though less refined item of " eles fresh and salt." [46]

In 1573 Elizabeth again endeavoured to suppress " the silk glittering with silver and gold lace," but in vain.

---

the price appears to have been half a crown an ounce.

" Eidem pro 2 li. 4 unc.' fili Sororis, ad 2s. 6d. per unciam, 4l. 10s.''—Eliz. 34 & 35.

[40] State Papers Domestic. Eliz. Vol. 84. The sum total amounts to 4,287.

[41] See BURGUNDY. " The naturalized French residing in this country are Normans of the district of Caux, a wicked sort of French, worse than all the English," writes, in 1553, Stephen Porlin, a French ecclesiastic, in his *Description of England and Scotland.*

[42] 1559. Oct. 20. Proclamation against excess of apparel. — State Papers Dom. Eliz. Vol. vii. 1566. Feb. 12.—*Ibid.* Vol. xxxix. 1579. Star Chamber on apparel.

[43] State Papers Dom. Eliz. Vol. xxiii. No. 8.

[44] *Ibid.* Vol. xlvii. No. 49.

[45] *Ibid.* Vol. viii. No. 31.

[46] The value of thread imported amounts to £13,671 13s. 4d.

The Queen was a great lover of foreign novelties. All will call to mind how she overhauled the French finery of poor Mary Stuart [47] on its way to her prison, purloining and selecting for her own use any new-fashioned article she craved. We even find Cecil, on the sly, penning a letter to Sir Henry Norris, her Majesty's envoy to the court of France, " that the Queen's Majesty would fain have a tailor that has skill to make her apparel both after the French and Italian manner, and she thinketh you might use some means to obtain such one as suiteth the Queen without mentioning any manner of request in the Queen's Majesty's name." His lady wife is to get one privately, without the knowledge coming to the Queen Mother's ears, " as she does not want to be beholden to her."

It is not to be wondered at, then, that the New Year's Gifts and Great Wardrobe Accounts [48] teem with entries of " doublets of peche satten all over covered with cut-work and lyned with a lace of Venyse gold,[49] kyrtells of white satten embroidered with purles of gold-like clouds, and layed round about with a bone lace of Venys gold." [50] This gold lace appears upon her petticoats everywhere varied by bone lace of Venys silver.[51]

That the Queen drew much fine thread point from the same locality her portraits testify, especially that preserved in the royal gallery of Gripsholm, in Sweden, once the property of her ill-fated admirer, Eric XIV. She wears a ruff, cuffs, tucker, and apron of geometric lace, of exquisite fineness, stained of a pale citron colour, similar to the liquid invented by Mrs. Turner, of Overbury memory, or, maybe, adopted from the saffron-tinted smocks of the Irish, the wearing of which she herself had prohibited. We find among her entries laces of Jean [52] and Spanish lace ; she did not even disdain bone lace of copper, and copper and silver

---

[47] Walsingham writes : In opening a coffer of the Queen of Scots, he found certain heades which so pleased certain ladies of his acquaintance, he had taken the liberty to detain a couple.

[48] " A mantel of lawn cutwork wrought throughout with cutwork of ' pomegranettes, roses, honeysuckles, cum crowns.' "

" A doublet of lawn cutwork worked with ' lez rolls and true loves,' &c."— G. W. A. Eliz. Last year.

[49] New Year's Gifts. By the Lady Shandowes. 1577-8.

[50] Marquis of Northampton.

[51] Lady Carew. " A cushyn of fine cameryk edged with bone lace of Venice sylver."

[52] " Laqueus de serico Jeano "— (Genoa). G. W. A. Eliz. 30-1.

at 18*d.* the ounce.[53]　　Some of her furnishers are English. One Wylliam Bowll supplies the Queen with " lace of crowne purle." [54]　　Of her sylkwoman, Alice Mountague, she has bone lace wrought with silver and spangles, sold by the owner at nine shillings.[55]

The Queen's smocks are entered as wrought with black work and edged with bone lace of gold of various kinds. We have ourselves seen a smock said to have been transmitted as an heirloom in one family from generation to generation.[56]

Fig. 122.

QUEEN ELIZABETH'S SMOCK.

It is of linen cloth embroidered in red silk, with her favourite pattern of oak-leaves and butterflies (Fig. 122). Many entries of these articles, besides that of Sir Philip Sidney's, appear among the New Year's Gifts.[57]

It was then the custom for the sponsors to give " chris-

---

[53] 1571.　*Revels at Court.*　Cunningham.

Some curious entries occur on the occasion of a Masque called " The Prince " given at court in 1600 :—

" For the tooth-drawer :

" To loope leace for his doublet and cassacke, 8*s.*

" For leace for the corne-cutters suite, 7*s.*

" For green leace for the tinkers suite, 2*s.*

" For the mouse-trapp-man :

" 6 yards of copper leace to leace *is* cloake, at 1*s.* 8*d.*, 10*s.*

" The Prophet merely wears fringe, 2 Ruffes and cuffes, 3*s.* 10*d.*"

The subject of the Masque seems lost to posterity.

[54] Lady Chandos, jun.　" A cushyn cloth of lawne, wrought with white worke of branches and trees edged with white bone worke wrought with crownes."—New Year's Gifts. 1577-8.

[55] 1572.　*Revels at Court.*

[56] In the possession of Mrs. Evans of Wimbledon.

[57] Sir Gawine Carew.　" A smock of cameryke wrought with black work and edged with bone lace of gold."

tening shirts," with little bands and cuffs edged with laces of gold and various kinds—a relic of the ancient custom of presenting white clothes to the neophytes when converted to Christianity. The "bearing cloth," [58] as the mantle used to cover the child when carried to baptism was called,[59] was also richly trimmed with lace and cut-work, and the Tree of Knowledge, the Holy Dove (Fig. 123), or the Flowerpot of the Annunciation (Fig. 124), was worked in "hollie-work' on the crown of the infant's cap or "biggin."

Fig. 123.   Fig. 124.

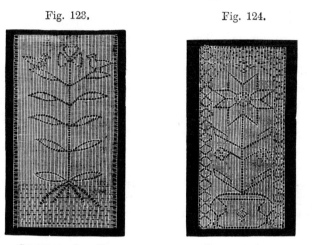

CHRISTENING CAPS, NEEDLE-MADE BRUSSELS.—Eighteenth century.

Aprons, too, of lace appeared in this reign. The Queen, as we have mentioned, wears one in her portrait at Gripsholm.[60]

> "Those aprons white, of finest thread,
>   So choicelie tied, so dearly bought;
>   So finely fringed, so nicely spread;
>   So quaintly cut, so richly wrought,"

writes the author of *Pleasant Quippes for Upstart Gentle-*

Lady Souche. "A smock of came-ryke, the ruffs and collar edged with a bone lace of gold."

The Lady Marquis of Winchester. "A smock of cameryke wrought with tanny silk and black, the ruffs and collar edged with a bone lace of silver." —New Year's Gifts. 1578-9.

[58] "A bearing cloth," for the Squire's child, is mentioned in the *Winter's Tale.*

[59] Many of these Christening robes of lace and point are preserved as heirlooms in old families; some are of old guipure, others of Flanders lace, and later of Valenciennes, or needle-point. The bib formed of guipure padded, with tiny mittens of lace, were also furnished to complete the suit.

[60] In 1584-5 Queen Elizabeth sends a most wonderful apron to be washed and starched, of cambric, edged with

women, in 1596. The fashion continued to the end of the eighteenth century.

Laced handkerchiefs now came into fashion. "Maydes and gentlewomen," writes Stowe, "gave to their favourites, as tokens of their love, little handkerchiefs of about three or four inches square, wrought round about," with a button at each corner.[61] The best were edged with a small gold lace. Gentlemen wore them in their hats as favours of their mistresses. Some cost sixpence, some twelvepence, and the richest sixteenpence.

Of the difference between purles and true lace it is difficult now to decide. The former word is of frequent occurrence among the New Year's Gifts, where we have "sleeves covered all over with purle," [62] and, in one case, the sleeves are offered unmade, with "a piece of purle upon a paper to edge them." [63] It was yet an article of great value and worthy almost of entail, for, in 1573, Elizabeth Sedgwicke, of Wathrape, widow, bequeaths to her daughter Lassells, of Walbron, "an edge of perlle for a remembrance, desirying her to give it to one of her daughters." [64]

We now turn, before quitting the sixteenth century, to that most portentous of all fabrications—Queen Elizabeth's ruff.

In the time of the Plantagenets Flemish tastes prevailed. With the Tudors, Katherine of Aragon, on her marriage with Prince Arthur, introduced the Spanish fashions, and the inventories from Henry VIII. downwards are filled with Spanish work, Spanish stitch, and so forth. Queen Elizabeth leant to the French and Italian modes, and during the Stuarts they were universally adopted.

The ruff was first introduced into England about the reign of Philip and Mary. These sovereigns are both represented on the Great Seal of England with small ruffs about

---

lace of gold, silver, and in-grain carnation silk, "operat' super oss'," with "pearl buttons pro ornatione dict' apron."—G. W. A. Eliz. 26 & 27.

[61] " A handkerchief she had,
   All wrought with silke and gold,
   Which she, to stay her trickling tears,
   Before her eyes did hold."
   —"Ballad of George Barwell."

[62] New Year's Gift of Lady Radcliffe. 1561.

[63] New Year's Gift of Lady St. Lawrence.

[64] Surtees' *Wills and Inv.* "Though the luxury of the court was excessive, the nation at large were frugal in their habits. Our Argentine of Dorset was called 'Argentine the Golden,' in consequence of his buckles, tags, and laces being of gold. Such an extravagance being looked on as a marvel in the remote hamlets of the southern counties."

their necks, and with diminutive ones of the same form encircling the wrists.[65] This Spanish ruff was not ornamented with lace. On the succession of Queen Elizabeth the ruff had increased to a large size, as we see portrayed on her Great Seal.

The art of starching, though known to the manufacturers of Flanders, did not reach England until 1564, when the Queen first set up a coach. Her coachman, named Gwyllam Boenen, was a Dutchman; his wife understood the art of starching, a secret she seems exclusively to have possessed, and of which the Queen availed herself until the arrival, some time after, of Madame Dinghen van der Plasse, who, with her husband, came from Flanders " for their better safeties," [66] and set up as a clear-starcher in London.

" The most curious wives," says Stowe, " now made themselves ruffs of cambric, and sent them to Madame Dinghen to be starched, who charged high prices. After a time they made themselves ruffs of lawn, and thereupon arose a general scoff, or by-word, that shortly they would make their ruffs of spiders' webs." Mrs. Dinghen at last took their daughters as her pupils. Her usual terms were from four to five pounds for teaching them to starch, and one pound for the art of seething starch.[67] The nobility patronised her, but the commonalty looked on her as the evil one, and called her famous liquid " devil's broth."

To keep the ruff erect, bewired [68] and starched though it be, was a troublesome affair—its falling a cause of agony to the wearer.

" Not so close, thy breath will draw my ruff,"

exclaims the fop. The tools used in starching and fluting

---

[65] Hence ruffles, diminutive of ruffs. " Ruff cuffs " they are called in the G. W. A. of James I., 11 & 12.

[66] Stowe's Chron.

[67] Endless are the entries in the Gt. W. Acc. for washing, starching and mending. The court laundress can have had no sinecure. We find " le Jup de lawne operat' cum stellis et aristis tritici Anglice wheateares " (Eliz. 42 & 43), sent to be washed, starched, etc. A network vail " sciss' totum desuper cum ragged staves."

(Leicester's device. *Ibid.* 29 & 30.) A diploid' (doublet) of cut-work flourished " cum auro et spangles " (*Ibid.*), and more wonderful still, in the last year of her reign she has washed and starched a toga " cum traine de la lawne operat' in auro et argento in forma caudarum pavorum," the identical dress in which she is portrayed in one of her portraits.

[68] " Eidem pro un ruff bon pynned sup' le wier Franc' cū rhet' aur' spangled, 70*s.*"—Eliz. 42 & 43.

ruffs were called setting-sticks, struts and poking-sticks : the two first were made of wood or bone, the poking-stick of iron, and heated in the fire.   By this heated tool the fold acquired that accurate and seemly order which constituted the beauty of this very preposterous attire.   It was about the year 1576, according to Stowe, the making of poking-sticks began.   They figure in the expenses of Elizabeth, who, in 1592, pays to her blacksmith, one Thomas Larkin, " pro 2 de lez setting-stickes at 2*s.* 6*d.*,"·the sum of 5*s.*[69]

We have frequent allusion to the article in the plays of the day :—[70]

" Your ruff must stand in print, and for that purpose, get poking-sticks with fair long handles, lest they scorch your hands."[71]

Again, in *Laugh and Lie Down*—[72]

" There she sat with her poking-stick, stiffening a fall."

When the use of starch and poking-sticks had rendered the arrangement of a ruff easy, the size began rapidly to increase.   " Both men and women wore them intolerably large, being a quarter of a yard deep, and twelve lengths in a ruff."[73]   In London this fashion was termed the French ruff ; in France, on the other hand, it was called " the English monster."[74]   Queen Elizabeth wore hers higher and stiffer than anyone in Europe, save the Queen of Navarre, for she had a " yellow throat," and was desirous to conceal it.[75]   Woe betide any fair lady of the court who dared let her white skin appear uncovered in the presence of majesty. Her ruffs were made of the finest cut-work, enriched with gold, silver, and even precious stones.   Though she consumed endless yards of cut-work, purle, needlework lace, bone lace of gold, of silver, enriched with pearls, and bugles,

---

[69] Gt. W. Acc. Eliz. 33 & 34.

[70] "B.: Where's my ruff and poker?" "R.: There's your ruff, shall I poke it?" "B.: So poke my ruff now."—Old Play by P. Dekker. 1602. Autolycus, among his wares, has " poking-sticks of steel." " Poked her rebatoes and surveryed her steel."—*Law Tricks.* 1608.

[71] Middleton's Comedy of *Blurt, Master Constable.*

[72] *Or, the World's Folly.* 1605.

[73] Stowe.

[74] *Ibid.*

[75] Therefore she wore " chin " ruffs. " Eidem pro 2 sutes de lez chinne ruffs edged cu' arg., 10*s.*"—Eliz. 42 & 43.

and spangles in the fabrication of the " three-piled ruff," [76]
she by no means extended such liberty to her subjects, for
she selected grave citizens and placed them at every gate
of the city to cut the ruffs if they exceeded the prescribed
depth. These " pillars of pride " form a numerous item
among the New Year's Gifts. Each lady seems to have
racked her brain to invent some novelty as yet unheard of
to gratify the Queen's vanity. On the new year 1559–60,
the Countess of Worcester offers a ruff of lawn cut-work set
with twenty small knots like mullets, garnished with small
sparks of rubies and pearls. [77]

The cut-work ruff is decorated or enriched with ornament
of every description. Nothing could be too gorgeous or too
extravagant. [78] Great was the wrath of old Philip Stubbes [79]
at these monstrosities, which, standing out a quarter of a
yard or more, " if Æolus with his blasts or Neptune with his
stormes chaunce to hit upon the crazie bark or their bruised
ruffes, then they goe flip flap in the winde like ragges that
flew abroade, lying upon their shoulders like the dishclout
of a slut. But wot ye what? the devill, as he, in the
fulnesse of his malice, first invented these great ruffes," etc.,
with a great deal more, which, as it comes rather under
the head of costume than lace, we omit, as foreign to our
subject.

Lace has always been made of human hair, and of this
we have frequent mention in the expenses of Queen Elizabeth. We believe the invention to be far older than her
reign, for there is frequent allusion to it in the early
romaunces. In the *Chevalier aux ij Epées* (MS. Bib. Nat.),
a lady requires of King Ris that he should present her with
a mantle fringed with the beards of nine conquered kings,
and hemmed with that of King Arthur, who was yet to
conquer. The mantle is to have " de sa barbe le tassel."

---

[76] Ben Jonson. *Every Man Out of His Humour.* 1599.

[77] Lady Cromwell. " Three sutes of ruffs of white cutwork edged with a passamayne of white.".
Lady Mary Se'm'. " 3 ruffs of lawne cutwork of flowers."

[78] " They are either clogged with gold, silver, or silk laces of stately price, wrought all over with needle-worke, speckeled and sparkled here and there with the sunne, the moone, the starres, and many other antiques strange to beholde. Some are wrought with open worke donne to the midst of the ruffe, and further some with close worke, some with purled lace so closed and other gewgawes so pestered, as the ruff is the leest parte of itself."
—Stubbe's Description of the Cut-work Ruff.

[79] *Anatomie of Abuses.* 1583.

The entries of Elizabeth, however, are of a less heroic nature ; and though we are well aware it was the custom of old ladies to weave into lace their silver-grey locks, and much as the fashion of hair bracelets and chains prevails, in Queen Elizabeth's case, setting aside all sentiment, we cannot help fancying the " laquei fact' de crine brayded cum lez risinge puffs," [80] as well as the " devices fact' de crine similiter les scallop shells," [81] to have been nothing more than " stuffings "—false additions, to swell the majesty of the royal " pirrywygge."

That point tresse, as this hair-lace is called, was known in her day, we have evidence in the Chartley inventory of Mary Stuart, in which is mentioned, " Un petit quarré fait à point tresse ouvré par la vieille Comtesse de Lennox elle estant à la Tour"; a tribute of affection the old countess would scarcely have offered to her daughter-in-law had she regarded her as implicated in the murder of her son. The writer saw at Chantilly an aged lace-maker employed in making a lace ground of hair on the pillow, used, she was informed, by wig-makers to give the parting of the hair ; but the fabric must be identical with the point tresse sent by the mother of Darnley to the Queen of Scots. Point tresse, when made out of the hair of aged people, is occasionally to be met with on the Continent, where, from its rarity, it fetches a high price. Some districts gained a reputation for their work, according to Turner :—" And Bedford's matrons wove their snowy locks." It may be detected by the glittering of the hair when held up to catch the sunbeams, or by frizzing when exposed to the test of fire, instead of blazing.

With this mention of point tresse we conclude the reign of Queen Elizabeth.

---

[80] " Eidem pro 3 dozin laquei fact' de crine brayded cum lez rising puffs de crine, ad 36s. le dd., £5 8s.."—Eliz. 31 & 32.

The entry occurs frequently.

In *Ibid.* 37 & 38 is a charge " pro 4 pirrywigges de crine," at 16s. 8d. each.

[81] In the G. W. A. of the last year of her reign, Elizabeth had a variety of devices in false hair. We have :—

" Eidem pro 200 invencionibus factis de crine in forma lez lowpes et tuftes," at 6d. each ; the like number in the form of leaves at 12d. ; 12 in form of " lez Peramides," at 3s. 4d. ; 24 of Globes, at 12d., with hair by the yard, made in lowpes, " crispat' curiose fact'," curle rotund', and other wonderful " inventions."

CHAPTER XXIV.

JAMES I. TO THE RESTORATION.

JAMES I.

" Now up aloft I mount unto the Ruffe,
Which into foolish mortals pride doth puffe;
Yet Ruffe's antiquity is here but small:
Within these eighty years not one at all.
For the 8th Henry, as I understand,
Was the first king that ever wore a Band,
And but a falling band plaine with a hem,
All other people knew no use of them."
Taylor, " Water-Poet." 1640.

THE ruff single, double, three piled, and Dædalian,[1] to the delight of the satirists, retained its sway during the early days of King James I. It was the "commode" of the eighteenth—the crinoline of the nineteenth century. Every play teems with allusions to this monstrosity. One compares it to

" A pinched lanthorn
Which schoolboys made in winter;"[2]

while a second[3] talks of a

" Starched ruff, like a new pigeon-house."

The lover, in the play of the *Antiquary*,[4] complains to his mistress in pathetic terms—

" Do you not remember how you fooled me, and set me to pin pleats in your ruff two hours together?"

---

[1] " Your trebble-quadruple Dædalian ruffes, nor your stiffe necked Rebatoes that have more arches for pride to row under than can stand under five London Bridges."—*The Gul's Horne-booke*, by T. Deckar. London, 1609.
[2] Beaumont and Fletcher. *Nice Valour.*
[3] *Ibid. The Blind Lady.* 1661.
[4] 1641.

Stubbes stood not alone in his anathemas. The dignitaries of the Church of England waxed wroth, and violent were their pulpit invectives.

"Fashion," emphatically preached John King,[5] Bishop of London, "has brought in deep ruffs[6] and shallow ruffs, thick ruffs and thin ruffs, double ruffs and no ruffs. When the Judge of quick and dead shall appear, he will not know those who have so defaced the fashion he hath created." The Bishop of Exeter, too, Joseph Hall, a good man, but no prophet, little wotting how lace-making would furnish bread and comfort to the women of his own diocese for centuries to come, in a sermon preached at the Spitel, after a long vituperation against its profaneness, concludes with these words: "But if none of our persuasions can prevail, hear this, ye garish popinjays of our time, if ye will not be ashamed to clothe yourselves after this shameless fashion, Heaven shall clothe you with shame and confusion. Hear this, ye plaister-faced Jezabels, if ye will not leave your daubs and your washes, Heaven will one day wash them off with fire and brimstone." Whether these denunciations had the effect of lessening the ruffs we know not; probably it only rendered them more exaggerated.

Of these offending adjuncts to the toilet of both sexes we have fine illustrations in the paintings of the day, as well as in the monuments of our cathedrals and churches.[7] They were composed of the finest geometric lace, such as we see portrayed in the works of Vinciolo and others. The artists of the day took particular pleasure in depicting them with the most exquisite minuteness.

These ruffs must have proved expensive for the wearer, though in James I.'s time, as Ben Jonson has it, men thought little of "turning four or five hundred acres of their best land into two or three trunks of apparel."[8]

---

[5] Called by James I. "the King of Preachers." Ob. 1621

[6] In the *Dumb Knight*, 1608, a woman, speaking of her ruff, says:—
"This is but shallow. I have a ruff is a quarter deep, measured by the yard."

[7] See the portraits in the National Portrait Gallery of Sir Dudley and Lady Carleton, by Cornelius Janssens, of the Queen of Bohemia, by Mirevelt, and of the Countess of Pembroke, by Mark Geerards. In Westminster Abbey, the effigies of Queen Elizabeth and Mary Queen of Scots, on their tombs.

[8] *Every Man Out of His Humour*, 1599.
Again, in his *Silent Woman*, he says:—

PLATE LXXIX.

No Spring Till now

MARY SIDNEY, COUNTESS OF PEMBROKE, IN 1614. 1555 ?–1621.—Probably by Marc Gheeraedts. National Portrait Gallery.
Photo by Walker and Cockerell.

PLATE LXXX.

HENRY WRIOTHESLEY, THIRD EARL OF SOUTHAMPTON, 1573–1624. – Probably painted in Holland about 1620, by Michiel Van Miereveldt. National Portrait Gallery.

Photo by Walker and Cockerell.

According to the Wardrobe Accounts,[9] " twenty-five yards of fyne bone lace" was required to edge a ruff, without counting the ground, composed either of lace squares or cut-work. Queen Anne, his consort, pays £5 for her wrought ruff, for "shewing" which eighteen yards of fine lace are purchased at 5s. 8d.[10]

The ruffs of the City ladye were kept downe by the old sumptuary law of Elizabeth.

"See, now, that you have not your 'city ruff' on, Mistress Sue," says Mistress Simple in the *City Match*.[11]

The Overbury murder (1613), and hanging of Mrs. Turner at Tyburn in 1615, are usually said, on the authority of Howel,[12] to have put an end to the fashion of yellow ruffs, but the following extracts show they were worn for some years later.

As late as 1620 the yellow starch, supposed to give a rich hue to the lace and cut-work of which ruffs were "built," gave scandal to the clergy. The Dean of Westminster ordered no lady or gentleman wearing yellow ruffs to be admitted into any pew in his church; but finding this "ill taken," and the King "moved in it," he ate his own words, and declared it to be all a mistake.[13] This fashion, again, gave great offence even in France. Since the English [14]

" She must have that Rich gown for such a great day, a new one
For the next, a richer for the third; have the chamber filled with
A succession of grooms, footmen, ushers,
And other messengers; besides embroiderers,
Jewellers, tire-women, semsters, feather men,
Perfumers; whilst she feels not how the land
Drops away, nor the acres melt; nor foresees
The change, when the mercer has your woods
For her velvets; never weighs what her pride
Costs, Sir."
[9] " Second Acc. of Sir John Villiers, 1617–8." P. R. O.
" 150 yards of fyne bone lace for six extraordinary ruffs provided against his Majesty's marriage, at 9s., 67s. 10d."

—Extraordinary Expenses. 1622–6. P. R. O.
[10] State Papers Dom., Jac. I. Vol. iii., No. 89. P. R. O.
[11] Jasper Mayne. 1670.
[12] " Mistris Turner, the first inventresse of yellow starch, was executed in a cobweb lawn ruff of that color at Tyburn, and with her I believe that yellow starch, which so much disfigured our nation and rendred them so ridiculous and fantastic, will receive its funerall."—*Howel's Letters*. 1645.
[13] State Papers Dom., James I. Vol. cxiii. No. 18.
[14] We read that in 1574 the Venetian ladies dyed their lace the colour of saffron. The fashion may therefore be derived from them.
" He is of England, by his yellow band." — *Notes from Black Fryers*. Henry Fitzgeffery. 1617.
" Now ten or twenty eggs will hardly suffice to starch one of these yellow bandes."—Barnaby Rich. *The Irish*

alliance, writes the *Courtisane à la Mode*, 1625,[15] "cette mode Anglaise sera cause qu'il pourra advenir une cherté sur le safran qui fera que les Bretons et les Poitevins seront contraints de manger leur beurre blanc et non pas jaune, comme ils sont accoutumés."

The Bishops, who first denounced the ruff, themselves held to the fashion long after it had been set aside by all other professions. Folks were not patriotic in their tastes, as in more modern days; they loved to go "as far as Paris to fetch over a fashion and come back again."[16]

The lace of Flanders, with the costly points and cut-works of Italy,[17] now became the rage, and continued so for nigh two centuries. Ben Jonson speaks of the "ruffs and cuffs of Flanders,"[18] while Lord Bacon, indignant at the female caprice of the day, writes to Sir George Villiers:—"Our English dames are much given to the wearing of costly laces, and if they may be brought from Italy, or France, or Flanders, they are in much esteem; whereas, if like laces were made by the English, so much thread would make a yard of lace, being put into that manufacture, would be five times, or perhaps ten or twenty times the value."[19] But Bacon had far better have looked at home, for he had himself, when Chancellor, granted an exclusive patent to Sir Giles Mompesson, the original of Sir Giles Overreach, for the monopoly of the sale and manufacture of gold and silver thread, the abuses of which caused in part his fall.[20]

James had half ruined the commerce of England by the granting of monopolies, which, says Sir John Culpepper, are "as numerous as the frogs of Egypt. They have got possession of our dwellings, they sip in our cups, they dip in our

---

Hubbub, or the English Hue and Cry. 1622.

Killigrew, in his play called *The Parson's Wedding*, published in 1664, alludes to the time when "yellow starch and wheel verdingales were cried down"; and in *The Blind Lady*, a play printed in 1661, a serving-man says to the maid: "You had once better opinion of me, though now you wash every day your best handkerchief in yellow starch."

[15] *La Courtisane à la Mode, selon l'Usage de la Cour de ce Temps.* Paris, 1625.

[16] Carlo, in *Every Man Out of His Humour.* 1599.

[17] "Eidem pro 29 virg' de opere sciss' bon' Italic', ad 35s., £68 5s."— Gt. W. A. Jac. I. 5 & 6.

[18] *The New Inn.*

[19] *Advice to Sir George Villiers.*

[20] See *Parliamentary History of England.*

Sir Giles was proceeded against as "a monopolist and patentee," and sentenced to be degraded and banished for life.

dish. They sit by our fire. We find them in the dye-vat, wash-bowl, and powdering-tub, etc. ; they have marked and sealed us from head to foot." [21] The bone-lace trade suffered alike with other handicrafts. [22] In 1606 James had already given a license to the Earl of Suffolk [23] for the import of gold and silver lace. In 1621, alarmed by the general complaints throughout the kingdom, [24] a proposition was made " for the erection of an Office of Pomp, to promote home manu-factures," and to repress pride by levying taxes on all articles of luxury. [25] What became of the Pomp Office we cannot pretend to say : the following year we are somewhat taken aback by a petition [26] from two Dutchmen, of Dort, showing " that the manufacture of gold and silver thread, purle, etc., in England " was " a great waste of bullion," the said Dutchmen being, we may infer, of opinion that it was more to their advantage to import such articles themselves. After a lapse of three years the petition is granted. [27] In the midst of all this granting and rescinding of monopolies, we hear in the month of April, 1623, how the decay of the bone-lace trade at Great Marlow caused great poverty." [28]

Though the laces of Flanders and Italy were much patronised by the court and high nobility, Queen Anne of Denmark appears to have given some protection to the fabrics of the country. Poor Queen Anne! When, on the news of Elizabeth's death, James hurried off to England, a correspondence took place between the King and the English Privy Council regarding the Queen's outfit, James consider-

---

[21] Speech in Parliament. *Rushout Papers*. Vol. xi., p. 916.

[22] " The office or grant for sealing bone lace was quashed by the King's proclamation, 1639, dated from his manour of York."—*Verney Papers*.

[23] B. M. *Bib. Lands.* 172, No. 59.

[24] 1604. Sept. 27. Patent to Ric. Dike and others to make Venice gold and silver thread for 21 years.—State Papers Dom., Jas. I. Vol. ix. 48.

1604. Dec. 30. Lease of the customs on gold and silver thread.—*Ibid.* Vol. x.

1605. Feb. 2. The same. *Ibid.* Vol. xii.

1611. May 21. Patent to Ric. Dike renewed.—*Ibid.* Vol. lxiii. 9.

In the same year (June 30) we find

a re-grant to the Earl of Suffolk of the moiety of all seizures of Venice gold and silver formerly granted in the fifth year of the King.—*Ibid.* Vol. lxiv. 66.

In 1622 a lease on the customs on gold and silver thread lace is given to Sir Edward Villiers. — *Ibid.* Vol. cxxxii. 34.

[25] *Ibid.* Vol. cxxi. 64.

[26] *Ibid.* Vol. cxxxii. 34.

[27] In 1624 King James renews his prohibition against the manufacture of " gold purles," as tending to the consumption of the coin and bullion of the kingdom.—*Fœdera*, Vol. xvii., p. 605.

[28] Petition. April 8, 1623. — State Papers, Vol. cxlii. 44. See Chap. xxx.

ing, and wisely—for the Scotch court was always out of elbows—that his wife's wardrobe was totally unfit to be produced in London.   To remedy the deficiency, the Council forwarded to the Queen, by the hands of her newly-named ladies, a quantity of Elizabeth's old gowns and ruffs, wherewith to make a creditable appearance on her arrival in England.   Elizabeth had died at the age of seventy, wizened, decayed, and yellow—Anne, young and comely, had but just attained her twenty-sixth year.   The rage of the high-spirited dame knew no bounds; she stormed with indignation—wear the clothes she must, for there were no others—so in revenge she refused to appoint any of the ladies, save Lady Bedford, though nominated by the King, to serve about her person in England.   On her arrival she bought a considerable quantity of linen, and as with the exception of one article,[29] purchased from a " French mann," her "nidell purle worke," her " white worke," her " small nidell worke," her " pece of lawin to bee a ruffe," with " eighteen yards of fine lace to shewe (sew) the ruffe," the " Great Bone " lace, and " Little Bone " lace were purchased at Winchester and Basing, towns bordering on the lacemaking counties, leading us to infer them to have been of English manufacture.[30]

The bill of laced linen purchased at the " Queen's lying down " on the birth of the Princess Sophia, in 1606, amounts to the sum of £614 5s. 8d.[31]   In this we have no mention of any foreign-made laces.   The child lived but three days.

---

[29] " Twoe payer of hande rebayters," i.e., cuffs.

[30] In the P. R. O. (State Papers Dom., James I. 1603, Sept.   Vol. iii. No. 89) is " A Memorandum of that Misteris Jane Drumonde her recyte from Ester Littellye, the furnishinge of her Majesties Linen Cloth," a long account, in which, among numerous other entries, we find :—

" It. at Basinge. Twenty four yeardes of small nidle work, at 6s. the yearde, £7 4s.

" More at Basinge. One ruffe cloth, cumbinge cloth and apron all shewed with white worke, at 50s. the piece, £7 10s.

" It. one pece of fine lawin to bee a ruffe, £5.

" Item, for 18 yeards of fine lace to shewe the ruffe, at 6s. the yearde, £5 8s.

" Item, 68 purle of fair needlework, at 20 pence the purle, £5 15s. 4d.

" Item, at Winchester, the 28th of September, one piece of cambrick, £4.

" Item, for 6 yards of fine purle, at 20s., £6.

" Item, for 4 yards of great bone lace, at 9s. the yard, 36s.

Queen Anne has also a fair wrought sark costing £6, and a cut-work handkerchief, £12, and 2 pieces of cutwork, ell wide and 2 yards long, at £2 the length, etc.

[31] *Lady Audrye Walsingham's Account.* 1606.—P. R. O.

Her little monument, of cradle-form, with lace-trimmed coverlets and sheets (Fig. 125), stands close to the recumbent effigy of her sister Mary [32] (Fig. 126), with ruff, collar,

Fig. 125.

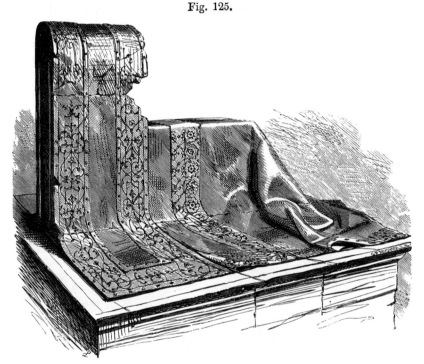

Monument of the Princess Sophia. + 1606. Fourth Daughter of James I.
(Westminster Abbey.)

and cap of geometric lace, in the north aisle of Henry VII.'s Chapel. [33]

After a time — epoch of the Spanish marriage [34] — the ruff

---

[32] Mary, her third daughter, died 1607, not two years of age. Mrs. Greene quotes from the P. R. O. a note of the "necessaries to be provided for the child," among which are six large cambric handkerchiefs, whereof one is to be edged with "fair cut-work to lay over the child's face"; six veils of lawn, edged with fair bone lace; six "gathered bibs of fine lawn with ruffles edged with bone lace," etc. The total value of the lace and cambric required for the infant's garments is estimated at £300.—*Lives of the Princesses of England.* Vol. vi., p. 90.

[33] England is rich in monumental effigies decorated with lace—too many to enumerate. Among them we would instance that of Alice, Countess of Derby, died 1636, in Harefield Church, Middlesex, in which the lace is very carefully sculptured.—Communicated by Mr. Albert Hartshorne.

[34] 1620–1. We have entries of "falling bands" of good cambric, edged with beautiful bone lace, two dozen

gave way to the "falling band," so familiar to us in the portraits of Rubens and Vandyke.

"There is such a deal of pinning these ruffs, when a fine clean fall is worth them all," says the Malcontent. "If you should chance to take a nap in the afternoon, your falling band requires no poking-stick to recover it." [35] Cut-work still continued in high favour; it was worn on every article of linen, from the richly-wrought collar to the nightcap. The Medicean ruff or gorget of the Countess of Pembroke

Fig. 126.

MONUMENT OF THE PRINCESS MARY. ✝ 1607. THIRD DAUGHTER OF JAMES I.
(Westminster Abbey.)

("Sidney's sister, Pembroke's mother"), with its elaborate border of swans (Fig. 127), is a good illustration of the fashion of her time.

Among the early entries of Prince Charles, we have four nightcaps of cut-work, £7,[36] for making two of which for his

---

stitched and shagged, and cut-work nightcaps, purchased for James I., in the same account, with 28s. for "one load of hay to stuff the woolsacks for the Parliament House."—G. W. Acc. Jac. I. 18 to 19.

In the same year, 1620, an English company exported a large quantity of gold and silver lace to India for the King of Golconda.

[35] *Malcontent.* 1600.

[36] Extraordinary expenses, 1622-26. P. R. O.

Highness, garnished with gold and silver lace, Patrick Burke receives £15;[37] but these modest entries are quite put to shame by those of his royal father, who, for ten yards of needlework lace " pro le edginge " of his " galiriculis vulgo

Fig. 127.

MARY, COUNTESS OF PEMBROKE. + 1621.
(From her portrait in Walpole's *Royal and Noble Authors.*)

nightcaps," pays £16 13s. 4d.[38] Well might the Water-Poet exclaim—

" A nightcap is a garment of high state." [39]

When Queen Anne died, in 1619, we have an elaborate

---

[37] " 2nd Acc. of Sir J. Villiers. 1617–18." P. R. O.

[38] Gt. W. A. Jac. I. 6 to 7.

[39] Taylor. 1640 :—

" The beau would feign sickness
   To show his nightcap fine,
And his wrought pillow overspread
   with lawn."—Davies. *Epigrams.*

account of her funeral,[40] and of the sum paid to Dorothy Speckart for dressing a hearse effigy with a large veil, wired and edged with peak lace and lawn, curiously cut in flowers, etc. Laced linen, however, was already discarded in mourning attire, for we find in the charges for the king's mourning ruffs, an edging at 14*d*. the piece is alone recorded.[41]

Towards the end of James I.'s reign a singular custom came into fashion, brought in by the Puritan ladies, that of representing religious subjects, both in lace, cut-work, and embroidery, a fashion hitherto confined to church vestments. We find constant allusions to it in the dramatists of the day. Thus, in the *City Match*,[42] we read—

> " She works religious petticoats, for flowers
> She'll make church histories. Her needle doth
> So sanctify my cushionets, besides
> My smock sleeves have such holy embroideries,
> And are so learned, that I fear in time
> All my apparel will be quoted by
> Some pious instructor."

Again, in the *Custom of the Country*—[43]

> " Sure you should not be
> Without a neat historical shirt."

[40] Acc. of Sir Lyonell Cranfield (now Earl of Middlesex), late Master of the Great Wardrobe, touching the funeral of Queen Anne, who died 2nd March, 1618 (*i.e.* 1619 N. S.). P. R. O.

[41] About this time a complaint is made by the London tradesmen, of the influx of refugee artizans, " who keepe theire misteries to themselves, which hath made them bould of late to device engines for workinge lace, &c., and such wherein one man doth more among them than seven English-men can doe, soe as theire cheape sale of those commodities beggareth all our English artificers of that trade and encricheth them," which becomes " scarce tolleruble," they conclude. Cecil, in consequence, orders a census to be made in 1621. Among the traders appears " one satten lace maker."

Colchester is bitterly irate against the Dutch strangers, and complains of one " Jonas Snav, a Bay and Say maker, whose wife selleth blacke browne, and white thredde, and all sorts of bone lace and vatuegardes, which they receive out of Holland. One Isaac Bowman, an Alyen born, a chirurgeon and merchant, selleth hoppes, bone lace, and such like, to the great grievance of the free burgesses."

A nest of refugee lace-makers, " who came out of France by reason of the late ' trobles ' yet continuing," were congregated at Dover (1621-2). A list of about five-and-twenty " widows, being makers of Bone lace," is given, and then Mary Tanyer and Margarett Le Moyne, " maydens and makers of bone lace," wind up the catalogue of the Dover " Alyens."

The Maidstone authorities complain that the thread-makers' trade is much decayed by the importation of thread from Flanders.—*List of Foreign Protestants resident in England*. 1618-88. Printed by the Camden Society.

[42] Jasper Mayne.

[43] Beaumont and Fletcher.

We find in a Scotch inventory [44] of the seventeenth century: " Of Holland scheittes ii pair, quhairof i pair schewit (sewed) with hollie work." [45]

The entries of this reign, beyond the " hollie work," picked [46] and seaming [47] lace, contain little of any novelty; all articles of the toilet were characterised by a most reckless extravagance.

"There is not a gentleman now in the fashion," says Peacham,[48] " whose band of Italian cut-work now standeth him not in the least three or four pounds. Yes, a semster in Holborn told me that there are of threescore pounds." We read how two-thirds of a woman's dower was often expended in the purchase of cut-work and Flanders lace.

In the warrant of the Great Wardrobe for the marriage expenses of the ill-fated Princess Elizabeth, on which occasion it is recorded of poor Arabella Stuart, the " Lady Arabella, though still in the Tower, has shewn her joy by buying four new gowns, one of which cost £1,500," [49] in addition to " gold cheine laze, silver spangled, silver looped, myllen bone lace, drawneworke poynte, black silk Naples lace," etc., all in the most astonishing quantity, we have the astounding entry of 1,692 ounces of silver bone lace.[50] No wonder, in

---

[44] " Valuables of Glenurquhy, 1640." Innes' *Sketches of Early Scotch History.*

[45] Collars of Hollie worke appear in the Inventories of Mary Stuart.

[46] " Thomas Hodges, for making ruffe and cuffes for his Highness of cuttworke edged with a fayre peake purle, £7."—2nd Account of Sir J. Villiers. Prince Charles. 1617–18. P. R. O.

" 40 yards broad peaked lace to edge 6 cupboard cloths, at 4s. a yard, £8."— *Ibid.*

[47] " Seaming " lace and spacing lace appear to have been generally used at this period to unite the breadths of linen, instead of a seam sewed. We find them employed for cupboard cloths, cushion cloths, sheets, shirts, etc., throughout the accounts of King James and Prince Charles.

" At Stratford-upon-Avon is preserved in the room where Shakspeare's wife Anne Hathaway, was born, an oaken linen chest, containing a pillow-case and a very large sheet made of homespun linen. Down the middle of the sheet is an ornamental open or cut-work insertion, about an inch and a half deep, and the pillow-case is similarly ornamented. They are marked E. H., and have always been used by the Hathaway family on special occasions, such as births, deaths, and marriages. This is still a common custom in Warwickshire; and many families can proudly show embroidered bed linen, which has been used on state occasions, and carefully preserved in old carved chests for three centuries and more."—*A Shakspeare Memorial.* 1864.

[48] *The Truth of the Times.* W. Peacham. 1638.

[49] State Papers Dom. Jas. I. Vol. lxxii. No. 28.

[50] Warrant on the Great Wardrobe. 1612–13. Princess Elizabeth's marriage.

after days, the Princess caused so much anxiety to the Palatine's Privy Purse, Colonel Schomberg, who in vain implores her to have her linen and lace bought beforehand, and paid at every fair.[51]　"You brought," he writes, "£3,000 worth of linen from England, and have bought £1,000 worth here," and yet "you are ill provided."[52]

CHARLES I.

"Embroider'd stockings, cut-work smocks and shirts."
—Ben Jonson.

Ruffs may literally be said to have gone out with James I. His son Charles is represented on the coins of the two first years of his reign in a stiff starched ruff;[53] in the fourth and fifth we see the ruff unstarched, falling down on his shoulders,[54] and afterwards, the falling band (Fig. 128) was generally adopted, and worn by all classes save the judges, who stuck to the ruff as a mark of dignity and decorum, till superseded by the peruke.[55]

Even loyal Oxford, conscientious to a hair's-breadth— always behind the rest of the world—when Whitelock, in 1635, addresses the Quarter Sessions arrayed in the new fashion, owned "one may speak as good sense in a falling band as in a ruff." The change did not, however, diminish the extravagance of the age. The bills for the King's lace and linen, which in the year 1625 amounted to £1,000, in

---

[51] Frankfort fair, at which most of the German princes made their purchases.

[52] German Correspondence. 1614– 15.—P. R. O.

We find among the accounts of Col. Schomberg and others :—

"To a merchant of Strasbourg, for laces which she had sent from Italy, 288 rix-dollars." And, in addition to numerous entries of silver and other laces :—

"Pour dentelle et linge karé pour Madame, 115 florins."

"Donné Madame de Caus pour des mouchoirs à point couppée pour Madame, £4."

"Une petite dentelle à point couppé, £3," etc.

Point coupé handkerchiefs seem to have been greatly in fashion. Ben Jonson, "Bartholomew Fair," 1614, mentions them :—

"A cut-work handkerchief she gave me."

[53] See *Snelling's Coins*. Pl. ix. 8, 9, 10.

[54] *Ibid.* Pl. ix. 5, 6, 11.

[55] Evelyn, describing a medal of King Charles I., struck in 1633, says he wears "a falling band, which new mode succeeded the cumbersome ruff; but neither did the bishops or the judges give it up so soon, the Lord Keeper Finch being, I think, the very first."

course of time rose to £1,500.[56] Falling bands of Flanders bone lace and cut-work appear constantly in the accounts.[57] As the foreign materials are carefully specified (it was one of these articles, then a novelty, that Queen Anne of Denmark " bought of the French Mann "), we may infer much of the

Fig. 128.

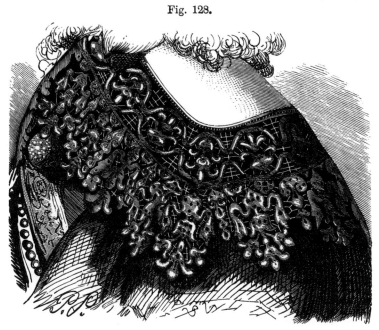

FALLING COLLAR OF THE SEVENTEENTH CENTURY.—(After Abraham Bosse.)

bobbin or bone lace to have been of home produce. As Ben Jonson says, " Rich apparel has strong virtues." It is, he adds, " the birdlime of fools." There was, indeed, no article of toilet at this period which was not encircled with lace— towels, sheets, shirts, caps, cushions, boots (Fig. 129), cuffs (Fig. 130)—and, as too often occurs in the case of excessive luxury, when the bills came in money was wanting to

---

[56] In 1633, the bills having risen to £1,500 a year, a project is made for reducing the charge for the King's fine linen and bone lace, " for his body," again to £1,000 per annum, for which sum it " may be very well done."— State Papers, Chas. I. Vol. ccxxxiv. No. 83.

[57] " Paid to Smith Wilkinson, for 420 yards of good Flanders bone lace for 12 day ruffes and 6 night ruffes ' cum cuffes eisdem,' £87 15*s.*

" For 6 falling bands made of good broad Flanders lace and Cuttworks with cuffs of the same, £52 16*s.*"— Gt. W. A. Car. I. 6 = 1631.

discharge them, Julian Elliott, the royal lace merchant, seldom receiving more than half her account, and in 1630— nothing.[58]　There were, as Shakespeare says,

"Bonds entered into
For gay apparel against the triumph day."[59]

The quantity of needlework purl consumed on the king's hunting collars, "colares pro venatione," scarcely appears credible.　One entry alone makes 994 yards for 12 collars and 24 pairs of cuffs.[60]　Again, 600 yards of fine bone lace is charged for trimming the ruffs of the King's nightclothes.[61]

The art of lace-making was now carried to great per-

Fig. 129.

Fig. 130.

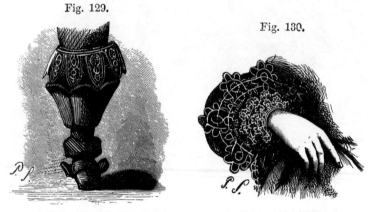

From an Engraving of Abraham Bosse.　　　From an Engraving of Abraham Bosse.

fection in England ; so much so, that the lease of twenty-one years, granted in 1627 to Dame Barbara Villiers, of the duties on gold and silver thread, became a terrible loss to the holder, who, in 1629, petitions for a discharge of £437 10s. arrears due to the Crown.　The prayer is favourably received by the officers of the Customs, to whom it was referred, who answer they "conceive those duties will decay, for the invention of making Venice gold and silver lace within the kingdom is come to that perfection, that it will be made here more cheap than it can be brought from

---

[58] See G. W. A., Mich., 1629, to April, 1630.
[59] *Twelfth-Night.*

[60] G. W. A. Car. I.　The Annunciation 9 to Mich. 11.
[61] *Ibid.* 8 and 9.

Fig. 131.

English Needle-made Lace.

Plate LXXXI.

Elizabeth, Princess Palatine, Granddaughter of James I., 1618–1680.—
Probably about 1638. By Gerard Honthorst. National Portrait Gallery.
Photo by Walker and Cockerell.

beyond seas." [62] The fancy for foreign articles still prevailed. "Among the goods brought in by Tristram Stephens," writes Sir John Hippisley, from Dover Castle, "are the bravest French bandes that ever I did see for ladies—they be fit for the Queen." [63]

Gold lace was exported in considerable quantities to India in the days of James I. ; [64] and now, in 1631, we find the "riband roses," edged with lace, notified among the articles allowed to be exported. These lace rosette-trimmed shoes were in vogue in the time of James I., and when first brought to that monarch he refused to adopt the fashion, asking, "If they wanted to make a ruffe-footed dove of him." They were afterwards worn in all the extravagance of the French court. (See France to Louis XIV.). Mr. Brooks, in his speech in the House of Commons against costly apparel (18 James I.), says, "Nowadays, the roses worn by Members of the House on their shoes are more than their father's apparel." Peacham speaks of "shoe ties, that goe under the name of roses, from thirty shillings to three, four, and five pounds the pair. Yea, a gallant of the time, not long since, paid thirty pounds for a pair. [65] Well might Taylor say they

> "Wear a farm in shoe-strings edged with gold,
> And spangled garters worth a copyhold."

It was not till the year 1635 that an effort was made for

---

[62] State Papers Dom. Charles I. Vol. cxlix. No. 31.

[63] In a letter to Mr. Edward Nicholas, Sec. of the Admiralty, March 7th, 1627 (afterwards Sec. of State to Chas. II.).—St. P. D. Chas. I. Vol. cxxiii. 62.

Among the State Papers (Vol. cxxvi. 70), is a letter from Susan Nicholas to her "loveing Brother," 1628. About lace for his band, she writes : "I have sent you your bootehose and could have sent your lase for your band, but that I did see these lasees which to my thought did do a greddeale better then that wh you did bespeake, and the best of them will cost no more then that which is half a crowne a yard, and so the uppermost will cost you, and the other will cost 18 pence ; I did thinke you would rather staye something long for it then to pay so deare for that wh would make no better show ; if you like either of these, you shall have it sone desptch, for I am promise to have it made in a fortnight. I have received the monie from my cousson Hunton. Heare is no news to wright of. Thus with my best love remembred unto you, I rest your very loving sister, "SUSANNE NICHOLAS.

"I have sent ye the lase ye foyrst bespoke, to compare them together, to see which ye like best."

[64] In 1620 an English company exported a large quantity of gold and silver lace to India for the King of Golconda.

[65] W. Peacham, *Truth of the Times.* 1638.

Hamlet says there are

"Two Provençal roses on my regal shoes."

the protection of our home fabrics, " at the request and for the benefit of the makers of those goods in and near London, and other parts of the realm, now brought to great want and necessity, occasioned by the excessive importation of these foreign wares." Foreign " Purles, Cutworks, or Bone-laces, or any commodities laced or edged therewith," are strictly prohibited. Orders are also given that all purles, cut-works, and bone laces English made are to be taken to a house near the sign of the " Red Hart " in Fore Street, without Cripple-gate, and there sealed by Thomas Smith or his deputy.[66]

An Act the same year prohibits the use of " gold or silver purles " except manufactured in foreign parts, and especially forbids the melting down any coin of the realm.

The manufacture of bone lace in England had now much improved, and was held in high estimation in France. We hear of Henrietta Maria sending ribbons, lace, and other fashions from England, in 1636, as a present to her sister-in-law, Anne of Austria ;[67] while, in a letter dated February 7th, 1636, the Countess of Leicester writes to her husband, then in France, who had requested her to procure him some fine bone lace of English make :—" The present for the Queen of France I will be careful to provide, but it cannot be hand-some for that proportion of money which you do mention ; for these bone laces, if they be good, are dear, and I will send the best, for the honor of my nation and my own credit."

Referring to the same demand, the Countess again writes to her lord, May 18th, 1637, Leicester House :—" All my present for the Queen of France is provided, which I have done with great care and some trouble; the expenses I cannot yet directly tell you, but I think it will be about £120, for the bone laces are extremely dear. I intend to

---

" When roses in the gardens grow,
And not in ribbons on a shoe ;
Now ribbon-roses take such place,
That garden roses want their grace."
—" Friar Bacon's Prophesie." 1604.
" I like," says Evelyn, " the boucle better than the formal rose."—*Tyran-nus, or the Mode.*
[66] This proclamation is dated from " our Honour of Hampton Court, 30th April, 1635."—Rymer's *Fœdera.* T.19, p. 690.
[67] When Anne of Austria was sus-

pected of secret correspondence with Spain and England, Richelieu sent the Chancellor to question the Abbess of the Val-de-Grâce with respect to the casket which had been secretly brought into the monastery. The Abbess (*Vie de la Mère d'Arbouse*) declared that this same casket came from the Queen of England, and that it only contained lace, ribbons, and other trimmings of English fashion, sent by Henrietta Maria as a present to the Queen.— *Galerie de l'Ancienne Cour.* 1791.

send it by Monsieur Ruvigny, for most of the things are of new fashion, and if I should keep them they would be less acceptable, for what is new now will quickly grow common, such things being sent over almost every week."

We can have no better evidence of the improvement in the English lace manufacture than these two letters.

An Act of 1638 for reforming abuses in the manufacture of lace, by which competent persons are appointed, whether natives or strangers, " who shall be of the Church of England," can scarcely have been advantageous to the community.

Lace, since the Reformation, had disappeared from the garments of the Church. In the search warrants made after Jesuits and priests of the Roman faith, it now occasionally peeps out. In an inventory of goods seized at the house of some Jesuit priests at Clerkenwell, in 1627, we find—" One faire Alb of cambric, with needle worke purles about the skirts, necke, and bandes."

Smuggling, too, had appeared upon the scene. In 1621 information is laid how Nicholas Peeter, master of the " Greyhound, of Apsom," had landed at Dover sundry packets of cut-workes and bone laces without paying the Customs.[68]

But the

> " Rebatoes, ribbands, cuffs, ruffs, falls,
> Scarfes, feathers, fans, maskes, muffs, laces, cauls," [69]

of King Charles's court were soon to disperse at the now outbreaking Revolution. The Herrn Maior Frau (Lady Mayoress), the noble English lady depicted by Hollar,[70] must now lay aside her whisk, edged with broad lace of needle point, and no longer hie to St. Martin's for lace :[71] she must content herself with a plain attire.

> " Sempsters with ruffs and cuffs, and quoifs and caules
> And falls," [72]

must be dismissed. Smocks of three pounds a-piece,[73]

---

[68] State Papers Dom. Vol. cxxiii. No. 65.
[69] " Rhodon and Iris, a Pastoral." 1631.
[70] " Ornatus Muliebris Anglicanus." 1645.
[71] " You must to the Pawn (Exchange) to buy lawn, to St. Martin for lace."—*Westward Ho.* 1607.
" A copper lace called St. Martin's lace."—Strype.
[72] Taylor, " Whip of Pride." 1640.
[73] In *Eastward Ho*, 1605, proud Gertrude says : " Smocks of three pound a smock, are to be born with all."

wrought smocks,[74] are no longer worn by all—much less those "seam'd thro' with cutwork,"[75] or "lace to her smocks, broad seaming laces,"[76] which, groans one of the Puritan writers, "is horrible to think of."

The ruff and cuffs of Flanders, gold lace cut-work and silver lace of curle,[77] needle point, and fine gartering with blown roses,[78] are now suppressed under Puritan rule.

The "fop" whom Henry Fitz-Geoffrey describes as having

> "An attractive lace
> And whalebone bodies for the better grace,"

must now think twice before he wears it.[79]

The officer, whom the poor soldier apostrophises as shining—

> " One blaze of plate about you, which puts out
> Our eyes when we march 'gainst the sunne, and armes you
> Compleatly with your own gold lace, which is
> Laid on so thick, that your own trimmings doe
> Render you engine proof, without more arms "—[80]

must no longer boast of

> "This shirt five times victorious I have fought under,
> And cut through squadrons of your curious Cut-work,
> As I will do through mine." [81]

In the Roundhead army he will scarce deign to comb his cropped locks. All is now dingy, of a sad colour, soberly in character with the tone of the times.

---

[74] " Bartholomew Fair." 1614.

[75] " She shewed me gowns and head tires,
Embroidered waistcoats, smocks seam'd thro' with cut-works."
    —Beaumont and Fletcher, " Four Plays in One." 1647.

[76] " Who would ha' thought a woman so well harness'd,
Or rather well caparison'd, indeed,
That wears such petticoats, and lace to her smocks,
Broad seaming laces."—Ben Jonson, *The Devil is an Ass.* 1616.

[77] A suite of russet " laced all over with silver curle lace."—" Expenses of Robt. Sidney, Earl of Leicester. Temp. Chas. I."

[78]   " This comes of wearing Scarlet, gold lace and cut-works; your fine gartering
With your blown roses."
            —*The Devil is an Ass.*

[79] *Notes from Black Fryers.*

[80] Jasper Mayne. " Amorous War." 1659.

[81] " The Little French Lawyer."

THE COMMONWEALTH.

The rule of the Puritans was a sad time for lace-makers, as regards the middle and lower classes : every village festival, all amusement was put down, bride laces and Mayings—all were vanity.

With respect to the upper classes, the Puritan ladies, as well as the men of birth, had no fancy for exchanging the rich dress of the Stuart Court for that of the Roundheads. Sir Thomas Fairfax, father of the General, is described as wearing a buff coat, richly ornamented with silver lace, his trunk hose trimmed with costly Flanders lace, his breastplate partly concealed by a falling collar of the same material. The foreign Ambassadors of the Parliament disdained the Puritan fashions. Lady Fanshaw describes her husband as wearing at the Court of Madrid, on some State occasion, " his linen very fine, laced with very rich Flanders lace." [82]

Indeed, it was not till the arrival of the Spanish envoy, the first accredited to the Protectorate of Cromwell, that Harrison begged Colonel Hutchinson and Lord Warwick to set an example to other nations at the audience, and not appear in gold and silver lace. Colonel Hutchinson, though he saw no harm in a rich dress, yet not to appear offensive, came next day in a plain black suit, as did the other gentlemen, when, to the astonishment of all, Harrison appeared in a scarlet coat so laden with " clinquaint " and lace as to hide the material of which it was made, showing, remarks Mrs. Hutchinson, " his godly speeches were only made that he might appear braver above the rest in the eyes of the strangers."

Nor did the mother of Cromwell lay aside these adornments. She wore a handkerchief, of which the broad point lace alone could be seen, and her green velvet cardinal was edged with broad gold lace.[83] Cromwell himself, when once in power, became more particular in his dress ; and if he lived as a Puritan, his body after death was more gorgeously attired than that of any deceased sovereign, with purple velvet, ermine, and the richest Flanders lace.[84] His effigy,

---

[82] *Memoirs.*
[83] *The Cromwell Family.*

[84] Sir Philip Warwick. 1640.

carved by one Symonds, was clad in a fine shirt of Holland, richly laced ; he wore bands and cuffs of the same materials, and his clothes were covered with gold lace.[85]

The more we read the more we feel convinced that the dislike manifested by the Puritan leaders to lace and other luxuries was but a political necessity, in order to follow the spirit of the age.

As an illustration of this opinion we may cite that in the account of the disbursements of the Committee of Safety, 1660, a political *jeu d'esprit* which preceded the Restoration, we find entered for Lady Lambert—

" Item, for seven new whisks lac'd with Flanders lace of the last Edition, each whisk is valued at fifty pound, £350."

Followed up by—

" Six new Flanders lac'd smocks, £300."

The whisk, as the gorget was now termed, was as great an object of extravagance to the women as was the falling band to the men. It continued in fashion during the reign of Charles II., and is often mentioned as lost or stolen among the advertisements in the public journals of the day. In the *Mercurius Publicus*, May 8th, 1662, we find : " A cambric whisk with Flanders lace, about a quarter of a yard broad, and a lace turning up about an inch broad, with a stock in the neck, and a strap hanging down before, was lost between the new Palace and Whitehall. Reward, 30*s*." Again, in *The Newes*, June 20th, 1664 : " Lost, a Tiffany whisk, with a great lace down, and a little one up, large Flowers, and open Work, with a Roul for the head and Peak."

---

[85] At the Restoration, it was removed from the Abbey and hung out of the window at Whitehall, and then broken up and destroyed.

PLATE LXXXII

JAMES HARRINGTON, Author of " Oceana," 1611–1677.   Between 1630–1640.
By Gerard Honthorst. National Portrait Gallery.
Photo by Walker and Cockerell.

PLATE LXXXIII.

JAMES, THE OLD PRETENDER, 1688–1766, WITH HIS SISTER PRINCESS LOUISA, 1692–1712. In 1695. By Nicolas de Largilliére. National Portrait Gallery.

Photo by Walker and Cockerell.

CHAPTER XXV.

CHARLES II. TO THE HOUSE OF HANOVER.

CHARLES II.

"The dangling knee-fringe, and the bib-cravat."
—Dryden. *Prologue.* 1674.

THE taste for luxury only required the restoration of th Stuarts to burst out in full vigour.

The following year Charles II. issued a proclamation [1] enforcing the Act of his father prohibiting the entry of foreign bone lace; but, far from acting as he preached, he purchases Flanders lace at eighteen shillings the yard, for the trimming of his fine lawn " collobium sindonis," [2] a sort of surplice worn during the ceremony of the anointment at the coronation.

The hand-spinners of gold wire, thread lace, and spangles of the City of London, no longer puritanically inclined, now speak out boldly. " Having heard a report the Parliament intend to pass an Act against the wearing of their manufacture, they hope it intends the reform, not the destruction of their craft, for by it many thousands would be ruined. Let every person," say they, " be prohibited from wearing gold, silver, and thread lace—that will encourage the gentry to do so." [3]

In 1662 is passed an Act prohibiting the importation of foreign bone lace, cut-works, etc., setting forth, " Whereas many poor children have attained great dexterity in the

---

[1] 1661, Nov. 20. State Papers. Dom. Charles II. Vol. xliv. P. R. O.

[2] " To William Briers, for making the Colobium Sindonis of fine lawn laced with fine Flanders lace, 33s. 4d.

" To Valentine Stucky, for 14 yards and a half of very fine Flanders lace for the same, at 18s. per yard, £12 6s. 6d."—" Acc. of the E. of Sandwich,

Master of the G. W. for the Coronation of King Charles II. 23 April, 1661." P. R. O.

[3] In the G. W. A. for 29 and 30 occurs a curious entry by the Master of the Great Wardrobe :—" I doe hereby charge myself with 5,000 Livres by me received in the realm of France for gold and silver fringes by me there

making thereof, the persons so employed have served most parts of the kingdom with bone lace, and for the carrying out of the same trade have caused much thread to be brought into the country, whereby the customs have been greatly advanced, until of late large quantities of bone lace, cut-work, etc., were brought into the kingdom and sold contrary to the former Statutes and the proclamation of November last; all such bone lace is to be forfeited, and a penalty of £100 paid by the offender." [4]

This same Act only occasioned the more smuggling of lace from Flanders, for the point made in England had never attained the beauty of Brussels, and indeed, wherever fine lace is mentioned at this period it is always of foreign fabric. That Charles himself was of this opinion there can be no doubt, for in the very same year he grants to one John Eaton a license to import such quantities of lace " made beyond the seas, as may be for the wear of the Queen, our dear Mother the Queen, our dear brother James, Duke of York," and the rest of the royal family. The permission is softened down by the words, " And to the end the same may be patterns for the manufacture of these commodities here, notwithstanding the late Statute forbidding their importation." [5] Charles had evidently received his lessons in the school of Mazarin. As the galleries of the cardinal were filled with sculptures, paintings, and majolica—rich produce of Italian art, as patterns for France, " per mostra di farne in Francia "—so the king's " pilea nocturna," pillow-beres, cravats, were trimmed with the points of Venice [6] and Flanders, at the rate of £600 per annum, for the sake of improving the lace manufacture of England.

The introduction of the flowing wig, with its long curls covering the shoulders, gave a final blow to the falling band;

---

sold, belon⁵ to a rich embroidered Bed of his said Majesty, which at one shilling and sevenpence ℔ lib. English, Being the value of the Exchange at that time, amounts to £395 16*s.* 8*d.*

　　　" (Signed)　R. MONTAGUE.

　" May 28, 1678."
[4] 14 Car. II. c. 13. Statutes at large. The Acts of Charles II. date from the death of his father; so the year of the Restoration, 1660, is counted as the thirteenth of his reign.

[5] 1662. State Papers Dom. Charles II. Vol. lv., No. 25. P. R. O.

[6] He pays £194 to his Laceman (Teneatori) for 3 Cravats " de poynt de Venez," and 24*s.* per yard for 57 yards of narrow point " teniæ poynt augustæ," to trim his falling ruffles, " manicis cadentibus," etc.—G. W. A. Car. II. 24 and 25.

Later (1676-7) we find charged for " un par manicarum, le poynt, £14."

the ends floating and tied in front could alone be visible. In time they diminished in size, and the remains are still seen in the laced bands of the lawyer, when in full dress, and the homely bordered cambric slips used by the clergy. The laced cravat now introduced continued in fashion until about the year 1735.[7]

It was at its height when Pepys writes in his diary : "Lord's Day, Oct. 19, 1662. Put on my new lace band, and so neat it is that I am resolved my great expense shall be lace bands, and it will set off anything else the more." The band was edged with the broadest lace. In the *Newes*, January 7th, 1663, we find : " Lost, a laced band, the lace a quarter of a yard deep, and the band marked in the stock with a B."

Mrs. Pepys—more thrifty soul—" wears her green petticoat of Florence satin, with white and black gimp lace of her own putting on (making), which is very pretty."

The custom, already common in France, of ladies making their own lace, excites the ire of the writer of *Britannia Languens*, in his " Discourse upon Trade."[8] " The manufacture of linen,"[9] he says, " was once the huswifery of English ladies, gentlewomen, and other women ;" now " the huswifery women of England employ themselves in making an ill sort of lace, which serves no national or natural necessity."

The days of Puritan simplicity were at an end.

" Instead of homespun coifs were seen
Good pinners edged with Colberteen."[10]

The laced cravat succeeded the falling collar. Lace handkerchiefs [11] were the fashion, and

" Gloves laced and trimmed as fine as Nell's." [12]

---

[7] When it was replaced by a black ribbon and a bow.

[8] London, 1680.

[9] Authors, however, disagree like the rest of the world. In a tract called *The Ancient Trades Decayed Repaired Again*, by Sir Roger L'Estrange (1678), we read : " Nay, if the materials used in a trade be not of the growth of England, yet, if the trade be to employ the poor, we should have it bought without money, and brought to us from beyond the seas where it is made as ' Bone lace.' "

[10] Swift. *Baucis and Philemon.*

[11] *Intelligencer.* 1665, June 5. " Lost, six handkerchers wrapt up in a brown paper, two laced, one point-laced set on tiffany; the two laced ones had been worn, the other four new."

London Gazette. 1672, Dec. 5-9. " Lost, a lawn pocket handkercher with a broad hem, laced round with a fine Point lace about four fingers broad, marked with an R in red silk."

[12] Evelyn. It was the custom, at a Maiden Assize, to present the judge with a pair of " laced gloves." Lord

Laced aprons, which even found their way to the homes of the Anglican clergy, and appear advertised as " Stolen from the vicarage house at Amersham in Oxfordshire : An apron of needlework lace, the middle being Network, another Apron laced with cut and slash lace."[13]

The newspapers crowd with losses of lace, and rarer—finds.[14]

They give us, however, no clue to the home manufacture. " A pasteboard box full of laced linen, and a little portmanteau with some white and grey Bone lace,"[15] would seem to signify a lace much made two hundred years ago, of which we have ourselves seen specimens from Dalecarlia, a sort of guipure, upon which the pattern is formed by the introduction of an unbleached thread, which comes out in full relief —a fancy more curious than pretty.

The petticoats of the ladies of King Charles's court have received due honour at the hands of Pepys, whose prying eyes seem to have been everywhere. On May 21 of the same year he so complacently admired himself in his new lace band, he writes down : " My wife and I to my Lord's lodging ; where she and I staid walking in White Hall Gardens. And in the Privy Garden saw the finest smocks and linnen petticoats of my Lady Castlemaine's, laced with rich lace at the bottom, that ever I saw ; and it did me good to look at them."

Speaking of the ladies' attire of this age, Evelyn says :—

" Another quilted white and red,
With a broad Flanders lace below ;

Campbell in 1856, at the Lincoln Lent Assizes, received from the sheriff a pair of white gloves richly trimmed with Brussels lace and embroidered, the city arms embossed in frosted silver on the back.

[13] *London Gazette.* 1677, Jan. 28–31. Again, Oct. 4–8, in the same year. " Stolen or lost out of the Petworth waggon, a deal box directed to the Lady Young of Burton in Sussex; there was in it a fine Point Apron, a suit of thin laced Night clothes," etc.

[14] *London Gazette.* 1675, June 14–17. " A right Point lace with a long musling neck laced at the ends with a narrow Point about three fingers broad, and a pair of Point cuffs of the same, worn foul and never washt, was lost on Monday last."

Ibid. 1677, Oct. 22–25. " Found in a ditch, Four laced forehead cloths. One laced Pinner, one laced Quoif, one pair of laced ruffels. . . . Two point aprons and other laced linen."

Intelligencer. 1664, Oct. 3. " Lost, A needle work point without a border, with a great part of the loups cut out, and a quarter of it new loupt with the needle. £5 reward."

[15] *London Gazette.* 1677, Oct. 8–11.

Four pairs of bas de soye shot through
With silver; diamond buckles too,
For garters, and as rich for shoe.
Twice twelve day smocks of Holland fine,
With cambric sleeves rich Point to joyn
(For she despises Colbertine);
Twelve more for night, all Flanders lac'd,
Or else she'll think herself disgrac'd.
The same her night gown must adorn,
With two Point waistcoats for the morn;
Of pocket mouchoirs, nose to drain,
A dozen laced, a dozen plain;
Three night gowns of rich Indian stuff;
Four cushion-cloths are scarce enough
Of Point and Flanders," [16] etc.

It is difficult now to ascertain what description of lace was that styled Colbertine.[17] It is constantly alluded to by the writers of the period. Randle Holme (1688) styles it, " A kind of open lace with a square grounding." [18] Evelyn himself, in his *Fop's Dictionary* (1690), gives, " Colbertine, a lace resembling net-work of the fabric of Monsieur Colbert, superintendent of the French King's manufactures ; " and the *Ladies' Dictionary*, 1694, repeats his definition. This is more incomprehensible still, point d'Alençon being the lace that can be specially styled of " the fabric " of Colbert, and Colbertine appears to have been a coarse production.[19] Swift talks of knowing

" The difference between
Rich Flanders lace and Colberteen." [20]

Congreve makes Lady Westport say—[21]

" Go hang out an old Frisonier gorget with a yard of yellow Colberteen."

And a traveller, in 1691,[22] speaking of Paris, writes :—" You shall see here the finer sort of people flaunting it in tawdry gauze or Colbertine, a parcel of coarse staring ribbons ; but ten of their holyday habits shall not amount to what a citizen's wife of London wears on her head every day."

---

[16] *Tyrannus, or the Mode.* 1661.

[17] It is written Colberteen, Colbertain, Golbertain, Colbertine.

[18] Colberteen, a lace resembling net-work, being of the manufacture of M. Colbert, a French statesman.

[19] A writer in *Notes and Queries* says : " I recollect this lace worn as a ruffle fifty years ago. The ground was square and coarse, it had a fine edge, with a round mesh, on which the pattern was woven. It was an inferior lace and in every-day wear."

[20] *Cadenus and Vanessa.* See also Young, p. 111.

[21] *Way of the World.*

[22] *Six Weeks in France.* 1691.

JAMES II.

The reign of James II., short and troubled, brought but little change in the fashion of the day; more prominence however, was given to the lace cravats, which were worn loosely round the throat, and with their ends hanging down over the upper part of the vest.

Charles II., in the last year of his reign, spends £20 12s. for a new cravat to be worn "on the birthday of his dear brother,"[23] and James expends £29 upon one of Venice point to appear in on that of his queen. Frequent entries of lace for the attendants of the Chapel Royal form items in the Royal Wardrobe Accounts.

Ruffles, night-rails, and cravats of point d'Espagne and de Venise now figure in Gazettes,[24] but "Flanders lace is still in high estimation," writes somebody, in 1668, "and even fans are made of it."

Then James II. fled, and years after we find him dying at St. Germains in—a laced nightcap. "This cap was called a 'toquet,' and put on when the king was in extremis, as a compliment to Louis XIV." "It was the court etiquette for all the Royals," writes Madame, in her *Memoirs*, "to die with a nightcap on." The toquet of King James may still be seen by the curious, adorning a wax model of the king's head, preserved as a relic in the Museum of Dunkirk.[25]

Out of mingled gratitude, we suppose, for the hospitality she had received at the French court, and the protection of the angels, which, she writes, "I experienced once when I

---

[23] Gt. W. A. Car. II. 35–36 = 1683–4.

[24] *Gazette*, July 20, 1682. Lost, a portmanteau full of women's clothes, among which are enumerated "two pairs of Point d'Espagne ruffles, a laced night rail and waistcoat, a pair of Point de Venise ruffles, a black laced scarf," etc.—*Malcolm's Anecdotes of London*.

The lace of James II.'s cravats and ruffles are of point de Venise.

Sex prælant cravatts de lacinia Venetiarum, are charged £141, and 9 yards lace, for six more cravats, £45.

£36 10s. for the cravat of Venice lace to wear on the day of his Coronation," etc.—G. W. A. Jac. II. 1685–6.

[25] A writer in the *Gentleman's Magazine* (October, 1745), mentions: "In the parlour of the monastery of English Benedictines at Paris, I was shown the mask of the king's face, taken off immediately after he was dead, together with the fine laced nightcap he died in." The cap at Dunkirk is trimmed with Flemish lace (old Mechlin). It must have

set fire to my lace night cornet, which was burned to the very head without singeing a single hair"—good Queen Mary of Modena, who shone so brightly in her days of adversity, died, *selon les règles,* coeffed in like fashion.

With this notice we finish the St. Germains reign of King James the Second.

WILLIAM III.

" Long wigs,
Steinkirk cravats."
—Congreve. *Love for Love.*

In William III.'s reign, the full shirt-sleeves, with their lace ruffles, were shown at the wrists, and the loose neck-cloths had long pendent ends terminating in lace, if they were not entirely made of that material. The hat, too, was edged with gold lace, and for summer wear the gloves were edged with lace.

Women's sleeves, at first short, wide and lace-edged, showing the delicate sleeves of the under garment, soon became tight, and were prolonged to the wrists, where they terminated in deep and wide upturned cuffs, whence drooped a profusion of lace lappets and ruffles.

The hair, combed up, and with an inclination backwards from the forehead, was surmounted by a strata of ribbon and lace, sometimes intermingled with feathers, and a kerchief or scarf of some very light material was permitted to hang down to the waist, or below it.

In 1698 the English Parliament passed another Act "for rendering the laws more effectual for preventing the importation of foreign Bone lace, Loom lace, Needlework Point, and Cutwork,"[26] with a penalty of 20*s.* per yard, and forfeiture. This Act caused such excitement among the convents and béguinages of Flanders that the Government, at that time under the dominion of Spain, prohibited, by way of retaliation, the importation of English wool. In consequence of the general distress occasioned by this edict

---

passed from Paris to the convent of English Benedictines at Dunkirk, who left that city in 1793. There is no record how it became deposited in the Museum.—Communicated by M. dem, Forçade, Conservator of the Museu la Dunkirk.

[26] 9 & 10 Will. III. = 1697–8.

among the woolstaplers of England, the Act prohibiting the importation of foreign lace into England was repealed,[27] so far as related to the Spanish Low Countries. England was the loser by this Custom-House war.[28]

Dress, after the Revolution, partook of the stately sobriety of the House of Nassau, but lace was extensively worn. Queen Mary favoured that wonderful erection, already spoken of in our chapter on France,[29] the tower or fontange, more generally called, certainly not from its convenience, the " commode," with its piled tiers of lace and ribbon, and the long hanging pinners, celebrated by Prior in his " Tale of the Widow and her Cat " :—

> " He scratch'd the maid, he stole the cream,
> He tore her best lac'd pinner."

Their Flanders lace heads, with the engageantes[30] or ruffles, and the dress covered with lace frills and flounces— " every part of the garment in curl "—caused a lady, says the *Spectator*, to resemble " a Friesland hen." [31]

Never yet were such sums expended on lace as in the days of William and Mary. The lace bill of the Queen, signed by Lady Derby, Mistress of the Robes, for the year 1694, amounts to the enormous sum of £1,918.[32] Among the most extravagant entries we find :—

	£.	s.	d.
21 yards of lace for 12 pillow beres, at 52s.	54	12	0
16 yards of lace for 2 toylights (toilets), at £12	192	0	0
24 yards for 6 handkerchiefs, at £4 10s.	108	0	0
30 yards for 6 night shifts, at 62s.	93	0	0
6 yards for 2 combing cloths, at £14	84	0	0

---

[27] 11 & 12 Will. III. = 1698–9.
[28] Smith's *Wealth of Nations*.
[29] See Louis XIV.
[30] See Louis XIV.
[31] *Spectator*, No. 129. 1711.
" Lost, from behind a Hackney coach, Lombard Street, a grounded lace night rail."—*London Gazette*. Aug. 8, 1695.
" Lost, two loopt lace Pinners and a pair of double laced ruffles, bundled up together."—*Ibid*. Jan. 6–10, 1697.
" Taken out of two boxes in Mr.

Drouth's waggon . . . six cards of piece lace looped and purled, scolopt heads to most of them . . . a fine Flanders lace head and ruffles, groundwork set on a wier," etc.—*Ibid*. April 11–14, 1698.

" Furbelows are not confined to scarfs, but, they must have furbelow'd gowns, and furbelow'd petticoats, and furbelow'd aprons; and, as I have heard, furbelow'd smocks too."—*Pleasant Art of Money-catching*. 1730.
[32] B. M. Add. MSS. No. 5751.

	£.	s.	d.
$3\frac{1}{2}$ yards for a combing cloth at £17 . . .	53	2	6
$3\frac{1}{8}$ do. at £14	42	0	0
An apron of lace	17	0	0

None of the lace furnished by Mr. Bampton, thread lace provider and milliner to the court, for the Queen's engageantes and ruffles, however, seems to have exceeded £5 10s. the yard. There is little new in this account. The lace is entered as scalloped,[33] ruffled, loopt: lace purle [34] still lingers on ; catgut, too, appears for the first time,[35] as well as raised point [36] and needlework.[37] The Queen's pinners are mentioned as Mazzarined ;[38] some fashion named in honour of the once fair Hortense, who ended her exiled life in England.

> "What do you lack, ladies fair,
> Mazzarine hoods, Fontanges, girdles ? " [39]

King William himself, early imbued with the Dutch taste for lace, exceeded, we may say, his wife in the extravagance of his lace bills ; for though the lace account for 1690 is noted only at £1,603, it increases annually until the year 1695–6, when the entries amount to the astonishing sum of £2,459 19s.[40] Among the items charged will be found :—

	£.	s.	d.
To six point cravats	158	0	0
To eight do. for hunting . .	85	0	0
54 yds. for 6 barbing cloths . . .	270	0	0
63 yds. for 6 combing cloths . . .	283	10	0
117 yards of " scissæ teniæ " (cut-work) for trimming 12 pockethandfs. .	485	14	3
78 yds. for 24 cravats, at £8 10s. .	663	0	0

---

[33] " Bought of John Bishop & Jer. Peirie, att y° Golden Ball, in Ludgate Hill, 26 April, 1693 :

" 3 yards 1/2 of Rich silver rufl'd scollop lace falbala, with a Rich broad silver Tire Orris at the head, at 7s. 3d. a yard, £25 0s. 6d.

" 8 yards of broad scollopped thread lace, at 25s.

" 3 yards Rich Paigning (?) Lace, 48s. 8d., £8 14s."

[34] " 9 1/2 Fine purle to set on the pinner. at 3s."

[35] " 5 3/4 of fine broad cattgutt border, at 20s."

[36] " 1 yard 7/16 Raised Point to put on the top of a pair of sleeves, at 30s."

[37] " 8 yards of Broad Needlework Lace, at 30s."

[38] " 3 yards of lace to Mazzarine y° pinners, at 25s."

Probably the same as the French " campanner."

[39] The Milliner, in Shadwell's *Bury Fair.* 1720.

[40] G. W. A. Will. III. 1688 to 1702. P. R. O.

In this right royal account of expenditure we find mention of " cockscombe laciniæ," of which the King consumes 344 yards.[41] What this may be we cannot say, as it is described as " green and white"; otherwise we might have supposed it some kind of Venice point, the little pearl-edged raised patterns of which are designated by Randle Holme as " cockscombs." More coquet than a woman, we find an exchange effected with Henry Furness, " Mercatori," of various laces, purchased for his handkerchiefs and razor cloths, which, laid by during the two years of " lugubris" for his beloved consort, the Queen—during which period he had used razor cloths with broad hems and no lace—had become " obsolete"—quite out of fashion. To effect this exchange the King pays the sum of £178 12s. 6d., the lace purchased for the six new razor cloths amounting to £270. In the same page we find him, now out of mourning, expending £499 10s. for lace to trim his twenty-four new nightshirts, " indusiis nocturnis."

With such royal patronage, no wonder the lace trade prospered, and that, within ten years of William's death, Defoe should quote the point lace of Blandford as selling at £30 the yard.

We have already told how the fashion of the laced Steinkirk found as much favour in England [42] as in France. Many people still possess, among their family relics, long oval-shaped brooches of topaz or Bristol stones, and wonder

---

[41] *Ibid.* vii. & viii.

[42] " I hope your Lordship is pleased with your Steinkerk."—Sir John Vanbrugh. *The Relapse.*

In Colley Cibber's *Careless Husband*, Lady Easy takes the Steinkirk off her neck and lays it on Sir Charles's head when he is asleep.

In *Love's Last Shift*, by the same author (1695), the hero speaks of being " Strangled in my own Steinkerk."

In *Love for Love*, by Congreve, Sir Novelty enumerates the Steinkirk, the large button, with other fashions, as created by him.

" I have heard the Steinkirk arrived but two months ago."—*Spectator*, No. 129.

The " modish spark" wears " a huge Steinkirk, twisted to the waist."—

1694. *Prologue to First Part of Don Quixote.*

Frank Osbaldeston, in *Rob Roy*, is deprived by the Highlanders of his cravat, " a Steinkirke richly laced."

At Ham House was the portrait of a Countess of Dysart, temp. Anne, in three-cornered cocked hat, long coat, flapped waistcoat, and Mechlin Steinkirk.

In the Account Book of Isabella, Duchess of Grafton, daughter of Lord Arlington, Evelyn's " sweet child"— her portrait hangs in Queen Mary's Room, Hampton Court—we have : " 1709. To a Stinkirk, £1 12s. 3d."

They appear to have been made of other stuffs than lace, for in the same account, 1708, we have entered : " To a green Steenkirk, £1 1s. 6d."

what they were used for. These old-fashioned articles of jewellery were worn to fasten (when not passed through the button-hole) the lace Steinkirk, so prevalent not only among the nobility, but worn by all classes. If the dialogue between Sir Nicholas Dainty and Major-General Blunt, as given in Shadwell's play, be correct, the volunteers of King William's day were not behind the military in elegance :—

" SIR NICHOLAS.—I must make great haste, I shall ne'er get my Points and Laces done up time enough.
" MAJ. GEN. B.—What say'st, young fellow ? Points and Laces for camps ?
" SIR NICH.—Yes, Points and Laces; why, I carry two laundresses on purpose. . . . Would you have a gentleman go undress'd in a camp ? Do you think I would see a camp if there was no dressing ? Why, I have two campaign suits, one trimmed with Flanders lace, and the other with rich Point.
" MAJ. GEN. B.—Campaign suits with lace and Point ! " [43]

In Westminster Abbey, where, as somewhat disrespectfully, say the Brothers Popplewell,[44] the images of William and Mary

" Stand upright in a press, with their bodies made of wax,
A globe and a wand in either hand and their robes upon their backs "—

the lace tucker and double sleeves of Queen Mary are of the finest raised Venice point, resembling Fig. 29 ; King William likewise wears a rich lace cravat and ruffles.[45]

In a memorandum (carta d' informazione) given to the Venetian ambassadors about to proceed to England, 1696, they are to be provided with very handsome collars of the finest Venetian point, which, it is added, is also the best present to make.[46]

Before concluding the subject of the lace-bearing heroes, we may as well state here that the English soldiers rivalled the cavaliers of France in the richness of their points till the extinction of hair-powder (the wearing of which in the army consumes, says some indignant writer, flour enough to feed 600,000 persons per annum), when the lace cravat was replaced by the stiff and cumbersome stock. Speaking of

[43] *The Volunteers, or the Stock Jobbers.*
[44] " The Tombs in Westminster Abbey," sung by the Brothers Popplewell. Broadside, 1775.—B. M. Roxburgh Coll.
[45] King Charles II.'s lace is the same as that of Queen Mary. The Duchess of Buckingham (the " mad " Duchess, daughter of James II.) has also very fine raised lace.
[46] Venice, Bib. St. Mark. Contarini Miscellany. Communicated by Mr. Rawdon Brown.

these military dandies, writes the *World*: "Nor can I behold the lace and the waste of finery in their clothing but in the same light as the silver plates and ornaments on a coffin; indeed, I am apt to impute their going to battle so trimmed and adorned to the same reason a once fine lady painted her cheeks just before she expired, that she might not look frightful when she was dead."

> "To war the troops advance,
> Adorned and trim like females for the dance.
> Down sinks Lothario, sent by one dire blow,
> A well-dress'd hero to the shades below."

As the justice's daughter says to her mamma, in Sheridan's *St. Patrick's Day* :—

> "Dear; to think how the sweet fellows sleep on the ground, and fight in silk stockings and lace ruffles."

Lace had now become an article worthy the attention of the light-fingered gentry. The jewels worn by our great-grandmothers of the eighteenth century, though mounted in the most exquisite taste, were for the most part false— Bristol or Alençon "diamonds," paste, or "Strass." Lace, on the other hand, was a sure commodity and easily disposed of. At the robbery of Lady Anderson's house in Red Lion Square during a fire, in 1700, the family of George Heneage, Esq., on a visit, are recorded to have lost—"A head with fine loopt lace, of very great value; a Flanders lace hood; a pair of double ruffles and tuckers; two laced aprons, one point, the other Flanders lace; and a large black lace scarf embroidered in gold."

Again, at an opera row some years later, the number of caps, ruffles, and heads enumerated as stolen by the pickpockets is quite fabulous. So expert had they become, that when first the ladies took to wearing powdered wigs, they dexterously cut open the leather backs of the hack coaches and carried off wig, head and all, before the rifled occupant had the slightest idea of their attack.[47] To remedy the evil, the police request all ladies for the future to sit with their backs to the horses.[48]

---

[47] *Weekly Journal.* March, 1717.   [48] *The Modern Warrior.* 1756.

QUEEN ANNE.

"PARLEY.—Oh, Sir, there's the prettiest fashion lately come over! so airy, so French, and all that! The Pinners are double ruffled with twelve plaits of a side, and open all from the face; the hair is frizzled up all round head, and stands as stiff as a bodkin. Then the Favourites hang loose upon the temple with a languishing lock in the middle. Then the Caule is extremely wide, and over all is a Cornet rais'd very high and all the Lappets behind."—Farquhar. *Sir Harry Wildair.*

Queen Anne, though less extravagant than her sister, was scarcely more patriotic. The point purchased for her coronation,[49] though it cost but £64 13s. 9d., was of Flanders growth. The bill is made out to the royal laceman of King William's day, now Sir Henry Furnesse, knight and merchant.

The Queen, too, in her gratitude, conferred a pension of £100 upon one Mrs. Abrahat, the royal clear-starcher; " because," writes the Duchess of Marlborough, " she had washed the Queen's heads for twenty pounds a year when she was princess."

In 1706 Anne again repeals the Acts which prohibit Flanders lace, with the clear understanding that nothing be construed into allowing the importation of lace made in " the dominions of the French King ";[50] an edict in itself sufficient to bring the points of France into the highest fashion.[51]

" France," writes an essayist, " is the wardrobe of the world ; " nay, " the English have so great an esteem for the workmanship of the French refugees, that hardly a thing vends without a Gallic name."[52]

To the refugees from Alençon and elsewhere, expelled by the cruel edict of Louis XIV., we owe the visible improvement of our laces in the eighteenth century.

Up to the present time we have had mention only of

---

[49] Acc. of Ralph, Earl of Montague, Master of the G. W., touching the Funeral of William III. and Coronation of Queen Anne. P. R. O.

[50] Statutes at large.—Anne 5 & 6.

[51] This edict greatly injured the lace trade of France. In the *Atlas Maritime et Commercial* of 1727, it states : " I might mention several other articles of French manufacture which, for want of a market in England where their chief consumption was, are so much decayed and in a manner quite sunk. I mean as to exportation, the English having now set up the same among themselves, such as bone lace."

[52] *History of Trade.* London, 1702.

" Flanders lace " in general. In the reign of Queen Anne
the points of " Macklin " and Brussels are first noted down
in the Royal Wardrobe Accounts. In 1710 her Majesty
pays for 26 yards of fine edged Brussels lace £151.[53] " Mais,
l'appétit vient en mangeant." The bill of Margareta Jolly,
for the year 1712, for the furnishing of Mechlin and Brussels
lace alone, amounts to the somewhat extravagant sum of
£1,418 14s. Taking the average price of the " Lace chanter
on Ludgate Hill," articles of daily use were costly enough.
' One Brussels head is valued at £40 ; a grounded Brussels
head, £30 ; one looped Brussels, £30." These objects, high
as the price may seem, lasted a woman's life. People in the
last century did not care for variety, they contented themselves with a few good articles ; hence among the objects
given in 1719, as necessary to a lady of fashion, we merely
find :—

	£	s.	d.
A French point or Flanders head and ruffles .	80	0	0
A ditto handkerchief	10	0	0
A black French laced hood	5	5	0

When the Princess Mary, daughter of George II.,
married, she had but four fine laced Brussels heads, two
loopt and two grounded, two extremely fine point ones, with
ruffles and lappets, six French caps and ruffles.[54]

Two point lace cravats were considered as a full supply
for any gentleman. Even young extravagant Lord Bedford,
who, at eighteen years of age, found he could not spend less
than £6,000 a year at Rome, when on the grand tour,
only charges his mother, Rachel Lady Russell, with that
number.[55]

The high commode,[56] with its lace rising tier upon tier,
which made the wits about town declare the ladies " carried
Bow steeple upon their heads," of a sudden collapsed in
Queen Anne's reign. It had shot up to a most extravagant
height, " insomuch that the female part of our species were

---

[53] " Pro 14 virgis lautæ Fimbr'
Bruxell' laciniæ et 12 virgis dict' laciniæ pro Reginæ persona, £151."—
G. W. A. 1710–11.
[54] *Letters of the Countess of Hartford to the Countess of Pomfret.* 1740.

[55] *Memoirs of Lady R. Russell.*
[56] " My high commode, my damask
    gown,
    My laced shoes of Spanish
    leather."
—D'Urfey. *The Young Maid's Portion.*

much taller than the men. We appeared," says the *Spectator*,[57] " as grasshoppers before them." [58]

In 1711 Anne forbade the entry of gold and silver lace,[59] of which the consumption had become most preposterous,[60] under pain of forfeiture and the fine of £100. Ladies wore even cherry-coloured stays trimmed with the forbidden fabric.[61] The point of Spain had the preference over thread lace for state garments, heads and ruffles excepted; and as late as 1763, when the Dowager Lady Effingham was robbed of her coronation robes, among the wonderful finery detailed there is no mention of thread lace.

The commerce of Flanders, notwithstanding the French taste, seemed now on a comfortable footing. "The Flanderkins," writes the *British Merchant* in 1713, " are gone off from wool, which we have got, to lace and linen. . . . We have learned better, I hope, by our unsuccessful attempt to prohibit the Flanders laces, which made the Flemings retaliate upon us, and lessened our exportation of woollen manufactures by several £100,000 per annum." [62]

Men looked upon lace as a necessary article to their wives' equipment. Addison declares that when the China mania first came in, women exchanged their Flanders point for punch-bowls and mandarins, thus picking their husbands' pockets, who is often purchasing a huge china vase when he fancies that he is buying a fine head for his wife.[63] Indeed, they could scarcely grumble, as a good wig cost from forty to fifty guineas—to say nothing of their own lace ties and

---

[57] No. 98. 1711.

[58] After fifteen years' discontinuance it shot up again. Swift, on meeting the Duchess of Grafton, dining at Sir Thomas Hanmer's, thus attired, declared she "looked like a mad woman."

[59] Statutes at large.

[60] In 1712 Mrs. Beale had stolen from her " a green silk knit waistcoat with gold and silver flowers all over it, and about 14 yards of gold and silver thick lace on it "; while another lady was robbed of a scarlet cloth coat so overlaid with the same lace, it might have been of any other colour.—*Malcolm's Anecdotes of the Manners and Customs of London in the Eighteenth Century.*

[61] *Post Boy.* Nov. 15, 1709. Articles Lost.

[62] *A Discourse on Trade*, by John Cary, merchant of Bristol. 1717. Again : " What injury was done by the Act 9-10 Will. III. for the more effectual preventing of importation of foreign bone lace, doth sufficiently appear by the preamble to that made 10–12 of the same reign for repealing it three months after the prohibition of our woollen manufactures in Flanders (which was occasioned by it) should be taken off; but I don't understand it be yet done, and it may prove an inevitable loss to the nation."

[63] *Lover.* No. 10. 1714.

ruffles.   Only an old antiquary like Sir Thomas Clayton could note down in his accounts :—" Lace and fal-lalls,[64] and a large looking-glass to see her old ugly face in—frivolous expenses to please my proud lady."

---

[64] The ornamental ribbons worn about the dress: " His dress has bows, and fine fallals."—Evelyn. Sometimes the term appears applied to the Fontanges or Commode. We read (1691) of " her three-storied Fladdal."

CHAPTER XXVI.

GEORGE I. AND II.

GEORGE I.

" Wisdom with periwigs, with cassocks grace,
Courage with swords, gentility with lace."—*Connoisseur.*

THE accession of the House of Hanover brought but little change either in the fashions or the fabrics. In 1717 the King published an edict regarding the hawking of lace, but the world was too much taken up with the Old Pretender and the court of St. Germains; the King, too, was often absent, preferring greatly his German dominions.

We now hear a great deal of lace ruffles; they were worn long and falling. Lord Bolingbroke, who enraged Queen Anne by his untidy dress—" she supposed, forsooth, he would some day come to court in his nightcap "—is described as having his cravat of point lace, and his hands hidden by exaggerated ruffles of the same material. In good old Jacobite times, these weeping ruffles served as well to conceal notes—" poulets "—passed from one wary politician to another, as they did the French sharpers to juggle and cheat at cards.

Lace continued the mania of the day. " Since your fantastical geers came in with wires, ribbons, and laces, and your furbelows with three hundred yards in a gown and petticoat, there has not been a good housewife in the nation," [1] writes an indignant dramatist. The lover was made to bribe the Abigail of his mistress with a piece of Flanders lace [2]—an offering not to be resisted. Lace appeared

---

[1] *Tunbridge Wells.* 1727.

[2] In *The Recruiting Officer* (1781), Lucy the maid says : " Indeed, Madam, the last bribe I had from the Captain

at baptisms,[3] at marriages, as well as at burials, of which more hereafter—even at the Old Bailey, where one Miss Margaret Caroline Rudd, a beauty of the day, tried for forgery, quite moved her jurors to tears, and nigh gained her acquittal by the taste of her elegantly-laced stomacher, the lace robings of her dress, and single lace flounce, her long pendulous ruffles, hanging from the elbow, heard, fluttering in her agitation, by the court; but, in spite of these allurements, Margaret Caroline Rudd was hanged.

Every woman, writes Swift,[4] is

> " In choosing lace a critic nice,
> Knows to a groat the lowest price."

Together, they

> " Of caps and ruffles hold the grave debate,
> As of their lives they would decide the fate."

Again, he says :—

" And when you are among yourselves, how naturally, after the first compliments, do you entertain yourselves with the price and choice of lace, apply your hands to each other's lappets and ruffles, as if the whole business of your life and the public concern depended on the cut of your petticoats." [5]

Even wise Mrs. Elizabeth Montague, who wrote epistles about the ancients, and instead of going to a ball, sat at home and read Sophocles, exclaims to her sister—" Surely

---

was only a small piece of Flanders lace for a cap." Melinda answers : " Ay, Flanders lace is a constant present from officers. . . . They every year bring over a cargo of lace, to cheat the king of his duty and his subjects of their honesty." Again, Silvio, in the bill of costs he sends in to the widow Zelinda, at the termination of his unsuccessful suit, makes a charge for " a piece of Flanders lace " to Mrs. Abigail, her woman.—Addison, in *Guardian*, No. 17. 1713.

[3] " In the next reign, George III. and Queen Charlotte often condescended to become sponsors to the children of the aristocracy. To one child their presence was fatal. In 1778 they ' stood ' to the infant daughter of the last Duke and Duchess

of Chandos. Cornwallis, Archbishop of Canterbury, officiated. The baby, overwhelmed by whole mountains of lace, lay in a dead faint. Her mother was so tender on the point of etiquette, that she would not let the little incident trouble a ceremony at which a king and queen were about to endow her child with the names of Georgiana Charlotte. As Cornwallis gave back the infant to her nurse, he remarked that it was the quietest baby he had ever held. Poor victim of ceremony! It was not quite dead, but dying; in a few unconscious hours it calmly slept away."—"A Gossip on Royal Christenings." *Cornhill Magazine.* April, 1864.

[4] " Furniture of a Woman's Mind.
[5] " Dean Swift to a Young . adv."

PLATE LXXXIV.

JOHN LAW, THE PARIS BANKER, Author of the Mississippi Scheme, 1671–1729.—
In cravat of Point de France, between 1708–20.   Painted by Belle.
National Portrait Gallery.

Photo by Walker and Cockerell.

your heroic spirit will prefer a beau's hand in Brussels lace to a stubborn Scævola without an arm."

In the middle of the nineteenth century it was the fashion that no young lady should wear lace previous to her marriage. In the reign of George II. etiquette was different, for we find the Duchess of Portland presenting Mrs. Montague, then a girl, with a lace head and ruffles.

Wrathfully do the satirists of the day rail against the expense of

> "The powder, patches, and the pins,
> The ribbon, jewels, and the rings,
> The lace, the paint, and warlike things
> That make up all their magazines," [6]

and the consequent distress of the lace merchants, to whom ladies are indebted for thousands. After a drawing-room, in which the fair population appeared in " borrowed," *i.e.*, unpaid lace,[7] one of the chief lacemen became well-nigh bankrupt. Duns besieged the houses of the great :—

> "By mercers, lacemen, mantua-makers press'd;
> But most for ready cash, for play distress'd,
> Where can she turn ? " [8]

The *Connoisseur*, describing the reckless extravagance of one of these ladies, writes :—" The lady played till all her ready money was gone, staked her cap and lost it, afterwards her handkerchief. He then staked both cap and handkerchief against her tucker, which, to his pique, she gained." When enumerating the various causes of suicide, he proposes " that an annual bill or report should be made out, giving the different causes which have led to the act." Among others, in his proposed " Bill of Suicide," he gives French claret, French lace, French cooks, etc.

The men, though scarcely coming up to the standard of Sir Courtly Nice,[9] who has all his bands and linen made in Holland and washed at Haarlem, were just as extravagant as the ladies.

---

[6] Cowley.

[7] 1731. *Simile for the Ladies, alluding to the laces worn at the last Birthday and not paid for.*

" In Evening fair you may behold
The Clouds are fringed with borrowed gold,
And this is many a lady's case
Who flaunts about in borrowed lace."

[8] Jenyns. " The Modern Fine Lady."

[9] Crown. *Sir Courtly Nice, or It Cannot Be*, a Comedy. 1731.

GEORGE II.

" ' How well this ribband's glass becomes your face,'
She cries in rapture ; ' then so sweet a lace !
How charmingly you look ! ' "
—Lady M. W. Montagu. *Town Eclogues.*

For court and state occasions Brussels lace still held its sway.

In the reign of George II. we read how, at the drawing-room of 1735, fine escalloped Brussels laced heads, triple ditto laced ruffles,[10] lappets hooked up with diamond solitaires, found favour. At the next the ladies wore heads dressed English, *i.e.,* bow of fine Brussels lace of exceeding rich patterns, with the same amount of laced ruffles and lappets. Gold flounces were also worn.

Speaking of the passion for Brussels lace, Postlethwait indignantly observes :—" 'Tis but a few years since England expended upon foreign lace and linen not less than two millions yearly. As lace in particular is the manufacture of nuns, our British ladies may as well endow monasteries as wear Flanders lace, for these Popish nuns are maintained by Protestant contributions." [11]

Patriotism, it would appear, did come into vogue in the year 1736, when at the marriage of Frederick, Prince of Wales, the bride is described as wearing a night-dress of superb lace, the bridegroom a cap of similar material. All the laces worn by the court on this occasion are announced to have been of English manufacture, with the exception of that of the Duke of Marlborough, who appeared in point d'Espagne. The bride, however, does not profit by this high example, for shortly after we read, in the *Memoirs of Madame Palatine*, of the secretary of Sir Luke Schaub being drugged at Paris by an impostor, and robbed of some money sent to defray the purchase of some French lace ruffles for the Princess of Wales.

---

[10] " 1748. Ruffles of twelve pounds a yard."—*Apology for Mrs. T. C. Philips.* 1748.

Lace, however, might be had at a more reasonable rate :—

" ' I have a fine lac'd suit of pinners,' says Mrs. Thomas, ' that was my great-grandmother's ! that has been worn but twice these forty years, and my mother told me cost almost four pounds when it was new, and reaches down hither.' "—" Miss Lucy in Town." Fielding.

[11] *Dictionary of Commerce.* 1766.

It was of native-made laces, we may infer, Mrs. Delany writes in the same year :—" Thanks for your apron. Brussels nor Mechlin ever produced anything prettier."

It appears somewhat strange that patriotism, as regards native manufactures, should have received an impulse during the reign of that most uninteresting though gallant little monarch, the second George of Brunswick.[12] But patriotism has its evils, for, writes an essayist, "some ladies now squander away all their money in fine laces, because it sets a great many poor people to work." [13]

Ten years previous to the death of King George II. was founded, with a view to correct the prevalent taste for foreign manufactures,[14] the Society of Anti-Gallicans, who held their quarterly meetings, and distributed prizes for bone, point lace, and other articles of English manufacture.[15]

This society, which continued in great activity for many years, proved most beneficial to the lace-making trade. It excited also a spirit of emulation among gentlewomen of the middle class, who were glad in the course of the year to add to a small income by making the finer kinds of needle-point, which, on account of their elaborate workmanship, could be produced only in foreign convents or by

---

[12] He was a martinet about his own dress, for his biographer relates during the last illness of Queen Caroline (1737), though the King was "visibly affected," remembering he had to meet the foreign ministers next day, he gave particular directions to his pages " to see that new ruffles were sewn on his old shirt sleeves, whereby he might wear a decent air in the eyes of the representatives of foreign majesty."

[13] " By a list of linen furnished to the Princesses Louisa and Mary, we find their night-dresses were trimmed with lace at 10s. per yard, and while their Royal Highnesses were in bibs, they had six suits of broad lace for aprons at from £50 to £60 each suit."—*Corr. of the Countess of Suffolk, Lady of the Bedchamber to Queen Caroline.*

Observe also the lace-trimmed aprons, ruffles, tuckers, etc., in the pretty picture of the family of Frederick, Prince of Wales, at Hampton Court Palace.

[14] The laws regarding the introduction of lace during this reign continued much the same until 1749, when the royal assent was given to an Act preventing the importation or wear of gold, silver, and thread lace manufactured in foreign parts.

[15] In the meeting of Nov. 10, 1752, at the " Crown, behind the Royal Exchange," the Hon. Edward Vernon, grand president, in the chair, it was agreed that the following premiums should be awarded: " For the best pair of men's needlework ruffles, to be produced to the committee in the first week of May next, five guineas ; to the second, three guineas ; to the third, two guineas. And for the best pair of English bone lace for ladies' lappets, to be produced to the committee in August next, fifteen guineas ; to the second, ten guineas ; to the third, five guineas." — *Gentleman's Magazine.*

persons whose maintenance did not entirely depend upon the work of their hands.

Towards the year 1756 certain changes in the fashion of the day now again mark the period, for—

"Dress still varying, most to form confined,
Shifts like the sands, the sport of every wind."

"Long lappets, the horse-shoe cap, the Brussels head, and the prudish mob pinned under the chin, have all had their day," says the *Connoisseur* in 1754. Now we have first mention of lace cardinals; trollopies or slammerkins [16] come in at the same period, with treble ruffles to the cuffs; writers talk, too, of a "gentle dame in blonde lace," blonde being as yet a newly-introduced manufacture.

Though history may only be all false,[17] as Sir Robert Walpole said to that "cynic in lace ruffles," his son Horace, yet the newspapers are to be depended upon for the fashion of the day, or, as Lady Mary would say, "for what new whim adorns the ruffle." [18]

The lace apron,[19] worn since the days of Queen Elizabeth, continued to hold its own till the end of the eighteenth century, though some considered it an appendage scarcely consistent with the dignity of polite society. The anecdote of Beau Nash, who held these articles in the strongest aversion, has been often related. "He absolutely excluded," says his biographer, "all who ventured to appear at the Assembly Room at Bath so attired. I have known him at a ball night strip the Duchess of Queensberry, and throw her apron on one of the hinder benches among the ladies' women, observing that none but Abigails appeared in white aprons; though that apron was of the costliest point, and cost two hundred guineas." [20]

---

[16] "Cardinal," a loose cloak after the fashion of a cardinal's "*trollopée*," a loose flowing gown open in the front, worn as a morning dress.—Fairholt. "Slammerkin," a sort of loose dress. This ugly word, in course of time, was used as an adjective, to signify untidy. Fortunately it is now obsolete.

[17] "Don't read history to me, for that I know to be false," said Sir R. Walpole to his son Horace, when he offered to read to him in his last illness.

[18] Lady M. W. Montagu. "Letter to Lord Harvey on the King's Birthday."

[19] "The working apron, too, from France,
With all its trim appurtenance."
—"Mundus Muliebris."

[20] Goldsmith. *Life of Richard Nash, of Bath*. London, 1762.

George II. did his best to promote the fabrics of his country, but at this period smuggling increased with fearful rapidity. It was a war to the knife between the revenue officer and society at large : all classes combined, town ladies of high degree with waiting-maids and the common sailor, to avoid the obnoxious duties and cheat the Government. To this subject we devote the following chapter.

CHAPTER XXVII.

SMUGGLING.

" May that mistaken taste be starv'd to reason,
    That does not think French fashions—English treason.
    Souse their cook's talent, and cut short their tailors;
    Wear your own lace; eat beef like Vernon's sailors."
                            —Aaron Hill.   1754.

WE have had occasional mention of this kindly-looked-upon
offence, in the carrying out of which many a reckless seaman
paid the penalty of his life in the latter part of the
eighteenth century.

From 1700 downwards, though the edicts prohibiting the
entry of Flanders lace were repealed, the points of France,
Spain and Venice, with other fabrics of note, were still
excluded from our ports. "England," writes Anderson,[1]
"brings home in a smuggling way from France much fine
lace and other prohibited fopperies." Prohibition went for
nothing; foreign lace ladies would have, and if they could
not smuggle it themselves, the smuggler brought it to
them. It was not till 1751 that the Customs appear to have
used undue severity as regards the entries, prying into
people's houses, and exercising a surveillance of so strict a
nature as to render the chance to evade their watchfulness a
very madness on the part of all degrees. In short, there
was not a female within ten miles of a seaport, writes an
essayist, that was in possession of a Mechlin lace cap or
pinner but they examined her title to it.

Lord Chesterfield, whose opinion that " dress is a very
silly thing, but it is much more silly not to be dressed
according to your station," was more than acted up to,
referring to the strictness of the Customs, writes to his son

---

[1] 1764.

in 1751, when coming over on a short visit: " Bring only two or three of your laced shirts, and the rest plain ones."

The revenue officers made frequent visits to the tailors' shops, and confiscated whatever articles they found of foreign manufacture.

On January 19th, 1752, a considerable quantity of foreign lace, gold and silver, seized at a tailor's, who paid the penalty of £100, was publicly burnt.[2]

George III., who really from his coming to the throne endeavoured to protect English manufactures, ordered, in 1764, all the stuffs and laces worn at the marriage of his sister, the Princess Augusta, to the Duke of Brunswick, to be of English manufacture. To this decree the nobility paid little attention. Three days previous to the marriage a descent was made by the Customs on the court milliner of the day, and nearly the whole of the clothes, silver, gold stuffs and lace, carried off, to the dismay of the modiste, as well as of the ladies deprived of their finery. The disgusted French milliner retired with a fortune of £11,000 to Versailles, where she purchased a villa, which, in base ingratitude to the English court, she called " La Folie des Dames Anglaises." In May of the same year three wedding garments, together with a large seizure of French lace, weighing nearly 100 lbs., were burnt at Mr. Coxe's refinery, conformably to the Act of Parliament. The following birthday, warned by the foregoing mischances, the nobility appeared in clothes and laces entirely of British manufacture.

Every paper tells how lace and ruffles of great value, sold on the previous day, had been seized in a hackney coach, between St. Paul's and Covent Garden; how a lady of rank was stopped in her chair and relieved of French lace to a large amount; or how a poor woman, carelessly picking a quartern loaf as she walked along, was arrested, and the loaf found to contain £200 worth of lace. Even ladies when walking had their black lace mittens cut off their hands, the officers supposing them to be of French manufacture; and lastly, a Turk's turban, of most Mameluke dimensions, was found, containing a stuffing of £90 worth of lace. Books,

---

[2] *Gentleman's Magazine.*

bottles, babies, false-bottomed boxes, umbrellas, daily poured
out their treasures to the lynx-eyed officers.

In May, 1765, the lace-makers joined the procession of
the silk-workers of Spitalfields to Westminster, bearing flags
and banners, to which were attached long floating pieces of
French lace, demanding of the Lords redress, and the total
exclusion of foreign goods. On receiving an answer that it
was too late, they must wait till next Session, the assemblage
declared that they would not be put off by promises ; they
broke the Duke of Bedford's palings on their way home, and
threatened to burn the premises of Mr. Carr, an obnoxious
draper. At the next levée they once more assembled before
St. James's, but, finding the dresses of the nobility to be
all of right English stuff, retired satisfied, without further
clamour.

The papers of the year 1764 teem with accounts of
seizures made by the Customs. Among the confiscated
effects of a person of the highest quality are enumerated :
" 16 black à-la-mode cloaks, trimmed with lace ; 44 French
lace caps ; 11 black laced handkerchiefs ; 6 lace hats ; 6 ditto
aprons ; 10 pairs of ruffles ; 6 pairs of ladies' blonde ditto,
and 25 gentlemen's." Eleven yards of edging and 6 pairs
of ruffles are extracted from the pocket of the footman.
Everybody smuggled. A gentleman attached to the Spanish
Embassy is unloaded of 36 dozen shirts, with fine Dresden
ruffles and jabots, and endless lace, in pieces, for ladies'
wear. These articles had escaped the vigilance of the
officers at Dover, but were seized on his arrival by the
coach at Southwark. Though Prime Ministers in those days
accepted bribes, the Custom-house officers seem to have done
their duty.[3]

When the body of his Grace the Duke of Devonshire was
brought over from France, where he died, the officers, to the
anger of his servants, not content with opening and searching
the coffin, poked the corpse with a stick to ascertain if it was
a real body ; but the trick of smuggling in coffins was too

---

[3] 1767. "An officer of the customs
seized nearly £400 worth of Flanders
lace, artfully concealed in the hollow
of a ship's buoy, on board a French
trader, lying off Iron Gate."—*Annual*
Register.
1772. "27,000 ells of French (Blois ?)
lace were seized in the port of Leigh
alone."—*Gentleman's Magazine.*

old to be attempted. Forty years before, when a deceased clergyman was conveyed from the Low Countries for interment, the body of the corpse was found to have disappeared, and to have been replaced by Flanders lace of immense value—the head and hands and feet alone remaining. This discovery did not, however, prevent the High Sheriff of Westminster from running—and that successfully—£6,000 worth of French lace in the coffin of Bishop Atterbury,[4] when his body was brought over from Calais for interment.

Towards the close of the French war, in the nineteenth century, smuggling of lace again became more rife than ever. It was in vain the authorities stopped the travelling carriages on their road from seaport towns to London, rifled the baggage of the unfortunate passengers by the mail at Rochester and Canterbury; they were generally outwitted, though spies in the pay of the Customs were ever on the watch.

Mrs. Palliser had in her possession a Brussels veil of great beauty, which narrowly escaped seizure. It belonged to a lady who was in the habit of accompanying her husband, for many years member for one of the Cinque Ports. The day after the election she was about to leave for London, somewhat nervous as to the fate of a Brussels veil she had purchased of a smuggler for a hundred guineas; when, at a dinner-party, it was announced that Lady Ellenborough, wife of the Lord Chief Justice, had been stopped near Dover, and a large quantity of valuable lace seized concealed in the lining of her carriage. Dismayed at the news, the lady imparted her trouble to a gentleman at her side, who immediately offered to take charge of the lace and convey it to London, remarking that " no one would suspect him, as he was a bachelor." Turning round suddenly, she observed one of the hired waiters to smile, and at once settling him to be a spy, she loudly accepted the offer; but that night, before going to bed, secretly caused the veil to be sewn up in the waistcoat of the newly-elected M.P., in such a manner that it filled the hollow of his back. Next morning they started, and reached London in safety, while her friend, who remained two days later, was stopped, and underwent

---

[4] The turbulent Bishop of Rochester, who was arraigned for his Jacobite intrigues, and died in exile at Paris. 1731.

a rigorous but unsuccessful examination from the Custom-house officers.

The free trade principles of the nineteenth century put a more effectual stop to smuggling than all the activity of revenue officers, spies, and informers, or even laws framed for the punishment of the offenders.

CHAPTER XXVIII.

GEORGE III.

"In clothes, cheap handsomeness doth bear the bell,
Wisdome's a trimmer thing than shop e'er gave.
Say not then, This with that lace will do well;
But, This with my discretion will be brave.
Much curiousnesse is a perpetual wooing,
Nothing with labour, fully long a doing."
—Herbert, "The Church Porch."

In 1760 commences the reign of George III. The King was patriotic, and did his best to encourage the fabrics of his country.

From the year 1761 various Acts were passed for the benefit of the lace-makers : the last, that of 1806, "increases the duties on foreign laces." [1]

Queen Charlotte, on her first landing in England, wore, in compliment to the subjects of her royal consort, a fly cap richly trimmed, with lappets of British lace, and a dress of similar manufacture.

The Englishman, however, regardless of the Anti-Gallicans, preferred his "Macklin" and his Brussels to all the finest productions of Devonshire or Newport-Pagnel.

Ruffles,[2] according to the fashion of Tavistock Street and St. James's, in May, 1773, still continued long, dipped in the sauce alike by clown and cavalier.[3]

"The beau,
A critic styled in point of dress,
Harangues on fashion, point, and lace."

---

[1] If imported in smaller quantities than twelve yards, the duty imposed was £2 per yard.

[2] "Let the ruffle grace his hand,
Ruffle, pride of Gallic land."
—"The Beau." 1755.

[3] "And dip your wristbands
(For cuffs you've none) as comely in the sauce
As any courtier."
—Beaumont and Fletcher.

A man was known by his "points"; he collected lace, as, in these more athletic days, a gentleman prides himself on his pointers or his horses. We read in the journals of the time how, on the day after Lord George Gordon's riots, a report ran through London that the Earl of Effingham, having joined the rioters, had been mortally wounded, and his body thrown into the Thames. He had been recognised, folks declared, by his point lace ruffles.[4]

Mr. Damer, less known than his wife, the talented sculptor and friend of Horace Walpole, appeared three times a day in a new suit, and at his death[5] left a wardrobe which sold for £15,000.[6] Well might it have been said of him—

> "We sacrifice to dress, till household joys
> And comforts cease. Dress drains our cellars dry,
> And keeps our larder bare; puts out our fires,
> And introduces hunger, frost, and woe,
> Where peace and hospitality might reign."[7]

There was "no difference between the nobleman and city 'prentice, except that the latter was sometimes the greater beau," writes the *Female Spectator*.[8]

> "His hands must be covered with fine Brussels lace."[9]

Painters of the eighteenth century loved to adorn their portraits with the finest fabrics of Venice and Flanders; modern artists consider such decorations as far too much trouble. "Over the chimney-piece," writes one of the essayists, describing a citizen's country box, "was my friend's portrait, which was drawn bolt upright in a full-bottomed periwig, a laced cravat, with the fringed ends appearing through the button-hole (Steinkirk fashion). Indeed, one would almost wonder how and where people managed to afford so rich a selection of laces in their days, did it not call to mind the demand of the Vicaress of Wakefield 'to have as many pearls and diamonds put into her picture as could be given for the money.'"

---

[4] He had retired to the country to be out of the way.
[5] August, 1776.
[6] The wardrobe of George IV. was estimated at the same sum.
[7] Cowper.
[8] 1757.
[9] "Monsieur à la Mode." 1753.

Ruffles were equally worn by the ladies :—[10]

> "Frizzle your elbows with ruffles sixteen;
> Furl off your lawn apron with flounces in rows." [11]

Indeed, if we may judge by the intellectual conversation overheard and accurately noted down by Miss Burney,[12] at Miss Monckton's (Lady Cork) party, court ruffles were inconvenient to wear :—

"'You can't think how I am encumbered with these nasty ruffles,' said Mrs. Hampden.

"'And I dined in them,' says the other. 'Only think !'

"'Oh !' answered Mrs. Hampden, 'it really puts me out of spirits.'"

Both ladies were dressed for a party at Cumberland House, and ill at ease in the costume prescribed by etiquette.

About 1770 the sleeves of the ladies' dresses were tight on the upper arm, where they suddenly became very large, and, drooping at the elbow, they terminated in rich fringes of lace ruffles. A few years later the sleeves expanded from the shoulders till they became a succession of constantly enlarging ruffles and lappets, and again, before 1780, they became tight throughout, with small cuffs and no lace at the elbows, when they were worn with long gloves.

Our history of English lace is now drawing to a close ; but, before quitting the subject, we must, however, make some allusion to the custom prevalent here, as in all countries, of using lace as a decoration to grave-clothes. In the chapter devoted to Greece, we have mentioned how much lace is still taken from the tombs of the Ionian Islands, washed, mended, or, more often, as a proof of its authenticity, sold in a most disgusting state to the purchaser. The custom was prevalent at Malta, as the lines of Beaumont and Fletcher testify :—

> "In her best habit, as the custom is,
> You know, in Malta, with all ceremonies,
> She's buried in the family monument,
> I' the temple of St. John." [13]

---

[10] "Let of ruffles many a row Guard your elbows white as snow." —"The Belle." 1755. "Gone to a lady of distinction with a Brussels head and ruffles." —*The Fool of Quality.* 1766.

[11] "Receipt for Modern Dress." 1753.

[12] *Recollections of Madame d'Arblay.*

[13] Beaumont and Fletcher. *The Knight of Malta.*

At Palermo you may see the mummies thus adorned in the celebrated catacombs of the Capuchin convent.[14]

In Denmark,[15] Sweden, and the north of Europe [16] the custom was general. The mass of lace in the tomb of the once fair Aurora Königsmarck, at Quedlenburg, would in itself be a fortune. She sleeps clad in the richest point d'Angleterre, Malines, and guipure. Setting aside the jewels which still glitter around her parchment form, no daughter of Pharaoh was ever so richly swathed.[17]

In Spain it is related as the privilege of a grandee : all people of a lower rank are interred in the habit of some religious order.[18]

Taking the grave-clothes of St. Cuthbert as an example, we believe the same custom to have prevailed in England from the earliest times.[19]

---

[14] In coffins with glass tops. Some of them date from 1700.

[15] In the vault of the Schleswig-Holstein family at Sonderburg.

[16] In the church of Revel lies the Duc de Croÿ, a general of Charles XII., arrayed in full costume, with a rich flowing tie of fine guipure ; not that he was ever interred—his body had been seized by his creditors for debt, and there it still remains.

The author of *Letters from a Lady in Russia* (1775), describing the funeral of a daughter of Prince Menzikoff, states she was dressed in a nightgown of silver tissue, on her head a fine laced mob, and a coronet ; round her forehead a ribbon embroidered with her name and age, etc.

[17] Alluding to this custom of interring ladies of rank in full dress, Madame de Sévigné writes to her daughter :—" Mon Dieu, ma chère enfant, que vos femmes sont sottes, vivantes et mortes ! Vous me faites horreur de cette profanation ! quelle profanation ! cela sent le paganisme, ho ! cela me dégoûteroit bien de mourir en Provence ; il faudroit que du moins je fusse assuré qu'on ne m'iroit pas chercher une coëffeuse en même temps qu'un plombier. Ah ! vraiment ! fi ! ne parlez plus de cela."—Lettre 627. Paris, 13 Déc., 1688.

[18] Laborde. *Itin. de l'Espagne.* Again, the Duc de Luynes says : " The Curé of St. Sulpice related to me the fashion in which the Duke of Alva, who died in Paris in 1739, was by his own will interred. A shirt of the finest Holland, trimmed with new point lace, the finest to be had for money ; a new coat of Vardez cloth, embroidered in silver ; a new wig ; his cane on the right, his sword on the left of his coffin."—*Mémoires.*

[19] That grave-clothes were lace-trimmed we infer from the following strange announcement in the *London Gazette* for August 12th to 15th, 1678 : " Whereas decent and fashionable lace shifts and Dressings for the dead, made of woollen, have been presented to his Majesty by Amy Potter, widow (the first that put the making of such things in practice), and his Majesty well liking the same, hath upon her humble Petition, been graciously pleased to give her leave to insert this advertisement, that it may be known she now wholly applies herself in making both lace and plain of all sorts, at reasonable prices, and lives in Crane Court in the Old Change, near St. Paul's Church Yard." Again, in November of the same year, we find another advertisement :—" His Majesty, to increase the woollen manufacture and to encourage obedience to the late act for burying in woollen, has granted to Amy Potter the sole privilege of making all sorts of woollen

Mrs. Oldfield, the celebrated actress, who died in 1730, caused herself to be thus interred. The lines of Pope have long since immortalised the story :—

> " Odious ! in woollen ! 'twould a saint provoke !
> (Were the last words that poor Narcissa spoke.)
> No, let a charming chintz and Brussels lace
> Wrap my cold limbs, and shade my lifeless face ;
> One would not, sure, be frightful when one's dead—
> And—Betty—give this cheek a little red."

" She was laid in her coffin," says her maid, " in a very fine Brussels lace head, a Holland shift with a tucker of double ruffles, and a pair of new kid gloves." Previous to her interment in Westminster Abbey she lay in state in the Jerusalem Chamber.[20] For Mrs. Oldfield in her lifetime was a great judge of lace, and treasured a statuette of the Earl of Strafford, finely carved in ivory by Grinling Gibbons, more, it is supposed, for the beauty of its lace Vandyke collar [21] than any other sentiment.

In 1763 another instance is recorded in the *London Magazine* of a young lady buried in her wedding clothes, point lace tucker, handkerchief, ruffles and apron ; also a fine point lappet head. From this period we happily hear no more of such extravagances.

Passing from interments and shrouds to more lively matters, we must quote the opinion of that Colossus of the eighteenth century, Dr. Johnson, who was too apt to talk on matters of taste and art, of which he was no competent judge. " A Brussels trimming," he declaims to Mrs. Piozzi, " is like bread sauce ; it takes away the glow of colour from the gown, and gives you nothing instead of it : but sauce was invented to heighten the flavour of our food, and trimming is an ornament to the manteau or it is nothing." [22] A man whose culinary ideas did not soar higher than bread sauce could scarcely pronounce on the relative effect and beauty of point lace.

If England had leant towards the products of France, in

---

laces for the decent burial of the dead or otherwise, for fourteen years, being the first inventor thereof."

[20] Betterton's *History of the English Stage.* Her kindness to the poet Savage is well known.

[21] This seems to have been a spéci-

alité of Gibbons ; for we find among the treasures of Strawberry Hill : " A beautiful cravat, in imitation of lace, carved by Gibbons, very masterly."— *Hist. and Antiquities of Twickenham.* London, 1797.

[22] Mrs. Piozzi's *Memoirs.*

1788, an Anglomania ran riot at Paris. Ladies wore a cap of mixed lace, English and French, which they styled the " Union of France and England." On the appearance of the French Revolution, the classic style of dress—its India muslins and transparent gauzes—caused the ancient points to fall into neglect. From this time dates the decline of the lace fabric throughout Europe.

Point still appeared at court and on state occasions, such as on the marriage of the Princess Caroline of Wales, 1795, but as an article of daily use it gradually disappeared from the wardrobes of all classes. A scrupulous feeling also arose in ladies' minds as to the propriety of wearing articles of so costly a nature, forgetting how many thousands of women gained a livelihood by its manufacture. Mrs. Hannah More, among the first, in her *Cœlebs in Search of a Wife*, alludes to the frivolity of the taste, when the little child exclaiming " at the beautiful lace with which the frock of another was trimmed, and which she was sure her mamma had given her for being good," remarks, " A profitable and, doubtless, lasting and inseparable association was thus formed in the child's mind between lace and goodness."

Whether in consequence of the French Revolution, or from the caprice of fashion, " real " lace—worse off than the passements and points of 1634, when in revolt—now underwent the most degrading vicissitudes. Indeed, so thoroughly was the taste for lace at this epoch gone by, that in many families collections of great value were, at the death of their respective owners, handed over as rubbish to the waiting maid.[23] Many ladies recollect in their youth to have tricked out their dolls in the finest Alençon point, which would now sell at a price far beyond their purses. Among the few who, in England, unseduced by frippery blonde, never neglected to preserve their collections entire, was the Duchess of

---

[23] A lady, who had very fine old lace, bequeathed her " wardrobe and lace " to some young friends, who, going after her death to take possession of their legacy, were surprised to find nothing but new lace. On inquiring of the old faithful Scotch servant what had become of the old needle points, she said : " Deed it's aw there, 'cept a wheen auld Dudds, black and ragged, I flinged on the fire."

Another collection of old lace met with an equally melancholy fate. The maid, not liking to give it over to the legatees in its coffee-coloured hue, sewed it carefully together, and put it in a strong soap lye on the fire, to simmer all night. When she took it out in the morning, it was reduced to a jelly ! Medea's caldron had not been more effectual !

Gloucester, whose lace was esteemed among the most magnificent in Europe.

When the taste of the age again turned towards the rich fabrics of the preceding centuries, much lace, both black and white, was found in the country farm-houses, preserved as remembrances of deceased patrons by old family dependants. Sometimes the hoard had been forgotten, and was again routed out from old wardrobes and chests, where it had lain unheeded for years. Much was recovered from theatrical wardrobes and the masquerade shops, and the Church, no longer in its temporal glory, both in Italy, Spain and Germany, gladly parted with what, to them, was of small value compared with the high price given for it by amateurs. In Italy perhaps the finest fabrics of Milan, Genoa, and Venice had fared best, from the custom which prevailed of sewing up family lace in rolls of linen to ensure its preservation.

After years of neglect lace became a "mania." In England the literary ladies were the first to take it up. Sydney Lady Morgan and Lady Stepney quarrelled weekly on the respective value and richness of their points. The former at one time commenced a history of the lace fabric, though what was the ultimate fate of the MS. the author is unable to state. The Countess of Blessington, at her death, left several chests filled with the finest antique lace of all descriptions.

The "dames du grand monde," both in England and France, now began to wear lace. But, strange as it may seem, never at any period did they appear to so little advantage as during the counter-revolution of the lace period. Lace was the fashion, and wear it somehow they would, though that somehow often gave them an appearance, as the French say, *du dernier ridicule*, simply from an ignorance displayed in the manner of arranging it. That lace was old seemed sufficient to satisfy all parties. They covered their dresses with odds and ends of all fabrics, without attention either to date or texture. One English lady appeared at a ball given by the French Embassy at Rome, boasting that she wore on the tablier of her dress every description of lace, from point coupé of the fifteenth to Alençon of the eighteenth century. The Count of Syracuse was accustomed to say : "The English ladies buy a scrap of lace as a souvenir of every town they pass through, till they reach Naples, then sew it on their dresses, and make one grande toilette of the whole to honour our first ball at the Academia Nobile."

The taste for lace has again become universal, and the quality now produced renders it within the reach of all classes of society ; and though by some the taste may be condemned, it gives employment to thousands and ten thousands of women, who find it more profitable and better adapted to their strength than the field labour which forms the occupation of the women in agricultural districts.   To these last, in a general point of view, the lace-maker of our southern counties, who works at home in her own cottage, is superior, both in education, refinement, and morality :—

> " Here the needle plies its busy task;
> The pattern grows, the well-depicted flower,
> Wrought patiently into the snowy lawn,
> Unfolds its bosom ; buds, and leaves, and sprigs,
> And curling tendrils, gracefully dispos'd,
> Follow the nimble fingers of the fair—
> A wreath that cannot fade, of flowers that blow
> With most success when all besides decay." [24]

---

[24] Cowper. " The Winter Evening."

CHAPTER XXIX.

THE LACE MANUFACTURERS OF ENGLAND.

" Yon cottager, who weaves at her own door,
Pillow and bobbins all her little store;
Content though mean, and cheerful if not gay,
Shuffling her threads about the livelong day:
Just earns a scanty pittance, and at night
Lies down secure, her heart and pocket light."—Cowper.

THE bone lace manufactures of England in the sixteenth and seventeenth centuries appear to have extended over a much wider area than they occupy in the present day. From Cambridge to the adjacent counties of Northampton and Hertfordshire, by Buckinghamshire, Bedfordshire, and Oxfordshire, the trade spread over the southern counties[1] of Wiltshire, Somersetshire,[2] Hampshire, and Dorset, to the more secluded valleys of Devon—the county which still sustains the ancient reputation of " English point"—terminating at Launceston, on the Cornish coast.

Various offsets from these fabrics were established in Wales.[3] Ripon,[4] an isolated manufactory, represented the

---

[1] Bishop Berkeley, in *A Word to the Wise*, writes of the English labourers in the South of England on a summer's evening " sitting along the streets of the town or village, each at his own door, with a cushion before him, making bone lace, and earning more in an evening's pastime than an Irish family would in a whole day."

[2] "Wells, bone lace and knitting stockings."—Anderson.

[3] "Launceston, where are two schools for forty-eight children of both sexes. The girls are taught to read, sew, and make bone lace, and they are to have their earnings for encouragement."—*Magna Britannia*. 1720.

Welsh lace was made at Swansea,

Pont-Ardawe, Llanwrtyd, Dufynock, and Brecon, but never of any beauty, some not unlike a coarse Valenciennes. " It was much made and worn," said an aged Wesleyan lady, " by our ' connexion,' and as a child I had all my frocks and pinafores trimmed with it. It was made in the cottages; each lace-maker had her own pattern, and carried it out for sale in the country."

[4] At what period, and by whom the lace manufactory of Ripon was founded, we have been unable to ascertain. It was probably a relic of conventual days, which, after having followed the fashion of each time, has now gradually died out. In 1842 broad Trolly laces of French design and fair work-

lace industry of York ; while the dependent islands of Man,[5] Wight[6] and Jersey,[7] may be supposed to have derived their learning from the smugglers who frequented their coast, rather than from the teaching of the Protestant refugees[8] who sought an asylum on the shores of Britain.

Many of these fabrics now belong to the past, consigned to oblivion even in the very counties where they once flourished. In describing, therefore, the lace manufactures of the United Kingdom, we shall confine ourselves to those which still remain, alluding only slightly to such as were

---

manship were fabricated in the old cathedral city ; where, in the poorer localities near the Bond and Blossom-gate, young women might be seen working their intricate patterns, with pillows, bobbins, and pins. In 1862 one old woman alone, says our inform-ant, sustains the memory of the craft, her produce a lace of a small lozenge-shaped pattern (Fig. 132), that earliest of all designs, and a narrow edging known in local parlance by the name of " fourpenny spot."

[5] Till its annexation to the Crown, the Isle of Man was the great smug-gling depôt for French laces. The traders then removed *en masse* to the Channel Isles, there to carry on their traffic. An idiot called " Peg the Fly " in Castletown (in 1842) was seen working at her pillow on a summer's evening, the last lace-maker of the island. Isle of Man lace was a simple Valenciennes edging.

[6] Isle of Wight lace was honoured by the patronage of Queen Victoria. The Princess Royal, reports the *Illus-trated News* of May, 1856, at the drawing-room, on her first presenta-tion, wore a dress of Newport lace, her train trimmed with the same.

The weariness of incarceration, when at Carisbrook, did not bring on Charles I. any distaste for rich apparel. Among the charges of 1648, Sept. and Nov., we find a sum of nigh £800 for suits and cloaks of black brocade tabby, black unshorn velvet, and black satin, all lined with plush and trimmed with rich bone lace.

Some bobbin lace was made in the island, but what is known as " Isle of

Wight " resembles " Nottingham " lace. It is made in frames on machine net, the pattern outlined with a run thread and filled in with needle-point stitches. Queen Victoria had several lace tippets made of Isle of Wight lace for the Royal children, and always chose the Mechlin style of rose pattern. Now (1901) there are only two or three old women workers left.

[7] Lace-making was never the staple manufacture of the Channel Islands ; stockings and garments of knitted wool afforded a livelihood to the natives. We have early mention of these articles in the inventories of James V. of Scotland and of Mary Stuart. Also in those of Henry VIII. and Queen Elizabeth, in which last we find (Gt. Ward. Acc., 28 & 29) the charge of 20*s.* for a pair of " Caligarum nexat' de factura Garneseie," the upper part and " lez clocks " worked in silk. At the beginning of the nineteenth century, when the island was inundated with French refugees, lace-making was introduced with much success into the Poor-House of St. Heliers. It formed the favourite occupation of the ladies of the island, some of whom (1863) retain the patterns and pillows of their mothers, just as they left them. Of late years many of the old raised Venetian points have been admirably imitated in " Jersey crochet work."

[8] The Puritans again, on their part, transferred the fabric to the other side of the Atlantic, where, says a writer of the eighteenth century, " very much fine lace was made in Long Island by the Protestant settlers."

once of note, and of which the existence is confirmed by the testimony of contemporary writers.

The " women of the mystery of thread-working " would appear to have made lace in London,[9] and of their complaints and grievances our public records bear goodly evidence. Of the products of their needle we know little or nothing.

Various Flemings and Burgundians established themselves in the City ; and though the emigrants, for the most part, betook themselves to the adjoining counties, the craft, till

Fig. 132.

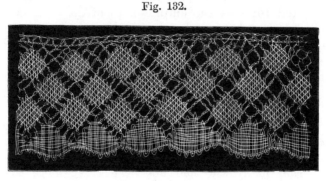

RIPON.

the end of the eighteenth century, may be said to have held fair commerce in the capital.

The London fabric can scarcely be looked upon as a staple trade in itself, mixed up as it was with lace-cleaning and lace-washing—an occupation first established by the ejected nuns.[10] Much point, too, was made by poor gentlewomen, as the records of the Anti-Gallican Society testify. " A strange infatuation," says a writer of the eighteenth century, "prevailed in the capital for many years among the class called demi-fashionables of sending their daughters to convents in France for education, if that could be so termed which amounted to a learning to work in lace. The Revolution, however, put

---

[9] See Chap. XXII.

[10] The richly-laced corporax cloths and church linen are sent to be washed by the " Lady Ancress," an ecclesiastical washerwoman, who is paid by the churchwardens of St. Margaret's, Westminster, the sum of 8d. ; this Lady Ancress, or Anchoress, being some worn-out nun, who, since the dissolution of the religious houses, eked out an existence by the art she had once practised within the convent.

an end to this practice." It is owing to this French education that the fine needle points were so extensively made in England ; though this occupation. however, did not seem to belong to any one county in particular ; for the reader who runs his eye over the proceedings of the Anti-Gallican Society will find prizes to have been awarded to gentlewomen from all parts—from the town of Leominster in Herefordshire to Broughton in Leicestershire, or Stourton in Gloucester.[11] Needle point, in contradistinction to bone lace, was an occupation confined to no special locality.

In 1764 the attention of the nobility seems to have been first directed towards the employment of the indigent poor, and, indeed, the better classes in the metropolis, in the making of bone lace and point ;[12] and in 1775, sanctioned by the patronage of Queen Charlotte, the Princesses, the Princess Amelia, and various members of the aristocracy, an institution was formed in Marylebone Lane, and also in James Street, Westminster, " for employing the female infants of the poor in the blond and black silk lace-making and thread laces." More than 300 girls attended the school. " They gave," says the *Annual Register*, such a proof of their capacity that many who had not been there more than six months carried home to their parents from 5s. to 7s. a month, with expectation of getting more as they improve."

From this time we hear no more of the making of lace, either point or bone, in the metropolis.

------

[11] In 1753 prizes were awarded for 14 pairs of curious needlework point ruffles.

[12] One society confers a prize of ten guineas upon a " gentlewoman for an improvement in manufacture by finishing a piece of lace in a very elegant manner with knitting-needles."

CHAPTER XXX.

BEDFORDSHIRE, BUCKINGHAMSHIRE, AND NORTHAMPTONSHIRE.[1]

BEDFORDSHIRE.

"He wears a stuff whose thread is coarse and round
But trimmed with curious lace." —Herbert.

IT would be a difficult matter now to determine when and by whom lace-making was first introduced into the counties of Bedfordshire and Buckingham. Authors, for the most part, have been glad to assign its introduction to the Flemings,[2] a nation to whose successive emigrations England owes much of her manufacturing greatness. Originally the laces were of old, wavy, graceful Flemish designs.

On the other hand, certain traditions handed down in the county villages of a good Queen who protected their craft, the annual festival of the workers—in the palmy days of the trade a matter of great moment — combined with the residence of that unhappy Queen, for the space of two years[3] at her jointure manor of Ampthill,[4] lead us rather to infer

---

[1] The lace of the three counties is practically equal—that is, it is all made in a similar fashion, and the same patterns are met with in each county. The " point " or " net " ground is met with in all, and worked level with the pattern in the same way with bobbins.

[2] Who fled from the Alva persecutions, and settled, first at Cranfield in Bedfordshire, then at Buckingham, Stoney Stratford, and Newport-Pagnel, whence the manufacture extended gradually over Oxford, Northampton, and Cambridge. Many Flemish names are still to be found in the villages of Bedfordshire.

[3] Queen Katherine died 1536.

[4] She retired to Ampthill early in 1531 while her appeal to Rome was pending, and remained there till the summer of 1533.

that the art of lace-making, as it then existed, was first imparted to the peasantry of Bedfordshire, as a means of subsistence, through the charity of Queen Katherine of Aragon. In the chapter devoted to needlework we have already alluded to the proficiency of this Queen in all arts connected with the needle, to the " trials of needlework " established by her mother, Queen ·Isabella, at which she, as a girl, had assisted. It is related, also, that during her [5] sojourn at Ampthill, " she passed her time, when not at her devotions, with her gentlewomen, working with her own hands something wrought in needlework, costly and artificially, which she intended for the honour of God to bestow on some of the churches." [6]

" The country people," continues her contemporary, " began to love her exceedingly. They visited her out of pure respect, and she received the tokens of regard they daily showed her most sweetly and graciously." The love borne by the peasantry to the Queen, the sympathy shown to her in her days of trouble and disgrace, most likely met with its reward ; and we believe Katherine to have taught them an art which, aided no doubt by the later introduction of the pillow and the improvements of the refugees, has now, for the space of nigh three centuries, been the staple employment of the female population of Bedfordshire and the adjoining counties. Until the latter half of the nineteenth century—though, like all such festivals in the present age, gradually dying out—the lace-makers still held " Cattern's day," [7] November 25th, as the holiday of their craft, kept, they say, " in memory of good Queen Katherine, who, when the trade was dull, burnt all her lace and ordered new to be made. The ladies of the court

---

[5] Lace of the heavy Venetian point was already used for ecclesiastical purposes, though scarcely in general use. The earliest known pattern-books date from fifteen years previous to the death of Katherine (1536).

[6] Dr. Nicolas Harpsfield. Douay, 1622. (In Latin.)

Again we read that at Kimbolton " she plied her needle, drank her potions, and told her beads."—*Duke of Manchester. Kimbolton Papers.*

[7] A lady from Ampthill writes (1863) :

"The feast of St. Katherine is no longer kept. In the palmy days of the trade both old and young used to subscribe a sum of money and enjoy a good cup of Bohea and cake, which they called 'Cattern' cake. After tea they danced and made merry, and finished the evening with a supper of boiled stuffed rabbits smothered with onion sauce." The custom of sending about Cattern cakes was also observed at Kettering, in Northamptonshire.

followed her example, and the fabric once more revived." " Ainsi s'écrit l'histoire"; and this garbled version may rest on as much foundation as most of the folk-lore current throughout the provinces.

Speaking of Bedfordshire, Defoe writes : " Thro' the whole south part of this country, as far as the borders of Buckinghamshire and Hertfordshire, the people are taken up with the manufacture of bone lace, in which they are wonderfully exercised and improved within these few years past " [8]— probably since the arrival of the French settlers after the Revocation of the Edict of Nantes. At the same period the author of the *Magna Britannia* [9] states that at Woburn, " lace of a high price is made in considerable quantities." Savary and Peuchet both declare the town of Bedford alone to have contained 500 lace-workers.

In 1863, as Mrs. Palliser wrote : " The lace schools of Bedfordshire are far more considerable than those in Devonshire. Four or five may frequently be found in the same village, numbering from twenty to thirty children each, and they are considered sufficiently important to be visited by Government inspectors. Their work is mostly purchased by large dealers, who make their arrangements with the instructress : the children are not bound for a term, as in the southern counties. Boys formerly attended the lace schools, but now they go at an early age to the fields."

These lace-schools are now things of the past. In some cases, however, in the lace counties, the County Council Technical Education Committee have supplemented private efforts with grants for classes to teach the lace industry.

The wages of a lace-worker average a shilling a day ; under press of business, caused by the demand for some fashionable article, they sometimes rise to one shilling and sixpence.

---

[8] *Tour through the whole Island of Great Britain*, by a Gentleman. 3 vols. 1724–27. Several subsequent editions of Defoe were published, with additions, by Richardson the novelist in 1732, 1742, 1762, 1769, and 1778. The last is " brought down to the present time by a gentleman of eminence in the literary world."

[9] *Magna Britannia et Hibernia, or a New Survey of Great Britain, collected and composed by an impartial hand*, by the Rev. Thos. Owen. Lond. 1720–31.

BUCKINGHAMSHIRE.

Though the first establishment of the fabric may have
been in the sister county, the workers of Buckingham appear
early to have gained the lion's share of public estimation for
the produce of their pillows, and the manufacture flourished,
till, suffering from the monopolies of James I., we read how
—In the year 1623, April 8th, a petition was addressed
from Great Marlow to the High Sheriff of Bucks, representing the distress of the people from "the bone-lace
making being much decayed." [10]

Three years later, 1626, Sir Henry Borlase founds and
endows the free school of Great Marlow for twenty-four boys
to read, write, and cast accounts ; and for twenty-four girls "to
knit, spin, and make bone lace " ; and here at Great Marlow
the trade flourished, all English, and even French authors [11]
citing its " manufactures de dentelles au fuseau" as the
staple produce of the town, and its surrounding villages,
which sold lace, however, they pronounce as " inférieure à
celle de Flandres."

During the seventeenth century the trade continued to
advance, and Fuller testifies to its once more prosperous
condition in Bucks, towards the year 1640. " No handicrafts of note," he writes, " (save what are common to other
countries) are used therein, except any will instance in bone
lace, much thereof being made about Owldney, in this
county, though more, I believe, in Devonshire, where we
shall meet more properly therewith." [12]   Olney, as it is now
written, a small market town, for many years the residence
of Cowper, known by its twenty-four-arched bridge, now no
more, " of wearisome but needful length " spanning the
Ouse—Olney, together with the fellow towns of Newport-
Pagnel and Aylesbury, are much quoted by the authorities
of the last century, though, as is too often the case in books
of travels and statistics, one writer copies from another the
information derived from a preceding author.   Defoe, however, who visited each county in detail, quotes " Ouldney
as possessing a considerable manufacture of bone lace ";

[10] State Papers Dom. Jac. I. Vol.
142. P. R. O.

[11] Savary and Peuchet.
[12] *Worthies*. Vol. i., p. 134.

while a letter from the poet Cowper to the Rev. John Newton, in 1780, enclosing a petition to Lord Dartmouth in favour of the lace-makers, declares that "hundreds in this little town are upon the point of starving, and that the most unremitting industry is barely sufficient to keep them from it." A distress caused, we may infer, by some caprice of fashion.

"The lace manufacture is still carried on," says Lysons,[13] "to a great extent in and about Olney, where veils and other lace of the finer sorts are made, and great fortunes are said to be acquired by the factors. Lace-making is in no part of the country so general as at Hanslape and in its immediate vicinity; but it prevails from fifteen to twenty miles round in every direction. At Hanslape not fewer than 800 out of a population of 1275 were employed in it in the year 1801. Children are put to the lace-schools at, or soon after, five years of age. At eleven or twelve years of age they are all able to maintain themselves without any assistance; both girls and boys are taught to make it, and some men when grown up follow no other employment; others, when out of work, find it a good resource, and can earn as much as the generality of day labourers. The lace made in Hanslape is from sixpence to two guineas a yard in value. It is calculated that from £8000 to £9000 net profit is annually brought into the parish by the lace manufacture."

The bone lace of Stoney Stratford [14] and Aylesbury are both quoted by Defoe, and the produce of the latter city is mentioned with praise. He writes: "Many of the poor here are employed in making lace for edgings, not much inferior to those from Flanders; but it is some pleasure to us to observe that the English are not the only nation in the world which admires foreign manufactures above its own, since the French, who gave fashions to most nations, buy and sell the finest laces at Paris under the name of 'dentelles d'Angleterre' or 'English laces.'" [15]

In the southern part of Buckinghamshire the hundreds of Burnham and Desborough were especially noted for the

---

[13] *Magna Britannia*, Daniel and Samuel Lysons. 1806-22.

[14] Describing the "lace and edgings" of the tradesman's wife, she has "from Stoney Stratford the first, and Great Marlow the last."—*The Complete English Tradesman*. Dan. Defoe. 1726.

[15] Edition 1762.

art, the lace-workers producing handsome lace of the finest quality, and about the year 1680 lace-making was one of the principal employments in High Wycombe.[16]

But Newport-Pagnel, whether from its more central position, or being of greater commercial importance, is the town which receives most praise from all contemporary authors. "This town," says the *Magna Britannia* in 1720, "is a sort of staple for bone lace, of which more is thought to be made here than any town in England; that commodity is brought to as great perfection almost as in Flanders." "Newport-Pagnel," writes Defoe, "carries on a great trade in bone lace, and the same manufacture employs all the neighbouring villages"; while Don Manuel Gonzales,[17] in 1730, speaks of its lace as little inferior to that of Flanders, which assertion he may have probably copied from previous writers.

At one of the earliest meetings of the Anti-Gallican Society, 1752, Admiral Vernon in the chair, the first prize to the maker of the best piece of English bone lace was awarded to Mr. William Marriott, of Newport-Pagnel, Bucks. The principal lace-dealers in London were invited to give their opinion, and they allowed it to be the best ever made in England. Emboldened by this success, we read how, in 1761, Earl Temple, Lord Lieutenant of Bucks, having been requested by Richard Lowndes, Esq., one of the Knights of the Shire, on behalf of the lace-makers, to present to the King a pair of fine lace ruffles, made by Messrs. Milward and Company, at Newport-Pagnel, in the same county, his Majesty, after looking at them and asking many questions respecting this branch of trade, was most graciously pleased to express himself that the inclination of his own

---

[16] In *Sheahan's History of Bucks*, published in 1862, the following places are mentioned as being engaged in the industry :—"Bierton (black and white lace), Cuddington, Haddenham, Great Hampden, Wendover, Gawcott (black), Beachampton, Marsh Gibbon, Preston Bisset, Claydon, Grendon, Dorton, Grandborough, Oving (black and white), Waddesdon, Newport-Pagnell, Bletchley, Hopton, Great Horwood, Bon Buckhill, Fenny Stratford, Hanslope (where 500 women and children are employed — about one-third of the population), Levendon, Great Sand-ford, Loughton, Melton Keynes, Moulsoe, Newton Blossomville, Olney, Sherrington, and the adjoining villages, Stoke Hammond, Wavendon, Great and Little Kimble, Wooleston, Aston Abbots, Swanbourne, Winslow, Rodnage."

[17] *The Voyage to Great Britain of Don Manuel Gonzales, late Merchant of the City of Lisbon.*—"Some say Defoe wrote this book himself; it is evidently from the pen of an Englishman." — *Lowndes' Bibliographers' Manual.* Bohn's Edition.

heart naturally led him to set a high value on every
endeavour to further English manufactures, and whatever
had such recommendation would be preferred by him to

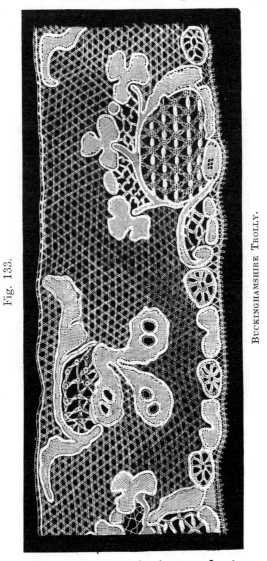

Fig. 133.

BUCKINGHAMSHIRE TROLLY.

works of possibly higher perfection made in any other
country.[18] From this period Newport-Pagnel is · cited as

_____

[18] *Annual Register.*

one of the most noted towns in the kingdom for making bone lace.[19]

As in other places, much complaint was made of the unhealthy state of the lace-working population, and of the injury sustained by long sitting in the vitiated air of the cottages.[20]

In Pennant's *Journey from Chester to London* (in 1782),

Fig. 134.

BUCKINGHAMSHIRE "POINT.

he notices in Towcester that, "this town is supported by the great concourse of passengers, and by a manufacture of lace, and a small one of silk stockings. The first was im-

---

[19] See *Britannia Depicta*, by John Owen, Gent. Lond. 1764, and others.
[20] In 1785 there appears in the *Gentleman's Magazine** "An essay on the cause and prevention of defor-mity among the lace-makers of Bucks and North Hants," suggesting im-proved ventilation and various other remedies long since adopted by the lace-working population in all countries.

---

* In 1761 appeared a previous paper, "to prevent the effects of stooping and vitiated air," etc.

ported from Flanders, and carried on with much success in this place, and still more in the neighbouring county" (Buckinghamshire).

At the end of the eighteenth century, the Revolution again drove many of the poorer French to seek refuge on our shores, as they had done a century before; and we find stated in the *Annual Register* of 1794: " A number

Fig. 135.

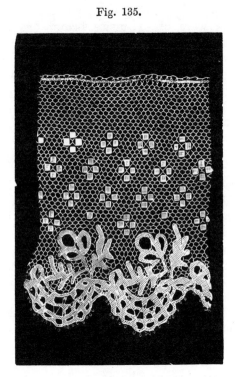

BUCKINGHAMSHIRE "POINT."

of ingenious French emigrants have found employment in Bucks, Bedfordshire, and the adjacent counties, in the manufacturing of lace, and it is expected, through the means of these artificers, considerable improvements will be introduced into the method of making English lace."

Figs. 134 and 135 represent the "point" ground, which won the laces of the midland counties their reputation. (See NORTHAMPTONSHIRE for additional matter.)

NORTHAMPTONSHIRE.

The laces of Northampton do not appear to have attracted the notice of the writers of the eighteenth century so much as those of the sister counties.

Anderson mentions that Kettering has " a considerable trade in lace "; and Lysons, later, observes that lace is made at Cheney. Certainly, the productions of this county a century back were of exquisite beauty, as we can bear testimony from the specimens in a pattern-book inherited by Mr. Cardwell, the well-known lace merchant of Northampton, from his predecessor in the trade, which we have had an opportunity of examining. We have also received examples from various localities in Bedfordshire and Buckinghamshire, and as there is much similarity in the products of the three counties, we shall, perhaps, better describe them by treating of them all collectively.

The earliest English lace was naturally the old Flemish, the pattern wavy and graceful, the ground well executed. Fig. 136, which we select as an example, is a specimen we received, with many others, of old Newport-Pagnel lace, given by Mrs. Bell, of that town, where her family has been established from time immemorial. Mrs. Bell could carry these laces back to the year 1780, when they were bequeathed to her father by an aged relative who had long been in the lace trade. The packets remain for the most part entire. The custom of " storing " lace was common among the country-people.

Next in antiquity is Fig. 137, a lace of Flemish design, with the fine Brussels ground. This is among the Northamptonshire laces already alluded to.

Many of the early patterns appear to have been run or worked in with the needle on the net ground (Fig. 138).

In 1778, according to M'Culloch,[21] was introduced the " point " ground, as it is locally termed, from which period dates the staple pillow lace trade of these counties. This ground is beautifully clear, the patterns well executed : we doubt if Fig. 139 could be surpassed in beauty by lace of

---

[21] *Dict. of Commerce.*

PLATE LXXXV.

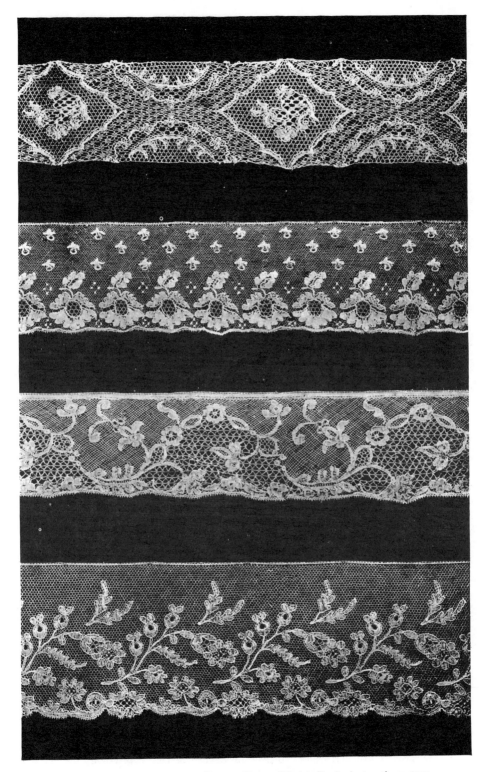

ENGLISH, BUCKINGHAMSHIRE. BOBBIN LACE.—First half of nineteenth century.
Widths: 3, 3, 3, 4 in. The property of Mrs. Ellis, The Vicarage, Much Wenlock.

PLATE LXXXVI.

ENGLISH, NORTHAMPTONSHIRE. BOBBIN LACE.—End of nineteenth century.
Widths: 1¾, 5¼ and 2 in.
Photo by A. Dryden from a private collection.

any foreign manufacture. Much of this point ground was made by men.

The principal branch of the lace trade was the making of " baby lace," as those narrow laces were called, most specially employed for the adorning of infants' caps (Figs.

Fig. 136.

OLD FLEMISH.—(Newport-Pagnel.)

140, 141, 142). The " point " ground was used, the patterns taken from those of Lille and Mechlin—hence the laces of Buckingham and Bedfordshire have often been styled " English Lille." Though the fashion in the mother-

Fig. 137.

OLD BRUSSELS.—(Northampton.)

country passed away, the American ladies held to the trimmed infant's cap until the breaking out of the Civil War; and up to that date large quantities of " baby lace " were exported to America, the finer sorts varying from five shillings to seven shillings and sixpence a yard, still retaining their ancient name of " points."

Many other descriptions of grounds were made—wire (Fig. 143), double, and trolly, in every kind of quality and

Fig. 138.

"RUN' LACE.—(Newport-Pagnel.)

width.   In the making of the finer sorts of edging as many as 200 threads would be employed.

Fig. 139.

ENGLISH "POINT."—(Northampton.)]

On the breaking out of the war with France, the closing of our ports to French goods gave an impetus to the trade, and the manufacturers undertook to supply the English

market with lace similar to that of Normandy and the
sea-coast villages of France ; hence a sort of " fausse "
Valenciennes, called the " French ground." But true

Fig. 140.

" BABY " LACE.—(Northampton.)

Valenciennes was also fabricated so fine (Fig. 144) as to
rival the products of French Hainault. It was made in

Fig. 141.   Fig. 142.

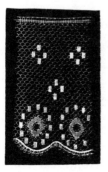

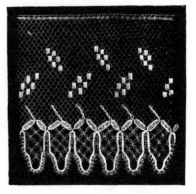

" BABY " LACE.—(Beds.   "BABY LACE.—(Bucks.)

considerable quantities, until the expertness of the smuggler
and the cessation of the war caused it to be laid aside.

One-third of the lace-workers of Northampton were

employed, previous to the introduction of machine-made net, in making quillings on the pillow.

During the Regency, a " point " lace, with the " cloth " or " toilé " on the edge, for many years was in fashion, and, in compliment to the Prince, was named by the loyal manufacturers " Regency Point." It was a durable and handsome lace (Fig. 145).

Fig. 143.

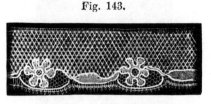

WIRE GROUND.—(Northampton.)

Towards the year 1830, insertions found their way to the public taste (Fig. 146).

Till the middle of the nineteenth century, in lace-making districts, almost the only schools were the lace schools—and there were several in most villages—where lace-making was

Fig. 144.

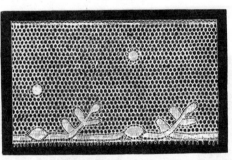

VALENCIENNES.—(Northampton.)

the principal thing taught and a little reading added. I am indebted to Mrs. Roberts, formerly of Spratton, near North-ampton, for the following description, which she kindly allows me to reprint.

" The following are the few particulars of the old lace school for which this village was at one time famous. Indeed, it may be borne in mind that, owing to the great interest taken in education by a former squire and a former vicar, Spratton fifty years ago was far ahead of its neighbours in the matter of education ; and the Spratton school

Fig. 145.

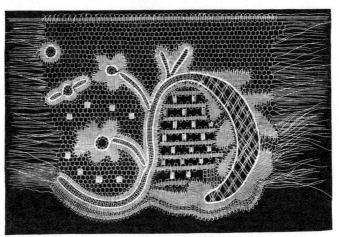

REGENCY POINT.—(Bedford.)

and Mr. Pridmore, the Spratton schoolmaster, with his somewhat strict discipline, were well known, not only to the children of Spratton, but to the boys and girls of most of

Fig. 146.

INSERTION.—(Bedford.

the adjacent villages. But the lace school was, no doubt, a commercial institution, and I think it will be admitted that the hours were long and the work severe. The girls left the day school at the age of eight years, and joined the lace school, and here the hours were from 6 A.M to 6 P.M. in the summer, and from 8 A.M. to 8 P.M. in the winter. Half an hour was allowed for breakfast and for tea, and one hour for dinner, so that there were ten hours for actual work. The girls had to stick ten pins a minute, or six hundred an hour ; and if at the end of the day they were five pins behind, they had to work for another hour. On Saturdays, however, they had a half-holiday, working only to the dinner-hour. They counted to themselves every pin they stuck, and at every fiftieth pin they called out the time, and the girls used to race each other as to who should call out first.

"They paid twopence a week (or threepence in winter) for lights, and in return they received the money realised from the sale of the lace they made, and they could earn about sixpence a day. Pay-day was a great event ; it came once a month.

"In the evenings eighteen girls worked by one tallow candle, value one penny ; the 'candle-stool' stood about as high as an ordinary table with four legs. In the middle of this was what was known as the 'pole-board,' with six holes in a circle and one in the centre. In the centre hole was a long stick with a socket for the candle at one end and peg-holes through the sides, so that it could be raised or lowered at will. In the other six holes were placed pieces of wood hollowed out like a cup, and into each of these was placed a bottle made of very thin glass and filled with water.[22] These bottles acted as strong condensers or lenses, and the eighteen girls sat round the table, three to each bottle, their stools being upon different levels, the highest nearest the bottle, which threw the light down upon the work like a burning-glass. In the day-time as many as thirty girls, and some-times boys, would work in a room about twelve feet square, with two windows, and in the winter they could have no fire for lack of room." The makers of the best laces would sit nearest the light, and so on in order of merit.

A "down" in Northamptonshire is the parchment

---

[22] In Flanders also these glasses were made and used. The "mediæval 'ourinals' are alike the retorts of the alchemist and the water-globes of the poor Flemish flax-thread spinners and lace makers." *Old English Glasses.* A. Hartshorne.

pattern, generally about twelve inches long. In Buckinghamshire they have two " eachs " ten inches long, and putting one in front of the other, so work round the pillow, which to many commends itself as a better plan than having one " down " and moving the lace back on reaching the end of the " down." The pillow is a hard round cushion, stuffed with straw and well hammered to make it hard for the bobbins to rattle on. It is then covered with the butcher-blue " pillow-cloth " all over ; a " lace cloth " of the same, for the lace to lie on, goes over the top ; then follows the lace-paper to pin it in as made, covered with the " lacing," which is a strip of bright print. The " hinder " of blue linen covers up all behind, the " worker " keeping the parchment clean in front where the hands rest. A bobbin bag and scissors are then tied on one side and a pin-cushion on the top ; a cloth " heller " is thrown over the whole when not used.

The pins are fine brass ones made on purpose ;[23] the bobbins are of various sizes and makes—very fine for fine lace, heavier and twisted round with strips of brass for coarser laces and gimp for the threads, which are the tracing ones, dividing the different characters of patterns ; some are of bone with words tattoed round in columns. The usual bobbin is plain turned wood, with coloured beads at the end for the necessary weight. The number varies from twenty to five hundred, according to the width of the pattern.[24]

---

[23] The larger pins had heads put to them with seeds of *galium* locally called **Hariffe** or goose-grass ; the seeds when fingered became hard and polished.

[24] Bobbins are usually made of bone, wood or ivory. English bobbins are of bone or wood, and especially in the counties of Bedford, Bucks, and Huntingdon, the set on a lace pillow formed a homely record of their owner's life. The names of her family, dates and records, births and marriages and mottoes, were carved, burnt, or stained on the bobbin, while events of general interest were often commemorated by the addition of a new bobbin. The *spangles, jingles* (or *gingles*) fastened to the end of the bobbin have a certain interest ; a waist-coat button and a few coral beads brought from overseas, a family relic in the shape of an old copper seal, or an ancient and battered coin—such things as these were often attached to the ring of brass wire passed through a hole in the bobbin. The inscriptions on the bobbins are sometimes burned and afterwards stained, and sometimes " pegged " or traced in tiny leaden studs, and consist of such mottoes as " Love me Truley " (*sic*), " Buy the Ring," " Osborne for Ever," " Queen Caroline," " Let no false Lover win my heart," " To me, my dear, you may come near," " Lovely Betty," " Dear Mother," and so forth.—R. E. Head. " Some notes on Lace-Bobbins." *The Reliquary*, July, 1900.

The Exhibition of 1851 gave a sudden impulse to the traders, and from that period the lace industry rapidly developed.   At this time was introduced the Maltese guipures and the " plaited " laces, a variety grafted on the old Maltese (Fig. 147).   Five years later appears the first specimen of the raised plait, now so thoroughly established in the market.   At the time Queen Victoria's trousseau was made, in which only English lace was used, the prices paid were so enormous that men made lace in the fields.   In those days the parchments on which the patterns were

Fig. 147.

PLAITED LACE.—(Bedford.)

pricked were worth their weight in gold ; many were extremely old and their owners were very jealous of others copying their patterns.   But, of late years, we hear of so little store being set by these parchments that they were actually boiled down to make glue.

The decay which threatened almost total extinction of the industry belongs to the last twenty years.   The contributory causes were several, chiefly the rapid development of machinery, which enabled large quantities to be sold at lower rates than the hand-workers could starve on, while the quality of the manufactured goods was good enough for the large public that required lace to last but a short time. Foreign competition, the higher wages required by all, and the many new employments opening to women took away the young people from the villages. In 1874 more than thirty young lace-women left a village of four hundred inhabitants to seek work elsewhere. The old workers gave up making good laces and supplied the popular demand with Maltese, which grew more and more inferior both in design and quality of thread, and gradually the old workers died out and no new ones took their places. The Lace Association has been started with the object of stimulating and

Fig. 148.

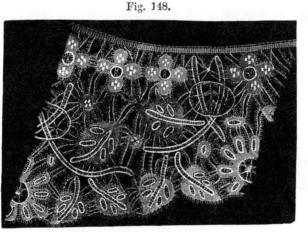

RAISED PLAIT.—Bedford.1

improving the local manufacture of pillow lace, of providing lace-workers with greater facilities for the sale of their work at more remunerative prices. Its aim is also to save the old designs of the " point " lace and discourage the coarse Maltese, to get new designs copied from old laces, and insist on only the best thread being used,[25] and good workmanship, and finally, to bring the lace before the public, and send it direct from worker to the purchaser, thus enabling the former to get the full value, saving the large profits which the dealers, buying for the shopkeepers, intercept for their own advantage,

Pillow lace was also made to some extent in Derbyshire.

[25] Too much stress cannot be laid on the importance of using fine linen thread. Many well-meant efforts are entirely ruined by the coarse woolly

SUFFOLK.

Suffolk has produced bobbin-made laces of little artistic value. The patterns in most of the specimens in the Victoria and Albert Museum collection are derived from simple Mechlin, Lille, and Valenciennes patterns. " The make of the lace resembles that of Buckinghamshire laces, and that of the Norman laces of the present time. The entire collection displays varied combinations of six ways of twisting and plaiting thread." [26]

---

cotton thread used for what ought to be a fine make of lace. That good thread can be got in Great Britain is evident from the fact that the Brussels dealers employ English thread, and sell it to Venice for the exquisite work of Burano. Needless to say, no Englishman has attempted to make a bid for the direct custom of the 8,000 lace-workers there employed.

[26] Catalogue of lace (Victoria and Albert Museum).

PLATE LXXXVII.

ENGLISH, SUFFOLK. BOBBIN LACE.—Nineteenth century. Resembling inferior Buckinghamshire, also Normandy and Saxony laces. Victoria and Albert Museum.

Fig. 149.

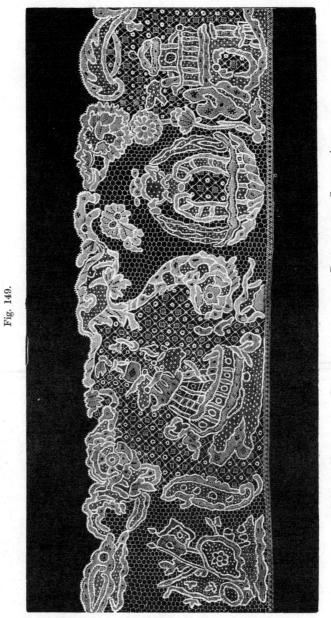

English Needle-made Lace, representing the Defeat of the Spanish Armada.

CHAPTER XXXI.

WILTSHIRE AND DORSETSHIRE.

FROM Wiltshire and Dorset, counties in the eighteenth century renowned for their lace, the trade has now passed away ; a few workers may yet be found in the retired sea-side village of Charmouth, and these are diminishing fast.

Of the Wiltshire manufactures we know but little, even from tradition, save that the art did once prevail. Peuchet alludes to it. When Sir Edward Hungerford attacked Wardour Castle in Wiltshire, Lady Arundel, describing the destruction of the leaden pipes by the soldiers, says, "They cut up the pipe and sold it, as these men's wives in North Wiltshire do bone lace, at sixpence a yard."

One Mary Hurdle, of Marlborough, in the time of Charles II., tells us in her "Memoirs"[1] that, being left an orphan, she was apprenticed by the chief magistrate to a maker of bone lace for eight years, and after that period of servitude she apprenticed herself for five years more.

Again, at the time of the Great Plague, cautions are issued by the Mayor of Marlborough to all parents and masters how they send their children and servants to school or abroad in making bone lace or otherwise, in any public house, place, or school used for that purpose.[2]

In the proceedings of the Anti-Gallican Society it is recorded that the second prize for needle point ruffles was, in 1751, awarded to Mrs. Elizabeth Waterman, of the episcopal city of Salisbury. Such are the scanty notices we have been able to glean of the once flourishing lace trade in Wiltshire.

---

[1] *The Conversion and Experience of Mary Hurll', or Hurdle, of Marlborough, a maker of bone lace in this* town, by the Rev. — Hughes, of that town.

[2] Waylem's *History of Marlborough.*

Dorset, on the other hand, holds a high place in the annals of lace-making, three separate towns, in their day —Blandford, Sherborne, and Lyme Regis—disputing the palm of excellence for their productions.

Of Blandford the earliest mention we find is in Owen's *Magna Britannica* of 1720, where he states : " The manu-facture of this town was heretofore ' band-strings,' which were once risen to a good price, but now times hath brought both bands themselves and their strings out of use, and so the inhabitants have turned their hands to making straw works and bone lace, which perhaps may come to nothing, if the fickle humour of fashionmongers take to wearing Flanders lace."

Only four years later Defoe writes of Blandford :—" This city is chiefly famous for making the finest bone lace in England, and where they showed us some so exquisitely fine as I think I never saw better in Flanders, France, or Italy, and which, they said, they rated above £30 sterling a yard ; but it is most certain that they make exceeding rich lace in this county, such as no part of England can equal." In the edition of 1762, Defoe adds, " This was the state and trade of the town when I was there in my first journey ; but on June 4, 1731, the whole town, except twenty-six houses, was consumed by fire, together with the church."

Postlethwayt,[3] Hutchins,[4] Lysons, and Knight (*Imperial Cyclopædia*) all tell the same story. Peuchet cites the Blandford laces as "comparables à celles qu'on fait en Flandres (excepté Bruxelles), en France, et même dans les Etats de Venise " ; and Anderson mentions Blandford as " a well-built town, surpassing all England in fine lace." More reliance is to be placed on the two last-named authorities than the former, who have evidently copied Defoe with-out troubling themselves to inquire more deeply into the matter.

It is generally supposed that the trade gradually declined after the great fire of 1731, when it was replaced by the

---

[3] " At Bland, on the Stour, between Salisbury and Dorchester, they made the finest lace in England, valued at £30 per yard."—*Universal Dict. of Trade and Commerce.* 1774.

[4] " Much bone lace was made here, and the finest point in England, equal, if not superior, to that of Flanders, and valued at £30 per yard till the beginning of this century."—*Hutchins' Hist. of the County of Dorset.* 2nd Edition, 1796.

manufacture of buttons, and no record of its former existence can be found among the present inhabitants of the place.[5]

Fig. 149 represents a curious piece of lace, preserved as an heirloom in a family in Dorsetshire. It formerly belonged to Queen Charlotte, and, when purchased by the present owner, had a label attached to it, " Queen Elizabeth's lace," with the tradition that it was made in commemoration of the defeat of the Spanish Armada, as the ships, dolphins, and national emblems testify. At this we beg to demur, as no similar lace was made at that period ; but we do not doubt its having been made in honour of that victory, for the building is decidedly old Tilbury Fort, familiar to all by the pencil of Stanfield. But the lace is point d'Argentan, as we see by the hexagonal " bride " ground and the workmanship of the pattern. None but the best lace-workers could have made it ; it was probably the handiwork of some English lady, or the pattern, designed in England, may have been sent to Argentan to execute, per- haps as a present to Queen Charlotte.

" Since the Reformation the clothing trade declined," writes Defoe, of Sherborne. " Before 1700, making buttons, haberdashery wares, and bone laces employed a great many hands " ; which said piece of information is repeated word for word in the *Imperial Cyclopædia*. Other authors, such as Anderson, declare, at a far later date, Sherborne to carry on a good trade in lace, and how, up to 1780, much blonde, both white and black, and of various colours, was made there, of which a supply was sent to all markets. From the latter end of the eighteenth century, the lace trade of Sherborne declined, and gradually died out.

The points of Lyme Regis rivalled, in the eighteenth century, those of Honiton and Blandford, and when the trade of the last-named town passed away, Lyme and Honiton laces held their own, side by side, in the London market. The fabric of Lyme Regis, for a period, came more before the public eye, for that old, deserted, and half-forgotten mercantile city, in the eighteenth century, once more raised its head as a fashionable watering-place. Prizes were awarded by the

---

[5] What this celebrated point was we cannot ascertain. Two samplars sent to us as Blandford point were of geometric pattern resembling the sam- plar, Fig. 5.

Anti-Gallican Society[6] to Miss Mary Channon, of Lyme Regis, and her fellow-townswoman, Miss Mary Ben, for ruffles of needle point and bone lace.　The reputation of the fabric, too, of Lyme Regis reached even the court ; and when Queen Charlotte first set foot on English ground, she wore a head and lappets of Dorset manufacture.　Some years later a splendid lace dress was made for her Majesty by the workers of Lyme, which, says the annalist of our southern coast,[7] gave great satisfaction at court.　The makers of this costly product, however, received but fourpence a day for their work.

The laces of Lyme, like all good articles, were expensive. A narrow piece set quite plain round an old woman's cap would cost four guineas, nor was five guineas a yard considered an exorbitant price.

It was a favourite custom at Lyme for lovers to have their initials entwined and worked together on a piece of ornamental lace.

The making of such expensive lace being scarcely found remunerative, the trade gradually expired ; and when the order for the marriage lace of Queen Victoria reached the southern counties, not one lace-maker was to be found to aid in the work in the once flourishing town of Lyme Regis.

---

[6] In 1752.　　　　　　[7] Roberts' *Hist. of Lyme Regis.*

CHAPTER XXXII.

DEVONSHIRE.

" Bone lace and Cyder."—*Anderson.*

" At Axminster, you may be furnished with fyne flax thread there spunne. At Honyton and Bradninch with bone lace much in request."—Westcote.

HONITON.

THE lace industry found its way to Devonshire, if the generally-accepted theory be correct, by the Flemish refugees flying from the persecutions of the Duke of Alva. There is much probability to support the theory, and some names,[1] of undoubted Flemish origin, appear among the entries of the church registers still preserved at Honiton, towards the latter end of the sixteenth century—names all handed down to their descendants in the present generation, and in these families the fabric has continued for a long lapse of years. On the other hand, if there had been any considerable number of Flemings in Devonshire, they would surely have founded a company of their Reformed Church, and no reference is found in the published books of the archives of the London Dutch Church of any such company in Devonshire, whereas references abound to places in the Eastern Counties and Midlands where Flemings were settled. Lace was made on the pillow in the Low Countries by the middle of the sixteenth century, so by the date of the Alva persecution (1568–77) the people might have learned it in sufficient numbers to start it wherever they set up their new home. Up to that date in England lace was made with the needle,[2]

---

[1] Burd, Genest, Raymunds, Brock, Couch, Gerard, Murck, Stocker, Maynard, Trump, Groot, etc.

[2] " We may rather infer that laces of silk and coarse thread were already fabricated in Devonshire, as elsewhere; and that the Flemings, on their arrival, having introduced the fine thread,

and it was not till we read of " bone-lace " that it may be
taken to mean pillow-lace.   The term " bone," according to
Fuller, was applied from the custom of using sheep's trotters
as bobbins.   In Devonshire, however, the tradition is that,
owing to the high price of pins, the lace-makers, being
within reach of the sea, made use of fish-bones, and thus
pillow-lace became " bone-lace."   The term " bobbin " came
into use soon afterwards, but was not so universal as
" bone " ; it occurs in the Wardrobe Accounts and Royal
inventories (where one entry runs, " In ye shoppe, 4 oz. and
½ of Bobbing lace, 6s. 4d.").

Although the earliest known MS.[3] giving an account of
the different towns in Devon makes no mention of lace, we
find from it that Mrs. Minifie,[4] one of the earliest-named
lace-makers, was an Englishwoman.

Queen Elizabeth was much addicted to the collecting and
wearing of beautiful clothes ; but no mention of English lace
by name seems to occur in the inventories and accounts, and
the earliest mention of Honiton lace is by Westcote, who,
writing about 1620, speaks of " bone lace much in request "
being made at Honiton and Bradninch ; and again referring
to Honiton.   " Here," says he, " is made abundance of bone
lace, a pretty toye now greatly in request ; and therefore the
town may say with merry Martial—

> " In praise for toyes such as this
> Honiton second to none is."

The oft-cited incription let into a raised tombstone, near
the wall of old Honiton church, together with Westcote,

---

then spun almost exclusively in their
own country, from that period the
trade of bone-lace-making flourished
in the southern as well as in the
midland counties of England " (Mrs.
Palliser, 1869).

[3] Ker's *Synopsis*, written about the
year 1561. Two copies of this MS.
exist, one in the library of Lord
Haldon at Haldon House (Co. Devon),
the other in the British Museum. This
MS. was never printed, but served as
an authority for Westcote and others.

[4] " She was a daughter of John Flay,
Vicar of Buckrell, near Honiton, who
by will in 1614 bequeaths certain
lands to Jerom Minify (*sic*), son of

Jerom Minify, of Burwash, Sussex,
who married his only daughter."—
Prince's *Worthies of Devon.* 1701.

Up to a recent date the Honiton
lace-makers were mostly of Flemish
origin. Mrs. Stocker, *ob.* 1769; Mr.
J. Stocker, + 1783, and four daughters ;
Mrs. Mary Stocker, + 179– ; Mr.
Gerard, + 1799, and daughter ; Mrs.
Lydia Maynard (of Anti-Gallican celebrity), + 1786 ; Mrs. Ann Brock,
+ 1815 ; Mrs. Elizabeth Humphrey,
+ 1790, whose family had been in the
lace manufacture 150 years and more.
The above list has been furnished to
the author by Mrs. Frank Aberdein,
whose grandfather was for many years

prove the industry to have been well established in the reign of James I.   The inscription runs—

"Here lyeth y° body of James Rodge, of Honinton, in y° County of Devonshire (Bonelace Siller, hath given unto the poore of Honinton P'ishe, the benyfitt of £100 for ever), who deceased y° 27 of July A° D¹ 1617 AETATAE SVAE 50.   Remember the Poore."

There have been traditions that Rodge was a valet who accompanied his master abroad, and there learning the fine Flemish stitches, taught some Devonshire women on his return home, and was enabled to make a comfortable competence by their work, bequeathing a sum of money to the poor of Honiton ; but it is more probable that he was an ordinary dealer.

Westcote,[5] who wrote about the year 1620, when noticing bone lace, does not speak of it as a new manufacture ; the trade had already taken root and flourished, for, including the above-mentioned Rodge, the three earliest bone lace makers of the seventeenth century on record all at their decease bequeathed sums of money for the benefit of their indigent townspeople, viz., Mrs. Minifie,[6] before mentioned, who died in 1617, and Thomas Humphrey, of Honiton, laceman, who willed in the year 1658 £20 towards the purchase of certain tenements, a notice of which benefaction is recorded on a painted board above the gallery of the old parish church.

By this time English lace had advanced in public estimation.   In the year 1660 a royal ordinance of France provided that a mark should be affixed to thread lace imported from England as well as on that of Flanders ; and we have already told elsewhere how the Earl of Essex procures, through his countess, bone lace to a considerable amount as a present to Queen Anne of Austria.

Speaking of bone lace, writes Fuller in his *Worthies*: " Much of this is made in and about Honyton, and weekly returned to London. . . . Modern is the use thereof in England, and that not exceeding the middle of the reign of

---

in the trade. Mrs. Treadwin, of Exeter, found an old lace-worker using a lace " Turn " for winding sticks, having the date 1678 rudely carved on the foot, showing how the trade was continued in the same family from generation to generation.

[5] *View of Devon.* T. Westcote.

[6] Her bequest is called " Minifie's Gift."

Queen Elizabeth. Let it not be condemned for a superfluous wearing because it doth neither hide, nor heat, seeing
it doth adorn. Besides, though private persons pay for it,
it stands the State in nothing ; not expensive of bullion like
other lace, costing nothing save a little thread descanted on
by art and industry. Hereby many children, who otherwise would be burthensome to the parish, prove beneficial
to their parents. Yea, many lame in their limbs and
impotent in their arms, if able in their fingers, gain a livelihood thereby ; not to say that it saveth some thousands of
pounds yearly, formerly sent over seas to fetch lace from
Flanders."

The English were always ready to protect their own
trades and manufactures, and various were the Acts passed
to prohibit the importation of foreign lace, for the encouragement of home workers. In 1698 it was proposed to repeal
the last preceding prohibition ; and, from the text of a
petition sent to the House of Commons, some interesting
light is thrown on the extent of the trade at that time.

"The making of Bone-lace has been an ancient Manufacture of England, and the Wisdom of our Parliaments all
along thought it the Interest of this Kingdom to prohibit its
Importation from Foreign Parts. . . . This has revived the
said Languishing Manufacture, and there are now above
one hundred thousand in England who get their living by it,
and earn by mere Labour £500,000 a year, according to the
lowest computation that can be made ; and the Persons
employed on it are, for the most part, Women and children
who have no other means of Subsistence. The English are
now arrived to make as good lace in Fineness and all other
respects as any that is wrought in Flanders, and particularly
since the last Act, so great an improvement is made that
way that in Buckinghamshire, the highest prized lace they
used to make was about eight shillings per yard, and now
they make lace there of above thirty shillings per yard, and
in Dorsetshire and Devonshire they now make lace worth six
pound per yard. . . .

". . . . The Lace Manufacture in England is the
greatest, next to the woollen, and maintains a multitude
of People, which otherwise the Parishes must, and that
would soon prove a heavy burthen, even to those concerned
in the Woollen Manufacture. On the Resolution, which

PLATE LXXXVIII.

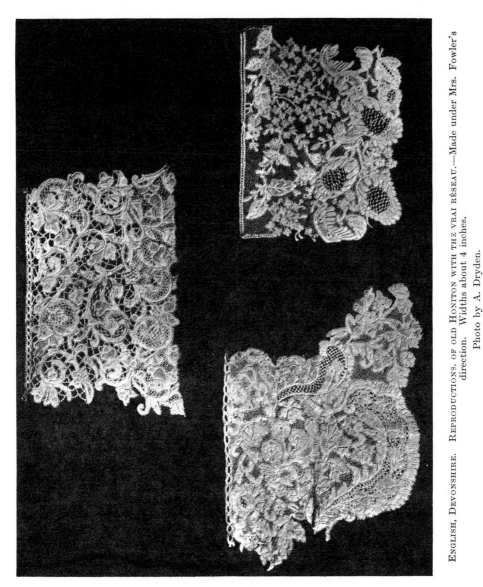

ENGLISH, DEVONSHIRE.   REPRODUCTIONS, OF OLD HONTON WITH THE VRAI RÉSEAU.—Made under Mrs. Fowler's
direction.   Widths about 4 inches.

Photo by A. Dryden.

shall be taken in this affair depends the Well-being, or ruin of numerous families in their Country. Many laws have been made to set our Poor on Work, and it is to be hoped none will be made to take away work from Multitudes who are already employed."[7]

Even in 1655, when the variety of points furnished matter for a letter from the members of the Baptist Church assembled at Bridgewater, the " Beleeven men," unwilling to injure so flourishing a commerce, merely censure " points and more laces than are required on garments," and these they desired might be proceeded against " with all sweetness and tenderness and long-suffering."[8] The conciliatory measures of the Puritans, maybe, affected the trade less than the doing of Lord Cambury and Lord Churchill's dragoons in the suppression of Monmouth's rebellion in 1680, by which time the lace-making art was carried on in many small country places in Devon. They pillaged the lace-makers right and left, and, when quartered at Colyton,[9] these unruly soldiers broke into the house of one William Bard, a dealer in bone lace, and there stole merchandise to the amount of £325 17s. 9d.[10]

" The valuable manufactures of lace, for which the inhabitants of Devon have long been conspicuous, are extending now from Exmouth to Torbay,"[11] writes Defoe in 1724.

---

[7] Here follows the numbers of the people in a few places who get their living by making lace. Among those quoted in Devonshire as interesting to compare with the present day are :—

" Coumbraligh 65, Sidmont 302, Axmouth 73, Sidbury 321, Buckerall 90, Farway 70, Utpotery 118, Branscombe Beare and Seaton 326, Honyton 1341, Axminster 60, Otery St. Mary, 814."

[8] Church Book of the Baptist Chapel of Lyme Regis.

[9] Colyton and Ottery St. Mary were among the first. Wherever the say or serge decayed, the lace trade planted itself.

In the church of Colyton, under a fine canopied tomb, repose back to back in most unsociable fashion the recumbent figures of Sir John and Lady Pole. " Dame Elizabeth, daughter of Roger How, merchant of London, ob. 1623," wears a splendid cape of three rows of bone lace descending to the waist. Her cap is trimmed with the same material. As this lace may be of Devonshire fabric, we give a wood-cut of the pattern (Fig. 150).

Sundry Flemish names may still be seen above the shop-windows of Colyton similar to those of Honiton—Stocker, Murch, Spiller, Rochett, Boatch, Kettel, Woram, and others.

[10] Don Manuel Gonzales mentions " bone lace " among the commodities of Devon.

[11] The lace manufacture now extends along the coast from the small watering-place of Seaton, by Beer, Branscombe, Salcombe, Sidmouth, and Ollerton, to Exmouth, including the Vale of Honiton and the towns above mentioned.

These must, however, have received a check as regards the export trade, for, says Savary, who wrote about the same date, "Depuis qu'on imite les dentelles nommées point d'Angleterre en Flandres, Picardie et Champagne, on n'en tire plus de Londres pour la France."

Great distress, too, is said to have existed among the Honiton lace-makers after the two great fires of 1756 and 1767. The second was of so devastating a character that the town had to be rebuilt. Shawe declares, writing at the end of the eighteenth century : "For its present condition Honiton is indebted to that dreadful fire which reduced three parts of it to ashes. The houses now wear a pleasing

Fig. 150.

aspect, and the principal street, extending from east to west, is paved in a remarkable manner, forming a canal, well shouldered up on each side with pebbles and green turf, which holds a stream of clear water with a square dipping place opposite each door, a mark of cleanliness and convenience I never saw before."

Three years previous to the Great Fire,[12] among a number of premiums awarded by the Anti-Gallican Society for the encouragement of our lace trade, the first prize of fifteen guineas is bestowed upon Mrs. Lydia Maynard, of Honiton, "in token of six pairs of ladies' lappets of unprecedented beauty, exhibited by her." About this time we read

---

[12] 1753.

in Bowen's *Geography* [13] that at Honiton "the people are chiefly employed in the manufactory of lace, the broadest sort that is made in England, of which great quantities are sent to London." "It acquired," says Lysons, "some years since, the name of Bath Brussels lace."

To give a precise description of the earliest Devonshire lace would now be impossible. The bone or bobbin lace at first consisted of a small and simple imitation of the beautiful Venetian geometrical cut-works and points, mere narrow strips made by coarse threads plaited and interlaced. They became wider and more elaborate as the workers gained experience. Specimens may be seen on two Devonshire monuments, though whether the lace of the district is imitated on the effigies is another matter; in any case similar patterns were probably made there at the time. One is on the monument of Lady Pole, in Colyton Church, where the lady's cape is edged with three rows of bone lace. The other, which is in excellent preservation, is on the recumbent effigy of Lady Doddridge (a member of the Bampfylde family) in Exeter Cathedral, her cuffs and tucker being adorned with geometric lace of a good pattern. Both belong to the first part of the seventeenth century.

In the same Cathedral is the monument of Bishop Stafford.[14] His collar appears to be of a net-work, embroidered in patterns of graceful design (Fig. 151).

Belgium was noted for her linens and delicately spun flax. In consequence the Flemings soon departed from the style of their Italian masters, and made laces of their own fine threads. They worked out their own designs also, and being great gardeners and fond of flowers, it naturally came about that they composed devices of blossoms and foliage.

These alterations in course of time found their way to England, there being much intercourse between their brethren here established and those remaining in Flanders. The lace continued to get finer and closer in texture, the flax thread being required so fine that it became necessary to spin it in damp underground cellars. That the workers in England could not compete successfully against the

---

[13] *Complete System of Geography.* Emanuel Bowen. 1747.

This extract is repeated verbatim in *England's Gazetteer*, by Philip Luckombe. London, 1790.

[14] Died 1398.

foreigner with their home-made threads we find over and over again. They also altered the Brussels designs, and instead of the beautiful "fillings" and open-work stitches, substituted heavy guipure bars. By this period "cordonnet" or "gimp" had come into use in Brussels lace. The "*vrai réseau*," or pillow-net ground, succeeded the "bride" about the end of the seventeenth century. This fashion enabled the flowers to be made separately and worked in with the net afterwards, or rather the net was worked into the flowers

Fig. 151.

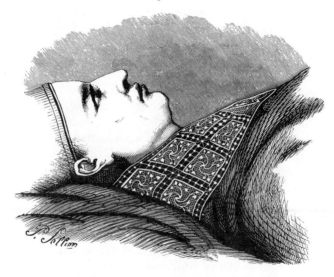

MONUMENT OF BISHOP STAFFORD, EXETER CATHEDRAL.

on the pillow. It was from the introduction of these separate sprigs that Honiton lace was able to compete with Brussels. The pattern in Fig. 153 is sewn on the plain pillow ground,[15] which was very beautiful and regular, but very expensive. It was made of the finest thread procured from Antwerp, the market price of which, in 1790, was £70 per pound,[16] and an old lace-maker told the author her father

---

[15] The best *réseau* was made by hand with the needle, and was much more expensive.

[16] Mrs. Aberdein, of Honiton, in-

formed Mrs. Palliser that her father often paid ninety-five guineas per lb. for the thread from Antwerp (1869).

had, during the war, paid a hundred guineas a pound to the smugglers for this highly-prized and then almost unattainable commodity.

Nor were the lace-worker's gains less remunerative. She would receive as much as eighteen shillings a yard for the workmanship alone of a piece of this elaborate net, measuring scarce two inches in width ;[17] and one of the old lace-dealers showed Mrs. Treadwin a piece of ground eighteen inches square, for the making of which she was paid fifteen pounds

Fig. 152.

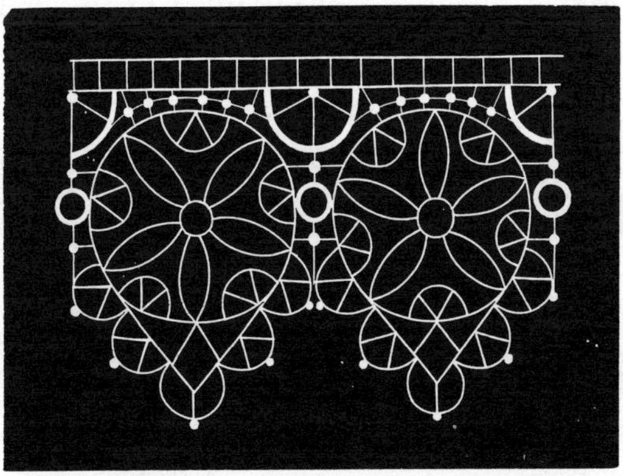

MONUMENT OF LADY DODDRIDGE. + 1614. (Exeter Cathedral.)

shortly before the establishment of the machine net manu-facture.[18] The price of lace was proportionately high. A Honiton veil would often cost a hundred guineas.

The Flemish character of Fig. 158 is unmistakable. The

---

[17] The manner of payment was somewhat Phœnician, reminding one of Queen Dido and her bargain. The lace ground was spread out on the counter, and the worker herself desired to cover it with shillings; and as many coins as found place on her work she carried away as the fruit of her labour. The author once calculated the cost, after this fashion, of a small lace veil on real ground, said to be one of the first ever fabricated. It was 12 inches wide and 30 inches long, and, making allowance for the shrinking caused by washing, the value amounted to £20, which proved to be exactly the sum originally paid for the veil. The ground of this veil, though perfect in its workmanship, is of a much wider mesh than was made in the last days of the fabric. It was the property of Mrs. Chick.

[18] "The last specimen of 'real' ground made in Devon was the marriage veil of Mrs. Marwood Tucker. It was with the greatest difficulty workers could be procured to make it. The price paid for the ground alone was 30 guineas" (1869).

design of the flower vase resembles those of the old Angleterre
à bride, and in execution this specimen may fairly warrant
a comparison with the productions of Brabant.   If really of
English make, we should place its fabrication at the beginning
of the eighteenth century, for it was long before the Devonshire lace-makers could rival in beauty the "cordonnet"
of the Flemish workers.

Fig. 154 is an example of the pattern worked in, the
favourite design of the butterfly and the acorn, already
familiar to us in the old point d'Angleterre and in the
smock of Queen Elizabeth.

The American War had an evil effect upon the lace trade,
and still worse was the French Revolution, which was followed

Fig. 153.

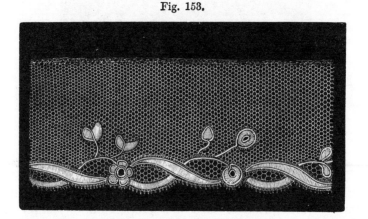

by the fashion of classical dress.   Lace became no longer
necessary to a lady's wardrobe, and the demand for it declined
to a serious extent for the workers.   Worse than these,
however, was the introduction of the machine net, the first
factory being set up at Tiverton in 1815.   Lysons writes
shortly afterwards in 1822 : "The manufactory of lace has
much declined, although the lace still retains its superiority.
Some years ago, at which time it was much patronised by
the Royal family, the manufacturers of Honiton employed
2,400 hands in the town and in the neighbouring villages,
but they do not now employ above 300."   For twenty years
the lace trade suffered the greatest depression, and the
Honiton lace-workers, forsaking the designs of their fore-
fathers, introduced a most hideous set of patterns, designed,

Fig. 154.

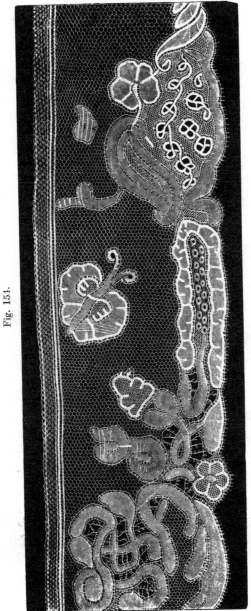

OLD DEVONSHIRE.

Fig. 155.

HONITON GUIPURE.

as they said, "out of their own heads." "Turkey tails," "frying pans," "bullocks' hearts," and the most senseless sprigs and borderings took the place of the graceful compositions of the old school. Not a leaf, not a flower was copied from nature. Anxious to introduce a purer taste, Queen Adelaide, to whom a petition had been sent on behalf of the distressed lace-makers, gave the order for a dress to be made of Honiton sprigs,[19] and commanded that the flowers should all be copied from nature. The order was executed by Mrs. Davey, of Honiton. The skirt was encircled with a wreath of elegantly designed sprigs, the initial of each flower forming the name of her Majesty.[20]

The example of the Queen found new followers, and when, in the progress of time, the wedding lace was required for Queen Victoria, it was with difficulty the necessary number of workers could be obtained to make it. It was undertaken by Miss Jane Bidney, who caused the work to be executed in the small fishing hamlet of Beer[21] and its environs. The dress cost £1,000. It was composed entirely of Honiton sprigs, connected on the pillow by a variety of open-work stitches ; but the patterns were immediately destroyed, so it cannot be described.

The bridal dresses of their Royal Highnesses the Princess Royal, the Princess Alice, and the Princess of Wales were all of Honiton point, the patterns consisting of the national flowers, the latter with prince's feathers intermixed with ferns, and introduced with the most happy effect.

The application of Honiton sprigs upon bobbin net has been of late years almost entirely superseded by the modern guipure (Fig. 155). The sprigs, when made, are sewn upon a piece of blue paper, and then united either on the pillow by "cut-works" or "purlings," or else joined with the needle by various stitches—lacet point, réseau, cut-work, and button-hole stitch (the most effective of all). Purling is made by the yard. The Honiton guipure has an original character almost unique. The large pieces surpass in richness and

---

[19] With the desire of combining the two interests, her Majesty ordered it to be made on the Brussels (machine-made) ground.

[20] AMARANTH, DAPHNE, EGLANTINE, LILAC, AURICULA, IVY, DAHLIA, EGLANTINE.

[21] The workers of Beer, Axmouth, and Branscombe, have always been considered the best in the trade.

perfection any lace of the same kind made in Belgium. The reliefs are embroidered with the greatest delicacy, and the beauty of the workmanship is exquisite ; and whereas the guipure applications of Belgium require to be whitened with lead, the Honiton workers give up their lace in all its original brilliancy and whiteness.[22] The fault in the Honiton lace has been its crowded and spiritless designs, but in these great improvement was manifested in the Exhibition of 1867.

Captain Marryat took much pains during a residence at Sidmouth to procure for the lace-makers new patterns of flowers, insects, and other natural objects. The younger members of the community accepted with gratitude these new patterns, and one even reproduced a piece of braidwork in imitation of Spanish point, and also a collar from Vecellio's book, in a manner most creditable to her ingenuity. In consequence of this movement, some gentlemen connected with the Bath and West of England Society[23] proposed that an exhibition should take place at the Annual Agricultural Show, held at Clifton, of Honiton lace, " designs strictly after nature." Prizes to the amount of £100 were given. The exhibition was most successful. Queen Victoria expressed a desire that the articles exhibited should be sent to Windsor for her inspection, and graciously commanded that two flounces with a corresponding length of trimming lace should be made for her. A design executed by Miss Cecilia Marryat having been approved of by her Majesty, the order for the lace was given to Mrs. Hayman, of Sidmouth. (Fig. 156 is from one of the honeysuckle sprigs selected.)

The Honiton lace-makers show great aptitude in imitating the Brussels designs, and[24] through the efforts of Mrs. Treadwin have succeeded in reproducing the ancient lace in

---

[22] Exposition Universelle de 1867. Rapport du Jury International, " Dentelles," par Felix Aubry.

[23] For the encouragement of Agriculture, Arts, Manufactures, and Commerce. The prizes were offered for the best Sprigs, Nosegays, Borders for shawls, veils, or collars, Lappets, collars and cuffs, Pocket-handkerchiefs, etc., " of good workmanship and design, worked either in Flowers, Fruits, Leaves, or Insects, strictly designed from nature." Three prizes were awarded for each description of article. The Society also offered prizes for small application sprigged veils, and for the best specimens of braidwork, in imitation of Spanish point.

[24] *Honiton Lace*, by Mrs. Treadwin. London, 1874. *Honiton Lace-making*, by Devonia, London, 1874.

the most wonderful manner. Fig. 158 is a lappet in the
Brussels style shown in the International Exhibition of 1874.
Mrs. Treadwin produced admirable specimens after the
pillow-made lace of Genoa and Flanders, and also a reproduction of the Venetian point in relief.

A new branch of industry has lately opened to the

Fig. 156.

HONEYSUCKLE SPRIG OF MODERN HONITON.

Devonshire lace-maker—that of restoring or re-making old
lace. The splendid mantles, tunics, and flounces which
enrich the shop-windows of the great lace-dealers of London
are mostly concocted from old fragments by the Devonshire
lace-workers. It is curious to see the ingenuity they display
in re-arranging the " old rags "—and such they are—sent
from London for restoration. Carefully cutting out the

designs of the old work, they sew them upon a paper pattern of the shape required. The "modes," or fancy stitches, are

Fig. 157.

OLD DEVONSHIRE POINT.

dexterously restored, any deficient flower supplied, and the whole joined together on the pillow.

TROLLY LACE.

Trolly lace comes next in order. It was quite different from anything else made in Devonshire, and resembled many of the laces made in the midlands at the present time. It was made of coarse British thread, and with heavier and larger bobbins, and worked straight on round and round the

Fig 158.

LAPPET MADE BY THE LATE MRS. TREADWIN, OF EXETER, 1864.

Fig. 159.

VENETIAN RELIEF IN POINT.—Reproduced by the late Mrs. Treadwin.

pillow. The origin of " Trolly " was undoubtedly Flemish, but it is said to have reached Devonshire at the time of the French Revolution, through the Normandy peasants, driven by want of employment from their own country, where lace was a great industry during the eighteenth century. The origin of " trolly " is from the Flemish " Trolle Kant," where the design was outlined with a thick thread, or, possibly, it may be derived from a corruption of the French *toilé*, applied to distinguish a flat linen pattern from the ground or *treille*, a general term for a net ground. It is now almost extinct in Devonshire, remaining in the hands of the midland counties,[25] where it more properly belongs.[26]

Trolly lace was not the work of women alone. In the flourishing days of its manufacture, every boy, until he had attained the age of fifteen, and was competent to work in the fields, attended the lace schools daily.[27] A lace-maker of Sidmouth, in 1869, had learned her craft at the village dame school,[28] in company with many boys. The men, especially the sailor returned from sea, would again resume the employment of their boyhood, in their hours of leisure, and the labourer, seated at his pillow on a summer's evening, would add to his weekly gains.

Mrs. Treadwin, in her younger days, saw some twenty-four men lace-makers in her native village of Woodbury, two of whom, Palmer by name, were still surviving in 1869, and one of these worked at his pillow so late as 1820.

Captain Marryat also succeeded in finding out a man of sixty, one James Gooding, dweller in Salcombe parish, near Sidmouth, who had in his day been a lace-maker of some reputation. " I have made hundreds of yards in my time," he said, " both wide and narrow, but never worked regularly at my pillow after sixteen years of age." Delighted to exhibit the craft of his boyhood, he hunted out his patterns,

---

[25] Lappets and scarfs were made of trolly lace from an early date. Mrs. Delarey, in one of her letters, dated 1756, speaks of a " trolly head." Trolly lace, before its downfall, has been sold at the extravagant price of five guineas a yard.

[26] " Fifty years since Devonshire workers still make a 'Greek' lace, as they termed it, similar to the 'dentelles torchons' so common through the Continent. The author has seen specimens of this fabric in a lace-maker's old pattern-book, once the property of her mother " (Mrs. Palliser, 1869).

[27] Though no longer employed at lace-making, the boys in the schools at Exmouth are instructed in crochet work (1869).

[28] Of Otterton.

and, setting to work, produced a piece of trolly edging, which soon found a place in the albums of sundry lace-collecting ladies, the last specimen of man-worked lace likely to be fabricated in the county of Devon.[29]

The lace schools of this time were a great feature, there being many in every village, and as few other schools existed, boys in addition to the girls of the place attended and learnt the industry. The usual mode of procedure was this. The children commenced attending at the age of five to seven, and were apprenticed to the mistress for an average of two years, who sold all their work for her trouble : they then paid sixpence a week for a time and had their own lace, then threepence, and so on, according to the amount of teaching they still required. The young children went first from ten to twelve in the morning, to accustom them to work by degrees. At Honiton the full hours were from eight to eight in the summer and in the depth of winter, but in the spring and autumn less, on account of the light as candles were begun only on September 3rd—Nutting day—till Shrovetide. The old rhyme runs :—

> " Be the Shrovetide high or low,
> Out the candle we will blow."

At Sidbury it was *de rigueur* that directly a young girl married, however young, she wore a cap, but till then the lace-makers were famous for the beautiful dressing of their hair. When school began they stood up in a circle to read the " verses." If any of them read " jokily," they were given a penalty, and likewise for idleness—so much extra work. In nearly all schools they were taught reading from the Bible, and in some they learnt writing; but all these are now things of the past.

Speaking of the occupation of lace-making, Cooke, in his *Topography of Devon*, observes : " It has been humanely remarked as a melancholy consideration that so much health

---

[29] In Woodbury will be found a small colony of lace-makers who are employed in making imitation Maltese or Greek lace, a fabric introduced into Devon by order of her late Majesty the Queen Dowager on her return from Malta. The workers copy these coarse geometric laces with great facility and precision. Among the various cheap articles to which the Devonshire workers have of late directed their labours is the tape or braid lace, and the shops of the country are now inundated with their productions in the form of collars and cuffs (1869.)

and comfort are sacrificed to the production of this beautiful though not necessary article of decoration. The sallow complexion, the weakly frame and the general appearance of languor and debility of the operatives, are sad and decisive proofs of the pernicious nature of the employment. The small unwholesome rooms in which numbers of these females, especially during their apprenticeship, are crowded together are great aggravations of the evil." He continues at some length, as indeed do many writers of the eighteenth century, to descant on this evil, but times are changed, sanitary laws and the love of fresh air have done much to remedy the mischief.[30] The pillows, too, are raised higher than formerly, by which means the stooping, so injurious to health, is avoided. Old lace-makers will tell stories of the cruel severities practised on the children in the dame schools of their day—of the length of time they sat without daring to move from the pillow, of prolonged punishments imposed on idle apprentices, and other barbarities, but these are now tales of the past.[31]

Ever since the Great Exhibition of 1851 drew attention to the industry, different persons have been trying to encourage both better design and better manufacture, but

---

[30] The Honiton pillows are rather smaller than those for Buckinghamshire lace, and do not have the multiplicity of starched coverings—only three "pill cloths," one over the top, and another on each side of the lace in progress; two pieces of horn called "sliders" go between to take the weight of the bobbins from dragging the stitches in progress; a small square pin-cushion is on one side, and stuck into the pillow is the "needle-pin"—a large sewing needle in a wooden handle, and for picking up loops through which the bobbins are placed. The pillow has to be frequently turned round in the course of the work, so that no stand is used, and it is rested against a table or doorway; and formerly, in the golden days, in fine weather there would be rows of workers sitting outside their cottages resting their "pills" against the back of the chair in front.

The bobbins used in Honiton lace-making are delicately-fashioned slender things of smooth, close-grained wood, their length averaging about three and a half inches. They have no "gingles," and none of the carving and relief inlayings of the Buckinghamshire and Bedfordshire bobbins; but some of them are curiously stained with a brown pigment in an irregular pattern resembling the mottlings of clouded bamboo or those of tortoise-shell.

[31] "The author has visited many lace-schools in Devon, and though it might be desired that some philanthropist would introduce the infant school system of allowing the pupils to march and stretch their limbs at the expiration of every hour, the children, notwithstanding, looked ruddy as the apples in their native orchards; and though the lace-worker may be less robust in appearance than the farm-servant or the Cheshire milkmaid, her life is more healthy far than the female operative in our northern manufactories" (1875).

the majority of the people have sought a livelihood by meeting the extensixe demand for cheap laces. Good patterns, good thread, and good work have been thrown aside, the workers and small dealers recking little of the fact that they themselves were ruining the trade as much as the competition of machinery and machine-made lace, and tarnishing the fair name of Honiton throughout the world, among those able to love and appreciate a beautiful art. Fortunately there are some to lead and direct in the right path, and all honour must be given to Mrs. Treadwin, who started reproducing old laces. She and her clever workers turned out the most exquisite copies of old Venetian rose point, Valenciennes, or Flemish. Her successor, Miss Herbert, carries it on; and while we have Msr. Fowler and her school at Honiton, and Miss Radford at Sidmouth, it would be easier to say what the heads and hands of the Devon lace-workers could not do than to enumerate the many beautiful stitches and patterns they achieve; needle-point or pillow, tape guipure or *vrai réseau*—there are able fingers to suit all tastes.[32]

Mrs. Fowler, of Honiton, has made a spirited attempt to teach some young people.[33] She employs women and girls all the year round, who work under the Factory Acts. The girls are taught needlework in addition, and to put together the sprigs made by the out-workers, the arrangement of which requires great taste and careful superintendence. The County Council grants courses of lessons in various places, some for all ages, others for children.[34] The

---

[32] "A good lace-maker easily earns her shilling a day, but in most parts of Devonshire the work is paid by the truck system, many of the more respectable shops giving one-half in money, the remaining sixpence to be taken out in tea or clothing, sold often considerably above their value. Other manufacturers—to their shame, be it told—pay their workers altogether in grocery, and should the lace-maker, from illness or any other cause, require an advance in cash, she is compelled to give work to the value of fourteen-pence for every shilling she receives. Some few houses pay their workers in money" (1875).

[33] Medals were won at the Chicago World's Fair for Devonshire lace by Mrs. Fowler and Miss Radford, of Sidmouth. The latter has also received the freedom of the City of London for a beautiful lace fan, her sprigs being the finest and most exquisite models of flowers and birds it is possible to produce in lace. A third medal was won by the Italian laces at Beer.

[34] Those held at Sidbury and Sidford are very successful, and the children, ranging in age from nine to fifteen, come regularly for their "lace." It is interesting to watch the improvement in the work of the "flys," the first

PLATE LXXXIX.

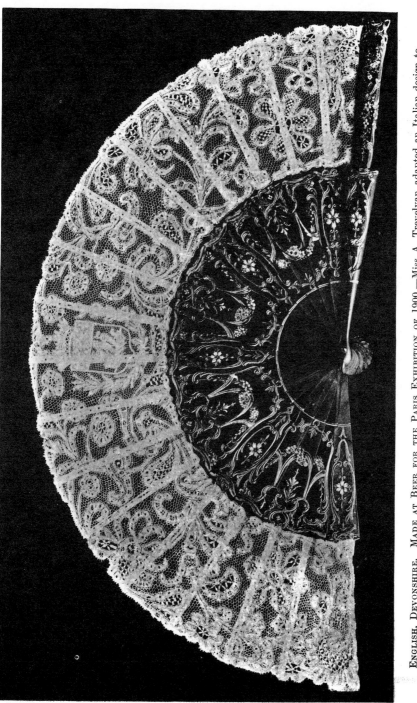

ENGLISH, DEVONSHIRE. MADE AT BEER FOR THE PARIS EXHIBITION OF 1900.—Miss A. Trevelyan adapted an Italian design to the old Honiton stitches.

Italian laces made at Beer is a new branch, established by Miss Bowdon, and ably carried on by Miss Audrey Trevelyan of Seaton. This Italian lace is made entirely on the pillow, and the way in which the women of Beer have picked up the stitches and mode of making speaks volumes for their skilfulness and adaptability. There are still a good number of workers left in this most picturesque village.[35]

A beautiful county and a beautiful art have come down to us hand in hand. Let us do our best to prevent the one being marred and the other lost, and keep them both together to be a joy and a pleasure for all time.

JAPAN.

The versatile Japanese have copied the Honiton method of making bobbin lace. The Government have encouraged a school at Yokohama for pillow lace making, under the supervision of an English lady, where they turn out lace of a distinctive Japanese character.

---

lesson, and as a rule each child makes forty to fifty before going on to anything further.

[35] At Beer, where fishing is the staple industry, in bad fish seasons the women can earn more than the men; and at Honiton in the hard winter of 1895 the lace-makers kept themselves and their families, and were spared applying for relief—all honour to their skill and self-helpfulness.

CHAPTER XXXIII.

SCOTLAND.

"With the pearlin above her brow."—Old Scotch Song.

"Pearlin-lace as fine as spiders' webs."—*Heart of Midlothian.*

FROM her constant intercourse with France, lace must have been early known in Scotland.

Of its use for ecclesiastical purposes, at a period when it was still unknown to the laity, we have evidence in the mutilated effigy of a crosiered ecclesiastic which once stood in a niche of the now ruined abbey church of Arbroath. The lace which adorns the robes of this figure is very elaborately and sharply chiselled, and when first discovered, still preserved some remains of the gold leaf with which it had been ornamented.

In the Inventories of King James V. we find constant mention of "pasment" of gold and silver,[1] as well as an entry of—"Ane gown of fresit clayth of gold, with pasment of perle of gold smyth wark lynit with cramasy sating."[2] And we have other proofs,[3] in addition to the testimony of Sir Walter Scott, as given in the *Monastery*,[4] that pasments of gold and silver as well as "purle," were already in daily use during King James's reign.

---

[1] "1539. Ane uther gowne of purpour satyne with ane braid pasment of gold and silver," etc.

"Twa Spanye cloikis of black freis with ane braid pasment of gold and silver."

"1542. Three peces of braid pasmentes of gold and silver."—*Inventories of the Royal Wardrobe and Jewel House. 1488–1606.* Edinb. 1815.

[2] 1542. Same Inv.

[3] In the Inv. of the Earl of Huntley, 1511–12, there is mention of dresses "passamenté d'or."

[4] Chap. X., note.

1537. James V. and Lord Somerville at Holyrood :—"Where are all your men and attendants, my Lord ? "

"Please, your Majesty, they are here"—pointing to the lace which was on his son and two pages' dress. The King laughed heartily and surveyed the finery, and bade him "Away with it all, and let him have his stout band of spears again."

Indeed, as early as 1575 the General Assembly of Scotland found necessary, as did the bishops in Denmark, to express its mind as to the style of dress befitting the clergy, and prohibit " all begares (gardes) of velvet on gown, hose, or coat, all superfluous cut-out work, all sewing on of pasments and laces."

A parchment, too, found in the cabinet of the Countess of Mar,[5] entitled " The Passement Bond," signed by the Duke of Lennox and other nobles, by which they engaged themselves to leave off wearing " passement," as a matter of expense and superfluity, shows that luxury in dress had early found its way into Scotland.

Notwithstanding these entries, it was not until the arrival of Mary Stuart in her northern dominions that lace in all its varieties appears. The inventory of the Queen's effects in 1567, printed by the Bannatyne Club, gives entries of passements, guimpeure d'or, and guimpeure d'argent,[6] with which her " robes de satin blanc et jaune " were " bordées " and " chamarées." Each style of embroidery and lace is designated by its special name. There is the " natte d'argent faite par entrelatz, passement d'or et d'argent fait à jour, chamarré de bisette," [7] etc.

The word dentelle, as told elsewhere,[8] occurs but once.

We have also alluded to the will made by the Queen previous to the birth of James VI., and her bequest of her " ouvrages maschés." [9] A relic of this expression is yet found in the word " mawsch," or " masch," as the pinking of silk and muslin is termed in Scotland, an advertisement of which

---

[5] Croft's *Excerpta Antiqua.*
The Countess of Mar, daughter of the first Duke of Lennox and grand-daughter by her mother's side to Marie Touchet. She was daughter-in-law to the preceptress of James VI., and in 1593 had the honour, at the baptism of Prince Henry, of lifting the child from his bed and delivering him to the Duke of Lennox. A portrait of this lady, in the high Elizabethan ruff, and with a " forepart " and tucker of exquisite raised Venice point, hung (circ. 1870) in the drawing-room of the late Miss Katherine Sinclair.
[6] " Une robe de velours vert cou-verté de Broderies, gimpeures, et cordons d'or et d'argent, et bordée d'un passement de même.
" Une robe veluat cramoisi bandée de broderie de guimpeure d'argent.
" Une robe de satin blanc chamarrée de broderie faite de guimpeure d'or.
" Id. de satin jaune toute couverte de broderye gumpeure, etc.
" Robe de weloux noyr semée de geynpeurs d'or."—*Inv. of Lillebourg.* 1561.
[7] " Chamarrée de bisette."—*Inv. of Lillebourg.* 1561.
" Ane rabbat of wolvin thread with passmentet with silver."
[8] Chap. III.
[9] See LACIS, Chap. II.

accomplishment " done here " was seen a few years ago in the shop-windows of the old town of Edinburgh.

In the Palace of Holyrood is still exhibited a small basket lined with blue silk, and trimmed with a bone lace of rudely-spun flax, run on with a ribbon of the same colour, recorded to be an offering sent by Queen Elizabeth to her cousin previous to the birth of her godchild. Antiquaries assert the story to be a fable. Whether the lace be of the time or not, as a work of art it is of no credit to any country.

How Queen Mary, in her youth, was instructed in the arts of point coupé and lacis, according to the works of Vinciolo, has been already related.[10] Of her talents as a needlewoman there is ample proof in the numerous beds, screens, etc., treasured as relics in the houses of the nobles where she was held captive. She knitted head-dresses of gold "réseille," with cuffs and collars[11] en suite,[12] to say nothing of nightcaps, and sent them as presents to Elizabeth,[13] all of which, we are told, the Queen received most graciously. Mary, in her early portraits as Dauphine of France, wears no thread lace. Much fine gold embroidered with passament enriches her dresses ; her sleeves are of gold rézeuil. In those of a later date, like that taken when in Lochleven Castle, her veil is bordered with a narrow bone lace—as yet a rarity —may be one of the same noted in the Inventory of 1578, as " Fyve litell vaills of wovin rasour (réseau) of threde, ane meekle twa of thame, passmentit with perle and black silk." [14]

When the Queen of Scots ascended the scaffold " she wore

---

[10] See NEEDLEWORK, Chap. I.

[11] Her lace ruffs Mary appears to have had from France, as we may infer from a letter written by Walsingham, at Paris, to Burleigh, when the Queen was captive at Sheffield Castle, 1578 : " I have of late granted a passport to one that conveyeth a box of linen to the Queen of Scots, who leaveth not this town for three or four days. I think your Lordship shall see somewhat written on some of the linen contained in the same, that shall be worth the reading. Her Majesty, under colour of seeing the fashion of the *ruffes*, may cause the several parcels of the linen to be held to the fire, whereby the writing may appear ; for I judge there will be some such matter discovered, which was the cause why I did the more willingly grant the passport."

[12] In 1575.

[13] There was some demur about receiving the nightcaps, for Elizabeth declared " that great commotions had taken place in the Privy Council because she had accepted the gifts of the Queen of Scots. They therefore remained for some time in the hands of La Mothe, the ambassador, but were finally accepted."—Miss Strickland.

[14] " Inventaire of our Soveraine Lord and his dearest moder. 1578."—Record Office, Edinburgh.

on her head," writes Burleigh's reporter, "a dressing of lawn edged with bone lace," and "a vest of lawn fastened to her caul," edged with the same material. This lace-edged veil was long preserved as a relic in the exiled Stuart family, until Cardinal York bequeathed it to Sir John Cox Hippisley. Miss Pigott[15] describes it of "transparent zephyr gauze, with a light check or plaid pattern interwoven with gold; the form as that of a long scarf."[16] Sir John, when exhibiting the veil at Baden, had the indiscretion to throw it over the Queen of Bavaria's head. The Queen shuddered at the omen, threw off the veil, and retired precipitately from the apartment, evidently in great alarm.

"Cuttit out werk," collars of "hollie crisp," quaiffs of woven thread,[17] cornettes of layn (linen) sewit with cuttit out werk of gold, wovin collars of threde, follow in quick succession. The cuttit out werk is mostly wrought in gold, silver, cramoisi, or black silk.[18] The Queen's "towell claiths" are adorned in similar manner.[19]

The Chartley Inventory of 1568[20] is rich in works of point coupé and rézeuil, in which are portrayed with the needle figures of birds, fishes, beasts, and flowers, "couppés chascune en son carré." The Queen exercised much ingenuity in her labours, varying the pattern according to her taste. In the list are noted fifty-two specimens of flowers designed after nature, "tirés au naturel;" 124 birds; as well as sixteen sorts of four-footed beasts, "entre lesquelles y ha un lyon assaillant un sanglier;" with fifty-two fishes, all of

---

[15] *Records of Life*, by Miss H. Pigott. 1839.

[16] Similar to the New Year's Gift of the Baroness Aletti to Queen Elizabeth:—

"A veil of lawn cutwork flourished with silver and divers colours."— *Nichols' Royal Progresses*.

[17] "Twa quaiffs ane of layn and uther of woving thread.

"Ane quaiff of layn with twa cornettes sewitt with cuttit out werk of gold and silver.

"Twa pair of cornettes of layn sewitt with cuttit out werk of gold.

"Ane wovin collar of thread passementit with incarnit and blew silk and silver."—*Inv. of* 1578.

[18] "Ane rabbat of cuttit out werk and gold and cramoisie silk with the handis (cuffs) thereof.

"Ane rabbat of cuttit out werk of gold and black silk.

"Ane rabbat of cuttit out werk with purpure silk with the handis of the same."—*Ibid.*

[19] "Twa towell claiths of holane claith sewitt with cuttit out werk and gold.

"Four napkinnes of holane claith and cammaraye sewitt with cuttit out werk of gold and silver and divers cullours of silk."—*Ibid.*

[20] Published by Prince Labanoff. "Recueil de Lettres de Marie Stuart." T. vii., p. 247.

divers sorts—giving good proofs of the poor prisoner's industry.   As to the designs after nature, with all respect to the memory of Queen Mary, the lions, cocks, and fishes of the sixteenth century which have come under our notice, require a student of mediæval needlework rather than a naturalist, to pronounce upon their identity.

James VI. of Scotland, reared in a hotbed of Calvinism, had not the means, even if he had the inclination, to indulge in much luxury in dress.   Certain necessary entries of braid pasmentis of gold, gold clinquant, braid pasmentis, cramoisi, for the ornamenting of clokkis, coittis, breikis, and roobes of the King, with "Twa unce and ane half pasmentis of gold and silver to werk the headis of the fokkis," made up the amount of expense sanctioned for the royal wedding; [21] while 34 ells braid pasmentis of gold to trim a robe for "his Majesties darrest bedfellow the Quene for her coronation," [22] gives but a poor idea of the luxury of the Scottish court.

Various enactments [23] were passed during the reign of James VI. against "unnecessary sumptuousness in men's apparel," by which no one except noblemen, lords of session, prelates, etc., were allowed to wear silver or gold lace. Provosts were permitted to wear silk, but no lace pearlin or pasmenterie, only a "watling silk lace" on the seams. [24]   No one but the above same privileged persons were to have pearlin on their ruffles, sarkis, napkins, and sokkis, and that pearlin to be made in the kingdom of Scotland.   This Act, dated 1621, is the first mention we have found of Scottish-made lace.

James VI. having granted to one James Bannatyne of Leith a patent for the "importing of foraine pearlin" into the country, in consequence of the great complaint of the embroiderers in 1639, this patent is rescinded, and the King forbids the entry of all " foraine pearlin."

The word lace does not exist in the Scotch language. "Pearlin " is the term used in old documents, defined in the

---

[21] *Marriage Expenses of James VI.*, 1589.   Published by the Bannatyne Club.

[22] *Accounts of the Great Chamberlain of Scotland.*   1590.—Bannatyne Club

[23] In 1581, 1597, and 1621.

[24] The same privilege was extended to their wives, their eldest sons with their wives, and their eldest daughters, but not to the younger children.

dictionaries to be " a species of lace made with thread." In the old Scotch songs it frequently occurs :—[25]

> " Then round the ring she dealt them ane by ane,
> Clean in her pearlin keck, and gown alane."
> —*Ross Helonora.*

Again—

> " We maun hae pearlins and mabbies and cocks,
> And some other things that ladies call smocks."

As the latter articles may appear more familiar to the world in general than " kecks," and " mabbies," and " cocks," we may as well explain a " pearlin keck " to signify a linen cap with a lace border ; a " mabbie," a mob ; a " cock," or cock-up, no more eccentric head-dress than the lofty fontanges or commode of the eighteenth century.

Again, in *Rob Roy* we have the term " pearlin :" when Bailie Nicol Jarvie piteously pleads to his kinswoman, Helen Macgregor, he says—

" I hae been serviceable to Rob before now, forbye a set of pearlins I sent yoursell when you were gaun to be married."

The recollection of these delicate attentions, however, has little effect on the Highland chieftainess, who threatens to have him chopped up, if ill befalls her lord, into as many square pieces as compose the Macgregor tartan, or throw him neck and heels into the Highland loch.

Montrose, we read, sent his lace ruffles to be starched and dressed before they were sewn on the embroidered sark he had made only to wear at his execution. " Pearlin " was provided for him which cost £10 an ell.

The close-fitting velvet cap, enriched with lace, appears in the seventeenth century to have been adopted by the lawyers of the Scotch courts. An example may be seen in the portrait of Sir Thomas Hope, Lord Advocate of Scotland, who died in 1646, which hangs in the Hall of the Advocates of Edinburgh. Another (Fig. 160) appears in the engraving of Sir Alexander Gibson, Bart., Lord Durie, one of the Lords of Session, who died two years previously.

In 1672, when lace—" point lace made of thread "—

---

[25] 1633. In the *Account of Expenses for the young Lord of Lorne,* we find :—
" 2 ells Cambridg' at 8s. the ell for ruffles. 16s.
" 2 ells of Perling at 30s., the uther at 33s. 4d., £3 3s. 4d."—Innes' *Sketches of Early Scotch History.*

came under the ban of the Covenanters, with a penalty of " 500 merks toties quoties," the wearing such vanities on liveries is strictly forbidden ; servants, however, are allowed to wear out their masters' and mistresses' old clothes.

In 1674, his Majesty, understanding that the manufacture of " pearlin and whyt lace made of thread (whereby many people gain their livelihood) was thereby much prejudiced and impaired, declares that from henceforth it shall be free to all and every person within this kingdom to wear ' whyt

Fig. 160.

Sir Alexander Gibson, Bart. (Lord Durie, Lord of Session. + 1644.)

lace,' as well as the privileged persons above mentioned." Finding these exclusions of little or no avail, in January, 1685, the Act remits the wearing of lace, both native and foreign, to all folks living.

The dead now came under the scrutiny of the Scotch Parliament, who order all lace or poynt, gold or silver, to be disused at interments, under the penalty of 300 pounds Scots.[26]

From the united effects of poverty, Covenanters and

---

[26] January, 1686.

legislation, after the departure of the court for England luxury, small though it was, declined in Edinburgh.

It was not till 1680, when James II., as Duke of York, accompanied by Mary of Modena and his " duteous " daughter Anne, visited the Scotch capital, that anything like gaiety or dress can be said to have surprised the strait-laced population.

Dryden, sneering at the barbarism of the Scotch capital, writes, in the prologue to a play delivered at Oxford, referring to a portion of the troop that accompanied the court to Scotland—

> " Laced linen there would be a dangerous thing;
> It might perhaps a new rebellion bring—
> The Scot who wore it would be chosen king."

The Highlander, however, when in full dress, did not disdain to adopt the falling band and ruffles of guipure or Flanders lace.

The advertisements and inventories of the first years of the eighteenth century give us little reason to imagine any change had been effected in the homely habits of the people.

At the marriage of a daughter of Thomas Smythe, of Methuen, in 1701, to Sir Thomas Moncrieffe, the bride had a head-suit and ruffles of cut-work which cost nearly six pounds ten shillings.[27] Few and scanty advertisements of roups of " white thread lace " appear in the journals of the day.[28]

And in such a state matters continued till the Jacobites,

---

[27] " In 1701, when Mistress Margaret, daughter of the Baron of Kilravock, married, ' flounced muslin and lace for combing cloths,' appear in her outfit." —Innes' *Sketches*.

[28] In a pamphlet published 1702, entitled, *An Accompt carried between England and Scotland*, alluding to the encouragement of the yarn trade, the author says : " This great improvement can be attested by the industry of many young gentlewomen that have little or no portion, by spinning one pound of fine lint, and then breaking it into fine flax and whitening it. One gentlewoman told me herself that, by making an ounce or two of it into fine bone lace, it was worth, or she got, twenty pounds Scots for that part of

it ; and might, after same manner, five or eight pounds sterling out of a pound of lint, that cost her not one shilling sterling. Now if a law were made not to import any muslin (her Grace the Duchess of Hamilton still wears our finest Scots muslin as a pattern to others—she who may wear the finest apparel) and Holland lace, it would induce and stir up many of all ranks to wear more fine ' Scots lace,' which would encourage and give bread to many young gentlewomen and help their fortunes." Then, among the products of Scotland by which " we may balance any nation," the same writer mentions " our white thread, and making laces."

" On Tuesday, the 16th inst., will

going and coming from St. Germains, introduced French
fashions and luxuries as yet unheard of in the then aristo-
cratic Canongate.

It sounds strange to a traveller, as he wanders among
these now deserted closes of Edinburgh, to read of the gay
doings and of the grand people who, in the last century,
dwelt within these poor-looking abodes. A difficult matter
it must have been to the Jacobite beauties, whose hoop (from
1725–8) measured nine yards in circumference, to mount the
narrow winding staircases of their dwellings ; and this very
difficulty gave rise to a luxury of underclothing almost
unknown in England or elsewhere. Every lady wore a
petticoat trimmed with the richest point lace. Nor was it
only the jupe that was lace-trimmed. Besides

"Twa lappets at her head, that flaunted gallantlie,"

ladies extended the luxury to finely-laced garters.

In 1720 the bubble Company " for the trading in Flanders
laces " appears advertised in the Scotch papers in large and
attractive letters. We strongly doubt, however, it having
gained any shareholders among the prudent population of
Edinburgh.

The prohibition of lace made in the dominions of the
French king [29] was a boon to the Jacobites, and many a lady,
and gentleman too, became wondrous loyal to the exiled
family, bribed by a packet from St. Germains. In the first
year of George II., says the *Gazette*,[30] a parcel of rich lace
was secretly brought to the Duke of Devonshire, by a mistake
in the similarity of the title. On being opened, hidden
among the folds, was found a miniature portrait of the
Pretender, set round with large diamonds. The packet was
addressed to a noble lord high in office, one of the most
zealous converts to loyalty.[31]

---

begin the roup of several sorts of mer-
chants' goods, in the first story of the
Turnpyke, above the head of Bells
Wynd, from 9 to 12 and 2 till 5.
'White thread lace.'"— *Edinburgh
Courant.* 1706.

[29] See Chap. XXV., Queen Anne.

[30] *Edinburgh Advertiser.* 1764.

[31] 1745. The following description
of Lady Lovat, wife of the rebel

Simon, is a charming picture of a
Scotch gentlewoman of the last century :—

" When at home her dress was a red
silk gown with ruffled cuffs and sleeves
puckered like a man's shirt, a fly cap
of lace encircling her head, with a mob
cap laid across it, falling down on the
cheeks ; her hair dressed and powdered ;
a lace handkerchief round the neck

Smuggling was universal in Scotland in the reigns of George I. and George II., for the people, unaccustomed to imposts, and regarding them as an unjust aggression upon their ancient liberties, made no scruple to elude the customs whenever it was possible so to do.

It was smuggling that originated the Porteous riots of 1736 ; and in his description of the excited mob, Sir Walter Scott makes Miss Grizel Dalmahoy exclaim—"They have ta'en awa' our Parliament. They hae oppressed our trade. Our gentles will hardly allow that a Scots needle can sew ruffles on a sark or lace on an owerlay." [32]

---

and bosom (termed by the Scotch a *Befong*)—a white apron edged with lace . . . . Any one who saw her sitting on her chair, so neat, fresh, and clean, would have taken her for a queen in wax-work placed in a glass case."—*Heart of Midlothian.*

Sir Walter Scott, whose descriptions are invariably drawn from memory, in his *Chronicles of the Canongate*, describes the dressing-room of Mrs. Bethune Balliol as exhibiting a superb mirror framed in silver filigree-work, a beautiful toilet, the cover of which was of Flanders lace.

[32] *Heart of Midlothian.*

CHAPTER XXXIV.

LACE MANUFACTURES OF SCOTLAND.

" Sae put on your pearlins, Marion,
　　And kirtle o' the cramasie."—Scottish Song.

DURING the treasonable year of 1745 Scotland was far too occupied with her risings and executions to give much attention to her national industry.　Up to that time considerable pains had been taken to improve the spinning of fine thread, prizes had been awarded, and the art taught in schools and other charitable institutions.

It was not till the middle of the eighteenth century that Anne, Duchess of Hamilton, known to Society by tradition as " one of the beautiful Miss Gunnings," seeing lace-makers at work when travelling on the Continent, thought employment might be given to the women of her own country by introducing the art into Scotland.　The Duchess therefore brought over women from France, and caused them to teach the girls in her schools how to make " bunt lace," as it was termed.

Sir John Sinclair thus notices the fabric :—" A small manufacture of thread lace has long been carried on here. At an early period it was the occupation of a good many women, but, from the fluctuation of fashion, it has fallen greatly into disuse.　Fashion again revived the demand, and the late Duchess of Hamilton, afterwards of Argyle, found still some lace-workers remaining, to whom her own demand, and that of those who followed her example, gave employment.　To these her Grace added twelve orphan girls, who were clothed, maintained, and taught at her expense.　Others learned the art, and while the demand lasted, the manufacture employed a good many hands.　Though the number is again diminished, there are still above forty at the business, who make handsome laces of different patterns, besides those who work occasionally for themselves or their friends. Perhaps, under the patronage of the present respectable duchess, the manufacture of Hamilton lace may again become as flourishing as ever." [1]

"The Duchess of Hamilton," says the *Edinburgh Amusement* of 1752, "has ordered a home to be set up in Hamilton for the reception of twelve poor girls and a mistress. The girls are to be taken in at the age of seven, clothed, fed, taught to spin, make lace, etc., and dismissed at fourteen."

The work of the fair Duchess throve, for, in 1754, we read how—"The Duchess of Hamilton has now the pleasure to see the good effects of her charity. Her Grace's small orphan family have, by spinning, gained a sum of money, and lately presented the Duke and Duchess with a double piece of Holland, and some suits of exceeding fine lace ruffles, of their own manufacture, which their Graces did them the honour to wear on the Duke's birthday, July 14, and which vied with anything worn on the occasion, though there was a splendid company present. The yarn of which the ruffles were made weighed only ten drops each hank." [2]

It was probably owing to the influence of this impulsive Irishwoman that, in the year 1754, was founded The Select Society of Edinburgh for encouraging the arts and manufactures of Scotland, headed by the Duke of Hamilton. This society was contemporary with the Anti-Gallican in England and the Dublin Society, though we believe, in this case, Dublin can claim precedence over the capital of North Britain.

At a meeting of the society it was moved that "The annual importation of worked ruffles and of bone lace and edging into this country is considerable. By proper encouragement we might be supplied at home with these ornaments. It was therefore resolved—

"That a premium be assigned to all superior merit in such work; such a one as may be a mark of respect to women of fashion, and may also be of some solid advantage to those whose laudable industry contributes to their own support.

---

[1] *Statistical Account of Scotland.*   Vol. ii., 198.
Sir John Sinclair. Edinburgh, 1792.   [2] *Edinburgh Amusement.*

"For the best imitation of Dresden work, or a pair of men's ruffles, a prize of £5 5s.

"For the best bone lace, not under twenty yards, £5 5s. The gainers of these two best articles may have the money or a gold medal, at their option."

As may be supposed, the newly-founded fabric of the Duchess was not passed over by a society of which the Duke himself was the patron. In the year 1757 we have among the prizes adjudged one of two guineas to Anne Henderson, of Hamilton, " for the whitest and best and finest lace, commonly called Hamilton lace, not under two yards " A prize had already been offered in 1755,[3] but, as stated the following year, " no lace was given in." Prizes continued in 1758 and 1759 to be given for the produce of Hamilton ; in the last year to the value of four guineas.[4]

The early death of the Duke of Hamilton, and the second marriage of the Duchess, did not in any way impede the progress of Hamilton lace, for, as late as 1778, we read in Locke's *Essays on the Scotch Commerce*—" The lace manufactory, under the patronage of the amiable Duchess of Hamilton (now Argyle), goes on with success and spirit."

With respect to the quality of this Hamilton lace, laudable as were the efforts of the Duchess, she succeeded in producing but a very coarse fabric. The specimens which have come under our notice are edgings of the commonest description, of a coarse thread, always of the lozenge pattern (Fig. 161) ; being strong and firm, it was used for nightcaps, never for dresses, and justified the description of a lady who described it as of little account, and spoke of it as "only Hamilton."

It appears that the Edinburgh Society died a natural death about 1764, but, notwithstanding the untimely demise of this patriotic club, a strong impetus had been given to the

---

[3] 1755. Premium £2 offered. " For the whitest, best, and finest lace, commonly called Hamilton lace, and of the best pattern, not under two yards in length and not under three inches in breadth."
[4] The Edinburgh Society did not confine their rewards to Hamilton lace ; imitation of Dresden, catgut lace,

gold, silver, and even livery lace, each met with its due reward.

1758. For imitation of lace done on catgut, for ruffles, a gold medal to Miss Anne Cant, Edinburgh.

For a piece of livery lace done to perfection to J. Bowie, 2 guineas.

To W. Bowie for a piece of gold and silver lace, 2 guineas.

lace-makers of Scotland.[5] Lace-making was introduced into the schools, and, what was better far, many daughters of the smaller gentry and scions of noble Jacobite houses, ruined by the catastrophe of 1745, either added to their incomes or supported themselves wholly by the making of the finer points. This custom seems to have been general, and, in alluding to it, Mrs. Calderwood speaks of the "helplessness" of the English women in comparison to the Scotch.

In the journals of the day we have constant advertisements, informing the public of the advantages to be gained by the useful arts imparted to their offspring in their

Fig. 161.

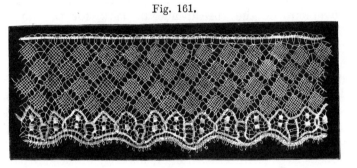

HAMILTON.

establishments, inserted by ladies of gentle blood—for the Scotchwomen of the last century no more disdained to employ themselves in the training of youth than does now a French dame de qualité to place herself at the head of the Sacré-Cœur, or some other convent devoted to educational purposes.[6]

The entry of all foreign laces was excluded by law. The

---

[5] 1769. Pennant, in his *Tour*, mentions among the manufactures of Scotland thread laces at Leith, Hamilton and Dalkeith.

[6] In 1762, Dec. 9, a schoolmistress in Dundee, among thirty-one accomplishments in which she professes to instruct her pupils, such as "waxwork, boning fowls without cutting the back," etc., enumerates, No. 21, "True point or tape lace," as well as "washing Flanders lace and point."

Again, in 1764, Mr. and Mrs. Mitchell advertise in their boarding-school "lacework and the washing of blonde laces; the pupils' own laces washed and got up at home. Terms £24."

At Miss Glen's boarding-school in the Trunk Close, 1768, young ladies are taught "white and coloured seam and washing of lace"—gratis.

These lady-teachers were not appointed in Scotland without giving due proofs of their capacity. In 1758 the magistrates and council of Aberdeen, being unanimous as to the "strict

Scotch nation of the Hanoverian persuasion were wrath at the frivolity of the Jacobite party. "£400,000 have been sent out of the country during the last year," writes the *Edinburgh Advertiser* of 1764, "to support our exiled countrymen in France, where they learn nothing but folly and extravagance." English laces were not included in the prohibition. In 1763, that "neat shop near the Stinking Style, in the Lukenbooths," held by Mr. James Baillie, advertises " Trollies, English laces, and pearl edgings." Four year later, black silk lace and guipure are added to the stock, " mennuet," and very cheap bone lace.[7]

Great efforts, and with success, were made for the improvement of the thread manufacture, for the purchase of which article at Lille £200,000 were annually sent from Scotland to France. Badly-spun yarn was seized and burned by the stamp master ; of this we have frequent mention.[8]

Peuchet, speaking of Scotland, says :—" Il s'est formé près d'Edinbourg une manufacture de fil de dentelle. On prétend que le fil de cette manufacture sert à faire des dentelles qui non-seulement égalent en beauté celles qui sont fabriquées avec le fil de l'étranger, mais encore les surpassent en durée. Cet avantage serait d'autant plus grand que l'importation de ce fil de l'étranger occasionne aux habitans de ce royaume une perte annuelle de £100,000."[9]

Whether about the year 1775 any change had taken place in the legïslation of the customs of Scotland, and they had become regulated by English law, we cannot say, but suddenly constant advertisements of Brussels lace and fine point appear in the *Gazette*, and this at the very time Loch

---

morality, Dresden work, modesty, and catgut lace-making," etc., of Miss Betsey Forbes, elected her to the office of schoolmistress of the city.

In *The Cottagers of Glenburnie* a lady, Mrs. Mason, tells a long story of the young laird having torn a suit of lace she was busied in getting up.

[7] *Edinburgh Advertiser.*

[8] 1774. " Several punds of badly-spun yarn was burnt by the stamp master in Montrose." This announcement constantly occurs.

[9] About this period a Mr. Brother-

ton, of Leith, seems to have made a discovery which was but a prelude to the bobbin net. It is thus described in the *Weekly Magazine* of 1772:—
" A new invention has lately been discovered by Mr. Brotherton, in Leith, for working black silk lace or white thread lace on a loom, to imitate any pattern whatever, and the lace done in this way looks fully as well as if sewed, and comes much cheaper. It is done any breadth, from three inches to three-quarters of a yard wide."

was doing his best to stir up once more Scotch patriotism with regard to manufactures.[10]

The Scotch Foresters set the example at their meeting in 1766, and then—we hear nothing more on the matter.

The *Weekly Magazine* of 1776 strongly recommends the art of lace-making as one calculated to flourish in Scotland, young girls beginning to learn at eight years of age, adding : "The directors of the hospital of Glasgow have already sent twenty-three girls to be taught by Madame Puteau,[11] a native of Lisle, now residing at Renfrew ; you will find the lace of Renfrew cheaper, as good and as neat as those imported from Brussels, Lisle, and Antwerp." David Loch also mentions the success of the young Glasgow lace-makers, who made lace, he says, from 10*d.* to 4*s.* 6*d.* per yard. He adds : "It is a pleasure to see them at work. I saw them ten days ago." He recommends the managers of the Workhouse of the Canongate to adopt the same plan : adding, they need not send to Glasgow for teachers, as there are plenty at the Orphan Hospital at Edinburgh capable of undertaking the office. Of the lace fabricated at Glasgow we know nothing, save from an advertisement in the *Caledonian Mercury* of 1778, where one William Smith, "Lace-maker," at the Greenhead, Glasgow, informs the public he has for some years "made and bleached candlewicks." Anderson and Loch did not agree on the subject of lace-making, the former considering it an unstable fabric, too easily affected by the caprices of fashion.[12]

---

[10] In 1775 Dallas, Barclay & Co., advertise a selling off of fine point, Brussels thread, blond, and black laces of all kinds, silver double edged lace, etc.—*Edinburgh Advertiser.*
1775. " Black blonde and thread laces, catguts of all sorts, just arrived from the India House in London in the Canongate."—*Caledonian Mercury.*
"Fashions for January ; dresses trimmed with Brussels point or Mignonette."—*Ibid.* Same year.

[11] " Madame Puteau carries on a lace manufacture after the manner of Mechlin and Brussels. She had lately twenty-two apprentices from the Glasgow Hospital. . . . . Mrs. Puteau has as much merit in this branch as has her husband in the making of fine thread. This he manufactures of such a fineness as to be valued at £10 the pound weight."—*Essays on the Trade, Commerce, Manufactures, Fisheries, etc., of Scotland.* David Loch. 1778.

[12] " If you look at the wardrobes of your grandmother, you will perceive what revolutions have happened in taste of mankind for laces and other fineries of that sort. How many suits of this kind do you meet with that cost amazing sums, which are now, and have long since been, entirely useless. In our own day did we not see that in one year Brussels laces are most in fashion and purchased at any price, while the next perhaps they are entirely laid aside, and French

Be that as it may, the manufacture of thread for lace alone employed five hundred machines, each machine occupying thirty-six persons : the value of the thread produced annually £175,000. Loch adds, that in consequence of the cheapness of provisions, Scotland, as a country, is better adapted to lace-making than England. In consequence of Loch's remarks, his Majesty's Board of Trustees for the Fisheries and Manufactures, after asking a number of questions, determined to give proper encouragement and have mistresses for teaching the different kinds of lace made in England and France, and oblige them to take girls of the poorer class, some from the hospitals, and the mistress for five years to have the benefit of their work. A girl might earn from 10*d*. to 1*s*. per day. They gave a salary to an experienced person from Lisle for the purpose of teaching the making of thread ; his wife to instruct in lace-making. With the records of 1788 end all mention of lace-making in Scotland.[13]

---

or other thread laces, or fine sewings, the names of which I know not, highly prized."—*Observations on the National Industry of Scotland.* Anderson. 1778.

[13] Lace-making at Hamilton is now a thing of the past, replaced in the nineteenth century by a tambour network for veils, scarfs and flounces.

CHAPTER XXXV.

IRELAND.

"The undoubted aptitude for lace-making of the women of Ireland."
—*Juror's Report, International Exhibition.* 1862.

"It is peculiarly interesting to note the various foreign influences which have done their part in the creation of Irish lace. Italian and Flemish, Greek, French and English, all have lent their aid."
—A. Loyd. *The Queen,* Feb. 6th, 1897.

LITTLE is known of the early state of manufactures in Ireland, save that the art of needlework was held in high estimation.

By the sumptuary laws of King Mogha Nuadhad, killed at the Battle of Maylean, A.D. 192, we learn that the value of a queen's raiment, should she bring a suitable dowry, ought to amount to the cost of six cows; but of what the said raiment consisted history is dark.

The same record, however, informs us that the price of a mantle, wrought with the needle, should be "a young bullock or steer."[1] This hooded mantle is described by Giraldus Cambrensis as composed of various pieces of cloth, striped, and worked in squares by the needle; maybe a species of cut-work.

Morgan, who wrote in 1588, declares the saffron-tinted shirts of the Irish to contain from twenty to thirty ells of linen. No wonder they are described—

"With pleates on pleates they pleated are,
As thick as pleates may lie."[2]

It was in such guise the Irish appeared at court before Queen Elizabeth,[3] and from them the yellow starch of Mrs. Turner may have derived its origin. The Irish, however,

---

Essay on the Dress of the Early Irish. J. C. Walker. 1788.
[2] *The Image of Irelande,* by Jhon Derricke. 1578.
[3] In 1562. See Camden. *Hist. Eliz.*

produced the dye not from saffron, but from a lichen gathered
on the rocks.   Be that as it may, the Government prohibited
its use, and the shirts were reduced in quantity to six ells,[4]
for the making of which " new-fangled pair of Gally-cushes,"
i.e., English shirts, as we find by the Corporation Book of
Kilkenny (1537), eighteenpence was charged if done with
silk or cut-work.   Ninepence extra was charged for every
ounce of silk worked in.

An Irish smock wrought with silk and gold was considered an object worthy of a king's wardrobe, as the
inventory of King Edward IV.[5] attests :—" Item, one Irishe
smocke wrought with gold and silke."

The Rebellion at an end, a friendly intercourse, as
regards fashion, was kept up between the English and the
Irish.   The ruff of geometric design, falling band, and cravat
of Flanders lace, all appeared in due succession.   The Irish,
always lovers of pomp and show, early used lace at the
interments of the great, as appears from an anecdote related
in a letter of Mr. O'Halloran :—" The late Lord Glandore
told me," he writes, " that when a boy, under a spacious
tomb in the ruined monastery at his seat, Ardfert Abbey
(Co. Kerry), he perceived something white.   He drew it
forth, and it proved to be a shroud of Flanders lace, the
covering of some person long deceased."

In the beginning of the eighteenth century a patriotic
feeling arose among the Irish, who joined hand in hand to
encourage the productions of their own country.   Swift was
hmong the first to support the movement, and in a prologue
he composed, in 1721, to a play acted for the benefit of the
Irish weavers, he says :—

> " Since waiting-women, like exacting jades,
> Hold up the prices of their old brocades,
> We'll dress in manufactures made at home."

Shortly afterwards, at a meeting, he proposed the
following resolution :—
" That the ladies wear Irish manufactures.   There is

---

[4] Henry VIII. 1537. Against Irish
fashions.   Not " to weare any shirt,
smock, kerchor, bendel, neckerchour,
mocket, or linen cappe colored or
dyed with saffron," and not to use
more than seven yards of linen in their
shirts or smocks.
[5] 4 Edw. IV., Harl MSS. No. 1419.
b.-g. 494.

PLATE XC.

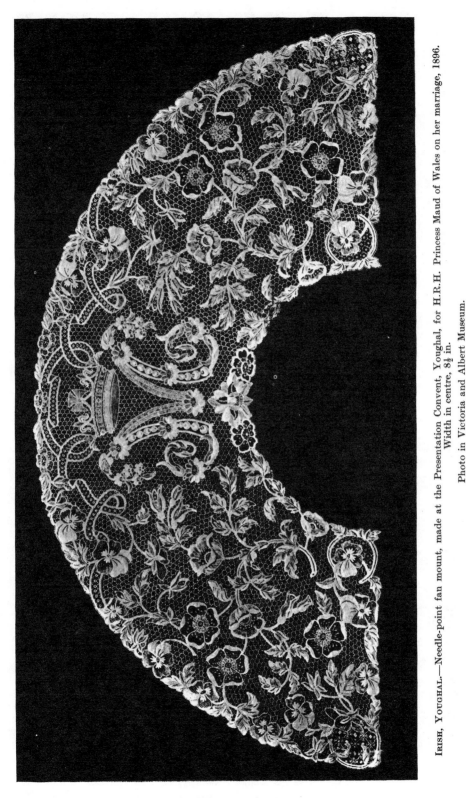

IRISH, YOUGHAL.—Needle-point fan mount, made at the Presentation Convent, Youghal, for H.R.H. Princess Maud of Wales on her marriage, 1896.
Width in centre, 8¼ in.

Photo in Victoria and Albert Museum.

Plate XCI.

Irish, Carrickmacross. Insertion and border of appliqué lace, made at the Bath and Shirley Schools. End of nineteenth century. Width of insertion, 6 in. ; border, 9¼ in.

Victoria and Albert Museum.

Plate XCII.

Irish. Limerick Lace. Tambour embroidery on net, made at Kinsale. End of nineteenth century. Width, 17 in.

Victoria and Albert Museum.

brought annually into this kingdom near £90,000 worth of silk, whereof the greater part is manufactured; £30,000 more is expended in muslin, holland, cambric, and calico. What the price of lace amounts to is not easy to be collected from the Custom-house book, being a kind of goods that, taking up little room, is easily run; but, considering the prodigious price of a woman's head-dress at ten, twelve, twenty pounds a yard, it must be very great."

Though a club of patriots had been formed in Ireland since the beginning of the eighteenth century, called the Dublin Society, they were not incorporated by charter until the year 1749; hence many of their records are lost, and we are unable to ascertain the precise period at which they took upon themselves the encouragement of the bone lace trade in Ireland. From their *Transactions* we learn that, so early as the year 1743, the annual value of the bone lace manufactured by the children of the workhouses of the city of Dublin amounted to £164 14*s*. 10½*d*.[6] In consequence of this success, the society ordain that £34 2*s*. 6*d*. be given to the Lady Arabella Denny to distribute among the children, for their encouragement in making bone lace. Indeed, to such a pitch were the productions of the needle already brought in Ireland, that in the same year, 1743, the Dublin Society gave Robert Baker, of Rollin Street, Dublin, a prize of £10 for his imitation of Brussels lace ruffles, which are described as being most exquisite both in design and workmanship. This Brussels lace of Irish growth was much prized by the patriots.[7] From this time the Dublin Society acted under their good genius, the Lady Arabella Denny. The prizes they awarded were liberal, and success attended their efforts.

In 1755 we find a prize of £2 15*s*. 6*d*. awarded to

---

[6] That lace ruffs soon appeared in Ireland may be proved by the effigy on a tomb still extant in the Abbey of Clonard, in which the Dillon arms are conspicuous, and also by paintings of the St. Lawrence family, *circ.* 1511, preserved at Howth Castle.

In the portrait at Muckruss of the Countess of Desmond she is represented with a lace collar. It was taken, as stated at the back of the portrait, " as she appeared at the court of King James, 1614, and in y⁰ 140th year of her age." Thither she went to endeavour to reverse the attainder of her house.

[7] At the end of the last century there lived at Creaden, near Waterford, a lady of the name of Power, lineal descendant of the kings of Munster, and called the Queen of Creaden. She affected the dress of the ancient Irish. The border of her coif was of the finest Irish-made Brussels lace; her jacket

Susanna Hunt, of Fishamble Street, aged eleven, for a piece of lace most extraordinarily well wrought. Miss Elinor Brereton, of Raheenduff, Queen's County, for the best imitation of Brussels lace with the needle, £7. On the same occasion Miss Martha M'Cullow, of Cork Bridge, gains the prize of £5 for "Dresden point." Miss Mary Gibson has £2 for "Cheyne Lace,"[8] of which we have scarcely heard mention since the days of Queen Elizabeth.

Bone lace had never in any quantity been imported from England. In 1703 but 2,333 yards, valuing only £116 13s., or 1s. per yard, passed through the Irish Custom House. Ireland, like the rest of the United Kingdom, received her points either from France or Flanders.

The thread used in the Irish fabric was derived from Hamburg, of which, in 1765, 2,573 lbs. were imported.

It was in this same year the Irish club of young gentlemen refused, by unanimous consent, to toast or consider beautiful any lady who should wear French lace or indulge in foreign fopperies.

During the two succeeding years the lace of various kinds exhibited by the workhouse children was greatly approved of, and the thanks of the Society offered to the Lady Arabella Denny.[9]

Prizes given to the children to the amount of £34 2s. 6d. ; the same for bone lace made by other manufacturers ; and one half the sum is also to be applied to " thread lace made with knitting needles."

A certain Mrs. Rachel Armstrong, of Inistioge (Co. Kilkenny), is also awarded a prize of £11 7s. 6d. " for having caused a considerable quantity of bone lace to be made by girls whom she has instructed and employed in the work." Among the premiums granted to " poor gentlewomen " we find : To Miss Jane Knox, for an apron of elegant pattern and curiously wrought, £6 16s. 6d., and silver medals to two ladies who, we suppose, are above

---

of the finest brown cloth trimmed with gold lace ; her petticoat of the finest scarlet cloth bordered with a row of broad gold lace ; all her dress was of Irish manufacture.

[8] *Gentleman's and Citizen's Almanack*, by G. Watson. Dublin, 1757.

[9] " The freedom of the city of Dublin was also conferred upon her, presented in due form in a silver box as a mark of esteem for her great charities and constant care of the Foundling children in the city workhouse."—*Dublin Freeman's Journal*, July 30th, 1765.

receiving money as a reward. The Society recommend that the bone lace made be exposed for sale in the warehouses of the Irish Silk Company. In consequence of the emulation excited among all classes, advertisements appear in the *Dublin News* of ladies " very capable of instructing young misses in fine lace-making, needlework point, broderie en tambour, all in the genteelest taste."

Lady Arabella stood not alone as a patroness of the art. In 1770 we read how " a considerable quantity of bone lace of extraordinary fineness and elegance of pattern, made at Castlebar in the Co. of Mayo, being produced to the Society, and it appearing that the manufacture of bone lace was founded, and is at present supported there by Lady Bingham, it was ordered that the sum of £25 be paid into the hands of her ladyship, to be disposed of in such encouragements as she shall judge will most effectually conduce to the carrying on and improvement of the said manufacture at Castlebar." The thanks of the Society are at the same time voted to her ladyship. In consequence of the large quantity fabricated, after the lapse of a few years the Society, in 1773, found themselves compelled to put some bounds to their liberality. No prizes are given for any lace exhibited at less than 11s. 4½d. the yard, and that only to those not resident in the city of Dublin or within five miles of it. Twenty per cent. will be given on the value of the lace, provided it shall not exceed £500 in value. The Society do not, however, withdraw the annual premium of £30 for the products of the " famishing children " of the city of Dublin workhouse,[10] always directed by the indefatigable Lady Arabella Denny.[11] From that period we hear no more of the Dublin Society and its prizes awarded for point, Dresden, Brussels, or bone lace.

The manufacture of gold and silver lace having met with considerable success, the Irish Parliament, in 1778, gave it their protection by passing an Act prohibiting the entry of all such commodities either from England or foreign parts.

---

[10] *Gentleman's and Citizen's Almanack*, by Samuel Watson. 1773.
[11] " The Lady Arabella Denny died 1792, aged 85; she was second daughter of Thomas Fitzmaurice, Earl of Kerry. The Irish Academy, in acknowledg- ment of her patriotic exertions, offered a prize of 100 guineas for the best monody on her death. It was gained by John Macaulay, Esq." — *Dublin Freeman's Journal*, July 20th, 1766.

And now for forty years and more history is silent on the subject of lace-making by the " famishing children " of the Emerald Isle.[12]

No existing Irish lace industry is as old as the appliqué lace which has been made in the neighbourhood of Carrickmacross since the year 1820. The process of its manufacture is simple enough, for the pattern is cut from cambric and applied to net with point stitches. Many accounts have been given of its origin. Some assign its genesis to India or to Persia, while the Florentine historian, Vasari, claims the artist Botticelli as its inventor. In any case, there can be no doubt that vast quantities were produced in Italy from the thirteenth to the seventeenth centuries. Such a specimen it was that Mrs. Grey Porter, wife of the then rector of Dunnamoyne, taught her servant, Anne Steadman, to copy, and also spread the art amongst the peasant women in the neighbourhood with such success that Miss Reid, of Rahans, gathered together the young women round Culloville and taught them to make lace on the same model. The girls flocked in from the surrounding districts to learn the work. It was, however, only dependent on private orders, and gradually suffered from over-production, and threatened to die out, until it was revived after the great famine of 1846. By Mr. Tristram Kennedy, the manager of the Bath estate, and Captain Morant, the agent of the Shirley estate, a vacant house was turned into a school, and this gave rise to the Bath and Shirley School, which has done so much to hand down this industry to the present day. Some samples of Brussels and guipure lace were brought to the school, where the teacher had them remodelled and placed in the hands of the best workers : and Carrickmacross became identified with some of the finest " guipure" that Ireland has produced.[13]

In the year 1829 the manufacture of Limerick tambour lace was first established in Ireland. Tambour work is of Eastern origin, and was known in China, Persia, India and

---

[12] Wakefield writes in 1812: " Lace is not manufactured to a large extent in Ireland. I saw some poor children who were taught weaving by the daughters of a clergyman, and Mr. Tighe mentions a school in Kilkenny where twelve girls were instructed in the art. At Abbey-leix there is a lace manufacture, but the quantity made is not of any importance."—*Account of Ireland. Statistical and Political.* Edw. Wakefield. 1812.

[13] *Pall Mall Gazette*, May 8th, 1897.

Turkey long before it spread to the United Kingdom. This work is still extensively carried on in the East, where it is much appreciated for its varied colours, as well as the labour expended upon it. Until the middle of the last century, tambour lace was unknown in Europe, with the exception of Turkey. It was about that time it was introduced into Saxony and Switzerland, but the knowledge of the art of making the lace did not reach England until 1820. Lace, in the strictest sense of the word, it cannot be termed. It is called tambour from the fact that the frame on which it is worked bears some resemblance to a drum-head or tambourine. On this is stretched a piece of Brussels or Nottingham net. A floss thread or cotton is then drawn by a hooked or tambour needle through the meshes of the net, and the design formed from a paper drawing which is placed before the worker. *Run* lace is of a finer and lighter character. The pattern is formed on the net with finer thread, which is not drawn in with the tambour, but run in with the point needle. (This description of lace was made in Nottinghamshire during the eighteenth century, and appears to have been copied from foreign designs, chiefly from those of Lille.) It came into fashion after Nottingham machine net had made the work possible, and is still called by old people Nottingham lace. This fabric was first introduced into Ireland by one Charles Walker,[14] a native of Oxfordshire, who brought over twenty-four girls as teachers, and commenced manufacturing at a place in Limerick called Mount Kennet. His goods were made entirely for one house in St. Paul's Churchyard, until that house became bankrupt in 1834, after which a traveller was sent through England, Scotland and Ireland to take orders. Her Excellency Lady Normanby, wife of the Lord Lieutenant, gave great encouragement to the fabric, causing dresses to be made, not only for herself, but also for Her Majesty the Queen of the

---

[14] Walker was a man of literary and artistic tastes, and educated for the Church, but, marrying the daughter of a lace-manufacturer, he set up in that business in Essex, working for the London wholesale trade. He removed next to Limerick, where he continued till 1841, when he sold the business, but his successor becoming bankrupt, he never received the purchase money, and died 1842, his ingenuity and industry ill-rewarded. In some work (we have lost the reference) it is stated that " Coggeshall, in Essex, made a tambour lace, a sort of medium between lace and embroidery." Could this be Walker's manufacture ?

Belgians, and the Grand Duchess of Baden. The subsequent history of Limerick laces bears a close resemblance to that of the other Irish lace industries. Mr. Charles Walker died in 1842. Many of his workers returned to England ; [15] the stimulus of constant supervision was gone ; old designs deteriorated from inferior copying, and new designs were not forthcoming. It was mainly due to the Convent of the Good Shepherd that this lace industry was saved from absolute extinction. Mrs. R. V. O'Brien has, however, done valuable service in its revival by her energy in establishing and maintaining the Limerick lace training school, which may be said to owe its origin to a lecture delivered by Mr. Alan S. Cole at the Limerick Chamber of Commerce in September, 1888, where photographs of ancient and modern lace and a loan collection of Limerick lace was shown. In this collection the work of the early days of Limerick, when the design was of the highest order, was contrasted with the more modern specimens. [16]

The first attempt to adapt the point de Venise to the necessities of the Irish people was made at Tynan, in Co. Armagh, on the borders of Tyrone. Mrs. Maclean, the wife of the Rev. William Maclean, then rector of the parish, was the owner of some old point de Venise, and she resolved to turn her collection to some practical use. " The lace was examined and re-examined, until the secret workings underlying every stitch, every picot, every filling, and every relief, had been grasped and understood. Steps were taken in 1849 to teach the people this industry, and by 1851 a

---

[15] In 1855 the number of workers employed numbered 1,500. In 1869 there were less than 500. In 1869 Mrs. Palliser writes of the tambour lace industry : " The existing depression of the trade has been partly caused by the emigration of girls to America and the colonies, while glove-making and army clothing employ the rest ; and indeed the manufacture aiming only at cheapness had produced a lace of inferior quality, without either novelty or beauty of design, from which cause Limerick lace has fallen into disrepute."

[16] No account of Limerick lace would be complete which does not make some reference to the work of the Sisters of Mercy at Kinsale, Co. Cork, where so much is now being done to revive those industries which were originally started with the object of coping with the famine of 1846. This revival is largely due to Mr. A. S. Cole, who originally suggested the establishment of an art class in connection with South Kensington, with Mr. Brennar, of the Cork School of Art, as its master. The studio is in connection with the workroom, which secures constant touch between the designing, alteration, and adaptation of patterns and their execution. (*Pall Mall Gazette*, May 8th, 1897.)

handsome flounce was ready, which was purchased by Lord John George Beresford, then Archbishop of Armagh and Primate of Ireland. It was exhibited at the great exhibition of that year in London, and attracted a large amount of attention, and brought many orders in its train. The business was thus considerably extended and enlarged, and the Primate and his nieces, Mrs. Eden and Mrs. Dunbar, did all they could to promote the sale of the work. The good fortune and prosperity of Tynan was, however, but of a temporary character. The Rev. William Maclean died in 1865, and, with his death, the local industry died out from want of supervision and organisation.

Irish point[17] also owes its genesis to the failure of the potato crop in 1846, and its original inspiration was given by a piece of point de Milan which fell into the hands of Mother Mary Ann Smith, of the Presentation Convent at Youghal, Co. Cork. She there conceived the idea of setting up an industry for the children attending the convent school. She studied the lace which had come into her possession, examined the process by which it had been made, unravelled the threads one by one, and at last succeeded in mastering its many details. She then selected some of the convent children who had shown a taste for fine needlework, and taught them separately what she herself learned. The convent school was opened in 1852. The main characteristic of this lace is that it is worked entirely with the needle.

Though Irish point lace owes its origin to Youghal Convent, its workers have done much to spread their art in other parts of Ireland, and in few districts more effectually than in the neighbourhood of Kenmare, Co. Kerry, where the late Mother Abbess O'Hagan introduced the industry into the Convent of the Poor Clares in 1861. The work is

---

[17] Various schools have been established throughout Ireland. Lady de Vere taught the mistress of a school on her own demesne at Curragh, Co. Limerick, the art of making application flowers, giving her own Brussels lace as patterns. The work was so good as soon to command a high price, and the late Queen of the Belgians actually purchased a dress of it at Harding's, and took it back with her to Brussels. The fabric is known by the name of "Irish" or "Curragh point."

The school set up at Belfast by the late Jane Clarke exhibited in 1851 beautiful imitations of the old Spanish and Italian points; amongst others a specimen of the fine raised Venetian point, which can scarcely be distinguished from the original. It is now in the Vict. and Albert Museum (1869).

based upon the same lines, though the Kenmare work claims as its speciality that it is entirely worked in linen thread, while at Youghal cotton is occasionally used. The Convent of the Poor Clares devote themselves chiefly to the production of flat point, appliqué, and guipure laces. Many other convents and lace centres in Ireland have had their teachers from Youghal and Kenmare. Flat point has been made for fifty years under the supervision of the Carmelite convent at New Ross, Co. Wexford, though the workers are now better known for their adaptation of Venetian rose point and the perfection to which they have brought their crochet than for their plain Irish point. For the first ten years the Carmelite nuns confined their attention to cut-work, flat point, and net lace. As the workers grew more expert, a heavy rose point was introduced. This style proved too heavy for the fashion; hence it was that, in 1865, the nuns turned their attention to finer work.

It was about that time that a travelling Jewish pedlar called at the convent with a miscellaneous assortment of antique vestments, old books, and other curiosities, among which were some broken pieces of old rose point lace. The then Prioress, the late Mother Augustine Dalton, purchased the specimens from the Jew, as she realised that they would give her the opportunity she wanted of varying the quality of the lace, and making the design finer and lighter in the future than it had been in the past. For weeks and for months she devoted herself to the task of ripping up portions, stitch by stitch, until she had mastered every detail. From this time dates the production of that fine rose point for which the convent at New Ross has deservedly earned so high a reputation. This rose point has gone on increasing in fineness of quality and in beauty of design. The defects in the earlier specimens were mainly due to the want of artistic culture in the girls, who could neither appreciate nor render the graceful sweeps and curves, nor the branching stems.

Irish crochet is another widespread national industry. Its main centres have been Cork in the South and Monaghan in the North of Ireland. The industry can be traced as far back as 1845, when the sisters of the Ursuline convent at Blackrock, Co. Cork, received £90 for the work done by the poor children in their schools. It may indeed be said that the growth of this great industry spread from this centre ; so much so, that within the space of a few years it formed part of the educational system of almost every convent in the land, and spread from the southern shores of Co. Cork to Wexford, to Monaghan and to Sligo.

Cork City was itself the natural centre of the industry, which extended so far and wide through the country that some thirty years ago there were no less than 12,000 women in the neighbourhood of Cork engaged in making crochet, lace collars, and edgings after Spanish and Venetian patterns. On the outbreak of the Franco-German war a further impetus was given to the industry, when the supply of Continental laces was cut off. Several years of unique prosperity followed, until the competition of the machine-made work of Nottingham and Switzerland ousted the Irish crochet from the market. At the present there has been a reaction against the usurpation by machinery of the place that art ought to occupy, and the Cork work is now once more coming to the fore.

As Cork has been the centre on the South, so is Clones in the North, and yet the industry which has for so many years done so much for the people of Monaghan owes its origin to the philanthropic efforts of Mrs. W. C. Roberts, of Thornton, Co. Kildare, who helped the poor to ward off the worst attacks of the famine of 1847 by the production of guipure and point de Venise crochet. After a few years of prosperity, the industry languished and disappeared from the neighbourhood, but twenty-four of the best-trained and most efficient of Mrs. Roberts's workers were sent out to other centres. One of these came to Mrs. Hand, the wife of the then Rector of Clones. This parish is the biggest in the county, and the poor from the surrounding mountains flocked down to learn the crochet ; and knotted and lifted as well as ordinary guipure, Greek and Spanish, and also Jesuit lace [18] has been produced with the crochet-needle in Clones, which still continues to be the most important centre of the industry.

At the Killarney Presentation Convent at Newton Barry,[19] and Cappoquin, drawn linen work in the style of

---

[18] From the tradition that a Jesuit procured the first Venetian lace pattern used in Ireland.

[19] It was in the famine period that

the Italian reticella, and at Parsonstown pillow laces of the
same character as Honiton are made.   In Ardee, a novel lace
is made with braid and cord.[20]

The rose point lace is often called "Innishmacsaint"
from the village in the county of Fermanagh where the
industry was transplanted on the death of the Rev. W.
Maclean, of Tynan, by his daughter, who went to live with
her sister, Mrs. George Tottenham, the wife of the rector.
What was Tynan's misfortune proved a boon to Innishmacsaint, and it became the chief centre of the Irish rose
point industry.   Both the heavier and finer kinds are
made there.   As at Tynan, the art of making the lace has
been learnt by the unravelling and close examination of
Venetian point.

As in English work, some of the Irish is spoilt by the
woolly cotton thread.   Foreign lace likewise in these days
suffers from the same fault.   The workmanship at the present
time can be so good that every effort ought to be made to
use only fine silky linen thread.   In Ireland, where flax can
be grown, there should be no excuse for employing any
other.

---

the Rector of Headford, Co. Galway, brought about a revival of the pillow lace, which was known to a few women in the county—taught, according to the tradition, by a soldier from foreign parts at some unknown date. This work is now reviving, thanks to the energetic care of Mrs. Dawson.

[20] Mr. A. S. Cole gives the following classification of Irish laces:—

There are seven sorts of Irish lace.

1. Flat needle-point lace.
2. Raised needle-point lace.
3. Embroidery on net, either darning or chain-stitch.
4. Cut cambric or linen work in the style of guipure or appliqué lace.
5. Drawn thread-work in the style of Reticella and Italian cut points.
6. Pillow lace in imitation of Devon lace.
7. Crochet.

PLATE XCIII.

IRISH. CROCHET LACE.—End of nineteenth century. Width of cuff, 5 in. ; length of plastron, 12 in. Victoria and Albert Museum.

CHAPTER XXXVI.

BOBBIN NET AND MACHINE-MADE LACE.

Fig. 162.

ARMS OF THE FRAME-WORK KNITTERS' COMPANY.

BOBBIN NET.

A SKETCH of the history of lace would be incomplete without a few words on bobbin net and machine lace, manufactures which have risen to so much importance both in England and France, and have placed lace within the reach of all classes of society. The subject has been so ably treated by Mr. Felkin that we refer our readers to his excellent work for its full history.[1]

This manufacture has its epochs :—

1768. Net first made by machinery.

1809. Invention of bobbin net.

1837. The Jacquard system applied to the bobbin net machine.

It has been already told how Barbara Uttmann made a plain thread net in Germany three centuries before any attempt was made to produce it by machinery.[2]

This invention is usually assigned to Hammond, a stocking framework knitter of Nottingham, who, examining one day the broad lace on his wife's cap, thought he could

---

[1] *History of Machine-Wrought Hosiery and Lace Manufacture.* W. Felkin. London, 1867.

[2] See GERMANY.

apply his machine to the production of a similar article.[3]
His attempt so far succeeded that, by means of the stocking-
frame invented the previous century,[4] he produced, 1768, not
lace, but a kind of knitting, of running loops or stitches, like
that afterwards known as " Brussels ground." In 1777, Else
and Harvey introduced at Nottingham the " pin " or point
net machine, so named because made on sharp pins or points.
" Point net" was afterwards improved, and the " barley-
corn " introduced : " square " and " spider net " appear in
succession.

But with all these improvements machinery had not yet
arrived at producing a solid net, it was still only knttting, a
single thread passing from one end of the frame to the
other ; and if a thread broke the work was unravelled ; the
threads, therefore, required to be gummed together, to give
stiffness and solidity to the net. To remedy this evil, the
warp or chain machine was invented, uniting the knitter's
and the weaver's machanism. Vandyke,[5] a Flemish workman, and three Englishmen dispute the invention. This new
machine was again improved and made " Mechlin net," from
which the machine took its name.

For forty years from Hammond's first attempt on the
stocking-frame, endless efforts were made to arrive at
imitating the ground of pillow lace, and there are few
manufactures in which so much capital has been expended,
and so much invention called forth. Each projector fancied

---

[3] An open stitch on stockings,
called the " Derby rib," had been
invented by Jedediah Strutt, in 1758.

[4] By Rev. William Lee, of Calverton
(Nottinghamshire). The romantic
story is well known ; but whether
actuated, as usually stated, by pique
at the absorbing attention paid to her
knitting by a lady, when he was urging
his suit—or, as others more amiably
affirm, by a desire to lighten the labour
of his wife, who was obliged to contribute to their joint support by knitting stockings—certain it is that it
was he who first conceived the idea of
the stocking-frame, and completed it
about 1589. His invention met with
no support from Queen Elizabeth, so
Lee went to France, where he was
well received by Henry IV. ; but the
same year Henry was assassinated,

and the Regent withdrawing her protection, Lee died of grief and disappointment. The arms of the Frame-
work Knitters' Company (Fig. 162)
are a stocking-frame, having for supporters William Lee in full canonicals
and a female holding in her hand
thread and a knitting-needle. After
Lee's death his brother returned to
England, where Lee's invention was
then appreciated. Stocking-making
became the fashion, everyone tried
it, and people had their portraits taken
with gold and silver needles suspended
round their necks.

[5] Vandyke had also appended the
chain to his stocking-frame, and the
zigzags formed by the ribs of his stockings were called " Vandyke," hence
the term now generally applied to all
indented edges.

he had discovered the true stitch, and patents after patents were taken out, resulting mostly in disappointment.

The machine for making "bobbin" net was invented by John Heathcoat, son of a farmer at Longwhatton (Leicestershire). After serving his apprenticeship he settled at Nottingham, and while occupied in putting together stocking and net machines, gave his attention to improving the Mechlin net frame.[6] In 1809, in conjunction with Mr. Lacy, he took out a patent for fourteen years for his new and highly ingenious bobbin net machine, which he called Old Loughborough, after the town to which he then removed.

"Bobbin net" was so named because the threads are wound upon bobbins.[7] It was "twisted" instead of "looped" net. Heathcoat began by making net little more than an inch in width,[8] and afterwards succeeded in producing it a yard wide. There are now machines which make it three yards and a half in width.[9]

In 1811 that vandal association called the Luddites[10] entered his manufactory and destroyed twenty-seven of his machines, of the value of £8,000. Indignant at their conduct he removed to Tiverton,[11] in Devonshire.

---

[6] Mechlin net was disused in 1819 from its too great elasticity.

[7] The "bobbins" on which the thread is wound for the weft consist of two circular copper plates riveted together, and fixed upon a small carriage or frame which moves backwards and forwards like a weaver's shuttle.

[8] The Old Loughboro' employed sixty movements to form one mesh—a result now obtained by twelve. It produced 1,000 meshes a minute—then thought a wonderful achievement, as by the pillow only five or six can be obtained. A good circular machine now produces 30,000 in the same time.

The quality of bobbin net depends upon the smallness of the meshes, their equality in size, and the regularity of the hexagons.

[9] Bobbin net is measured by the "rack," which consists of 240 meshes. This mode of counting was adopted to avoid the frequent disagreements about measure which arose between the master and the workmen in consequence of the elasticity of the net.

The exchange of linen to cotton thread was the source of great regret to the Roman Catholic clergy, who by ecclesiastical law can only wear albs of flax.

[10] This association was formed by Ludlam, or General Ludd, as he was called, a stocking-frame worker at Nottingham in 1811, when prices had fallen. The Luddites, their faces covered with a black veil, armed with swords and pistols, paraded the streets at night, entered the workshops, and broke the machines with hammers. A thousand machines were thus destroyed. Soon the net-workers joined them and made a similar destruction of the bobbin net machines. Although many were punished, it was only with the return of work that the society disappeared in 1817.

[11] Heathcoat represented Tiverton from 1834 to 1859, colleague of Lord Palmerston.

Steam power was first introduced by Mr. J. Lindley in 1815-16, but did not come into active operation till 1820; it became general 1822-23.

In 1818 the first power machines were put to work, and the year 1823 is memorable for the "bobbin net fever." Mr. Heathcoat's patent having expired, all Nottingham went mad. Everyone wished to make bobbin net. Numerous individuals, clergymen, lawyers, doctors, and others, readily embarked capital in so tempting a speculation. Prices fell in proportion as production increased; but the demand was immense, and the Nottingham lace frame became the organ of general supply, rivalling and supplanting in plain nets the most finished productions of France and the Netherlands.[12] Dr. Ure says: "It was no uncommon thing for an artisan to leave his usual calling and betake himself to a lace frame, of which he was part proprietor, and realize, by working upon it, twenty, thirty, nay, even forty shillings a day. In consequence of such wonderful gains, Nottingham, with Loughborough and the adjoining villages, became the scene of an epidemic mania. Many, though nearly void of mechanical genius or the constructive talent, tormented themselves night and day with projects of bobbins, pushers, lockers, point-bars, and needles of every various form, till their minds got permanently bewildered. Several lost their senses altogether, and some, after cherishing visions of wealth as in the olden time of alchemy, finding their schemes abortive, sank into despair and committed suicide." Such is the history of the bobbin net[13] invention in England.[14]

---

[12] McCulloch.

[13] The most extraordinary changes took place in the price of the finished articles. Lace which was sold by Heathcoat for 5 guineas a yard soon after the taking out of his patent can now be equalled at eighteenpence a yard; quillings, as made by a newly-constructed machine in 1810, and sold at 4s. 6d., can now be equalled and excelled at 1½d. a yard; while a certain width of net which brought £17 per piece 20 years ago is now sold for 7s. (1843). Progressive value of a square yard of plain cotton bobbin net:

	£	s.			s.	d.
1809	. .	5	0	1830	. . 2	0
1813	. .	2	0	1833	. . 1	4
1815	. .	1	10	1836	. . 0	10
1818	. .	1	0	1842	. . 0	6
1821	. .	0	12	1850	. . 0	4
1824	. .	0	8	1856	. . 0	3
1827	. .	0	4	1862	. . 0	3

Histoire du Tulle et des Dentelles mécaniques en Angleterre et en France, par S. Ferguson fils. Paris, 1862.

"Bobbin net and lace are cleaned from the loose fibres of the cotton by the ingenious process of gassing, as it is called, invented by the late Mr. Samuel Hall, of Nottingham. A flame of gas is drawn through the lace by means of a vacuum above. The sheet of lace passes to the flame opaque and obscured by loose fibre, and issues from it bright and clear, not to be distinguished from lace made of the purest linen thread, and perfectly uninjured by the flame."—*Journal of the Society of Arts.* Jan., 1864.

[14] In 1826 Mr. Huskisson's reduction of the duty on French tulle caused so much distress in Leicester and Nottingham, that ladies were desired to wear only English tulle at court; and in 1831 Queen Adelaide appeared at one of her balls in a dress of English silk net.

We now pass on to

FRANCE.

" To the great trading nation, to the great manufacturing nation, no progress which any portion of the human race can make in knowledge, in taste for the conveniences of life, or in the wealth by which these conveniences are produced, can be matter of indifference."—Macaulay.

Since the failure [15] of Lee, in 1610, to introduce the stocking-frame into France, that country remained ignorant of a manufacture which was daily progressing in England, on whom she was dependent for stockings and for net.

In 1778 Caillen attempted a kind of net " tricot dentelle," for which he obtained a gratuity from the Academy of £40, but his method did not succeed ; it was, like the first efforts of our countrymen, only knitting.

In 1784 Louis XVI. sent the Duke de Liancourt to England to study the improvements in the stocking and net machinery, and to bring back a frame. He was accompanied by Rhumbolt, who worked in a manufactory at Nottingham, and having acquired the art, returned to France. Monarchy had fallen, but the French Republic, 1793–4, granted Rhumbolt the sum of 110,000 francs (£4,400). The machine he brought with him was the point net. [16]

The cessation of all commercial intercourse prevented France from keeping pace with the improvements making in England ; yet, singularly enough, at the beginning of the nineteenth century more net was manufactured in France than in England. At the time of the Peace of Amiens (1802) there were 2,000 frames in Lyons and Nîmes, while there were scarcely 1,200 in England ; but the superiority of the English net was incontestable, so, to protect the national manufacture, Napoleon prohibited the importation. This of course increased its demand ; the net was in request in proportion as it was prohibited. The best mart for Nottingham was the French market, so the Nottingham net trade took every means to pass their produce into France.

---

[15] John Hindres, in 1656, first established a stocking-frame in France.

[16] The net produced was called "Tulle simple et double de Lyon et de Vienne." The net was single loops, hence the name of " single press," given to these primitive frames.

Hayne, one of the proprietors of the " barley-corn " net, had gone to Paris to make arrangements for smuggling it over, when the war broke out, and he was detained. Napoleon proposed that he should set up a machine in France ; but he preferred continuing his illicit trade, which he carried on with great success until 1809, when his own agent informed against him, his goods were seized and burned, and having in one seizure lost £60,000 (1,500,000 fr.), he was completely ruined, and fled to England.[17]

The French manufacturers took out various patents for the improvement of their " Mechlin " machines, and one was taken, in 1809, for making a crossed net called " fond de glace " ; but the same year Heathcoat producing the bobbin net machine, the inventors could not sustain the competition.

Every attempt was made to get over bobbin net machines; but the export of English machinery was punished by transportation, and the Nottingham manufacturers established at their own expense a line of surveillance to prevent the bobbin net machines from going out. In spite of all these precautions, Cutts, an old workman of Heathcoat's, contrived to elude their vigilance, and, in 1815, to import a machine to Valenciennes, whence he removed it to Douai, where he entered into partnership with M. Thomassin. In 1816 they produced the first bobbin net dress made in France. It was embroidered by hand by a workwoman of Douai, and presented by the makers to the Duchesse d'Angoulême. About the end of the year 1816 James Clark introduced a machine into Calais, which he passed in pieces by means of some French sailors. These two were the first bobbin net machines set up in France.

It is not within our limits to follow the Calais lace manufacturers through their progress ; suffice it to say that it was in 1817 that the first bobbin net machine worked, concealed from all eyes, at Saint-Pierre-lez-Calais, now, if not the rival of Nottingham, at least the great

---

[17] In 1801 George Armitage took a " point net " machine to Antwerp, and made several after the same model, thus introducing the manufacture into Belgium. He next went to Paris, but the wholesale contraband trade of Hayne left him no hope of success. He afterwards went to Prussia to set up net and stocking machines. At the age of eighty-two he started for Australia, where he died, in 1857, aged eighty-nine.

centre of the bobbin net and machinery lace manufactures in France.[18]

St. Quentin, Douai, Cambrai, Rouen, Caen, have all in turn been the seats of the tulle manufacture. Some of these fabrics are extinct; the others have a very limited trade compared with Saint-Pierre and Lyons.

At Lyons silk net is mostly made.[19] Dating from 1791, various patents have been taken out for its manufacture. These silk nets were embroidered at Condrieu (Rhône), and were (the black especially for veils and mantles) much esteemed, particularly in Spain.

In 1825 the " tulle bobine grenadine," black and white, was brought out by M. Doguin, who afterwards used the fine silks, and invented that popular material first called " zephyr," since " illusion." His son, in 1838, brought out the " tulle Bruxelles."

BELGIUM.

In 1834 [20] eight bobbin net machines were set up in Brussels by Mr. Washer, for the purpose of making the double and triple twisted net, upon which the pillow flowers are sewn to produce the Brussels application lace. Mr. Washer devoted himself exclusively to the making of the extra fine mesh, training up workmen specially to this minute work. In a few years he succeeded in excelling the English manufacture; and this net, universally known as " Brussels net," has nearly superseded the expensive pillow ground, and has thereby materially decreased the price of Brussels lace. It is made of English cotton, stated, in the specimens exhibited in 1867, as costing £44 per pound.

---

[18] The great difficulty encountered by the French manufacturers consisted in the cotton. France did not furnish cotton higher than No. 70; the English ranges from 160 to 200. The prohibition of English cotton obliged them to obtain it by smuggling until 1834, when it was admitted on paying a duty. Now they make their own, and are able to rival Nottingham in the prices of their productions. A great number of Nottingham lacemakers have emigrated to Calais.

[19] The Caen blond first suggested the idea.

[20] The first net frame was set up at Brussels in 1801. Others followed at Termonde, 1817; Ghent, 1828; Sainte Fosse, etc.

MACHINERY LACE.

" Qui sait si le métier à tulle ne sera pas un jour, en quelque sorte, un vrai coussin de dentellière, et les bobines de véritables fuseaux manœuvrés par des mains mécaniques."—Aubry, in 1851.

If England boasts the invention of bobbin net, to France must be assigned the application of the Jacquard system to the net-frame, and consequently the invention of machinery lace. Shawls and large pieces in " run lace," as it is termed, had previously been made after this manner at Nottingham and Derby. The pattern proposed to be " run in " is printed by means of engraved wood blocks on the ground, which, if white, is of cotton ; if black, of silk. The ground is stretched on a frame ; the " lace-runner" places her left hand under the net, and with the right works the pattern. The filling up of the interior is termed either " fining" or " open-working," as the original meshes of the net are brought to a smaller or larger size by the needle.[21]

In 1820 Symes, of Nottingham, invented a pattern which he called " Grecian" net. This was followed by the " spot," or " point d'esprit," and various other fancy nets—bullet-hole, tattings, and others.

The Jacquard system had been used at Lyons with the Mechlin frame in 1823–4 for making patterned net and embroidered blondes. This suggested the possibility of applying the Jacquard cards to making lace, and in 1836 to 1838 Mr. Ferguson,[22] by applying it to the circular bobbin net frame, brought out the black silk net called " dentelle de Cambrai," an imitation of Chantilly. The pattern was woven by the machine, the brodé or relief " run in."

Various patents [23] were immediately taken out in England and France. Nottingham and Saint-Pierre-lez-Calais rival

---

[21] D. Wyatt.

[22] Mr. Ferguson, the inventor of the bullet-hole, square net (tulle carré), and wire-ground (point de champ ou de Paris), had transferred his manufacture, in 1838, from Nottingham to Cambrai, where, in partnership with M. Jourdan, he made the " dentelle de Cambrai," and in 1852 the " lama " lace, which differs from the Cambrai inasmuch as the weft (*trame*) is made of mohair instead of silk. Mr. Fer-

guson next established himself at Amiens, where he brought out the Yak, another mixed lace.

[23] The first patents were :—

1836. Hind and Draper took out one in France, and 1837 in England.

1838. Ferguson takes a patent at Cambrai under the name of his partner Jourdan.

1839. Crofton.

1841. Houston and Deverill, for the application of the Jacquard to the

each other in the variety of their productions. At the International Exhibition of 1867 Nottingham exhibited Spanish laces, most faithful copies of the costly pillow-made Barcelona ; imitations of Mechlin, the brodé and picot executed by hand ; Brussels needle-point ; Caen blondes, and Valenciennes rivalling those of Calais ; also Cluny and the black laces of Chantilly and Mirecourt.

The French, by adopting what is technically termed eight " motives," produce their lace of a finer make and more complex pattern. The Calais lace is an admirable copy of the square-grounded Valenciennes, and is the staple trade of the manufacture. Calais also produces blondes, black and white, silver and gold, the white nearly approaching in brilliancy and whiteness the famed productions of Caen, which, by their cheapness, they have expelled from competition. She also imitates the woollen laces of Le Puy, together with black and white laces innumerable.

" Broadly speaking, lace-making by machinery is more nearly like the pillow lace-making process than that of needle-point. The machine continues to twist any desired threads around one another. In pillow lace-making, besides twisting, we have plaiting, and this plaiting has not been reproduced by the majority of lace machines. Quite recently, however, a French machine, called the ' Dentellière,' has been invented to do the plaiting. A description of this machine has been published in *La Nature* (March 3rd, 1881).

" Whilst the ordinary lace-making machine belongs to the family of weaving machines, the Dentellière more nearly resembles the pillow of a lace-worker with the threads arranged over the pillow. In general appearance it looks something like a large semicircular frame-work of iron— with thousands of threads from the outer semicircle converging to the centre, representing the table or pillow. Over this central table is the apparatus which holds the end threads side by side, and which regulates the plaiting of them. The cost of producing lace in this manner is said to be greater at present than by hand." [24]

Leaver machine. The great manufactures of Nottingham and Calais are made on the Leaver Jacquard frame.

The first patterned net was produced, 1780, by R. Frost, the embroidery made by hand.

[24] Cantor Lectures on the Art of Lace-Making. A. S. Cole. 1880.

Almost every description of lace is now fabricated by machinery;[25] and it is often no easy task, even for a practised eye, to detect the difference. Still, we must ever be of opinion that the most finished productions of the frame never possess the touch, the finish, or the beauty of the laces made by hand. The invention of machine-made lace has this peculiarity—it has not diminished the demand for the finer fabrics of the pillow and the needle. On the contrary, the rich have sought more eagerly than ever the exquisite works of Brussels and Alençon, since machinery

Fig. 163.

THE LAGETTA, OR LACE-BARK TREE.

has brought the wearing of lace within the reach of all classes of society.

The inner bark of the Lagetta, or Lace-bark tree[26] of Jamaica, may be separated into thin layers, and then into distinct meshes, bearing some resemblance to lace (Fig. 163). Of this material a cravat and ruffles were presented to King Charles II. by the Governor of Jamaica; and at the Exhibition of 1851 a dress of the same fibre was presented to Queen Victoria, which her Majesty was graciously pleased to accept.

---

[25] The machines now in use are the Circular, Leaver, Transverse Warp and Pusher. Out of 3,552 machines computed to be in England in 1862 2,448 were at Nottingham."—*International Exhibition, Juror's Report.*

[26] *Daphne lagetta.*

Caterpillars have been made to spin lace veils by the ingenious contrivance of a gentleman of Munich.[27] These veils are not strong, but surprisingly light—one, a yard square, would scarcely weigh five grains, whilst a patent net veil of the same size weighs 262.

Asbestos has also been woven into lace : and a specimen of this mineral lace is, we have been told, in the Cabinet of Natural History at the Garden of Plants, Paris.

---

[27] He makes a paste of the plant which is the usual food of the caterpillar, and spreads it thinly over a stone or other flat substance ; then with a camel's-hair pencil dipped in olive oil he draws upon the coating of paste the pattern he wishes the insects to leave open. The stone being placed in an inclined position, the caterpillars* are laid at the bottom, and the animals eat and spin their way up to the top, carefully avoiding every part touched by the oil, but devouring the rest of the paste.—*Encyclopædia Britannica.*

---

* *Phalæna pandilla.*

APPENDIX.

The Notes marked with an * show that the works referred to have been examined by the Author.[1]

I.

Eyn new kunstlich boich, dair yn. C. vnd. xxxviij. figuren, monster ad' stalen befonden, wie man na der rechter art, Lauffer werck, Spansche stich, mit der nålen, vort vp der Ramen, vnd vp der laden, borden wirckenn sall, wilche stalen all etzo samen verbessert synt, vnd vyl kunstlicher gemacht, dā dye eirsten, &c. Sere nutzlich allen wapen sticker, frauwen, ionfferen, vnd met ger, dair uns solch kunst lichtlich tzu leren.

D Gedruckt tzu Collen vp dem Doemhoff dwrch Peter Quentell.

Anno. M. D. XXXVJJ.[2]

1527.
Cologne.
P. Quen-
tell.

Small 8vo, 22 ff., 42 plates.

Title in Gothic letters; beneath, woodcuts representing women at work. On the back of the leaf, a large escutcheon, the three crowns of Cologne in chief; supporters, a lion and a griffin. Below, "O Fœlix Colonia. 1527."

The patterns consist of mediæval and arabesque borders, alphabets, etc., some on white, others on black grounds. Some with counted stitches.

Quentell refers to a previous edition. Brunet and the Marquis d'Adda mention a copy, 1529, with the portrait of Charles V., and a second edition 1532.

2.

Liure noveau et subtil touchant lart et sciēce tant de brouderie fronssures, tapisseries cōme aultres mestiers quō fait alesguille, soit au petit mestier, aultelisse ou sur toille clere, tresvtile et necessaire a toutes, gens usans des mestiers et ars

1527.
Cologne.
P. Quinty.

---

[1] Two interesting papers were published in the *Gazette des Beaux Arts* for 1863 and 1864, entitled, "Essai bibliographique sur les anciens dessins de dentelles, modèles de tapisseries, patrons de broderies et publiés le xvi. et le xvii. siècle," &c., by the Marquis Girolamo d'Addo, of Milan.

[2] Cambridge University Library.

dessuld, ou semblables, ou il y ha C. et. xxxviij patrons de diuers ouvraiges faich per art et proportion.

En primere a culoge (Cologne) par matrepiere quinty demorāt denpre leglie de iii roies.[3]

The same cut as the preceding, with the arms of Cologne, which seems to have been engraved for a great Bible printed by Quentell, in 1527, and is no guide for the date. Figs. 164, 165.

Fig. 164.

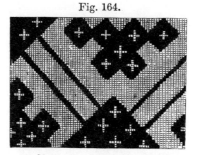

METRE P. QUINTY.—Cologne, 1527.

Fig. 165.

METRE P. QUINTY.—Cologne, 1527.

3.

1530.
Venice.
A. Tag-
lienti.

Opera nuova che insegna a le Dōne a cuscire : a raccāmare e a disegnar a ciascuno : Et la ditta opera sara di grande utilita ad ogni artista : per esser il disegno ad ogniuno necessario : la qual e ititolata esempio di racāmi.[4]

4to, 23 ff., 36 plates.
Title in red Gothic letters ; beneath four woodcuts representing women at work. Two pages of dedication to the ladies, by Giovanni Antonio Taglienti, in which he says his book is for the instruction of each " valorosa donna & tutte altre donzelle, con gli huomini insieme & fanciulli, liquali si dilettarano de imparar a disegnar, cuscir, & raccammar."

---

[3] Paris, Bibliothèque Nat. Gravures, L. h. 13 d.*

[4] Bib. Nat. V. 1897.*—Genoa.
Cav. Merli, 1528 (?).

Then follows a most miscellaneous collection of what he terms, in his dedication, " fregi, frisi, tondi maravigliosi, groppi moreschi et arabeschi, ucelli volanti, fiori, lettere antique, maiuscoli, & le francesche," etc., three pages very much like the pictures in a child's spelling book, rounds (tondi) for cushions, and two pages representing hearts and scrolls ; hearts transfixed, one with an arrow, another with a sword, a third torn open by two hands, motto on the scroll :—

> " La virtù al huomo sempre li resta
> Nè morte nol pò privar di questa."

On the other page hearts transfixed by two arrows, with two eyes above : " Occhi piangete accompagnete il core. Inclita virtus." Then follow six pages of instructions, from which we learn the various stitches in which these wonderful patterns may be executed, " damaschino, rilevato, a filo, sopra punto, ingaseato, Ciprioto, croceato, pugliese, scritto, incroceato, in aere, fatto su la rate, a magliata, desfilato, & di racammo," to be sewn in various coloured silks, gold and silver thread, or black silk, for " collari di huomo & di donna, camisciole con pettorali, frisi di contorni di letti, entemelle di cuscini, frisi di alcun boccassino, & scufie," etc. On the last page, " Stampa in Vineggia per Giovan Antonio Tagliente & i Fratelli de Sabbio. 1530." Brunet gives an edition dated 1528.

4.

La fleur de la science de pourtraicture et patrons de broderie. Facon arabicque, et ytalique. Cum priviligio regis.

1530. *Paris.* *F. Pelegrin.*

Frontispiece. Title in Gothic letters. A large figure of Sol (?), with a yoke, his feet chained, a ball, maybe the Earth, at the end of the chain. In one hand he holds a scroll with the legend, " Exitus acta probat." Privilege of " Francoys par la grace de Dieu roy de France," to " Francisque pelegrin de Florence," to publish " ung livre de fueillages, entrelatz et ouvraiges moresques, et Damasquins," for six years. " Dōne a bordeaulx le xvii. jour de Juing. L'an de grace mil cinq cens trēte Et de nostre regne le seiziesme."

Ce present livre a este imprime a paris par jaques nyverd. Le iv. jour daoust. Lan de grace mil cinq cēs xxx. Pour noble hōme messire Francisque Pelegrin de florence.

On les vend a paris En la grant rue sainct Anthoyne devant les tournelles. Au logis de monseigneur le comte de Carpes. Par messire Frācisque pelegrin de florence.[5]

Small fol., 62 ff., 58 plates, consisting of graceful moresque patterns, no animals or natural objects represented. At plate 33, surrounded by arabesques, is an N, the initial of the printer.

5.

Esemplario di lavori : dove le tenere fanciulle & altre donne nobile potranno facilment imparare il modo & ordine di lavorare, cusire, racamare, & finalmente far tutte quelle gentillezze & lodevoli opere, le quali pò fare una donna virtuosa con laco in

1529. *Venice.* *N. Zoppino.*

---

[5] Paris, Bib. de l'Arsenal. 11,952.*

mano, con li suoi compasse & misure.　Vinezia, per Nicolo
D'Aristotile detto Zoppino MDXXIX.　8vo.[6]　46 plates.

The Cav[re] Merli quotes another edition, date 1530, in the possession of
the Avvocato Francesco Pianesani, and another he believes of 1529.

6.

1532.
Venice.
N. Zop-
pino.

Convivio delle belle Donne, dove con li.　Nuovi raccami,
&c.　In fine: Finisce il convivio delle, &c.　Nuovamente
stampato in Vinegia, per Nicolo d'Aristotile, detto Zoppino del
mese d'Agosto.　MDXXXII.

In 4to, ff. 24.[7]

7.

1537.
Venice.
N. Zop-
pino.

Gli universali de i belli Recami antichi, et moderni, ne i
quali un pellegrino ingegno, si di huomo come di donna potra in
questa nostra eta con l'ago vertuosamente esercitar si.　Non
ancora da alcuni dati altri inluce.

Frontispiece, two ladies at work; dedication to "gli virtuosi Giovani
et gentilissime Fanciulle."　At the end styles himself "Nicolo d'Aristotile
detto Zoppino."　March, 1537.
In 4to, ff. 25, printed on both sides.[8]

8.

1534.
Augsburg.
Schartzem-
berger.

Ain New Formbüchlin bin ich gnandt
Allen Künstlern noch vnbekandt
Sih mich (lieber kauffer) recht an,
Findst drefftlich in diser kunff stan
Schön gschnierlet, geböglet, auf gladt,
Und gold, auch schön von premen stadt,
Es gibt dir ain prem unb ain kledyt.
Wenn mans recht aussainander schneydt,
Das kanst schneyden auss der Ellen,
Von Samat, Seyden, wie manss wolle,
Ich mag braucht wern in allem landt,
Wen man mich ersücht mit verstandt.

(At the end.)

Gedruckt in der Kaiserlichen Riechstatt, Augspurg, durch
Johan Schartzemberger.　Formschneyder.　1534.[9]

Small obl., 20 ff., 38 plates.
Frontispiece.　Title in black Gothic letters, at the foot three subjects
of women at work, printed in red.
The patterns, consisting of graceful arabesque borders, are also in red
(Figs. 166, 167, 168).

---

[6] Oxford, Bib. Bodleian.
[7] Milan, Cavaliere Bertini.

[8] Venice, Library of St. Mark.
[9] Bib. Nat.　Grav. L. h. 13. e.*

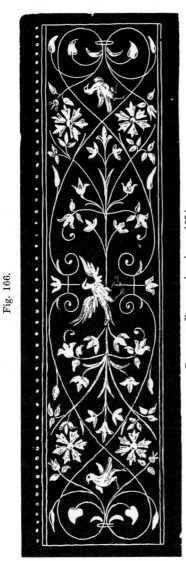

Fig. 166.

PATTERN BOOK.—Augsburg, 1534.

Fig. 167.

PATTERN BOOK.—Augsburg, 1534.

Fig. 168.

AUGSBURG. 1534.

9.

A neawe treatys : as cōcernynge the excellency of the nedle *N. D.* worcke spânisshe stitche and weavynge in the frame, very *Antwerp.* necessary to al theym wiche desyre the perfect knowledge of *sterman.* seamstry, quiltinge and brodry worke, côteinynge an cxxxviij figures or tables, so playnli made & set tout in portrature, the whiche is difficyll ; and natôly for crafts mē but also for gentle-wemē & and iôge damosels that therein may obtayne greater conynge delyte and pleasure.

These books be to sell at Andwarp in the golden Unycorne at Willm̄ Vorstermans.

Gheprent tot Antwerpen in die camerstrate in den gulden eenhoren bey Willem Vorsterman.[10]

8vo, 24 ff., 46 plates.
Title in Gothic letters, with figures.
P. 1, dorso : Woodcut of a woman at work and a man sitting by her side.
Patterns mediæval, small black squares, arabesques, etc.
Vorsterman worked from 1514 to 1542.[11]

10.

Giardinetto novo di punti tagliati et gropposi, per exercitio *1542* et ornamento delle donne. Ven. 1542, in 4to.[12] *Venice.*

[10] Bib. de l'Arsenal. 11,951.*
[11] Silvestre, *Marques Typogra-phiques des Imprimeurs en France,* depuis 1470. Paris, 1853-61.
[12] Quoted in Cat. Cappi, of Bologna, 1829.

11.

1543.
Venice.

Esemplare che insegna alle donne el modo di cucire. Venetia, 1543.[13]

12.

1544.
Venice.

Il Specchio di pensiere (*sic*), delle belle donne dove si vede varie sorti di punti, cioè, punti tagliati, gropposi, &c. Venetia, 1544.

In 4to.[14]

13.

1544.
Venice.

Ornamento delle belle donne et virtuose : Opere in cui troverai varie sorti di frisi con li quali si potra ornar ciascun donna. Ven. 1544.[15]

14.

1546.
Paris.
Gormont.

Le livre de moresques, tres utile et necessaire à tous orfevres, tailleurs, graveurs, painctres, tapissiers, brodeurs, lingieres et femmes qui besongnent de l'aiguille. Paris. Gormont, 1546. Fig. en bois.[16]

15.

1549.
Lyon.
P. de Ste.
Lucie.

La fleur des patrons de lingerie, a deux endroitz, a point croise, a point couche, et a point picque, en fil dor, fil dargēt, & fil de soye, ou aultre en quelque ouvraige que ce soit, en comprenant lart de broderie et tissuterie. Imprimees a Lyon, en la maison de Pierre de saincte Lucie (dict le Prince, Pres nostre Dame de Confort).[17]

(At the end.)

Imprimé à Lyon par Piarre de saincte Lucie, dict le Prince. 1549.

8vo, 12 ff., 21 plates.
Frontispiece. Title in Gothic letters, with woodcuts representing people at work. Below, two women sitting at frames ; above, two others ; and between, a man with a frame in his hand. On each side a shield, one with crowned heart, on the other a lion, three fleurs de lys in chief. Patterns mediæval. At the end, the device of the printer, a mountain, on the top of which is a city against which a youth is placing his hand : motto, "Spero." At the foot of the mountain a cavern in which is seated a Fury. This device is engraved No. 616 in Silvestre, who gives 1530 to 1555 as the date of Pierre de Saincte Lucie.

---

[13] Quoted in Cat. Cappi, of Bologna, 1829.
[14] *Ibid.*
[15] *Ibid.*
[16] Cat. Bib. Heber., part vi., p. 258. No. 3,514.
[17] Paris, Bib. Sainte-Geneviève.

V. 634.* Bound in one volume with the three following. (Nos. 16, 17, and 18.)—Catalogue de Livres provenant de la Bibliothèque de M. L. D. D. L. V. (Duke de La Vallière). Paris, 1763. T. xi., No. 2,204.

16.

Livre nouveau, dict patrons de lingerie, cest assavoir a deux endroitz, a point croise, point couche & point picque, en fil dor, dargent, de soye & autres, en quelque ouvrage que ce soit: comprenant lart de Broderie & Tissoterie. Imprimees a Lyon, chez Pierre de Saincte Lucie, pres nostre Dame de Confort.[18]

N. D. Lyon. P. de Ste. Lucie.

8vo, 24 ff., 44 plates.
Frontispiece. Title in Gothic letters; the same shields as the preceding; two women at work. Patterns mediæval. At the end the same device.
The copy of the Arsenal is a different impression. Instead of " Imprimees," &c., we have, " On les vend," etc.

17.

Patrons de diverses manieres
Inventez tressubtilement
Duysans a Brodeurs et Lingieres
Et a ceusy lesquelz vrayement
Veullent par bon entendement
User Dantique, et Roboesque,
Frize et Moderne proprement,
En comprenant aussi Moresque.
A tous massons, menuisiers, & verriers
Feront prouffit ces pourtraictz largement
Aux orpheures, et gentilz tapissiers
A ieunes gens aussi semblablement
Oublier point ne veuly auscunement
Cõtrepointiers & les tailleurs dymages
Et tissotiers lesquelz pareillement
Par ces patrons acquerront heritages.

N. D. Lyon. P. de Ste. Lucie.

Imprimees a Lyon, par Pierre de Saincte Lucie, dict le Prince, pres nostre Dame de Confort.[19]

8vo, 16 ff., 31 plates. Title in Gothic letters. Patterns mediæval.
The copy at the Arsenal is a later impression. " On les vend a Lyon, par Pierre de saincte Lucie, en la maison du deffunct Prince, pres," etc. It has only 12 ff., and 23 plates.

18.

Sensuyuent lis patrons de messire Antoine Belin, Reclus de sainct Martial de Lyon. Item plusieurs autres beaulx Patrons nouveaulx, qui ont este inventez par Jehan Mayol Carme de Lyon.
On les vend à Lyon, chez le Prince.[20]

N. D. Lyon. Le Prince.

---

[18] Bib. Ste. Geneviève. V. 634.* —Bib. de l'Arsenal. No. 11,953.*— Cat. d'Estrées. Paris, 1740-46. No. 8,843. 3.
[19] Bib. Ste. Geneviève. V. 634.*

—Bib. de l'Arsenal. No. 11,953.*— Cat. d'Estrées. No. 8,843. 1.
[20] Bib. Ste. Geneviève. V. 634.* —Bib. de l'Arsenal. No. 11,953.*

Small 8vo, 6 ff., 85 plates. Copy at the Arsenal has 12 ff.

The same device of the printer in the frontispiece and at the end of the book. " Finis."

One of the patterns represents St. Margaret holding the cross to a dragon, but in these four books the designs are copied from each other, and are many of them repetitions of Quinty.

19.

N. D.
Lyon.
D. Celle.

Ce livre est plaisant et utile
   A gens qui besongnent de leguille
Pour comprendre legèrement
   Damoyselle bourgoyse ou fille
Femmes qui ont l'esperit agille
   Ne scauroint faillir nullement
Corrige est nouvellement
   Dung hoñeste hoɱe par bon zelle
Son nom est Dominicque Celle
   Qui a tous lecteurs shumylie
Domicille a en Italie.
   En Thoulouse a prins sa naissance.
Mise il a son intelligence
   A lamender subtillement
Taillé il est totallement
   Par Jehan coste de rue merciere
A Lyon et consequemment
   Quatre vingtz fassons a vrayement
Tous de differente maniere.[21]

28 ff., 27 plates. Title in Gothic letters. Dedication to the Reader, in which it states the book is for the profit of " tant hommes que femmes." Patterns mediæval. At the end of the Preface, " Finis coronat opus."

20.

N. D.
Venice.
G. A. Va-
vassore.

Esemplario di lavori : che insegna alle dōne il modo e ordine di lavorare : cusire : e racāmare : e finalmēte far tutte q̄lle opere degne di memoria : lequale po fare una donna virtuosa con laco in mano. Et uno documento che insegna al cōpratore accio sia ben servito.[22]

In 8vo, 25 ff., printed on both sides, 48 plates. Title in red Gothic characters, framed round by six woodcuts similar to that of Vorsterman ; at the foot, " fiorio Vavasore fecit."

Then follows the " Documento per el compratore," and an Address to Ladies and Readers, by " Giovandrea Vavassore detto Guadagnino," saying that he had already " fatti alcuni libri di esempli di diverse sorte."

There is no date to this copy ; but in the library of Prince Messimo, at Rome, is a copy dated Venice, 18 Feb., 1546, containing 50 plates ; and Brunet quotes an edition, " Stampato in Vinezia, 1556 ; " Cav. Merli also possesses an edition of the same date. Mr. E. Arnold has also a copy with the same date.

The patterns are mediæval, on black grounds, with counted stitches, a large flower pot, mermaid, Paschal lamb, and a double plate representing Orpheus playing to the beasts.

---

[21] Paris, Bib. Baron Jérôme Pichon.*   [22] Bib. Nat. Grav. L. h. 4.*

21.

Essemplario novo di piu di cento variate mostre di qualunque orte bellissime per cusire intitolato Fontana di gli essempli.

N. D.
Venice.
G. A. Va-
vassore.

Oblong 8vo. No date. 16 ff., 28 plates.

In the frontispiece is a fountain with the motto, " Solicitudo est mater divitiarum," and on each side of the fountain—

"Donne donzelle ch
El cusir seguite

Per farvi eterne alla
Fonte venite."

On the back of the frontispiece is the Dedication, headed, "Il Pelliciolo alla molta magnifica Madona Chiara Lipomana;" the page finished by a sonnet; in the last! leaf, "Avviso alle virtuose donne et a qualunque lettore Giovanni Andrea Vavassore detto Guadagnino." Says he has "negli tempi passati fatto imprimere molto e varie sorte d'essemplari di mostre," etc. At the foot, "Nuovamente stampato."[23] This work is also described by Count Cicognara with the same title, only with the date 1550. In the Bibliotheca Communitativa, Bologna, is a copy of the same date. In this last edition the author writes his name Valvassore.

22.

Vavassore Gio. Andrea. Opera nova Universal intitulata corona di ricammi; Dove le venerande donne e fanciulle: troveraño di varie opere p fare colari di camisiola & torniaēnti di letti ēternelle di cuscini boccasini schufioni: cordlli di piu sorte ; et molte opere per recāmatori p dipitore poreuesı : (*sic*) de lequale opere o vero esempli ciascuno le potra pore in opera secōdo el suo bisogno: con gratia novamente stampata ne la inclita citta di vineggia per Giovanni Andrea Vavassore detto Guadagniō. 36 pp., sm. 4to.

N. D.
Venice.
G. A. Va-
vassore.

13 ff., 52 designs, none of which are repetitions of the preceding.[24]

23.

Vavassore Gio. Andrea detto Guadagnino. Opera nova, etc. . . . dove le venerande donne et fanciulle trovaranno di varie opere et molte opere per recamatori et per dipintori, etc. Nuovamente stampata, etc.[25]

N. D.
Venice.
G. A. Va-
vassore.

Quite a different collection from the preceding. A little of everything in this volume.

Zoan Andrea Vavassore was the pupil in drawing and engraving of Andrea Mantegna. Towards the beginning of the sixteenth century, he worked on his own account, and his engravings are much sought after. So greedy was he of gain as to obtain for him the name of Guadigno, in Venetian patois, " covetous." He lived to a great age.

---

[23] Bib. Nat. Grav. L. h. 4. a.*— Catalogo ragionato dei libri posseduti dal Conte di Cicognara. Pisa, 1821. No. 1,818.

[24] Library V. and A. Museum. —Venice, Lib. St. Mark.—Milan, Bib. Marquis d'Adda.

[25] Milan, Bib. Marquis G. d'Adda.

24.

N. D.
A. Paga-
nino.

Libro questo di rechami per el quale se impara in diversi modi l'ordine e il modo de recamare, cosa non mai più fatta n' è stata mostrata.

By Alessandro Paganino.[26]

20 plates, with a long explanation how these works are done. (Communicated by Prince Massimo.)

25.

N. D.
Paris.
Vve.
Ruelle.

Patrons pour Brodeurs, Lingieres, Massons, Verriers, et autres gens d'esprit. A Paris. Pour la Veuve Jean Ruelle, rue S. Jacques, à l'enseigne Sainct Nicolas.[27]

4to, 23 ff., 32 plates of mediæval designs. Ornamented title-page.

26.

1548.
Venice.
M. Pagan.

Il specchio di pensieri delle belle et virtudiose donne, dove si vede varie sorti di Punti, cioè punti tagliati, punti gropposi, punti in rede, et punti in Stuora. MDXLVIII. Stamp. in Venetia, per Mathio Pagan in frezzaria, in le case nove Tien per insegna la fede.[28]

16 ff.

27.

1551.
Venice.
M. Pagan.

1. L'honesto Essempio del vertuoso desiderio che hanno le donne di nobile ingegno circa lo imparare i punti tagliati e fogliami. In Venetia per Mathio Pagan in Frezaria al segno della Fede, M.D.L.[29]

In the V. and A. Museum is a copy dated 1550.

28.

1551.
Venice.
M. Pagan.

Giardineto novo di Punti tagliati et gropposi, per esurcitio et ornamento delle donne. At the end, Venetia, Mathio Pagan in Frezzaria, in le case nove (tien per insegna della Fede) MDLI. Dedication, Alla signora Lucretia, Romana Mathio Pagan, salute.[30] See also No. 38.

29.

1554.
Dubois.

Variarum protractionum quas vulgo Maurusias vocant omnium antehac excusarum libellus longe copiasissimus pictoribus, aurifabris, polymilariis, barbaricariis variisque id genus

[26] Rome, Bib. Prince Massimo.
[27] Bib. de l'Arsenal. 11,954 (with D. de Sera).*
[28] Genoa, Cav. Merli.
[29] Quoted by Cav. Merli.
[30] Florence. M. Bigazzi.

artificibus etiam acu operantibus utilissimus nuncque primen in lucem editus anno 1554. Balthazar Sylvius (Dubois) fecit. Jo. Theodoret, Jo. Israel de Bry excud.[31]

In 4to, ff. 23, copperplate.

30.

Triompho di Lavori a Fogliami de i quali si puo far ponti in aere; opera d' Fra Hieronimo da Cividal di Frioli, de l'Ordine de i Servi di Osservantia. Cum gratia et privileggio per anni xi.[32]

1555. *Padua.* *Fra Hiero-* *nimo.*

Obl. 4to, 14 ff., 22 pl.
Ornamental title-page. On the top, a female seated in a triumphal car drawn by unicorns, with attendants. On each side of the title are women teaching children to work.
P. 1, dorso. Dedication of the author, "Alla Magnifica & Illustre Signora Isabella Contessa Canossa," whose "Immortal Triompho" is represented in the above woodcut. Fra Hieronimo speaks of preparing "più alte e divine imprese."
Then follow three pages of verses in terzette, and p. 8, dorso, the impresa of the printer, a lion rampant, holding a sword in his fore paws. Below, "In Padou per Jacobo Fabriano, ad instantia de Fra Hieronimo da Cividal di Frioli: de l' Ordine de i Servi di Osservantia 1555."

31.

Lucidario di ricami di Guiseppe Torello. Venezia, 1556.

In 4to.

1556. *Venice.* *Torello.*

32.

New Modelbüch, allen Nägerin, unnd Sydenstickern sehr nutzlich zü branchē, vor nye in Druck aussgangen durch Hans Hoffman, Burger und formschneider zu Strassburg. At the end, Zu Strassburg Gedruckt am Kommarckt durch Jacob Frölich. 1556. 4to.[33]

1556. *Strasburg.* *H. Hoff-* *man.*

4to. A to G in fours. (28 leaves.)
Title printed in red and black. On it a woodcut of two women, one engaged in embroidery, the other fringing her some stuff. The last leaf (Giiii.) has on the recto a woodcut of a woman at a frame, the verso blank.

33.

Nüw Modelbüch, allerley gattungen Däntelschnür, so diser zyt in hoch Tütschlanden geng und brüchig sind, zu underricht jren Leertöchteren unnd allen anderen schurwirckeren zu Zurych

N. D. *Zurich.* *C.Froscho* *ver.*

---

[31] Paris, Bib. Nat. Milan, Bib. Belgiosa and Marquis d'Adda.
[32] Bib. de l'Arsenal. 11,953.*—

Bologna, Bib. Comm.—Cat. d'Es- trées. 8843. No. 2.
[33] Mr. E. Arnold.

und wo die sind, yetz nüwlich zübereit, und erstmals in truch verfergket durch R. M.[34]

No place or date, but as appears, both from the title and preface, to be printed at Zurich, by Christopher Froschover. The date probably from 1530 to 1540.

4to. Signatures A to F in fours. 24 leaves. On the title a woodcut of two women working at lace pillows.

34.

N. D.
Frankfort. Modelbüch Welscher, Ober und Niderlandischer Arbait. Getruckt zü Franckfort.

No date, but probably at least as early as 1530. 4to. Signatures A to D in fours. 20 leaves.
Title enclosed in an elegant woodcut border.

35.

1537.
Frankfort.
C. Ege-nolffs. Modelbüch, von erhabener unnd flacher Arbait, Auff der Ramen, Laden, und nach der Zale.
Getruckt zu Franckfort, Bei Christian Egenolffs, Erben.

The date, 1537, occurs on one of the patterns. 4to. AA to HH in fours. 32 leaves. Title in a woodcut border. 178 patterns.

36.

1571.
Frankfort
on the
Mayn.
N. Baseus. New Modelbüch.
Von allerhandt Art, Nehens und Stickens, jetzt mit viellerley Welscher Arbeyt, Mödel und Stahlen, allen Steinmetzen, Seiden-stickern und Neterin, sehr nützlich und kunstlich, von newem zugericht.

Getruckt zu Frankfurt am Mayn, 1571.
Device and motto of Nicolas Baseus on title-page. Sm. 4to. (Library V. and A. Museum.)

37.

1568.
Frankfort
on the
Mayn.
N. Baseus. Das new Modelbüch, &c.

Franckfurt am Mayn, 1568, 4to. Printer, Nicholas Baseus, ff. 40.

38.

1569.
Frankfort
on the
Mayn. Modelbüch ; Zweiter Theil : Franckfurt am Mayn, 1569.

4to, ff. 44. Nos. 36 and 37 are cited by the Marquis d'Adda.

---

[34] Royal Library, Munich.

39.

La Gloria et l' honore de ponti tagliati et ponti in aere
Venezia per Mathio Pagan in Frezzeria al segno della Fede.
1558.[35]

1558.
Venice.
M. Pagan.

16 plates. Dedicated to Vittoria Farnese, Duchess of Urbino.

40.

Il Monte. Opera nova di recami intitolata il monte, nella
quale si ritrova varie, & diverse sorti di mostre, di punti in aiere,
à fogliami. Dove le belle & virtuose Donne protranno fare ogni
sorte di lavoro, accommodate alle vera forma misura & grandezza,
che debbono essere ne mai piu per l' adietro da alcuno vedute.
Opera non men bella che utile, & necessaria.[36]

N. D
Venice.

Below, the impresa of the printer, an eagle with its young ; motto,
" Virtute parta sibi non tantum." In Venetia.
4to, 16 ff., 29 plates of bold scroll borders.

41.

Il Monte (libro secondo) Opera dove ogni bella donna potrà
fare ogni sorte di lavori cioè colari, fazzoletti, maneghetti. avertadure (berthes), &c., in Venetia, 1560.[37]

1559.
Venice.
G. A. Bin-
doni.

Printer's mark and motto as No. 39 : afterwards the dedication dated
1559, " à Vittoria da Cordova Gio. Ant. Bindoni," in which he states
" Ho preso arditamente di presentarvi questo secondo Monte." 4to,
ff. 16.

42.

Bellezze de recami et dessegni opera novo non men bella che
utile, e necessaria et non più veduta in luce. Venezia, 1558.[38]

1558.
Venice.

Ob. 4to. 20 plates of patterns.

43.

Lo Splendore delle virtuose giovani con varie mostre di
fogliami e punti in aere. Venezia. Per Iseppo Foresto in calle
dell' acqua a S. Zulian all' insegno del Pellegrino, 1558.[39]

1558.
Venice.
I. Foresto.

16 plates.

---

[35] Cat. Cicognara. 1583. No. 4.
[36] Bib. de l'Arsenal. No. 11,953.*
—Mr. E. Arnold.
[37] Florence, M. Bigazzi.

[38] Cat. Cicognara. 1583. No. 1.
Bound in one volume. with six
others.
[39] *Ibid.* 1583. No. 5.

44.

Trionfo di Virtù Libro novo da cucir, con fogliami, ponti a fili, ponti cruciati, &c.   Venezia, 1559.[40]

16 plates.

45.

N. D.   Burato.

Consisting of four leaves, with patterns of canvas (tela chiara), in squares, for works in " punta " of various widths, with instructions how to increase or diminish the patterns.   See CUTWORK.

On the back of the last page is printed in large characters, " P. Alex. Pag. (Paganinus).   Benacensis F. Bena. V. V." [41]

46.

N. D.   Burato . . . . con nova maestria, gratiose donne, novo artificio vi appoito.

A second edition without date.   4to, ff. 59; frontispiece, ladies at work, verso, Triumph of Fame.   Four books of designs of great elegance and taste.   The Marquis d'Adda assigns them to Vavassore.

47.

N. D.
A. Pas-
serotti.   Passerotti Aurelio Pittore Bolognese dissegnatore e miniatore figlio di Bartolommeo Passerotti circa al 1560.   Libro Primo di lavorieri alle molto illustre et virtuosissime gentildonne Bolognesi.   Libro secondo alle molto magnifici et virtuosissimi signori.[42]

In fol. obl.

67 ff., including two dedications and a frontispiece.   Designs for embroidery, etc., drawn with a pen.   In the title-page of the first book is the device of a sunflower, " Non san questi occhi volgere altrove."

48.

Le Pompe.   Opera nova di recami dove trovansi varie mostre di punto in aere.   Venezia, 1557.[43]

Probably an earlier impression of the following.   4to, ff. 16.

49.

1559.   Le Pompe, opera nova nella quale si ritrovano varie, & diverse sorti di mostre, per poter far Cordelle over Bindelle, d' Oro, di Seta, di Filo, overo di altra cosa di Dove le belle et virtuose donne potranno fare ogni sorte di lavoro, cioè merli di diverse sorte, Cavezzi, Colari, Maneghetti, & tutte quelle cose

---

[40] Cat. Cicognara.   1583. No. **6.**
[41] *Ibid.*   1583. No. 7.

[42] Cat. Cicognara.   No. 1 7
[43] *Ibid.*   1583.   No. 3.

che le piaceranno. Opera non men bella, che utile, & necessaria. E non più veduta in luce. 1559.[44]

Below, the same impresa of the eagle, as in "Il Monte," Nos. 39 and 40.

8vo, 16 ff., 30 plates.

A great variety of borders and indented patterns (merli). (Fig. 169.) "Si vendeno alla Libraria della Gatta."

Fig. 169.

LE POMPE, 1559.

In the Cat. d'Estrées is noted, "Le Pompe, Opera nella quale si retrovano diverse sorti di mostse per poter far cordelie, Bindelle, d' oro di seta, di filo. 1559, fig." Probably the same work.

50.

Le Pompe, Libro secondo. Opera nuova nella quale si ritrovana varie e diverse sorti di Mostre, per poter fare Cordelle, ovver Bindelle, d'Oro, di Seta, di Filo, ovvero di altra cosa. Dove

1560.
Venice.

---

[44] Bib. de l'Arsenal. 11,953.*

le belle & virtuose Donne potranno far ogni sorte di lavoro, coèi
Merli di diverse sorte, Cavezzi, Colari, Maneghetti & tutte quelle
cose che li piaceno. Opera hon men bello che utile & necessaria
e non più veduta in luce.

> Impresa of the printer, "Pegasus," and below, In "Venetia 1560."
> Obl. 8vo, 16 ff., 29 plates.[45]
> Mrs. Stisted's copy is dated 1562, and there is one at Vienna, in the
> Imperial Library, of the same date.

51.

**1563.
Venice.
J. Cale-
pino.**

Splendore delle virtuose giovani dove si contengono molte, &
varie mostre a fogliami cio è punti in aere, et punti tagliati,
bellissimi, & con tale arteficio, che li punti tagliati serveno alli
punti in aere. Et da quella ch' è sopragasi far si possono,
medesimamente molte altre.
In Venetia Appresso Jeronimo Calepino, 1563.[46]

> 8vo, 20 ff., 35 plates of scroll patterns in the style of "Il Monte."
> Dedication "Alla molto honorata M. Anzola ingegniera suocera mia
> digniss." Francesco Calepino, wishing, he says, to "ristampare la
> presente opera," he dedicates it to her. In Bib. Melzi, Milan, a copy
> dated 1567.

52.

**1563.
Venice.
J. Cale-
pino.**

Lucidario di recami, nel qual si contengono molte, & varie
sorti di disegni. A punti in aere et punti tagliati, & a fogliami,
& con figure & di più altre maniere, come al presente si usano
non più venute in luce Per lequali ogni elevato ingegno potrà
in diversi modi commodissimamente servirsi. In Venetia,
Appresso Ieronimo Calepino, 1563.[47]

> 8vo, 16 ff., 29 plates of flowing borders like the preceding.

53.

**1564.
Venice.**

I Frutti opera nuova intitulata i frutti de i punti in stuora,
a fogliami, nella quale si ritrova varie, et diverse sorti di mostre
di ponti in Stuora, a fogliami, & punti in gasii & in punti in
Trezola.[48] Dove ogni bella et virtuosa donna potrà fare ogni
sorte di lavoro, cioè fazoletti, colari, maneghetti, Merli, Frisi,
Cavezzi, Intimelle, overo forelle, avertadure da camise, & altre
sorti di lavori, come piu a pieno potrai vedere, ne mei per
l' adietro d' alcun altro fatte & poste in luce.

---

[45] Bib. de l'Arsenal. 11,953.*—
Mrs. Stisted. Bagni di Lucca.
[46] Bib. Nat. V. 1901.*—Bib. de
l'Arsenal. 11,973.*—Cat. d'Estrées.
[47] Bib. Nat. V. 1901.*—Bib. de
l'Arsenal. 11,973.*—Cat. d'Estrées.
[48] Trezola, in the Riviera dialect,
signifies a plait-tresse. "Porta i
capei in trezola." ("She wears her
hair plaited.")

Opera non men bella, che utile et necessaria a ciascuna virtuosa gentildonna. In Vinegia, 1564.[49]

Obl. 8vo, 16 ff., 30 plates of patterns either in dots or small squares.

54.

Patrons pour brodeurs, lingières, massons, verriers, et autres gens d'esperit; nouvellement imprimé, à Paris, rue Saint-Jacques, à la Queue-de Regnard M.DLXIIII.[50]

1564.
Paris.

55.

Fede (Opere nova) intitulata: Dei Recami nella quale si contiene varie diverse sorte di mostre di punti scritto, tagliato, in Stuora, in Rede, &c. In Venetia, appresso Domenico de Franceschi in Frezzaria, all' insegna della Regina. M.DLVIII.

1564.
Venice.
D. de
Frances-
chi.

in 4to, ff. 16. In his *Avis au Lecteur*, Franceschi alludes to three other works he had published, styled *La Regina*, *La Serena*, and *La Speranza*.

56.

Serena opera nova di recami, nella quale si ritrova varie et diverse sorte di punti in stuora et punti a filo. In Venetia, Domenico di Franceschi, 1564.

1564.
Venice.
D. de
Frances-
chi.

Obl. 4to, ff. 16. Nos. 55 and 56 cited by Marquis d'Adda.

57.

Le trésor des patrons, contenant diverses sortes de broderies et lingeries, pour coudre avec grande facilité et pour ouvrer en diverses sortes de piquer avec l'ésguille, pulveriser par dessus et faire ouvrages de toutes sortes de points &ct par Jean Ostans. Lyon, Ben. Rigaud. 1581, in 4-to.[51]

1581.
Lyon.
J. Ostans.

58.

Ostans Giovanni. La vera perfettione del disegno di varie sorti di Recami, et di cucire, &c. . . . punti a fogliami punti tagliati punti a fili et rimessi punti in cruciati, punti a stuora, et ogni altra arte che dia opera a disegni. Fatta nuovamente per Gio. Ostans. Vittoria, con gratia et privilegio dell' Illus.

1567.
Venice.
J. Ostans.

---

[49] Bib. de l'Arsenal. 11,955 *bis*,* with *Vera Perfettione* and *Fiori* of F. Franceschi, and *Corona* of Vecellio.

[50] Quoted by Willemin.
[51] Quoted in Art. "Tricot et Travaux des Dames."

Senato Venetiano per anni.[52]   In Venetia appresso Gio. Ostans,
1567.

> 4to obl., 4 cahiers of 8 ff., 74 plates. Letter of Ostans to Lucretia
> Contarini; verso, an engraving of Lucretia Romana, surrounded by her
> women, signed Jose. Sal. (Joseph Salviati), who furnished the design,
> two sonnets, and Aves. A striking example of the borrowing between
> France and Italy in the sixteenth century, probably of the school of
> Fontainebleau. Grotesques like A. du Cerceau, scrolls after E. de Laulne,
> fresco of figures from G. Tory. Brunet describes a copy dated 1591.

59.

1584.
Venice.
Valvas-
sore's
heirs.

Ostans. La vera perfettione del desegno &ct.   Venetia
M.DLXXXIIII., presso gli heredi Valvassori e Gio. Dom.   Micheli
al segno dell' Ippogrifo.

> In 4to obl. (Cited by Marquis d'Adda.)

60.

1582.
B. Tabin.

Neues Künstlicher, Modelbuch von allerhand artlichen und
gerechten Mödeln, &c., bei B. Tabin.[53]

61.

Paris.
1584.
D. de Sera.

Le livre de Lingerie, composé par Maistre Dominique de
Sera, Italien, enseignant le noble & gentil art de l'esguille, pour
besongner en tous points : utile & profitable à toutes Dames
& Damoyselles, pour passer le temps, & euiter oysiveté.

Nouvellement augmenté, & enrichi, de plusieurs excelents &
divers patrons, tant du point coupé, raiseau, que passement, de
l'invention de M. Jean Cousin, Peintre à Paris.

A Paris.   Chez Hierosme de Marnef, & la veufve de Guil-
laume Cauellat, au mont S. Hilaire à l'enseigne du Pelican.
1584.   Avec privilege du Roy.[54]

> In the Cat. d'Estrées, No. 8848, is *Livre de Pourtraicture de Jean
> Cousin*. Paris, 1637, in 4 fig.
> 4to, 28 ff., 51 plates of mediæval design.
> Frontispiece, three women and a child at work, on each side of the
> title a man and a woman at work under a trifoliated canopy.
> Privilege for three years to H. de Marnef, " juré libraire en l'Univer-
> sité de Paris."
> " L'auteur aux lecteurs." He takes his pen to portray what he has
> seen " en Italie, Espagne, Romanie, Allemagne, & autre païs, dont je ne
> fais aucune mention à cause de trop longue plexite," that he gives at

---

[52] Bib. M. d'Adda.   Mr. Gruner.
[53] Dresden, New Museum for Art   [54] Bib. de l'Arsenal. 11,954.*
and Industry. Communicated by

least eighty designs for the use and singular profit of many, " hommes tant que femmes." Below, " Finis coronat opus."

Then follows a " Balade " of 28 lines. On the last page, the impresa of Cavellat, a pelican in its piety, " Mors in me vita in me."

62.

Frano Gio. Libro delle mostre da ceuser per le donne.

16 engravings on wood and 8 on copper. (Cited by Marquis d'Adda.)

1596.
G. Frano.

63.

Danieli Bartholomeo Recamatore libro di diversi disegni per Collari, punti per Fazzoletti et Reticelle divarie sorte. Agostino Parisini forma in Bologna.

Bologna.
A. Pari-
sini.

15 leaves obl. 8vo, entirely engraved au burin, towards the end of the sixteenth century.[55]

64.

Ornamento delle belle et virtuose donne opera nova nella quale troverrai varie sorti di frisi, con li quali si potra ornar ciascuna donna, & ogni letti con ponti tagliato, ponti gropposi, & ogni altra sorte di ponti per fare quelle belle opere che si appartengono alle virtuose & lodevoli fanciulle.

N. D.

On a scutcheon, with 3 figures below, " Libro Primo." Lib. Victoria and Albert Museum.

65.

Les singuliers et nouveaux pourtraicts et ouvrages de Lingerie. Servans de patrons à faire toutes sortes de poincts, couppé, Lacis & autres. Dedie a la Royne. Nouvellement inventez, au proffit & cōtentement, des nobles Dames & Damoiselles & autres gentils esprits, amateurs d'un tel art. Par le Seigneur Federic (*sic*) de Vinciolo Venitien. A Paris. Par Iean le Clerc le ieune, ruë Chartiere, au Chef Sainct Denis. 1587. Avec privilege du Roy.[56]

1587.
Paris.
1st Edit.
1st Part.
F. Vin-
ciolo.

Les singuliers et nouveaux pourtraicts et ouvrages de Lingerie ou est representé les sept planettes, & plusieurs autres figures & pourtraitz servans de patrons à faire de plusieurs sortes de Lacis. Nouvellement inventez, au proffit & cōtentement des nobles Dames & Damoiselles & autres gentils esprits, amateurs d'un tel art. Par le Seigneur Federic de Vinciolo Venitien. A Paris. Par Iean le Clerc le ieune, ruë Chartiere, au Chef Sainct Denis. 1587. Avec privilege du Roi.

(At the end.)
Privilege for nine years to " Iean le Clerc le ieune, ' tailleur d'histoires,' à Paris," signed 27 June, 1587. " De l'Imprimerie de David le Clerc Rue Frementel à l'Estoille d'Or."

---

[55] Milan. Bib. Marquis Giro-lamo d'Adda.

[56] Bib. Rouen. No. 1313. Both Parts in one vol.*

4to.

The first part consists of 40 ff., 36 of patterns and 4 preliminary pages.

P. 1.　The title-page with decorated border, in which are two ladies at work.　(See Title-page of this work.)

P. 2.　Dedication of " Le Seigneur Federic de Vinciolo aux Benevolles Lecteurs," in which he sets forth that several authors before him having published certain patterns for work that " les Seigneurs, Dames, & Damoyselles ont eu pour agréable," he, to show " la bonne volonté que je porte à la France, laquelle m'ayant été douce et favorable, depuis certain temps que j'ay quitté Venize, païs de ma nativité," wish to portray the present " pourtraicts d'ouvrages magnifiques tous differēs, & non encor usitez en cette cōtree ni aultres, & que j'ay tenus cachés & incōgnus jusques à maintenant," feeling assured that if the first you had seen " on engendré quelque fruit & utilité, ceux cy en aporteront d'avantage," and if I see this my invention pleases you, I will " vous faire participer d'un aultre seconde bande d'ouvrages."

P. 3.　Dedication " A la Royne," Louise de Vaudemont, by Le Clerc, saying that having received from Italy some rare and singular patterns, and " ouvrages de l'ingerie & en ayāt invēte quelques uns, selon mon petit sçavoir, j'ay pensé puis que ces choses là appartienent principallement aux Dames," that he cannot do better than present them to the Queen, as if these patterns are useful (as he hears some less perfect and more rudely sketched have served and profited before), they ought to be offered to her Majesty.　Signed last day of May, 1587.

P. 4.　A sonnet

Aux Dames et Damoiselles.

" L'un sefforce à gaigner le cœur des grāds seigneurs
　Pour posséder enfin une exquise richesse,
　L'autre aspire aux Estats pour monter en altesse,
　Et l'autre par la guerre alléche les honneurs.

　Quand à moy, seulement pour chasser mes langueurs,
　Je me sen satisfait de vivre en petitesse,
　Et de faire si bien, qu'aux dames je délaisse
　Un grand contentement en mes graves labeurs.

　Prenez doncques en gré (mes Dames), je vous prie,
　Ces pourtrais ouvragez lesquelz je vous dédie,
　Pour tromper vos ennuis, et l'esprit employer.
　En ceste nouveauté, pourrés beaucoup apprendre,
　Et maistresses en fin en cest œuvre vous rendre.
　Le travail est plaisant.　Si grand est le loyer."

　　　　　" *Morir assidouamente per virtu,*
　　　　　　Non morirè."

Then follow the 36 patterns set off in white on a black ground, viz., 20 " Ouvrages de point Couppé," the first plate with the double λλ, according to the fashion introduced by Francis I. of using Greek monograms, standing for Queen Louise.　On the second page are two escutcheons, one of France, the other with the letter H for Henry III.　Then follow eight " Passemens de point Couppé," which are succeeded by eight more " Ouvrages de point Couppé."

Part 2, 24 ff.　Same decorated frontispiece and 22 plates of subjects in squares for stitches like the German patterns of the present day.　These consist of the Seven Planets, Sol, Luna, Mars, Mercury, Jupiter, Venus and Saturn.　Four in squares of various designs ; two of Amorini shooting stags and birds ; Neptune and the winds ; an arabesque with impresa of a column with circle and double triangle ; five borders and squares, and two "bordures à carreaux," diamond-shaped meshes. The last page contains the Extract from the Privilege.

This is the original edition of Vinciolo, of which we know but one copy existing—that in the Library at Rouen.

It was followed the same year by two other editions, with alterations.[57]

66.

Les singuliers et nouveaux pourtraicts pour les ouvrages de Lingerie. Nouvellement augmentez de plusieurs differens pourtraits servans de patrons à faire toutes sortes poincts couppé, Lacis, et autres reseau de poinct conté. Dedié à la Royne. Le tout inventé, au proffit & contentement des nobles Dames & Damoiselles & autres gentils esprits, amateurs d'un el art. Par le Seigneur Federic de Vinciolo Venitien. **A**. Paris. Par Iean le Clerc le ieune, ruë Chartiere, au Chef Sainct Denis, pres le college de Coqueret. Avec privilege du Roy. 1587.

[margin: 1587. 2nd Ed. 1st Part. F. Vinciolo.]

Les singuliers et nouveaux pourtraicts pour les ouvrages de Lingerie ou avons augmēté plusieurs nouveaux & differens portraitz de reseau, tout point conté, plusieurs nouvelles bordures et autres sortes differentes.

[margin: 2nd part.]

Nouvellement inventez au proffit & cōtentement des nobles Dames & Damoiselles & autres gentils esprits amateurs d'un tel art. Par le Seigneur Federick de Vinciolo Venitien. **A** Paris. Par Iean le Clerc le ieune, Ruë Chartiere, au Chef Sainct Denis, pres le college de Coqueret. Avec privilege du Roy. 1587.[58]

1st Part, 40 ff. The same frontispiece, dedications, date, and sonnet, as the first, the same number of patterns, only the eight styled in the first "Passemens" are here all called, like the others, "Ouvrages" de point couppé. (See Fig. 4.)

2nd Part, 32 ff. This part has 30 patterns, comprising the 24 of the first edition, and six additional ones, consisting of squares and two hunting subjects.

67.

Les singuliers et nouveaux Pourtraicts, du Seigneur Federic de Vinciolo Venitien, pour toutes sortes d'ouvrages de Lingerie. Dedie a la Royne. Derechef et pour la troisieme fois augmentez Outre le reseau premier et le point couppé et lacis, de plusieurs beaux et differens portrais de reseau de point côté avec le nombre des mailles, choze non encor veue ni inventée.

[margin: 1587. 3rd Edit. No. 1. Parts 1 and 2.]

---

[57] We have received notice of there being a copy of the original edition at Turin, in the Library of the University.

[58] Bib. Nat. Grav. L. h. 2.* (with Part I.) : " Ex Bibliotheca illustrissimi Johannis d'Estrées Cameracensis Archiepiscopi designati quam Monasterio St. Germani à Pratis legavit. Anno 1718."

A Paris. Par Iean le Clerc le ieune, ruë Chartiere, au Chef
Sainct Denis, pres le College de Coqueret. Avec privilege du
Roy. 1587.[59]

This must be the first impression of the third edition.

1588.
3rd Edit.
No. 2.
1st Part.

Les singuliers et nouveaux pourtraicts, du Seigneur Federic
de Vinciolo Venitien, pour toutes sortes d'ouvrages de Lingerie.
Dedié a la Royne. Derechef et pour la troisiesme fois
augmentez, outre le reseau premier & le point couppé & lacis, de
plusieurs beaux et differens portrais de reseau de point côté,
avec le nombre des mailles, chose non encor veuë, ny inventée.
A Paris. Par Iean le Clerc le ieune, au mont Saint Hilaire, du
Chef Sainct Denis, pres le Clos Bruneau. Avec privilege du
Roy. 1588.[60]

68.

2nd Part.

Les singuliers et nouveaux pourtraicts, du Seigneur Federic
de Vinciolo Venitien, pour toutes sortes d'ouvrages de Lingerie.
Dedié a la Royne. Derechef et pour la troisiesme fois
augmentez, outre le reseau premier & le point couppé & lacis, de
plusieurs beaux et differens portrais de reseau de point côté,
avec le nombre des mailles, chose non encor veuë, ny inventée.
A Paris. Par Iean le Clerc le ieune, au mont Saint Hilaire,
au Chef Sainct Denis, pres le Clos Bruneau. Avec privilege du
Roy. 1588.[61]

This must be subsequent to the Brussels impression, as Jean le Clerc
has changed his address.

In the third edition, dorso of pp. 1 and 2, we have the addition of
portraits of Louise de Vaudemont and Henry III., with a complimentary
stanza of four lines under each.

In his Advertisement au lecteur, Vinciolo says that having promised,
since the first impression of his book, to give a " nouvelle bande d'ouvrages,"
and not to disappoint certain ladies who have complained that he has not
made " du reseau assez beau à leur fantaisie," I have wished for the third
time to place before their eyes many new and different patterns of " reseau
de point conté que j'ay cousus et attachez à la fin de mes premières
figures," beneath which I have put the number and quantity of the
stitches. Same dedication and sonnet as before. Privilege for nine years
dated Paris, 25 May, 1587. " De l'Imprimerie de David le Clerc, ruë
S. Jacques, au petit Bec, devant le College de Marmouttier."

1st Part, 40 ff., 36 plates, 27 of point couppé, two stomachers, and
seven " Passemens " de point couppé ; the same lettered " Ouvrages " as
in the preceding impression.

2nd Part, 36 ff., 50 plates. The thirty already published in the second
edition, after which follow the twenty additional of " reseau de point
conté," announced in the Preface, consisting of " 6 Quarrés, 2 Coins de

---

[59] Brussels, Bib. Roy. M. Alvin,
Conservateur en Chef.
[60] Bib. Ste. Geneviève. V. 634.*
—Bib. Nat. Grav. L. h. 2. b.*

[61] Bib. Ste. Geneviève (with 1st
Part).*—Bib. Nat. Grav. L. h. 2. b.
(with 1st Part).*

Mouchoir, 2 Bordures, 6 animals : Lion, Pelican, Unicorn, Stag, Peacock, and Griffon " ; and the Four Seasons. " Déesse des fleurs, representant le Printemps," etc.

These last twenty have the number of stitches given. (See Fig. 5.)

On the last page is an escutcheon with the arms of France and Poland.

69.

A later impression still.

Same title, date, portraits, dedication, and sonnet, only the Privilege is dated " ce douzième jour de Novembre 1587. De l'Imprimerie de David le Clerc, Rue S. Jaques, aux trois Mores." [62]

34 ff. 30 plates, 1st part ; 50 plates in 2nd.

1588.
3rd Edit.
No. 3.
Parts 1
and 2.

70.

Les singuliers et nouveaux pourtraicts, du Seigneur Frederic de Vinciolo, Venitien, pour toutes sortes d'ouvrages de Lingerie. Dedie à la Royne Douairière de France.

De Rechef et pour la troisiesme fois augmentez, outre le reseau premier & le point couppé & lacis, de plusieurs beaux & differens portrais de reseau de point côté, avec le nombre des mailles, chose non encore veuë ny inventée.

A Paris. Par Iean le Clerc, ruë Saint Jean de Latran, à la Salemandre. Avec privilege du Roy. 1595.[63]

1595.
3rd Edit.
No. 4.
Parts 1
and 2.

This impression is dedicated to Louise de Vaudemont, now " Reine Douairière," Henry III. having died in 1589.

71.

The same title as that of 1595—differing only in date.[64]

Privilege for six years, " donné à Mantes, le 3 Juillet 1593." At the foot, " De l'Imprimerie de David le Clerc au Petit Corbeil 1606."

The 1st part has 32 ff. and 36 plates ; 32 " Ouvrages de poinct couppé," and 4 stomachers.

The 2nd part 46 plates, same as those of 1588, only four less.

On the last page the escutcheon of France and Navarre.

1606.
3rd Edit.
No. 5.
Parts 1
and 2.

72.

Les singuliers et nouveaux pourtraicts, du Seigneur Federic de Vinciolo Venitien, pour toutes sortes d'ouvrages de Lingerie. Dedie a la Royne. Derechef et pour la quatrieme fois augmentez, outre le reseau premier et le point couppé et lacis, de plusieurs beaux et differens portrais de reseau de point conté, avec le nombre de mailles, chose non encore veue ni inventee. A Thurin. Par Eleazaro Thomysi. 1589.[65]

1589.
4th Edit.
Turin.

and 2.

Described in Cat. Cicognara with the date 1658. The 1st part 44 ff. and 39 plates ; the 2nd with 36 plates.

---

[62] Bib. de l'Arsenal. 11,954 *bis.**

[63] British Museum. Grenville Lib. 2584.*

[64] Bib. Nat. Grav. L. h. 1. a.*

[65] Brussels, Bib. Roy.—Cat. Cicognara. No. 1822.

The editions of 1613 and 1623 are described in their chronological order. Nos. 64 and 71.

That of 1603 we have not seen; but M. Leber states it to be equally rich with that of 1623.

The copies of Vinciolo in the Bodleian bear the dates of 1588, 1603, and 1612.

Baron Pichon has a copy of an impression of 1612.

One at Bordeaux, in the Bib. de la Ville, is dated 1588.

In a book sale at Antwerp, March, 1864, there was sold the following :—

Lot 528. *Livre de Patrons de Lingerie dedié a la Royne, nouvelle-ment invente par le seign^r Frederic de Vinciolo, Venitien.* Paris, Jean le Clerc, 1598.—*Les singuliers et nouveaux pourtraicts pour toutes sortes d'ouvrages de Lingerie.* Paris, *Ibid.*, 1598.—*Les secondes œuvres et subtiles inventions de Lingerie.* Paris, *Ibid.*, 1598.—*Nouveaux pour-traicts de Point coupé et Dantelles en petite moyenne et grande forme.* A. Montbeliard, Jacques Foillet, 1598. 4 tom. 1 vol. in-4. v. anc. fig. sur bois.

It went for 440 francs to a Mr. Ross. We do not know the editions of 1598.

As M. Leber observes, the various editions of Vinciolo, published by Le Clerc and his widow, from 1587 to 1623, and perhaps later, are only impressions more or less varied of the two distinct books, the one of point coupé, the other of lacis.

The work of Vinciolo has been reprinted in several countries. In England it has been translated and published by Wolfe. (See No. 72.) At Liege, by Jean de Glen. (See No. 79.) Mr. Douce says that it was reprinted " at Strasburg, 1596, and at Basle, 1599, with a second part, which is rare, and sometimes contains a portrait by Gaultier of Catherine de Bourbon."

In the Bib. Nat. (Grav. B. c. 22), a volume headed *Vinciolo (Federigo) Peintre Venitien et ses imitateurs*, contains, with " La pratique," etc., of Mignerak (See No. 93), a German copy of the " nouveaux pourtraits," the work printed by Ludwig Künigs, at Basle, 1599 (See No. 85); and a German work headed " Broderies sur filet," 50 plates engraved upon copper.

73.

1591.
London.
Wolf.

New and singular patternes and workes of Linnen. Serving for patterns to make all sortes of Lace edging and Cut-workes. Newly invented for the profite and contentment of Ladies, Gentlewomen, and others that are desirous of this Arte. London : Imprinted by J. Wolfe and Edward White, 1591.[66]

EPISTLE TO THE READER.

Having framed a body of the best and rarest manner in true perfection of sundrie sortes of deuises or workes, as well for frame-workes as other needle-workes, I devised with all diligence and industrious studie to sattisfy the gentle mindes of vertuous women by bringing to light things never before as yet seene nor committed to print; All which devises are soe framed in due proportion as taking them in order, the one is formed or made by the other, and soe proceedeth forward ; Whereby with more

---

[66] Quoted in Watt's *Bibliographai Britannica.*

ease they may be sewed and wrought in Cloth, and keeping true accompt of the threads, maintaine the bewtey of the worke. And more, who desyrith to bring the worke into a lesser forme, let them make the squares lesse. And if greater, then inlarge them, and so may you worke in divers sortes, either by stitch, pouncing, or pouldering upon the same as you please. Alsoe it is to be understood that these squares serve not onely for cut-workes, but alsoe for all other manner of seweing or stitching, noteing withall that they are made to keepe the work or deuise in good order and even proportion—And even if ye will that squares be greater, make of two, one, four, two, and soe they will be larger. And in this manner may you proceed in all.

God prosper your desires.

Then follows the dedication :

To the Right Worshipful Gentlewoman, Mistress Susan Saltonstall, wife to the right Worshipfull Mr. Richard Saltonstall, Alderman of the City of London (afterwards Lord Mayor, and knighted in 1597).

It being my chance (Right Worshipfull) to lighten upon certaine paternes of cut-worke and others brought out of Foreign Countries which have bin greatly accepted of by divers Ladies and Gentlewomen of sundrie nations and consequently of the common people ; This seemed unto mee a sufficient instance and argument to bestowe likewise some paines for the publishing thereof, But being in suspense of the dedication two causes induced mee to imbolden myselfe to present it unto your acceptation and patronage : First because that rare devises and inventions are for the most part more agreeable and gratefuller accepted, than ordinarie and common things, although of great price and value, Secondlie because these workes belong chiefly to Gentlewomen for to passe away their time in vertuous exercises Wherefore to fit and accommodate the dedication aright to the contents and subject of the book I thought it not amisse to offer it unto your worship in token of thankfullness for so many benefites which I have received so bountifullie at your hands Assuring myselfe moreover that as these patternes will bring sufficient content-ment and profite to all well-willers, that are desirous of this Arte, soe they shall for ever acknowledge themselves to be beholden chiefly unto you, being the chiefest occasion of the publishing and setting forthe thereof. And therefore uppon hope that you will take these inventions in good parte, which in time I am purposed (If God permit) to increase and augment with more paternes of worke. In the meantime I pray God give to your Worship a happie prosperous and long life with a full accomplishment of all your vertuous desires.

Your worshipps most dutiful
Servant and Kinsman,
ADRIAN POYNTZ.

74.

Fiori di ricami nuovamente posti in luce ne i quali sono varii, et diversi dissegni di lavori ; Come Merli, Bauari, Manichetti, & altre sorti di opere, che al presente sono in uso, utilissimi ad ogni stato di Donne. Seconda Impressione.

1591.
Bologna.
T. Pasini.

Impresa of Mercury. Below—

In Bologna, per Giovanni Rossi. MDXCI. Ad instanza di Tomaso Pasini.[67]

---

[67] Bib. de l'Arsenal. No. 11,954 *ter*.*

Obl. 8vo, 20 ff., 18 plates like Vecellio, one " bavaro."
Dedicated by the author to " La Signora Silveria Rossi Ghisolieri."
Mostly indented patterns on black grounds.

75.

1591.
Venice.
F. di
Frances-
chi.

Prima Parte de' fiori, e disegni di varie sorti di Ricami moderni come merli, bavari, manichetti, & altri nobili lavori che al presente sono in uso.

A figure of Peace. Below—

In Venetia, Appresso Francesco di Franceschi Senese all' insegna della Pace 1591.[68]

Obl. 8vo, 20 ff., 17 plates in the style of Vecellio.
Dedication to "La Signora Gabriella Zeno Michele," signed "Di Venetia alli 19 di Marzo, 1591, Giovanbattista Ciotti." The last plate a figure of Fortune, with " Finis in Venetia 1591. Appresso Nicolo Moretti, ad instantia di Francesco di Franceschi."

76.

1591.
Venice.
F. di
Frances-
chi.

La vera perfettione del disegno di varie sorti di ricami & di cucire ogni sorti de punti à foglami, punti tagliati, punti a fili & rimessi, punti incrociati, punti à stuoro & ogn' altre arte, che dia opera à disegni. E di nuovo aggiuntovi varie sorti di merli, e mostre, che al presente sono in uso & in pratica.

Impresa of Peace differing from the preceding.

In Venetia, Appresso Francesco di Franceschi Senese all' insegna della Pace. 1591.[69]

Obl. 8vo, 36 ff., 72 plates.
Dedicated to "Signora Lucretia Contarini, per matrimonio Priula Nobile Gentildonna Venetiana," by Giovanni Ostans.
A woodcut of Lucretia working with her maidens, signed Jose Sol, 1557.
Patterns, Small Squares, Gorgets, Youth, Paris, Pyramus and Thisbe, Arabesques, Grotesques, and an Alphabet.
On the last leaf, dorso, A. B. C. D. "tutte sono quaderni." A figure again of Peace, and " In Ven. 1590."

77.

1592.
Venice.
1st Book.
C. Vecellio.

Corona delle nobili et virtuose donne. Libro primo. Nel quale si dimostra in varij Dissegni, tutti le sorti di Mostre di punti tagliati, punti in aria, punti à Reticello, e d' ogni altra

---

[68] Bib. de l'Arsenal. 11,955 *bis.**   [69] *Ibid.*
—Bib. Bodleian.

sorte cosi per Freggi come per Merli, & Rosette, che con l'
Aco si usano hoggidì per tutta l' Europa. Et molte delle quali
Mostre possono servire anchora per Opere à Mazzette. Aggiuntivi
in questa Quarta impressione molti bellissimi dissegni non mai
più veduti.

Then follows the printer's impresa of the stork and serpent. "Volup-
tatum et malorum effetuu dissipatio," with a lady at work on each side,
and below—

Con privilegio. In Venetia, Appresso Cesare Vecellio in
Frezzaria nelle Case de' Preti. 1592.[70]

Which is repeated in the 2nd and 3rd Books.
   Obl. 4to, 32 ff., 28 plates.
   Dedication of Vecellio "Alla Clarissima, et Illustrissima Signora,
Viena Vendramina Nani, dignatissima Consorte dell' Illust^{rmo} Sig. Polo
Nani, il Procurator di S. Marco," in which he refers to his work on
costume, and says that he dedicates this book to her for the delight
she takes in these works and "in farne essercitar le donne di casa
sua, ricetto delle piu virtuose giovani che hoggidì vivano in questa città."
Signed: Venice, Jan. 20, 1591.
   Beautiful designs, among which are three corners for handkerchiefs,
the last lettered: "Diverse inventioni p. cantoni dee fazoletti."
   On Plate 3, within a point coupé border, is a statue of Venus standing
upon a tortoise, with other figures, and above, "Conviensi, che della
Donna la bontà, & non la bellezza sia divulgata," and underneath :—

"Veneer io son, de le mirabil mani
   Del dotto Fidia d' un bel marmo finta.
In me vedete atti gentili, e humani,
   Ch' esser dè Donna à gentilezza accinta.
Io sopra una Testugine dimora,
   Perchè stia in Casa, e sia tacita ogn' hora."

Corona delle nobili et virtuose donne.   Libro secondo.   *2nd Book.*
   Nel quale si dimostra in varij Dissegni, tutte le sorti di
Mostre de punte tagliati, punti in aria, punti à Reticello, e d'
ogni altra sorte, cosi per Freggi, come per Merli, & Rosette, che
con l' Aco si usano hoggidì per tutta l' Europa. Et molti delle
quali Mostre possono servire anchora per Opere à Mazzette.
Aggiuntivi in questa Quarta Impressione molti bellissimi
dissegni non mai più veduti. Con Privilegio. In Venetia,
Appresso Cesare Vecellio, in Frezzaria nelle Case de' Preti.
1592.

28 ff., 26 plates.
   The dedication of this and the next book, though differently worded,
are addressed to the same lady as the first. This is dated Jan. 24, 1591.
   Among the patterns are two designs for handkerchiefs, and on the last
plate a statue of Vesta, within a point coupé border.

Corono delle nobili et virtuose donne. Libro terzo. Nel *3rd Book.*

---

[70] Bib. de l'Arsenal. **11,955*** (with Books 2 and 3). *Mazzette* means
detached bouquets—sprigs.

quale si dimostra in varii dissegni molte sorti di Mostri di
Punti in Aria, Punti tagliati, Punti a reticello, and ancora di
picciole; cosi per Freggi, come per Merli, & Rosette, che con l'
Aco si usano hoggidi per tutta l'Europa.   Con alcune altre
inventione di Bavari all' usanza Venetiana.   Opera nouva e
non più in luce.   Con privilegio.   In Venetia Appresso Cesare
Vecellio, stà in Frezzaria nelle Case de' Petri.   1592.

Dedication dated June 15, 1591.   Vecellio says he has added "alcune
inventioni di bavari all' usanza nostra."   In the copy (Bib. de l'Arsenal,
11,955 *bis*) are added instructions to transfer the patterns upon parchment without injuring the book.   The last plate shows how to reduce the
patterns and how to prick them (Fig. 170).   This is sometimes given at
the end of the first book instead of the third.

28 ff., 26 plates, two of bavari.

On Pl. 27, woman with a torch and Cupid.   At Pl. 28, in a point

Fig. 170.

MANNER OF PRICKING THE PATTERN.—(Vecellio.)

coupé border, is a fox holding the bust of a lady, the conceit of which is
explained by the verses to be, that sense is better than beauty :—

"Trovò la Volpe d' un Scultore eletto
Una testa sì ben formata, tale,
Che sol le manca Spirito havresti detto,
Tanto l' industria, e l' arteficio vale,
La prende in man, poi dice; O che perfetto
Capo, e gentil; ma voto è d' inteletto."

78.

1594.
Venice.
C. Vecellio. Gioiello della corona per le nobili e virtuose donne.   Libro
quarto.   Nel quale si dimostra altri nuovi bellissimi Dissegni
di tutte le sorte di Mostre di Punti in Aria, Punti tagliati &
Punti à Reticello; così per Freggi, come per Merli, & Rosette,
che con l' Aco si usano hoggidì per tutta l' Europa.   Et molte
delle quali mostre possono servire anchora per opere à Mazzette
Nuovament posto in luce con molte bellissime inventioni non
mai più usate, nè vedute.   Con privilegio.   In Venetia, Appresso
Cesare Vecellio, in Frezzaria nella Casa de i Preti.   1594.

Same impresa of the stork and serpent.
Dedicated to the Sign. Isabella Palavicina Lupi Marchesa di Soragana,
dated "Venetia alli 20 Novembrio 1592."   Cesare Vecellio.   30 plates.[71]

---

[71] Rouen, Bib.   Bound in one vol. with the three parts of the *Corona.**

Vecellio, author of the *Corona* and *Gioiello*, also published a work on costume styled *Degli Habiti Antichi et Moderni. In Venezia*, 1590. *Presso Damian Zenero.* In the frontispiece is a salamander; on the last leaf a figure of Vesta. It has been reproduced by F. Didot, Paris.

He was not, as is often incorrectly stated, a relation, or even of the same family as Titian.

These are the earliest impressions we have had an opportunity of examining of Vecellio's works, which appear to have been widely circulated. The Bib. de l'Arsenal possesses two copies of the *Corona* (No. 11,955), from which we have described. In the other (No. 11,155 *bis*), Book 1 "ultima," Book 2 "quarta," are both dated 1593; and Book 3 "nuovamente ristampata la quarta volta," 1592. The plates all the same.

The Library of Rouen (No. 1,315) has a volume containing the *Corona* and *Gioiello.* Book 1 "quarta Imp.," Book 2 "ultima," both dated 1594; and Book 3 "quinta," 1593. The *Gioiello*, 1593.

In the Bodleian is a copy of the three books, date 1592; and another, date 1561, was in the possession of the late Mrs. Dennistoun of Dennistoun.

At Venice, in the Doge's Library, is a volume containing the three books of the *Corona* and the *Gioiello*, dated 1593.

Mrs. Stisted, Bagni di Lucca, also possesses the three books of the *Corona*, dated 1597, and the *Gioiello*, 1592.

At Bologna the Library has one volume, containing the first and second books only, evidently the original impressions. The titles are the same as the above, only to each is affixed, " Opera nuova e non più data in luce," and " Stampata per gli Hered' della Regina. 1591. An instantia di Cesare Vecellio, Stà in Frezzaria."

The same Library also possesses a volume, with the three books of the *Corona*, the first and third "ottava," the second "quarta," and the *Gioiello*, " nuovamente posto in luce." All " In Venetia appresso gli heredi di Cesare Vecellio, in Frezzaria. 1608."

At Vienna, in the new Museum for Art and Industry, is a copy of the five books, dated 1601.[72]

Cav. Merli cites from a copy of the four books, dated 1600.

The various impressions, therefore, date from 1591 to 1608.

We see these different parts, like those of Vinciolo and all these old collections, have been printed and reprinted independently of each other, since the third part was at its fifth impression in 1593, while the first, which ought to have preceded it, was only at its fourth in 1594.[73]

79.

New Model Buch darinnen allerley Gattung schöner Modeln der newen aussgeschitnen Arbeit auff Krägen, Hempter, Jakelet und dergleichen zu newen, so zuvor in Teutschlandt nicht gesehen. Allen thugentsamen Frawen und Jungkfrawen, Nätterinnen, auch allen audern so lust zu solcher kunstlichen Arbeit haben, sehr dienstlich.

1593.
St. Gall.
G. Strauben.

---

[72] Communicated by Mr. Gruner.
[73] Note of M. Leber, who gives the dates of the dedication of the Rouen copy as follows :—B. 1, 20 Jan. ; B. 2, 24 Jan. ; B. 3, 15 June, all 1591. The *Gioiello*, 10 Nov., 1592. The vol. containing the two works has 101 plates, in addition to 10 leaves of titles, dedications etc.

Getruckt in uerlegung George Strauben, von S. Gallem, Anno 1593.[74]

Translation.

New Patternbook, in which are all sorts of beautiful patterns of the new cutwork for collars, shirts, jackets, and such like, such as never before were seen in Germany. Most useful to all virtuous dames and such artistic works, very respectfully dedicated.

Printed for the publisher, G. Strauben.

A reprint of the third book of Vecellio's *Corona.*

80.

N.D.
Lindau
am
Bodensee.

Neu Model-Buch, darinnen allerley gattung schöner Modeln der neuen, etc.

Probably a reprint of No. 79.
27 plates.

81.

1597.
Liége.
J. de Glen.

Les singuliers et nouveaux pourtraits, pour toutes sortes de lingeries de Jean de Glen, dediés à Madame Loyse de Perez ; à Liége, chez Jean de Glen, l'an 1597.[75]

Obl. 4to, 39 plates, mostly borrowed from Vinciolo, as well as the title.

82.

1596.
Florence.
M. Florini.

Fior di Ricami nuovamente porti in luce. Fiorenze, 1596, ad instanza di Mattheo Florini.

4to obl., 24 plates and 2 leaves of text.[76]

83.

1603.
Siena.
M. Florini.

Fiori di Ricami nuovamente porti in luce nei quali sono varie et diversi disegni di lavori, como merli, bavari, manichetti e altre sorte di opera. Siena, appresso Matteo Florini, 1603.

4to obl., 24 pages.[77]

84.

1603.
Siena.
M. Florini.

Giojello, &c. Nel quale si di mostra altri novi bellissimi disegni di tutte le sorte, di mostre &c. . . . di punti &c., cosi

---

[74] Victoria and Albert Museum.
[75] Brussels, Bib. Royale. Jean de Glen is also author of a work entitled *Des Habits, Mœurs, Ceremonies, Façons de faire, anciennes & modernes du Monde, par J. de Glen, Linger.* Liége. J. de Glen. 1601. In-8.
[76] Lyon. M. Yemenis.
[77] Turin, Count Manzoni.

per fregi come per merli et rosette che con l' aco si usanno hoggi di per tutte l' Europa. Opere a Mazzetto nuovamente posta in luce con motte bellissime inventioni non mai più usate ne vedute. In Siena, Matteo Florini MDCIII.

4to obl. (Cited by Marquis d'Adda.)

85.

Schön neues Modelbuch von allerley lüstigen Mödeln naczunehen zu würken un zu sticke ; gemacht im Jar Ch. 1597, zu Nürmberg, bey Balthaser Laimoxen zu erfragen.[78]

1597.
*Nurem-
berg.*
*B. Lai-
moxen.*

Translation.

Fine new Patternbook of all sorts of pleasant patterns for sewing, working, and embroidering: made in the year of Christ 1597, at Nurmberg : to be had of Balthasar Laimoxen.

Obl. fol., 27 ff.
5 sheets, title-page, and poem, signed J. S. (Johann Sibmacher.)
Mr. Gruner has communicated to us a work with the same title, dated 1591.[79]

86.

Nouveaux pourctraicts de point coupé et dantelles en petite moyenne et grande forme nouvellement inventez & mis en lumiere Imprimé a Montbéliard par Jacques Foillet cbɔlɔxciix (1598).[80]

1598.
*Montbé-
liard.*
J. Foillet.

Small 4to, 82 ff., 78 plates.
Frontispiece with borders composed of squares of point coupé.
" Avertissement aux dames," of three pages, stating these works are all composed of " point devant l'esguille, de point en toille, en bouclages, & de cordonnages." The writer gives patterns of roses of all sizes, " very little, middling, large, and very large," with from one to nine *pertuis*, or openings, holes. Also Carreaux in different forms, and lastly *dantelles*. " Je n'ay voulu omettre de vous dire que pour faire des dantelles, il vous fault jetter un fil de la grandeur que desiré faire vos dantelles, & les cordonner, puis jetter les fils au dedans, qui fera tendre le cordon & lui donnera la forme carrée, ronde, ou telle forme que desires, ce qu'estant faict vous paracheverès facilement. Enoultre vous verrez qu'estant bien petites deviennent peu a peu bien grandes jusques a la fin. Elles vous enricheront & embelliront vos ouvrages en les applicant aux bords d'iceux." Directions, we confess, perfectly enigmatical to us. The author finishes by exhorting the ladies to imitate Minerva and Arachne, " qui ont acquis un grand renom, pour avoir (cõme à l'envie l'une de l'autre) travaillé de l'esguille."
The avertissement is followed by an " Exhortation aux jeunes filles," in verse, of 21 lines, beginning—

" Si nuisible est aux humains la paresse," etc.

---

[78] Berlin, Royal Library.
[79] Dresden, New Museum of Art and Industry.

[80] Bib. Nat. V. 1902,* and Grav. L. h. 3.* — Bib. de l'Arsenal. 11,956.*—Bib. Ste. Geneviève.*

40 patterns of " roses," of point coupé.
And 18 of " Carreaux," variously disposed.
Then follow 20 patterns of lace, of " bien petites, petites, moyennes,
& grosses," all " au point devant l'Esguille." (See Figs. 8 to 12.)
At the end : " La fin courone l'œuvre." This is the earliest pattern-
book in which the word " dantelle " occurs.

87.

1598.
Mont-
béliard.
J. Foillet.

New Modelbuch darinnen allerley ausgeschnittene Arbeit,
in kleiner, mittelmässiger und grosser form erst neulich erfun-
den. Allen tugenden Frawen vnnd Júngfrawen sehr nutzlich.
Gedruckt zu Mumpelgarten durch Jacob Foillet, 1598.[81]

88.

1599.
Basle.

Fewrnew Modelbuch von allerhandt Künstlicher Arbeidt,
nämlich Gestricht, Aussgezogen Aussgeschnitten, Gewiefflet,
Gesticht, Gewirckt, und Geneyt : von Wollen, Garn, Faden,
oder Seyden : auff der Laden, und Sonderlich auff den Ramen,
Jetzt Erstmals in Teutschlandt an Tag gebracht : Zu Ehren und
Glücklicher Zeitvetreibung allen dugentsamen Frawen, und
Jungfrawen Nächerinen, auch allen andern, so lust zu solcher
Kunstlicher Arbeit haben sehr dienstlich. Getruckt zu Basel.
In verlegung Ludwig Kūnigs MDXCIX.[82]

Small obl., 33 ff., 32 plates.
Frontispiece border of point coupé. Title in Gothic red and black.
Patterns, mostly borders, number of stitches given, " Mit xxxxvii.,
Bengen," etc. " Ende dieses modelbuchs."

89.

1601.
Paris.

Béle Prérie contenant divers caracters, et differentes sortes de
lettres alphabetiques, à sçavoir lettres Romaines, de formes,
lettres pour appliquer sur le reseuil ou lassis, et autres pour
marquer sur toile et linges, par Pier. le Bé. Paris, 1601.[83]

In 4to obl.

90.

1601.
Nurem-
berg.
Sibmacher.

Modelbuch in Kupfer gemacht, Nürmberg, bei Michel
Kuisner, 1601, by J. Sibmacher.[84]

91.

1604.
Nurem-
berg.
J. Sib-
macher.

Newes Modelbûch fûr Kûpfer gemacht, darinnen allerhand
art newen Model von dem Mittel und Dick ausgeschniden duer

---

[81] Victoria and Albert Museum.
[82] Bib. Nat. Grav. B. c. 22.
Vinciolo.*

[83] Catalogue des Livres de feu
M. Picard. 1780. No. 455.
[84] Brussels, Bib. Royale.

Arbeit auch andern kunstlichen Nahework zu gebrauchen mit Fluss fur druck verfertigt. Mit Röm. Kais. Maj trentich Nürmberg 1604.[85]

Translation.

New book of patterns (on copper) in which are copied out all kinds of new patterns for thick and thin materials, to be used also in the making of other artistic needlework. . .

Obl. 4to, 58 plates carefully engraved upon copper.

Title-page surrounded by a richly ornamented border, with two figures, one sewing, the other at embroidery; also a second ornamented frontispiece, dedication to Maria Elizabeth, Electress Palatine, dated 1601. Nuremberg, J. Sibmacher, citizen and engraver.

Then follow five pages of dialogue, given page 6, note 24, and 227.

A printed title to the next plate. "The following pattern may be worked in several different ways, with a woven seam, a flat, round, or crossed Jew stitch."[86] It is probably meant for cut-work made on thin materials.

Then follow 58 leaves of patterns, the greater number of which have the number of rows written over each pattern. Pl. 38, with two patterns, is inscribed, "The following patterns are for thick cut-work." In the upper pattern, on the first leaf, are the arms of the Palatine; on the second, those of Juliers and Mark.

92.

Pretiosa gemma delle virtuose donne dove si vedono bellissimi lavori di ponti in aria, reticella, di maglia e piombini disegnati da Isabella Catanea Parasole. E di nuovo dati in luce da Luchino Gargano con alcuni altri bellissimi lavori nuovamente inventati. Stampata in Venetia ad instantia di Luchino Gargano MDC.[87] See also No. 99.

1600. Venice. I. C. Parasole.

93.

Allerhand Model zum Stricken un Nähen.[88]

N. D.

Obl. 4to, 64 plates. No date.

94.

A book of models for point coupé and embroidery, published at Padua, October 1st, 1604, by Pietro Paolo Fozzi, "Romano."[89]

1604. Padua. P.P. Fozzi.

95.

Schön newes Modelbuch von 500 schönen aussor wählten, Kunstlichen, so wol Italiähnischen, Frantzösischen, Nieder-

1605. Frankfort on the Mayn. S. Latomus.

---

[85] Nuremberg, German Museum.
[86] Jew's stitch is given both by Sibmacher and Latomus. (No. 95.) We do not know what it is.

[87] Cited by Cav. Merli, in his *Origine delle Trine.*
[88] Cat. Evans, Strand.
[89] Paris, Musée de Cluny.*

ländischen, Engelländischen, als Teutschen Mödeln, Allen, Näher. . . . hstichern, &c., zu nutz. (*Some of the words are illegible.*)

Livre des Modelles fort utile à tous ceux qui besoignent à l'esguille.

At the foot of last page recto is, " Franckfurt am Mayn, bey Sigismund Latomus, 1605." [90]

Small obl. 100 plates (Fig. 171), and coloured title-page with figures.

Fig. 171.

FRANKFORT-ON-THE-MAIN, 1605.

In the first plate is an escutcheon with this monogram (Fig. 172) surrounded with embroidery.

Fig. 172.

Monogram.

In the Nuremburg copy it is at p. 83.

96.

1607.
Frankfort on the Mayn. S. Latomus.

    Schön newes Modelbuch, Von hundert vnd achtzig schönen kunstreichen vnd gerechten Mödeln, Teutsche vnd Welsche, welche auff mancherley Art können geneet werden, als mit Zopffnath, Creutz vnnd Judenstich, auch auff Laden zu wircken : Dessgleichen von ausserlesenen Zinnigen oder Spitzen. Allen Seydenstickern, Mödelwirckerin, Näderin, vnd solcher Arbeitgeflissenen Weibsbildern sehr dienstlich, vnd zu andern Mustern

---

[90] Bib. Nat. Grav. L. h. 4. b*.—Nuremberg, German Museum.

anleytlich vnd verstendig. Franckfurt am Mayn, In Verlegung Sigismundi Latomi. M.D.C.VII.[91]

Small 4to obl. 180 patterns.

Sheets A-O (the last has only 3 leaves). On the title-page are two ladies, one working at a pillow, the other at a frame; in the back-ground, other women employed at various works. Another copy dated 1629. Mr. Arnold and Mr. F. S. Ellis.

97.

La pratique de l'aiguille industrieuse du très excellent Milour Matthias Mignerak Anglois, ouvrier fort expert en toute sorte de lingerie ou sont tracez Divers compartimens de carrez tous differans en grandeur et invention avec les plus exquises bordures, desseins d'ordonnances qui se soient veux jusques à ce jourd'hui tant poetiques historiques, qu'au tres ouvrages de point de rebord. Ensemble Les nouvelles invencions Françoises pour ce qui est de devotion et contemplation. A la Tres-Chrestiene Roine de France et de Navarre. Avec privilege 1605 du Roy.[92]

A Paris, par Jean Leclerc, rue St.-Jean de Latran, à la Salamandre roialle.

1605.
Paris.
M. Migne-rak.

EXTRACT FROM "DISCOURS DU LACIS."

" Ce chef d'œuvre divin n'est pas à l'adventure
Mais par art composé, par nombre, et par mesure;
Il commence par un, et va multipliant
Le nombre de ses trouz qu'un nœud va reliant,
Sans perdre aucunement des nombres d'entresuitte,
Croissant, et decroissant d'une mesme conduitte:
Et ainsi qu'il commence il acheve par un,
Du monde le principe et le terme commun.
Si l'on veut sans faillir cet ouvrage parfaire,
Il faut multiplier, adjouster, et soustraire:
Il faut bien promptement assembler, et partir,
Qui veut un beau Lacis inegal compartir.
Mais se peut il trouver, souz la voute azurée,
Chose plus justement en tous sens mesurée?
Ouvrage ou il y ait tant de proportions,
De figures, de traicts et de dimensions?
D'un point premièrement une ligne l'on tire,
Puis le filet courbé un cercle va descrire,
Et du cercle noué se trouve le quarré
Pour lequel retrouver tant d'esprits ont erré.
De six mailles se faict une figure egale,
De trois costez esgaux, pour forme pyramidale:

---

[91] Stockholm. Royal Library. (Communicated by the librarian, Mr. H. Wieselgren.) In the same library is a work, without title-page or date, for " broderies et de tous autres besongnant à l'aiguille," by Hieronymus Cock, containing, with designs of every description, a few patterns for Spanish point of great beauty.

[92] Bib. Baron J. Pichon, 2 copies.* — Cat. d'Estrées. — Bib. Nat. Grav. B. c. 22.* (Title-page wanting.)

Et l'ouvrage croissant, s'en forme promptement
Une autre dont les deux sont egaux seulement.
Si l'on tire un des coings, se forme une figure.
D'un triangle en tout sens, d'inegale mesure.
Le moule plus tiré faict les angles pointuz,
Et l'ouvrage estendu faict les angles obtuz.
De mailles à la fin un beau quarré se faict,
Composé de quarrez, tout egal, et parfaict,
Quarré qui toutesfois se forme variable,
Or en lozange, et or en figure de table.
La bande de Lacis recouvert, à nos yeux,
Est comme un beau pourtraict de l'escharpe des cieux,
Dont chaque endroit ouvré nous represente un signe,
Le milieu, les degrez de l'Ecliptique ligne ;
　　Le quarré, des vertus le symbole, et signal
De science du livre et bonnet doctoral,
Nous va representant l'Eglise et la Justice.
La façon de lacer figure l'exercice
D'enfiler une bague ou bien l'art d'escrimer.

　　　　　.　　　　　.　　　　　.　　　　　.

Le lacis recouvert sert de filet aux dames
Pour les hommes suprendre et enlacer leurs ames,
Elles en font collets, coiffures, et mouchoirs,
Des tentures de lits, tauayoles, pignoirs,
Et maint autre ornement dont elles les enlacent,
C'est pourquoi en laçant les femmes ne se lassent."

In 4to, 76 ff., 72 plates.

Frontispiece: Two ladies, with frames in their hands, labelled "Diana" and "Pallas." On the top, an escutcheon per pale France and Medicis, supported by Cupids. Beneath, Cupids with distaff and winding reels. Between the sides of a pair of scissors is a cushion on which is extended a piece of lacis, a "marguerite" in progress. (See Fig. 6.) Above, "Petrus Firens fecit, I. le Clerc excud." Below, "A Paris par Jean le Clerc Rue St. Jean de Latran à la Salamandre royalle."

Dedication of Jean le Clerc "A la royne," then Marie de Medicis, stating: "J'avois recouvré d'un personnage Anglois tres-expert en toute sorte de Lingerie;" but who this Milour Mignerak may be, history tells not.

Then follows the "Discours du Lacis," a poem, of which we give an extract.

The privilege is signed Aug. 2, 1605.

The patterns consist of the Queen's arms and cypher, 4 Scripture subjects: Adam and Eve, the annunciation, Ecce Homo, and Magdalen; 4 Elements, 4 Seasons; Roman Charity, Lucretia, Venus, and "Pluye d'or;" 6 Arbes à fruit, 6 Pots à fleurs, 30 Carrés grands, moyens et petits; 6 Bordures, and, what is quite a novelty, 6 "Passements faits au fuseau." (See Fig. 13): the first mention of pillow lace in any of the French pattern-books.

98.

1613.
Paris.
F. Vin-
ciolo.

Les secondes œuvres, et subtiles inventions de Lingerie du Seigneur Federic de Vinçiolo Venitien ; nouvellement augmenté de plusieurs carrez de point de rebort. Dediée à Madame, sœur unique du roy. Ou sont representees plusieurs figures de Reseau, nombres de Carrez et Bordures tous differents, le tout de poinct conté, avec autres sortes de Carrez de nouvelles inventions non encore vues.

A Paris. Par Jean le Clerc, rue sainct Jean de Latran, à la Salemandre, 1613. Avec privilege du Roy.[93]

A scarce and valuable volume, the fullest edition of the second part of Vinciolo's work.

4to, 68 ff., 61 plates.

It contains a—

SONNET AUX DAMES & DAMOYSELLES.

" Esprits rarement beaux qui fuyez la paresse,
Je vous fais un present qui la pourra chasser,
Quand vous desirez de gayement passer
Vostre temps, et monstrer de vostre main l'adresse.

Le present est utile et plein de gentillesse,
Il monstre les moyens de bien entrelasser.
Et faire au point couppé tout ce qu'on peut penser.
Cet exercise plaist à Pallas la Deesse.

Par ses enseignemens, avec l'esguille on fait
Des fleurons, des oyseaux, en ouvrage parfait,
Des chiffres et des nœuds, tels que l'amour desire.

Aymez cet exercise, et vous y occupez,
Et puis vous cognoistrez que sur les points couppez
En diverses façons quelque portrait se tire."

The author's address to the reader, and a

Dedication to " Madame, sœur unique du roy " (Catherine de Bourbon, sister of Henry IV., married, 1599, to the Duc de Bar), signed by Le Clerc.

On the second plates are her arms, a lozenge, France and Navarre with crown and cordelière, and the same lozenge also surmounts the decorated frontispiece, supported on either side by a genius (?) working at a frame and point coupé drapery.

7 Scripture subjects : The Salutation, St. Sacrement, Passion, Crucifixion, Adoration of the Kings, etc. ; the number of the stitches given to each.

2 Stomachers, and various patterns of " carrez " and borders. 2 of " Point de rebort."

At the end is the " Discours du Lacis," already printed by Mignerak.

99.

Teatro delle nobili et virtuose donne, dove si rappresentano varij disegni di lavori novamente inventati e disegnati da Elisabetta Catanea Parasole Romana.

1616
Rome.
E. C. Parasole.

Dedicata alla Serenissima Principessa Donna Elisabetta Borbona d' Austria, Principessa di Spagna, da E. C. Parasole. Data di Roma a di 5 Marzo 1616.[94] Other editions, 1620, 1625, and 1636. The last is dedicated to the Grand Duchess of

---

[93] Bib. Rouen. No. 1,314.*—Bib. Baron J. Pichon.*

[94] Florence, Bib. Prof. Santerelli. —Rome, Bib. Prince Massimo.

Tuscany, and has the Medici and Della Rovere arms in the title-page.

Obl. 4to, 47 ff., 46 plates (44 in Prince Massimo's copy) beautifully executed, the titles printed to each plate, as "Lavori di punti in aria, Merletti di ponti reticella, Merletti a piombini," etc. (See Fig. 15.

IOO.

1600.
Venice.
I. C.
Parasole.

Pretiosa gemme delle virtuose donne dore si vedono bellisimi lavori di ponto in aria, reticella, dimaglia e piombini disegnati da Isabella Catanea Parasole. E di nuovo dati in luce da Luchino Gargano con alcuni altri bellisimi lavori nuovamente inventate. Stampata in Venetea ad instantia de Luchino Gargano MDC.[95]

IOI.

1625.
Rome.
I. C.
Parasole.

Gemma pretiosa delle virtuose donne, dore si vedono bellisimi lavori de Ponti in Aria, Reticella, di Maglia, e Piombini disegnatida Isabella Catanea Parasole.

In Rome, appreso Guliegno Facciotti, 1625.

102.

1618.
Frankfort on the Mayn.
D. Meyer.

Zierat Buch, von allerhandt Kutschnur, Schleyer deckel, Krägen, Leibgürtel, Passmenten, Händschug, Wehrgeheng und Schubenehen, Messerscheyden, Secklen, Früchten, Blumen und ands. mehr.

Allen Perlenbefftern, Nederin, Lehrinngen und andern welche lust zu dieser Kunst tragen, sehr nützlich.

Inn diese Format zusammen ordiniert und gsetzt durch Daniel Meyer Mahlern. 1ster Theil.

Franckfuhrt am Mayn, bey Eberhardt Kusern zu finden.

11 ff., 9 plates.

Translation.

Decoration book of all sorts of Cords, Veil covers, Collars, Belts, Laces, Gloves, Shoulder knots, shoe-seams (?), Knife sheaths, Bags, Fruit, Flowers, and other things besides. Very useful to all Beadworkers, Seamstresses, Apprentices, and others, who take a pleasure or are fond of this art. Arranged and put into this form by D. M. M. 1st part.

103.

1619.
Leipsic.
A. Bret-schneider.

New Modelbuch Darinnen allerley kunstliche Virsirung und Müster artiger Züege und schöner Blümmen zu zierlichen Ueberschlagen, Haupt Schurtz Schnüptüchern Hauben Handschuhen, Uhren (?) gehenzen, Kampfüttern ünd dergleichen auf Muhler naht und Seidenstücker arbeit gantz Kunstlich gemahlt

---

[95] Cat. Evans, Strand.

und vorgerissen, dergleichen sie bevorn noch nie in Druck ausgegangen. 16 Leipzicht 19.

Inn Verlegŭng Henning Grosseren, de Jŭngeren Andreas Bretschneider Mahller.[96]

Translation.

New pattern-book, in which all sorts of artistic ornamentations and patterns of pretty stuffs and beautiful flowers for covers for Head, Aprons, and Pocket-handkerchiefs, Caps, Gloves, Clock cases, Comb Cases, and such like, artistically sketched from painter and silk embroiderer's work, and which have never before gone out of print.

Small folio, 53 plates, and half a sheet of text, containing the dedication of the work to Madame Catherine von Dorstats, née Löser. There appear to be 3 plates wanting.

104.

A Schole House for the Needle. 1624.[97]

Obl. 4to. Was sold at the White Knight's sale for £3 15s.

1624.
London.

105.

Corona delle nobili et virtuose donne. Libro terzo. Nel quale si dimostra in varii dissegni tutte le sorti di Mostre di punti tagliati e punti in aria, punti Fiamenghi, punti a Retcello, e d' ogn' altra sorte, Cosi per Fregi, per merli e Rosette, che con Aco si viano hoggidi per lutta l'Europa. E molte delle quali Mostre porsono Serviri ancora per opera à Mozzete. Con le dichiarationi a le Mostre a' Lavori fatti da Lugretia Romana. In Venetia, appresso Allessandro de Vecchi, 1620.[98]

27 ff., obl. 8vo.

1620.
Venice.
Lugretia
Romana.

106.

Corona delle Nobili et Virtuose Donne, Libro primo, nel quale si dimostra in varij Dissegni tutte le sorti di Mostre di punti tagliati, punti in Aria, punti Fiamenghi, punti a Reticello, e d' ogni altre sorte, cosi per Freggi, per Merli, e Rosette, che con l' Aco si usano per tutta l'Europa. E molte delle quali Mostre possono servire ancora per opere a Mazzete. Con le dichiarazioni a le Mostre, a Lavori fatti da Lugretia Romana.

In Venetia appresso Alessandro de Vecchi MDCXXV. Si vendono in Venetia al Ponte de' Baretteri alla libreria delle tre Rose.[99]

1625.
Venice.
Lucretia
Romana.

Lady Wilton, in her *Art of Needlework*, quotes a copy dated 1620.

Obl. 4to, ff. 27. Portrait of Maria d'Aragon.

---

[96] Hesse-Cassel, Public Library. Communicated by Mr. N. R. Bernhardi, the head Librarian.

[97] Lowndes, *Bibliographer's Manual.* New edit. by Henry Bohn.

[98] Victoria and Albert Museum.

[99] Vienna, Imperial Library.

107.

N. D.
Venice.
Lucretia
Romana.

Ornamento nobile, per ogni gentil matrona, dove si contiene bavari, frisi d' infinita bellezza, lavori, per Linzuoli, Traverse, e Facuoli, Piena dì Figure, Ninfe, Satiri, Grotesche, Fontane, Musiche, Caccie di Cervi, Uccelli, ed altri Animali. Con ponti in aria, fiamenghi, et tagliati, con Adornamenti bellissimi, da imperare, per ogni Virtuosa Donna, che si diletta di perfetta-mente cucire. Opera, per Pittori, Scultori, e disegnatori giovevole alle lor professioni, Fatta da Lucretia Romana, il quinto volume di Suoi lavori. Dedicato alle Virtuose donne, in Venetia.[100]

Fol., 20 plates.

Frontispiece, in point coupé frame. A woman in classic attire is represented under a Doric porch, standing on a tortoise, symbol of a home-loving woman. (See No. 77.) She holds a ball of thread in her hand. Behind, on the left, are two women at work; on the right, a sculptor chiselling a statue of Minerva.

The plates, which are rich and beautiful, are each accompanied by a short explanation, as " Degna de esser portata de ogni imperatrice; " " Hopera bellissima che per il piu il Signora Duchesa et altre Signore si servano per li suoi Lavori; " " Questa bellissima Rosette usano auco le gentildonne Venetiane da far traverse," etc. (Fig. 173.)

The bavari are executed in three different stitches: punto d' aieri, p. fiamingo, and p. tagliato. This author and Vecellio give Flemish patterns (punti Fiamenghi). They consist mostly of rosettes and stars (gotico).

108.

1623.
Paris.

Les excellents eschantillons, patrons et modelles du Seigneur Federic de Vinciolo Venitien, pour apprendre à faire toutes sortes d'ouvrages de Lingerie, de Poinct couppé, grands et petits passements à jour, et dentelles exquises. Dediez à la Royne. A Paris. Chez la Veufve Jean le Clerc, ruë Sainct Jean de Latran, à la Salamandre Royalle. Avec Privilege du Roy, 1623.[101]

In 4to, 56 ff.

The old frontispiece and same "Avertissement."

Dedication to the Queen, Anne of Austria.

The Goddess Pallas invented " les ouvrages de lingerie, le poinct couppé, les grands and petits passements à jour, toutes sortes de dentelles, tant pour se desennuyer que se parer, par l'artifice de ses ingenieuses mains. Araciné s'y adonna, and bien qu'inferieure se voulant comparer à elle & en venir à l'experience, mais sa presomption fut chastiée." Many illustrious ladies have delighted in this "honneste exercise." Fastrade and Constance, wives of the Emperor Charlemagne and of King Robert, " s'employèrent de cette manufacture, & de leurs ouvrages ornèrent les églises & les autels." This royal "mestier" has reached perfection through the works of Vinciolo. I reprint and again increase his work, which I dedicate to your Majesty, to whom I presume they will be agree-

---

[100] Brussels, Bib. Roy. 　　　　　Brussels, Bib. Roy.—Cat. d'Estrées
[101] Bib. Imp. Grav. L. h. 2. a.*— 　　8847.

Fig. 173.

BAVARO DI PONTO D'AIERE, DI GRAN BELLEZZI.—Con figure di moiti strumenti che sonano a musica, con rosete d'intorno di bellia e vaga vista per ogni Principessa.

BAVARO DI PONTO D'AERE.—Con belissime figure ed altri fiori.

BAVARI."—From *Ornamento nobile* of Lucretia Romana.

able; the subject of which it treats is " une invention de déesse & une occupation de Royne—vous estant autant Royne des vertus que vous l'estes de deux royaumes." Signed, " la Veufve de feu Iean le Clerc."

Same sonnet.

Privilege for six years, dated Paris, last day of March, 1623.

55 ff., 58 plates, 24 ouvrages de point couppé and 8 of " Passements au fuzeau " (see Figs. 14 and 15), and alphabet.

109.

A Schole Howse for the Needle. Teaching by sundry sortes of patterns and examples of different kindes, how to compose many faire workes ; which being set in order and forme according to the skill and understanding of the workwoman will, no doubt, yield profit unto such as live by the needle and give good content to adorne the worthy. London printed in Shoe Lane at the " Faulcon " by Richard Shorleyker, 1632.

To the Reader.

Gentle Reader, I would have you know that the Diversities of Examples which you shall find in this " Schoole-howse for the Needle " are only but patternes which serve but to helpe and inlarge your invention. But for the disposing of them into forme and order of Workes that I leave to your own skill and understanding. Whose ingenious and well prac-tised wits will soe readily (I doubt not) compose them into such beautiful formes as will be able to give content, both to the workers and the wearers of them. And againe for your behoafe I have in the end of this booke made two scales or checker patternes which by enlarging or con-tracting into greater or lesser squares you may enlarge or make lesser any of the saide patternes and examples in the booke or any other whatever.

Vale !

And because I would not have any one mistaken in any of these patternes contayned in this Booke, for some peradventure will look to find workes set out in order as they should be wrought with the needle or florished upon the Tent, &c. But as I have said before in the beginning of this Booke, that, that is here published are only but diver-sitie of patternes, out of which the workwoman is to take her choice of one or more at her pleasure and so have them drawne out into forme and order of worke. Of which skill if it may be I would have serving-men (such as have time enough) to practice and be skilful in which will be quickly learned if they would, with a little patience applie their mindes to practise it. A quarter of the time that they spend in playing at cards, tables, quaffing and drinking would make them excellent in this know-ledge especially such as are ingenious and indued with good wits, as for the most part all of them have ; Againe it is a thing that no doubt would yield them both praise and profit, beside the pleasure and delight it would be unto them, and a good inducement to drawe on others of their own ranke and qualitie to the like practice and imitation.

110.

Here followeth certaine patternes of Cut-workes ; and but once Printed before. Also sundry sorts of Spots, as Flowers, Birds, and Fishes, &c., and will fitly serve to be wrought, some

1632. *London*

with Gould, some with Silke, and some with Gewell (*sic*) or otherwise at your pleasure.

London ; Pinted (*sic*) in Shoe-lane, at the signe of the Faulcon, by Richard Shorleyker. 1632.[102]

Obl. 4to.

The copy in the Bodleian is probably due to the above. It has no date and varies in title : " Newly invented and never published before," with " crewell in coullers," etc. ; and " Never but once published before." Printed by Rich. Shorleyker.
33 patterns and title.

III.

The needles excellency, a new booke wherein are divers admirable workes wrought with the needle. Newly invented and cut in copper for the pleasure and profit of the industrious Printed for James Boler, &c., 1640.[103]

" Beneath this title is a neat engraving of three ladies in a flower garden, under the names of Wisdom, Industrie, and Follie. Prefixed to the patterns are sundry poems in a commendation of the needle, and describing the characters of ladies who have been eminent for their skill in needlework, among whom are Queen Elizabeth and the Countess of Pembroke. These poems were composed by John Taylor, the Water Poet. It appears the work had gone through twelve impressions. . . . From the costume of a lady and gentleman in one of the patterns, it appears to have been originally published in the reign of James I."— (Douce.) From this description of the frontispiece, it seems to be copied from Sibmacher.

" The Needle's Excellency, or a new Book of Patterns, with a poem by John Taylor, in Praise of the Needle." London, 1640. Obl. 4to, engraved title, and 28 plates of patterns. Sold, 1771, £6 17s. 6d. (Lowndes, *Bibliographer's Manual.* New edit., by H. Bohn). Another copy of the same date, marked 12th edition, is in the Library of King's College, Cambridge. It consists of title, four leaves with the poem, subscribed John Taylor, and 31 leaves of copper cuts of patterns.

112.

1642.
Pistoja.
P. A. For-
tunato.

Le Pompe di Minerva, per le nobili e virtuose donne che con industriosa mano di trattenersi dilettano di far Rezze, maglia quadra, punti in aria, punti in tagliati, punti a reticello, cosi per fregio come per merletti e rosette di varie sorti, si come oggidi con l'aco di lavorar usati per tutto l' Europa, arrichite di bellissimi et vaghi intagli cavati da più celebri autori di tal professione. In Pistoja, per Piero A. Fortunato.

In 8vo obl., dedicated to Caterina Giraldini, in Cellesi. August 20 1642.[104]

---

[102] In the possession of Mrs. Marryat. " Maes y dderwen."— Bib. Bodleian.

[103] Quoted by Mr. Douce (*Illustrations of Shakspeare*).

[104] S. Marino. M. P. Bonella.

113.

Dass Neue Modelbuch von schönen Nädereyen, Ladengewerk und Soterleins arbeit. Ander theil. Nürnberg, bey Paulus Fürsten Kunsthändler.

1666.
Nurem-
berg.

Obl. 4to, 3 sheets of text, 50 plates.
Dedicated to the Princess Rosina Helena. Nürnberg, March 20, 1666.[105]

114.

In the Bib. Imp. (Gravures, L. h. 4. c.) is a vol. lettered "Guipure, gravures burin," containing a collection of patterns engraved on copper, 43 plates, four of which are double, pasted in the book, without title or date. Pomegranates, narcissus, lilies, carnations, most of them labelled "Kreutzstick, Frantzösischenstick, and Fadengewürck" (thread work), the number of stitches given, with Clocks (Zwickel) of stockings and other patterns.

115.

Model Buch, dritter Theil von unterschiedlicher Vögeln, Blumen und Früchten &cte. Von und in Verlegung Rosina Helena Fürtin. Nürnberg, Christoff Gerharts, 1676.

1676.
Nurem-
berg.
C. Ger-
harts.

4to obl., engraved title and printed list; 42 wood plates, 4 large.

116.

Methode pour faire une infinité de desseins differens, avec des carreaux mi-partis de deux couleurs par une ligne diagonale ou observations du père Dominique Donat, religieux carme de la province de Touleuse sur une mémoire inserée dans l'histoire de l'Académie royale des sciences à Paris, l'année 1704, presenté par le Rev. Père Sebastien Truchet. Paris, 1722.[106]

1722.
Paris.

72 geometric squares, with directions how to make them useful to architects, painters, embroiderers, "tous ceux qui se servent de l'aiguille," and others.

117.

Neues Neta- und Strickbuch fur das schöne Geschlecht, worinnen allerhand Zierrathen, wie auch viele neue Zwickel, nebst Buchstaben und Zahlen, sowohl zum Nähen als Stricken in zierlichen Nissen und Mustern befindlich sind. Mit vielen Kupfertafeln. Nürnberg und Leipzig, der Christoph Weigel und Schneider. 1784.[107]

1784.
Nurem-
berg and
Leipzig.
Christoph
Weigel.

---

[105] Berlin, Roy. Library.
[106] Bib. de l'Arsenal. 11,956 *bis.**
[107] Victoria and Albert Museum.

118.

N.D.
Nurem-
berg.
F. M.
Helmin.

Continuation der kunst- und fleisz-übenden Nadel-Ergötzung oder des neu ersonnenen besondern Nehe-Buchs dritter Theil, worinnen fleiszige Liebhaberinnen deeser nöthig und nützlichen Wissenchaft, ihr kunstliches Nadel-Exercitium, beij unterschiedlich vorfallenden Belegenheiten zu haben allerhand noch nie vorgekomene Muster zu Deso gebrauch, vorlegt und en die Hand gegeben werden von Fr. Margaretha Helmin, zu finden in Nürnberg bei Joh. Christoph Weigel. Nürnburg. No date.[108]

Oblong fol.

119.

N.D.
Nurem-
berg.
J. Chr.
Weigel.

Zierlich webende Minerva, oder neu erfundenes Kunst- und Bild-Buch der Weber- und Zeichner-Arbeit, worinnen treue Anweisung geschieht, wie man kunstlich wirken und schöne Arbeit verfertigen soll, von der vierschäfftigen an, bis auf zwey und dreissig-schafftige. Nurnberg (Johann Christoph Weigel). No date.[109]

49 plates in sheets.

---

[108] Victoria and Albert Museum.　　[109] *Ibid.*

GLOSSARY OF TERMS

Bars. See *Brides.*

Bead Edge. A simple heading for pillow lace.

Bobbins. Small elongated wooden or bone reels on which the thread is wound for the purpose of lace-making. They are frequently ornamented with patterns pricked or stained, and polished. They are weighted with "gingles" or "jingles" (*i.e.*, beads, coins, seals, seeds, or various articles).

Brides. A small strip or connection (1) of threads overcast with buttonhole stitches, or (2) of twisted or plaited threads. It is used instead of a ground-work of net; the word is French, its English equivalent being *pearl-tie.* The French word is chiefly employed.

Brides ornées = brides ornamented with picots, loops, or pearls.

Buttonhole Stitch. One of the chief stitches in needle-made lace; also known as *close stitch, Point noué,* and *Punto a Feston.*

Cartisane. A strip of parchment or vellum covered with silk or gold or metal thread, used to form a pattern.

Close Stitch = Buttonhole stitch.

Cordonnet. The outline to ornamental forms. The cordonnet consists (1) of a single thread, or (2) of several threads worked together to give the appearance of one large thread, or (3) of a thread or horsehair overcast with buttonhole stitches. In England called *gimp.*

Couronnes. Ornaments to the cordonnet. When they ornament the raised cordonnet in the body of the pattern they are known as *fleurs volantes.*

Coxcombs = Bars.

Dentélé = Scalloped border.

Droschel. Flemish word used in Belgium for net-ground made with bobbins.

Dressed Pillow. A term used by bobbin-lace makers to intimate that all accessories necessary are in their proper positions.[1]

---

[1] *A History of Hand-made Lace.* Mrs. Nevill Jackson and E. Jesurum. 1900.

Edge. There are two edges to lace; the outer, which in trimmings and flounces is either scalloped or ornamented with picots, and the *engrêlure* or *footing.*

Engrêlure = Footing, or heading, of a lace, used to sew the lace on to the material it is to decorate.

Entoilage. French term for a plain mesh ground or galloon.[1]

Fil de Crin. A thick or heavy outline or cordonnet.[1]

Fil de Trace. The name by which the outlines of needle-made laces are distinguished.[1]

Fillings. A word occasionally used for *modes* or *jours*; fancy stitches employed to fill in enclosed spaces in needle-made and bobbin laces.[1]

Flax. Is composed of the filaments of the fibrous portion of *Linum usitatissimum*, an annual, native of Europe, and from it linen thread is spun. That of Flanders is the best for lace-making.

Fleurs Volantes. See *Couronnes.*

Fond. Identical with *champ, entoilage,* and *treille.* The ground-work of needle-point or bobbin lace as distinct from the toilé or pattern which it surrounds and supports. Grounds are divided into *fonds claires, brides claires,* and *brides ornées.* The *fond claires* include the *Réseau* or net-patterned grounds. *Fond de Neige* is also known as *Œil de Perdrix.*

Fond Simple. Sometimes called *Point de Lille;* is the purest, lightest, and most transparent of all grounds. The sides of the meshes are not partly plaited as in Brussels and Mechlin, nor wholly plaited as in Valenciennes and Chioggia; but four of the sides are formed by twisting two threads round each other, and the remaining two sides by simply crossing of the threads over each other. [See *Grounds.*][1]

Footing. See *Engrêlure.*

Gimp. The *pattern* which rests on the ground or is held together by brides. The work should not, however be confounded with the material gimp, which was formerly called *guipure.*

　　　In Honiton and the Midlands, the word denotes the coarse glazed thread used to raise certain edges of the design.[1]

Gingles. A name given in Buckinghamshire, etc., to the bunches of coloured beads hung on to bobbins by means of brass wire, in order to give extra weight and so increase the tension of the threads.[1]

---

[1] *A History of Hand-made Lace.* Mrs. Nevill Jackson and E. Jesurum. 1900.

Groppo [Italian]. A knot or tie.

Grounds. The grounds of laces are divided into two classes, one being called the *bride*, the other the *Réseau*. The *bride* ground is formed with plain or ornamental bars, in order to connect the ornaments forming the pattern. The *Réseau* ground is a net made with the needle or with bobbins, to connect the ornaments forming the pattern.

Guipure. A lace-like trimming of twisted threads. The word is now used to loosely describe many laces of coarse pattern. *Guipure d'Art* is the name given to modern darned netting.[1]

Heading = Footing, engrêlure.

Jours. Ornamental devices occurring in various parts of a piece of lace. The earliest forms of *jours* may be seen in Venetian point lace, where they are introduced into the centre of a flower or other such device. [*Modes* are identical with *jours.*]

Legs = Bars.

Mat, or *Math.* The closely-plaited portions of flowers or leaves in bobbin-made lace ; also the closely-worked portion of any lace.[1]

Modes. See *Jours.*

Œil de Perdrix. See *Fond.*

Orris. A corruption of Arras. The term is now used to denote galloon for upholstering purposes. In the eighteenth century it was applied to laces of gold and silver.[1]

Passement. Until the seventeenth century, laces, bands, and gimps were called *passements à l'aiguille;* bobbin laces, *passements au fuseau.* At present the word denotes the pricked pattern on parchment upon which both needle-point and bobbin laces are worked.

Passementerie. Now used for all kinds of fringes, ribbons, and gimp for dress trimmings.

Pearls, or *Purls =* Bars.

Pearl edge, or *Purl edge.* A narrow thread edge of projecting loops used to sew upon lace as a finish to the edge.[1]

Pearlin, or *Pearling* [Scotch]. Lace.

Picot. Minute loops worked on to the edge of a *bride* or *cordonnet,* or added as an enrichment to a flower—as in the case of rose point, in which *picots* play an important part.

---

[1] *A History of Hand-made Lace.* Mrs. Nevill Jackson and E. Jesurum. 1900.

Pillow Lace. Lace made on the pillow, by twisting and plaiting threads. The French term is *dentelle au fuseau.*

Pizzo [Italian]. Lace.

Ply = A single untwisted thread.

Point Lace. Lace made with the point of the needle. The French term is *Point à l'aiguille.* The term point has been misused to describe varieties of lace, such as *Point d'Angleterre, Point de Malines,* etc., which are laces made on the pillow, and not with the point of the needle.

Point de Raccroc. A stitch used by lace-makers to join *réseau* ground.

Point Noué = Buttonhole stitch.

Point Plat. A French term for flat point executed without a raised cordonnet or outline cord.[1]

Pricked. The term used in pillow lace-making to denote the special marking out of the pattern upon parchment.

Pricker. A short instrument used in bobbin lace to prick holes in the pattern to receive the pins.[1]

Punto a Feston = Buttonhole stitch.

Purls = *Brides.*

Purlings = A stitch used in Honiton guipure to unite the bobbin-made sprigs.[1]

Réseau. Ground of small regular meshes made on the pillow in various manners, and made by the point of the needle in fewer and less elaborate manners. The French term, as here given, is generally used in preference to any English equivalent.

Réseau Rosacé. See *Argentella* (Ch. ARGENTAN).

Rouissage. The process of steeping the flax preparatory to its being spun for lace-making.

Rezél, Reseuil. See LACIS, Chap. II.

Runners. The name by which the bobbins which work across a pattern in bobbin lace are known.

Sam cloth. Old name for a sampler.

---

[1] *A History of Hand-made Lace.* Mrs. Nevill Jackson and E. Jesurum. 1900.

INDEX

Aberdeen, qualifications of schoolmistress of, 431 n[6]

Aberdein, Mrs. Frank, cited, 400 n[4]

Abrahat, Mrs., pensioned by Queen Anne, 347

Abrantès, Duchesse d', 105, 128 n[27], 185 n[12], 186 and n[15], 237 n[21]

Abruzzi, the, lace-making in, 68

Addison, cited, 349

Addo, Marquis d', 459 n[1]

Adelaide, Queen, 409 and n[19], n[20]

Adélaïde de France, 182

Adelhaïs, Queen (wife of Hugh Capet), 5

Agriculture, women employed in, lace-makers contrasted with, 370

Aquesseau, Chancellor d', quoted, 264

Alb lace, at Granada, 92

Albert, Archduke of Austria, 113 n[10]

—— Museum (Exeter), tallies in, 78 n[97]

Albissola, lace manufacture at, 75, 77 and n[95], 78, 79 and n[101]

Alcuid, embroidery taught by, 6

Alenches, 249

Alençon

  numbers of lace-workers at Chantilly and, (1851), 257 n[24],

  refugees from, in 18th century, 347

  ——, Duke d', 140 n[3]

  —— lace (see Point d'Alençon)

Alice, Princess, bridal dress of, 409

Almagro, lace industry at, 102 and n[32], 103 n[40]

Aloe thread, Florentine use of, 93 n[8]

—— thread lace

  Greek, 86

  Italian, 79 and n[100]

  Portuguese, 107

  Spanish, 91, 93, 99, 101

Alost Valenciennes, ground stitch of, 133

Altar-cloths,

  alternate designs on, 24

  Bock collection, in, 23

  Prague, at (by Anne of Bohemia), 9

Altar frontal in point conté, (Mrs. Hailstone's), 23

Altenburg, 268

Alva, Duke of, 366 n[18]

Alvin, M., 480 n[59]

Amelia, Princess, 128

America,

  impulse given to lace industry by U.S., 187

America—*continued*

  lace imported to, from—

    Bailleul, 241

    England (baby lace) 385

    Grammont, 134

    Italy, 75, 79

    Mirecourt, 253

    Portugal, 106

    Saxony, 263

    Spain, 102

  Puritan lace-makers in, 372 n[8]

  war with, effect of, on lace trade, 408

Amsterdam, establishment of lace fabric at, 259

Anderson, quoted, 74, 83, 101, 124, 271, 288, 371 n[2], 384, 396; cited, 264 n[21], 265 n[25], 286, 397

——, Lady, robbery at house of, 346

Angoulême, Duchesse d', 196

Anne of Austria,

  influence of, on French fashions, 147, 150

  Mechlin veil of, 125–126 and n[40]

  pattern-book dedicated to, 144, 498

  pilgrimage to Thierzac, 248

  presents of English lace from Henrietta Maria to, 330 and n[67], 401

—— of Bohemia, Queen (wife of Richard II.), altar-cloth by, 9

—— of Denmark,

  cost of lace of, 317 and n[10], 320 and n[31]

  Elizabeth's old clothes presented to, 320

  English home industries encouraged by, 319

  foreign lace purchased by, 327

  funeral of, 325 and n[40]

—— of England (Queen Anne)

  household management of, 174 n[15]

  Mechlin lace of, 126 and n[44]

  period of, 347–350

Anspach, 265

——, Margrave of, 178

Anti-Gallican Society

  Edinburgh and Dublin Societies contemporaneous with, 429

  prizes awarded by, 119, 262, 297, 355 and n[15], 374 and nn, 380, 395, 398, 404

  records of, cited, 373

Antwerp

  book sale at (1864), 482

  Brussels lace made at, 130

  Mechlin lace made at, 125